In Pursuit of Justice

MW00526997

"John Albion Andrew is a little-known American hero. He led with courage and principle in pursuit of equality. In this new biography, Stephen D. Engle has given us a thoroughly engaging portrait of the man, his times, and his leadership."

—DEVAL L. PATRICK, professor of the practice of public leadership and co-director of the Center for Public Leadership, Harvard Kennedy School

"John Andrew is one of the unsung heroes of the Civil War, and Stephen D. Engle has captured this Massachusetts governor in his complexity and his passion for justice in such a perilous time. Engle brings tremendous research to this gracefully written re-creation of a life that had been waiting for its biographer. Engle tells a remarkable story of the uses of power—for a lawyer and especially a governor—to protect fugitives, free the enslaved, and build a more equal society. One hopes for a broad readership; Andrew was the real article—a genuinely abolitionist white state leader who walked the walk of Black emancipation."

—DAVID W. BLIGHT, Sterling Professor of History at Yale University and author of the Pulitzer Prize–winning *Frederick Douglass: Prophet of Freedom*

"This moving biography of John Albion Andrew demonstrates the power of passionate crusaders to reshape society, including the most intransigent forces of racial injustice. Engle traces Andrew's career from its roots in Christian faith and a liberal education through the courtroom, Republican politics, the Massachusetts governorship, and the searing crises of Civil War and Reconstruction."

—NANCY HEWITT, author of *Radical Friend, Amy Kirby Post and Her Activist Worlds,* winner of the 2018 James Bradford Best Biography Prize, Society for Historians of the Early American Republic

"Stephen D. Engle's biography of John A. Andrew closes a glaring gap in the literature on mid-nineteenth-century U.S. history. As governor of Massachusetts throughout the Civil War, Andrew pushed tirelessly for emancipation, the enrollment of Black men in U.S. military service, and applying relentless pressure against the Confederacy. This book superbly assesses

Andrew's life and career, while also reminding us that state leaders played a central role in waging a war to save and improve the republic."

—GARY W. GALLAGHER, author of *The Union War* and John L. Nau III Professor of History Emeritus, University of Virginia

"Stephen D. Engle reintroduces us to one of the nineteenth century's leading political reformers, abolitionists, and citizens. John Andrew deserves to be more widely known, and this book is the kind of biography he deserves. Through the story of Andrew's life, Engle illuminates the contentious and exhilarating era in which Andrew played such a pivotal role."

—ROBERT ALLISON, author of *The American Revolution: A Very Short Introduction*

"In an engagingly written book, Stephen D. Engle traces Andrew's trajectory from young idealistic student and abolitionist lawyer to his career as Lincoln's most effective ally among the Civil War governors. A first-class biography, Engle's book is also a comprehensive history of the one of the most consequential governorships in American history. It will be read by many; it will be essential reading for those working in the political history of the Civil War."

—JOHN L. BROOKE, author of *"There Is a North": Fugitive Slaves, Political Crisis, and Cultural Transformation in the Coming of the Civil War*

IN
PURSUIT *of*
JUSTICE

IN
PURSUIT *of*
JUSTICE

||||||||||||||||||||||||||||||||||||||||||||||||||||||||||||||||||||||||||||||||||||||

THE LIFE OF JOHN ALBION ANDREW

Stephen D. Engle

UNIVERSITY OF MASSACHUSETTS PRESS—*Amherst and Boston*

Copyright © 2023 by University of Massachusetts Press
All rights reserved
Printed in the United States of America

ISBN 978-1-62534-745-9 (paper); 746-6 (hardcover)

Designed by Sally Nichols
Set in Freight Pro and Futura
Printed and bound by Books International, Inc.

Cover design by Sally Nichols
Cover photo: Unknown photographer, *The governor of Massachusetts, John Albion Andrews.*
Courtesy of Special Collections, Fine Arts Library, Harvard University.

Library of Congress Cataloging-in-Publication Data

Names: Engle, Stephen Douglas, author.
Title: In pursuit of justice : the life of John Albion Andrew / Stephen
Engle, University of Massachusetts Press.
Description: Amherst and Boston : University of Massachusetts Press, [2023]
| Includes bibliographical references and index.
Identifiers: LCCN 2023013418 (print) | LCCN 2023013419 (ebook) | ISBN
9781625347459 (paperback) | ISBN 9781625347466 (hardcover) | ISBN
9781685750329 (ebook)
Subjects: LCSH: Andrew, John A. (John Albion), 1818–1867. | Lawyers—United
States—Biography. | Lawyers—Massachusetts—Boston—Biography. |
Abolitionists—Massachusetts—Boston—Biography. | Racial
justice—Massachusetts—Boston. | Antislavery
movements—Massachusetts—Boston—History—19th century. |
Massachusetts—History—Civil War, 1861–1865.
Classification: LCC KF368.A47 E54 2023 (print) | LCC KF368.A47 (ebook) |
DDC 340.092 [B] —dc23/eng/20230712
LC record available at https://lccn.loc.gov/2023013418
LC ebook record available at https://lccn.loc.gov/2023013419

British Library Cataloguing-in-Publication Data
A catalog record for this book is available from the British Library.

Portions of the epilogue were previously published in *Final Resting Places: Reflections on the
Meaning of Civil War Graves,* ed. Brian Matthew Jordan and Jonathan W. White (Athens:
University of Georgia Press, 2023). Some information from this text was previous pub-
lished in "'Under Full Sail': John Andrew, Abraham Lincoln, and Standing by the Union,"
Massachusetts Historical Review 19 (2017): 43–81.

CONTENTS

List of Illustrations ix

Preface xi

Acknowledgments xv

CHAPTER 1 *Windham Origins: 1818–1833* 1

CHAPTER 2 *The Bowdoin College Years: 1834–1837* 14

CHAPTER 3 *The Poor Man's Lawyer: 1837–1845* 24

CHAPTER 4 *The Emerging Politician: 1846–1849* 39

CHAPTER 5 *On the Right Side of God: 1850–1854* 53

CHAPTER 6 *The Republican Tide: 1855–1856* 69

CHAPTER 7 *The Radical Champion: 1857–1858* 85

CHAPTER 8 *Republican Star Rising: 1858–1859* 100

CHAPTER 9 *The Governorship: 1860* 118

CHAPTER 10 *Man for the Hour: January–April 1861* 135

CHAPTER 11 *A Grand Era Has Dawned: April–May 1861* 148

CHAPTER 12 *Communities at War: June–September 1861* 156

CHAPTER 13 *The Politics of Command: October–November 1861* 168

CHAPTER 14 *The Lord Is Marching On: November 1861–January 1862* 178

CHAPTER 15   *The Changing War: January–July 1862*   192

CHAPTER 16   *Emancipation: July–November 1862*   207

CHAPTER 17   *Slaves No More: December 1862–May 1863*   228

CHAPTER 18   *Opening Eyes of North and South: May–December 1863*   247

CHAPTER 19   *The Promise of a New Year: January–June 1864*   263

CHAPTER 20   *This Justice: July–December 1864*   280

CHAPTER 21   *Thirteenth Amendment: January–June 1865*   297

CHAPTER 22   *Last Months in the Statehouse: July–December 1865*   315

CHAPTER 23   *Working for the Ages: January–April 1866*   335

CHAPTER 24   *Postwar Yankee: May 1866–May 1867*   350

EPILOGUE   *Children Will Call You Blessed: April 1866–October 1897*   365

Notes   385
Bibliography   467
Index   503

I know not what record of sin awaits me in the world to come—I cannot tell—but this I do know, I never despised a man because he was poor, because he was ignorant, or because he was black.

—John Albion Andrew
Oak Bluffs, Martha's Vineyard, August 1862

ILLUSTRATIONS

FIGURE 1. Bowdoin College in the 1830s   18

FIGURE 2. George Thompson   20

FIGURE 3. Leonard Grimes   32

FIGURE 4. James Freeman Clarke   35

FIGURE 5. Charles Sumner   41

FIGURE 6. Lewis Hayden   43

FIGURE 7. Governor Andrew in Boston   198

FIGURE 8. The governor of Massachusetts   210

FIGURE 9. Slave collar sent to John Andrew   255

FIGURE 10. John Andrew's library   373

FIGURE 11. John Andrew's statue   380

PREFACE

John Albion Andrew embraced one profoundly radical idea: that all men truly are created equal. He championed lost causes, loathed America's racial prejudices, and sought justice for the lowly, even when the fight was wholly unpopular. His story places slavery and abolition at the center of America's history and affirms that a life driven by justice and conviction can be timeless. Yet it is also a reminder of the national tragedy that ensued from standing up for such beliefs, as opposing factions shaped divergent paths toward their vision of the "more perfect Union" that the founding fathers had charted in the Constitution.

Throughout his life Andrew watched as the expanding republic struggled to endure half slave and half free. He recognized that slavery was incompatible with the Christian notion of inalienable human rights, yet he lived in a strident era when an emerging sectionalism was shaping questions of territorial development and challenging Americans to decide whether God or man had relegated African Americans to human chattel. Issues around slavery, abolition, the *Amistad* case, the press, and the Mexican American War heightened the young idealist's political awareness. Along with this political and cultural tumult, he was shaped by books, sermons, and a bucolic landscape. At Bowdoin College, Andrew found his true calling, not from his professors but from the British abolitionist and human rights activist George D. Thompson, who passed through Brunswick, Maine, one afternoon and delivered a fiery sermon: "I hesitate not to say that in Christian America, a land of Sabbath schools, of religious privileges, of temperance societies and rivals there exists the worst institution in the world, there is not an institution which the sun in the heaven shines upon, so fraught with woe to man as American slavery."[1] Andrew never forgot those powerful words.

As a budding Thompson disciple and reformist crusader, Andrew expressed his Christian principles through social and legal activism, working at the bar against racial injustice in Boston's public spaces and schools. He was also engaged in extralegal efforts to help fugitive slaves. Known as the "poor man's lawyer," Andrew sought to strengthen the weak, lift the fallen, comfort the downtrodden, and, especially, prevail over prejudice; and his work demonstrated that a small, rabble-rousing, but passionate faction could bring about change. He lived the axiom that Theodore Parker had made famous in his sermon "Of Justice and the Conscience" published in 1853: "I do not pretend to understand the moral universe," said Parker. "The arc is a long one, my eye reaches but little ways. I cannot calculate the curve and complete the figure by the experience of sight; I can divine it by conscience. But from what I see I am sure it bends towards justice."[2]

Eventually, however, Andrew came to believe that fundamental change could not come from the courtroom; it must come from the ballot box. He helped to establish the Free-Soil Party and the Republican Party in Massachusetts, and when elected governor, relied on his abolitionist fervor to lead his state through the Civil War. In pressing for emancipation as well as for African American enlistment and equal pay in the Union ranks, he advanced the nation's racial progress. In this way, he reflected Abraham Lincoln's belief that Americans must "think anew, and act anew" about slavery and emancipation. "We must disenthrall ourselves" from the past; "we must rise with the occasion."[3]

Andrew had spent his life rising with the occasion, as his contemporaries, including Lincoln, well knew. A Republican abolitionist, he won five successive gubernatorial elections by historic margins, which was a monumental achievement. In his view, slavery had brought on the South's rebellion; thus, the conflict must end the institution. From the beginning he saw the crisis as an opportunity to advance African Americans' status in a reunified nation dedicated to freedom for all. Neither the Union nor the Constitution could remain the same, he believed. He hoped that the war would correct the errors of previous generations and ensure a future free from shackles and racial prejudice, though he recognized that reversing decades of federal policy would be a herculean endeavor. With Lincoln, he focused on combining military and legal emancipation in Union-occupied territory, an approach that ultimately culminated in passage of the Thirteenth Amendment.

Tragically, the Commonwealth's war governor died a century before the nation could realize his vision of racial equality. For several decades after his death, commemorative gatherings honoring the war governors, the African American regiments, and Union veterans and the dead kept Andrew's significance alive. As years passed, however, this popular and beloved Bostonian faded into obscurity. Henry Greenleaf Pearson, a Portland, Maine, native and Harvard graduate, who taught English composition at the Massachusetts Institute of Technology brought Andrew into the light of day in 1904 with the publication of *The Life of John A. Andrew, Governor of Massachusetts, 1861–1865*. Percy Bicknell reviewed it for *The Dial: A Semi-monthly Journal of Literary Criticism, Discussion, and Information*, noting that "in the rather surprising lack of any previous biography of Andrew . . . Mr. Pearson's work will be welcomed as supplying a want and as probably the final and authoritative life of Massachusetts' famous war governor."[4]

Though he had been highly esteemed in his time, later historians apparently lost sight of him. Beyond a brief acknowledgment that he had raised African American regiments for the Union army, his name now hardly registers in the nation's master narrative. One exception is his brief but significant appearance in the 1989 award-winning movie *Glory* about the famed 54th Massachusetts Infantry Regiment, based on Peter Burchard's novel *One Gallant Rush* (1965) and Lincoln Kirstein's long essay "Lay This Laurel" (1973). Another is Russell Duncan's *Blue-Eyed Child of Fortune: The Civil War Letters of Robert Gould Shaw* (1992), which sheds significant light on the relationship between Shaw and Andrew. Still, the governor's legacy remains in the scholarly attic.

In 2007, Governor Deval Patrick referenced to Andrew when he became the first Black person to ascend to Massachusetts' highest state office. The Commonwealth's governors customarily hang a former governor's portrait in their chambers, someone from whom to draw inspiration. "I chose the portrait of Governor John Andrew," he said in his state of the Commonwealth address, "who came to office just before the outbreak of the Civil War and who, among other things, gave freed black men their first opportunity to serve their country as soldiers":

> It was not a popular thing for Governor Andrew to do, or for legislators then to support, but it showed political courage, and that act of courage meant something to those men, to this Nation, and to future generations. At a time of great divide in America, [Andrew] demonstrated a willingness to change the status quo and encourage others to do the same. I am proud to display his portrait, and hope that I may govern with the same compassion and foresight that he demonstrated."[5]

Why such an extraordinary American, renowned in his day as a reformer and a crusader for African American equality, been essentially forgotten remains to be seen. The renowned abolitionist, writer, and activist Julia Ward Howe called Andrew the nation's "champion in our hour of need, a prophet armed with forethought wise," and was confident his story and importance would be central to the historical contours that shaped America's most profound historical narrative.[6] In this book, I seek to bring that legacy to life. *In Pursuit of Justice* is an intimate portrait of a dedicated humanitarian and abolitionist, who governed during a defining crisis while spearheading racial change and prodding Lincoln to accept his vision. It is a remarkable story.[7]

ACKNOWLEDGMENTS

In Pursuit of Justice would never have seen the light of day without the many people who helped me along the way. Truth be told, the best thing about Florida Atlantic University is the students, and I am privileged to be teaching them about the past in hopes that they find it useful in understanding the present. My thesis students and faithful HIS 5060 Seminar disciples continue to impress me every fall, not only by their willingness to indulge my "three kinds of history" exercises but also by demonstrating their methodological showmanship in tracking scholarly change over time.

For more than three decades at Florida Atlantic University, I have called upon my colleagues to support my research, and they never disappoint me. Patty Kollander, Ben Lowe, and Doug Kanter, who succeeded me as department chair, have allowed me the time to continue my scholarship, and I am grateful to them. Hugh Ripley befriended our department when I was chair and made it possible for us to purchase the John Albion Andrew Papers on microfilm. I remain indebted to his generosity. My colleagues Sandy Norman, Boyd Breslow, Mark Rose, Eric Hanne, and Michael Zager have saved me from myself on more than one occasion. Our departmental collegiality confirms why students appreciate that learning from our faculty is as much about community and kinship as it is about teaching and scholarship. Oliver Buckton, an esteemed scholar of British literature, has been patient with my intrusions upon his time in talking about Andrew. Our conversations have benefited me more than he knows.

The unsung heroes in any project are the librarians, archivists, and staff who help scholars bring a past to life. I thank Vicky Thur,

Teresa Van Dyke, and Maris Hayashi at Florida Atlantic University, who have made my scholarly life here so pleasant. My gratitude also goes to Michelle Krowl and the entire staff of the Manuscript Division at the Library of Congress; Lisa Caprino at the Huntington Library; Cara Gilgenbach at the Kent State University Library; Mary Haegert, Noah Sheola, and Emily Walhout at Harvard University's Houghton Library; Marieke Van Der Steenhoven of the George J. Mitchell Department of Special Collections and Archives at Bowdoin College; Anne E. Deschaine at the Peabody Essex Museum's Phillips Library; Sierra Dixon and Tasha Caswell at the Chicago Historical Society and Museum; Beth Carroll-Horrocks, Catherine Gaggioli, and Elizabeth Bouvier at the Massachusetts State Archives; Michelle Ganz at the Lincoln Memorial University Archives; Diana Harper at the University of Chicago's Special Collections; Anne Dalton at the Hingham Public Library; Anne Causey at the University of Virginia Special Collections Library; Caroline White at the Robert S. Cox Special Collections and University Archives Research Center, University of Massachusetts, Amherst; Laurin Penland and Megan O'Connell at Duke University; Thai Jones at Columbia University; Brianna Cregle at Princeton University Library's Special Collections; Kimberley Reynolds and Aaron Schmidt at the Boston Public Library; Gretchen Grozier at the Jamaica Plain Historical Society; Carolle Morini of the Boston Athenaeum Society; Judy Lucey at the New England Historic Genealogical Society; Michael Achille at the Hingham Historical Society; Susan Krueger and Lee Grady at the Wisconsin Historical Society; Natalie Kelsey and Eisha Neely at Cornell University Library's Special Collections; Lindsay McGrath at the Hingham Public Library; and Thomas Knoles, Brianne Barrett, and Kimberly Toney at the American Antiquarian Society. Rebecca M. Beit-Aharon conducted research for me in the Massachusetts State Archives during the Covid pandemic, and I am thankful for her expert skills and uncanny attention to detail.

I am also indebted to those repositories, libraries, and philanthropic organizations that supported my research for this book. Several research trips were funded by Florida Atlantic University's Osher Lifelong Learning Institute and the Virginia Center for Civil War Studies, which allowed me to spend time in Blacksburg, Virginia, and study an important manuscript collection. The Gilder Lehrman Institute of American History has been a terrific supporter of my research and provided funding for this project. I am especially indebted to the Andrew Mellon Foundation for making possible my research in New England, where I spent research trips at the region's rich repositories. I was fortunate to spend many cold months in residence at the Massachusetts Historical Society in Boston, where I enjoyed the warm hospitality of its fine staff. Conrad Wright supported my work from the beginning and helped steer my way to Boston. When Conrad retired from the historical society, Kanisorn (Kid) Wongsrichanalai, replaced him and became another tremendous asset to my project.

Others who assisted me over the years deserve special thanks, including Richard P. Hawkins, Stephen Pinkerton, Kevin Caprice, Ellen Miller, and David Williams. When I discovered a cache of correspondence between Elizabeth Van Lew and Andrew, I reached out to Liz Varon for assistance in deciphering that relationship. Beyond her perceptive assessment and gracious hospitality, Liz connected me with the novelist Lois Leveen, who shared her keen insights about Van Lew. Jon White and Bill Marvel have always offered their research assistance, and I am grateful for their generosity.

I remain indebted to a small circle of dear friends. Jim Marten, Gary Gallagher, Bill Blair, Joan Waugh, Carrie Janney, Nina Silber, and Matt Gallman befriended me many years ago, and I have gained so much from our long connection. David Coles, perhaps the most learned scholar on the Civil War, has remained my friend since graduate school, and I am thankful he allows me to intrude on his time. I am also thankful to Mary McLaughlin, who invited me into the Smithsonian Institution's Associates Program, where I shared my thoughts on the Civil War and John Andrew while lecturing on various Civil War topics to very learned Washington audiences. Richard F. Miller knew John Andrew long before I did and deserves a medal for agreeing to read an initial draft of the manuscript. This book found a home with the University of Massachusetts Press because Mark Simpson-Vos introduced me to Mary Dougherty, who took an interest in Andrew from the beginning and gave me space while gently prodding me forward. *Superb* is the word that defines both Mark and Mary. I am also grateful to the staff and especially Dawn Potter, whose editing skills made this not simply a shorter work but also a better book. The manuscript's anonymous readers also deserve thanks for challenging me to expand my conclusions, even while pressing me to shorten the text. All deserve the accolades in bringing Andrew to life; the errors are mine alone.

I remain indebted to my professors Jim Jones, Joe Richardson, John E. Stealey III, and especially Hans L. Trefousse, a World War II veteran, distinguished historian, and dear friend for many years. It is said that after encountering racism in New York City in the 1950s, Hans moved his scholarly focus away from the Second World War to bring attention to the failure of America's first civil rights crusade during the nineteenth century. He devoted his life to the world the freedmen made during Reconstruction and reckoned with a sordid past that Americans found unflattering. Making sense of the years following the Civil War reminded him of his native Germany and its attempt to reunify in 1989. Hans used the period as historical architecture to establish a blueprint of the past to demonstrate a path forward in the United States. In his assertive but jovial way, he convinced me that John Andrew, like many abolitionist Republicans, had been left in the dustbin because he was too progressive for his times. It was Hans who encouraged me to write Andrew's biography, and I regret that his eyes will not fall upon these pages.

Unearthing Andrew's story allowed me to explore New England's bucolic countryside with my wife Stephanie, whose voracious reading, expansive intellect, and insightful commentary are a humbling reminder that an elementary school teacher is the real scholar in a family of veterinarians, lawyers, and professors. Our two children, Claire and Taylor, are grown now; but by being part of the solution in their own professional lives, they confirm that a life devoted to educating is a noble and honorable way of paying the advantage forward.

Stephen D. Engle
Boca Raton, Florida

IN
PURSUIT *of*
JUSTICE

CHAPTER 1

WINDHAM ORIGINS

1818–1833

John Quincy Adams and Faneuil Hall

Walking from Charles Street to Faneuil Hall, a winded John Albion Andrew hurried against a sturdy Boston gale as quickly as his stubby legs would carry him. Papers tucked in his satchel, the cold wind blowing back his swallowtail frockcoat and his curly hair, he was determined to arrive on time. The evening promised to be extraordinary. Recent events had stirred the young barrister, and he did not want to be late to the indignation meeting and miss the public address by John Quincy Adams. Adams's legendary career had inspired Andrew, not least his recent skillful argument before the Supreme Court in support of releasing the African slaves aboard the *Amistad*.

Yet tension was running through Andrew's veins. His family and friends knew him as a devout Unitarian who never missed Sunday service or weekday Bible studies, but his new social circles were exposing him to radical people and ideas. The fight against slavery was ongoing, and it distressed him. Influential abolitionists had shown him extralegal ways to work against slavery, and Andrew was becoming involved in these underground fugitive activities. Though a legal disciple, he adhered to rigid constitutional principles, he also cared deeply for the less fortunate, the underprivileged, and the downtrodden. Andrew was torn between kinship to his fellow man and his sacred oath to uphold the Constitution.[1]

The year was 1846, and recent events were polarizing the country politically. In May the United States had declared war on Mexico. By

1

August, Pennsylvania congressman David Wilmot had amplified anti-war tensions when he resolved to prohibit slavery from the territories that the United States would acquire in the presumed victory. His legislative proposition was unsuccessful, but Wilmot's name became currency among northerners who were attempting to contain slavery. By September, Bostonians found themselves protesting another congressional mandate, this one involving the abduction of a fugitive slave named George. Horrified, Henry Ingersoll Bowditch, a distinguished physician and abolitionist, invited twenty friends to his home on the evening of September 13 to gather facts and mount a response. After the guests arrived, Samuel Gridley Howe, another renowned physician, presented the details. Listening amid these antislavery stalwarts was twenty-eight-year-old Andrew, whom Bowditch had asked to chronicle the proceedings.

According to Howe, the brig *Ottoman*, owned by the Boston merchant John H. Pearson, had arrived in Boston Harbor on Tuesday, September 8. Five days after the ship had sailed from New Orleans, its captain, James W. Hannum, had discovered a stowaway named George. (The press mistakenly recorded his name as Joseph.) Louisiana law held ship captains liable for transporting people who were escaping slavery, and the only means to avoid the penalty was to return the fugitive or spend between two to ten years in jail and pay a fine equal to the enslaved person's value. Given Boston's abolitionist proclivities, the captain feared a protest, so before docking in the early morning hours, he deposited George on Spectacle Island in Boston Harbor, guarded by a trusted sailor. He then entered the harbor, went into the city, and arranged his return trip to New Orleans. He also met with the shipowner. Pearson told Hannum that he had no choice but to return George to New Orleans. He instructed the captain to move George from the island to the *Niagara*, which Pearson also owned and was about to set sail for Louisiana.[2]

In the meantime, according to Bowditch, George stole a pilot boat and headed for South Boston's Shirley Point. When the captain discovered the fugitive's escape, he tracked him down, falsely accused him of stealing a pocket watch, and told onlookers that he was taking him to jail. Instead, the captain planned to carry him onto the *Niagara* bound for New Orleans. By this time, a small but vocal crowd was following the captors and spreading the news. Bowditch explained that the abolitionist lawyer Samuel Edmund Sewall had obtained a writ of habeas corpus from Samuel Hubbard, a judge on the state's supreme court.

But the fugitive could not be found, so the court had ordered a criminal warrant against the captain under the kidnapping provision. The press reported that considerable efforts were made by "friends of freedom, by employing boats, steamers, &c., to obtain the liberation of the man, but the commercial spirit threw too many obstacles in their way, and they were defeated." Pearson declared that "he would get that man back to New Orleans if it cost him a hundred thousand dollars," wrote a reporter for the *Daily Evening Traveller*, "and the whole commercial community and the commercial press evidently sympathsie [*sic*] with him and sustain him!"[3]

Bowditch's twenty guests formally voted to revitalize Boston's Vigilance Committee. As chair, they named Boston abolitionist and Massachusetts Anti-Slavery Society member Francis Jackson, and they assigned the newcomer John Andrew to secretarial duties. Howe motioned for members to call a public meeting at Faneuil Hall, and attendees nominated Howe, Andrew, Bowditch, the journalist and writer Richard Hildreth, and Elbridge Gerry, Jr., the oldest son of founding father Elbridge Gerry, to organize the meeting. Jackson agreed to invite John Quincy Adams to preside, and Andrew sent invitations to Boston's most prominent abolitionists requesting their attendance at a September 24 indignation meeting. Ralph Waldo Emerson agreed to attend and, in his acceptance, expressed outrage at Boston merchants whose trade with the slaveowners made them accomplices in shameful crimes: "It is high time our bad wealth come[s] to an end. I shall very willingly turn to the mountains to chop wood and seek to find for myself and my children labors compatible with freedom and honor."[4]

Faneuil Hall was densely crowded, and Adams, now seventy-eight years old, was impressive. He had spent his last years in Congress working to create the Smithsonian Institute for the "increase and diffusion of knowledge," but tonight he focused on increasing and diffusing human rights. Boston was ablaze with outrage over George's case, and some 5,000 attendees cheered Adams when he took the podium, not knowing it would be his final appearance before a public audience. "Forty years ago," he said, "I stood, by the suffrages of your fathers and perhaps your grandfathers, in this same situation." He recalled an incident in which "a seaman had been taken out of an American frigate by the crew of a British man-of-war, and a similar meeting was called." At that time, he told his listeners, the question was whether the Commonwealth would maintain its independence as a state. Now he softly asked, "whether your and my native Commonwealth [are] capable of protecting the men who are under its laws, or not."[5]

Andrew found himself in the midst of a movement. As secretary, he was seated near Adams's son, Charles Francis Adams, and close to Theodore Parker, Charles Sumner, Wendell Phillips, Stephen C. Phillips, Henry Wadsworth Longfellow, and Emerson. At this event, his job was to record transactions, draft resolutions, and secure witness testimony to present evidence to a grand jury. The young attorney was eager to defend Massachusetts's laws against slavery, and he closely studied the facts, speeches, energy, and courage displayed by his fellow freedom defenders.

Rising to speak on this autumn night, Parker, a renowned reformer, abolitionist, transcendentalist, and Unitarian minister declared that "legislatures could make and unmake laws, but "there is a law of God, written on the heart, that cannot be altered or revoked,—that we should do unto another as we would that others should do unto us." Parker, Phillips, and Sumner all made the case that southerners should be held accountable. After these speeches, Howe called on Andrew to present resolutions that declared it to be the first duty of all governments to guarantee the personal safety of every individual upon their soil—that there was nothing in the institutions and laws of any foreign state or nation that could justify or excuse any violation of the smallest right or privilege of the humblest individual within Massachusetts. Members resolved to enlist citizens whose "duty it shall be to take all needed measures to secure the protection of the laws to all persons who may hereafter be in danger of abduction from this Commonwealth."[6]

Within a week, forty members of the Vigilance Committee convened at Bowditch's home for a second meeting. They reconfirmed Jackson as chair, named Bowditch secretary, and established a five-member executive committee, chaired by Howe, and a five-member finance committee, managed by Andrew. The young barrister was tasked with raising $1,000 for a general fund and offering a $100 reward to anyone who offered new information about fugitive slaves being held secretly in Boston. But they were too late to save George. While the committee was raising money and collecting testimony against the *Ottoman*'s owners, local authorities were boarding George onto the *Niagara* and returning him to his enslaver. The abolitionists had failed in their public quest, and Andrew was beginning to understand why so many took part in the moonlit work of the vast Underground Railroad.

It would be an understatement to say that these ominous times needed new leaders to fight injustice. Years later, Frank Sanborn, a noted journalist, teacher, and abolitionist, recalled that it was at these meetings that Andrew "came prominently forward" in Boston. The moment and the cause baptized a new disciple. His name was John Andrew.[7]

Windham

According to Julia Ward Howe, John Andrew was born in the Massachusetts wilderness. By that, she meant the District of Maine, then part of the Commonwealth. His birthplace was Windham, in Cumberland County, near Sebago Lake, fifteen miles from Portland. The novelist Harriet Beecher Stowe once described it as "a little, cold, poor, barren mountain town where the winter rages for six months of the year."[8] Gilbert Haven, a Methodist bishop, journalist, and long-time Andrew family friend, recalled Andrew's boyhood home as one story high and unpainted, with a flat stone step, a door in the middle, and high steep roof—"the usual sort of an old-fashioned poorish New England farmhouse."[9]

English in origin, Andrew's father, Jonathan, was both a farmer and a merchant who ran the local general store. Virtuous, frugal, and independent, the family was self-sufficient and well respected in the community. Andrew's life-long friend, Peleg Whitman Chandler, recalled Jonathan as a "man of marked character," who possessed "great intelligence" and was "judicious" by nature.[10] His general store served as a local gathering place for market exchange, news, and gossip.

Before her marriage, Nancy Pierce, Andrew's mother, taught at nearby Fryeburg Academy, one of the oldest private college preparatory schools in the United States. She was intellectually gifted, well educated, and cultured; and, as the story goes, Jonathan and Nancy enjoyed a "pretty little old-fashioned romance." On horseback to visit relatives in North Bridgton, she was trotting through Naples, a lakeside village, when the mare stumbled and threw her to the ground in front of the Chute-Church Tavern and Hotel. Onlookers rushed to her aid and brought her into the hotel. Her injuries forced her to convalesce there for days, during which time she met a guest from South Windham named Jonathan Andrew, who was visiting his brother-in-law John Chute, the hotel owner. It was love at first sight.[11]

On May 31, 1818, Nancy gave birth to her first child, John Albion Andrew, named after a maternal uncle, Albion K. Pierce. According to the essayist and popular Boston literary critic Edwin Percy Whipple, the child came from that good New England stock "in which conscience seems as hereditary as intelligence, and in which the fine cumulative results of the moral struggles and triumphs of many generations of honest lives appear to be transmitted as a spiritual inheritance." He was, Whipple declared, "in the best sense of the word, well born."[12] In 1819 Andrew's brother, Isaac Watson, was born, followed by sisters Sarah Elizabeth in 1822 and Nancy Alfreda in 1824.[13]

Andrew was a round, diminutive, blue-eyed child with curly blond hair and pale, delicate features. He was active and inquisitive but feeble, and his mother was constantly worried about his health. During his many illnesses she read to him, and he absorbed words easily, learning to talk at an early age. Nancy poured herself into his intellectual training, drilling him daily. Early on he demonstrated an aptitude for reading and was soon familiar with *The New England Primer* and the King James Bible. While Andrew had little to say about his mother in his later correspondence, others recall her as nurturing, kind, and musical, though, like her son, she was frail and chronically sick. Peleg Chandler characterized her as "altogether prepossessing in appearance ... admirable in her domestic arrangements, judicious, sensible, energetic, and a rigid disciplinarian of her children. There was a rare union of gentleness and force in this woman, which made her generally attractive, and especially endeared her to all who came under her influence."[14]

Jonathan, who tended to be stern and pious, was softened only by his beloved wife's influence. He adored Nancy, staying close, attending to her needs, and always deferring to her council. He was dismayed by his eldest son's small stature and fragile health, although Andrew never detected this disappointment. Years later Jonathan remarked that his "little governor," dwarfed by other children his age, "did not look as tho' he was worth raising." Even as a man Andrew never stood more than five feet, six inches tall, yet he was always supremely confident, thanks to those fireside readings with his mother and his family's close companionship.[15]

Andrew and his siblings spent their winters working in their father's store, sleighing in the surrounding hills, and devising ways to lighten the long, cold months. In the spring, the brothers often meandered to the Presumpscot River, where they watched the river drivers, clad in their red flannel shirts, maneuvering logs over the dam and downstream toward the sawmill. Stowe later described a "sunny-faced, curly-headed boy," always "full of fun and frolic and kind-heartedness." She recounted stories of him "patter[ing] bare-footed after the cows in the dim grey of summer mornings, how he was forward to put on the tea-kettle for mother, and always inexhaustible in obligingness, how in winter he drew the girls to school on his sled, and was doughty and valiant in defending snow forts, and how his arm and prowess were always for the weak against the strong and the right against the wrong."[16]

Jonathan Andrew was a good and honest businessman, but he was less successful as a farmer, unsuited to managing oxen and without the mechanical ability even "to make a respectable cider-trap." Shy and reticent, he was nonetheless a firm disciplinarian, with pronounced ideas about education, a contempt for meanness, and a hatred of injustice. He required rigor and obedience from his children, and the slightest transgressions fired his wrath. Shortly before her death in 1897, Andrew's sister Sarah recalled that her father had believed in "a place for everything, and everything in its place." She said, "A pitchfork in common use for foddering the cattle was always to be kept standing in a certain corner of the barn, where he could lay his hand on it in the night, without a lantern." Sarah remembered that, on one occasion, he had felt for the fork in vain and had called the boys to account. With a mixture of chagrin and amusement, they reported that "father was might particular, for that fork wasn't more'n two inches out of place."[17]

As a young boy, Andrew swept the store floor, stocked the shelves, and ran errands. When the temperance movement swept through Windham, Nancy demanded that Jonathan stop selling liquor to keep the family in the church's good graces. He agreed. As a deacon and the owner of twenty pews, he frequently opened his home to traveling ministers, and he was happy to save face with them.

He was less happy with the district school. Worried that his children were not learning what they should, he built a small schoolhouse on his farm, where Nancy served as teacher, instructing her own children along with those of her neighbors. In this humble building, painted yellow with pine benches and seats, the parents oversaw Andrew's instruction. Early on, Nancy had recognized his penchant for literature and his exceptional oratorical skills. Elias Nason, a Congregational minister, and teacher, boarded with the Andrews during those years, and he recalled Nancy's "superior intellectual ability." Yet, like her husband, she was a strict disciplinarian. Her daughter Sarah recalled an incident in which Nancy, who suffered from chronic illness, summoned Andrew home from school. When he arrived, she merely pointed at his cap, which he had carelessly left on the floor. "The hint was enough," Sarah said; "without a word he picked up the cap, hung it on the proper peg, and promptly went back to school."[18]

As Andrew matured, Nancy exposed him to the poetry of Robert Burns, Thomas Moore, and William Cowper. Among those works was

Cowper's *The Task: A Poem in Six Books*, meant to reinforce the child's Christian piety. Literature and morality served as a counterweight to grammar and mathematics. To teach the latter subjects, she enlisted her friends Almira P. Baker and Sibyl Ann Farnsworth. The boy reveled in learning, poring over Caleb Bingham's anthology, *The Columbian Orator*, which contained rules on oratory as well as texts for reading and recital. Reverend Nason remembered that books were always Andrew's inclination, not "running, leaping, boating, gunning."[19] By the time he was eleven years old, he was doing more than just devouring them; he was digesting and retaining what he had read. Eager to encourage their son, his parents put him under the tutelage of Portland Academy principal Barzillai Cushman, who taught him Latin in preparation for college.[20]

During the following summer, Jonathan became the Windham postmaster. The appointment changed his son's world. As he helped his father sort the mail, Andrew encountered pamphlets, magazines, and newspapers that reported on Andrew Jackson's contentious presidency and the lofty democratic tendencies swirling about the young republic. He learned about local political happenings and read stirring editorials about the damnable institution of slavery. He began supplementing his history, poetry, and Latin studies with the newspapers that chronicled contemporary society. In the fall of 1829, congressional debate reflected the crystallized divisions between northerners and southerners over slavery and the tariff. Jackson was not popular among New Englanders, yet Andrew saw how difficult it would be to combat the unyielding affection that many Americans had for Old Hickory. Still, despite his absorption in his reading, the boy was never aloof. Hannah Whittier, a neighbor, and a classmate, remembered him as a "bright, cheerful, amiable, and affectionate boy," often a "peacemaker."[21]

That year Nancy decided that Andrew needed a new school and sent him twenty miles away to North Yarmouth Academy. During his eleven-week session, he lived with Grenville Mellen, a lawyer, a budding poet, and a Bowdoin College trustee. Mellen had recently lost his wife and only child, and he had fallen into a deep melancholy, so Andrew's presence was a boon. After the Yarmouth term, the boy enrolled at Bridgton Academy, twenty-five miles from Windham, where he remained until the winter of 1831. It was the farthest he'd ever been from home. There he began studying French with Reverend Thomas Treadwell Stone, a Bowdoin graduate and, at that time, Bridgton's headmaster.

Andrew arrived at Bridgton as Stone's conversion to abolitionism was beginning to become evident in his sermons, and his teacher's convictions made a significant impact on the impressionable adolescent. Stone recognized that young Andrew was already "a decided politician," one who despised injustice. At Bridgton, the boy matured quickly. He was drawn to his older peers and displayed a flair for extemporaneous speaking on topics of the day. Like his father, he admired John Quincy Adams, calling himself an "Adam's man" and often arguing with local Jacksonian Democrats.[22] He enjoyed the French literature he read in Stone's classes—in particular, *The Adventures of Gil Blas*, a picaresque satire by Alain-René Lesage recounting the adventures of a poor young man who becomes a landed nobleman. Andrew thrived at the academy, enjoying its surroundings, his classmates, and his studies. Meanwhile, his younger siblings were following in his footsteps, each of them in turn attending the area's finishing schools.[23]

But there were challenges ahead. In the winter of 1831–32, Nancy became ill, and thirteen-year-old Andrew and his brother Isaac had to leave school to help with their sisters and father. Bedridden when they arrived, Nancy's condition worsened, and the family recognized that she would not recover. The boys helped at the store, did farm chores, and took care of their sisters, doing their best to keep up with their studies as they watched their mother deteriorate. On March 7, she died.

If Andrew grieved, he did so privately. There is no record of his reaction, yet we know it was an enormous loss. Gone was the affection, the gentle spirit that had defined her and comforted him. Now the boy had to soldier on, caring for his sisters, his brother, even his father, who was broken by the loss of his wife. In her absence, Jonathan worked to become a more compassionate counselor, companion, and friend to his children, especially to the boys. Nancy's influence had softened his stoicism, and her departure transformed him into a more gracious parent. It also brought out the man in his eldest son, imbuing Andrew with the emotional fortitude to lead the family. While relatives from nearby Salem stepped in to manage the post office and the store, the boy attended to his father's correspondence and his family's care. Yet his mother's death remained a profound blow, and Andrew would return to her grave at least once every year until he died.[24]

Andrew's mother had nurtured him intellectually and emotionally. His father was girding him for an unforgiving world, one that demanded self-reliance, self-restraint, and self-discipline. Amid the Jacksonian fever sweeping across the United States, Jonathan saw himself as a protector of values, a voice of restraint in the face of moral corruption, and his sons embraced their father's moral tenets, including his antislavery views. As Andrew matured intellectually, he also gained confidence in his ability to share and expand these views. When speaking to others, he was candid, blunt, and curious about the currents of social reform swirling throughout New England. He pored over the *Christian Mirror*, a weekly religious newspaper published by the Maine Missionary Society under the editorship of Asa Cummings. Isaac later recalled that "to go for the mail in which [the paper] was due became the chief excitement of his week."[25] Cummings was Harvard-educated, a former Bowdoin College tutor, and a pastor at North Yarmouth Congregational Church. He was a revered preacher, and members of the Andrew family frequently sat in his congregation. Under his leadership, the *Christian Mirror* became the region's antislavery and temperance organ, and it helped Andrew develop a firm enmity to the peculiar institution.[26]

America in the early 1830s was a republic in search of a national identity. Thus, it was a time filled with fervent voices. Among them was the printer-journalist William Lloyd Garrison, a prominent social reformer and abolitionist who was zealous in his work to drive slavery out of the republic. In 1831, at the age of twenty-five, he launched his newspaper, the *Liberator*, with the goal of attracting national attention to the slaves' cause. Biblically inspired, Garrison used his paper to advance antislavery democracy, and he covered all relevant recent events and publications, among them David Walker's *Appeal to the Colored Citizens of the World*, Virginia's legislative debates over slavery, and Nat Turner's rebellion in South Hampton, Virginia. At age fifteen, Andrew was a decade younger than Garrison, but he read the *Liberator* and it reinforced his convictions. Preachers had shown him that God was a God of justice for all creatures. This "truth," as his brother Isaac remembered him characterizing it, was "mighty and would prevail."[27]

Contemporary literature was also addressing the issue of slavery, and this, too, attracted Andrew's interest. When the poet John Greenleaf Whittier's antislavery pamphlet *Justice and Expediency; or Slavery Considered with a View to its Rightful Remedy, Abolition* appeared in 1833, it influenced the teenager significantly. That same year, Lydia Maria Child published *An Appeal in Favor of That Class of Americans Called Africans*, which advocated immediate abolition without compensation to enslavers. Because her message was aimed specifically at white American prejudices, Andrew gave a copy to his younger sisters with an inscription that captured his thoughts on humankind and enslavement:

> To my two sisters, this little volume is affectionately presented, with the fervent aspiration that the instruction contained in it, and inculcated by one of the gifted ones of their own sex, may prompt their hearts to

pity for the oppressed African, may uproot all prejudice that may be implanted there against those immortal beings, whose only crime is that of being unfortunate and having a skin of a darker hue than their own, and may teach them to remember that "of one blood, God made all the nations of the earth."[28]

Gorham Academy

In the fall, the Andrew brothers were ready to enter school again, so Jonathan arranged to keep them close to home, enrolling them at nearby Gorham Academy. It was an excellent choice. The school's alumni included men of distinction such as Henry Ward Beecher and Calvin Stowe, and Longfellow had briefly worked there. Founded in 1806, it served as the college preparatory academy for Bowdoin College, teaching boys English, Greek, Latin, geography, astronomy, and other subjects, including moral instruction. Gorham's admission qualifications were simple: candidates had to demonstrate high moral character and pay tuition for one quarter in advance of matriculation.[29]

Albion enrolled in September 1832 and came under the tutelage of Reuben Nason, a Harvard-educated minister and former Bowdoin president, whose eccentric personality and strong disciplinary style made a lasting impression on him. Nason's pupils received instruction in reading, writing, arithmetic, English grammar and composition, speaking, geography, the use of globes, and mathematics. In addition, he lectured them weekly on Christian doctrine. Although Nason was genial to those who followed the academy's strict codes, he was quick to physically punish idle and mischievous students. An enthusiastic classicist, he drilled the boys in Latin and Greek so that they could pass Bowdoin's oral entrance examination.

Pupils spent all day in school but enjoyed three week-long vacations annually, in August, January, and May. To ensure that "the minds of the students may not be diverted from those pursuits which ought, during the hours of study, to engage their undivided attention," the school declared that "no prints, playthings, books of amusements, etc., shall be brought into the Academy under penalty of forfeiture." Both in school and in public boys were to conduct themselves as gentlemen, "abstain from all quarreling and contention among themselves, [and] from insulting or abusive language," and "cultivate a spirit of concord and unanimity, and to consider each other as brothers of one common family, remembering 'to do to others as they wish others to do to them.'" Students honored the Sabbath by attending both morning and evening services.[30]

At Gorham Academy, the brothers honed their skills for college, the future for which their mother had prepared them. Andrew entered the academy as one of just thirty-three students, but he was poised, confident, and enthusiastic. He embraced the headmaster's rigor and the classical curriculum, diving into the work of Latin poets, historians, and statesmen. He read Frederic Jacob's *Greek Reader* as well as the Greek Testament. Contemporaries remembered him as an inquisitive student, adept at tackling complex problems by asking his teachers the "why and wherefore and the reason of the things they taught him."[31]

Except during the harshest winter weeks, the boys were day students, driving to school in a yellow-bodied chaise pulled by a white horse or riding on horseback, always remembering to take along their dinners and hay. These were enchanting days; Isaac recalled that, on their journeys, they took turns driving or studying and that, when not driving, Andrew read books or recited poetry. Among his favorites were Charles Sprague's *Curiosity: A Poem* and *Fifty Years Ago*, a Fourth of July celebration. Years later Isaac remained impressed by his brother's extraordinary memory and dramatic oratory. On Sundays, at the old meetinghouse on the hill where the family worshipped, Andrew was fascinated by the eloquent minister Elijah Kellogg. The reverend was captivating, recalled Isaac, his brother's "admirable power of mimicry" could reproduce those sermons almost verbatim in words, style, and manner. Kellogg often cited scriptures about being thy brother's keeper and honoring the Sabbath. Andrew's versions were so impressive that, on rainy Sundays, local children would come together to listen to him preach his own sermons in Kellogg-like fashion.[32]

The boy became known locally for his eloquence, verbal mastery, and debating skills, so much so that temperance leaders invited him to give an address at the Windham church. Isaac recalled an afternoon scene in front of a packed house, when his brother "rose to his feet, cool, calm and collected, with the dignity of a man, and the modesty of a child, and began." Andrew drew a stark comparison between the child "who is early taught to partake of alcoholic drinks and following him along his downward career he pictured his wretched end" and those who chose temperance early on and lived a long and upward life. Still a "short, fat, chubby, curly headed little fellow," the boy "stood in that old church and with earnestness and eloquence gesticulating with his right arm, he advocated the cause of temperance and besought the young as well as the old, to beware of strong drink." Isaac said that "the company was held almost spell-bound"; and when Andrew finished, one church elder commented, "Albion beats us all."[33]

Such moments demonstrated that the household was recovering its equilibrium after the loss of Nancy. In the words of family friend Clara Bancroft Beatley, "the comfort of the father in the companionship of this son was great and cheer was gradually restored to the bereaved household." She continued: "From just such devotion to a mother's memory, appreciation of a father's need, and willingness to sacrifice his own pleasures for the good of brothers and sisters, the character of the great man was made."[34]

Andrew thrived at Gorham, in part because he became friendly with Cyrus Woodman, a native of Buxton, who had returned from a brief stint at Bowdoin to hone his preparatory skills for readmission. Quiet and reserved, Woodman was drawn to Andrew's affable demeanor, yet in appearance and character they made a curious pair. Woodman was tall, lean, impeccably dressed, an exterior that belied his gloom, insecurity, and pessimism. Andrew's chubby, slovenly appearance gave little indication of his dramatic, extroverted confidence, which often dispelled Woodman's disconsolate outlook. When it came to politics, the two were polar opposites. Though Andrew looked like a heedless Democrat, his father had raised him with national-republican principles. Woodman resembled a cosmopolitan sophisticate but came from by a Jacksonian family. Despite their differences, however, Andrew took the lead in cultivating a friendship that would last a lifetime. When Woodman graduated from the academy and moved on to Bowdoin, Andrew worked harder than ever to prepare for his collegiate future in Brunswick. In a note to Woodman in the fall of 1833, he said, "I have got more than half of 80 pages of the first book of Livy, some in Xenophon, and I am now going at Algebra, and I have been reviewing [the] Greek reader a little." He begged, "Please to find out what they are doing," and if "any one asks for me, just tell them I am in the land."[35]

CHAPTER 2
||||||||||||||||||||||||||||||||

THE BOWDOIN COLLEGE YEARS
1834–1837

Parade Grounds

As Andrew reviewed his Greek lessons, the country was changing all around him. In the early 1830s, the cotton industry was booming in the South, paralleled by the demand for weaving labor in the North. Slavery was overspreading the young nation, as evidenced by the slave pens and auction blocks near Capitol Hill. As punishment for his 1831 insurrection, and to deter future uprisings, Nat Turner was hanged, then drawn, quartered, and beheaded, and his skin was flayed for souvenirs. Jackson won reelection in 1832, but at a high price, as the nullification crisis with South Carolina pushed the nation toward open warfare. The president had objected to extending federal powers beyond what the Constitution allowed, yet there were spirited debates about the enforcement of the federal tariff over a state's right to nullify such a mandate. The impasse ended in compromise in 1833, the same year the British abolished slavery in their empire. That fall, some 1,500 anti-abolitionists rioted in New York City to protest William Lloyd Garrison's lecture at Arthur and Lewis Tappan's Anti-Slavery Society. The situation was so serious that the military had to suppress them. Even in free territories, dismantling slavery was a herculean undertaking, one that aggravated not only southerners but also the many northerners who had not coalesced against the institution. Nonetheless, the anti-slavery chorus was intensifying in New England, and Andrew followed its call.

By 1834, Senator Henry Clay of Kentucky had founded a new party in opposition to the Jacksonian Democrats and the president's veto of the Second National Bank. These self-proclaimed Whigs took their name from the English party that had opposed King George III in the eighteenth century. Led by Clay and Massachusetts senator Daniel Webster, who had had a distinguished career as a lawyer before the Supreme Court, the Whigs favored the interventionist economic program known as the American system, which endorsed protective tariffs, a national bank, and federal subsidies for internal improvements.[1]

Meanwhile, Gorham Academy had prepared Andrew for college, and in February 1834, the nearly sixteen-year-old freshman arrived at Bowdoin College's tiny campus in Brunswick, Maine. The college was embroiled in politics when he arrived. Just the year before, Supreme Court Justice Joseph Story had presided over the landmark case *William Allen v. Joseph McKeen*, which had settled a long, ambiguous dispute over whether Maine legislators had governance power over Bowdoin. The situation had begun in 1831, when William Allen, president of the college and a Congregational minister, refused to resign after quarreling with the board of trustees. Influential board members had succeeded in getting the legislature to pass a law forbidding any college president in the state to continue in office unless reelected by his college board with a two-thirds majority. In the Supreme Court decision, however, Justice Story applied the 1819 Dartmouth College ruling that asserted a college's autonomy as a private corporation, and Allen retained his position.[2]

When Andrew arrived, Allen was presiding over 240 students, a hundred of whom were studying medicine. Haughty, pious, and arrogant, he was unpopular on campus, but graduates of his practical curriculum were well equipped in both mind and soul. The college had six professors, including Longfellow, a Bowdoin alumnus who had graduated a decade earlier and had just completed his first book. Recently returned from Europe, he was now compiling short essays about his exploits, a collection titled *Outre-Mer: A Pilgrimage beyond the Sea*, styled after Washington Irving's *The Sketch Book of Geoffrey Crayon*. However, he was absent during most of Andrew's second year, preparing for his new professorship at Harvard College, so the new student had little exposure to the esteemed teacher.[3]

Gorham had schooled Andrew well for Bowdoin's admission requirements, which also compelled candidates to produce certificates of good moral character. In September, proctors administered entrance examinations on the day before the college's commencement ceremony, which opened the fall term. Bowdoin divided their semesters into three terms, fall, spring, and summer, with vacations in September, the third week of December, and the last two weeks of May.[4]

Like most New England colleges, Bowdoin catered to the sons of wealthy conservatives and the political elite, and Andrew felt out of place. Annual tuition in the 1830s was $119, which must have been a significant financial burden for his family. Some classmates remembered his arrival on campus and watching his family unpack a crude country wagon. As the he alighted from the cart, they commented on his "immense corporosity." Even his familiar name changed: though he had been known at home as Albion, people at Bowdoin began calling him John, and the new moniker stuck.[5]

More than five hundred men had graduated from Bowdoin, and many of its distinguished alumni had gone on to become professors and college presidents. Yet the campus was not impressive. Massachusetts Hall was a simple, three-story brick structure, flanked by a two-story wooden chapel whose second floor contained the college library. Two other large buildings in the quadrangle, Maine Hall and North College Hall, housed the undergraduates. The college was dominated by a rigid Calvinist climate, which emphasized predestination and justification by faith alone. Students' daily regimen was strict. It began at 6 a.m., when chapel bells summoned students to a fifteen-minute service, and ended at 5:30 p.m., when they collected students for evening prayer. The freshmen had a demanding course load. Their first-term readings included the *Anabasis* of Xenophon, Titus Livius' monumental *History of Rome*, Sylvestre Lacroix's *Arithmetic*, and William Smyth's *Algebra*. Second-term studies included Alexander Adam's *Roman Antiquities* as well as more algebra and Roman history texts. The third term required yet more algebra, Levi Hedge's *Logic*, Herodotus' *History of the Persian Wars*, and the historical works of Marcus Velleius Paterculus and Quintus Curtius Rufus. First-year students translated English into Latin weekly; second years translated Latin into English weekly. The Bowdoin library was one of New England's finest but was open for only one hour per day and did not loan books, so Andrew spent his time studying either in his room or outdoors.[6]

Though he was intellectually prepared for Bowdoin's academic rigor, Andrew, like many freshmen, did not work hard at his studies. Instead, he occupied his time with religious and social activities. He joined the praying circle, which no doubt made his father happy, but he soon found the group's discussions and fundamental doctrines to be boorish. He attended chapel but lost interest and instead was drawn to Brunswick's Unitarian church, where Longfellow taught Bible classes.

He was a work in progress—intellectually, spiritually, and socially—and he did not always adhere to proper etiquette. After he sent his first letter to his father, beginning with "Dear Father" and ending with "Yours Affectionately," Jonathan edited and returned it, reminding his son that he should have written "Honored Sir" and "Your dutiful son." Andrew never made that mistake again.[7]

Andrew was popular among his classmates and developed several close friendships, including with his roommate, Ammi Bradbury from Auburn. Another friend was Dorchester, Massachusetts, native Henry Gardner, who recalled that Andrew was "even fatter" in college than he was later in life but had a "beautiful face." Except "for rather pronounced spectacles which he always wore, it would have been strikingly handsome." Gardner recalled, "his hair was wonderful, it was very abundant, of a rich auburn tint, and was a mass of curls."[8] Andrew grew closest to Jordan G. Ferguson of South Berwick and to his old friend Cyrus Woodman. Though classes and lectures consumed the day, the three found time for fun, which often meant pranking their classmates. One night, Woodman and fellow classmates, of which Andrew was surely one, disguised themselves with burnt cork and old clothes and built a bonfire of wood shavings and other flammable materials (including college property) inside an old tar barrel. Andrew may also have belonged to a secret club of pranksters known as the "Old Dominion" who occasionally dressed in costumes and raided local farms, once even the president's garden. Woodman recalled that Andrew was at his best when outfitted in an apron, with sleeves rolled up "and his curly blond hair tumbling across his forehead," hatching some scheme. Despite the temperance fervor of his younger days, Andrew now sometimes partook of the "good creature rum," and the classmates dubbed their dormitory "Sodom."[9]

Andrew was aware of his father's expectations, but he also reveled in the new social opportunities at Bowdoin as well as the opportunity to pursue his interests in history, poetry, music, debate, and free thought. He enjoyed lounging with his friends, talking and reading. Every day he committed several poems to memory, and he even published a poem of his own in the *Juvenile Reformer*, a short-lived Portland periodical. Andrew frequented the college's literary societies, among them the Peucinian Society, one of the nation's oldest, which hosted fortnightly debates on statesmanship, culture, and political thought. Its chief rival on campus was the Athenaean Society, which, according to legend, was founded by a disgruntled Peucinian, who, after failing to graduate, formed a subscription library and purchased books with the dues.

FIGURE 1. Bowdoin College in the 1830s. Courtesy of George J. Mitchell Department of Special Collections, Bowdoin College Library.

The Athenaean Society was less orthodox than the Peucinian Society but had similar intellectual and literary standards, and an intense rivalry existed between the two. By 1836, Andrew's poetic talents had so impressed his classmates that he was invited to join the Athenaean Society and deliver a poem on its anniversary.[10]

Andrew had less interest in other campus activities. Although he was a gifted orator and drawn to righteous argument, he did not participate in the debate club known as the Theological Society. He found the topics mundane and narrow. Indeed, despite his aptitude for preaching, he was suffocated by Bowdoin's denominational atmosphere. Instead, he devoted his energy to issues of slavery, abolition, and politics. During these years he even wrote a poem titled "Hymn to Peace." His views so impressed Thomas Cogswell Upham, a professor and philosopher, that Upham encouraged the young man to establish a chapter of the American Peace Society on campus. Andrew also came under the spell of Samuel Phillips Newman, a professor of rhetoric and oratory, studies that embraced literature.[11]

In his free time Andrew played checkers, backgammon, and whist. At one point he attended a show by the traveling circus Saltando. Some classmates later recalled that, in 1837, he organized the famous "mock mustering" protest to highlight the Maine legislature's decision to force students into militia training. When students appeared on the parade grounds for their required "May training," "there was an amazing diversity of uniform from the commander down to the meekest Freshman in the extreme rear rank." The tactic of having them all dress in costume was "at once extraordinary and impressive," recalled an observer, "while the addresses of those in command were marvelous forays on all known vocabularies." The mandate soon faded, but the "pomp and circumstance" was so popular that an annual burlesque continued as a Bowdoin tradition for twenty years. Andrew had left his mark, as silly as it seemed.[12]

George Thompson

Though Andrew was indifferent to academic honors, he rapidly matured intellectually, in large part because of his participation in Bowdoin's social advocacy clubs. There were several on campus, including the conservative Colonization Society, but Andrew's particular focus was the Anti-Slavery Society, a smaller group that endorsed abolition. Always an admirer of fiery and charismatic preaching, he came to recognize that a virtuous message and powerful rhetoric were ways to engage an audience. He learned this firsthand in October of his freshman year, when the Anti-Slavery Society assembled to hear a speech by the British minister and abolitionist George Thompson, who was touring New England. Following his address, Thompson sat with students and discussed his views on slavery. The minister's passion so enthralled Andrew that the young student copied out Thompson's words and memorized them.[13]

One passage particularly resonated. "Sirs," Thompson had thundered, "I hesitate not to say, that in Christian America, the land of the Sabbath schools, of religious privileges, of temperance societies and revivals, there exists the worst institution in the world. There is not an institution which the sun in the heaven shines upon, so fraught with woe to man as American slavery."[14] Afterward Andrew "dreamed by night, and mused in leisure hours, and read and thought by day, and wondered" if this terrible American institution "would forever last, and if it would cleave like the dead carcass to the living body, to the name and fame, and fortunes, and future of my country."[15]

FIGURE 2. George Thompson. Courtesy of Special Collections, Fine Arts Library, Harvard University.

Andrew was just sixteen years old that fall, but he had already chosen a reformer's path. According to his classmate Elias Bond, on more than one occasion Andrew would stand outside in the grounds or in the open window of his room and regale listeners with a reprise of Thompson's lecture. Bond said that "it was generally agreed that listening to these soliloquies, the re-delivery of the lecture was scarcely a whit inferior to the original presentation in its rhetorical finish."[16] Another contemporary recalled, "John Albion Andrew allied himself very early to principles of eternal truth and justice, and lived by them loyally, to the end." In an album kept by a Bowdoin classmate, Richard Pike, Andrew wrote, "Pike: May you ever be the poor man's friend, the champion of the slave, a preacher of righteousness and a son of God."[17]

In 1836, Andrew entered his third year at Bowdoin. His first-term studies included Horace, Homer's *Iliad*, James Wood's *Principles of Mechanics*, and Greek. In his second term he explored calculus, electricity, magnetism, optics, and Marcus Tullius Cicero's *Tusculan Questions*. In his final term, he continued to study Homer and calculus and added William Rawle's *View of the Constitution of the United States* and Emmerich de Vattel's *Law of Nations*. Juniors and seniors were required to engage in forensic disputations, write English compositions, and deliver public declamations, all of which played to Andrew's strengths. His performance earned him an invitation to deliver a Commencement Day poem to the seniors:

> The Road to Honor—
> Straight and narrow as the way to heaven
> Soon shall we take each other's hand,
> And speak the sad good bye,
> And we may roam o'er sea and land,
> Far from each of our College Band
> Of warmest, purest, truest friends:
> But all shall meet,
> Where never ends communion sweet;
> And pleasure high,
> Where friends ne'er part,
> Nor say good bye.[18]

The Bowdoin years had solidified the friendship between Andrew and Woodman; but when Woodman graduated in 1836, he decided to move to Boston and make law his profession. He took an apprenticeship in the office of William Hubbard and Francis Watts, matriculated at Harvard Law School, and was eventually admitted to the Suffolk County bar.[19] Meanwhile, Andrew spent one more year at Bowdoin. It was his most difficult year, and he struggled without his best friend. In his first term he studied astronomy, mathematics, William Paley's *Natural Theology or Evidences of the Existence and Attributes of the Deity*, and

Upham's *Mental Philosophy*. In the second term he studied chemistry with Parker Cleaveland, a renowned and popular professor, and also undertook courses on Hebrew, political economy, and moral philosophy, which required him to read Dugald Stewart's *The Active and Moral Powers of Man*, Joseph Butler's *Analogy of Religion, Natural and Revealed*, and Upham's *A Philosophical and Practical Treatise on the Will*.[20]

Andrew continued his affiliation with the Praying Circle, as recorded by a classmate, Dean Andrews, who kept the group's journal. Its entries for that spring include notes on a lively lecture presented by Alpheus Spring Packard, Sr., a Bowdoin graduate and a professor of ancient language and classical literature. But Andrew still engaged in mischief, teaming up with another senior, the New Yorker Fordyce Barker, in transgressions such as cutting chapel, missing meetings, allegedly singing obscene songs, and using profane language. Their behavior was so blatant that the board of trustees required them to explain their overall "unseemly levity in speech and behavior."[21] Andrew appeared before the board to answer the accusations, but "rose before they were presented, stated that he was obliged to leave in a few minutes, and, by permission, read a formal protest." Then he left the room. He refused to be publicly admonished, and his colleagues in the Prayer Circle were incensed, though he later agreed to effect a reconciliation. Louis Clinton Hatch, who became a historian of the college, defended Andrew's actions, recalling that there were no recorded instances of his use of obscenities and explaining that he was "barely nineteen." As "a jolly, fun-loving youth . . . he may have allowed himself to use indecent language, but such conduct does not seem in accordance with his nature; and doubtless the Circle, which disapproved of going to the post office on Sunday, was easily shocked." By this time, Andrew was regularly attending Brunswick's Unitarian church, which no doubt also infuriated his circle colleagues.[22]

Bowdoin had challenged Andrew, but he made his way through to the end and was one of forty-one seniors to graduate in 1837. At that time, Bowdoin required each graduate to take part in the ceremony, but Andrew disliked the accompanying elitist pomp. He was among the many students who petitioned against fulfilling these parts unless the president dispensed with making distinctions in rank. Andrew's collegiate record had been less than stellar, yet he came away with a sense of purpose: to pursue a legal career that would allow him to advance the humanitarian reforms he embraced. One observer recalled that Andrew's mind was on the world beyond Bowdoin, not on his class standing. As he had done throughout his life, he strolled through the local countryside, observing his surroundings and engaging with everyone he met. "His mirthful love knew no bounds," a friend remembered. "He made everybody happy around him, and frequently the boys would sit up till midnight around the open fire to listen to his stories."[23] He had ripened his thoughts about justice and injustice, right and wrong, morality and immorality, and that summer he gave a Fourth of July speech in the Brunswick Unitarian church on the antislavery cause, his first public address on the topic.[24]

Classmates recalled Andrew's "ready wit, good nature, fair scholarship, [and] easy style of speaking." He was a "social, genial, warm-hearted-lad," always content with himself and true to his morals. Friends treasured his charm, his skills with words, and his budding public ambitions. He loved debate, possessed a quick mind, and was fearless in advocating against injustice. To one classmate he penned a few profound words in his graduation album: "Stand fast, hold on, fear not; a few bullet-holes through the body of reformers, though they destroy mortal life, are only so many sky-lights for the truth to shrine through,—and so much the sooner will its light illumine the nations."[25]

With confidence and determination, he wrote to his brother that he was eager to pursue a law career. "You would not change places with me, nor I with you perhaps, having each chosen the path best suited for us," he told Isaac. "However, if when I get to studying law, hard work, close attention and all the effort I am capable of making will do anything, I shall give my friends no reason to blush."[26] Woodman returned to Bowdoin to see his best friend graduate. After the ceremony, Andrew packed his trunk, and the two headed south. When they reached Portland, the former classmates parted ways, but they would soon meet again in Boston, where John Andrew would begin a new chapter.[27]

CHAPTER 3

THE POOR MAN'S LAWYER

1837–1845

Boston Lawyer

As Andrew developed his intellect, his spirituality, and his quirks at Bowdoin, his siblings, Isaac, Sarah, and Alfreda, carried on the family business and did what they could to comfort their widowed father. Isaac became the head of the family and shifted his focus from the farm to the store in order to pay for Andrew's tuition and the girls' schooling. By the time Andrew graduated in 1837, Isaac had persuaded his father to sell the store and move to Boxford, Massachusetts, twenty-five miles north of Boston, where Jonathan's extended family lived. After leaving Brunswick, Andrew joined them briefly in Boxford and for a while considered studying law with his cousin John Forrester Andrew, a prominent lawyer in Salem. Woodman's influence, however, was stronger, and so was the prospect of studying in Boston. "I know of nothing that would make me more happy," Andrew told his friend, "than to study and live near you."[1]

When Andrew arrived in Boston, he was confident about his future in the bustling city. Yet a financial panic had seized the country: banks were failing, unemployment was soaring, and ethnic tensions had flared. Boston became a flashpoint. In June, violence erupted between Irish-Catholic immigrants and the city's Protestant firemen. In what became known as the Broad Street Riot, more than 800 residents vandalized homes and stores and terrorized their occupants. Although no one died, a Boston *Atlas* reporter described it as a scene "seldom witnessed in the streets, much less in the dwellings of a civilized Christian city."

That summer, Bostonians were also caught up in numerous abolitionist demonstrations, some of which included mixed groups of white activists and African American radicals. They loudly protested Texas annexation and independence, which they feared would expand slavery and skew the congressional balance of power in the South's favor. The tumult that summer was not simply linked to ethnic tensions and opposition to slavery but also arose from the infamous gag rule in the House of Representatives, which forced congressmen to table discussions and petitions related to slavery. John Quincy Adams opposed this act, but neither he nor other northerners could prevail over southern leaders.[2]

Andrew landed in a city that was in an identity crisis over slavery. Garrison's *Liberator* had been steadily attacking southern enslavers and their northern enablers, and his sustained offensive was fueling a conservative backlash that often turned violent. In 1835, Garrison himself had barely escaped death when an anti-abolitionist mob in Boston had attempted to lynch him. The editor was badgering northerners to call for racial equality and an immediate end to slavery, arguing that anyone "not with us is against us." As a result, conservatives called him a radical and an instigator and maintained that his inflammatory approach would embolden enslavers and disrupt the economic ties between New England and the South. Seeking common ground, the Unitarian minister William Ellery Channing had composed a compelling and widely circulated pamphlet condemning both slavery and the abolitionists' tumultuous means of ending it, recommending instead a milder, more thoughtful approach. Dubbed a "gradualist," he came under severe attack from the "immediatists" who wanted to publicly shame enslavers into ending the institution at once.[3]

Andrew quickly found himself in a political and cultural fray. He grasped that the new abolitionist activism was not popular in the electoral culture and that it had hardened northern conservative opinion against the antislavery movement. Even more alarming was the radical turn to violence. In November 1837, newspapers reported that a pro-slavery mob had attacked and killed Elijah Lovejoy, a Presbyterian minister and abolitionist newspaper editor in Alton, Illinois. Lovejoy was a Maine native, well known in Boston abolitionist circles, and the murder had deep local and national repercussions. When Ohio resident John Brown, later to become famous in the Harpers Ferry raid, learned of it during a church prayer meeting, he vowed, "Here, before God, in the presence of these witnesses, from this time, I consecrate my life to the destruction of slavery."[4]

This was not Andrew's first time in Boston. Still, navigating the city was a far greater challenge than wandering among Brunswick's sleepy streets. At this period Boston was the nation's fifth largest, a thriving port and manufacturing center, and its 90,000 residents represented a wide spectrum of classes and backgrounds. Andrew's own background was modest, rural, and democratic, but Boston was ruled by an aristocratic elite who towered above commoners such as himself. It was also far more diverse than rural Maine. Not only did Andrew encounter his first African American community in Boston, but he also witnessed intense urban poverty. Still, he recognized the advantages of his good education, which would give him the ability to assist the less fortunate. He felt a responsibility to heed his father's advice to attend to "thy Christian neighbor."

As soon as Andrew arrived in Boston, Woodman walked him to the Court Street law office of Fuller and Washburn and introduced him to Henry H. Fuller, who took on the newcomer as an apprentice.[5] It was an ideal situation. Forty-six years old, Fuller was an accomplished lawyer who had graduated second in his class from Harvard. He was rumored to have argued more cases than any other Massachusetts lawyer of his age and was known for his legal ingenuity and his devotion to his clients. Like Andrew, Fuller had a passion for reading and speaking, and he had contributed Greek and Latin verse and English prose to the *Harvard Lyceum*, a literary magazine. His legal knowledge was vast, his judgment sound, and his courtroom prowess unrivaled. The son of a clergyman, Fuller squared his life by his Unitarian precepts. He was incorruptible and conscientious to a fault, but what influenced Andrew most was his charity and generosity. His Court Street office served as a kind of halfway house for young lawyers, where he was both a disciplinarian and an exacting mentor. Andrew felt privileged to have come under his tutelage. Yet there was one glaring divide between them: Fuller was a staunch conservative, and thus the two seldom discussed politics, concluding that the law was above their political differences. Andrew gained great insight from this relational experience, and in later years it helped him better manage conservatives as he was pulling together a new political party.[6]

Andrew lodged with Woodman, sharing a tiny attic room at Mrs. Blodgett's Howard Street boardinghouse. There he reunited with his Bowdoin classmate Peleg Whitman Chandler, and the three aspiring lawyers settled into bachelor life. Despite noisy arguments in their attic and Andrew's jokes and early morning singing, the "Bowdoin Boys" became favorites with Mrs. Blodgett. Andrew's finances were spartan: he had little money to waste on entertainment so instead spent his time studying, analyzing the legal texts and opinions that Fuller had assigned him, and discussing briefs with his friends. The three devoured the daily news and debated current events, politics, and antislavery issues, their talk often triggered by the lectures they attended at the Lyceum. But primarily Andrew focused on work. He would arrive at the office early, and Fuller would quiz him daily on his studies. Then he would spend the morning hours reading, take a break for lunch, and read again until dark.[7]

Given Andrew's proclivities, it seems likely that he soon became familiar with Boston's reformist circles, which drew visionaries such as Henry Ingersoll Bowditch, Samuel Gridley Howe, Julia Ward Howe, Theodore Parker, Thomas Wentworth Higginson, Charles Sumner, Richard Henry Dana, Jr., and Wendell Phillips. Most were fervent, even radical, abolitionists, who supported racial equality and actively recruited trustworthy newcomers into their fold. As Andrew made his way into these circles, members welcomed him, aware of his concern for the downtrodden and the disadvantaged.[8] Even as he ground away at his law studies, his connections to the antislavery movement grew. He followed the news closely and took a notable interest in Angelina and Sarah Grimké's work. The daughters of a wealthy South Carolina slaveholder, the sisters spent 1837 traveling throughout Massachusetts, speaking about their experiences with slavery and convincing 20,000 women to sign a petition calling for an immediate end to the institution. Angelina presented the petition to the Massachusetts legislature in February 1838—the first woman to address a legislative body. Whether onlookers were appalled or spellbound, her actions showed the public that abolitionist women were "turning the world upside down."[9] Impressed by the sisters' advocacy for abolition and women's rights, Garrison published many of their letters in the *Liberator*. That same fall he moved his family and the newspaper to Boston, where they found a renewed reformist spirit as well as a virulent coalition of oppositionists.[10]

In 1840, Andrew passed his examinations and was admitted to the Suffolk County bar. Confidently he stepped out onto his own, taking a second-floor office at 19 Court Street, which he shared with the eccentric lawyer Neal Dow. The new firm focused on litigating civil cases, and Fuller observed his protégé's work. In October 1841, impressed with what he saw, he invited Andrew to rejoin his office as a partner. Andrew agreed, and the two embarked on a fruitful working relationship, thriving despite their political differences. Andrew's position at the firm brought him into contact with Fuller's pioneering niece,

Margaret Fuller, who had moved to Boston in 1836 to teach Latin, French, and Italian. In 1840, Emerson invited her to edit his transcendentalist journal, *The Dial*. During her time as editor, she lived with her uncle and likely visited the law office. Eight years older than Andrew, she was already famed as a journalist and a women's suffrage activist, and the young lawyer was surely familiar with her work.

As a lawyer, Andrew was drawn to tenant-landlord disputes, and he quickly developed a kinship with the renters, who were often impoverished. Meanwhile, Henry Fuller honed his junior partner's skills, transforming the untidy, impulsive student into a professional public servant. According to Chandler, the partners became like brothers, despite their vast age difference. Andrew took direction from Fuller, appreciating his partner's strong opinions and sharing his legal views. Slavery was the issue on which they differed. A gradualist, Fuller "stood by the ancient ways," Chandler recalled, "even in the cut of his coat and the shape of his hat."[11]

As an adult, Andrew remained physically small. At five feet, six inches tall, he was "an inch shorter than the average height for a man." Acquaintances recalled his "round, good-humored face, with keen penetrating eyes beneath a brow as finely sculptured as that of a Greek statue, and closely curling hair above it." "He was broad-shouldered, remarkably so," noted a friend, "and had a strong figure but not a strong constitution." Friends remember that "his hands were soft and as white as a woman's; and though his step was quick and elastic, he disliked walking long distances and was averse to physical exercise generally." He retained his father's moral rectitude: according to Frank Preston Stearns, son of the abolitionist George Luther Stearns, who later became one of Andrew's closest friends, he "considered the saving of a human soul more important than rescuing a human life."[12] Yet he was charming, frank without being arrogant, and kind-hearted. Not surprisingly, he was a Whig, though more because of the party's reform philosophy than because of its slavery stance. He joined a political club in Cambridge; and in the 1840 presidential election, he was one of the few Bostonians to vote for the Kentucky abolitionist James G. Birney. During the Birney campaign, Henry J. Gardner, a Bowdoin classmate, and a future Massachusetts governor, invited Andrew to give an address in Hopkinton, twenty-five miles west of Boston. The speech was so memorable that Phillip Greely, Jr., the Whig Party's state committee chair, invited him to speak elsewhere as well. Andrew's involvement in politics had begun, and his distinctive role was starting to take shape.[13]

Unfortunately, he was also beginning to suffer from debilitating headaches, which affected his work with Fuller. He was overweight, possibly diabetic or suffering from a thyroid problem. His caseload began to suffer, and he turned for relief to books and conversations. As always, he was interested in discussing social and philosophical issues, but he also liked to read aloud to his colleagues. The office library contained Charles Dickens's *Oliver Twist* and a "well-thumbed copy of Byron." Like many of his contemporaries, Andrew was captivated by Byron's romantic, revolutionary verse.[14] He confessed to Woodman:

> The truth is, I am a terrible procrastinator, . . . by nature, irregular, averse to labor, *always thinking of something else*; I am forever dreaming about doing, but half my time I am either insufferably lazy or too unwell with my old enemy (if I have a right to call anything so that is so much by me), the headache, for any exertion. As for real work, what may rightly be called so, it is not for me to pretend that I spend a great many hours, taking the days together, in any steady occupation; and yet time steals over me, it runs past me, I grow tired and sleepy and go to bed.[15]

Nonetheless, Andrew snapped into focus in the courtroom. He reveled in displaying his debating skills. Before a jury, he was resolute but at ease, distilling points, determined not to waste time on peripherals. Judges found him quick and thorough; his opponents found him dangerous, adept, and frighteningly well prepared. Despite his behind-the-scenes struggles, his performance in court was always polished, dramatic, and dominant.[16]

Colleagues believed he had the potential to become one of Boston's great lawyers, but his philanthropic work often lured him away from the office. He continued to live frugally, devoting his Sundays to visiting the city prisons. He took on pro bono cases and represented poor women seeking divorce. The law office became a halfway house for clients in need of free legal advice and representation. Because of this, he struggled financially, yet he found solace in his humanitarian work.[17]

Still, Andrew's zeal needed a focus; so, for him, it was serendipitous that, in 1839, the antislavery theologian James Freeman Clarke decided to return to Boston after a stint spent in Kentucky preaching against slavery. After joining Emerson's transcendentalist club and befriending Margaret Fuller, Clarke established the Church of the Disciples, hoping to bring together a congregation that would apply Christianity to contemporary social problems. He blurred the distinction between himself and his followers, encouraging his parishioners to become ministers and activists themselves. All would be united, conforming action with belief.[18]

A Burgeoning Spiritual Life

Clarke's impact on Andrew's spiritual life was immediate and profound, and it took place just as many Boston churches were closing their doors to antislavery advocates. Eight years older than Andrew, Clarke was an electrifying preacher and a writer of hymns and essays, contributing to the *Christian Examiner*, the *Christian Inquirer*, *The Dial*, *Harper's*, the *Index*, and the *Atlantic Monthly*. Andrew was instantly attracted to Clarke's free-church movement, which embraced social reform and tolerance. The minister had reconceptualized Unitarianism to respond to contemporary political and moral challenges. Like transcendentalists, he believed that the distribution of labor was a way to work for God's greater good. His congregants became a disciple-like community, both as worshipers and as community stewards. Clarke's services initially took place on Sundays in Boston's Amory Hall, but he then decided to hold church services throughout the week so that congregants could transform scriptural teachings into daily community service. Andrew recalled, "In the first place I liked the flavor of the *man*. He carried his service as though he felt it a good thing to worship God and wanted the people to feel the same. I liked his sermon thoroughly. It was . . . [a] well-seasoned speech."[19]

In 1842, Andrew joined the church and shared his enthusiasm with Woodman, who was then living in Wisconsin. Whereas most churches required membership fees, Clarke's was based "entirely on the voluntary principle, and is always to remain so, there being no taxation or letting out of seats." Andrew wrote, "There is much more zeal and earnestness among the people than is often found, [and] I think you would be greatly pleased if you were here." Clarke, he said, "has the best mind, style, and everything for a minister that there is a-going, he is logical, sensible, earnest, pious, forcible, solemn, quiet and calm, in fine, my *beau ideal* of a pulpit orator and a private gentleman & Christian. This is high eulogy, but deserved."[20]

Andrew enrolled in and then led a large Bible class, often conducting its proceedings in the presence of Clarke, who recalled his new parishioner as a curly-haired, rosy-cheeked man who looked younger than he was. As Clarke had intended, this turn toward religion became manifest in Andrew's daily life, binding intellect to conscience and spiritual labor to service for humanity. He attended weekly social-religious meetings, led prayer services, and referred to fellow parishioners as brothers and sisters. According to a church member, Andrew would embrace even those with whom he disagreed, reinforcing the Christian belief that the "true way to treat all whom we supposed to be in error was not go *from* them but to go *to* them—not shut them out, but to take them in."[21]

Andrew was attracted to the democratic nature of religious experiences, and he relished the chance to worship with other congregations so as to compare ministers and messages. After beginning to work in Boston's African American community, he attended the Twelfth Baptist Church, led by Leonard Grimes, an escaped Virginia slave, whose stories inspired his parishioners. Andrew was so taken with Grimes that he often taught Bible classes at the church. Worshipping at Twelfth Baptist drew Andrew more deeply into Boston's Black community and into connections with the Underground Railroad.

He also ventured to the wharves to worship with the sailors who attended the Methodist Bethel mission. Its pastor, Edward Thompson Taylor, had preached in ports around the world and was known for his eloquent extemporizing. (He may have inspired Herman Melville's Father Mapple in *Moby-Dick*.) Pacing back and forth, his hands clasped behind him, he frequently used nautical metaphors to dramatize the soul's journey.[22]

These experiences taught Andrew how to lead—whether in the pulpit, in a Bible class, or at Sunday school. His community work enhanced his philanthropic legal work and expanded his humanitarian awareness. He became a regular at the Boston Port Society, serving as its secretary until his death. He read Unitarian publications such the *Christian Register* and the *Christian World*, which focused on inculcating the principles of rational religion and genuine piety. He even contributed to them, writing book reviews and essays and reporting on Unitarian conventions.[23]

Given his activity in Boston's reformist and faith circles, it is no surprise that Andrew became involved in the travails of George and Rebecca Latimer. In 1842, the couple escaped from a Norfolk, Virginia, slaveowner and arrived in Boston as fugitives. That October, a former employee of the owner spotted George Latimer in the city and contacted the owner, James Gray, who had the fugitive arrested on a charge of larceny. On October 19, Gray applied to the courts to have Latimer returned to bondage. Supreme Court justice Joseph Story, who had freed the *Amistad* slaves the year before, gave Gray ten days to stake his claim. Fearing a mob, Gray paid the city jailer to keep Latimer in custody until the court's decision. Meanwhile, African American activists, while keeping Rebecca hidden, gathered to protest Latimer's arrest. The radical Black abolitionist William Cooper Nell took the lead in

FIGURE 3. Leonard Grimes. Prints and Photographs Division, Library of Congress, LC-DIG-ppmsca-53262.

organizing a defense and recruiting white allies, including Andrew. But Latimer remained in jail, which his defenders declared was illegal use of a public facility, and they called on the sheriff to dismiss the jailer.

The case dominated the Boston press for weeks. Finally, the self-appointed Latimer Committee offered to pay Gray $400 for Latimer's freedom. Gray conceded defeat and accepted the money, but the case ignited a larger political movement to prevent future seizures in Massachusetts. In 1843, some 65,000 signatories petitioned the state legislature to pass the Latimer Law, which would prohibit state judges from hearing cases under the 1793 Fugitive Slave Act, forbid law officers from taking part in the arrest of fugitives or from lodging them in public buildings, and establish penalties for violators, including removal from office. These became the basis for what would become a series of personal liberty laws.[24]

In Massachusetts, the Latimer case was a turning point in the struggle for African American freedom. The local lawyers who gathered to talk at Taft's Cornhill Coffeehouse were riveted by Justice Story's reading of the law. Andrew, too, followed the case closely and surely joined the crowds at a Faneuil Hall "Human Rights" meeting in late October. The list of attendees included the reformer Henry Ingersoll Bowditch, well known for his dedication to the less fortunate. Bowditch was a cultivated gentleman of property and standing, who had trained as a doctor in Paris and then returned to Boston in the mid-1830s. Now, with William Francis Channing and Frederick Cabot, he founded the *Latimer Journal and North Star*, a short-lived triweekly paper devoted to abolitionism.[25]

Although Bowditch and Andrew came from vastly different social circles, their paths would cross frequently, and Andrew's reformist fervor was garnering attention. In September 1844, Bowdoin invited him to address the Athenaean Society, a notable honor for someone so early in his career. Andrew's speech was a well-crafted introspection on the journey toward maturity. "The highest office of scholarship," he argued, was "to observe what is, and to inquire what ought to be." He continued, "If I were to give a name to the greatest evil to the individual, and of inefficiency to his influence in the world, for all good and noble things, I should call it, *the want of a devoted enthusiasm*." Because "America's rugged individualism sowed selfishness to personal ambition, . . . young men must abandon this notion and reach for a higher purpose by helping their fellow neighbor." In his view, "the genuine man must follow the path to truth and reason, and that progress should not be measured by individual success, but rather by the

collective good and moral heroism. . . . The true scholars and philoso-
phers are servants to their neighbors and not bought by a price, but by
their humanity to the disadvantaged and underprivileged."[26]

That fall, the Fuller-Andrew partnership moved their firm to a larger
office at 6 State Street. They took on several more apprentices, including Cyrus Woodman's younger brother Horatio. One of those students
recalled Andrew's "pauper clientage" as a "ragged set, of which most
young lawyers would have been ashamed, but whom he cherished quietly and discreetly." Some of these clients sought Andrew out because
of his reputation as a defender of the needy; others were sent to him
by fellow philanthropists. In the office Andrew was always cheerful,
demonstrating an "unpretentious kindness" but also regaling the students with jokes and reminiscences. According to one apprentice, he
would read aloud the essays, often arguments against slavery, which he
had written for the *Christian World* or the *Christian Register*. This worried the conservative Fuller, yet many of his colleagues believed that
Andrew had a meteoric future. Andrew himself did not agree. As one
student recalled, he assumed "he was destined to live and die simply
as a plain, honest, and moderately successful lawyer, a useful citizen, a
zealous philanthropist, and a sensible party constituent."[27]

In May 1845, Andrew found himself in the middle of a congregational
schism when a theological controversy threatened to split Clarke's
church. Clarke had arranged to conduct a pulpit exchange with the radical theologian Theodore Parker, who had already delivered a controversial sermon, "The Transient and Permanent in Christianity," that
had divided the Unitarians. In it Parker had argued that Christianity's
historic traditions did not reflect the truth. The Bible was full of contradictions, he said, and Christian beliefs should be rooted in personal
faith and a relationship with God, not in scripture. While Clarke was
skeptical of Parker's theology, he was bold enough to take part in the
exchange, maintaining that he communed with people because of their
character, not their creed. Andrew agreed, so he was surprised when
several prominent families left Clarke's church in protest. Leaping into
the doctrinal fray, he argued that Parker's denial of biblical authority
was no different from the views of Roman Catholics, Quakers, and
Swedenborgians. None of these sects had forfeited their rights as
Christians. Clarke's daughter, Lillian, remembered Andrew saying:

> I shall not leave because a majority differ from me on this or any other
> question. This is my religious home. If you turn me out of your meetings,

I will stand on the outside and look in through the window and see you. If I cannot do this, I will come the next day and sit in the place where you have been, and commune with you. I belong to your communion and must belong to it always."[28]

FIGURE 4. James Freeman Clarke. Courtesy of Special Collections, Fine Arts Library, Harvard University.

Eventually, the furor died down, and Andrew soldiered on. He continued to focus his legal practice on Boston's neediest, though Fuller tried to pull him toward loftier clients. He often assisted other lawyers with their briefs, especially those involving capital punishment, which he vehemently opposed. In the summer of 1845, he aligned himself with Robert Rantoul, Jr., a distinguished lawyer and political leader, and the Unitarian ministers John Murray Spear and Robert F. Walcutt in debating a case concerning a poor nineteen-year-old named Orinn De Wolf, who had been sentenced to death for murder in the central Massachusetts city of Worcester. The victim's wife had seduced De Wolf, who, while drunk, had killed her husband. De Wolf's advocates held a meeting at Boston's Ritchie Hall in early August, appointing a committee to visit the governor in hopes of procuring a commutation. Andrew was a member of the committee, along with Rantoul, Spear, Wendell Phillips, Walter Channing, and Ellis G. Loring; and they managed to convince the governor to commute the death sentence to life in prison.[29]

Andrew was drawn to Rantoul, a Harvard graduate, and a champion of justice in both the state legislature and his law office. Famous as a reformer of divorce and usury laws, Rantoul was an outspoken critic of capital punishment and was instrumental in recodifying Massachusetts common law. Rantoul was a model for using the law and the political system to advance humanitarian reform. Recently he had won the case *Commonwealth v. John Hunt & Others*, representing the Boston Journeymen Bootmaker Society, a labor union that was seeking higher wages for its members. In a landmark decision, Judge Lemuel Shaw of the Massachusetts supreme judicial court declared that labor unions, which used legal means to achieve legal ends, were lawful and struck down attempts to illegalize them as "conspiracies."[30]

The Prisoner's Friend

By 1846, Rantoul had been appointed U.S. attorney for Massachusetts, and he was no longer engaging with Andrew on local legal issues. Still, the friends remained connected via their interest in prison reform and their mutual hatred of the death penalty. They worked alongside John Murray Spear and his brother Charles Spear, also a Universalist minister, whose weekly magazine, the *Prisoner's Friend*, was perhaps the nation's first publication wholly devoted to prison reform. The four were instrumental in the creation of the Massachusetts Society for the Abolition of Capital Punishment. Members included Francis

Jackson, Robert F. Wallcut, William Lloyd Garrison, Ellis Gray Loring, John Greenleaf Whittier, Wendell Phillips, and Reverend Clarke.

At the same time Andrew was working more closely with the African American community in service of the antislavery cause. Fuller's concerns increased: though he may have admired elements of his partner's progressivism, he worried that the cost to the firm would be severe. He decided to make a change in the office. In December 1846, his nephew, Richard Frederick Fuller, was admitted to practice. Richard was an orphan, and Fuller had played a significant role in his nephew's life for years. Though Andrew understood what was coming, he encouraged Richard to join the firm and announced his own departure. The split saddened both partners. "I can hardly bring myself to think of dissolving the partnership between yourself and me," Fuller wrote to Andrew. "It has been in all respects so happy and agreeable,—you have been ever so acceptable, so worthy, so just what I would have you to be,—and that I feel great pain and melancholy, at the thought of dissolving our connexion."[31]

Andrew entered the law office of Theophilus Parsons Chandler, the older brother of his friend Peleg, who also worked in the office. The Chandler name was prominent in legal circles. In 1838, Peleg had founded the nation's first successful law magazine, the *Law Reporter*, and Theophilus had argued cases against Daniel Webster. Before settling in Boston, the brothers had worked in their father's Bangor, Maine, practice. Their office at 4 Court Street was just a few blocks away from Faneuil Hall. There, on Beacon's Hill, "the paradise of Boston lawyers," the firm's attorneys came into daily contact with progressive luminaries such as Charles Sumner, George S. Hillard, Rufus Choate, Theophilus Parsons, Horace Mann, Edward G. Loring, Richard Henry Dana, Jr., and Luther S. Cushing. There was a great deal of business conducted in this office and the lawyers became familiar with one another's cases. Andrew was immediately drawn to Sumner's legal mind and Howe's altruistic heart.[32]

As Andrew was settling into his new firm, national affairs were in turmoil. President John Tyler's annexation of Texas reinforced the American commitment to manifest destiny, the notion that God wanted the nation to spread democracy's blessings westward, whether that also spread slavery. Yet there were critics of Tyler's move, which took place just as he was leaving office. They saw it as one more calamity of his "accidental presidency," further damaging Mexican American relations and likely to affect voters' decisions in upcoming elections.

Abolitionists declared that the time had come for northerners to halt slavery's westward expansion. They found support for their activism in the writings of Frederick Douglass, whose newly published memoir, *Narrative of the Life of Frederick, An American Slave*, detailed his journey from bondage into freedom. By this time Douglass was living in Lynn, near Boston, so Massachusetts abolitionists were particularly active in promoting his voice.[33]

The Commonwealth's conservatives, many of them dependent on the cotton industry, continued to support western expansion. Thus, reformers, eager for change at the ballot box, worked to attract Whigs to their cause. The party had emerged as a viable opponent to Jacksonian Democrats, championing a pro-business use of governmental agency, a protective tariff, and the elevation of the laboring classes. These Whigs were populists, who, while largely avoiding discussions about slavery, advocated self-improvement, self-discipline, and self-made men. Andrew had already aligned himself with the party and in 1844 assumed a small leadership role in the national movement, when voters elected him as the party director for Boston's Fourth Ward. His focus in that position was on ending the unpopular congressional gag rule.

Though Andrew was becoming more politically active, he remained dedicated to his reformist work, and the two often overlapped. Most Whigs believed that society could be improved only through self-reform and soul change. Thus, with Charles Spear, Louis Dwight, Walter Channing, John Browne, Samuel Howe, and Henry Bowditch, Andrew established the Boston Society for Aiding Discharged Convicts, aimed at helping former prisoners chart a moral path forward. The association raised funds for clothing, tools, and board, and members mentored and monitored candidates for several months after release.

By this time the Whigs had established themselves as the dominant party in Massachusetts. Since 1834, they had controlled the governor's office for all but two of the past ten years, and they owned the legislature. Yet the Boston party was fractured. Many voters were morally indifferent "cotton" Whigs, who supported the looming war with Mexico, in contrast to the high-minded "conscience" Whigs who opposed it. Andrew and his reformist colleagues sided with the latter. He saw the party as the most practical way to link his Christianity with his budding political activism; and keeping company with the conscience wing drew him deeper into political affairs, especially as they related to halting slavery's expansion.[34]

CHAPTER 4

THE EMERGING POLITICIAN

1846–1849

Young Whigs

In May 1846, the United States declared war on Mexico. Then, on a sweltering August evening, Pennsylvania congressman David Wilmot lit a partisan fuse. Rising in the House chamber, he proposed an amendment to the appropriation's bill that would support American expansion into regions where slavery already existed. But, he declared, if Americans were to acquire free territory because of the war, then "God forbid that we should be the means of planting this institution upon it." It was unclear, for now, if this proviso would prove "to be of any great consequence." With overwhelming northern support, the House passed Wilmot's resolution, so "loathsome to Southern eyes," but the Senate rejected it. For the moment nothing had changed. Clearly, however, a storm was brewing.[1]

Andrew had long recognized that slavery was at odds with the nation's democratic principles. The brewing political divisions increased the tension he felt between his professional legal responsibilities and the extralegal world of the radical abolitionists. While he had spent his young career working to uplift and defend the poor, the incarcerated, and the fugitive, he had not become a militant Garrisonian. Reading the *Liberator* had certainly reinforced his hatred of slavery, and he may also have read Whitter's *Voices of Freedom*, a verse argument for the abolitionist cause. Still, he tried to temper his enthusiasm and observe his legal limits. Unlike Garrison and others, he did not advocate disunion but believed in focusing on the political culture and changing the electorate. He knew this approach would take longer but was optimistic that it could bring about a permanent solution. Thus, he preferred to help seasoned politicians take over the state's Whig Party rather than publicly support the Garrisonians.

By September, he and his Whig colleagues were refashioning the party's platform to emphasize freedom and equality and were engaged in choosing a candidate to run against the incumbent congressman, Robert C. Winthrop, a wealthy disciple of Daniel Webster who had endorsed the Mexican American War. He attended the party's state convention, which took place just before the great Faneuil Hall meeting about George, the escaped slave from the *Ottoman*. For Andrew, both events were transformative. At the convention Sumner, who had declined to run as a Whig candidate for Congress, announced that the party should not compromise on slavery and said he was prepared for the consequences of such a stance. Though conservatives argued that slavery could be abolished only through constitutional means, Andrew and other young Whigs believed they could create change at the polls.[2]

Andrew was assigned to prepare resolutions and nominate a candidate, and he was disappointed that Sumner had refused to stand for the seat. He had come to know his Court Street colleague well and had pressed him to accept the nomination. Though Sumner had refused, Andrew was swept away by his luminescent rhetoric and distressed by the recent attacks on him by Boston's pro-Democratic *Daily Atlas*. He and the other young Whigs believed that Sumner was "especially worthy at the present crisis to represent the interests of the city, and the cardinal principles of truth, justice, liberty, and peace, which have not died out in the breasts of her citizens."[3] So Andrew fired off a letter, hoping to sway him: "Are we not all of us high and true sense—*providential* men? Does not an unerring finger point us, visibly and often, to a duty at once irksome and dangerous, but still as certain and clear, as the fiery cross of Constantine? Are you not *the* man, if there is or can be one, for this crisis in our affairs?"[4]

He failed to persuade Sumner, and in early November, he guided delegates to accept the physician and abolitionist Samuel Howe's nomination. Sumner and Charles Francis Adams spoke at the meeting, endorsing Howe and the antislavery platform, but Howe lost the election in a landslide. These zealous reformers were not daunted. Instead, they formed a new political movement in Massachusetts, which, by 1848, was known as the Free-Soil Party. "Men who know their ground so well as these 'young Whigs' appear to do," wrote a correspondent to

FIGURE 5. Charles Sumner. Courtesy of the Boston Public Library.

the Boston *Chronotype*, "have commenced this work with so much earnestness, [and] will not cannot stop, short of their aim." He predicted, "The days of slavery are numbered."[5]

Andrew was hard at work on voting efforts when the *Ottoman* case redirected his attention and energy. At the meeting at Faneuil Hall on

September 24, Andrew saw the aged John Quincy Adams for the first and last time. Adams delivered a remarkable address, and Andrew, who was recording the resolutions for presentation to a grand jury, never forgot the impassioned atmosphere of the hall. Yet for all their energy and public voice, these reformers remained a quasi-underground group, quietly working on behalf of the fugitives passing through Boston.[6] As Andrew's political and reformist worlds converged, he came to understand that antislavery and abolition were not synonymous. Antislavery was a more popular stance because it did not insist upon the immediate eradication of slavery or on racial equality. He understood that equality before the law could be politically and constitutionally mandated, but racial equality was a different matter. A color line could not easily be erased by laws or the courts. Still, he was determined to uphold the standards of equality in his work with the African American community. The fact that the Constitution presided over matters of slavery and fugitives magnified the politics of the institution, as Andrew recognized during his work with the Boston Vigilance Committee, yet he was also naturally drawn to equality in his personal dealings with others.[7]

As a regular attendee at Reverend Grimes's church, Andrew became friends with several of its African American congregants. One was Lewis Hayden, a former Kentucky slave, who had escaped and fled to Canada. In early 1846 he had moved to Boston and joined Grimes's church, which connected him to the city's Underground Railroad activists. Andrew had met Hayden even before he had moved to Boston, when he and John M. Brown had visited Reverend Clarke's church to advocate for the newly founded Liberty Party and solicit aid for a meetinghouse in Detroit that would serve the city's growing but destitute African American population. The two young men were kindred spirits and became life-long friends. Andrew saw Hayden as a valued colleague and a respected community leader. Hayden saw Andrew as a Christian disciple of justice for all. Andrew did more than simply befriend African Americans, sit in their church, and read the *Liberator*. He fought slavery and racism in the courts and the political culture, working to bend local justice where he could and move the state's politics toward antislavery. Through Hayden, Andrew saw slavery's cruel effects first hand and learned why his friend so valued having been transformed from "a thing to a man."[8]

Andrew's social and political growth had expanded, not reduced, his antislavery passions. A letter he received from Woodman at about this time shows how far he had matured into his reformist convictions.

FIGURE 6. Lewis Hayden. Courtesy of the Houghton Library, Harvard University. CC BY 4.0, https://creativecommons.org/licenses/by/4.0/.

Woodman chided his old friend for his foolish humanitarian endeavors: "I presume you are still exerting yourself in [*sic*] behalf of the 'downtrodden humanity' striving to free the slave from his bonds and the felon from the halter." He continued, "The principal subject of your discourse is now, I imagine, the unlawfulness of war in general and of the war in Mexico in particular." But the person that Woodman mocked as an idealist had become a rising star among the young Whigs.[9] Andrew had also recently assumed associate editorship of the *Christian World*, where he pressed forward his political and spiritual agenda, urging ministers to evangelize against the expansion of slavery and condemn America's actions in Mexico.

Boston was the home ground of the moral absolutists who led the antislavery movement, yet their fervor had not spread everywhere in the state. Although slavery had died out in Massachusetts decades earlier, citizens did not necessarily endorse legislation that would remove racial barriers or promote racial harmony. Conservative citizens and legislative statutes made it clear that, in the Commonwealth, African Americans were not equal to whites.[10] Meanwhile, even as Andrew became ever more engaged in Boston's political culture and the fight against slavery, his law career and his finances remained shaky. He confessed to Woodman that he had "no business capacity to speak of . . . except to spend what I can find in my pockets." Much of what he spent went to charity. Still, his daily interactions with Sumner and others in his legal circle helped him understand the importance of balancing his worlds. As much as he wanted to help people via the courtroom, he knew that political change had far greater reformist implications. Yet politics could also promote cruelty, selfishness, and a divide-and-conquer attitude. For the moment, he was content to stand behind others, like Sumner, who were richer and more intellectually confident. For now, he had to make his law career pay.[11]

Although the conscience Whigs were defeated in the November 1846 congressional race, the loss laid the ground for the Free-Soilers in Massachusetts. Andrew was learning that ideology could prevail over practicality when developing a coalition of constituents. Over the next few months, he became active in a group of lawyers and reformers, including the Chandlers, Sumner, Charles Francis Adams, Sr., and Howe, who wanted more than just to end slavery. They wanted racial justice. Many were wealthy and distinguished, yet they welcomed the twenty-eight-year-old Andrew into their leadership circle. Many worked at the 4 Court Street offices, and despite their eclectic differences, they were bound by a common cause.[12]

As the group's junior colleague, Andrew was assigned to preside over state meetings, report on resolutions, and stump for their cause. He also learned more about his colleagues. In Sumner, for instance, he saw not only an antislavery advocate but also an inspired crusader—sometimes polished but sometimes a bully. He became close to other Court Street lawyers as well, including Richard Henry Dana, Jr., and George Stillman Hillard. Dana, a distinguished expert in maritime law, had graduated from Harvard Law School in the same year that Andrew had graduated from Bowdoin, and they were admitted to the Suffolk County bar together. Dana later went on to write the memoir *Two Years before the Mast* as well as *The Seaman's Friend*, which became the standard reference on sailors' legal rights. Hillard was a Maine native, Harvard-educated, who served in the Massachusetts General Assembly. He had edited the *Christian Register* and, by the time he met Andrew, was co-editing the *American Jurist*, a leading legal journal.[13]

What the coalition lacked in members it made up for in unity and determination. Because Massachusetts state elections often served as a political weathervane, Whigs across the nation followed them closely. Thus, local Whigs were determined to prevent their state party from ever again supporting an enslaver for president, and they also began working closely with the Commonwealth's African American community. Charles Francis Adams agreed to edit the Boston *Whig*, the movement's mouthpiece, and spent two years blasting the cotton Whigs for deserting their principles in favor of self-interest. As the Whig Party began to dissolve, antislavery men took the lead in forging a new coalition whose chief goal was to prevent or exterminate slavery from the western territories.[14]

Andrew believed that the Constitution and the political culture were slavery's chief supports, and he wanted to use those same instruments to end the institution. Yet he tempered his assertiveness. Critics charged that Garrison's inflammatory rhetoric had done the cause more harm than good, so he focused his legal and editorial labor on the practical application of political power. Even as he collaborated with other leaders to elevate antislavery issues and unseat conservatives, he avoided aligning himself with Garrison, even as they socialized. Instead, he increased his involvement with the African American community, becoming close to William Nell, Charles Lenox Remond, and other Black activists. Grassroots reformers, both Black and white, often assembled in Andrew's law office, where they plotted how to navigate the split between the state's conscience Whigs and national leaders. Andrew also encouraged Reverend Clarke to assume the *Christian World*'s editorship, believing that his spiritual influence would help steer the readership into an antislavery course. Though Andrew offered to continue editing and writing for the paper, his migraines had returned, and he was ill or convalescent for days on end.[15]

Free-Soil Politics

By September 1847, as General Winfield Scott was closing in on Mexico's capital city, Boston's antislavery activists were focusing on the sixty-six Black men, women, and children who had just arrived in the city from Brandon Plantation in Prince George County, Virginia. They had been the slaves of Carter H. Edloe, whose will emancipated them; and in early September they sailed north on the *Thomas H. Thompson*. Andrew, along with Garrison, Phillips, and the Unitarian minister Samuel May, was waiting at Boston's Long Wharf to welcome them. Peter Randolph, the leader of the new arrivals, said their reception was overwhelmingly hospitable. The abolitionists and Reverend Grimes's congregation helped the newcomers assimilate into Boston's African American community and find places to live and work. Andrew quickly became close to Randolph, eager to hear stories of slave life in Virginia, of how Randolph had learned to read and write, and especially of his religious conversion. Andrew later often remarked that Randolph's definition of faith was one of the best he had ever heard. Likewise, for Randolph, Andrew's generosity was a welcome change. "I speak of this, simply to show the noble spirit of the man toward the unfortunate," he recalled in his memoirs. "I, born an ignorant slave, he, an educated lawyer, yet he did not disdain to talk with me on the great subject of religion."[16]

Several transcendentalist clubs and enterprises had recently disbanded, among them Brook Farm, a communal utopian experiment in West Roxbury, and the Hedge Club, named after the Unitarian minister Frederic Henry Hedge. To fill the void, Parker inaugurated a new one, the Conversational Club, at his home, and Andrew joined, along with his friends Samuel and Julia Howe and Reverend Clarke. Members met biweekly to explore such topics as "woman," "evil: is human sinfulness a positive or merely negative matter?," "what explanation can be given of the existence of evil?," and "what shall we do to elevate the laboring classes?" His engagement in this club enlarged his circle of friends and associates who affirmed the high value of applying Christian principles to social circumstances.[17]

In February 1848 Mexico and the United States signed a treaty, and the war ended. Now Andrew was ready to roll up his sleeves and start shaping an antislavery course among the voters. But then John Quincy Adams collapsed in the House and died soon thereafter. Washington mourned the loss of the great statesmen, and Boston was crushed. Without Adams to carry the antislavery banner, who would emerge to lead the fight? As people around the nation mourned, Congress struggled to find a unified path forward now that the war was over. Adams may have understood that manifest destiny was a complex and dangerous notion, but few Americans recognized that it was leading to another political and civil crisis.

For the moment, conquest of Mexican lands had sated America's expansionist appetite. Yet settling the new land meant finding an answer to the slavery question. The war had redefined not only America's borders but also its political culture, and these changes played out in the 1848 presidential election, as many voters opted for moderation on national issues and rejected northern antislavery aspirations. Massachusetts Whigs remained divided, and conscience Whigs came to believe they had no future in a party dominated by the prominent cotton Whigs Abbott Lawrence and Nathan Appleton, who supported the slaveholder Zachary Taylor's nomination for president.[18]

Sumner had predicted that a new party would be needed to carry freedom's mantle into the territories, and Andrew was eager to bring this about. He and other idealists sought to garner support from antiwar Whigs, antislavery Democrats, and abolitionist Liberty men, who considered the war a moral abomination. Before the Whig Party's national convention, Andrew and his colleagues met in Charles Francis Adams's office and resolved that if Taylor or any pro-slavery candidates appeared on the ballot, they would launch a new opposition party, the Free-Soilers. The bold step was aided by the Democrats, who nominated Michigan's Lewis Cass in May and adopted a doctrine later dubbed *popular sovereignty* that allowed territorial residents to determine slavery's future. The Whigs skirted antislavery rhetoric in their Philadelphia convention, nominated Taylor, and sought to maintain North-South economic alliances in New England. Angry over both parties' moves, the state's conscience Whigs called a late June convention in Worcester to organize a new party and align political developments in Massachusetts with antislavery movements in other states. Sumner and Adams engineered the meeting and enlisted political leaders such as Henry Wilson, Francis Bird, and Amasa Walker to stump for the party throughout the state, fighting off the "unhallowed union" between "the lords of the lash and the lords of the loom," as Sumner put it.[19]

Andrew helped to put the Free-Soil Party on firm footing in the Bay State. He saw it as an opportunity to bring together politics and Christian morality to advance the antislavery cause. During these long weeks of work, Andrew, Sumner, and the Howes grew even closer as friends. They all attended Clarke's Church of the Disciples, and together they raised funds to establish the Boston Temporary Home for the Destitute. Andrew frequented the Howes' Boston home and was often a guest at their Newport retreat. Julia Howe later recalled him as charming, witty, and genial.[20]

The postwar chaos that realigned party politics in Massachusetts also transformed politics in other states. The national Free-Soil Party took shape in Buffalo that August, when enthusiastic delegates nominated the New Yorker Martin van Buren for president. Known as "Old Kinderhook," he had ridden Andrew Jackson's coattails to the presidency in 1836, and now, twelve years, later he stood alongside a vice presidential candidate from Massachusetts, Charles Francis Adams, whose father, John Quincy, had famously opposed Jackson in 1824.

Van Buren's road to the Free-Soilers was circuitous, yet the splintering political culture had allowed him to reemerge as an antislavery man.

The Massachusetts Free-Soilers were the guiding force behind these choices for national leadership. In addition to Sumner, Andrew, and Adams, Francis William Bird played a major role. Tall and spare, Bird had been educated at Brown and was a wealthy paper manufacturer in East Walpole. Nicknamed the "Sage of Walpole," he was famously charitable and sociable, forming a Saturday-afternoon club in Boston affectionately known as the Bird Club. Andrew and Bird frequently dined together at the Cornhill Coffeehouse and became close friends. Older than Andrew, Bird saw great leadership potential in the young lawyer but knew that his charming demeanor would need to harden if he were to seek public office. Bird had deep pockets, abundant political credibility, and influential connections. More importantly, he was keenly aware of Boston's unforgiving voters. Bird maintained friendly relationships with the city's powerbrokers, including the ward boss James W. Stone, the businessman Henry L. Pierce, and the editor of the *Daily Whig* William S. Robinson. They were the Bird Club's core originators; but with the rise of the Free-Soil Party, its membership increased, and many became Andrew's life-long friends.[21]

Despite the Massachusetts influence, Free-Soil convention leaders in Buffalo avoided the issue of African American equality. Outrage over slavery's expansion may have unified them, but it did not translate into an endorsement of racial equality. At home, however, Andrew continued to work for votes, getting his name into the papers for his service on the rallying committee for Boston's seventh ward. Charles T. Condon of the New York *Tribune* later recalled him as an "original Abolitionist, or Liberty party man," one who "could always say, as Theodore Parker did, 'when the laws of Massachusetts or the laws of the Union conflict with the laws of God, I would keep God's law in preference, though the heavens should fall.'"[22] Still, Andrew knew that voters generally remained morally and racially conservative. There would be repercussions if he and his colleagues moved too fast or far from the base.

In the 1848 election, most voters saw the Van Buren-Adams ticket as a righteous crusade that was long on oratory and short on popularity. The Free-Soilers received just 10 percent of the vote: they did not carry a single state or capture even one electoral vote. As a result, the antislavery contingent found itself isolated, its members perceived as dangerous zealots in both the North and the South. Nonetheless, the party had made inroads in Massachusetts; having outpolled the Democrats, it became the state's second party. As Sumner said, the Commonwealth's voters had "been stirred on the subject of slavery to depths never before reached." Thanks to the work of Andrew and others, "much information with regard to the Slave-Power [had] been diffused in quarters heretofore ignorant of the enormous tyranny."[23] An editorial in the *Massachusetts Quarterly Review* declared that "the Free Soil party . . . cannot go back . . . they cannot not stand still . . . they must go forward . . . with this as their motto: NO SLAVERY IN AMERICA."[24]

Zachary Taylor's victory further polarized the national political culture. Hardened sectional disputes remained as the Thirty-first Congress convened in December. House members took more than a week and fifty-nine ballots to elect a speaker—an ominous sign—and nine Free-Soilers, including Representative Charles Allen of Worcester, were players in this struggle. Allen was a prominent Whig activist—a lawyer, a judge, and a delegate to the Whigs' national convention in Philadelphia. Yet after Taylor's nomination, he had publicly called for the party's dissolution. Undoubtedly, Andrew was aware of the tenuous nature of party politics in both the state and the nation. Allen was just one example of the sea change.

Andrew had come to understand that politics was as much about power as about principle, and the shifting fortunes of the Free-Soilers also showed that voters were not one-dimensional but were influenced by a multitude of issues. To win over the electorate, party activists needed to broaden their base: they needed to steer moderates and even some conservatives into their antislavery corner. Locally, this meant that Free-Soil leaders needed to negotiate with the politicians of opposing parties who worked in Boston's wards. As Andrew had learned, strategy and messaging were crucial, but so was remaining in tune with the voters, even while prodding them.[25]

As he pondered his party's next steps, Andrew continued his daily legal round. His professional and social worlds were an extraordinary blend of Boston's wealthy intelligentsia and the city's pauper class. "I thank God," a lawyer once exclaimed to him, "that there is one man at the bar to look out for the poor devils of criminals who are guilty enough and have no friends and no money." Yet though his charity work centered on women, felons, and the poor, his political activities gave him access to the state's elite reformist community.[26] By this time, he had earned significant acclaim among these activists. Thus, when the town of Boxford opened a lyceum, its council invited him to give the inaugural lecture. It was a rousing address, borrowed from a speech Andrew had presented years before at Bowdoin's Athenaean Society. Afterward he had the pleasure of spending time with his father and siblings. His friend Cyrus Woodman attended the affair, as did the Chandler brothers. Peleg recalled "the merriment of the . . . evening." He wrote, "After the lecture, we drove home in the cold and bracing air, about as full of fun as mortals can be. . . . There was cider, the inevitable doughnuts, and all the Yankee 'fixings,' with a blazing fire that it is good to think about. What a time it was! What shouts of laughter at our own jokes!" Andrew's father was immensely proud. One of his sisters told her brother that "father seems to look upon your lecture as the *only one* ever delivered and that nothing *can equal it*. He is greatly stirred up by it."[27]

Andrew's daily work was in Boston, but he was never far from his family in spirit. He wrote frequently to his siblings about numerous subjects, including railroad investments for their father. He gave Isaac $50 in store credit to ensure that he had properly tailored clothes. He kept Alfreda apprised of national and local news, knowing that she, too, was fascinated by current events. Though Isaac and Sarah usually remained on the farm, Alfreda often visited Andrew in Boston.[28]

Meanwhile, Andrew had made another important connection via his antislavery activism—Eliza Jones Hersey. She was from Hingham, a hamlet on the south shore of Massachusetts Bay. The Herseys were prominent Unitarians, and their family name was listed among the Pilgrim fathers who had arrived in 1620. Andrew first met Eliza at an antislavery meeting in Hingham in 1846. "I was pleased with her from the first time I ever saw her face," he told his sister Sarah. "I like Eliza better, the more I see her." The two continued to meet "accidentally" when she came to Boston for church services or public lectures, and Andrew sensed a "certain 'internal harmony'" between them. He wrote to her and, without proposing an engagement, said that he wanted a proper courtship so that they could become friends. "I was certain she had rather a good opinion of me," he told Sarah, "and I became more positive of what were our true relations to each other."[29] Yet just two years earlier, Andrew had confessed to Woodman that he was destined to be "an old bachelor," unlikely to find someone "to regulate and straighten out the irregular & crooked parts of my character."[30]

Eliza was reserved, warm-hearted, and affectionate. Andrew admired her strong convictions, her honesty with herself, and her independent thought. "She has a good womanly mind; i.e., a woman's tact and insight," he wrote. "She is not what would be called a literary person. . . . Nor is she the reverse of that. . . . If she really lacks anywhere, it is in training and discipline." Eliza was quick to appreciate Andrew's literary and legal flare, and she had little patience for "silly or empty" persons. "The truth is," he told Sarah, "I think Eliza is extremely well adapted to me." After a two-year courtship, he proposed, and the two were married on Christmas Eve 1848 at the New North Church in Hingham, where he had taught Sunday school. A close friend, Reverend Oliver Stearns, presided, and the marriage announcement appeared in the Boston press.[31]

The Andrews began their life together in an unpretentious boardinghouse in Boston's West End. That same year, however, Andrew's father died, and Eliza became pregnant. The couple decided to return to Hingham and moved into the Hersey family home, where Eliza gave birth to their first child, Charles Albion, on October 28, 1849. "From the moment the little hero blew his trumpet," wrote the proud father, "all was well.... We are all so pleased, that it is hard to tell which of us seems the most silly. Eliza lies and laughs [and] looks at him, calling him 'so cunning,' and all that.... Eliza's mother says he is the prettiest baby she ever saw; and that she would say so if it had no relation to her."[32] Eliza was soon pregnant again, but then tragedy struck: the infant Charles died just two months before the birth of his brother, John Forrester, on November 26, 1850. Andrew turned to Reverend Clarke for consolation:

> I feel as if the dear possession was not wholly lost. The sweetness of his earthly life did more than any bitterness in his temporary loss. I long sometimes, to hear that little cheerful voice, to see that fair face, with its large, soft, blue thoughtful eyes, those golden curls which were the delight of us all, those smiles always ready for every one; to fondle him in my arms, until a sense of loss comes over me, as if some part of my being is gone.

Eliza took the death hard and fell into a deep melancholy, but Andrew's winter train rides to Boston gave him time to redirect his depression into his everyday challenges.[33] In the summer, he commuted by ferry, but he spent much of those warm months in Hingham. He reveled in walking the family to church, singing familiar hymns, and teaching Sunday school. After ten years as a city bachelor, he basked in small-town life. As he increased his practice, he gained some lucrative new clients, and he and Eliza were able to live comfortably. Yet his pleasure in a genteel country life did not affect his zeal as an activist. With Josiah Quincy, Jr., George Emerson, Samuel Howe, and others, he petitioned the legislature for a school for "Idiotic and Feeble-Minded Youth," winning approval and substantial funding. He continued to attend and lead programs at Clarke's church, sit in on the Twelfth Street Baptist services, and work intimately with Boston's abolitionist leaders to aid and defend fugitive slaves.[34]

Andrew's involvement in one of Boston's most famous capital punishment trials added luster to his reputation. In the winter and spring of 1849, he assisted fellow barristers William Aspinwall and Edgar Hodges in attempting to rescue Washington Goode from execution. Goode was an African American sailor who had been found guilty of murdering a fellow sailor over a romantic rivalry. In handing down the verdict, Chief Justice Lemuel Shaw made note of Goode's drinking problems and his habit of frequenting wharfside taverns and brothels. Hoping to stay the execution, which was scheduled for January 1850, death penalty abolitionists and members of the Massachusetts Society for the Abolition of Capital Punishment mounted an intense clemency campaign, led by Andrew, Ralph Waldo Emerson, Reverend Clarke, Charles Spear, Robert Rantoul, Wendell Phillips, Frederick Douglass, Lydia Maria Child, and Henry David Thoreau. There had not been an execution in Boston for thirteen years, and hundreds of citizens signed a petition for mercy.

Andrew loathed the racial prejudice in Boston, which was rampant in lyceums, schools, jury boxes, and especially prisons. In public addresses and in conversations with Goode's defense team, he made the case that Goode was unschooled, without religion or parents to teach him; that he had been raised ignorant in the Louisiana rice swamps. In Andrew's view, Goode was being hanged not because of his crime but because of his complexion. White people who had committed far worse crimes had escaped the gallows, he argued, but Goode had been treated as guilty even before standing trial.[35] His pleas were unsuccessful. "The old law of Noah . . . once more triumphed," said Spear. On a rainy May morning, the "clouds wept in sadness" over the large crowd in the private jail yard. Goode was so feeble that prison guards were forced to strap him onto a chair and carry him to the gallows. They placed a white hood over his head, adjusted a noose around his neck, and pulled the lever that dropped him to his death. It was a tragic scene, one that further divided Bostonians over the issue of race equality.[36]

CHAPTER 5

ON THE RIGHT SIDE OF GOD
1850–1854

Vigilance and Justice

As Andrew pulled himself out of depression over his son's death and Goode's execution, the national press was feverishly focused on western expansion and the California gold rush. In 1848–49, hundreds of ships carried thousands of eager gold hunters from Atlantic ports to California. Meanwhile, the Taylor administration continued to wrangle over the reward that had come with victory over Mexico—more land for settlers and Pacific Coast connections for expanding a global economy—and thus had lost the support of the South. By 1850, Congress was still undecided about what to do with the western territories the nation had acquired.

That spring and summer, Senator Henry Clay of Kentucky managed to engineer a political compromise, which he presumed would finally settle sectional differences. In a concession to the North, California was admitted as a free state, and the slave trade was abolished in Washington, DC, along with settling the Texans' debts and establishing territorial governments in the newly acquired lands. However, the Compromise of 1850 established more aggressive federal machinery for the return of fugitive slaves. Enslavers with an affidavit of identity could now appear before a federal commissioner and reclaim their property. As Andrew saw it, this did more than simply take power from local judicial tribunals. Because slaves had no civil rights, they would not be able to take court action to reverse this ruling, which meant that free African Americans were likely to be kidnapped into slavery.[1]

In New England, this new version of the Fugitive Slave Law provoked a storm of protest over slavery's constitutional legitimacy. As a result, it triggered a power struggle, one pitting southern enslavers who sent agents north to reclaim their property against abolitionists who sought to prevent them. The Wilmot proviso had been a slow-burning fuse, but the Fugitive Slave Law was a sudden flame. It, more than any other event thus far, shaped Andrew's generation's approach to fighting slavery. His cohort abhorred the directive. Even Andrew, who had always been careful of others' views, became militant about the issue. Throughout his career, he had worked to be the people's voice—in the courtroom, in prisons, in churches, and beside the ballot box. Now, once again, he was forced to reckon with how laws intended to protect human rights could also destroy human life. He saw that obedience to a higher moral code must sometimes mean defiance of established laws. Thus, he was aghast when Daniel Webster conceded to Clay's resolutions. Remarking, in his "Seventh of March" speech, that Massachusetts would need to overcome its prejudice against the new law, Webster assured enslavers that law-abiding northerners had a moral and constitutional duty to help recapture runaways. Andrew was not alone in his horror at the senator's capitulation: Garrison spent weeks railing against the speech.[2]

The law spurred Boston's abolitionists to action. Black activists formed the League of Freedom, a grassroots group that pledged to guard against moral abuse. It joined ranks with the rejuvenated Boston Vigilance Committee to protect fugitives from federal marshals. These united efforts established routes along the Underground Railroad in and out of Boston. At night fugitives would typically travel by cart or carriage to the next station, and Andrew offered legal, financial, and administrative assistance for these exchanges. He worked closely with Leonard Grimes and Lewis Hayden to protect runaways, including William and Ellen Craft, who had fled from Georgia in disguise, made their way to Boston, and subsequently escaped to England. The pair became celebrities, embarrassing conservatives, who wanted to make an example of other escapees.[3]

In mid-October, Andrew attended an indignation meeting in Faneuil Hall, presided over by Charles Francis Adams. While Adams advised "no measures of violence or excess," he challenged attendees to commit to the labor required to repeal the odious law. "Words . . . are of little avail in this struggle," he declared. "We must act, . . . placing ourselves on the impregnable basis of Right." At the meeting, Frederick Douglass told the story of a female runaway, then in New Bedford, "who [had] hid herself in the hold of a vessel." He said, "They smoked the vessel, as was the custom, and the woman lay there in the hold, almost suffocated but she resolved to die rather than come forth." As punishment, her master "took her out, tied her up, and stripping her to the waist, laid on the lash until the warm blood dropped at her feet, he then washed her back in brine, and nailed her by her right ear to a fence rail, and in her agony, she tore off the outer rim of her ear." Andrew had heard such horror stories before, but this one turned his stomach.[4]

That fall, Reverend Clarke fell ill and took a leave of absence from his congregation. The church leaned on parishioners such as Andrew to conduct services, set the worship schedule, and arrange Bible studies. The assignment drew him more deeply into the church community, and his temporary leadership assignment fused his morality with his politics. He was working closely with Bird Club colleagues, knowing that now was the time to make a moral impression on voters. The junto had expanded to include Charles Sumner, Charles Francis Adams, William Garrison, Samuel Gridley Howe, Ralph Waldo Emerson, Charles W. Slack, John G. Palfrey, Franklin Sanborn, George L. Stearns, Elizur Wright, James Russell Lowell, Louis Agassiz, Nathaniel Hawthorne, Henry Wadsworth Longfellow, and John Greenleaf Whittier. They were bound by "a common need and love of good fellowship" as well as a commitment to antislavery.[5] Journalists, abolitionists, lawyers, ward bosses, literary figures: they had become the heart of Boston's antislavery machine.[6]

If Clarke, Grimes, and Hayden served as Andrew's religious triumvirate, the Bird associates were his political coterie. Bird himself was highly visible in state politics, spurning the Compromise of 1850 and, in the fall, winning a seat in the state legislature. Boston's Free-Soil counselors, as they were locally known, strategized over which political reforms would be necessary to wrest power from the Whigs. They also worked to publicize their arguments. In January 1851, they merged several existing political journals—the *Chronotype*, the *Emancipator*, and the *Boston Republican*—into a new organ called the *Commonwealth*, under the editorship of Elizur Wright. They hoped that the new Free-Soil daily would channel constituents to their cause, yet they failed to recognize that the bulk of the voters were not sophisticated readers.[7]

Andrew was active both above and below ground. During those days, he worked with his Court Street colleagues to forge a strong antislavery coalition. At twilight he quietly assisted Hayden and his associates to transport fugitives through the city. As he commuted from Boston to Hingham, he remained aware of the growing disparity between urban and rural Massachusetts. By 1850, Boston's population had increased tremendously. After the widespread revolutionary outbreak in western Europe, starting in 1848, a mass of immigrants had arrived, and they now formed half of the city's 130,000 residents. Boston had become one of America's most pluralistic societies. Yet the influx had created myriad municipal problems, with the poor packed into disease-ridden cellars even as the elite enjoyed opulent homes on beautifully land-scaped streets. Most of Boston's 2,500 African American residents lived on Beacon Hill. Fugitives could easily blend into that community, and Andrew's office served as a legal halfway house for them.[8]

Then, in mid-February 1851, an escaped Virginia slave named Shadrach Minkins gave Boston's antislavery community its first oppor-tunity to test the Fugitive Slave Law. Federal authorities apprehended Minkins at the Cornhill Coffeehouse, rushing him immediately to the federal courthouse, where George Ticknor Curtis, then a magistrate judge, was forced to comply with U.S. judicial commissioners and held him under guard to await a hearing. The Boston Vigilance Committee swung into action, quickly collecting $1,300 for a defense team com-posed of Richard Dana, Jr., Charles Davis, and Elizur Wright. The law-yers presented themselves at the courthouse; but as Wright and Davis were leaving the courtroom, African American activists surged past them, seized Minkins from federal officers, and hustled him down the steps and out the door. As the group raced down the street, two men, Hayden and Robert Morris, managed to guide Minkins into the Fourth Ward, where they secreted him in a neighbor's attic. That night, Under-ground Railroad conductors drove him to Watertown, and he eventually made his way to Canada.

The nation went into an uproar. Newspapers ranted, and President Millard Fillmore called for the conspirators to be indicted. Andrew wrote to Clarke, confirming the reportage and explaining that his friend Hayden was in custody for aiding and abetting the escape. "I hate war and love peace," he said, "but I should regret less the death of a hundred men defending successfully the sacred rights of human nature, and the blood-bought liberties of freemen, alike cloven down by this infernal law, than I should return to bondage a single fugitive."[9]

Before long, Boston was embroiled in another fugitive situation. Twenty-three-year-old Thomas Sims had sneaked aboard the *M & J. C. Gilmore* when it was docked in Savannah, Georgia. During the journey to Boston, crew members discovered him, and the captain locked the runaway slave into a cabin. But as the ship neared its destination, Sims escaped, stole a rowboat, and paddled to shore and freedom. On the evening of April 3, two police officers apprehended him on Richmond Street, claimed that he was disturbing the peace, and arrested him for theft. Authorities wanted to avoid a repeat of the Minkins escape. So, because Massachusetts law forbade prisons to be used as slave pens, they incarcerated Sims on the courthouse's third floor, "the door fastened with four two inch bolts, and [guarded by] sixty ferocious men, willing to be the tools of injustice, and enemies of liberty."[10]

To Andrew's astonishment, the governor mobilized more than 250 militia and police to guard the building. Boston Vigilance Committee members debated whether to use violence or allow the law to take its course. Wendell Phillips later claimed that the failure to rescue Sims was linked to the committee's inability to act decisively. Hayden, Grimes, and Thomas Wentworth Higginson, a militant white minister, argued for action and plotted Sims's escape. Yet others, including Andrew, recognized that bringing Sims to trial might place the issue before the public in a way that an escape would not. They supported a legal defense. Charles Loring, Robert Rantoul, Jr., Samuel Sewall, and Charles Sumner volunteered to defend him. So, in March, committee members petitioned the state supreme court for a writ of habeas corpus. When that was denied, they produced more petitions, arguing that the federal judicial commissioner was wielding unconstitutional power. Again, they were denied, and Sims's case went before Judge Lemuel Shaw, who ruled against him. On April 12, more than three hundred police, armed with swords and clubs, escorted him to Boston's wharf, where he set sail for Savannah. The editor of Boston's *Semi-Weekly Advertiser* noted: "It is gratifying to observe that, not withstanding the excited tone of the declamation on these occasions, and the disorganizing recommendations which are occasionally embraced in resolutions of these assemblies, the legal proceedings go on in an orderly and quiet manner, and the laws which are so much decried we have no doubt will be executed."[11]

The Sims case was front-page news, but the Boston Vigilance Committee had failed. Though Andrew was stricken silent, Theodore Parker was not. He wrote, "What a change from the Boston of John Hancock, to the Boston of the Fugitive Slave Bill; from the town which hung Grenville and Huske in effigy, to the city which approved Mr. Webster's speech in defence of slave-catching! . . . Massachusetts, all New England, has been deeply guilty of slavery and the slave-trade."[12]

The Politics of Man Hunting

Garrison's *Liberator* described the Sims's disaster as "one of the most disgraceful scenes ever witnessed in this city," but conservative papers lauded the result. Boston had been redeemed, claimed the *Herald*, "from the opprobrious epithets which have been denounced against her for her supposed inability and disinclination to yield to the laws of the Union, and the South will please accord us all the credit which is due therefor[e]."[13] Disgusted, Andrew watched conservatives celebrate what they saw as a major victory over abolitionists. Yet the antislavery coalition did not slacken in its work. Dana and Sumner spent weeks drawing up a bill to combat the Fugitive Slave Law, which was published in the Boston *Daily Commonwealth*. Though the bill was debated in the state legislature, lawmakers voted it down, refusing to condemn federal authority. An irate Ralph Waldo Emerson declared, "I will not obey, by God." He told a crowd in Concord, "This is a case of conscience, a call for compassion, a call for mercy. Slavery poisons and depraves everything it touches."[14]

Meanwhile, Hayden had been taken into custody for his part in Shadrach Minkins's escape. Dana, who was defending him, called on Andrew for legal advice and asked him to serve as a character witness. Eventually, Hayden was acquitted of aiding and abetting. That spring the tide began to turn for the abolitionists. In a historic electoral victory, a coalition of Free-Soilers, antislavery Whigs, and Democrats took control of the General Court and the governorship. Nathaniel Banks became the state's speaker of the house, Henry Wilson became the state's speaker of the senate, and, in a close race, Sumner was sent to the U.S. Senate to replace the retiring Daniel Webster. Andrew and his colleagues had gained an ally on the national stage, and this brought them directly into the complex politics around slavery in the United States. Much more than ice jams were breaking open that spring, as Bostonians listened to a one-hundred-gun salute on the Common in honor of the Free-Soil victory.

Andrew continued to ponder the Minkins case and the Fugitive Slave Law's constitutionality. His thoughts focused on the Latimer laws, which prevented Massachusetts officials from helping to detain suspected fugitive slaves and banned the use of state facilities to confine suspects. They had become the basis for the state's personal liberty laws. Andrew wrote to Sumner that the Fugitive Slave Law was "no law to a freeman. And no free man but a coward would even submit to it—having the means of effectual resistance. The answer is right, not only in morality, but also in legality, and . . . if it [is] right for any one man in Massachusetts, it is right for every man in Massachusetts." Andrew never wavered from the view that this really did mean "every man," regardless of color.[15]

Notably, the drama surrounding the Minkins and Sims cases fully entered into public consciousness via a work of fiction: the novel *Uncle Tom's Cabin; or, Life Among the Lowly*, published in March 1852 by the Connecticut abolitionist and teacher Harriet Beecher Stowe. The daughter of a New England preacher, Stowe was already a well-known writer. Nonetheless, she and her publisher were completely unprepared for *Uncle Tom's* popularity. The novel sold 3,000 copies on the day it appeared. Within a year, sales would top more than 300,000 copies, and the novel's plot had sparked a national debate on slavery. With her graphic descriptions of human torment, Stowe's portrayal of slavery triggered a massive reaction among northern readers. Richard Henry Dana, Jr., who pored over the novel during a train ride to New Haven, recalled, "It was a singular fact that four persons [in the railcar] were reading this book, each unconnected with the other."[16] *Uncle Tom's Cabin* had suddenly become the greatest single indictment against slavery.[17]

Andrew's correspondence does not mention the novel, but he surely read and discussed it with his Court Street and coffeehouse associates. Stowe's story was impressive, unforgettable, not least because her villain, Simon Legree, was a Yankee. Yet Andrew remained convinced that voters could bring about change. In May, he turned his sights toward the fall elections, hopeful that the Free-Soilers could capitalize on their previous year's victory and infuse the antislavery impulse into the national body politic. In a letter to Sumner, he expressed reluctance about supporting Winfield Scott's candidacy for president. He was incensed by the general's support for the Compromise of 1850 and remained grateful for Sumner's staunch abolitionism. After Robert Winthrop, a congressman from Massachusetts, attacked Sumner for his views, Andrew reassured his friend: "Does he not know that your very presence, as a free-soiler, in the Senate, is more than a speech?"[18]

Andrew was not a Garrison-style dis-unionist; but, like several of his Bird Club associates, including Sumner, he knew he needed to channel his reformer-activist ends through political means. Garrison's recently founded American Anti-Slavery Society included only a handful of African Americans in leadership roles. Because of this and other reasons, Frederick Douglass split with Garrison, and others, including Andrew, followed suit, preferring to associate with the Black reformers' grassroots groups. In the meantime, Andrew quietly corresponded with Sumner to gain a better sense of his own political course.

By the summer of 1852, many Americans, their outrage triggered by Stowe's novel, could not continue to overlook the contradictions between slavery and constitutionally guaranteed freedoms. As debate in Massachusetts swirled around the Fugitive Slave Law, Andrew labored at his growing legal practice and strategized for the coming election. But there were also important matters taking place in his family: on July 29 Eliza gave birth to their third child, Elizabeth Loring, known as Bessie. Andrew joyfully took up his fatherly duties again.[19]

Massachusetts Free-Soilers knew they had an uphill battle in the election; conservatives appeared to command a practical, compromise-based lead. So that summer a number of Andrew's colleagues convened a broad-based coalition that would eventually become the state's Republican party. For now, however, Free-Soilers were positioning themselves for the national convention in Pittsburgh. They wanted a no-compromise-with-slavery platform and even went so far as to rename themselves the Free Democratic Party. In the process of this work, Andrew struck up correspondence with the journalist Robert Carter, a New York native, who had moved to Boston in 1841. By 1852, Carter had joined the local Free-Soilers and for the moment was serving as editor of the Bird Club's Boston-based journal *Commonwealth*. Andrew asked him to publish the letter that John Van Buren, a son of Martin Van Buren, had sent to the Vermont Democratic Convention in 1851, declaring that the Fugitive Slave law was unconstitutional. Andrew told Carter, "It seems to me, in the present aspect of affairs, that [the letter] ought to be published & widely circulated among the Democracy, especially in the State of New York. . . . [Van Buren] took the highest ground against the Fugitive Act," offering to "resist it, *by force*."[20] As Andrew knew, journalists had great power in shaping political opinion, and he relied on sympathetic editors to promote his cause among the people.

The fall presidential election pitted the Whig candidate, Winfield Scott, against the Democrat Franklin Pierce, a former New Hampshire senator. Unsurprisingly, both had adopted platforms that skirted the slavery issue. The Free-Soilers, now known as the Free Democratic Party, nominated another New Hampshire senator, John Hale. Yet their vigorous antislavery platform did not attract voters. Having been burned in the previous election, barnburner Democrats and conscience Whigs who had once been attracted to that platform now realigned with their parties. Still, Andrew, like Sumner, refused to support Scott or Pierce and voted for Hale, though he knew his candidate had no chance.

A few weeks before the election, Daniel Webster died. Wendell Phillips wrote, "If the Fugitive Slave Law died with him, he would indeed have slept in blessings."[21] His passing marked the end of an era. Gone was New England's most celebrated Whig, the last of Congress's "Great Triumvirate," which had included the enslavers Henry Clay and John Calhoun. Together, the three men had shaped the contours of a party ideology that had made no apology for slavery and had transformed capitalistic development, nationalism, and conservatism into Whig cornerstones. Now, although the Whigs were able to carry Massachusetts for Scott, they remained deeply fractured as a party. Meanwhile, the Free-Soilers had performed well, and they hoped to use this Whig division to their advantage in future races.[22]

Andrew experienced a more personal loss that fall when his friend and mentor Henry Fuller died. Despite their political differences, Fuller had polished Andrew's public persona, transforming him into a shrewd and eloquent courtroom presence. In a tribute to his friend, Andrew recalled Fuller as a consummate servant-leader who had dedicated himself to clients from every class. Thanks to his mentor, the young lawyer had matured into intellectual and political confidence, and he sorrowed over the loss.[23]

In November, Franklin Pierce was elected president. After his victory, he centered his expansionist impulses on building a transatlantic railroad to California. But in Massachusetts politicians remained fixated on slavery. As the legislature convened in January 1853, members prepared to debate amendments to the state constitution that would disempower the Fugitive Slave Law. Andrew had hoped to be part of this cohort. Though he remained busy in Boston and Hingham, he had allowed his name to go forward as a candidate for the Plymouth County state senate seat. Thanks to a coalition between Democrats and Free-Soilers, he, along with the political veteran Horace Collamore, had been put forward as antislavery candidates. Yet neither pulled enough votes to win, and the Whigs Aaron Hobart and Matthias Ellis were duly elected to the legislature.[24]

Anti-Nebraska and Anthony Burns

In early January 1854, Senator Stephen A. Douglas presented what he called the "Nebraska Bill," which he saw as a solution for managing western expansion in a way that would allow the federal government to complete the transcontinental railroad. The bill concerned the vast tract of land between the Missouri River and the Rocky Mountains. At question was how the slavery issue would be handled in the new territories of Nebraska and Kansas. Douglas's bill presumed that Nebraska would be settled as free and Kansas would be settled as slaveholding, but it left the choice to the voters, a notion that Douglas promoted as popular sovereignty. The resulting political storm further widened the nation's sectional divide.[25]

Enacting the Nebraska Bill would require repealing the Missouri Compromise, which had prohibited slavery's expansion in the Louisiana Purchase territories. This incited a congressional debate that had little to do with the railroad and everything to do with slavery's expansion. Eager to awaken a broad-based antislavery countermovement, a number of congressmen turned to the press, hoping that a flurry of editorials on the issue would draw concerned northern voters into the fray. A group of Free Democratic and antislavery representatives, including Sumner, fanned the flames by publishing an anti–Nebraska Bill manifesto, "An Appeal of the Independent Democrats in Congress to the People of the United States." In late January, Douglas amended the bill to include specifics about the organization of two separate territorial governments, renaming his proposal the Kansas-Nebraska Act. The oratorical combat continued for weeks in the House and Senate. Finally, on March 5, after a night-long debate, senators passed the bill at five o'clock in the morning. A correspondent for the New York–based *Christian Inquirer* described the scene as "a sad spectacle," and "an undignified debate . . . brought to an undignified close."[26]

The congressional uproar reverberated across the country. Yet few Americans understood the notion of popular sovereignty better than the antislavery activists of Massachusetts, who had long been the underdogs in the fight against the Fugitive Slave Law and slavery's expansion. Now Boston abolitionists began holding anti-Nebraska meetings to publicize their opposition to the new act. In February Andrew's friend Richard Dana attended one in Faneuil Hall, noting in his diary that "the Nebraska question is now the great question before the country."[27] Josiah Quincy, once the mayor of Boston and a former member of Congress also attended, offering an anecdote that was fitting for the moment. He recalled telling the Virginia legislator John Randolph, "If you push these measures much farther, you will produce Union at the North. Union at the North!"[28]

On April 5, another daughter, Edith, was born into the Andrew family. But despite the exhaustions of work and home, Andrew closely followed the congressional proceedings and their aftermath. The House had yet to vote on the act, but members were aware of the growing national rancor. In response, members postponed other bills to ensure that the Kansas-Nebraska Act came to a vote before Congress adjourned in May. Late on the night of May 23, the House passed the act by a vote of 113 to 100, and Pierce signed it a week later. "The deed is done," wrote Garrison. "The Slave Power is again victorious."[29] Yet the ink had barely dried before Josiah Quincy's prediction came to pass: northerners did unite.[30]

In Massachusetts, the tipping point was, unsurprisingly, another run-in with the Fugitive Slave Law. In these days, when congressmen were about to sign the Kansas-Nebraska Act into law, Judge Edward Loring, a federal judicial commissioner, and an anti-Nebraska Whig, issued an arrest warrant for the fugitive slave Anthony Burns. A year earlier, the twenty-three-year-old had escaped from a Virginia plantation to Boston, where he found employment in a clothing store and became a congregant at Reverend Grimes's church. Using a false pretext, marshals apprehended Burns on Court Street and took him to the courthouse. His owner, Charles Suttle, demanded that the fugitive be returned to Virginia. For legal help he turned to Edward Parker and Seth Thomas, who had worked with claimants in the Craft and Sims cases. Dana and Robert Morris, a prominent African American lawyer, mediated on Burns's behalf, and the pair managed to delay the case until May 27. Simultaneously, the Boston Vigilance Committee, led by Andrew, took action to defend the fugitive. As these supporters worked to free Burns legally, the mayor of Boston called out the city's entire 1,800-member militia, a show of strength against the 5,000 antislavery activists who had demonstrated against Burns's incarceration and were staging a rally in Faneuil Hall.[31]

On the night of May 26, a crowd of African American and white abolitionists, including Lewis Hayden and Thomas Higginson, stormed the courthouse to free Burns. Using a beam as battering ram, they forced their way through a door but were met by more than fifty policemen. During the pandemonium, shots rang out, killing James Batchelder, a Boston truckman who had been appointed as one of the guards. Several people were injured, including Dana, and some were arrested, among them Hayden and Albert Browne, Jr., a young lawyer in Andrew's office, who had attempted to rescue Higginson. Additional forces were called in overnight and the next morning a crowd of 2,000 people gathered in protest. Pleading for calm, the mayor ordered police to barricade all the roads leading to the courthouse. The affair at the courthouse undermined the abolitionists' cause, highlighting their violent tendencies and marking them as anarchists. These were exactly the tactics that worried Andrew and his closest friends. Though he was deeply involved with the Burns case, he remained aloof from the violence—not only because of his pacifist convictions but also because he needed to be available as legal defense.[32]

That same May, Theodore Parker delivered an address aptly titled "Some Thoughts on the Progress of America" to attendees of the Anti-Slavery Convention in Boston. While Parker praised the Anglo-Saxon colonists for bringing what he saw as their superior Teutonic characteristics to the New World, he denounced the reign of terror over African Americans, excoriating southerners, and their assumptions about racial inferiority. Andrew knew that many northerners shared the same prejudices, but he continued to align his own thinking with the moral assumptions that Parker had earlier outlined in his sermon "Of Justice and the Conscience"—that civilization was predicated on a "continual and progressive triumph of the right." As Parker said, "I do not pretend to understand the moral universe, [for] the arc is a long one, but from what I see I am sure it bends towards justice." He was an optimist: "Things refuse to be mismanaged long," he argued.[33] Andrew trusted in this axiom.

On May 31, the Burns case came before Judge Loring, who yielded to the law. The defense could not overcome a decree that granted commissioners the power to issue arrest warrants, hold hearings, and issue certificates of removal. For instance, according to the law, any man arrested in Boston and charged with a crime under, say, Virginia laws would not be tried in Massachusetts but in Virginia. This law applied to slaves and non-slaves alike, though opponents of the Fugitive Slave Law argued that a white accused criminal would eventually get a trial whereas an accused slave would not. Burns's defense advocated that every legal means should be available for constitutional protection, but to no avail. The *Boston Post* described the law as a "ministerial, and not a judicial act"; thus, the fugitive's arrest was seen as constitutional.[34] Fearing violence after his decision, Loring solicited federal support from President Pierce, who dispatched three companies of regulars to Boston. The city police was out in force as thousands of citizens lined the street to the wharf, held back by marshals' guards armed with drawn bayonets, but this did not deter some crowd members from singing, "Oh! Carry Me Back to Old Virginia," to the waiting ship.[35]

Standing inside Andrew's office, Clarke observed the crowd on the corner of Court and Washington streets. He later recalled:

> I saw . . . the lawyers' offices hung in black. I saw the cavalry, artillery, marines, and police, a thousand strong, escorting with shotted guns one trembling colored man to the vessel which was to carry him to slavery. I heard the curses, both loud and deep, poured on these soldiers; I saw the red flush in their cheeks as the crowd yelled at them, Kidnappers! Kidnappers![36]

Nearby, the headquarters of the journal *Commonwealth* displayed a coffin inscribed with the word "Liberty" dangling by ropes from the top of the building.[37] Andrew himself refused to watch the procession; instead, he sat writing at his desk, the only calm man in the room. If his soul was on fire, few could tell. He had done all he could to prevent the rendition; "now he could do no more, and sat at his desk as serene as if no such events were taking place around him."[38] But the event left its mark on the citizens. Mary Blanchard, the daughter of Benjamin Seaver, a former mayor who also served as congressman, told her father that "the last week will long be remembered as a sad one by the citizens of Boston."[39] The editor of the *Monthly Religious Magazine* was blunter: "It is not that Virginia has conquered Massachusetts—that our necks are under the heel of the oppressor . . . [but] that our prophecies have failed, and our wishes are disappointed."[40]

Federal commissioners indicted Parker, Phillips, Higginson, Martin Stowell, and three others for their roles in the courthouse riot. Parker asked former presidential candidate John Hale to serve as his lead counsel; the other defendants retained Andrew, his protégé William Burt, Charles Ellis, and Henry Durant. Andrew may have restrained his emotions on Burns's rendition day, but he was vigorous in his defense of the accused. He offered the dramatic argument that Loring should be removed from his position, claiming that the warrant was illegal because it had originated from a jurisdiction without legal authority and that the indictment had not sufficiently particularized the offense with which the defendants were charged. In their rebuttal, prosecutors declared that the government had no object in mind other than maintaining the law.

As Andrew saw it, the problem was not necessarily Loring but the laws he was dutifully bound to execute. Though he was a devoted constitutionalist, Andrew's compassion for the fugitives had overcome his better judgment. But the law was clear, and Dana surprised his colleagues by defending Loring. In the end, the state's house and senate voted to remove the judge, but Governor Henry Gardner kept him in office, arguing that there was no state law that prohibited a state judge from returning a fugitive slave. Sidelined, Andrew observed Dana's admirable defense of a law he despised. Loring's detractors needed to wait until the fall elections would provide a political opening to move against him. In the meantime, Bostonians vilified the judge, burning him in effigy and barring him from his social affiliations. Harvard Law School even debated about whether to remove him from the faculty. Meanwhile, amid this excitement and acrimony, Reverend Grimes, working quietly through intermediaries, raised enough money to purchase Burns, who returned to Boston as a free man.[41]

Andrew had no illusions about the strength of the Boston Vigilance Committee's influence. Its efforts to protect fugitives paled in comparison with Congress's titanic power to ensure their return to bondage. Nonetheless, he was deeply shocked by the Burns's decision and its aftermath, which highlighted the South's ever-increasing stronghold on national politics. Compliance with the law was one thing, yet he was repulsed by the idea of adhering to immorality through injustice. And when he learned about the political collusion on Capitol Hill that had resulted in the passage of the Kansas-Nebraska Act and the repeal of the Missouri Compromise, his blood boiled. That Senator Douglas had engineered a way to undo congressional prohibitions on slavery for the sake of a transcontinental railroad made the compromise all the more repugnant.

Outraged Free-Soilers convened in Boston's Music Hall to promote the idea of a Free Democratic state convention. Among the fiery speakers was Andrew, who argued that the time had come for northern voters to unite their political interests to promote freedom against slavery's expansion. In his view, this was Christian democracy at work, a notion that Clarke had beautifully conceptualized in his recent "Discourse on Christian Politics." He had declared, "Cast down but not destroyed, fraud and force, allied with fear and cupidity, may conquer much, but they cannot conquer God Almighty." "Let us work in his cause," Clarke had challenged his brethren. Andrew was in the audience that day, and he embraced the challenge.[42]

Not just in New England but across the North, a new popular sovereignty was unfolding as antislavery Democrats, Whigs, and Free-Soilers
forged an anti-Nebraska coalition in reaction the Kansas-Nebraska
Act. In Massachusetts, this fusion took shape in the summer of 1854 as
activists worked to chart a new course. Andrew called them together
for a meeting in Worcester in July, where representatives appointed a
provisional state committee to undertake the new coalition's vision.
They named Andrew chairman and christened themselves the Republican Party. In their view, Sumner would be the likeliest champion of
their cause. Yet while he was flattered by the invitation, he recognized
that the movement remained feeble.[43]

Sumner cast a large shadow in Boston's political world, and Andrew
was content to stand in his shade. But he, too, was a powerful per-
suader. Now he told the senator that the moment for conciliation had
passed. It was time for a political transformation, and Sumner was
best positioned to lead this new party in the national arena. He told his
friend:

> I think, in spite of strong opposition from the Whig presses and fugle-
> man, which cannot bear to give up their factious powers and influence,
> that there is a great popular movement commenced, which may—under
> proper cultivation—disclose a splendid result in the fall. . . . Your recent
> battles in the Senate have shut the mouth of personal opposition, wrung
> applause from the unwilling, excited a State pride and gratitude, such as
> rarely it is the fortune of any one to win. . . . I want you to write to me at
> once, permitting me to say to any of our friends that you *will* attend the
> meeting.[44]

To buoy the Republican alliance at the September convention,
Andrew invited the New York journalist Horace Greeley, editor of the
Tribune, to speak. Greeley declined the invitation but praised the new
fusion party as a coalition of "united defenders of Free labor and Free
soils throughout the Union."[45] In the meantime, Sumner accepted
Andrew's invitation to lead the party and gave an impassioned speech
that fashioned its identity, demanding that voters "place freedom
above party, and their country above politicians." "Such an organization," he said, "is now presented by this Republican Convention." "As
republicans," he declared, "we go forth to encounter the *oligarchs* of
slavery."[46]

Sumner's speech was captivating, but he was savvy enough to avoid
committing himself to this frail crusade. If Washington had taught the
senator anything, it was that traditional party lines were too rigid for

such far-reaching antislavery principles. Andrew understood, though he was disappointed. He next attempted to lure Henry Wilson to stand as the Republican Party's candidate for Massachusetts governor and managed to place his name on the ballot that fall. But like Sumner, Wilson saw the pitfalls ahead, especially with the rise of a new political movement about to envelop Commonwealth voters.[47]

CHAPTER 6

THE REPUBLICAN TIDE

1855–1856

The Politics of Reform

The name *Republican* suggested visionary ambitions, but for now they resonated in only limited circles in Massachusetts. By the fall of 1854, the emerging Republican party was trying to extend its reach further into the state, even as its activists were dealing with another tide of prejudice. This one linked to the migratory swell that had brought thousands of German Protestants and Irish Catholics into the local workforce. Under the mantra "Americans must rule America," a secret anti-Catholic nativist group known as the Supreme Order of the Star-Spangled Banner began its "mysterious political career, as the Know Nothings. It sought to prohibit Catholics from holding public office and to prevent immigrants from voting by extending the period before naturalization. The group required its members to be "twenty-years of age, to believe in the existence of a God, and to obey without question, the will of the Order." Although clearly xenophobic, Know Nothings supported the regulation of industry, women's rights, working-class improvements, and educational and temperance reform, all of which held wide appeal. With the collapse of the Whig Party, the movement became powerful in Boston and emerged as a major political alliance known as the American Party.[1]

Days before the election, Henry Wilson betrayed his loftier impulses. He pulled out as the Republican gubernatorial candidate and instead accepted the Free-Soil nomination as governor. Some newspapers charged that he had made an arrangement with the Know Nothings not to run as a Republican in exchange for election to the U.S. Senate, should they carry the legislature. He was not alone in bolting from the Republicans: many pragmatic Free-Soilers-turned-Republicans made the same leap to the Know Nothing's American Party. Now Andrew was caught in a difficult spot. Though he loathed the Know Nothing's anti-immigrant impulses, he sensed a Republican loss. Thus, lured by the promise of social and school reform, he followed several of his close colleagues, including his friend Lewis Hayden, who closed ranks behind gubernatorial candidate Henry J. Gardner, a moderate Whig who had moved into the Know Nothing camp and won by an over-whelming majority. Like Andrew, Gardner was a Bowdoin alumnus, a reformer, an antislavery activist, but not a nativist. In November the Massachusetts Know Nothings captured the governorship, all state-wide offices, every state senate seat, and most of the state house seats. Unsurprisingly, the new legislature elected Wilson to fill the retiring Edward Everett's vacancy in the U.S. Senate. On the sidelines, skeptics such as Andrew and Sumner took great care not to offend the new political order, even while they remained suspect about its longevity. Both sensed that the movement would be short-lived, and they were biding their time.[2]

Massachusetts Know Nothings not only opposed slavery but also promised to modernize society, regulate railroads and insurance companies, improve schools, expand women's and laborers' rights, and revise regulatory laws to improve working-class conditions. Though Andrew appreciated such humanitarian ideals, he was not blind to the party's discriminatory tactics and beliefs. For instance, now that the Know Nothings controlled the legislature, they were able to enact a prohibition law in 1855, and its enforcement became both a political and legal issue over the use and abuse of alcohol. Still, despite its prejudicial actions, the party had unified Boston's abolitionist culture, allowing the antislavery platform to find its way into mainstream politics and give Andrew an unexpected victory.[3]

It also gave him the hope of ending capital punishment in the state. He had already been involved in establishing the Society for the Abolition of Capital Punishment. In early 1855, as part of his service on the standing committee that annually brought anti–death penalty resolutions to the legislature, he had presented such a brilliant case that Garrison decided to print it verbatim in the *Liberator*. Legislators were impressed by his exceptionally conceived argument and impassioned oratory. He described these deaths in detail, revealing what had been mostly hidden from the public:

Somebody goes into the jail and blind[fold]s the victim; two or three others take him between them, and they march to the scaffold; somebody else adjusts the fatal machinery; somebody else puts him in the position in which the act may be consummated; and at last, so far we have refined, that no man's hand perpetrates the last act which results in the felon's death. No, sir, the Sheriff leaves him as he stands there, and by a cunning device, the machinery is so adjusted, that his *foot*, in the natural course of his retreat, may touch a fatal spring. Every individual does as little as he can, and at last, it seems as if nobody hangs the victim. We skulk all round; and dare not face the awful responsibility in its dark and abhorrent form.[4]

For Andrew, this work against the death penalty was as emotionally transformative as his work for fugitive slaves. The same adrenaline that raced through the condemned prisoner, he imagined, certainly ran through escaped slaves.

By the spring of 1855, he had joined the Boston Anti-Man Hunting League, a radical group that included several members of the Boston Vigilance Committee and involved secret handshakes, grips, codes, and passwords. Andrew, along with Henry Bowditch, Samuel Howe, James Clarke, Ellis Loring, Henry Prentiss, and others, drew up the organization's constitution. Members trained themselves in extralegal tactics to stop fugitive kidnappings, including, if necessary, abducting slave catchers. Andrew was continuing to suffer from chronic health problems, which kept him from participating in the league's more labor-intensive activities, so he focused on fundraising for equipment (including billy clubs and a boat named *Moby Dick*) and expansion. "Wrong-headed and absurd as the plan may seem to many, if not all, 'reasonable' persons," said Bowditch, "I am proud to remember that I was among the first of those who advocated physical resistance to slavery as we saw it in the North." By this time Andrew and his associates had come to know most of Boston's fugitives personally, and the "Budget for Destitute Fugitives," which he administrated, served more than four hundred transient families in the 1850s.[5]

Andrew's client list continued to expand. Fugitives knew they had a friend in him, and they often hung around his office, seeking advice and comfort. Among them was Father Josiah Hansen, who had escaped years before from a Kentucky farm. He would share his history with other fugitives, who told similarly heart-wrenching stories. Yet even as Andrew remained tied to his reform work, he was attentive to state and local politics. The Bird Club kept him close to the inner circles of power, and he took note of how volatile local politics could be. The trick, he believed, was to remain devoted to cause and principle. This was complicated because even in Boston pervasive racial discrimination highlighted the contradictions within those who opposed slavery but did not advocate equality. Yet the antislavery activists continued to gain ground and visibility. At a recent Massachusetts Anti-slavery Society meeting, Garrison had publicly burnt the Fugitive Slave Law, Judge Loring's decision in the Burns case, and the U.S. Constitution. Even more impressive than these inflammatory acts, however, were the words that the writer and naturalist Henry David Thoreau offered to the crowd: "The law will never make men free. It is men who have to make the law free."[6]

Seth Botts and Mary Botts

Andrew and Thoreau both demonstrated the truth of those words when they became involved in the case of the fugitive slave Seth Botts. Botts had escaped from a Stafford County, Virginia, plantation in September 1850. After making his way to Boston, he changed his name to Henry Williams and found lodging at the home of Isabella Holmes, the daughter of Samuel Snowden, a Methodist minister and antislavery activist. Botts took a job as a barber; but when he learned that federal marshals were on his trail, the Vigilance Committee sent him to Thoreau's house in Concord. To authenticate his story, Botts gave Thoreau letters from Garrison and Reverend Joseph Cammett Lovejoy. He told Thoreau that he had been corresponding with his owner, James Tolson, to negotiate not only his own manumission but also his family's. He had saved $500 of the $600 needed for himself but he needed legal assistance to purchase his family. A heartbreaking side note was that Tolson was also Botts's father.

On October 1, 1851, Thoreau recorded in his diary that he had put Botts onto the train heading for Canada and freedom.[7] But that December he returned to Boston, eager to help his family. More than likely Thoreau had mentioned Andrew's name to him. Possibly Botts struck up a conversation with the lawyer at the barbershop where he worked, near the Cornhill Coffeehouse. However they met, Andrew listened to Botts's complicated story and offered to help him. The situation would take years to unravel legally, though Andrew was hoping to depend on Sumner as a liaison in executing the legal transactions, given that Tolson's property was close to Washington. He began corresponding with Christopher Neale, a wealthy Alexandria judge, who represented the estate that held some members of Botts's family, and he wrote to Sumner about his client.[8]

In January 1852, Andrew sent Sumner $500, asking the senator to give the money to John Clark, a mediator, who had agreed to serve on Tolson's behalf. Despite his pro-slavery stance, Clark was a congenial clergyman, and the tone of his letters had convinced Andrew that he was sympathetic to the situation. In early February, Sumner sent Andrew good news: a manumission document verifying that Botts had bought his freedom. Furthermore, given the "love and affection" Tolson felt for his son, the slaveowner had agreed to allow him two more years to raise the remaining $100. Unfortunately, this gesture put Botts at risk of reenslavement until he received his official manumission papers. (He finally did on July 28, 1854.)[9]

Meanwhile, in August 1852, Andrew had asked Sumner to help him obtain the freedom of Botts's wife, Elizabeth, as well as their three children, his mother-in-law Prudence Bell, and her other children. Complicated by questions of ownership, the case involving his mother-in-law was stalled in the circuit court for months before reaching the Virginia Supreme Court in 1854. As that case pended, Andrew continued his correspondence with Judge Neale, managing in this way to get the litigating parties to allow Elizabeth and her children to leave Virginia. As he had done for Seth, he offered cash—$800—toward "the expenses of a suit of freedom."[10] But he could not initiate their passage until October, when the higher court finally ruled that Prudence Bell belonged without condition to John Cornwell. Now Andrew enlisted the help of Boston attorney Charles Ingersoll, then visiting Washington, asking him to meet personally with Neale. Ingersoll reported to Andrew that Neale had agreed to travel to Prince William County, retrieve Elizabeth and the children, and bring them to Alexandria. This took place in mid-January 1855. A week later Cornwell arrived in Alexandria with the manumission deeds.

To pay for Neale's traveling expenses and for the family's trip north, Andrew sent additional funds to Sumner, which arrived in early March. Neale then released the family to Sumner, who would care for them for a few days until they could be transported to Boston. In a letter to Andrew, the senator described the children as light-skinned, noting that one daughter, seven-year-old Mary, was so white that it was difficult to detect African blood. He wondered if Andrew might consider photographing her for publicity purposes. Andrew agreed, arranging with Sumner to have a daguerreotype made of Mary before she left for Boston. It might not only aid his quest to free her relatives but also "add impressiveness to the appeal made for state action" against the Fugitive Slave Law.[11]

The daguerreotype was made at Julian Vannerson Studio in Richmond, and Sumner sent a copy to Andrew while the family was enroute to Boston. After showing it to several friends, Andrew told the senator that people had begun "asking for it."[12] Sumner also sent several copies to other friends, in one letter speaking of Mary as a "second Ida May," referring to the kidnapped heroine of Mary Langdon's antislavery novel *Ida May: The Story of Things Actual and Possible*. He mentioned the daguerreotype and its subject in a letter to the Boston-based *Telegraph*: "She is bright and intelligent. . . . I think her presence among us (in Boston) will be more effective than any speech I can make." He hoped that it would be exhibited to the members of the legislature: "Let a hardhearted Hunker look at it and be softened."[13] Sumner's letter and Mary's picture circulated throughout the press in Boston and New York, garnering significant attention. Andrew took advantage of the publicity to solicit donations for the family. In a letter to Longfellow asking for help, he emphasized, "Seven persons get their freedom for $1300."[14]

On March 9, forty-four days after their manumission, the Botts family was reunited in Boston before a cheering crowd. It had been several years since Seth had seen his wife and children, and the scene was moving. Andrew wrote to Sumner, "You may be assured that I contemplated the happy and complete re-establishment of this poor family, restored to each other, no more as slaves, but in full freedom and peace, with more thankfulness than I can tell." He even arranged the parents' official marriage.[15]

By bringing Mary Botts's apparent whiteness into public discussion, Andrew and Sumner highlighted the paradoxes of racial categorization and segregated schooling. The resulting interest in her portrait became so intense that Andrew was able to use it to fundraise for the manumission of Prudence Bell and her children. He published a broadside titled "History of Ida May," which he offered for sale in portrait galleries, bookstores, and stationery shops. The funds for manumission, he told Sumner, would "be raised by the profits on the sale of little Ida May's picture, whose youth, beauty, and innocence, rescued from all the horrible contingencies of the bond-woman's lot, have touched many hearts and moistened many eyes."[16] Mary became known as the "white slave," and the newspapers used her image to reinforce a sentimental, but effective, vision of universal childhood. Covering her visit to the state capitol, a reporter for the *Worcester Daily Spy* wrote that her "eyes sparkled just like those of any other little girl when she saw the big cod-fish hanging in the hall."[17] In late March, with Andrew's approval, Sumner brought her with him to Boston's Tremont Temple.

She and Anthony Burns sat beside him while he spoke on "The Necessity, the Practicability, and the Dignity of the Anti-Slavery Enterprise." The publicity campaign was extremely effective. Andrew's broadside sold so well that he secured the Bells' manumission. From beginning to end, the process, which he later described to Sumner "as the siege of Troy," would take nine years to complete.[18]

As Andrew's fame increased, so did his workload. It was time to reduce his travel, so he and Eliza purchased a small brick home on Charles Street in Boston. He had loved Hingham's slow pace and pastoral surroundings, but eliminating the commute meant he could spend more time with his young children while continuing to engage deeply with his moral activism. He continued to puzzle over the conundrums of prejudice. The Botts case had confirmed that complexion more than race was determining white attitudes. Race, as he understood it, was the condition of belonging to a group that shared qualities or characteristics inherited from a common ancestor. It was an oddity that the complexion which made humans less valuable as slaves made them more acceptable in free society.[19]

By now Andrew had been practicing law for fifteen years. Although, to this point, he had had few international or maritime clients, the Crimean War, which had been raging in the Balkans since 1853, now drew him into a case that expanded his legal knowledge. Early in 1855, Charles Henry Stanley, the British consul in New York, asked him to defend Louis Kazinski, a Polish sailor, and his three associates for violating neutrality laws. The British had allied with the Ottoman Empire, France, and Sardinia against the Russians. In need of troops, they had sent agents to America to search for British subjects, with the goal of conscripting them, sending them to Halifax in Nova Scotia, and then transporting them to the Balkans for military duty. American authorities, however, interpreted this as the illegal recruitment of men in the United States, and federal marshals were ordered to seize several British brigs. Among them was the *Buffalo*, bound for Halifax. U.S. Attorney Benjamin Hallett ordered Kazinski's party, who had been forcibly conscripting the men, to Boston, where they were held under arrest.

Assisted by his partner, William Burt, Andrew worked for months on the case, which went to trial in mid-July. The prosecutor argued that a concerted arrangement to procure men for the war existed between the officers at Halifax and the British vice-consul at New York. Kazinski, he maintained, had forcibly retained the men on the brig, refusing to land those begging for discharge. Andrew countered that there was no way to prove the consent of the men who had been hired to enlist in

Massachusetts and that facts proved that the British officers had grossly deceived Kazinski and his associates. After a long week in federal court, Andrew won a not-guilty verdict, and Judge Peleg Sprague ordered the defendants to be discharged.[20] Andrew's handling of the complicated international laws was impressive. Moreover, by the time he finished up the Kazinski case, the defendants in his Burns case had already escaped criminal prosecution, thanks to the work of his co-counsel.

Given their work on behalf of both fugitive slaves and equal rights for "Colored Children" in the public schools, Andrew and Lewis Hayden were invited in February 1855 to address the legislature. Andrew used the occasion to offer his views on the Fugitive Slave Law's constitutionality and urged members to enact a personal liberty law comparable to the ones in Vermont and Connecticut. After he had finished, the committee chair invited John Githell to speak. Born in Pennsylvania and raised in an abolitionist district in Ohio, Githell now owned fifty slaves in Alabama. He told his listeners, "If any of mine get here, you may keep 'em," but he claimed that they liked home so well that they would not run away. "We are hospitable," he said, "[and we] think for our niggers." Hayden then rose in response. "Now, sir," he addressed the chair, "you have all seen Frederick Douglass, Mr. Brown, and other fugitive slaves, and if they are the worst specimens then you need have no fear of letting loose those now in bondage!" Githell, in turn, declared that he had a clear conscience as an enslaver. Yet he was willing to sell his slaves and abolish the institution; he believed that God would "work it out" in the end.[21]

At about this time African American activists had solicited Andrew to examine the statutes that were segregating Massachusetts schools. For decades, Black community members had been forced to manage their children's formal education. By the late 1840s, however, a movement had begun to end segregation and allow African American children to attend schools in their home district. After several defeats, they turned to Sumner, who, in December 1849, assisted by his Black co-counsel, Robert Morris, argued the case before the Massachusetts Supreme Judicial Court. Sumner and Morris declared that school segregation violated equality before the law because racial distinctions were not permissible in the state. In response, the court ruled that segregated schools were constitutional because they were equally provisioned. In answering the charge that segregation perpetuated race prejudice, justices argued that "this prejudice, if it exists, is not created by law, and probably cannot be changed by law," and the precedent stood.

Now, along with Sumner, Morris, Hayden, and the African American integrationist William Cooper Nell, Andrew undertook the challenge of desegregating Boston's private lyceums and public schools. In order to redefine how Americans were conceptualizing race, Black and white abolitionists and communal organizations began to develop an African American intellectual movement to advance the notion of school integration. Their work caught national attention. The New York–based *Herald* asked if putting "children of the African race on a footing of equality with the children of the original Puritans" would be a national standard of the American Party. In response, the Boston-based *Telegraph* maintained that "the public schools of Massachusetts are her peculiar institution, as slavery is the peculiar institution of Virginia, and she claims the right to regulate them in her own way."[22]

In the spring of 1855, the Boston integrationists joined ranks with school committee members Henry Bowditch, Edmund Jackson, and others to demand an end to separate schools. With Sumner back in Washington, they turned to Andrew, asking him to review and revise the existing statutes. Charles Slack, a Know Nothing legislator and the editor of the *Commonwealth*, had prepared a report proposing desegregation, which Andrew revised and presented to the legislature. It read, "In determining the qualifications of scholars to be admitted into any public school or any district school in this Commonwealth, no distinction shall be made on account of the race, color, or religious opinions, of the applicant or scholar." Andrew recognized that maintaining separate schools would have consequences, not only because of inferior conditions in Black schools but also because of long-term psychological and sociological damage. A fairer education system would not erase racial prejudice, but it would be a start.

With little opposition, legislators passed a school desegregation law, which the governor signed on April 28. The Commonwealth had become the first state to pass an act outlawing public school segregation; and on September 1, African American children were permitted to attend the public schools near their homes. To celebrate, Black parents met at the Twelfth Baptist Church, affectionately known as the "Church of the Fugitive Slaves," where they expressed their appreciation and pledged to have their "children [arrive] punctually at school, and neat in their dress, and in all other ways will aid their instructors in the task that which has been assigned them."[23]

The new law was a triumph for Andrew. To add to his joy, legislators also overrode Governor Gardner's veto of the Personal Liberty Law, which he and his colleagues had designed to thwart the Fugitive Slaw

Law. This bold new law forbade state courts, state jails, and state militia from being used in the apprehension of any African American fugitive. It also ordered that no one serving as U.S. judicial commissioner could hold a state-managed judicial office. Southerners were outraged; their papers dubbed the law the "Massachusetts Nullification" and highlighted it as a step closer to disunion. The Washington-based *National Intelligencer* maintained that the law would be "inoperative," given that the governor, "not believing it constitutional," had not given the "requisite order to insure its administration." The *North Star* noted that it remained to be seen if Judge Loring would resign as either judge of probate or slave commissioner.[24]

Andrew spent much of the summer of 1855 focusing on how to vitalize the Republican Party. In Massachusetts, a political realignment had begun at the local level, and Nathaniel Banks had agreed to chair the Republican state convention. (Though Democrats had nominated him, he was in actuality a Know Nothing.) Andrew wanted to design a platform that would bring together antislavery Whigs, Free-Soilers, independent Democrats, and Know Nothings, and Sumner emboldened him in this task. The state's Republican convention took place in Worcester in September, with attendees supporting the antislavery platform and nominating Julius Rockwell, a Whig from Pittsfield, as their candidate for governor. Yet Whiggery and Know Nothingism had not run their course in Massachusetts. As the Republicans set their own slate, Samuel Walley accepted the Whig nomination, and the incumbent Gardner agreed to serve as the Know Nothing candidate for another term. The nativist movement continued to attract a broad spectrum of conservatives and xenophobes, and it easily prevailed again in November. Still, even as Republicans lost another battle, they were slowly winning the war. The election results revealed a clear choice going forward. Would voters continue to opt for Know Nothing nativist conservatism or choose the antislavery principles of the Republican Party?

As the Kansas-Nebraska Act and the Burns's case crystalized the republic's sectional divide, Massachusetts political culture was struggling with change. Writing about this shift, Boston's *Daily Advertiser* made two fundamental observations. First, the Republican Party, "like its predecessors," had proven "again to be successful in nothing but bragging." Second, Gardner's supporters "may chiefly be found among those who[m] newspaper articles and public arguments do not even reach—much less convince," and thus "unjust prejudices, skillfully manipulated—wrong impressions studiously indulged—determine their votes." To win an election, Sumner agreed with the editor, saying that "the best men, with the best characters & best talents ... devoted to the best cause," as he described, would have to draw voters toward a single party with a narrow definition of antislavery. Whether abolitionists liked this or not, they needed a leader with such appeal.[25]

Andrew had no illusions about the Republican Party's prospects. He knew that tough work lay ahead. The party was luring Whigs and Free-Soilers into its ranks, but leaders would need to find a way to separate conservatives from their anti-abolitionism. Recent elections had provided lessons in how to navigate these antislavery shoals, and Republicans would need to take advantage of them, especially now that the American Party's popularity was waning. Candidates were turning away from its appalling nativism to acknowledge a higher moral ground. Yet as this transformation was happening in Massachusetts, turmoil was escalating in Kansas between pro- and antislavery forces, a chaotic situation that had spawned two separate territorial governments. Reading Garrison's Kansas updates in the *Liberator*, Andrew understood that the storm was fast approaching.[26]

Let It Be Vacant

When members of the House and the Senate gathered in December to open the Thirty-fourth Congress, they knew they would have to address slavery's future in Kansas. Andrew and his Bird Club associates paid close attention to the proceedings, poring over the newspapers, writing to acquaintances in Washington, and sharing what they had learned. Sumner was an important resource. "You will note," he wrote to Longfellow, "how Slavery has absorbed every thing in the Senate! ... The feeling is intense towards [New York senator William Henry] Seward & myself. I accept this as a tribute to our position."[27]

The Republican position was rising that winter, and Boston supporters were delighted when, after a record-breaking two months of balloting, Nathaniel Banks, one of their own, won the House speakership. Not a single southern representative voted in his favor, but democracy was about majority rule, not sectional rule. As Andrew saw it, the tide was turning. Banks was officially listed as a member of the American Party, but the coalition of Massachusetts Republicans and Know Nothings celebrated his success as a northern victory. Banks now had the patronage power to appoint antislavery representatives to important committees. Many of these congressmen, who had, till now, remained prudently quiet about the slavery issue, saw Banks's ascension as an omen, and the Massachusetts reformers were jubilant. On the evening of February 28, Andrew presided over a banquet at the Revere House in honor of Banks's victory. In his opening address, however, he, too, exercised restraint. Mindful of his audience's mixed political stances, he merely said, "His election to the Speakership of the National House of Representatives is a triumph of free labor, and of free principles of the Republic."[28]

This joy was tempered by the terrible news coming from Kansas. The Boston newspapers lamented the violence and depredations, and the narratives of first-person witnesses were horrifying. Andrew's law partner, Theophilus Chandler, shared information from his sister, Hannah Anderson Ropes, who had traveled to Lawrence with the New England Aid Society, which was working to support antislavery settlers. She was so alarmed for her life that she kept pistols and a knife on her nightstand and loaded rifles leaning against the walls. "We have to thank the pitiless winter for our *safety* thus far," she wrote. "Nobody goes to bed here without some preparation for an attack before morning. You at home can't get the *whole measure* of a 'border ruffian' quite yet."[29]

As Congress and President Pierce bungled their way through the Kansas situation, Sumner kept his Boston friends apprised of the government's vexing "popular sovereignty" approach to democracy. The acrimony between the pro- and antislavery contingents created a feverish atmosphere. Sumner, who spoke constantly in favor of abolitionism, was hounded by journalists but remained unbowed. On May 19, standing before his Senate colleagues, he launched into a rebuke of slavery and its bullying proponents. The oration was a tour de force of scholarship and passion, a two-day-long torrent of stunning prose and damning content. Later known as "The Crime against Kansas," Sumner's harangue exposed slavery as a heinous crime against humanity. He excoriated Senator Ambrose Butler of South Carolina (who was conspicuously absent) as the Don Quixote of slavery and Senator Stephen Douglas of Illinois as the "Squire . . . , its very Sancho Panza, ready to do all its humiliating offices." His speech made a sensation in the Washington press, and southern legislators were incensed. A few days later, Preston Brooks, a congressman from South Carolina and a cousin of Butler's, made his way into the Senate chambers in search of Sumner and beat him with a cane. A witness, Dr. John Bunting of Montreal, happened to be in the Senate gallery and witnessed the assault. He recalled that Douglas, standing within five feet of Sumner, watched in silence, "in a free and easy position, with both hands in his pockets, his hat on, and making no movement towards the assailant."[30]

Brooks was beside himself with fury—so much so that when Massachusetts senator Henry Wilson came to Sumner's defense, the congressman challenged him to a duel. The southern press was galvanized, hailing Brooks as a hero and suggesting that all abolitionists should be lashed into submission. For their part, northerners were outraged by the act. Beyond the barbarism of the beating, they were shocked by the violence that lay behind the South's so-called honorable code of conduct. The assault, so contradictory to democratic principles, shattered northern conservatives' racist complacency. By beating Sumner, Brooks had displayed the wrath that was being inflicted on Africans Americans every day. For citizens across the North, the "blood-spot in the Senate Chambers" became a memorial to the "Southern hostility to freedom."[31]

In response to the attack, Andrew and other Republican leaders organized an indignation meeting at Faneuil Hall. Whether or not they had previously approved of Sumner or his speech, attendees now saw him as a martyr for the antislavery cause. "Shall the South prevail in this kind of warfare?" Andrew challenged the audience. "The battle is no longer for the down-trodden slave, but for the preservation of the rights of freemen—for the maintenance of liberty at the North."[32]

Equally disheartening was news that the violent pro-slavery attack on the free-state town of Lawrence, Kansas, on May 21 had provoked a bloody response. The *Liberator* published story after story of the violence, and Hannah Ropes released a memoir, *Six Months in Kansas by a Lady*, describing the atrocities. "Lawrence is dead," she wrote, "but surely as there is justice in Heaven, this by violence, wholly unprovoked, will be avenged."[33] Less than a week later, John Brown and his abolitionist band retaliated against the pro-slavery activists whom he believed had sacked Lawrence. During a two-day rampage, the posse murdered several people, touching off a firestorm in what the press had now dubbed "Bleeding Kansas."[34]

As Sumner struggled to recover from his injuries, Republicans focused on Kansas and his assault, distributing nearly a million copies of his speech throughout the North in order to build momentum for the party. By the summer, the senator, still weak, was moved to Silver Spring, Maryland, where he spent several weeks convalescing at the home of Francis Blair, Sr. A native of Kentucky, Blair had once owned slaves and had served as an unofficial advisor to Andrew Jackson. But he had come to abhor the notion of expanding slavery so had left the Democratic Party and joined the Free-Soilers. Now he was a key figure in the development of the new Republican Party. Sumner had built a strong connection with Blair and, via letters, had introduced him to Andrew. Now the two of them were also close friends.

Both northerners and southerners avidly followed the news of Sumner's recovery. At issue was his Senate seat: would he be well enough to serve again? For the moment Andrew suggested that the seat remain unfilled. As he and his Republican colleagues debated this question, they were also preparing for their first national convention, to be held in Philadelphia in mid-June. Delegates poured into the city for the event. In his opening address, Edwin Morgan of New York called the meeting to order and reminded them that they had gathered to "give direction to a movement which is to decide whether the people of the United States are to be hereinafter and forever chained to the present national policy of the extension of human slavery." Speaker of the House Banks brought forward the nomination of the party's presidential and vice-presidential candidates: John Frémont of California and William Dayton of New Jersey. Delegates then approved an antislavery platform calling for congressional sovereignty in the territories.[35]

By this time, Andrew and his Bird Club associates were exerting an immense, if informal, influence in Massachusetts politics and the national Republican party.[36] That summer Andrew gave several addresses around the state, including a fiery speech at Abington on a rain-soaked Fourth of July: "Let him who has a ballot to give, a brain to think, or a heart to feel, be prepared to do his duty. Every man counts [as] one. No argument is needed to prove the worth of freedom. It is one of the self-evident truths of the Declaration of Independence."[37] In the meantime, he had taken on another high-profile fugitive case. In Mobile, Alabama, William Jones had escaped onto the barque *Growler*, ready to sail for Boston. The captain discovered the fugitive in the hold, nearly dead from heat exhaustion. He intended to turn Jones over to authorities in Boston; but as the ship approached the city on July 16, the desperate man jumped overboard. Though the captain retrieved him, the affair attracted onlookers, who notified the Vigilance Committee, which, in turn, contacted Andrew.

Now the state's new Personal Liberty Law entered the action. John Oliver, an African American carpenter, appeared before Judge Theron Metcalf to certify that Jones was a fugitive slave. He then petitioned for a writ of habeas corpus under the new law, which the judge granted. Authorities served the writ to the captain and brought Jones to the courthouse. By this time, a large group of African American activists had packed the chambers, and Andrew was present as Jones's defense. He read the return notice, moving that Jones be discharged, and Judge Metcalf consented. It was a stunning moment. Attendees broke into applause, sent up three cheers for Andrew, and escorted the fugitive outside. Suddenly, "as if by previous concert, one group ran one way and one another, and the identity of the fugitive was not thereafter a thing to be easily picked up again."[38]

As Andrew absorbed himself in these affairs, the Democratic convention took place in Cincinnati. Its delegates were ready for a change in leadership: instead of nominating the incumbent, Franklin Pierce, for president, they chose James Buchanan of Pennsylvania and John Breckinridge of Kentucky as their presidential and vice-presidential candidates. Although party members were divided over slavery, they endorsed the obtuse "popular sovereignty" formula as the method for determining the slavery question in newly admitted states. Meanwhile, the American Party nominated Millard Fillmore of New York and Andrew Donelson of Tennessee. While it was attempting to present itself as the one party capable of bridging the sectional divide, its platform failed to take a fundamental stand on the slavery issue. Its only clear goal was to weaken Republicans by attracting conservatives.[39]

In the fall of 1856, news about Bleeding Kansas was still filling the newspaper columns. Clearly, it would be the election's central issue. Andrew, who was now the Republican Party's official representative for Boston's Sixth Ward, remained avidly involved in politics. But trouble was brewing in the local party. Massachusetts Republicans, under the aegis of Banks and Wilson, had agreed not to run a gubernatorial candidate against Gardner. However, a group of antislavery radicals, led by Frank Bird, refused to support the compromise and, in protest, hastily pulled together an "Honest Man's Ticket," promoting Josiah Quincy as candidate for governor and Andrew as candidate for attorney general. The schism was a bold rebuke to Gardner's opportunism and Know Nothing nativism, but Andrew was dismayed. Days before the election, he published a notice in the *Daily Advertiser* saying that his name had appeared on this ticket without his permission and that he would not be a candidate. On election day, Frémont, the Republican candidate for president, swept Massachusetts. Republicans did well at all levels in the state, a decisive shift from the previous two elections, though Bird's party garnered more than 6,000 votes. On the national level, all three parties attracted northern support, but Republicans surged massively in the polls, a remarkable result, given that they had virtually no backing in the South. In the end, however, Buchanan won a popular plurality as well as the electoral vote.[40]

Weeks after the election, despite the Jones triumph, Andrew wrote to Sumner, reporting that he had no good news about the local political situation and the Know Nothings. But he was glad to know that the senator was recovering and hoped that nothing would induce him to resign his seat. In a short, but prophetic note, Andrew wrote, "Sit in yr seat—if you can, if you can't; let it be vacant."[41] It would be months before Sumner could return to work, and for northerners his vacant seat became a metaphor for the antislavery cause. Though the election results had given Republicans reason for hope, Buchanan's victory had been a triumph for violent frontier democracy and southern arrogance. There was work to be done; and though Andrew had refused Bird's nomination, he continued to use the club as a barometer for gauging Boston's changing political culture. His friends' encouragement had induced him to imagine his eventual political ascent.[42]

CHAPTER 7

THE RADICAL CHAMPION

1857–1858

The Politics of Abolition

William Garrison commenced the New Year of 1857 by changing the *Liberator*'s masthead, but his message remained radically defiant: only disunion from the slave states would push the public to end human bondage. Though Andrew respected Garrison and believed in the editor's goals, he resisted attempts to draw him into that orbit. Politics and passive resistance remained his path to ending slavery.

On March 4, the Supreme Court's chief justice, Roger B. Taney, administered the oath of office to the new president, James Buchanan. By this time the Republican-dominated Massachusetts legislature had voted overwhelmingly to send Charles Sumner back to the Senate for a second term. Still feeble from his injuries, he had returned to Washington, which was full of speculations about whether the Supreme Court would settle the matter of slavery's expansion. But Sumner was unable to serve; his health broke down after one day, and physicians recommended a European convalescent. Andrew was heartbroken. Republicans had gained significant ground in the recent election, and he had been hopeful that the new cohort in Congress could capitalize on those gains. It remained to be seen if the southern stronghold on the Democratic Party could persevere against the rising Republican wave in the North.[1]

On March 6, the Supreme Court rendered its landmark verdict in *Dred Scott v. Sandford*: five judges concurred with Chief Justice Taney that the rights and privileges enshrined in the U.S. Constitution did not include citizenship for African Americans, either free or enslaved. Andrew was stricken. He later told Garrison that the *Dred Scott* decision had emboldened southern enslavers. Only by bringing political power to expose the "cheapening of human cattle" could reformers "teach the dumbest tongue to cry out, the coldest heart to feel, and the blindest incarnation of respectable nonchalance to see, that the only remaining inquiry for the American people is, whether all poor men shall be slaves, or all slaves shall be made free?"[2]

The court's decision unhinged New England abolitionists, but they found some relief in the knowledge that their government allies did not remain silent. Justice Benjamin Curtis's dissent in the *Dred Scott* case drew praise. The Washington correspondent for Boston's *Daily Advertiser* praised the Massachusetts native, declaring that "all the great lawyers here are enthusiastic in their eulogiums." Curtis had maintained "that native born colored persons can be citizens of the State and of the United States, and that Congress has power to exclude slavery from the territories." The reporter declared that the dissent "cannot be too highly praised. It is an impregnable breastwork of solid granite against the political heresies which have taken possession of the federal judiciary." Andrew wholly agreed.[3]

Taney's opinion presented Republicans with a dilemma. If they took a noble stand on African American citizenship, they would be labeled "black Republicans" and alienate the southerners even further. But the Court's decision negated the party's core platform—no territorial slavery—and was therefore a threat to the party itself. The party had reached a crisis point, but both Sumner and Andrew saw this as an advantage; it meant that the course ahead was becoming clearer.

When the Court's ruling came down, Sumner was traveling to Paris, but Andrew was still in Boston, in the midst of his own *Dred Scott* tussle. Though he did not realize this at the time, he was preparing what may have been the nation's first lawsuit to reach any state supreme court concerning a business owner's right to exclude or segregate patrons. Andrew's case was a public amusement discrimination suit, which he was bringing on behalf of an African American who had been denied access to Howard Athenaeum, one of Boston's most famous cultural institutions. In December 1856, Julian McCrea, a barber, had purchased tickets in the theater's upper balcony, known as the "family circle," for the Robert Marsh show *Juvenile Comedians*. When he and his party attempted to ascend the stairs, the doorman stopped them, refusing to admit the group because of McCrea's race. He, in turn, declared that he would not be denied his civil rights on account of his color, which prompted authorities to escort him from the building. McCrea turned to Andrew, who sued Marsh in superior court for assault and sought damages for "injury" and "indignity." Andrew argued that McCrea's ticket had given him the right to sit in the balcony. Invoking the common-law governance of public accommodations, he maintained that Marsh was operating a public exhibition for money and had no right to discriminate among members of the public. Though Andrew's argument had a sound legal and humanitarian basis, Judge Josiah Abbott deferred to legislative authority. Marsh, he said, was not "prevented from making it a regulation of admission to his exhibition that no black persons should be admitted to certain portions of it." Because Marsh had a license, the judge said, he was entitled to make and enforce business rules. The court ruled that patron segregation was a reasonable business regulation. Andrew brought an appeal to the Massachusetts Supreme Judicial Court, which, not surprisingly, upheld the decision. The case reinforced Andrew's conviction that, until the political culture was transformed at the highest levels, African Americans would never be entitled to the constitutional rights and privileges of white Americans.[4]

Andrew's friendship with Lewis Hayden and William Nell, his regular attendance at Reverend Grimes's church, and his local Republican activism had made him a familiar face in the African American Sixth Ward. In previous elections the Whig Party had dominated the ward, but now there were rumors that Hayden was scheming to get Andrew's name onto the Republican ticket in the coming state election. Fatigued by Gardner's nativism, political leaders were coming to believe that Know Nothingism had run its course in Massachusetts. Many were chafing about new legislative recommendations, including an extended waiting period for immigrant naturalization and an amendment requiring voters to be able to read the U.S. Constitution and write their names. After the *Dred Scott* decision, voters were ready for a change.[5]

As Andrew concentrated on his caseload that spring, he continued to follow the news from Kansas. Several of his friends were associated with the state committee raising funds for Kansas settlers, and he himself had spent time working for a writ of habeas corpus that would test the legality of the Kansas freedom fighters' imprisonment. The Taney decision had emboldened proslavery ruffians, and they routinely used tactics such as fraudulent census taking, political fraud, and border skirmishes to terrorize their antislavery victims. Without outside support, these settlers were prey.

That spring John Brown arrived in Boston, armed with references from the New York State abolitionist Gerrit Smith and Ohio's Free-Soil governor Salmon P. Chase. Known for his Kansas exploits, Brown was looking to raise money to equip and defend antislavery communities. His host was George Stearns, a wealthy manufacturer, who was a stationmaster on the Underground Railroad and a financial backer of the Emigrant Aid Company, which supported the Free-Soil settlement in Kansas. Stearns ushered Brown into gatherings in Concord and Boston, and Andrew probably met him in May at a Sunday-evening reception at Theodore Parker's home.[6]

By the summer of 1857, as press coverage of Kansas affairs ebbed and flowed, the state party conventions were drawing considerable attention. There was bitter division between conservative nativists and antislavery advocates. In Massachusetts the fiery Frank Bird had already appeared at a "Disunion Convention" in Worcester, urging voters to abandon Garrison-style radicalism, to fight *Dred Scott* and slavery at the ballot box, not in the courts. "My only hope is in framing a public opinion at the North as true as to freedom as that of the South is to slavery," he said, "and then that public opinion will find an effective form of expression."[7]

Andrew was an obvious choice for Republican leadership. After he was elected as an at-large member for the party's state convention, the press began to hint that this "straight Republican" might be a formidable opponent to Nathaniel Banks in the gubernatorial race. When Judge Josiah Abbott announced his retirement from the Suffolk County Superior Court that summer, the newspapers clamored for Andrew as a replacement. These paeans likely convinced Hayden, just days before the November election, to put him on the ticket as the Sixth Ward's Republican candidate for the state legislature. Though Andrew had taken no part in the campaign and was nominated very late, he was elected to a seat. He and George Clapp, a tailor, easily defeated their opponents as the ward's representatives. Banks won the governorship, and the Republicans were in full command of the state's political future.

In retrospect, Andrew's passivity about the process seems odd. Given that he had been so involved in shaping the state's progression of reformist parties, he had never shown an interest in running for office but had passively allowed his name to appear as a candidate. Perhaps he was still modest about his fitness. He had always believed that politicians arose from the elite, yet he was surely aware of how formidable he had become as a leader. Whatever his private feelings, with encouragement from the African American community, he was about to embark on a new journey.[8]

Shortly after the election, the newspapers announced that Andrew had taken up a new case, one involving a twenty-five-year-old slave named Betty Sweet. Her owners, Lewis Sweet and his family, were touring the northern states with their five-year-old and had been living for several weeks in Lawrence, Massachusetts. During this period Betty had told someone that she did not want to return to Tennessee. The information was relayed to the Vigilance Committee, which solicited Andrew's services. He drew up a writ of habeas corpus, asked a deputy sheriff to retrieve her, and brought her into court before Judge Lemuel Shaw. Using information from unnamed sources, Andrew declared that Betty was being held against her will. Defense counsel countered, arguing that the Sweets had allowed her to come and go freely. In fact, said the defense, her owners had declared that if she wanted her liberty, they would "abide by . . . [her] wishes." Both sides stated their belief that Betty should make the decision herself. [9]

Judge Shaw took Betty into an adjourning room. There, she told him that the Sweets had raised her from infancy, that they loved her, and that she had a husband and children whom she would not leave. The judge reported back to the attorneys: given her circumstances, Betty had chosen to stay with her masters. At this point, several African American attendees, including Reverend Grimes, urged her to choose freedom. As tensions increased, Andrew took the group aside and advised them to respect her decision. In the meantime, he made clear to the Sweets that Shaw's ruling had allowed Betty to choose freedom, even after her return to Tennessee, and they agreed. Still, Andrew had trouble accepting her decision. The case haunted him, though several conservative papers trumpeted it as a victory. One noted:

> "Betty," is a sensible girl, [and] we have no doubt her choice was dictated by a common sense view of the relative condition of the poor classes at the North, and slave population of the South. . . . She has a home, and a master and mistress to look after her, which cannot be said of twenty thousand poor and friendless wanderers in New England alone, who are now out of employment, with no comforts laid in store for the coming dreary winter.[10]

In New York, the *Herald* gleefully headlined the story "Slave Excitement in Boston: A Tennessee Negro Girl Spurns the Abolitionists."[11]

Still, the editor's assessment of New England's bleak forecast was no exaggeration. That fall the worst financial panic in twenty years was gripping the nation, the result of a collapse in Nebraska land sales, a slowing economy, the Crimean War, and the *Dred Scott* decision. Newspapers encouraged the wealthy "to feel for those who bear the burden of constant poverty," and Andrew's work to keep debtors out of prison was a testament to this reality. The economic collapse was suffocating the North's working classes; there was some truth to the notion that these so-called "white slaves" were no better off than the Blacks in servitude, and southerners used the comparison to boost confidence in slave-based capitalism. Moreover, as Andrew was well aware, disillusion and alienation among the working classes, especially among the Boston Irish, was transforming into resentment against abolitionists and Republicans. By year's end, the nation was heading into a full-scale depression, deepening the sectional chasm.

At this fraught moment, Massachusetts Republicans worked to rally their forces. Though the radical abolitionists had protested against his candidacy, Nathaniel Banks was an astute politician, bringing a lifetime of experience—as congressman, as House speaker, as convention chair—to his new position as governor. He was more than qualified to pull the state out of financial turmoil. Still, as a former Whig and Know Nothing, he was emblematic of the crisis in the Republican Party, where high-minded conservatives contended with high-minded progressives for control. He had little in common with reformists such as Andrew, other than the fact that they both called themselves Republicans.[12]

It was not an easy moment to assume political office. "Had I known that I would have been elected," Andrew later chided Hayden, "I never would have allowed the use of my name."[13] Nonetheless, he resolved to make the most of his tenure and spent the winter poring over the procedures and issues of the General Court. The ailing Charles Sumner, who had returned from Europe, urged Andrew to rely on his own political voice: "Pray banish from your mind the counsels you rec'd from Washington & then judge for yourself."[14] This advice, along with his encyclopedic constitutional and legal knowledge, would serve him well in his new role.

Sixth Ward Legislator

When Andrew arrived at the General Court in January 1858, Hayden, Grimes, and others were hopeful that the "poor man's" lawyer would be able to lift their cause from the underground into mainstream politics.

Yet the Bird Club had already prepared him for the unforgiving nature of politics, girding him for what lay ahead. Though he had intended to focus his legislative energies on African Americans' civil rights, he was quickly sidetracked into a quarrel that had little to do with governance and much to do with settling scores. Early in the session, legislators were poised to deny the Massachusetts Anti-Slavery Society's request to use the Hall of Representatives for a meeting. Newburyport's representative, Caleb Cushing, a proslavery Democrat who had been President Pierce's attorney general, objected to the request, claiming that the society was hostile to the Constitution and the Union. Members promoted disorder and sedition, he argued, and their purposes were "pernicious to the material as well as the religious and moral interests of the people, to the states, the Union, and the slaves themselves."[15] In response, Andrew argued that representatives, in the past, had granted members use of the hall as a matter of courtesy. "In the old Whig times," he noted, "when the Society was compelled to hold its meetings in a stable, the State House was opened to them, and one of its orators said in this Hall, Boston furnishes with a stable, but Massachusetts opens her State House." Then he made his move: aware that Cushing and several of his allies would be absent from the legislature for several days, he called for another vote. The house narrowly backed his argument: eighty-five to eighty-one.

Amid his legislative and legal work, Andrew found time in February to attend a "Meeting of the Colored Citizens of Boston" at the Joy Street Church, where members resolved to memorialize the one-year anniversary of the *Dred Scott* decision on March 6. At the meeting, William Nell resolved that Andrew be entrusted to deliver the memorial to the legislature as an affirmation of their citizenship. He welcomed the assignment, but he knew he would have to deal with legislators who were bent on defending slavery. He consulted Sumner, who was now in Boston: "If you can give me anything you would like to see rammed down into the gun, I shall receive it thankfully."[16] In the meantime, he sat quietly among the lawmakers, day after day, and observed their back-and-forth arguments, then returned to his office and poured himself into research on Taney's *Dred Scott* opinion.

During these weeks, the legislature was dealing with thousands of petitions demanding the removal of Edward Loring, the slave commissioner and probate judge who had returned Anthony Burns to his Virginia enslaver three years before the *Dred Scott* verdict. Garrisonian lawmakers defended the petitioners, who had every right to expect that their requests would be addressed "in a spirit full of Puritan pluck and Revolutionary backbone."[17] But Cushing railed against efforts to remove Loring. He launched a series of verbal assaults against the Massachusetts Anti-Slavery Society, calling the attorney Wendell Phillips, known as abolitionism's "golden trumpet," a "whipped spaniel crouching at the [society's] feet." Cushing accused legislators of attempting to destroy the judiciary by abolishing the probate court, all for the sake of one man's removal. But few responded to his tirades, except to offer occasional resolutions denouncing the Democratic Party and the pro-slavery Lecompton Constitution in Kansas and others that reasserted the rights of freedmen.[18]

In a letter to Sumner, Andrew acknowledged that Republicans disagreed about slavery issues, but he believed that Commonwealth citizens did not wish "to lie down in the silence of Pharaoh and his host, beneath the waters of the Dead Sea; and let the waves of advancing despotism roll over them forever." He spent weeks gathering his ammunition. Then, on February 26, he stood before the house and delivered the African American community's memorial on the *Dred Scott* decision. He announced that the document would be printed, for the purpose of "giving to these our fellow citizens an opportunity of being heard, touching their own views of their own interests in their own cause."[19]

On March 4, Andrew rose again, this time offering two resolutions. First, he asked the assembly to agree that "we hold it to be a self-evident truth, that all men are endowed with the unalienable right to life, liberty, and the pursuit of happiness, and that we are opposed to slavery in every form and color and in favor of freemen and free-soil wherever man lives throughout God's heritage." Second, he requested them to resolve that,

> by common law and by common sense, as well as by the decision of the Supreme Court of the United States (in *Prig v. Pennsylvania*) "the state of slavery is a mere municipal regulation founded upon and limited to the verge of the territorial law," that is to the limits of the State creating it, and we deny the power of Congress, or of any territorial legislature, or any man or men, to give it a legal existence in any territory of the Union while the federal constitution shall be maintained.

He asked representatives to "resist by all constitutional means" attempts by the federal government to nationalize slavery and to reject the political frauds in Kansas and the state constitution.[20] Legislators overwhelmingly rejected both resolutions.

On March 5, Andrew proposed a motion to print representatives' reasons for voting against his resolutions. When legislators rejected his request, he launched into a refutation of the *Dred Scott* decision. He opened by declaring that his African American friends, whose memorial he had read days before, were on the right side of God. Then he launched into an oration challenging Justice Taney's view that Black men in the United States had no rights that white men were bound to respect. The *Dred Scott* decision was not law, he declared, but merely a judicial verdict that did not reflect the framers' intentions:

> I denounce it as unjust to the colored men, because it assumes that the white men of America, for many generations, and so closely, connected with the sons of Africa, had been compelled, by their observation of them and their experience with them, to the conclusive opinion, that men descended from African slaves could never, by possibility, be fit for the enjoyment of political rights. What a terrible comment is that upon a whole continent of humanity. I quarrel with that decision for an assumption so sweeping and so monstrous. I quarrel with it because the assumption contradicts all the facts of our history, contradicts the fact that colored men were citizens of my own State of Massachusetts, before the adoption of the Federal Constitution, that slavery had been abolished by the Constitution of Massachusetts as contrary to the declaration of rights . . . because it overlooks the fact that in four other States of these United States colored men, the descendants of slaves, were citizens of the United States before the adoption of the Federal Constitution—because it overlooks the fact, that by the very Articles of Confederation, those colored men, of African descent and of servile origin, were citizens of the confederate States. I quarrel with that opinion, because it is unjust to the memory of our fathers, as well as to the colored race, and the public history of our country.[21]

Andrew reminded his listeners that he had been charged with the duty of presenting a memorial by men "who felt afflicted in their souls, as they are crossed in their interests and cut down in their rights, by the supposed adjudication of the highest tribunal known to the American laws."

> They are humble men, they are men of sable hue, of African origin, and I suppose, of servile descent. But they are men. True they are black, [but] this war, made by the Court for political purposes by Presidents and Cabinets, upon colored men, is no war declared against race. It is not a war against color, nor a war against race, nor a demonstration in the interest of white men. *It is a war against Freedom.*

Line by line, the new representative dissected the Taney opinion. Then, in closing, he proclaimed, "I care not how small may be the minority with which to-day I am associated in the opinions I have the happiness to own, [but] the sun of that morning begins to dawn—I see its foreshine already on the mountain tops—when they will be accepted and justified by the great heart and intellect of regenerated America."[22]

Thunderous applause broke out in the General Court. Andrew's argument was impressive, and his oratorical presence was astounding. Some legal scholars have since called his speech "the best and clearest, and most incisive analysis ever made of the *Dred Scott* decision."[23] It stands as one of the greatest defenses of African American citizenship and civil rights ever uttered in the Massachusetts legislature.

Yet Sumner worried that no speech, no matter how thrilling, could change attitudes about the decision. The real issue before legislators, he maintained, was the removal of Judge Loring. He told Samuel Howe that Massachusetts "seems stifled": "Not a voice against {*Edward*} Loring, not a voice against the Kansas Usurpation—not a voice against the Dred Scott diabolism. . . . Where is the Republican Party. . . . Where is {*John*} Andrew?" Though Sumner acknowledged that "Andrew has done grandly," he knew that the new representative could not rest: "[he] must fight his last battle & if need be, 'hold the bridge' alone against the conservative forces headed by a Republican governor."[24] It was time for Andrew to embrace his role at center stage.

Yet Andrew was cautious. He had already shared with Sumner his concerns about attracting supporters to oust Loring. Those high-ranking representatives "have, from the start, looked on me as a dangerous character. They have *watched* me at every step, [and] I have . . . on two or three occasions had to face all of them on matters not political but of progressive legislation." He told Sumner that he had been waiting for the right moment to wade into deeper political waters: "And now, after two months, having got known by and acquainted with the most of them, so that I do not fear being thought a mere intruder, I have begun 'to speak for myself."[25]

It was clear that, to advance action against the Fugitive Slave Law and Judge Loring, Andrew would need to be persistent and deeply persuasive. On March 10, Cushing launched into another tirade about abolitionists: "There exists in this Commonwealth a handful of perverted persons, foolish women, and still more foolish men, black men and white men, black women and white women . . . [whose] perpetual cry is for the overthrow of the constitution of the United States." Andrew, unmoved by Cushing's vitriol, asked if Loring had, at the time of his federal judicial appointment, any power to act in the rendition of slaves. He then declared that all judicial officers of the state ought to be disconnected from the federal government, that the people would soon demand as much. He referred the issue to a special committee of the legislature. The house speaker immediately assigned Andrew to chair that group, the House Committee on Probate and Chancery.[26]

Over the next several days, Andrew's rebuttal touched off an acrimonious debate in the legislature, and the visitors' gallery was soon packed. As the newly installed chair of the special committee, Andrew now proposed a resolution to remove the judge by eliminating his position. Cushing opposed this, arguing that Loring had not been guilty of misconduct or of any violation of the law and therefore could not be impeached. He maintained that Loring was the victim of legislative outrage.

Governor Banks, who had dreams of a presidential run, understood that removing the judge risked alienating him from conservative supporters. Yet he needed to placate the radicals, in hopes that they might acquiesce to his nomination. So he devised a scheme: he proposed merging the probate and insolvency court systems, which, if legislatively approved, would eliminate Loring's position. The plan was unpopular, but it gave him a passage forward. Andrew had already concluded that this would be the best solution, and he now worked to rally lawmakers to his camp. As Banks anxiously sent messengers to the legislature, Andrew labored to organize support. In a letter to Sumner, Theophilus Chandler reported, "He is working nobly. By prudence, industry, and good judgment, he has done very much towards bringing the members up to the point."[27] Bird, too, was impressed. He told Sumner, "We lack a few brave men in our Legislature. Andrew alone fights."[28]

Each day, Cushing stood up in the house to attack the plot to remove Loring. Each day, when he returned to his seat, the room became painfully quiet; no Republican rose in response. Cushing thought this meant that he had the votes to keep the judge in his place. Yet after listening to evidence, both the house and the senate favored Loring's removal. They recommended that a joint committee, consisting of five house members and two senate members, be appointed to present this request to the governor. On March 19, Banks complied with the recommendation and asked that Loring be removed from the office of judge of probate for Suffolk County. Repeating the argument that Andrew had outlined weeks before, Banks explained that the lines of power separating state and federal jurisdictions meant that the judicial functions of the two governments should not be represented in the same officer.

The measure carried in the General Court. Cushing had been defeated. Rising from his seat, he addressed the speaker: "And now, sir, the deed is done!" "Amen!" cried a member, stirring the assembly to laughter. Even Cushing chuckled.[29] But when the speaker restored quiet, Cushing launched a final attack on the Commonwealth's Personal Liberty Law, defending the primacy of law and order and adherence to constitutional standards. Listeners were driven into silence by the tirade.

One observer, Charles Creighton Hazewell, a political editor for the Boston-based *Traveller*, remarked to state senator Eben Stone that "the man who can successfully reply" to Cushing "ought to be made Governor of Massachusetts."[30] Stone later recalled that Andrew stood, remained silent for a moment, and then "proceeded somewhat hesitatingly." Members listened intently. "I knew the stuff was in him," Stone said, "and that he only needed to be excited to a point where he could overcome a certain diffidence, to make an effective speech." After a few minutes, Stone said to a fellow senator, "'Andrew is getting warm; he is turning up his coat sleeve; now you will have it.' In a moment his voice broke out in a higher key, and struck a note beyond the compass of its natural tones, penetrating, resonant, triumphant; and for more than half an hour, he spoke with a rapid, vehement and overpowering eloquence, which I never heard equaled before, or since."[31]

Before a packed gallery, Andrew veered into a condemnation of the southern policies that Cushing had promoted. "They may go on," he declared, "but the day of reckoning is at hand. Behind that party stalks the headsman! 'Because sentence is not speedily executed against an evil work, therefore the hearts of the sons of men have it fully set in them to do evil.' But the judgment will come." Praising Governor Banks, he celebrated the state's prominent role in the fight: "We have grown more than the life-time of a generation of men since the inauguration of Governor Gardiner." Andrew ridiculed Cushing's "offer to do service as a Massachusetts militiaman in behalf of slave-owners," exclaiming:

> When the Sheriff of Massachusetts holds in his hand the writ of personal replevin, or of *habeas corpus*, issued out of the Supreme Judicial Court of Massachusetts, to take into his possession . . . a man who, on the soil of Massachusetts, was in actual possession of his freedom, up to the time of his seizure—*prima facie*, presumptively free— . . . and when the sheriff of the county calls upon the *posse comitatus* to assist in the service of that writ, and when the Governor orders out the troops to protect that officer in the performance of his duty, I expect with pleasure [to be] . . . walking arm in arm with my learned friend from Newburyport.[32]

The speaker interrupted Andrew to ask if he were nearly finished. Immediately, members shouted, "Go on, go on," but Andrew replied that he was done, merely concluding, "I echo the declaration of the gentleman from Newburyport, that *the deed is done!* Yes, sir! It was *well* done—and it was done *quickly.*" He sat down to deafening laughter and applause. Akin to Sumner's "Crime against Kansas" speech, Andrew's rebuttal had cemented his position as the Republicans' new leader.[33] Even Cushing congratulated him. The abolitionist Frank Sanborn, who had met Andrew years before at one of Theodore Parker's Sunday-evening receptions, recalled now that the "ruddy and cheerful young lawyer, in no very large practice," had even then been "spoken of by Parker and Wendell Phillips as 'the future chief justice.' But this speech, in his view, was revealing a different destiny: it was what would lead Andrew to become governor.[34] Boston's *Post*, which loathed the abolitionists, editorialized that Andrew had advanced the slaves' cause more effectively than the radical antislavery contingent ever had. "[He] ruled supreme because he had not only some ability and knowledge" but also "hesitate[d] to keep step to the music of Garrison and Company." He was the "only champion upon the floor of the house."[35] The Boston correspondent for the *New York Times* wrote that Andrew had "made the best speech of the session."[36]

Andrew had entered legislative lore. Florence Howe Hall, the daughter of Samuel Gridley and Julia Howe, recalled him as "a young advocate," moved, "like another David, to attack his Goliath."[37] Newspapers reprinted his words:

> There is one purpose which animates and inspires every heart, and that is the purpose to preserve and protect liberty. If any gentleman on this floor expects that one single provision of that infernal statute [the Fugitive Slave Law] shall ever become, for a single moment, other than hated by Massachusetts, I reply to him in the language of the poet: "Lay not that flattering unction to your soul."[38]

Witnesses said "it was a scene never to be forgotten." The oratorical battle between Cushing and Andrew reminded many "of the scripture story of David and Goliath, for Cushing was in the height of his fame, and Andrew was of most youthful appearance and comparatively unknown."[39] Several Boston papers carried portions of the speech, but Garrison devoted two pages of the *Liberator* to reprinting every word. Even the *Boston Herald* saw the speech as a "struggle to defend the rights and honor of Massachusetts—the rights and honor of one of the sovereign States of this confederacy."[40] Stone commented, "If a speech is to be measured by its effects upon its hearers, [then Andrew's was] . . . beyond all comparison the most eloquent and the most remarkable that has been made in Massachusetts in this generation."[41]

By coming to the defense of the African American community, Andrew had connected civil rights to debates over the Personal Liberty Law's constitutionality. The changes he had set in motion forbade attorneys from serving in state courts if they had appeared as counsel against African Americans who were being held under the Fugitive Slave Law. On the last day of the legislative session, however, Andrew announced that he would not be returning. In response, the representatives paid tribute to the historic session. Cushing and Andrew offered complimentary resolutions to one another. Andrew commented that, as much as he disagreed with Cushing, he was nonetheless thankful to be parting as "personal friends," though he knew he would never trust him.[42]

Andrew had earned his colleagues' esteem through his eloquence and his careful, learned analysis. The British jurist and historian Frederick Harrison later wrote that his rapid rise in the house was without precedent: he "won his way into the popular favor" and became "the leader of the House" in a single session.[43] Though eighteen years at the Boston bar had cemented Andrew's reputation as a lawyer, his few months in the General Court catapulted him into public prominence. Sumner, who had been traveling, congratulated him: "Till I reached Washington, I did not know the half you had done." He wrote of reading his "complete & admirable speech" on the Dred Scott case "& yr. first speech on the removal of Loring—both of which filled me with delight." He added, "I do enjoy a good speech . . . on the right side."[44]

That April Andrew returned to his law office, but the legislative session had taxed him, and his severe headaches reappeared, keeping him close to home. His son Henry Hersey was born on April 26, and amid his new family responsibilities he attempted to resume a normal life. He took up his usual social and reformist activities, which included teaching a group of African American youth at a local church. Yet his celebrity status had brought him many more cases as well as an increased income. He needed to recover his strength, and he spent much of the early summer with his family, recuperating.[45]

As Andrew's star was ascending, Sumner's seemed to be waning. His Senate seat remained vacant, and his European trips elicited complaints that he was "shamming" and had lost interest in representing Massachusetts citizens. A number of progressive leaders believed he ought to resign, accept life as an invalid, and perhaps allow Andrew to become his replacement. Andrew, however, remained steadfast in his support of this friend who had always been loyal to him. When Banks attempted to remove Sumner, on the grounds that he had been absent from sessions, Andrew and Bird foiled the plot. Sumner refused to resign, yet his health continued to prevent him from returning to his duties, and he secluded himself from the news.[46]

CHAPTER 8

REPUBLICAN STAR RISING

1858–1859

Slavery Has No Business to Exist Anywhere

By the end of the summer of 1858, the nation's attention had shifted from Kansas to the upcoming political conventions. At question was the ability of northerners to break the southern grip on the presidency, Congress, and the Supreme Court. In Massachusetts, Republican Party chiefs hoped to stay in power in the fall elections and possibly help trigger a national takeover in the presidential election in 1860. In the meantime, the press followed the oratorical contrast between Illinois senate candidates Abraham Lincoln and Stephen Douglas. Andrew, always drawn toward speech making, must have been captivated by the luminescent rhetoric.

Though Andrew had stepped away from political office, his Bird Club associates convinced him to stump the Bay State to rally voters to the party. Republican leaders rewarded him by choosing him to preside over the 1,200-member convention, which met in Worcester that September. So popular was the Boston lawyer that even the *New York Times* correspondent covering the event reminded readers that Andrew was "the same gentleman who took the lead in the legislative war that was carried on against Judge Loring, last winter, and who more than conquered Gen. Cushing, in that memorable context."[1]

By choosing Andrew as convention president, state Republicans were confirming their antislavery platform and honoring his skills. As Eben Stone recalled, the convention itself had excited no special interest. But after members concluded their business, delegates began calling for their favorite speakers, including Henry Wilson and Nathaniel Banks. Then someone shouted for Andrew. Embarrassed, he nonetheless rose and spoke for the next half-hour. An observer commented on the impact of his words, which "elevated and by his fervor and force transported delegates to another level." Andrew told his listeners, "Slavery has no business to exist *any where*," predicting that one day the sun would "rise upon no master, and act upon no slave."[2] Though the speech was unplanned and unrehearsed, it was impressively delivered. His eloquence, Stone believed, was "superior to [that of] any man of his time in this state, except [for Wendell] Phillips." It "gushed forth from his mind like a flood of delirious music, in obedience to an irrepressible law of his organization."[3]

Republicans staged several rallies that autumn, and Andrew traveled from town to town, stumping for the cause. Everywhere he told voters that moral conscience, rather than political expediency, should guide the nation toward the goal of abolishing slavery. To steer a new northern course, he worked to attract disparate voters without making it appear as if the Garrisonians had seized party control. If Republicans were to change the nation's direction on slavery, it was vital that abolitionists become Republicans, not vice versa. It was a judicious but effective distinction. By the November election, it was clear that Andrew had done his job. Massachusetts voters had thoroughly denounced the Buchanan administration's pro-slavery policies in Kansas, and Republicans were triumphant: Banks was reelected governor by an overwhelming majority, and Anson Burlingame, Eli Thayer, Henry Dawes, and Charles Adams, were sent to Congress. In the *Liberator*, Garrison declared that the antagonistic systems of free labor and slave labor were on a collision course; and Burlingame, in a post-election speech to a crowd at the Parker House, reminded his listeners, "Fellow-Citizens, you have fought a great battle, and won a great victory, [but] . . . I wish here and now to enlist you for the war of 1860."[4]

By the time the Congress assembled in December 1858, Andrew had returned to his legal work, but he remained attentive to the news from Capitol Hill. Democrats controlled the Senate and although the Republicans lacked a majority in the House, they cooperated with smaller parties in unifying against the Fugitive Slave Law and slavery's expansion, which was affecting nearly every legislative decision. Yet Andrew's electioneering had revived his hopes. He had another pleasure that autumn. His old friend Cyrus Woodman had been living in Wisconsin and then Germany, but now he and his family had returned to the United States, and they spent some weeks with the Andrews. The two men reveled in this reunion, reminiscing about college and their nomadic early years in Boston. It was clear to Woodman that Andrew had come far since those days.[5]

Andrew began 1859 by collecting signatures for a petition he planned to bring before the Commonwealth's lower house, in hopes of correcting the problems that had contributed to his loss in *McCrea v. Marsh* two years earlier. He wanted to demonstrate to legislators that, even though Massachusetts might boast of its antislavery convictions, Commonwealth laws still allowed racial discrimination in public places. In late January, he appeared before the legislature with 275 signatures urging passage of a law "prohibiting any person licensed to exhibit any public show, or to open or maintain any theatrical exhibition, or other public amusement, in this Commonwealth, from excluding any person from any seat or place occupied by audience or spectators, on account of his race, opinion or color." As Andrew expected, however, legislators did not address his proposition and moved on to more mundane matters, such as deciding on the proper place for the Daniel Webster statue.[6]

Disheartened but not surprised, Andrew continued to coordinate with the Vigilance Committee to raise funds to aid fugitives who were trying to live and work in Boston. He was taking a great interest in educational issues, speaking in churches and at African American meetings about the importance of educating poor children and adolescents. He became involved with the Warren Street Chapel Association, which promoted free evening classes for teaching young people practical skills. He also continued as treasurer for the Boston Port Society and as a trustee for the Massachusetts School for Idiotic and Feeble-Minded Youth. With Louis Agassiz, a Harvard professor and a renowned scholar of natural history, he addressed a March 17 gathering at the statehouse, hoping to secure funds for the Louis Agassiz Museum of Comparative Zoology. In April, he joined his Bird Club associates in hosting a festival at the Parker House to honor Thomas Jefferson's birthday. George Boutwell presided, and Andrew did not expect to speak; but after the crowd petitioned him, he said he was "always ready, by word or blow, to speak or strike for liberty." His eloquence quickly enraptured the audience.[7]

Recognizing Andrew's popularity, Governor Banks offered him a seat on the Massachusetts Superior Court that May—a judicious move, no doubt meant to deter him as a political competitor. Andrew, however, declined the offer. The Lowell-based *Daily Citizen* reported that "a score of disappointed judicial candidates will admire his taste and puzzle their brains as to the *probabilities*. We do not know Mr. A's reasons, but suppose he thinks a judge must be too dignified and reserved, and that he prefers to remain his own master and be a *'merry'* Andrew."[8]

Andrew explained his reasons to Woodman. "You will probably have seen," he told his friend "that,—contrary to what was your reasonable inference from the fact of my nomination,—I did not accept the judgeship." Not only was he unwilling to give up his freedom for the bench, but he also disagreed with the many laws that engendered racial prejudice. Likewise, he would not wholly commit to politics, which, he said, were "mainly accidental to me; not of the substance and woof of my conscious scheme of life." Politicians, he believed, were too often driven by special interests rather than progress or morality. He recognized that his views were popular only within a small circle of humanitarians. "But," he told Woodman, "when if ever I am thought by others worthy to take any place where I see a chance to be useful and to do some good, [which] I want to see done and to which I feel called,—I may not refuse."[9]

Yet despite his unofficial status, Andrew had tremendous sway in many Boston neighborhoods, including the wharfside streets near the Bethel Chapel. Thus, it was no surprise that by the summer of 1859 he was drawn into a thrilling sea-related case involving the steersman Cyrus Plumer, a ringleader in an 1857 mutiny on the New Bedford whaler *Junior*, sailing between Australia and New Zealand. The *Junior*'s crew had been at sea for six months without sighting a whale, and they were living in wretched conditions. On Christmas Day they had seized the ship, killed the captain and the third mate, and severely injured others. But without navigational skills, the mutineers could not sail safely in the treacherous Tasman Sea, so Plumer had made a deal with a wounded officer, Nelson Provost, who had guided the ship to Australia's southeastern coast in exchange for his life. In making this agreement, Provost had asked Plumer to dictate a testimonial that would absolve any innocent crewmembers. By the time they reached land, Plumer had dictated a full confession to an officer named William Herbert, who entered it into the ship's log. Then the mutineers and the survivors rowed to shore and went their separate ways.

The press ran wild with the tale, and within weeks authorities apprehended Plumer and his band. They were returned to Boston, where they were arraigned on August 21, 1858, and indicted for murder and piracy. Benjamin Butler and Charles Chandler served as defense counsel, and the trial was set for November. Convinced that he would lose the case,

Butler moved to have the charges reduced from murder to manslaughter. He then focused his defense not on the murders but on the crew's miserable living conditions and wretched treatment. In a five-hour-long address, he declared that laws should be revised to protect seamen from abuse. Comparing shipboard horrors to slavery, he argued that Congress should pause its concentration on the enslaved and focus its efforts on protecting white sailors. Butler succeeded in saving some of the assailants but not Plumer, and the judge delayed his sentencing until those other charges were resolved. Finally, in April, the judge ruled that Plumer was guilty of murder and would hang on June 24.

Butler's brilliant comparison between the sailors' miserable conditions and the sufferings of the slaves depicted in *Uncle Tom's Cabin* became a legal legend. Andrew agreed that the merchant marine laws needed to be reformed and that Plumer's retaliation may have been justified. In his view the death sentence would serve no purpose in deterring future mutinies. In fact, he believed that commuting the sentence to imprisonment for life might encourage shipowners to improve onboard conditions. He was not alone in his anger. Rancor about the issue was rife in Boston, so much so that a cordage merchant refused to sell a federal marshal a gallows rope for Plumer, arguing that three-quarters of the ship's murdered officers had deserved their fates.

A number of concerned citizens implored Andrew to petition President Buchanan to commute Plumer's sentence to imprisonment for life. Andrew quickly acquired more than 21,000 signatures and set out for Washington with a group of Plumer's friends and family. On July 3 he met with Buchanan and handed him the petitions, telling the president that dread of life imprisonment would be a stronger deterrent than dread of death. After consulting with his cabinet, Buchanan agreed and commuted the sentence. Andrew immediately returned to Boston and, with the federal marshal and a few others, went straight to the jail to tell Plumer the news.[10]

For years afterward, Andrew retold the tale of spending that Fourth of July in Washington. During the visit, he had met a southern cabinet member who had told him, "with the twang and the peculiarity of emphasis which used to mark the conversation of the apostles and leaders of incipient treason: You Yankees are a singular people." Andrew claimed to have replied, "Indeed we are sir." In his version of the interaction, he had then launched into a speech:

> In Boston, the metropolis of Yankeedom, . . . [this] anniversary of American Liberty has been ushered in by a chorus of bells and of cannon. . . . [It

is the] Sabbath day of Freedom. . . . By processions, civic and military, by solemn praise, and by a patriotic oration in the presence of the authorities and father of the city; by cheerful reunion of the representatives of the people and of every branch of the public service around the hospitable board where the Mayor in person presides by festivities and games for children of every class; by sundown guns and evening fireworks . . . these "singular Yankees" are remembering and celebrating this day.

Glaring at the southerner, he had then remarked, "Here at the seat of the Federal Government, I perceive only a few colored children of the Sunday Schools marching in procession, alone and almost without human sympathy. I hope to see the day, when something of our *singularity* may strike as high as the city of Washington."[11]

Andrew returned to Boston a hero. People everywhere clamored to hear him speak, including those in his Maine homeland. In Gorham, he gave a graduation speech at the Maine Female Academy that celebrated the place's familiarity: "the walks, the playground, the daily ascent to school, the quiet nooks, where friendly trees defended us from the summer's sun, the very dust of summer and the snow-drifts of the winter, as well as the dear companions of those innocent and more careless days." But amid these homely wanderings, his speech returned to his customary moral concerns. He emphasized that good character was what made the "plain man look noble, and the proud man mean." He drew on historical figures such as Napoleon to emphasize that moral people show their real mettle in moments of despair.[12]

In the summer of 1859 Andrew took on another fugitive case, this one involving the slave Maria Gaskins, who came to his attention via the abolitionist Nathaniel Spooner. Spooner had been riding with friends in Plymouth when they came up to the home of William Brown, an African American. Brown shouted out to them, "There is a slave in my house, who wants to be free." The company went inside and met the thirty-five-year-old Gaskins, who was traveling in New England with her masters, William and Mary Holmes. Gaskins explained that they had purchased her in her hometown, Savannah, Georgia, and had brought her to New Orleans. Then, under the pretense of returning her to friends in Savannah, they had instead taken passage up the Mississippi River, traveling across the Midwest to New England. In Plymouth, her mistress did not allow her to go out except to church, and that was where she had found friends and shared her story.[13]

Gaskins told the visitors that she did indeed wish to be free. So Spooner acquired a writ of habeas corpus from Judge Thomas Russell and proceeded to the house where Gaskins was residing. Her owners protested, and the scene grew ugly, but Spooner and a deputy sheriff managed to extract her and bring her to Boston. By this time, the Vigilance Committee had gone to work, securing Andrew and his partner William Burt as her counsel. In the state supreme court, Andrew argued that Gaskins's masters had taken her beyond the reach of Louisiana's slave code. Judge Theron Metcalf concurred; he advised her to return to Plymouth, retrieve her belongings, and prepare for life as a free woman. To avoid potential reenslavement, Andrew asked the judge to prepare a record of these proceedings that she could produce in a subsequent arrest. The case drew national attention, and Gaskins became a media darling. The *Daily Citizen* described her as "quite an intelligent looking negress, with a bright eye, and looks as able to earn her own living out of slavery as that of her owners in it." Yet editors worried about repercussions, with one fretting that Andrew had shaken "the pillars of the Union."[14]

In late summer, Garrison and other Boston abolitionists invited Andrew to take part in a celebration to mark the British liberation of more than 800,000 slaves in the British West Indies. Andrew was unable to attend, but he sent a letter in honor of the occasion:

> It is, in my judgment, beyond reasonable doubt that sound political economy, as well as national security and tranquility, requires that the people who inhabit every country should be free to enjoy their natural rights. . . . Into whose souls, even now, does the iron of slavery in America enter with the bitterest pain and the deepest wound? . . . The only remaining inquiry for the American people is, *whether all poor men shall be slaves, or all slaves shall be made free!*"[15]

This may have been Andrew's first use of a phrase that later became a signature expression in his political life.

Andrew was vacationing with Samuel Howe that summer, who continued to be impressed by his friend's talents. In Howe's view, this "poor man's lawyer" was "one of the few men left in the Republican party to save it from utter discredit." Writing to Theodore Parker, he continued: "He and all like him will, I think, soon cleave off, and carry a large portion . . . of the people [with them]." Howe saw Andrew as a solution to "Banks and his adherents [who] use their power for its own increase and perpetuation, rather than for advancement of human freedom and good."[16]

John Brown at Harpers Ferry

In Virginia, the morning of October 17 was cool and drizzly. Alexander Boteler, a plantation owner and businessman in Shepherdstown, was finishing breakfast when his daughter arrived to tell him that a "negro insurrection" had begun overnight in Harpers Ferry, ten miles away. Boteler, who became one of the first chroniclers of the uprising, immediately rode to the river village. There he met "a little old darky" who was obviously running away from something. "Who's doing the killing?" Boteler asked. According to his account, the slave replied, "I hearn tell dis mornin' dat some of de white folks allowed dey was abolitioners, come down for ter raise a ruction 'mong de colored people." Boteler soon learned that John Brown was the "abolitioner" responsible for triggering what the New England reformer Frank Sanborn later described as "an act of war" against slavery.[17] Harpers Ferry was located at the confluence of the Potomac and Shenandoah rivers, and its arsenal was the nation's second largest. Over the course of thirty-six hours, Brown and nineteen other men had stormed it, fighting against townspeople, militia, and federal troops before being captured or killed. Though not one slave was freed, seventeen people died. Brown, who was wounded, was taken to jail in nearby Charles Town, where he and the surviving conspirators waited to be arraigned. Two of his sons, Oliver and Watson, would die soon after the raid, while another, Owen, would survive, escaping to Ohio and later moving to California.

The press exploded with news about the failed insurrection. In Boston, Andrew mobilized an ad hoc committee of to raise money for Brown's defense—unaware that some of his enlistees may have had connections with the incident. Meanwhile, newspapers reported that Colonel Robert E. Lee's aide-de-camp, Lieutenant Jeb Stuart, had confiscated a cache of documents at the Maryland farmhouse where Brown had prepared for the raid. These included letters from the "secret six," a group of northern abolitionists who included Andrew's friends Frank Sanborn, Samuel Howe, Thomas Higginson, Theodore Parker, and George Stearns as well as Gerrit Smith, a friend of Frederick Douglass.

The press made much of these northern supporters, and claims of a conspiracy may have some truth. That spring Brown had visited Boston on a fundraising mission for his Kansas antislavery campaign but also for another undisclosed scheme. At that time he met with Sanborn, Higginson, Parker, Stearns, and Howe, who may have introduced him to Andrew. Brown eventually set his sights on Harpers Ferry, hoping to lure local slaves from their masters and arm them at the arsenal. As he prepared, he cultivated the support of Harriet Tubman, who herself had rescued hundreds of slaves from bondage. Yet some of Brown's initial supporters grew wary of his bloody intentions and distanced themselves. Even Douglass told Brown that his plan was suicidal.[18]

In Boston, Andrew had been drawn toward the magnetic Brown and his mission. But he had also felt sorry for the old man, giving him $25 and hoping he would use the funds for his family as well as for his cause. If Andrew had been privy to any talk of a Virginia raid, he never mentioned it. But when the press reported that Brown had had accomplices, Douglass was so concerned that he fled to England. Within a few days Sanborn visited Andrew's office and admitted that he might be implicated. Horrified, Andrew called Sanborn a fool and urged him to go to Canada. Howe, too, was anxious. After he appeared at Stearns's home, raging about the tragedy, he told his friend that they both needed leave the country. Stearns suggested they visit Andrew first, and the two did so the next morning, though without revealing their full involvement with Brown. Thanks to Sanborn, however, Andrew was already prepared. He explained the legalities of conspiratorial culpability: despite their foolishness, they were safe from prosecution. "I see no possible way in which any one can have done anything in Massachusetts for which he can be carried to any other state," Andrew told Stearns.[19]

Andrew remained concerned about Brown's situation. He solicited a Maryland friend, Montgomery Blair, to defend him or to recommend another high-profile lawyer. Blair suggested Thomas Chilton, and Andrew agreed to pay for Chilton's services as well as for those of his co-counsel William Green. As Andrew was working out these details, Howe dispatched a young Boston lawyer, George Sennott, to report on the case, and Higginson's friend John LeBarnes sent another young lawyer, George Hoyt, to do the same. But the wheels of justice were turning quickly. The Buchanan administration and Virginia's governor Henry Wise had arranged to have Brown and his accomplices arraigned for murder by the state of Virginia and for treason by the U.S. government. On October 25, the bailiff read the charges. Each person involved was to be tried separately by the presiding judge, Richard Parker, who set Brown's trial to begin on October 27. Until Andrew's hired lawyers could arrive, the magistrates assigned two local attorneys, Thomas Green and Lawson Botts, to serve as defense counsel. Andrew Hunter, a Virginia legislator who was devoutly pro-slavery, was the prosecutor, and the twelve-member jury would all be locals. Andrew presumed that Brown would accept the insanity plea that Botts had argued in his defense. But Brown did not trust his local counsel team, and the feeling was mutual.[20]

When Hoyt arrived in Charles Town a day into the trial, he was ready to assist, though many onlookers mistook him for an abolitionist spy rather than an attorney. Nevertheless, Judge Parker allowed him to serve as co-counsel with Botts and Green. On the trial's second day, however, Brown accused his Virginia lawyers of mishandling his case and dismissed them. Now Hoyt, just twenty-one years old, found himself in charge of conducting a defense for the nation's most notorious criminal. From a distance, Andrew exerted his legal influence to help, urging Hoyt to induce Brown to accept an insanity plea. "That he is a maniac can probably be proved," he wrote. If the defendant would accept that plea, Andrew had funds to pay for his counsel. Despite these upheavals among the defense lawyers, Judge Parker accelerated the trial's pace, ordering closing arguments to begin on October 31. But finally Samuel Chilton and a Cleveland attorney named Hiram Griswold arrived to take the defense out of Hoyt's hands.[21]

Throughout the trial, Brown, convalescing from his injuries, had been lying on a cot in the courtroom. There, after five days, he heard the jury return a guilty verdict within forty-five minutes. Two days later, guards carried him into the courtroom for sentencing. When Judge Parker asked Brown if he wanted to explain why he should not be sentenced, the prisoner launched into a five-minute argument claiming that God was on his side:

> I see a book kissed, which I suppose to be the Bible, or at least the New Testament, which teaches me that all things whatsoever I would that men should do to me, I should do even so to them. It teaches me, further, to remember them that are in bonds as bound with them. I endeavor to act up to that instruction. I am yet too young to understand that God is any respecter of persons. I believe that to have interfered as I have done, as I have always freely admitted I have done, in behalf of His despised poor, I did no wrong, but right. Now, if it is deemed necessary that I should forfeit my life for the furtherance of the ends of justice, and mingle my blood further with the blood of millions in this slave country whose rights are disregarded by wicked, cruel, and unjust enactments, I say, let it be done.[22]

Northern reporters pounced on Brown's prophetic speech, using it to batter at the claim that slavery was constitutionally sound. As they described the scene in the courtroom, they also worked to portray it as a metaphor for the nation itself, on trial for its sins. On the day of the sentencing, the correspondent for the *New York Herald* noted that "not the slightest sound was heard in the vast crowd as the verdict was thus returned and read." In the eerie silence, Parker ordered Brown to be hanged. The next day he sentenced the rest of the conspirations to be hanged as well.[23] The executions were set for December 2.

With Brown's execution date scheduled, the nation now had a month to ponder the gravity of this historical moment. Northerners remained ambivalent about Brown's raid. Massachusetts politicians Henry Wilson and Charles Sumner feared that his recklessness might destroy the Republican coalition, allowing critics to accuse party members of abetting and martyring a fanatic. Indeed, the timing was awkward. The raid had taken place just two weeks after Massachusetts legislators had overturned a law prohibiting African Americans from joining the state militia, the last of the Commonwealth's laws that specifically discriminated against Black residents. Yet Andrew, Chilton, and Greene persisted in their defense of Brown, lobbying for a new trial in a U.S. court and seeking to obtain a writ of error before Virginia's Supreme Judicial Court of Appeals. Andrew told Green that he would have happily become publicly involved in the case but knew that, as a Republican lawyer from Massachusetts, he would be "quite as much on trial as my client would be. Besides that, I would be a stranger to the local jurisprudence and practice of Virginia."[24] Moreover, though he hoped for a new trial, he knew this would mean that the people who had had knowledge of Brown's plan would be summoned to court. Brown had refused to name his backers, but the evidence of co-conspirators was overwhelming. Stearns wired Andrew from Montreal: "When will the act [that is, obtaining a writ of error] be perfected? Will it protect us?"[25] He and other members of the "secret six" turned to Andrew for advice and reassurance. Should they remain in Boston and potentially be arrested, or should they, like Howe and Stearns, flee the country.[26]

Sanborn remained in Boston, as did Higginson, who hated the notion of desertion. But Andrew's hopes for a new trial went nowhere, so he turned his attention to raising funds for Brown's family. Writing to Green about their dashed plans, he said:

> I esteem it a great blunder of the court . . . that they did not allow an argument, and place their own reasons before the world. . . . I can understand and can sympathize with your feelings, position, and attitude, and I am sure that if the question of slavery rested, for its solution, solely with gentlemen of education, culture, and refinement, instead of being managed by speculators in politics, land, and negroes, who take no thought for the future of men and nations, I should have no fears. But slavery must be the ultimate ruin, I hold, of *any* people, however grand

and virtuous otherwise, by whom it is treated as if it were a normal institution, or as the normal condition of any of the human race.[27]

He told Green that, while the condemned man's conduct was inde-
fensible, he recognized "great and admirable properties in Brown,
of both mind and character, and an apparent consciousness of self-
sacrificing and noble purpose, and a heroic devotedness to his own
long-cherished view of truth; which, while they may stamp him a
fanatic, can never allow him, in calm history, to be regarded as a *felon*."
Andrew believed that sparing Brown's life would reflect well on Virginians; without such charity, history would not forgive them. He was
opposed to slavery not "simply as one of the obstacles in the way of
human progress," but also because he saw "a better hope for all races
than that." He told Green, "It cannot be perpetual; nor can any unnatu-
ral thing or social wrong be immortal. The ages will conquer it. Shall it
conquer *us* too?" Then the tone of his letter became sermonlike:

> The stone will grind to powder him on whom it falls. Shall it fall on slav-
> ery, and crush us, the American people, in the fall? God knows how much
> I believe in the force and conquering power of the truth itself. I feel sure
> that our general freedom to think, to know and to utter will secure the
> ultimate triumph of truth and justice, and ultimate freedom and happi-
> ness to the whole.[28]

A few days after Brown's sentencing, his children began digging
graves in North Elba, New York, for their father and two brothers.
Meanwhile, the Republican press hardly mentioned that Banks had
been reelected governor of Massachusetts. As the state's radicals were
praising Brown and raising money for his family, conservatives and
moderates were condemning him as a madman and throwing their
support behind Banks, who soundly defeated Ben Butler and George
Briggs. When Stearns and Howe returned to Boston, they received a
cold reception from many of their friends and colleagues. But Andrew
stood by them. He understood that they had wanted to inspire people
to do their religious duty, even as he deplored their association with
Brown's violent means.[29]

Bostonians were deeply divided by the Brown saga. Some saw his
act as noble, while others were convinced that violence could not end
slavery. For his part, Andrew knew it would take a herculean effort to
eliminate racial discrimination, but he believed that championing racial
justice at the ballot box was better than using the sword. This, however,
required walking a tightrope between the conservative majority and the
progressive minority. He was aware that this was not a popular view

among most Massachusetts voters. Still, as much as he hated slavery, Andrew never publicly derided enslavers in the way Garrison did. He wanted slavery to end, but he did not want it to end with bloodshed.[30]

Crimes of This Guilty Land

On November 19 Andrew presided over a meeting at Tremont Temple, with the goal of raising funds for Brown's family. A number of prominent abolitionists refused to attend, though both Ralph Waldo Emerson and Wendell Phillips were there. Charles Francis Adams, declined to appear but said he would contribute to the family fund. At the meeting Andrew carefully avoided praising Brown's actions and said that he had taken no part in igniting the events. Yet, he told his listeners, there was "an irrepressible conflict between Freedom and Slavery, as old and as immortal as the irrepressible conflict between right and wrong." He paused for a moment, then apologized for what he was about to say: "[It is] wholly outside the duty of this assembly to-night," to judge "whether the enterprise of John Brown and his associates in Virginia was wise or foolish, right or wrong. I only know that, whether the enterprise itself was the one or the other, John Brown himself is right." The crowd erupted in applause, and Andrew continued:

> I sympathize with the man. I sympathize with the idea because I sympathize with and believe in the eternal right. They who are dependent upon him, and his sons and his associates in the battle at Harper's Ferry have a right to call upon us who have professed to believe, or who have in any manner or measure taught the doctrine of the rights of man as applied to the colored slaves of the South, to stand by them in their bereavement, whether those husbands and fathers and brothers were right or wrong.[31]

There was nobility in bending the arc of the moral universe toward justice. But even this had its critics. Boston press was harsh in its response to Andrew's declaration. The *Post* directly asked all Republicans to consider if they, too, believed that Brown was right.[32] Yet many of those present were electrified. Frank Preston Stearns, the son of George Stearns, was a teenager when he attended the meeting. Though Andrew was small and boyish, his presence was larger than life. "Nothing," recalled the young Stearns, "could have been more daring [than this speech] or more likely to make him unpopular, [yet] . . . his whole appearance was resolute and intrepid. He had set his foot down, and no power on earth could induce him to withdraw it." As Stearns recollected, a clergyman had been invited to speak at the meeting and had at first accepted, until his parishioners complained. He then declined with the excuse that he had supposed there would be two sides to the question. Andrew wanted nothing to do with such moral cowardice. "As if," he said, "there could be two sides to the question [of] whether John Brown's wife and daughters should be permitted to starve."[33]

The Harpers Ferry raid may have commenced Brown's canonization but it sounded the Union's knell, and both southerners and northerners were challenged to respond to the raid. Now Andrew's declaration seemed to group him among the accomplices; some critics went so far as to call him the "secret seventh" conspirator. As Brown lay in a Charles Town jail cell, Andrew had taken up the gauntlet, continuing in his own way what the condemned man had begun in October.[34]

As December 2 neared, a prison guard asked Brown for his autograph. The abolitionist consented, on one condition: that the guard should not make a spectacle of it. Keeping his promise, on the morning of his hanging, Brown sent for the guard and, as he left the jail, handed the man a short communication with his signature. The guard immediately opened the note, which read: "I John Brown am now quite *certain* that the crimes of this *guilty land* will never be purged *away*; but with Blood. I had *as I now think*; vainly flattered myself that without *very much* bloodshed; it might be done."[35] Still, Brown found peace on that sunny morning. "This is a beautiful country," he remarked, sitting atop his coffin as he was driven to his death. "I never had the pleasure of seeing it before."[36] At 11:15 he mounted the gallows, his steps firm, a white muslin hood covering his face. Minutes later the trapdoor dropped, and Brown was dangling at the end of a rope. Thirty-five minutes later, after his pulse had ceased, he was cut down and laid in the coffin. The governor of Virginia had allowed his body to be sent to New York, and Brown's martyrdom took shape as his remains began their journey northward.

Northerners commemorated the execution by ringing church bells in unison at the hour of Brown's death. Henry Wadsworth Longfellow wrote in his diary: "This will be a great day in our history; the date of a new revolution,—quite as much needed as the old one."[37] Samuel Bowles, the editor of the *Springfield Republican*, noted, as the execution hour approached, that "the calmest man in all Virginia to-day will be he who knows that he will be in another world before the sun has reached its meridian."[38] Close to 4,000 people gathered at Tremont Temple. Andrew, too, had the hour etched in his mind. That morning he got into his carriage with a few friends and drove about town. Just before noon, he tugged on the reins, came to a stop, pulled out his pocket watch, and said, "John Brown is dead." When they came upon a gunsmith, he allowed that he had never fired a gun and probably never struck a blow in his life, but a new day was about to dawn, and a spirit of activism had fallen upon him. Unable to go back to work, he continued to drive through Boston. Later in the day, he probably attended a prayer meeting at Reverend Grimes's church, where the African American community had congregated to mourn Brown.[39]

Andrew defended Brown's cause long after his execution. In his correspondence with Green, he continued to discuss slavery and racial prejudice, declaring that he never wished to "hide or to forget the wrongs of my own section toward descendants of Africans, & those immediately brought thence as slaves." Yet, he explained, "I do not desire to make a case against the South. I do not believe the question ought to assume that phase, at all." The question at hand, he maintained, was a matter of "simple right or wrong between the African race & *all* of us who have oppressed, & do oppress them,—& second, in relation to the modified powers & duties of the states & people, severally & respectively, inter sese, under the Federal Constitution":

> I do not regard society as perfect anywhere. I hope not to be a block in the way of my own nearest friends and neighbors; even in the way of those more remote. . . . [Yet] I am convinced of the substantial equality of Men, & as to their fundamental rights, I include colored men in the citizenry of Humanity, and I accept the logical consequences of the inclusion. . . . My head & heart, my reading, my reasoning & my knowledge & experience of men, of both races combine to teach me that creed.

He mentioned his work for the fugitive slave Seth Botts:

> I asked myself, is there any difference in the right of that man & of myself to be free? And, if there is,—then running the question along from the thoroughbred negro, through various shades, including a hazel-eyed, brown-haired, fair-skin'd girl, (once even on the auction block,)—I asked: Where—in this chain, did the right to freedom end and the door to slavery begin?[40]

When legislators returned to Washington, Senator James Mason of Virginia, who had authored the 1850 Fugitive Slave Law, expected Congress to determine if Brown had had co-conspirators and, if so, to bring them to justice. He introduced a resolution asking that a committee be appointed. After it passed, he was named chair, and Senator Jefferson Davis of Mississippi was named chief inquisitor.[41] Montgomery Blair, the Maryland lawyer who had helped Andrew find legal defense for Brown, was following these Senate proceedings closely, and he warned Andrew that southern "mischief makers" might conspire to have a northerner arrested to placate their constituents. But Sumner encouraged his friend to appear before the committee, if he were called. In the meantime, Andrew wrote to Senator William Pitt Fessenden of Maine, declaring that, in his view, the senatorial inquiry was purely political. He argued that Mason should allow committee members to travel to meet witnesses and record testimony, thus saving citizens the inconvenience of traveling. He also noted that several potential witnesses had declined to testify, for fear that admitting to any knowledge of Brown would make them appear to be conspirators. In a return letter, Fessenden confessed that, while he disapproved of Brown's methods, "I cannot help feeling a certain [amount] of sympathy with the man." The thought resonated with Andrew.[42]

The New Year came and went without fanfare. As winter settled upon Boston, Andrew worried about his friends. Sanborn wrote to say that Mason's committee had summoned him to Washington, and he wanted Andrew's advice about whether he should appear before the committee. Howe had decided not to testify, which had further implicated him. "You know my view about the old man," he had written to Andrew; "he was . . . not mad, but *intensified* to the verge of madness." Howe claimed that the financed arms in Brown's possession had been intended for the Kansas freedom fighters. He said that the New England committee supporting abolitionists' efforts in Kansas "gave him no authority to take those arms to Va., but on the contrary, gave him express orders to do otherwise with them."[43] Eventually, however, Howe's conscience got the better of him, and he did appear before Mason's committee, telling members that he had had no knowledge of Brown's plan to attack Harpers Ferry and had believed that his donations would be used to defend freedom in Kansas.[44]

Mason's summons to Andrew arrived in early February. Andrew immediately consulted Sumner about scheduling logistics, as he was currently involved in an important case in Boston. The senator assured him committee members would accommodate him, so Andrew quickly made his way to Washington and appeared in the Senate on February 9. Members' initial questions focused on his connections to Brown's attorneys Chilton and Green but then turned to Andrew's own association with Brown.[45] Andrew was outraged by the rapid pace of this interrogation: "It was wholly unlike anything I had ever known or heard of in my practice as a lawyer. When some persons had been indicted for kidnapping, in Massachusetts, last September, the court gave General Cushing, their counsel, two or three months after the arraignment before he was required even to file a plea." However, he explained his reasons for not going to Virginia to defend Brown himself and clarified why he had employed Chilton and Green instead. The committee pressed on, questioning him about the money he had raised for Brown's defense and for his family. Mason asked if this fundraising had been affected by an assumption that Brown would not receive a fair trial or if it had been a way to show support for his abolitionist career. In reply, Andrew denounced the Kansas murders and then asserted his belief that Brown would not have received a fair trial and reiterated his concerns about the destitution of Brown's family.[46]

Mason challenged Andrew to explain the $25 he had personally given to Brown and asked if he had had motives to offer more. Andrew explained why he had concluded that "John Brown himself" was "right." He told the committee he had met the man at a gathering in Massachusetts, where he had listened to his story: "I did not know how to understand the old gentleman fully, because when I hear a man talk upon great themes, touching which I think he must have deep feeling, in a tone perfectly level, without emphasis and without any exhibition of feeling, I am always ready to suspect that there is something wrong in the man's brain." He did not seem to be a "dangerous man," but "his sufferings and hardships and bereavements had produced some effect upon him." Andrew knew that Brown was poor and thus, in parting, "expressed my gratitude to him for having fought for a great cause with earnestness, fidelity, and conscientiousness, while I had been quietly at home earning my money and supporting my family in Boston under my own vine and fig tree, with nobody to molest or make me afraid."[47]

Senator Davis badgered Andrew, asking if he believed that Brown's "useful services . . . for the preservation of good order and government" included the Kansas murders, the incursions into Missouri to run off slaves, and alleged horse stealing. Andrew replied that he had been unaware of these details until they were brought up at Brown's trial and then turned the tables on Davis:

> Since the gentleman has called my attention again to that subject, I think the attack which was made against representative government in the assault upon Senator Sumner, in Washington, which, so far as I could learn from the public press, was, if not justified, at least winked at throughout the South, was an act of very much greater danger to our liberties and to civil society than the attack of a few men upon our neighbors over the borders of a State.

In the end, Andrew was able to make made the point that, for all his faults, Brown had invaded Virginia in retaliation for Missouri's invasion of Kansas.[48] After he returned to Boston, the editor of Lowell's *Daily Citizen* called him a man of "large heart and unquestionable backbone."[49]

The Brown raid had infused antislavery ideals more deeply into the Commonwealth's political culture. Yet it had also changed southern attitudes. For the South, the crisis no longer centered around Kansas statehood but had moved closer to the nation's capital. Brown's insurrection had forced Americans of all stripes to consider deliberately if the United States could remain half-slave and half-free. As Henry Thoreau told a crowd in North Elba, New York, "years are no longer required for a revolution of public opinion," emphasizing that "days, nay hours, produce marked changes in this case." Andrew was not in attendance, but he would have agreed with those words. He had been profoundly shaken by Brown's raid and his execution. Indeed, he kept a sketch of Brown on the gallows for the rest of his life. Yet in these critical years he had shown his mettle, and Howe, among many others, was impressed. He remarked to his wife, "Andrew is going to be governor of Massachusetts."[50]

CHAPTER 9

THE GOVERNORSHIP
1860

"Give Me My Boots"

Though he was busier than ever that winter, Andrew found time to advance a cause that was close to his heart: establishing the Home for Aged Colored Women, a project led by Reverend Clarke and Reverend Grimes. In 1850, Andrew Bigelow had founded the Home for Aged Women for respectable, native-born, white Protestant women, seeing it as a way to keep them out of public almshouses. But even public shelters would not admit indigent African American women, who were typically forced to find assistance in institutions for the insane. The first meeting to found the Home for Aged Colored Women took place in January 1860 in Clarke's church vestry.[1] Andrew had prepared the legal documents necessary to charter the home, and he also helped to fund the enterprise. His friend William Claflin, a Republican antislavery activist, later said that he had never known anyone else like Andrew: "His devotion to the colored race knew no bounds, not because of their color, but simply because they were hated, oppressed, and down-trodden."[2]

Though journalists hardly ever recorded Andrew's work for "the lowly," the press had devoted much attention to his work on behalf of Brown's family and the Republican Party, and this coverage, both good and bad, had elevated his name around the state. But attitudes about slavery were hardening in both the North and the South, and Brown's raid had shaken the North's conscience. Though the insurrection had failed, that failure and Brown's Christ-like execution had buoyed the antislavery cause far more than his success would have done. Andrew hoped his party could capitalize on this emotional Christian resonance in the November election.

Close friends saw Andrew as the republican ideal: a man who lived an unassuming, self-made, Christian life; who squared his morality with his aspirations. Though parties, not personalities, drove the political culture, Frank Bird was determined to make this talented and devoted counselor the next governor of Massachusetts. And he had the clout for the mission. Massachusetts voters went to the polls annually to elect their governor, and Andrew's ascent began in early March, at the state Republican convention, when Bird orchestrated his nomination as a delegate to the national convention in Chicago. Members voted overwhelmingly for him over the other candidates. "No poor power of speech" could express Andrew's gratitude. For now, Massachusetts Republicans were firmly behind presidential candidate William Seward, but they trusted Andrew to guide the rest of the national delegates toward the best decision. For his part, Andrew told Cyrus Woodman that he liked the other potential candidates, Salmon Chase and William Fessenden, just as well as Seward.[3]

Meanwhile, he focused on defending Frank Sanborn. On the night of April 3, five federal marshals attempted to arrest Sanborn in Concord, on a charge of conspiring with John Brown. They were led by Silas Carleton, recently deputized as a marshal by the Senate's sergeant-at-arms. As Sanborn's family incited a gathering crowd, a violent struggle ensued, and townspeople managed to wrest Sanborn away from the officers, hiding him until a writ of habeas corpus could be produced. The following morning the news sped to Boston. H. Burr Crandall, a lawyer apprenticing in Andrew's firm, recalled that day. For hours the office was besieged by Sanborn's supporters, all of them clamoring for counsel, and the "coolest person in it was Andrew." Crandall wrote, "He had no time for exultation, but standing at his high desk, was pulling down book after book, and occasionally with a quick, nervous movement, accompanied by a little sniff, adjusting his spectacles, passing his fingers through his curly hair, writing with running pen, and preparing a case he was soon to argue." Into the office crowded men, "black and white[,] to congratulate him" on this opportunity, including Wendell Phillips, who stopped in to encourage the "judge," as Andrew was known to his friends—the nickname they had given him after he had declined an appointment to the Supreme Judicial Court of Massachusetts.[4]

As soon as he had pulled together his materials, Andrew darted from the office to the home of state supreme court judge Ebenezer Rockwood Hoar, where he obtained a writ of habeas corpus, to be executed by Concord's deputy sheriff. On April 5, the next day, Sanborn appeared before a packed Boston courtroom and a full bench of judges, with Lemuel Shaw presiding. Andrew, along with attorneys John Keyes, Samuel Sewall, and Robert Paine, asked that Sanborn be released, arguing that the Senate's power to arrest could not be delegated to someone deputized by the sergeant-at-arms. Andrew further contended that no congressional act had ever created the office of sergeant-at-arms, which nullified Sanborn's arrest. The court agreed, and Sanborn returned to Concord.[5]

In early May, Andrew put his work in Boston behind him and headed for Chicago by train to attend the Republican National Convention, the longest trip he had ever made. He traveled with twenty-five other Massachusetts delegates, including Seth Webb, Jr., George W. McLellan, J. A. Sidwell, and Charles Hale. The party stopped briefly in Albany before heading to Niagara Falls, where they crossed into Canada and visited the site of the Battle of Lundy's Lane, made famous in the War of 1812. When he finally arrived in Chicago, he wrote to his wife, "Here I am at last, more than 1000 miles from home."[6] The experience made a lasting impression on him. At the convention he met politicians from all over the country, including the New York delegates, who, according to the Cincinnati journalist Murat Halstead, "can drink as much whiskey, swear as loud and long, sing as bad songs, and 'get up and howl' as ferociously as any crowd of Democrats you ever heard, or heard of."[7]

Into this maelstrom, the Massachusetts delegation arrived armed for battle. From what Andrew could learn, Seward seemed most likely to take the nomination, but the Commonwealth colleagues worried that he could not win the general election in November. So on the convention's eve, Andrew led the New England delegates to join ranks with those in Pennsylvania, New Jersey, Illinois, and Indiana—states that he believed were crucial to a national victory. To gather preliminary information, he proposed that these delegates hold a small caucus to see if they could rally behind one candidate; by now he was hopeful it would be Lincoln. Andrew had been impressed by the Illinois lawyer's unsullied fame, his fearless defense of Republican principles in the great debate with Stephen Douglas two years before, and his status as a self-made man. From what he had read and learned from colleagues, he believed that Lincoln's principles, devotion to the new party, and popularity made him the better candidate for the presidency. When the twelve-member caucus met to report, however, members failed to agree. Andrew was taken aback. Indeed, he worried about his own delegation. By the end of the first balloting on May 18, it had become clear that many Massachusetts delegates favored Seward, but some also favored Lincoln. In the second balloting, the state's delegates gave Seward twenty-two votes and Lincoln four. By the third ballot, however, Andrew had managed to move sixteen votes to Lincoln, giving him a total of eighteen and leaving Seward with eight. The final balloting revealed that Lincoln had won not only the Massachusetts delegation's votes but also the convention's presidential nomination. When the chair announced the result, Andrew rose to second to the motion. He then gave a short, memorable speech. Harkening back to the days of Bunker Hill and the Battle of Concord, Andrew referred to Massachusetts as the bastion of American liberty, "where under judicial decision, human slavery was banished from the venerable soil of the ancient commonwealth, before the colonies were a united people":

> We have come from the shadows of the Old South Church, where American liberty was baptized in the waters of religion, and we hold the purpose firm and strong, as we have through the tedious struggle of years now gone by, to rescue, before we die, the holy ark of American liberty from the grasp of the Philistines who hold it.

If, as Andrew declared, the Revolutionary War had been the "manifest destiny" of democracy, then now was the time for Republicans to save the nation from itself. Deafening applause followed Andrew's eloquence, which, as Boston's *Daily Advertiser* reported, was "much admired by the immense concourse of fair women and gallant patriots who crowded the vast Wigwam."[8]

A committee of national delegates journeyed from Chicago to Springfield, Illinois, to inform Lincoln of his nomination. Andrew was part of this group; and as soon as he saw Lincoln in person, he understood "in a flash that here was a man who was master of himself." He wrote, "For the first time, . . . [the delegates] understood that he whom they had supposed to be little more than a loquacious and clever State politician, had force, insight, conscience, that their misgivings were in vain."[9] When Andrew shook hands with the nominee, he said, "We claim you, Mr. Lincoln, as coming from Massachusetts, because all the old Lincoln names are from Plymouth County." Lincoln replied humorously, "We'll consider it so this evening."[10]

Andrew's trip to Illinois had been a welcome change from his daily round, but it also taxed his health. Yet he was unable to rest. As soon as he wearily returned to Boston, friends and colleagues greeted him eagerly, anxious to learn about the convention and Lincoln. To this point, the new Republican nominee had not been a popular choice among New England voters, so Andrew needed to forestall quickly Seward's supporters. So when state Republicans met in Faneuil Hall to ratify the Chicago nominations, he gave a speech justifying the decision to endorse Lincoln. "Old Faneuil Hall was not only crowded," according to the *Daily Citizen*, "but surrounded by such a throng of people as have seldom been seen ever there."[11] Andrew's listeners were rapt, and he was quick to share his impressions of the new candidate:

> You ask me what Abraham Lincoln is like. There we saw him, and all there was of him, and it was not a difficult matter to catch a sight of that honest and intellectual face, for he stood like Saul among his brethren, head and shoulders above every other man. . . . I would trust my case with the honesty and with the intellect and with the heart and with the brain of Abraham Lincoln as a lawyer, and I would trust my country's cause in the care of Abraham Lincoln as its chief magistrate, while the wind blows and the water runs.[12]

Though Andrew had grand visions for the Republican Party as the instrument for ending slavery, he knew his party's base was conservative, so he was careful to cloak his enthusiasm within political realism. Yet he could not hide his passionate desire to break the shackles of servitude, and he cared little for critics who disagreed with that great purpose. Even as his popularity grew, he felt compelled to explain the differences between the Garrisonians and himself, working to justify his practical, peaceful, constitutional abolitionism. He wrote directly to Garrison, reminding him that political parties placed limitations on individual thinking and chiding him for his attacks: "I have been so often pained at the unremitting and I think unjust assaults by persons upon your platform on men whom I greatly respect, and whose services in the cause of rational and impartial liberty I highly prize." Andrew remained convinced that the ballot box was the only route to abolishing slavery.[13]

Andrew had continued to deny his fitness for political office, but many Bostonians thought otherwise. The lawyer John Dodge wrote to Cyrus Woodman in July, reporting that "our old friend Andrew still rides on the high waves of popularity. I verily believe that he is this day the most popular man in Massachusetts."[14] The attention did not lead him to sugarcoat his beliefs. At the annual First of August celebration in Abington, where abolitionists and antislavery activists gathered to celebrate British Emancipation Day, Andrew repeated a comment he had made the year before in a letter to Garrison: the only remaining inquiry for the American people was "whether all poor men shall be slaves, or all slaves shall be made free."[15]

The *Worcester Spy* declared that "no man in the state has been more talked of, as our next candidate for governor, than John A. Andrew. He is one of the truest representatives of Massachusetts republicanism."[16] Observers found him genuine and accessible but also logical and persuasive. Like his party, he promoted Free-Soiler ideals but was wise enough to promote free labor as well. Though Andrew was not a rigid doctrinaire, free labor ideology resonated with northerners who believed that the South was different from and inferior to the free states and was an impediment to their material progress. Nonetheless, Governor Banks remained the favorite for reelection, despite the fact that he had catered to the Know Nothings, endorsed anti-immigrant measures, and vetoed bills that would have allowed Black residents to serve in the state militia. Radicals had been unable to overturn his veto, and the fallout from Brown's raid still smoldered in the political consciousness.[17]

Although most governors were little more than figureheads in the antebellum era, the Republican Party's very existence was evidence that a gale was sweeping across the electoral landscape. To southerners, the Republicans seemed almost mutinous. In this climate, Andrew understood that party unity was vital. With sectional tensions growing ever more acrimonious, he refused to permit his name to go forward as a gubernatorial candidate, in part because he believed that Banks was a more appropriate fit for the party, in part because politicians generally needed to be wealthy and he could not afford a loss of income.

But Andrew's friends had other plans, and William Robinson, known as "Warrington," went to work for them that summer. Writing for the *Springfield Republican*, he helped steer readers toward supporting Andrew's gubernatorial candidacy. Although he recognized the lawyer's reluctance to stand, he insisted, "We have never yet had a genuine, 'regular built' anti-slavery man for governor of this state, 'clear down to his boots,' as the saying is. We have had men who have yielded to the anti-slavery sentiment of the state, but none who have led it and heartily sympathized with it. Gov. Banks is no exception." Andrew, he believed, would stand up for the Republican Party platform without going beyond it. "The stormy time for Massachusetts republicanism," he prophesied, "will be in 1861, and not in 1860."[18]

For the moment, however, Andrew remained focused on his law firm. He had recently undertaken another international maritime case, this time one involving the yacht *Wanderer*. In 1859, the *Wanderer* had been docked in Port Jefferson, New York, when local authorities seized it under suspicion that it had been illegally transporting slaves from Africa to the United States. The yacht was moved to New York City and then to Boston. There, after months of legal battles, the yacht's owner, a Savannah cotton planter named Charles Lamar, asked Andrew to reclaim the ship so he could sell it. Lamar shamelessly contended that he had had no knowledge that the boat had been used to transport slaves. The case, which dragged out for two years, excited national interest, especially in Boston and New Yorker.

Somewhat surprisingly, Andrew agreed to take up the case; and in early June, after he had returned from the Republican National Convention, it was set for trial in the U.S. District Court of Massachusetts. Andrew threw himself into his final arguments, contending that Lamar had not ordered or known that the *Wanderer* was engaged in slaving and laying all blame on the captain. In his view, it was unjust that a vessel should be forfeited to the government for a crime for which the owner was innocent, and he maintained that this conflicted with the system of forfeitures under U.S. revenue laws. Andrew was not victorious. Later that month, the court decreed that Lamar had put an agent in possession of his ship and thus could not say that he was innocent of that agent's acts.[19]

The Next Massachusetts Governor

By the summer of 1860, the gulf between conservatives and radicals showed no signs of narrowing. Southerners were convinced that a Lincoln presidency would necessitate immediate secession, yet their divided Democratic Party seemed destined for a heavy loss in the elections. Meanwhile, Republican newspaper editors in Massachusetts were struggling to distance their party from Garrison-style abolitionism. Then, in August, Nathaniel Banks accepted a position as president of the Illinois Central Railroad. He quietly planned to pass the gubernatorial torch to Congressman Henry Dawes, a western Massachusetts conservative loathed by Bird Club associates. Quickly, Republican Party operatives arranged to publish news of Banks's railroad job, planning to release to the papers late on August 24, five days before the state convention was scheduled to open in Worcester. The goal was to circumvent any chance of Andrew's candidacy: the publishing arrangement meant that weekly newspapers in districts where he was popular would not learn the news until the convention was taking place, when it would be too late to nominate him. But on the morning of the 24th, as Banks traveled from New York to Boston with William Claflin, chair of the Republican State Committee, he revealed he would not be a candidate for reelection. Claflin, a Bird Club member, was startled; and when he arrived in Boston that night, he dashed to Charles Sumner's house and told him the story. Sumner immediately stood up. "Give me my boots," he exclaimed. "John A. Andrew must be the next governor of Massachusetts."[20]

Andrew was at the Parker House with Eben Stone, Frank Bird, and several other friends when they discovered the conservative Republicans' plot. Though Andrew had not coveted the governor's office, he was indignant about being treated unfairly, and the Bird Club sprang into action, determined to place his name before the voters. Bird labored tirelessly behind the scenes, and Warrington trumpeted Andrew's candidacy in the *Springfield Republican*: "To-day the politicians are all alive with excitement. The republican headquarters are well filled. Nearly everybody there is for John A. Andrew, . . . a man of solid and shining qualities." Not only did he make "admirable speeches," but he was "a thinker and an able man in every sense of the word." Even better, he was "a good man and an honest man, and true man to his friends and his enemies."[21]

Warrington was first and foremost a political gadfly, yet his endorsement reflected the widespread affection that so many people felt for Andrew. Knowing that Andrew needed conservative votes to win, he reminded readers of his candidate's support for both the conservative Seward and the moderate Lincoln. State Republicans responded, with large crowds arriving in Worcester on August 29, determined to help Andrew ascend to power. By day's end, he had received an unprecedented 723 votes of the 1,074 cast on the first ballot. The *New York Herald* called it a "waterloo victory of the radical over the conservative wing of the party. Andrew is one of the most ultra of the Massachusetts Republicans. He is an earnest, thorough going abolitionist, with not the least love for the 'peculiar institution.'"[22]

Andrew had spent much of the summer stumping for the Republican Party throughout New England. When he passed through Hingham in early September, the townspeople gathered to receive him at his summer residence. On a cool evening, 2,000 men, women, and children processed from Loring Hall to his front lawn, where a band played "Hail to the Chief." Andrew thanked them eloquently. "How dear to my heart are these fields, these hills, these spreading trees," he said, paying tribute to Samuel Woodworth's poem "The Old Oaken Bucket":

This verdant grass, this sounding shore before you, where, now for fourteen years, through summer heat, and sometimes, through winter storms, I have trod your streets, rambled your woods, sauntered by your shores, sat by your firesides, and felt the warm pressure of your hands; sometimes teaching your children in Sunday school, sometimes speaking to my fellow citizens . . . always with the cordial friendship of those who differed from oftentimes in what they thought the radicalism of my opinions . . . speaking [to] willing ears—very much more willing to hear than my words were worthy to be listened to,—on topics most interesting to your minds and convictions.[23]

There is a political axiom that candidates do not pick the moment; the moment picks the candidate. Andrew had been plucked from the courtroom for a higher purpose, or so it seemed.

When Andrew returned to Boston, thousands gathered to celebrate the Republican nominee for governor. He used the opportunity to emphasize his party's commitment to free men, free soil, and free labor:

Wherever slavery gains a foothold in any territory, the same men who own the slaves, also own the land. By owning slaves they crowd out and drive away, discourage and put down, all experiments at successful free white labor. Owning the labor and owning the land, they subsidize the press, they silence the pulpit . . . and they make the laws, taking care to apportion the taxes so as to protect slavery and discourage freedom.

The issue of slavery was not a "Negro question," he asserted; for if the Supreme Court had erased the rights of African Americans from the Constitution, it could wipe out white men's as well. Andrew told the crowd that he did not intend to wait for God to "perform the work assigned to human instrumentality."[24] Already he was using "free soil, free men" rhetoric to persuade white voters that they, too, had a stake in the slavery question.

Exposing Banks's scheme had not hurt Andrew's candidacy. Indeed, the governor's departure from the race had opened a favorable path for him, especially when combined with Sumner's enthusiastic endorsement. Many newspapers quickly hailed his fitness for office, and Andrew now set out to convince those that had remained silent. After he asked his friend Charles Winslow why the *Boston Journal* had not refuted claims against his candidacy, Winslow wrote to its editor, James Dix. Arguing that Andrew was "the most prominent representative of the purely republican idea in Massachusetts," Winslow asserted that he was "an honest man;—& whether politician or civilian—an honest man is the noblest work of God & can be entrusted with the liberty & highest interests of his fellowmen anywhere & in any situation with the gift of the State or the republic."[25] The appeal swayed Dix, who replied: "It is of course no secret that we were opposed to the nomination of Mr. Andrew, not upon personal grounds, for I know of no politician for whom I have a higher respect, but because of his surroundings. His nomination so far as it was a personal triumph is to me rather a matter of rejoicing than otherwise for I believe John A. Andrew 'himself is right.'" Andrew thanked Winslow for his aid. If voters were to elect him in November, he said, "may God give me grace, protect me from all unworthy motives, and guide me in the way of truth."[26]

State Republicans ratified their party nominations in Boston's Music Hall on September 11. It was a triumphant scene: crowds filled the chamber, music played, and party leaders offered resounding speeches. Congressman Anson Burlingame held court, emoting that Republicanism would soon find "a safe haven of rest in Abraham's bosom" and with Andrew: "There was not a stain upon his character, and his ability was unquestioned. There was but one charge against him, and that was that he had a heart."[27] Even Andrew's enemies, though sour, could not deny that he had the experience and temperament for the governorship, despite his devotion to the antislavery cause. Writing to Henry Dawes, Samuel Bowles called him a "dogmatic" politician who "lacks breadth and tact for government" but is "withal one of the cleverest, good-naturedest, and heartiest fellows alive."[28]

Still, Andrew needed to win the support of conservatives. As Warrington wrote in the *Springfield Republican*, "his John Brown sympathies and speeches, his Garrisonian affiliations, his negro-training predilections and all that sort of extreme anti-slaveryism will be trumpeted far and wide in the state to injure him."[29] George Lunt, the editor of the *Boston Courier*, led the charge, frequently misquoting Andrew, attacking his defense of Brown, and deriding his devotion to civil rights for African Americans. "Commercial men, merchants, Christians, mechanics, farmers," asked his October 1 editorial, "what say you to this thirst for the blood of your brothers? Do you endorse John Brown?" Democrats decried Andrew for leading "the canonization of the half-demented traitor, murderer, and robber, John Brown, the Abolitionist St. John."[30] The old Whigs also refused to be swayed, turning instead to Amos Lawrence, a textile manufacturer, as their candidate for governor. But that choice fell "like a wet blanket" onto the party's rank and file, for Lawrence himself had abolitionist credentials. He had chaired the Kansas Emigrant Aid Committee, which had provided the rifles that Brown had used at Harpers Ferry. Still, the conservatives were hopeful. At one point, one accosted Andrew on a Boston street: "Well, Andrew, you are a good fellow; but we will whip you like a sack!" Andrew stepped aside and, with a "peculiar twinkle" in his eye, said, "S—, it don't lie in your breeches to do it."[31]

Andrew's opponents were frightened by his "dangerous" abolition, but for many others his candidacy was, in Garrison's words, "a cheering sign of the times," not only because of his "exemplary character and great moral worth" but also because he represented the "highest phase of political anti-slavery feeling as yet developed." With Andrew as candidate, Massachusetts "takes no steps backwards" but "steadily advance[es] in the cause of humanity and freedom," though Garrison was quick to point out that the candidate was not an "ultraist or a radical."[32] Garrison did not limit himself to these paeans in the Liberator. He even paid for an advertisement in the Boston Post: "We take it for granted that no one who intends to cast a vote at the approaching election, and who has a particle of anti-slavery feeling or sentiment in his breast, will fail to record it in favor of the election of John A. Andrew."[33]

Hoping to sway voters, the Republican State Committee encouraged Andrew to stump around the state, and it published and disseminated a pamphlet of his letters and speeches. To diffuse his critics, his political managers advised him to strictly align with the Republican platform, which called only for an end to slavery's expansion, and he agreed. In a mid-September speech in the southeastern Massachusetts town of Berkley, he reiterated his commitment to the Union: "The real danger is not to the Union, but to the people. . . . In what condition must they be who in the South are watching for the dawn of Freedom's day; when slave masters and free laborers may unite to lift the heaviest bond, which white as well as black men ever bore."[34] For state Republicans Andrew's nomination felt like a turning point. In his diary Charles Winslow called him a "remarkable man & fit to be the leader of the great benevolent & patriotic idea which lies at the foundation of the republican party in this State. I have never been more impressed with the combination of intellectual & moral strength than was apparent in the speech of the present candidate for governor."[35] The scientist William Rogers wrote to his brother Henry that slavery's expansion would be wiped out by this election: "Mr. Andrew, whom you know, will be the next Governor,—an honest, fearless, clearheaded and humane man."[36]

In Sunshine and in Storm

Andrew's health and energy improved that fall, and he was ready to "give new vigor to the political contest," as the editor of the *New Hampshire Statesman* remarked.[37] Lowell's *Daily Citizen* was a constant champion, celebrating both his eloquence and his personality:

> To unaffected simplicity and frankness of manners, [he] adds the graces of high intellectual culture and the power of forensic oratory of the first order, while his acknowledged honesty and genial and generous nature make him a fitting representative of genuine manhood.... His fidelity to truth and justice has caused the temporizing to regard him as impractical, [but] ... he is the same John A. Andrew in sunshine and in storm, the same after as before receiving the gubernatorial nomination, [and] ... such a character the people delight to honor.

Yet as Andrew made clear, the "day is not distant, if the people of Massachusetts do not prove themselves apostates from the faith of the fathers.[38] The "storm" was approaching, and Andrew knew it.

November 6 was Election Day, but it was stormy, and the gale disrupted the telegraph. Massachusetts voters waited anxiously for news. Finally, the word came through: Lincoln had received 40 percent of the popular vote and an overwhelming majority of the electoral college vote. His only real competition was Stephen Douglas, who had polled second-highest among northerners but had garnered only twelve electoral votes and had carried the popular vote in only Missouri and New Jersey. John Breckinridge had lost to Lincoln by 1 million votes but had received seventy-two electoral votes.

In Massachusetts, Andrew had been just one contender in a crowded race. The Cotton Whig Amos Lawrence was running as a Constitutional Unionist, Erasmus D. Beach as a Douglas Democrat, and Benjamin Butler as a Breckinridge Democrat. Nonetheless, he prevailed by the largest margin in Massachusetts history. Andrew received 104,527 votes, compared to a combined 65,007 for the other three candidates. Andrew's lieutenant governor would be John Goodrich, a Sheffield native, who had served in the state senate and as a U.S. congressman.[39]

Contrary to the predictions of many Boston papers, the Republican Party could now celebrate a resounding victory throughout the North—an ominous sign for the slave states. Voters opposed to slavery's expansion had cracked the institution's political armor. The Massachusetts Republicans were a large part of this change. The Boston correspondent for the *New York Times* wrote that conservatives had been "in convulsions over Mr. Andrew's nomination," and his election served notice of "the growth of great truths and great ideas in the minds of a free people, from a first germ of thirty years ago to a present ripe maturity."[40] In a post-election speech at Tremont Temple, Andrew did not emphasize such divisions. Instead, he spoke of unity and freedom, promising that the new Republican government would "guarantee justice to all the states in the confederacy; and this equality will endure to the last. . . . Injustice in every form will disappear before the growing intelligence of the free people in every state. That is my prophecy."[41]

Time would tell if the election would lead to such profound changes. For now, abolitionists rejoiced, hoping their new governor would do for Massachusetts what Sumner had done for the nation. Yet Andrew's majority win also proved that conservatives had played a part in electing him and would hold him accountable to his constitutional convictions. Not all of them were confident. In early December, Richard Faye, a wealthy Boston manufacturer, told Banks that he feared the worst: "[Andrew] has neither your eyes nor your ears . . . [but has] committed body & soul to abolitionism pure & simple, right or wrong, constitutional or otherwise." In the coming weeks, Faye, along with others, including Colonel Jonas French of the state militia, publicly pushed back against the state's antislavery politicians. "Tell John Andrew, Tell John Andrew, Tell John Andrew, John Brown is Dead" was their motto. They hoped it would goad the governor-elect into fanning secessionist flames.[42]

Bird Club members now controlled the Republican State Committee and the most important state offices, but they, too, worried. Their party had triumphed, but its new leadership belonged not to Boston's conservative elite but to resourceful and dedicated antislavery activists. This meant that they were vulnerable. Andrew was aware of their anxieties, so he deputized Bird, Sanborn, Stearns, Howe, Sumner, and others as his unofficial cabinet. This decision to surround himself with colleagues more politically skilled than himself was a smart move. Andrew was able to air opinions and disagreements without fear of recrimination, and they protected him in Boston as they had shielded Sumner in Washington. The group focused on consolidating state political power and ensuring that constituents remained in step with national and state party leaders. They were not alarmed by post-election secession threats: like Andrew, they suspected that any war would inevitably end slavery. Disrupting the economy was a different matter, especially for northern elites with southern ties. Yet if northerners were accused of risking economic damage by ignoring southerners' earnest concerns, short-sighted secessionists were now failing to appreciate northerners' growing determination to preserve the Union and contain slavery.[43]

One evening after his election, Andrew met former governor Henry Gardner on Beacon Street in Boston. Gardner congratulated him, and the two men walked arm in arm up the street. They had known each other at Bowdoin, and Gardner was aware that Andrew had established the college's Peace Society. With southern secession now appearing imminent, he asked Andrew if he would wear a uniform if war were to break out.

"Do you think a peace man like me would make such an infernal fool of himself as to put on that nonsensical toggery?" Andrew replied.

Gardner retorted, "Well, you will appoint staff, won't you?"

Andrew asked, "Of what earthly use would they be?"

Gardner insisted, "You will attend the military reviews, won't you, as Governors usually do?"

Andrew said, "Not if I can find or invent any reasonable excuse to avoid it. I don't believe in the whole trumpery thing." Gardner recorded that the word Andrew really used "wasn't trumpery." Yet within months, he recalled, this peace man would be working twenty hours a day, helping to manage the nation's bloodiest conflict.[44]

In letters to Sumner, Andrew made it clear that he was aware that Lincoln's election had provoked talk of secession, but he believed that the president-elect would prevent dissolution. Nonetheless, the Republican win was inarguably a sectional victory, and it hastened the deteriorating relations between southern and northern congressional leaders. In Massachusetts, Lincoln, Brown, and Andrew were inextricably linked in the minds of voters and politicians, and events on the first anniversary of Brown's execution displayed the animosity between radicals and conservatives. African American abolitionists commemorated December 2 as a notable day in the fight against slavery and scheduled a December 3 meeting at Boston's Tremont Temple where speakers would address the question "How Can American Slavery be Abolished?" Anti-abolitionist merchants, however, sent a message to the South that they, too, saw Brown's raid as shameful. In their view, no law-abiding Massachusetts citizen "ought to countenance, sympathize with, or hold communion" with anyone who thinks that the raiders and the abettors were right. Rowdies calling themselves "union men" sympathetic to the anti-abolitionists attempted to disrupt the meeting, and a violent melee ensued, lasting until police arrived and restored order. By day's end, the mayor had ordered the hall to be cleared.[45]

The autumn campaign had been arduous, and Andrew's health had deteriorated significantly. He had been overweight for years, and his migraines had recently grown worse, bringing on nausea, vomiting, and terrible nosebleeds. Fearing he was in danger of a stroke, his doctor prescribed prolonged rest and warned him that overexertion of his brain might kill him. Convalescing at home, he had declined the invitation to the meeting, calling it "injudicious and unnecessary," given how furiously the South was goading the nation to war. Yet he wrote a letter to Moses Kimball, a Republican candidate for Boston mayor, supporting the abolitionists' right to free speech. Quoting John Milton, he proclaimed their "right to think, to know and to utter." This, he wrote, "is the dearest of all liberties. Without this right, there can be no liberty of any people; with it, there can be no slavery."[46]

As Republicans rose to power in the state, their political enemies fought back. Among them was Caleb Cushing, Andrew's nemesis when he was in the legislature. Now Cushing declared that "a band of drunken mutineers" had seized the Commonwealth, "so the good ship of state drifts,—drifts, with the storm still howling around her,—drifts into the gulf of perdition, with the black flag of the pirate hoisted at the mizzen."[47] Such sentiments echoed the fears of Massachusetts conservatives with southern business interests, who hoped to avert disunion. To placate those interests, state representatives organized a petition to repeal the state's Personal Liberty Law. The *Springfield Republican* and the *Boston Daily Advertiser* endorsed it and circulated it throughout state. These and other moves toward conciliation gave Andrew much to ponder before his inauguration.[48]

Andrew was scheduled to leave for Washington in early December. He was exhausted, and rumors were spreading that he was dangerously ill and not expected to live. Still, he soldiered on. He told Sumner to expect him in the capital within a few days and to avoid all compromises in the meantime. Before leaving, he wrote to Nathaniel Banks, the outgoing governor, asking for advice in preparing an inaugural speech: "Any facts or views which might tend to illustrate the successes which have attended your own efforts at reform, I should be happy to present, both for the truth's sake and as a fit tribute to your administration." Mid-month, he and George Stearns finally left Boston together, stopping on the way in New York City and Philadelphia to meet fellow Republicans. Andrew confided to his friend John Murray Forbes that he was anxious to ascertain the mood in Washington[49]

Sumner and other colleagues welcomed Andrew to Washington but quickly cautioned him to keep his radical opinions quiet during public conversations. Among themselves, however, they talked freely, advising him to stand by his state's antislavery record. In the weeks and months to come, they thought, it might become a rallying point against those seeking to compromise with the South.[50] George Loring, a Boston physician and politician, was in Washington at this time and recalled walking down Pennsylvania Avenue with Andrew. As they passed the Treasury Department, Andrew's eyes were attracted to someone across the street. "I am looking at that old man descending the hill beneath the shadow of the Treasury building," he said. It was James Buchanan, frail and careworn. The contrast between the grizzled president and the baby-faced governor-elect was not lost on Loring. He wrote that Buchanan was "passing down to the close of another chapter, unfortunate in, and unequal to, his hour"; with him, "one era of our history went out," carrying "the painful record of our national compromises." Yet beside Loring walked Andrew, with a glowing countenance and a bright future, a promise of "freedom and national integrity" in a new era.[51]

A New Era

Andrew and Stearns talked at length on the train back to Boston. As governor, Andrew wanted to shore up local defenses, and Stearns emphasized that, to do so, he would need to sway the state's farmers and mechanics to the Republican cause. Lincoln's election, Stearns said, had convinced the American people that slavery's expansion in the territories had been settled, so he thought that Andrew would have considerable support, even from conservatives, in leveraging the state against disunion. Though Andrew and his colleagues knew that any potential war would be about slavery, he would need to present it to his constituents simply as a way to preserve the Union and nothing more.

It was no secret, Stearns later wrote, that he and Andrew had gone to Washington to stiffen Republicans' backbones and to ascertain if war preparations were imminent.[52] Andrew had spoken with several southern politicians about the possibility of secession, even visiting with James Mason, who had led the Senate's investigation into Brown's northern collaborators. On December 20, South Carolina seceded from the United States, and Mason told Andrew that more southern states would follow. It remained to be seen if northerners would compromise their principles to succumb to southern demands or if the nation would go to war.[53]

In Boston, Andrew found a letter waiting for him from his friend Charles Winslow. The doctor and Andrew had long been pondering how free-market enterprise might revitalize the South, and they were convinced that northern and southern commerce must be fused and wrested away from its dependency on slavery. At the very least, Winslow wrote, "the gradual abolition of slavery, must be as clear to your mind as it is to mine. The fullness of time has now arrived when the great blow must be struck to bring about the national results contemplated by the framers of the constitution."[54]

As Andrew was pondering such thoughts, he received a curious invitation from George Ticknor Curtis, a distinguished jurist who had served as co-counsel for Dred Scott. At Curtis's Boston home, the judge read Andrew a letter from a man in Georgia, who explained that he and many other loyalists wanted to remain in the Union. He asked Curtis to press Andrew to recommend, in his inaugural speech, removing the Personal Liberty Law from the state's statutes. Otherwise, the South could not be placated. Curtis now turned to his visitor. "Mr. Andrew," he said, "this is a matter that rises above all party considerations." When Andrew refused to make such a statement, Curtis went on: "But, my dear sir, you see the situation: South Carolina has already seceded; if Georgia secedes, other Gulf States will follow, and sooner or later there will be a civil war. You do not, I know, wish to see a civil war. Why will you not advise our Legislature to make this very small concession?"

Rising to his feet, Andrew replied, "Sir, if it pleases the Lord to strike those people down there with judicial blindness, I am not going out of my way to help them. If they choose to secede, let them, and if there is to be a civil war, let it come." Compromise had thus far failed to wash out slavery's stain, and he refused to cower before the separatists. Curtis was forced to tell the man from Georgia that the governor-elect would not oblige him.[55]

CHAPTER 10

MAN FOR THE HOUR

January–April 1861

The Life of Every Man Is Lengthened by Trial

Andrew wanted to mobilize his war resources quietly so as to avoid any pretense of goading southerners into conflict. This was difficult because state laws had designated local communities as the lawful administrators over residents. As in most states, "chief executive" was just a title in Massachusetts, and in the nineteenth century the governor's role was more ceremonial than official. Most previous governors had been elites, and the name John Andrew barely resonated alongside the likes of John Hancock, Samuel Adams, Elbridge Gerry, and Edward Everett. The General Court had always held the state's the political reins. Only since the election of Nathaniel Banks had the governor's office expanded its power and authority. Now, with Andrew's advent, conservative Republican papers such as the *Daily Advertiser* prepared readers for the calamity that was surely coming. Editors begged incoming legislators to rescind the Personal Liberty Law and help hold together a dissolving Union: "Let us show the world that in Massachusetts at least a State legislature is not a boy's debating society, that practical sense guides the deliberations of the assembly, and that order, system and moderation prevail."[1] For Andrew, such pressure was hardly reassuring.

As he began his work in the state, he remained in close contact with congressional matters via his colleagues in Washington. Closer to home, he enlisted his friend John Forbes to help supervise war procurement. This move did not assuage those who worried about

Andrew's antislavery radicalism. Though Forbes was a prominent Boston businessman, he was also a rare Republican among a cadre of conservatives. Like Andrew, he believed that the party needed to rely on not only Boston's wealthy classes but also on the state's rural commoners. Yet he, too, disagreed with Andrew about the Personal Liberty Law. Governor Banks, on his way out of office, had done his part in muddying those political waters. By urging the repeal of all legislation obnoxious to southerners, "Banks has delivered an execrable thing," Andrew told Sumner, "but it doesn't disturb my soul at all."[2] Yet he told Forbes that any silence about the Personal Liberty Law might look like agreement with repeal. That was not true, so he needed to determine a judicious path forward.[3]

Andrew was not a typical politician, but he quickly demonstrated that he was intellectually and administratively suited to be a war governor. As conservatives heightened their inflammatory rhetoric, he refused to compromise. He displayed, according to Peleg Chandler, a "union of intellectual ability, enthusiasm, firmness, unflinching courage and undoubting religious faith, which enable him to meet every trying emergency as it arose."[4] The Massachusetts General Court convened on January 2; and three days later, Banks passed the executive torch to Andrew. In his inaugural speech, the new governor focused on hope:

[It] will be too terrible, the sacrifice too momentous, the difficulties in our path are too slight, the capacity of our people is too manifest, and the future too brilliant, to justify forebodings, or to excite permanent fears. The life of every man is lengthened by trial, and the strength of every government must be tested by revolt and revolution.[5]

The *Daily Advertiser* observed, "Few Governors of Massachusetts have ever had a more attentive audience than Andrew had" on that snowy day.[6]

In his address, he highlighted the Commonwealth's historic loyalty to the Union and its determination to preserve it. He reviewed the state's finances and the militia's condition, reporting that more than 155,000 men had enrolled but that fewer than 6,000 were ready for service. He reminded listeners of the state's prominent international ports—in Boston and New Bedford—of its excellent railroads, of its booming manufacturing sector. The Commonwealth was home to six federal arsenals, which held the nation's largest inventory of smoothbore muskets, the second-largest inventory of rifles, and hundreds of artillery pieces. Massachusetts, he said, was one of the more progressive states when it came to governance. Yet there was room for improvement. Andrew called for the revision of bank legislation, the modification of usury and divorce laws, and the repeal of capital punishment. Perhaps anticipating the looming war effort, he called for the repeal of voting restrictions for recent immigrants. He expressed confidence that the judiciary would protect the constitutionality of the Personal Liberty Law and directed the legislature to repair any errors in it without compromising the rights of free African Americans. Throughout his speech, he advanced his view of a progressive society.[7]

"There is but one issue before the country now," Andrew told his listeners: "shall a government, organized under constitutional forms, be subverted." The people of Massachusetts would never permit this, he maintained. He deplored slavery's grip on the nation and predicted that the Republican Party would spell its doom. By way of their dissent, he said, the secessionists had in fact unified the North. The brutalities in Kansas and in Congress were burned into American memory. Throughout its history, he declared, Massachusetts had always been on the right side. Drawing upon Revolutionary War imagery, he proclaimed that those who "till the soil, who drive the mills, and hammer out their own iron and leather on their own anvils and lapstones are honest, intelligent, patriotic, independent, and brave. They know that simple defeat in an election is no cause for disruption of a government." Massachusetts citizens, "confiding in the patriotism of their brethren in other States, accept this issue, and respond, in the words of Jackson, 'The Federal Union, it must be preserved!'"[8] The Revolutionary analogy had become a rallying cry for New Englanders. Longfellow's newly published poem "Paul Revere's Ride" was reviving the spirit of the Minute Men, and now Andrew's address was reverberating across New England, awakening northerners to the Union cause.[9]

But darkness was continuing to encroach. After his speech, Andrew found a confidential letter from Congressman Adams on his desk. The "revolutionists," Adams reported, had determined to take the Capitol before Lincoln's inauguration. To counter this move, he advised Andrew to direct state legislators to take provisional measures to protect the federal government. But care was necessary: because Virginia and Maryland still hung in the balance between secession and loyalty, Andrew would need to mask his moves to avoid tipping the scale toward secession. It was important to make these Union-saving measures seem to have emerged "spontaneously" from the states, to avoid the appearance that Washington had engineered them. That afternoon, Andrew met Frank Bird in front of Parker's Hotel and relayed Adams's news. "My letters from Washington convince me that we are to have war," he told Bird, yet "our people do not dream of such a possibility" so they "need to be accustomed to the smell of gunpowder." As a first step, he proposed that salutes be fired to commemorate the upcoming anniversary of the Battle of New Orleans in the capital of every New England state. The following day, messengers headed out in a dreadful snowstorm for Montpelier, Concord, Augusta, Hartford, and Providence to alert the other governors.[10]

In Sumner's view, Andrew's approach was "clear, strong & right. I feel happy that Mass. at last has found her voice."[11] Though only a few southern states had so far seceded, Sumner and other Washington observers painted a grim picture of the future. "The cotton states are doomed," predicted the senator. "*They will all go.* If possible, we must avoid civil war; indeed, to avert this dread calamity, I will give up, if necessary, territory & state; but I will not give up our principles."[12] He told Charles Loring, "Andrew has spoken like a jurist & a Governor of Mass. There can be no doubt that the first & most sacred duty of Govt. is to protect the lives & liberties of subjects." Sumner was convinced that the new governor would do all in his power to take care of his people.[13]

Andrew's confidence reassured his alarmed citizenry. Increase Smith of Dorchester called his inaugural speech a "glorious address," declaring that Andrew was "*the man for the hour.*"[14] Edward Pierce of Boston, a lawyer and a delegate to the Republican National Convention, told Andrew that he knew of no one "who could have caught so well the sentiment which became the hour. How good it is that Providence sends a man when one is wanted to suit a critical period."[15] Emily Howland of New York, an abolitionist and educator who taught at the Normal School for Colored Girls in Washington, D.C., implored Andrew to rebuke Massachusetts journalists who supported secession and "charge them with being the real enemies of freedom." "Daylight is near," she wrote, and soon "the people of Mass will appreciate the wisdom which I am sure you will bring into her counsels."[16]

Andrew threw himself into his executive duties. He hired personal secretaries to handle the steady stream of mail into the statehouse. As his senior aide, he chose Horace Sargent, who had been Banks's secretary and had since made it clear that he supported Andrew's vision for preserving the Union. For another senior aide, Andrew chose Henry Lee, Jr., an outspoken Free-Soiler with useful ties to commercial and social conservative elites. As private secretary, he brought in Albert Browne, Jr., who had worked in his law office; and as jack-of-all-trades, he relied on Joseph Spear, a former client whom he had saved from jail. Afterward Spear had taken a job in his law office, and Andrew seemed to cling to him like a father to a son, favoring him and often loaning him money.[17]

As states continued to secede from the Union, the governor's chambers transformed into a war room. Andrew evaluated the state militia and eliminated soldiers and officers whom he deemed unable to serve. In this he was aided by Banks, who had ordered the state's adjutant general, William Schouler, to overhaul the militia before Andrew took office. The Scottish-born Schouler had previously been Governor Salmon P. Chase's adjutant general, and he had since become an editorial writer for Whig and Republican papers. He had a stellar reputation.[18]

As newspapers bewailed the national crisis, most militiamen quickly readied themselves for duty, though some resented the preemptive call to combat and boycotted Andrew's orders. Meanwhile, Sumner told Andrew that he and his northern congressional colleagues would not call for repeal of the Personal Liberty Law to please the border states. As much as they wanted to preserve the Union, they refused to submit to secessionary blackmail. Sumner feared that such a reaction would threaten every future presidential election "with the menace of secession by the defeated party."[19] In this atmosphere, the Massachusetts Anti-Slavery Society rose to new heights of abolitionary fervor, abandoning all pretense of Union-saving decorum, which infuriated conservatives. Critics of the society blamed its leaders for provoking secession, and even Andrew's patience was tested. Still, when advertisements announced that James Clarke, Wendell Phillips, and Ralph Waldo Emerson would be speaking at the society's annual meeting at Tremont Temple, he asked Boston's mayor, Joseph Wightman, to protect attendees from anti-abolitionist mobs, especially in light of the previous month's John Brown anniversary fiasco. Wightman, a Democrat, reluctantly agreed to maintain peace. When January 24, the day of the society's meeting, arrived, rowdies packed the galleries and harangued the presenters. As Phillips spoke, agitators tossed seat cushions onto the crowd below and sang, "Tell John Andrew John Brown's dead." Phillips had to pause in his speech, waiting several minutes as taunts and disruptions continued. Then he took off his coat to resounding applause and commented, "I may have to stand here a while."[20]

During a midday break, the meeting chair, Francis Jackson, sent Phillips and his coterie into the statehouse for security, and by late afternoon the mayor had cleared the gallery. That evening he closed Tremont Temple. Meanwhile, Andrew was powerless to intervene unless the mayor were to determine that the police could not handle the violence. The governor had dispatched his aides to persuade

Wightman, but now he could do no more. It was a hard situation because these were Andrew's friends. They were frustrated too. When they proposed appealing to the House of Representatives and asking for the use of its hall, he had to discourage them because he had no state police to keep order. When they protested, he responded, "Show me my authority. Tell me what law of the State of Massachusetts you ask me to enforce." Phillips was deeply disappointed, but Andrew was unshakeable. "Well, sir," he said to his friend, "if this be the attitude you stand in to the Government we need converse no longer." Yet before Phillips left the room, the two men managed to reconcile; their "pleasant, personal feelings were not interrupted."[21]

Andrew gave no public reason for his refusal to step in, but privately he confided to friends that if he had conceded he would have placed himself in opposition to the courts, "which would be an evil." He said, "I prefer to bear the misrepresentation myself. My back is broad enough for that." Principle came before everything, especially constitutional principle. Amid the furor, Sumner and other friends applauded his actions. Clarke went so far as to invite him to tea, as his aged mother wanted Andrew to "reassure her about the state of the country."[22]

Andrew regretted his dust-up with Phillips, but he knew there would be plenty of opportunities to demonstrate his devotion to his abolitionist friends. One of them arrived in late January, when he spoke at the presentation of two revolutionary-era muskets, which Theodore Parker had given to the Commonwealth. During an emotionally charged speech, Andrew raised a musket, pressed his lips to the barrel, and said, "Preserve it as the Jews of old did the table of the Law in the Ark of the Covenant!" Such theater brought the crowd to its feet. Henry Lee, Jr., noted the "cold chills" that came over the spectators: and "the fervor which was natural to him . . . and which burst forth at times in a way which made some of us who were fastidious shiver, was precisely what inspired and kindled the people." Writing to Sumner, Andrew said that he had spent considerable time composing his speech and had hoped to use the opportunity to "bring souls under conviction." Although critics ridiculed his emotionalism, Julia Howe, seated in the gallery that day, remembered it as a "most impressive" scene.[23]

Nationally, any desire to avoid war was fading. As congressional compromise measures went down in flames, Lincoln remained in Springfield, Illinois, writing letter after letter and refusing to step aside as president-elect. By January's end, the Virginia legislature had proposed a conciliatory measure to end the congressional standoff, which Secretary of State William Seward hailed as a "Peace Convention." Northern and southern members were invited to meet at Washington's Willard's Hotel in February; and before the meeting, Congressman Adams circulated a petition among his fellow state representatives asking Andrew to appoint a delegation to the conference. Sumner, however, was sick of conciliation and refused to sign it. Should Andrew move in that direction, the senator advised him to appoint high-minded, principled men who would not compromise.[24]

Despite such disagreements, both Adams and Sumner kept Andrew informed about the backdoor machinations in Washington, which appeared to be moving toward a compromise that would keep Congress from interfering with slavery. Andrew hesitated about appointing a delegation to the conference, believing it should be postponed until after Lincoln's inauguration. He was aware of Sumner's and Adams's differences over slavery and was disappointed that Adams had sponsored a proposal to admit New Mexico to the Union as a slave state. He and Sumner saw this as a betrayal. Adams, however, was convinced that delaying war by admitting a state where the institution clearly would not expand gave the appearance of conceding nearly everything to avoid conflict. He thought it would be wise for Massachusetts to participate in the conference as a gesture to save face. "I am a little afraid," Adams told Andrew, that our "absence would confirm the charge of indifference which is much used against us," and he feared Massachusetts might have "volunteer representation . . . that would scarcely express our class of opinion."[25] Peleg Chandler agreed and encouraged Andrew to allow the legislature to appoint commissioners. "Time is everything now," he warned.[26]

Adams's willingness to concede concerned Andrew, but he told Sumner that Amos Lawrence, Edward Everett, and other conservative "Union-savers" were now in Washington presenting a "State Street" petition with 14,000 signatures in favor of compromise measures. According to Warrington, this "dough-face" petition had created an uproar in Massachusetts, dividing citizens just when they should be coming together. Still, pressed by legislators, Andrew agreed to send a delegation to the meeting in Washington, choosing John Forbes, Richard Waters, John Goodrich, Francis Crowninshield, Charles Allen, and Theophilus Chandler, all of them strongly opposed to any concession on slavery. "If these men come home and report in Faneuil Hall that New England must stand *alone*," he told Sumner, "ALONE we can stand there."[27]

The Bird Club understood that Adams had swayed Andrew. Yet he had had good reasons for giving in. He did not want Massachusetts to be singled out for goading southerners into war, and he had chosen delegates who would not surrender power. It pained him that his friends could not see this. To smooth matters, he wrote to Bird: in the future, "when I am clearly wrong—don't be too serious and look as if I was going straight to the devil—but treat me as if there might be a remaining relish of salvation, and a chance of doing better the next time."[28] Bird assured Andrew that he would never doubt his judgment or his devotion to the cause.[29] Sumner, too, was confident in the governor. "In God's name stand firm!" he said. "Don't cave, Andrew!"[30] He remarked that he had long been wanting to tell him how much he had "enjoyed & admired yr *old musket speech*."[31]

Bird's response relieved him, but it did not diminish his anxiety about the war clouds hovering over Washington. Sumner reported a conversation with Edwin Stanton, Buchanan's attorney general, who confided that he was "surrounded by secessionists." Stanton warned Sumner that the peace effort was a smoke screen and would come to nothing, "that Virginia would most certainly secede—that the conspiracy there was the most wide-spread & perfect." Sumner agreed with Stanton's assessment that "we are in the midst of a revolution."[32] Three days later Stanton told Sumner that he did "*not think it probable, hardly possible* that we shall be here [on] the 4th March," the day of Lincoln's inauguration.[33]

Other Washington observers confirmed Sumner's fears. Two members of Stanton's inner circle, John Clifford and Stephen Phillips, dispatched a late-night communiqué to Andrew, with Stanton's permission, apprising him of their concerns. Andrew shared the telegram with legislators, who voted to give him an emergency fund to defend the nation's capital. Andrew quickly assembled his staff and mobilized for war. He dispatched an aide to Washington to confer with Sumner and General Winfield Scott about necessary military arrangements. He assigned Henry Lee, Jr., to collect information about transporting troops to Washington if Maryland should secede. He solicited reports on the state's military condition and summoned military experts to the statehouse. Within days, he pulled together a war council comprised of high-ranking military authorities, staff secretaries, military aides, and financiers. To Forbes, he gave the financial responsibility of transporting troops to Washington. Terrible times were ahead, and that knowledge dominated the governor's every hour.[34]

Even before Lincoln left Springfield for Washington, Andrew had begun shaping a nation-state alliance that would prove beneficial to both governor and president. He took the lead by offering the president-elect his views on possible candidates for the cabinet. Appointing Salmon Chase, he advised, would "encourage and strengthen the Republicans of Massachusetts. It will assure them of an incorruptible administration of the Department, and of a wise, sincere, and sagacious Counsellor in the Cabinet." He was less enthusiastic about Simon Cameron, an old Jacksonian Democrat who had migrated to the Republican party in 1856: "[he] would have been a weight about as hard to bear as any I can conceive of,—no one here thinks him honest. And that is fatal." Despite his disagreements with Adams, Andrew hoped the congressman might be a candidate for a cabinet post, but he declared that Banks was utterly unworthy of any position. Although he was not personally acquainted with Gideon Welles of Connecticut, Andrew believed he was "a true man & one of ability." He was delighted to learn that Lincoln had decided to bring his long-time friend Montgomery Blair into the cabinet, a move that would give the governor inside access to cabinet conversations and perhaps some influence.[35]

For himself, Andrew sought nothing more from Lincoln than his partnership in the approaching storm. This modest charm won the president's favor. "If at any time I can serve the cause by any word of mine, I am at your service," Andrew wrote. "I may sometimes venture to speak frankly, as I have done in this letter," but "only for the sake of one of the dearest objects. I have in life, viz, the triumph and perpetuation of a party of principle devoted to the realization of the best hopes of patriots and good men." Andrew had great faith in the "fresh heart of the Northwest" and admitted to Lincoln that "our Eastern city life represses enthusiasm, even while it ministers to culture." In his view,

> the heart and hope and enterprise of the West are most needful for the Country; and I trust that while you will be comprehensive in your States-manship, you will be seen always characteristically [as] a Western man. Every good man of intelligence always does well, when he "acts himself." We fail, when we try to please others and meet their wishes instead of following out our own best judgment.

Andrew emphasized that Massachusetts Republicans had long fought against slavery's expansion and were willing do whatever was required to free the Union from that evil. "We will stand by you as we would, if you had been born and reared on Bunker Hill," Andrew assured him and promised that he "would be faithful to [Lincoln's] . . . administration and maintain his cause against all comers."[36]

Washington residents believed that their city would be safe so long as the surrounding states of Virginia and Maryland remained in the Union. Thus, their fears were heightened on February 6, when the southern states formally formed the Confederacy. This seemed to shatter all hope of reconciliation. Though his aide, John Ritchie, reported back to Andrew from the capital, telling him that there was "not the slightest probability of an immediate call" for troops, Andrew knew better and continued war preparations.[37] A few days later, he wrote to Woodman that he was "as quiet and calm as a philosopher; but I stand surprised beyond measure at the content with which others received the efforts of traitors to break up the government."[38]

Conflict was coming, and Andrew did not want it to be wasted on settling old scores but be a route to shaping the nation's new political and racial contours. Violence, even of John Brown's sort, may have encouraged people to believe that insurrection could inspire change, but he knew that actual change began by electing leaders, such as Lincoln, who could bring it forth. As Congress certified the electoral votes legalizing his election, an anxious public imagined the secessionists' next moves, especially in the border states. If Virginia seceded, Adams had warned Andrew, so would Maryland, and Washington would be surrounded. He recommended that Andrew have a provisional force ready. In the meantime, Ritchie returned from Washington with instructions from General Scott, who had concluded that a sea route would be the best means to land troops in Baltimore or Annapolis. Like the Minute Men, Andrew was prepared.[39]

Within a few weeks in the statehouse, Andrew had transformed from a peacetime civic figurehead into a war-ready commander-in-chief. Yet he maintained his simple ways, his humility, his faith. He was often seen pacing through his chambers, his hands clasped behind him, looking upward, as if toward God. "Never have I known a man," said Theophilus Chandler, "who lived so near the golden rule of Christ as Mr. Andrew."[40] "He worked," observed Reverend Clarke, "like the great engine in the heart of a steamship."[41] Preserving the Union required an indestructible federal-state bond, and this took shape as Andrew mobilized for war. His willingness to work in tandem with Lincoln's administration gave him considerable sway, and the residents of Massachusetts looked to him for leadership as they had done to no other governor. He laid the foundation for what would become an enduring, active partnership between state and nation.

Antebellum governance had been legislatively centered and regionally driven because of a decentralized political system. Many Massachusetts conservatives accepted the idea of states' rights, though they rejected the presumption of state sovereignty over national sovereignty. Southern secession gave them the opportunity to emphasize the mutual respect and kinship among states that obliged their citizens to preserve the Union—even one that contained slavery. As he raised militia, Andrew functioned as an agent attached to national and regional coalitions that stressed governmental activism. This had the appearance of nationalism, yet it required governors to play crucial roles in the war effort. Andrew was well suited to the task; for as John Greenleaf Whittier told Sumner, "our good governor" was elected because of "his great and deserved popularity" but also because of a "universal conviction of his integrity."[42]

Many of his colleagues found it oddly prophetic that such a person should be serving as governor at this national moment. Though Andrew was confident and determined, he could not have prevented the coming conflict if he had tried. He had learned during his December visit to Washington that southern leaders and slaveowners had driven common folk into a secessionist whirlwind that would cripple them. "From his insight sprang his foresight," wrote his friend, the essayist Edwin Whipple. He was always ahead of the people because he believed it was his duty to be their guardian, to go first and carve a path.[43]

Still, there were those who feared that too much power was concentrated in the hands of a radical. Here, too, Andrew showed foresight. Though as a lawyer he was an advocate for the poor, as governor he enlisted the aid of Boston's elite families, some of whom had southern commercial connections. He drew upon these wealthy, highly educated clans for his secretaries, his military aides, and his militia officers. In these extraordinary times he reached across the political and cultural divide to establish his war machinery. This required him to establish credibility by making judicious decisions that revealed he was above partisanship. Then he appointed men who were free to disagree with him but who knew better than to carry such disagreements to the streets or the press and thus undermine the people's confidence.[44]

As it turned out, he was sager than Adams in predicting that the peace convention would fail. Yet critics assailed him for frightening Commonwealth residents into premature mobilization, which, they argued, had contributed to the convention's failure. In fact, Andrew's preparations proved to be not only necessary but timely. In sending delegates to the convention, he had seemed to yield to conservative clamor, but the incident had taught him to balance his impulse to forge ahead against slavery with the need to preserve the Union via practical measures. He was unaccustomed to such delicate responsibility, but he was quickly finding his way. Julia Howe wrote years after the war that Andrew "was gifted with that political sagacity which results from a knowledge of principles, and corresponding faith in them."[45] At the time, however, her husband was less confident. Howe told Bird that Andrew "was like a noble horse harnessed in with mules; how long he will retain his virility, I know not." If he disappointed the expectations of his overzealous friends, that was because he had overzealous enemies. The current of the times, Andrew told Blair, forced wise men to find other means to move African Americans toward their freedom.[46]

Andrew was convinced that the southern states' decision to form the Confederacy had doomed slavery as an institution. Yet southerners were preparing to fight for their right to maintain it, and this paralyzed the Buchanan administration. Northerners were shocked, but they were willing to defend Washington at all costs. In Andrew's view, if southerners were making a fuss about Lincoln's election by leaving the Union, then northerners should make a fuss about preserving it. Still, the sides maneuvered, waiting to see who would strike the first blow. "*All* of our opponents await only the final disruption of the States to bring up a general charge that we desired it to happen and to that end refused all conciliation," Adams wrote to Andrew. "I hold the dissolution of the union, if in any way promoted by us, as in this stage of the slave question, a great political blunder, if not a crime."[47]

Andrew wanted to prepare his constituents for the coming war, but he could not share confidential information, so he remained publicly focused on shoring up the nation's defense. He was unnerved when Seward asked him to have a provisional force ready for Lincoln's inaugural. "I wish we were back where we were last year," he told Sumner, "and had a good 20 yrs. fight before us. I fear *our beard* is not yet grown, and that we'd better stayed a while longer in Jericho."[48] Fortunately, Lincoln's inauguration on March 4 came off peacefully, and John Goodrich wrote to Andrew from Washington that "again we have a Government!" As Goodrich admiringly described the president's speech as "bring[ing] the nation up," another Massachusetts politician, Linus B. Comins, remained worried, mentioning that several southerners were predicting "*war in thirty days*." He reported Lincoln was for "ploughing out all traitors & sprinkl[ing lime] upon their bones as soon as possible."[49] Andrew was relieved to learn that Sumner had been elected chair of the Senate Committee on Foreign Relations and Henry Wilson chair of the Committee on Military Affairs and the Militia.

Andrew prorogued the General Court on April 11, and legislators left Boston, having put the state on a firm footing for war. This had been accomplished in slightly more than three months. Already the new governor had acquired near legendary status. According to one story, he had begun preparing for war even before taking office. The Boston Democrat Ben Butler claimed to have had a conversation with Senator Jefferson Davis, who had convinced him that war was imminent. Butler returned to Boston in December, went to the statehouse to urge the governor-elect to prepare for war, and secured $25,000 to have 20,000 overcoats made for the troops. Andrew had called a secret legislative session, reported the conversation and the looming crisis, and secured additional funds for equipment and coats. Soon to be known as "Andrew's overcoats," the heavy blue woolen outerwear was manufactured in Butler's mill.[50]

By the time Andrew took office, his friend Lewis Hayden was working as a messenger in the Massachusetts secretary of state's office. It was not a lofty appointment, but it was a milestone for African Americans: Hayden was the first to serve as a state government employee, and he remained in that position for thirty years. His employer, Oliver Warner, arrived at the statehouse when Andrew did, in January 1858, and Andrew may have mentioned Hayden to him. However the job was acquired, it allowed the two to socialize frequently, and Hayden became an ever-more important conduit between the governor and the African American community. When Andrew called up the militia, Hayden and Robert Morris addressed Boston's African American citizens, and 125 men joined a drill company to prepare for military service. Several Massachusetts legislators introduced resolutions urging the federal government to enlist men of African descent. The measure passed the Senate but was narrowly defeated in the House. Thus, even as war loomed across the republic, Andrew was still fighting his personal war against injustice, the war he had been fighting since he had arrived in Boston more than twenty years before. Hayden understood this about the governor, and soon many other Americans would as well.[51]

CHAPTER 11
‖‖‖‖‖‖‖‖‖‖‖‖‖‖‖‖‖‖‖‖‖‖‖‖‖‖‖

A GRAND ERA HAS DAWNED

April–May 1861

Each Day an Epoch

That spring, through newspapers and letters, Massachusetts citizens watched the seventy-three-year-old nation break apart. On April 14, they read that South Carolina soldiers had besieged the garrison at Fort Sumter, bombarding it for thirty-three hours and forcing a humiliating federal surrender. The southern uprising had commenced, and Andrew paced his executive chambers, contemplating his next move. Secessionists were determined to pursue independence, but critics decried their act as no less insurrectionary than John Brown's. Northerners were galvanized into action. Howe wrote to Andrew, "Since they will have it so, in the name of God,—Amen! Now let all of the Governors and Chief men of the people see to it that war shall not cease until Emancipation is secure. If I can be of use anywhere, in any capacity (save that of a spy) command me."[1] John D. Andrews, a friend from Dedham, wrote to the governor from the National Hotel in Washington: "We have reached a grand era. "Each day an Epoch. The people must have faith & patience. We are in for it, & must go on, and we can never have more reason for a nobler cause."[2]

Andrew, as Howe's daughter later wrote, was "perhaps the only man in the country who was ready for war."[3] Yet he had been forced to strike a balance between his abolitionist impulses and their local unpopularity, and this stifled his true feelings. Such balancing acts were the virtue and vice of politics, but he was not disheartened. Though he agreed with the radical Republicans who were determined to turn the conflict into an emancipation enterprise, Andrew knew he needed to proceed judiciously toward that end. It was an irony that a man who loathed violence, championed passive resistance, and had even composed peace poems had now become a war governor. Yet Andrew had confidence in his principles and was determined to defend them. Already he had worked to get African Americans elected to the legislature, and he had hopes that representatives would elect Reverend Leonard Grimes as their senate chaplain. Still, in one important wartime matter, his hands were tied. When Lewis Hayden brought him a petition signed by a hundred African Americans who were offering to serve in the ranks, he had to tell his friend that the government had denied them the right to die for their country.[4]

On April 15, Andrew received a wire from Senator Henry Wilson warning him that Lincoln would be ordering out the northern states' militias. Minutes later, he received official word from the War Department: the president was asking for 75,000 men, contracted for ninety days of service, who would be used to defend Washington and reclaim the seized forts. The Massachusetts quota was 1,500 men, and citizens responded instantly and fervently to this call to arms. Andrew immediately summoned the Third, Fourth, Sixth, and Eighth Militias to proceed to the nation's capital and called for more men to ensure that only the strongest companies would be sent forth. The journalist James Bowen recalled that in Boston "every house displayed the emblems of loyalty; man and woman, child and old age wore rosettes of red, white and blue; the stars and stripes were unfurled from every flag-staff. The naturally cool blood of the North, which had shrunk from the prospect of fratricidal strife now burned to avenge the insult to the nation and is flag."[5]

Crowds overran the adjutant-general's office at the statehouse. Military-age males poured in from all corners of the state, eager to take part in the glorious cause. Already Andrew was worried about uniform and equipment shortages, so he directed his war council to procure the necessary supplies. He refused to wait for instructions from Lincoln's secretary of war, Simon Cameron, who had struggled to administer even peacetime affairs in his short stint. Guessing that the facility at Harpers Ferry was certain to be attacked, Andrew advised the armory in Springfield, Massachusetts, to double its production. He asked Cameron to allow him to raise a regiment to defend Boston Harbor. "Our people are alive," he telegraphed, suggesting that the secretary would be wise to capitalize on the state's patriotism.[6]

Governors throughout New England were looking to Massachusetts for advice and support, so Andrew quickly established a regional wartime administration, developing a broad scheme for raising troops, procuring supplies, negotiating loans, and developing strong federal-state alliances. His emergency work with the Boston Vigilance Committee and the Underground Railroad had trained him well, as had his legal research and analysis. By the time Cameron had wired him with instructions to send his troops south via the railroad, Forbes had already chartered a passage that would land troops at Fort Monroe, at the end of the Virginia peninsula and on to Washington. In April rain, would-be soldiers sloshed into Boston, where Andrew made sure they were organized, inspected, outfitted, armed, and properly officered. Amid these hasty preparations, he appointed Benjamin Butler to lead the Massachusetts brigade. Wilson and Sumner had recommended against this appointment: Butler had lost the governorship to Andrew and was known to be haughty and a shrewd maneuverer. Indeed, it was said, that he owed his brigadier generalship to local bankers who advanced funds (with the legislature out of session) to Andrew to finance the expedition south, provided Butler received the promotion that came with being brigade commander. But he was well liked in the militia, opposed nativist laws, was innovative and immensely popular with a wide variety of people—from bankers to immigrants, and especially the Irish, whose help Andrew would need. Appointing Butler allowed him to reach across the aisle and place the Union's preservation above partisan politics. He encouraged the commander to establish military headquarters in the statehouse so that civil and military authorities could confer.[7]

Boston streets were thronged with people, excited and anxious for news. On April 17 Andrew spent time working in his chambers, then strolled onto Boston Common, moving from company to company, visiting with the men. On the capitol steps, he handed the Sixth Regiment's flag to Colonel Edward Jones and assured the men that he would take care of their families. "So help me God," replied Jones, accepting the flag, "I will never desert it."[8] On the following day, the Eighth Regiment, under Butler's leadership, gathered at the statehouse. "Go forth to battle," Andrew told the men. "We remain behind to watch over and protect those you hold most dear." Butler then spoke, promising that "we will not turn back till we show those who have laid their hands upon the fabric of the Union there is but one thought in the North,— the Union of these States." Quoting Daniel Webster, he declared the Union "now and forever, one and inseparable."[9]

Andrew and Butler stood together on the steps, surrounded by regimental flags, a visible sign that military mobilization and civic advocacy were in lockstep. By the end of the week, Massachusetts had met its quota. Andrew shared words with each departing unit: "Yesterday you were citizens; to-day you are heroes. I speak to you as citizens and soldiers, not of Massachusetts, but of the American Confederate Union." To deafening applause he proclaimed, "While we live, that Union shall last."[10] One observer called the governor's eloquence "inspiring enough to last the regiment through the campaign."[11] Meanwhile, other northern states were doing their part. The governors of Rhode Island, New York, and Pennsylvania had already put regiments in motion, and within forty-eight hours Union soldiers were occupying Washington and Fort Monroe.

In Massachusetts lore, April 19, the beginning of the Revolutionary War, had long been a day of reckoning. Now, on the evening of April 19, 1861, Andrew learned that a pro-secession mob had attacked the Sixth Regiment as it passed through Baltimore, marching from one train station to another. Several men had been killed. It was an ominous turn of events: Andrew had raced to get his troops to Washington, and now Massachusetts blood was the first to be shed. Butler wired the details, informing the governor that the rest of the regiment would continue to the capital. Andrew received communiqués throughout the night. At 2 a.m., he wired Baltimore's mayor, George Brown, asking that the bodies be placed in ice and shipped to Boston. The mayor responded that he could not: egress from Baltimore had been cut off. Explaining the deaths, he told Andrew that Marylanders had "viewed the passage of armed troops to another State through the streets as an invasion of our soil and could not be restrained."[12] By 4 a.m., Butler had wired the governor again, saying that he would move his troops by steamer from Perryville on the Susquehanna River to Annapolis and then march to Washington.[13]

Without disclosing confidential operations, Andrew made his military correspondence available to the press, with the goal of keeping the public informed and maintaining support. He enlisted secretaries to compose these formal communications. Meanwhile, he wrote copious personal letters and continued to focus on military matters, receiving legislative approval to borrow $200,000 to cover emergency expenses, including the purchase of arms from Europe. To acquire them, he sent the Boston attorney Francis Crowninshield and the armorer Charles McFarland abroad and advised them to communicate with other New England governors for orders. At the same time, he established a quartermaster department to expedite the procurement and distribution of military supplies among the regiments. The Bay State had become a war machine. But in Washington, all remained quiet along the Potomac. The city had essentially been cut off from the loyal states, except for rail travel through Baltimore. It was an embarrassment that so vast a nation had so few roads into its most prominent city. Communication out of Washington was sporadic, and Andrew waiting anxiously for updates from Sumner, who kept a close watch on the White House.[14]

Taking Up the War

As Washington remained isolated, Boston was abuzz. "Everybody in Massachusetts seems to be congratulating himself that he is a citizen of such a state," wrote Warrington in the *Springfield Republican*. "I suppose the people of each state were equally ready, but their leaders were not. Governor Andrew's praise is in the mouth of everybody."[15] The governor and his staff "took up the war" and forged ahead "as if there was not an inch of red tape in the world."[16] And Andrew did not limit himself to fortifying his troops. When Mrs. Francis Wright of Foxboro wrote to him, asking what she could do for the war effort, he responded, "Inspire your brothers, your fathers, your husbands with a spirit of self-sacrifice. Cheer the fireside of the families of those who have marched to war."[17]

Women became important allies in the effort, and Andrew made great use of their efforts. They formed several relief societies, including the New England Women's Auxiliary Association Supply Department, to support the men in the ranks. Older statesmen and businessmen also offered aid. When the conservative Boston merchant William Gray offered Andrew $10,000 for soldiers' families, he praised the governor's nonpartisan decision making: "I feel very great gratification at the designation of Brigadier General Butler. It offers to the people of the whole country the highest evidence that Massachusetts knows no party, but stands as one man, when the liberties of the Union, and the perpetuity of the Government are assailed."[18] Even former Whig governor Edward Everett, who had chided abolitionists for standing in the way of compromise, offered the governor his services. Andrew showed his gratitude, inviting Everett to attend important legislative addresses and appointing him to a committee tasked with erecting a monument to the Declaration of Independence in Philadelphia.[19]

Even Andrew's nemesis, Caleb Cushing, offered his services. Yet though Andrew had great respect for the Democrat, he could not bring him into the fold:

> Your frequently avowed opinions touching the ideas and sentiments of Massachusetts, your intimacy of social, political, and sympathetic intercourse with the leading secessionists of the Rebel States, . . . forbid my finding you any place in the Council or the Camp. . . . Were I to accept your offer, I should dishearten numerous good and loyal men, and tend to demoralize our military service.[20]

He later told former governor Henry Gardner that no one in Massachusetts was "so responsible for this war as [Cushing]," and Andrew could not allow citizen soldiers to come under his command.[21] Forbes surmised as much. "Our Govr. turns up a *trump*, full of decision and having no Presidential aspirations, he has acted with a single eye to the public good, and has brought *in* all parties around him. His snub of Caleb Cushing, who wanted to *ride in* on the storm, is said to be delicious."[22]

As war governor, Andrew's true character shone through. The crisis demanded conviction, resolve, problem solving, energy, and intellect. As he had for his legal clients, he worked tirelessly for the people of Massachusetts. He started the day early, pored over the mail, read departmental reports, and held interviews with cabinet officials, businessmen, and military officers. Just before noon, he left his office and retired into a neighboring room, where he ate a small lunch of bread, cheese, and black tea, a drink he believed would nourish his nerves. At noon he threw open his doors to the public. He routinely worked a twelve-hour day and then walked home to Charles Street, where his family saw him only in the early mornings and on Sundays, although his children often paid him a visit at the office in the early afternoon. Andrew made sure his staff worked as hard and long as he did. Yet he retained his sweet disposition toward all, commonly quoting passages from the works of Whittier, Byron, Longfellow, and Milton to relieve tension among visitors, disarm opponents, or feed his own soul. Massachusetts soldiers soon came to appreciate his charm, even as they recognized that he was always thinking of their welfare. Once a man with a special knapsack appeared among the many important visitors who were waiting to see the governor. After the man stated that several soldiers had told him they preferred this new model, Andrew drew him out from the crowd, asked for the knapsack, strapped it to his own back, and marched around the chambers until he had convinced himself that his men should have it too.[23]

Day after day, the war machine grew, and money was a constant concern. Bankers loaned the legislature several million dollars to support soldiers' families, and Andrew donated freely from his modest $3,500 salary. He wrote personal letters to civic and social leaders involved in the war effort, and he also wrote to the soldiers. Responding to a woman in Cambridge who had been aiding them, he mused:

> In glancing over the list of their names, I realize most completely how deep a hold the cause, in behalf of which those troops are mustered, has upon every social class in our community,—that there are no hands in Massachusetts too delicate to contribute something to the work. Almost the next letter which I opened, after breaking the seal of yours, was from a poor needle-woman, saying she had but little, but desiring to give something from that little in the same behalf; and surely a cause which so appeals both to the garret and the drawing-room cannot be other than *national* and *just*.[24]

To support the growing number of benevolent organizations, he assigned Josiah Quincy, Jr., as their point person and asked the press to notify citizens that all money contributed to the war effort would be placed with the Committee of One Hundred, an association composed of city and political leaders from around the state, which would administer a soldiers' and families' fund. Andrew served as the committee's president.[25]

Andrew centralized all war-related decisions in his office, including out-of-state troop transport. Without directives from Washington, he went looking for the help he needed—for instance, by enlisting the New York Union Defense Committee and General John Wool, commander of the Department of the East, when he needed to move Massachusetts soldiers through New York City. Now seventy-seven years old and infirm, Wool nonetheless responded; and with former Massachusetts governor George Boutwell he established methods for moving and assisting soldiers on their way to the front. Boutwell told Secretary of War Cameron that the "whole North is wild and determined in its enthusiasm" and asked the War Department to requisition more arms and steamers.[26]

On April 25, Andrew learned that telegraph communication had been restored between Washington and Boston, but his morning mail contained no instructions from the White House or the War Department. Andrew turned to Montgomery Blair, now Lincoln's postmaster general, to discuss operational moves. Blair said that he did not have much faith in General Scott's military policy, especially in establishing Washington's defense. But Andrew refused to lose hope. "We are enlisted for the war," he said, and "have put ourselves, or rather, keep ourselves where we belong under the National lead of the President and his Cabinet—under the folds of the flag our fathers helped to raise."[27] The letters that poured into his office confirmed that his constituents supported his vigor. "All this is glorious—just as God intended it to be," wrote Charles Winslow. "The Red Sea is opening," and "I am glad you are at the head of affairs just now." He urged the governor to keep pushing forward; though the war would cost much in money and in blood, it would ultimately save lives and the Union. Andrew agreed.[28]

Toward that end, Andrew urged Cameron to accept additional troops for service, including the Irish, the Germans, and "other tough men." Shortly before Fort Sumter was attacked, the governor had reversed a nativist policy disbanding militia companies composed of foreign-born soldiers, and this paved the way for recruitment in what became the First and Second German Massachusetts Volunteers. But Cameron would not come to a decision on the need for additional troops. The vacillation annoyed Andrew, and he assured other state governors that he would loan them arms and equipment to get their own troops to the front. When Archibald Campbell, the Unionist editor of the *Wheeling Intelligencer*, wrote to him, soliciting weapons for Union loyalists in western Virginia, Andrew saw to it that 2,000 rifles went south to the mountaineers.[29]

With each passing day, Andrew confronted uncertainties, but he rose above the bureaucratic rubbish and focused on coordinating regional affairs with the other northern governors. A wire from Boutwell reassured him that Lincoln's cabinet, except for Seward, favored a vigorous war. He also reported that the crisis in Washington had passed, and that Butler's presence would allow Maryland's governor to keep the state from seceding. In the meantime, Butler had pledged to cooperate with Maryland laws so long as the state remained in the Union. In his heart Andrew felt that Union soldiers should not suppress slave uprisings because they would weaken the enemy. Maryland still hung in the balance, and he knew that Butler was wise to tread judiciously. Nonetheless, their disagreement was a portent of things to come.[30]

CHAPTER 12

||||||||||||||||||||||||||||||||||||

COMMUNITIES AT WAR

June–September 1861

"The Rawness of It All"

Andrew's forethought paid dividends as Massachusetts mobilized for war. His aide, Colonel Henry Lee, recalled that the statehouse team worked day and night:

> [They assumed] the roles of armorers, quarter-masters, commissaries, to obtain from raw officers the list of arms, clothing equipments [sic] and rations required: to collect and distribute or pack and forward and invoice these, to organize a Medical Board to examine surgeons and provide them with their instruments and supplies, to engage streamers and railroads to transport the troops, and finally to accompany the Governor as he presented to them the standards under which they were sent forth and spoke words of encouragement and thanks.

Considering "the rawness of it all," it was "wonderful that the preparations were so complete," and Lee believed this helped fuse "the whole country into a glow of patriotism."[1] At one point, supplies were so abundant that Andrew boasted to Lincoln that he had arranged to have about half of the provisions intended for the Massachusetts men at Fort Monroe to be freely distributed among all of the soldiers, and he noted that there were boxes of fresh salmon packed in ice for the president, General Scott, and General Butler.[2]

"The governor's toil in these first throes of national anguish knew no distinction of hours, or night or day," remembered his military aide Horace Sargent:

Long after midnight, or when the gas would blend its sticky flame with the first gray of morning, he would still be busy with his pen; or, if worn out with the night's mental labor, he would suddenly appear in Faneuil or some other hall, where regiment or company, quartered overnight and trying to sleep amid the tumult of wagon deliveries and the opening of boxes, was hurrying on the new accoutrements and straggling into line.

When the soldiers recognized him, "the rousing cheer that would greet him from the *blue-coated* men swelled his heart, and took away all the sting from the derision which his practical foresight had excited among those, and they are many, who 'to party gave up what was meant for mankind.'"[3]

Andrew's cheer lightened the labor of these grueling days. Sargent recalled:

In the offices, crammed to suffocation with every applicant and contrast— the charitable and the selfish, the sublime and the grotesque, there was food for mirth as well as for sadness. There were sutlers seeking an outfit, and saints with bandages and lint, English officers tendering their service and our regulars giving good advice; inventors of new-fangled guns, pistols, and sabers . . . which the inventors threatened to sell to the Confederacy if we did not buy them. . . . [There were] gentlemen far gone in consumption, desiring gentle horseback exercise in cavalry; ladies offering to sew for us; needlewomen begging us not to let ladies take the bread from soldiers' wives; philanthropists telling us that Confederate workmen, in our arsenals were making up cartridges with black sand instead of powder; saddlers proposing sole leather cuirasses shaped like the top of a coffin; bands of sweet-eyed, blushing girls bringing in nice long nightgowns "for the poor soldiers."[4]

One observer wrote, "The people stood aghast with a deeper realization than before of the seriousness of the situation, but to the tireless toilers at the State House there came only the call to renewed exertions and a graver responsibility."[5] Harvard University's president, Cornelius Felton, wrote to Andrew days after the Baltimore affair, telling him that students were clamoring to prepare themselves for battle. "Our proper business here is to educate the young," he said, "& prepare men for the great duty of citizenship in a free country." Felton thanked Andrew for the energy that he had generated in Massachusetts.[6] William Rogers, a founder of the Massachusetts Institute of Technology, said that Andrew had "shown himself as wise as he is patriotic and just minded. I believe there has rarely been a public functionary here, so entirely pure, so humane, and at the same time so discreet and so perfectly honest and fearless."[7]

The governor's leadership and convictions deeply affected the soldiers. Charles Bowers, serving in the Fifth Massachusetts, wrote to his wife from Washington: "We leave the old Bay State to do what we can to sustain her character for heroic deeds untarnished and give utterance to the deeply held convictions of her sons that human slavery shall not curse another inch of the territory of this great country."[8] Andrew spoke at King's Chapel on Tremont Street after the bodies of the men killed in Baltimore were returned to Boston, and his military secretary, Albert Browne, Jr., recalled the governor's "vow, that so long as he should govern Massachusetts, and so far as Massachusetts could control the issue, [the war] ... should not end without freeing every slave in America."[9]

Nonetheless, dealings with the federal War Department continued to be problematic. Tasked with raising new volunteers while supporting his existing ranks far away in a hostile state, Andrew needed immediate answers, but Secretary Cameron's bureaucratic approach was stifling and slow. At one point, the governor wired Colonel Robert Cowdin at Washington's National Hotel, asking, "Why don't Secretary Cameron communicate directly to me?"[10] He had to rely on Forbes, Boutwell, Howe, and others to serve as his eyes and ears in the cabinet and Congress.

As state representatives passed legislation enabling banks to purchase government securities, providing aid to soldier's families, and establishing drill camps for soldiers awaiting orders, Andrew relied on a vast volunteer network to assist him in overseeing the soldiers' welfare, both corporeal and spiritual. Via letter, he introduced Lincoln to Nicholson Broughton, then visiting Washington on behalf of the American Tract Society, which wanted to circulate evangelical publications among the troops. He supervised the supply ships and the volunteer field agents who ensured that food and other necessities would reach the soldiers. His aides in Boston were equally busy. Howe, who was focusing on soldiers' sanitary conditions, lamented, "Soap, Soap, Soap. There is more need of a *health officer* than of a chaplain." Judge Rockwood Hoar was negotiating with Washington officials to commission Boston-based steamers as federal vessels, which would relieve the state of some financial burden. To oversee troop welfare, Andrew dispatched Charles Dalton, Harrison Ritchie, and Charles Russell Lowell, Jr., to Washington.[11]

Managing affairs in Boston and Washington required round-the-clock telegraphs. When Senator Wilson wired that Massachusetts uniforms and equipment were inferior to that of soldiers from other states, Andrew wired back to explain that officer inefficiency and inexperience and a lack of federal assistance had contributed to the problem. Despite these issues, Massachusetts troops, on the whole, did well in Washington, chiefly because Andrew took steps to ensure that they were well fed. To keep track of troop conditions at Fort Monroe, he enlisted Edward Pierce, a friend of Sumner's, to draft a report, and he asked Howe to compile his regimental findings into a document for dissemination to the press. The data in these reports confirmed that soldiers were adjusting well to army life. Andrew continued to make sure that the public had access to news, authorizing the reporter Charles Coffin to serve as a war correspondent for the Massachusetts troops. Soon critics stopped complaining that Commonwealth soldiers had too few supplies and began complaining that they had too many. "The invoice of articles," Forbes told Andrew, "contains articles hardly dreamed of even by general officers in actual war." Among the donations were hundreds of pounds of beef, donated by Quincy Market butchers, as well as 320 tons of ice, donated by a Boston firm to keep the meat fresh. Forbes had to find a way to transport those perishables to Fort Monroe quickly.[12]

Convinced that the war might be long, Andrew shored up the state's resources. He secured funds to pay and equip troops for several months, sold several vessels to the federal government, and pressed Treasury Secretary Salmon Chase to count the state's debt as federal expenses. In addition, he convinced legislators to establish a $3 million fund for war expenses, and convinced representatives that he could be trusted with a several-million-dollar emergency fund to be used at his own discretion. He also pressed Lincoln and Cameron to accept regiments beyond the allotted quota, arguing that they would soon be needed.[13]

On May 14 Andrew called the legislature into special session to make these necessary arrangements. As he prepared his legislative address, he considered whether he should focus on pragmatic matters or infuse loftier goals into his speech. In his mind, the war was, at heart, a conflict between those who defended slavery and those who did not. But when he sought Montgomery Blair's advice, Blair bluntly replied, "Drop the nigger." He argued that the war was young and that residents of the loyal states, no matter what their views, needed to stand united to preserve the Union as it now existed, not as the governor imagined it should be. So Andrew restrained his antislavery eloquence. "The occasion," he told the legislators, "demands action, and it shall not be delayed by speech":

A grand era has dawned . . . and soon, emerging from the apparent gloom, will breathe a freer inspiration in the assured consciousness of vitality and power. This is no war of sections, no war of North and South.

It is waged to avenge no former wrongs. . . . It is a struggle of the people to vindicate their own rights, to retain and invigorate the institutions of their fathers . . . and therefore while I do not forget, I will not name to-day that *"subtle poison"* which has always lurked in our national system.[14]

A correspondent for the *New York Herald* remarked that Andrew's speech "hits the nail on the Head."[15] As the legislature moved forward into its decision-making tasks, the governor remained careful. He even prorogued the legislature when representatives made a motion to strike the word *white* from the militia laws so that African Americans could serve. Andrew wanted to avoid adding another burden to the Lincoln administration, and the expediency of the moment was used to justify the measure's failure.[16]

Modifying his language to legislators did not mean that he had modified his goals. Andrew understood that the war had made slavery the nation's central issue, and he wanted to use every possible means, including liberating and arming slaves, to win the conflict. But he would wait till the time was right. For now, he focused on preparing the thousands of civilians who had stepped forward to fight. In early May, Lincoln had called for an additional 42,000 volunteers to expand the regular army. Andrew believed that this number was insufficient to crush the rebellion, and he told Cameron so. He beseeched the president and the war secretary to set up military camps where men could train.[17] Others shared his urgency, among them General Hiram Walbridge, a radical New York Democrat, who had been petitioning the president for weeks to expand the army and accept more regiments. By mid-June, the War Department acquiesced and allowed Massachusetts to form ten more regiments. This was an encouraging sign. "I trust we shall see the end of the war in a year,"[18] Andrew wrote to Walbridge, and "that its conclusion will demonstrate the vitality of democratic republican government. The beginning of an end, grand, glorious and sublime, is already here." With sixteen regiments committed, Andrew was confident about expanding mobilization, especially as the first batch of recruits was due to muster out soon.

Over the course of the next few weeks, soldiers streamed out of Boston, many of them singing "the John Brown song," an indication that some of them saw the war as Andrew did.[19] In a sense he believed that the United States had commenced a national reconstruction. As much as he wanted to preserve what the founders had established, he also saw the war as a civil rights crusade. Nothing could remain the same, he believed, not soldiers, civilians, communities, or institutions. As he walked among the units on Boston Common, he reminded the soldiers that each regiment, like a community, depended on individual effort: "A lynch pin out of a cart wheel and not supplied is fatal to the whole load, loses the cargo, and makes the cart and team as useless as if there were none."[20] These were words reminiscent of his father.

War Governor

By summer, Forbes was worried that the governor was "killing himself with attention to military details."[21] He seemed to have his finger in every pie, even establishing civilian rifle clubs so that future soldiers would understand military drill. He was proud of "the work of his own state and . . . the devotion of her sons," wrote an observer.[22] As he searched for regimental staff, officers, and surgeons, he always considered how politics and character affected each person's fitness for the position. Even those who were dissatisfied by his appointments respected his process. In his view, training and loyalty were key to leadership, and he was difficult to sway. When friends requested a commission for Jonas French, an attorney and a Democrat, Andrew barked, "Gentlemen, if he was as good a soldier as Julius Caesar, and you should bring an angel from heaven to indorse him, knowing what I do [about him], I would not commission him."[23] It was not easy for Andrew to maintain these standards, however, as there was a short-age of qualified officers. To compensate, the legislature allowed him to appoint military staff, many of whom he found in the militia. As quartermaster general, he chose John Reed, who had served on Banks's staff; for surgeon general, William Dale, modest but with a scrupulous sense of honor. James Marshall served as paymaster, Joseph Day as provost marshal general, Richard Peirce as inspector general, and William Burt, his longtime law partner, as judge advocate general.[24]

In the early months of the war, Andrew made mistakes, but he soon became more judicious in commissioning officers. Thus, according to Harrison Ritchie, he was gradually able to "chang[e] a town meeting into a regiment." Andrew wrote:

> My experience thus far has taught me . . . that I must do my own thinking—that no other mortal *will* do it for me; that others, in advising me, almost invariably, unconsciously or otherwise, do it from an entirely different point of view from my own,—which is that of my own personal, unavoidable and ever pursuing sense of responsibility for the safety, suc-cess and honor of our soldiers, and the credit of the State.[25]

As he democratized regiments, he also learned to discern how each unit's political and ethnic makeup might add or detract from its cohesion. He recognized that saving the Union on the battlefield required a bipartisan approach, so he worked to strengthen the military across party lines.[26]

Complaints poured forth, however, not so much about his military appointments but about his reliance on Boston's elite. There was some truth to this accusation. Educated men impressed him, and he deliberately commissioned officers from this class, hoping to show his constituents that the wealthy were sharing the war burden. Still, against his better judgment, he sometimes allowed the soldiers to choose their officers. On at least one occasion this had unfortunate results: on a hot day, one was seen parading his men through the Washington streets, all of them weighed down by tattered woolen overcoats. The "overcoat march" made Washington headlines, and Sumner and other Massachusetts representatives visited the camp to demand the colonel's resignation. "I made an inexcusable blunder in appointing him," Andrew told Sumner. "I knew better, because my own opinion was against it; and I did not follow *my own* judgment but the prevailing opinion about me."[27]

When Congress convened in special session in early July, representatives found themselves, in the words of the *Daily Advertiser*, at the "very threshold of a duty which has fallen to the lot of no preceding Congress in our history."[28] Lincoln's message for them that day was brilliant. He couched the conflict as a "People's Contest" and emphasized that Americans were struggling to "maintain in the world, that form, and substance of government, whose leading object is, to elevate the condition of men—to lift artificial weights from all shoulders—to clear the paths of laudable pursuit for all—to afford all, an unfettered start, and fair chance, in the race for life." Andrew agreed, for he had recognized even before his inauguration that the Union's preservation would require the cooperative self-governing of nation and state. In appearances around the Commonwealth, he rallied the citizens onward. In the meantime, he appointed William Bullock, a banker who had recruited the Twentieth Massachusetts Harvard Regiment, to head a statewide effort to fill the ranks.[29]

Many northerners had assumed that, once they defeated the secessionists on the battlefield, the ninety-day regiments would disband, the soldiers would return home, and the South would return to the United States. But the war dragged on. More than 150,000 soldiers and sailors poured into Washington that summer, and Sumner told Andrew that there was great pressure on the administration "for active aggressive measures." The senator warned of coming battles at Fort Monroe and Harpers Ferry, and the daily news confirmed as much. The New York and Boston papers had essentially become the national press, and they had a vast readership in the North. Thus, though he was far from Washington, the governor often had more information than its residents had.[30]

Butler and his regiment were reeling from the debacle at Bethel Church, where, on June 10, the Confederates had repulsed the general's attempt to drive them from their advanced positions on the Virginia peninsula. A month later, Confederates had destroyed the bridges into Harpers Ferry, marching out of the Shenandoah Valley crying, "Forward to Richmond," as the Yankees advanced from Newport News. Meanwhile, Andrew was preoccupied with home-front formalities. On July 17, Harvard conferred on him and on General Winfield Scott the degree of honorary doctor of laws for having distinguished themselves in preparing the nation for war. A large crowd gathered for the occasion, and the college president called on Andrew to speak. Remarking that he could say nothing that would capture the Commonwealth's war spirit, the governor instead turned to Scott: "You have given him a degree in the North; he will presently take several degrees in the South—where as a Doctor of the Laws, he will teach the rebels obedience." The crowd erupted in cheers and laughter. Caroline Healey Dall, who was in the audience, recalled that "the Governor was applauded, till he had to rise & bow," and the graduating students tossed their hats in the air. "Governor Andrew—caught the thrill, while it quivered on the air—and sent it from his pencil's end to the Telegraph Office," she said. "There has not been such a Commencement *Dinner* within the memory of man. President Quincy, at 90—spoke with the freshness of youth, Everett with the padlock off, Andrew with the steam *on*, Phillips & Garrison present!!"[31] Afterward, the governor printed up Scott's "new degree" and sent it out to encourage the soldiers.

Days later, on July 21, the armies clashed in Manassas, a village along Bull Run, a meandering tributary of the Occoquan River, separating Loudoun and Prince William counties. The battle began at dawn, raging furiously until late afternoon, when the Confederates forced General Irvin McDowell's Federals from the rain-soaked field. The Union's defeat stunned northerners, who had been confident that their citizen-soldiers would return home as heroes. When the news came over the wires, Andrew was in Hingham, recovering from a migraine. He gathered himself together and returned to Boston, where he received details about the battle and the soldiers' humiliating retreat to Washington.

Rumors about a Confederate offensive on Washington abounded, and Andrew worried that circumstances were worse than reported. But there was a bright spot. Butler's camps at Fort Monroe had attracted hundreds of slaves, and the general had asked Secretary Cameron for guidance on what to do with them. After all, unlike Maryland, Virginia had joined the Confederacy, so Butler was not bound by its slave codes. As Cameron and Congress spent weeks debating if the slaves were "persons" or "property," Butler put the adult men to work, and Andrew applauded his decision and helped him find old uniforms to clothe them.

Butler had advanced a defense of emancipation simply by asking for instructions about what rights the men had as contraband. Though the dilemma had its ironies, Andrew thought that it also had the potential to help the Union: these men could do more than dig trenches; they could serve as soldiers. As always, the governor was eager to push the issue further. If the nation was willing to wage a war with slavery advocates, why not make African American freedom a condition of reunion? Still, he restrained himself, for he knew that any attempt to weaken the Confederacy would also test, perhaps fatally, northerners' racial complacency. In the meantime, he did what he could. He wrote to Charles Adams, now a minister in London, and introduced him to John Martin, a Boston clergyman who had escaped slavery in Alabama and had since worked on abolitionist issues with Andrew in Boston. Martin was now in England, representing the American Missionary Association and lecturing widely against slavery. Andrew asked Adams to help Martin in this work, recognizing that it was a way to glorify the Union cause in the eyes of the British.[32]

For northerners, the Battle of Bull Run was a terrible awakening, in large part because the Union forces were undertrained. Andrew is said to have described the forces as "a collection of town meetings. The army meant well, but it did not know how to obey."[33] He was not entirely wrong. The war fervor that had swept Massachusetts in April had transformed into gloom, and complaints arrived from the field about the officers Andrew had drawn from the militia. Incensed by the rout, Charles Bowditch, the son of the governor's close friend Henry Bowditch, complained to his father that northerners were in "a torpor from which nothing can wake them except some terrible disaster ten times as severe as that which we received. The country must be aroused to the sense of its dangers." He urged his father to "go and see Gov. Andrew, and Edwd. Everett . . . and make them get up a meeting in Faneuil Hall where patriotic addresses shall be made to rouse the people from their stupor."[34]

By August, heat and stress were taking a toll on Andrew's health, and he withdrew to Hingham for several days to recover. When he returned to the statehouse, he learned that Lincoln had summoned George McClellan to Washington to replace Irvin McDowell as commander in chief of the Army of the Potomac. The hope was that the new commander, spoiled and haughty, would look and act like a leader who could win his soldiers' devotion while also improving military discipline. Lincoln was now asking for an additional 500,000 volunteers, which would increase the Massachusetts quota by nearly 35,000 men. The call sparked not only anxiety but also renewed determination. Andrew quickly needed to find a way to reenlist his ninety-day veterans for three years, for Sumner had informed him that McClellan was fretting over Washington's safety and wanted the additional regiments soon. Changes also needed to be made at the officer level. The debacle at Bull Run had demonstrated that states needed to establish examining boards to determine if young regular officers should be allowed to transfer to volunteer regiments. Andrew had been petitioning for such boards, against the wishes of Cameron and Scott. McClellan, however, wired Cameron to say that Andrew's recommendation was a good one and should "be at once granted."[35] At the same time, Congress passed the First Confiscation Act, authorizing court proceedings for the military confiscation of any Confederate property, including slaves. Although this was an internationally recognized law of war, Andrew saw it as an instrument of liberation.

With McClellan's arrival, the Union army expanded precipitously, from 75,000 troops to more than a half million. Boston overflowed with mustering regiments awaiting transport to Washington. Struggling to fill his quota, Andrew asked Cameron to include the 10,000 Massachusetts sailors serving in the navy. Still, finding soldiers was easier than finding competent officers. As the War Department established a military review board to evaluate officer fitness, the governor scoured the state for competent options. He was annoyed to find that several regiments were electing their officers, an approach that politicized the ranks by emphasizing popularity over competence. As much as he appreciated such democratic tendencies, he feared that this would lead to unnecessary casualties. Meanwhile, Cameron authorized him to raise a cavalry regiment and to furnish General Thomas Sherman with five regiments to take part in a North Carolina expedition, though the secretary made it clear that the main army should be supplied before Sherman's force.[36]

Andrew used every avenue he could to attract volunteers into the ranks, and he leaned on friends who could help him. James Cabot, a lawyer who edited the *Massachusetts Quarterly Review*, published an open appeal on the governor's behalf. In it, he took the dangerous step of stressing that the conflict was not only about preserving the Union but also about ending slavery. He told Andrew, "It is time that the true issues of this contest were clearly put. Let the cant about the 'Union' cease. If the Union means anything, it means consent in principles, it means a common standard of right and civilization." He implored Andrew to cut through the fog in Washington and move earnestly against slavery, as he had at the beginning of the war. George Boutwell also encouraged him: "As in April, . . . we must rely upon your energy and forethought to supply the manifest deficiencies in the conduct of affairs at Washington."[37]

Andrew found himself managing overlapping interactions among multiple players: the statehouse, the War Department, soldiers in the field, and home-front organizations. He kept a close eye on the regimental rolls, tracking vacancies and sickness. Even before Congress enacted a federal allotment system to reserve a third of soldiers' pay for their families, Andrew was working with state legislators to establish an Act in Aid of the Families of Volunteers, hoping to prevent soldiers from wasting their pay in camp. He enlisted Massachusetts banks to supplement the system so that families would not suffer from sluggish federal bureaucracy. As more men volunteered, he expanded his operations to meet their needs. Later in August, when his health improved, he traveled to New York City to confer with Governor Edwin Morgan and Colonel Frank Howe, who had outfitted a Manhattan factory as barracks space for Massachusetts soldiers. In these "New England Rooms," as they were known, a massive relief effort fed and housed the soldiers as they went back and forth.[38]

By late summer Andrew had grown tired of skirting that "'*subtle poison*' which has lurked always in our national system." In letter after letter, soldiers stationed in Virginia wrote that the Union army had become a magnet for runaway slaves. Though Lincoln was trying hard to keep the slavery issue out of the war, officers in the field had to take a practical approach, as Butler had already demonstrated. But when John Frémont was appointed commander of the army's Western Department, he showed every sign of upending Lincoln's strategy. He arrived in St. Louis, eager to turn the war in the Union's favor; and in an astonishing proclamation on August 30, he declared martial law, confiscated property, freed the slaves of all Confederate activists, and instituted the death penalty for guerrillas. Though Missouri was a slave state, it had remained in the Union, and Lincoln feared that Frémont's assault on civilian rule might thwart attempts to maintain a loyal government in both Missouri and Kentucky. Yet Frémont's controversial actions gave voice to the yearnings of abolitionists such as Andrew.

Lincoln moved quickly to stifle Frémont, enlisting Montgomery Blair to tell Andrew and others that he had asked the commander to walk back his orders, shoot no guerrillas, and free no slaves. Andrew may have disagreed with Lincoln's limited goals, but he understood his reaction to Frémont. After all, lawmakers, not generals, made federal policy. He knew from Sumner that Lincoln shared his views about slavery, but he also understood that the president had a nation to lead, not just one New England state.[39]

Still, the governor did all he could to infuse a moral purpose into the war. He missed Prince Napoleon's visit to Massachusetts that summer, instead staying in New York City to greet the Harvard boys in the Twentieth Massachusetts as they made their way to the front. One soldier recalled that the governor was the "first man I saw going up the ship at the landing, with a basket of bread on his arm, a loaf for every man, which he gave to them as they passed by."[40] During a regimental dinner, Andrew took the opportunity to stoke the fire that Frémont had lit in Missouri. He reminded his listeners that the war was not merely a sectional conflict but a contest to preserve humanity's God-given rights, and he boldly promoted African American enlistment in the Union army. "This war," he told the soldiers, was not a sectional one. "It is a war of ideas, I grant you; but ideas are universal, not sectional." He doubted that "our Generals, when any man comes to the standard and desires to defend the flag, will find it important to light a candle to see what is the complexion of his face, or to consult the family Bible to ascertain whether his grandfather came from the banks of the Thames or the banks of the Senegal."[41]

Whether or not the soldiers appreciated Andrew's remarks, he had nonetheless expressed his true beliefs about the war. The question of contraband status, initiated by Butler at Fort Monroe and taken up by Frémont in Missouri, was poised to play a critical part in the Union's potential embrace of emancipation and abolition. Yet northerners, including Andrew's constituents, vacillated. Frémont's proclamation had offended conservative political leaders and startled the president, but Lincoln's retraction had drawn equally spirited responses. Andrew had made his speech on the eve of the Massachusetts Republican Convention, knowing that he might be damaging his chances for reelection. It remained to be seen how voters would respond.[42]

CHAPTER 13

THE POLITICS OF COMMAND

October–November 1861

War and Society

As autumn transformed the Massachusetts landscape into a riot of color, Andrew's war room was changing too. His secretary, Horace Sargent, resigned to take a commission in the First Cavalry, and Harrison Ritchie took over as his senior aide. As a favor to his friend Charles Adams, Andrew offered his son, John Quincy Adams II, a staff position, delighted to bring the young lawyer into his purview. For support, he continued to lean on Colonel Frank Howe and his old friend Samuel Howe. The pair supervised his soldier-relief efforts; and because the doctor lived close to the statehouse, Andrew often retreated to his parlor when migraines overcame him.[1]

By now the entire statehouse had become a war depot. Around the governor's chambers hung uniform samples and equipment, ranging from weapons to medical supplies to food-storage options, all left by vendors hoping for a governmental contract. When he was not at work behind his desk, Andrew walked around the room, hands clasped behind him, inspecting these various materials. To expose unscrupulous contractors, he would show their shoddy products to visitors. He would arrive at the statehouse before dawn, first passing by the offices of the adjutant general and the surgeon general to gather the latest intelligence about the regiments. His workdays were long. When John Forbes was in town, he would summon Andrew to dine with him at the Parker House, as a way to lure him from the chambers. On monthly visits to the Bird Club, he often arrived late, breathless, and "so full of force that he seemed as much like a steam-engine as a man." His friends would applaud, but he would pay no attention. "Waiter, bring me some minced fish with carrots and beets," he would say.[2]

Andrew had expected public enthusiasm for the war to wane after Bull Run, so he focused on maintaining popular confidence. Yet he had his own reasons to be downhearted. On August 8 Congress passed the Crittenden-Johnson Resolution, declaring that the war's purpose was limited to preserving the Union. This confirmed Andrew's instinct to downplay abolition as a war aim; yet combined with the Bull Run loss, it was dispiriting. Still, he refrained from publicly criticizing Congress and concentrated on practical issues. General Thomas Sherman arrived in Boston in early September, armed with Cameron's directive and asking for three regiments from Massachusetts. Andrew was on board with raising additional men, but he was concerned that the War Department had granted Sherman's request for an independent command and undisclosed operation without the state's knowledge or consent. This violated the congressional act authorizing states to be the sole authority for raising and officering volunteer regiments. Though he agreed to raise the troops, he sent envoys to Washington to tell Lincoln that no more independent permissions would be granted.[3]

On September 11, however, a telegraph jointly signed by Lincoln and Cameron caught Andrew off guard. General Butler was heading to Boston to raise six New England regiments for a special coastal assignment. Worried that Republicans alone were driving the war effort, he sought, for political reasons, to muster 5,000 Democrats to serve in a New England division. Lincoln, who could not resist the notion of converting political opponents into loyal soldiers, had authorized him to move forward, as long as he could recruit and officer his regiments through the region's governors. The telegraph seemed to suggest that Butler's military authority was more influential than Andrew's state authority, and the governor was incensed. Eventually, Andrew consented, but only on the condition that he could fill Sherman's quota first and that the power to raise additional regiments would be left entirely to the state. He also refused to commission political opponents. Butler tried to go around him, lobbying everyone he could think of, including Andrew's friend Montgomery Blair, and the venture rapidly became a civil-military quagmire.[4]

As autumn advanced, Andrew traveled among the state's military camps, often journeying at night so as to have the day for business and review. In addition to inspecting the arsenals in Cambridge and

Springfield, he visited the Hoosac railroad tunnel, an ambitious engineering project in western Massachusetts intended to link Boston with the Hudson River. Governor Banks had left office before signing the payment order for the continued work on the tunnel, and Andrew refused to endorse payment until he and legislators had studied the matter more closely to ensure that funds were not being wasted. Though the contractors were angry and accused him of opposing the project, he in fact supported the enterprise and was willing to fund it, if it came under the control of a state commission. State funds, he argued, must be dispensed by state agents who are responsible only to the state, not by corporate agents.[5]

During the previous summer Andrew had attended numerous events around the region, including the agricultural fair at Brook Farm in Roxbury and commencement ceremonies at several colleges and normal schools that summer. These travels helped him become intimately familiar with the people and places of Massachusetts. He also enjoyed visiting soldiers in the field or in camp. Julia Howe recalled, "How well I have in mind the governor's appearance as, in his military cloak, wearing scrupulously white kid gloves, he walked from rank to rank, receiving the salute of the men and returning it with great good humor!" When he wanted to escape the burdens of the war, he and his friends would drive far out into the countryside and meander along the back roads. He often walked Boston's streets with the quartermaster general, John Reed, and on Sundays he might dine at Peleg Chandler's home on Mount Vernon Street. He took time to visit the Howes at their home in Portsmouth, Rhode Island, and to visit Forbes at his home on Naushon Island.[6]

Always he remained aware of history. As a child, he had relished finding relics of the past, and now he took special delight in knowing that he held the same office that had been graced by John Winthrop and Samuel Adams. His love for the state's history helped bring him closer to the soldiers and their families, especially when they were suffering. The statehouse became a halfway house for the downtrodden, just as his law office had been.[7]

Andrew had always had a knack for endearing himself to people, and this remained an important aspect of his governing. Despite its radical abolitionists, its antislavery societies, and its Republican governance, Massachusetts was still dominated, both politically and economically, by its wealthy, old-blood elite. Class divisions led to squabbles between Republicans and the Old Whig establishment, yet Andrew consistently bridged these chasms. "Gov. Andrew drew around him troops of new supporters," wrote Frank Bird, "but the 'old guard'"—his longtime political and abolitionist allies—"never wavered, either through jealousy or lack of confidence, in their support and love of him, and he never wavered in his faith in them."[8]

Andrew always had faith that the people would do the right thing, and this may have made him seem to be larger and more inclusive than the Republican Party. He attracted people who, like him, believed in safeguarding social reforms and ending the war quickly through whatever means were necessary. But he also attracted people who disagreed with his opinions about abolition but were drawn by his frankness and sincerity. When the Republican State Convention met in Worcester on October 1, no one was surprised when Andrew was again nominated as the party's candidate for governor, with support from a coalition of conservative Whigs and Democrats. In his address, the committee chair, Henry Dawes simply reaffirmed the Republicans' commitment to the war effort and the soldiers. Sumner, however, went further, applauding Andrew's efforts to push the Lincoln administration toward a more vigorous war policy. Sumner titled his speech "Emancipation: The Cure for the Rebellion," which, as the *Boston Post* noted, was a direct challenge to Lincoln:

> All will unite in sustaining the Government, and in driving back the Rebels, but this cannot be done by half-way measures, or by lukewarm, conduct. Do not hearken to the voice of Slavery, no matter what its tones of persuasion. Believe its friendship is more deadly than its enmity. If you are wise, prudent, conservative, practical you will strike quick and hard—strike, too, where the blow will be most felt—strike at the mainspring of the rebellion.[9]

Critics decried Sumner's mad "John Brown" speech. According to the *Daily Advertiser*, such an argument "has a tendency to weaken the confidence of the people in the management of the war." Andrew agreed, though reluctantly. He understood that neither soldiers nor money would be forthcoming if the public believed that abolition was at the root of the war, even though he burned for this. His own "John Brown" transgressions had been forgiven; editors of the *Daily Advertiser* conceded that Andrew had proven to be a great war leader and had discharged his duties with "such fidelity and singular zeal" that it would be foolish not to reelect. But a wrong step could jeopardize his popularity and influence, as well as his ultimate path forward.[10]

All Not Quiet on the Potomac

On October 21, musket fire opened outside of Leesburg, Virginia, the beginning of the Battle of Ball's Bluff, another excruciating Union defeat. Of the 1,900 troops that crossed the Potomac River from Maryland, close to nine hundred were killed, wounded, or missing. As the troops retreated across the river, nearly a hundred more Union men were drowned or shot as they attempted to reach Harrison's Island. The disaster crushed the northern buoyancy that had returned after Bull Run. Even worse for the Commonwealth was the fact that Brigadier General Charles Stone, the commander of the Union forces, was a Massachusetts man, who had sparked the fight when he ordered the Fifteenth Massachusetts to send a patrol across the river. Searching for an explanation, Andrew dispatched several men to Poolesville, Maryland, to investigate. Their report made it clear that there had been problems with leadership, particularly with Lieutenant Colonel Francis Palfrey, the commander of the Twentieth Massachusetts (known as the Harvard Regiment), whom Andrew had appointed despite the unanimous opposition of his military aides. While Palfrey might prove to be a good a soldier, he was unsuited to lead, and Andrew needed to make changes.

Andrew remained in Boston poring over reports. But when George Boutwell shared complaints that Colonel Charles Devens's soldiers had been sent into battle with inferior guns, he took offense. Such untruths, he said, "wounded [the] hearts of many of our people who now mourn the loss of friends who have fallen on the field."[11] Meanwhile, he sent supplies to Richmond for the captured soldiers; and when the bodies began to return, he made painful visits to the families. He accompanied William Putnam's body as it was carried to his mother's home in Roxbury, where she lay convalescing from an illness. At the door, Putnam's sister said, "Governor Andrew, we thanked you when we got Willie's commission and we thank you now." Andrew broke down and cried. Willie had been a Harvard law student, recently commissioned as a second lieutenant in the Twentieth Massachusetts, and his death filled Andrew with melancholy.[12] He wrote to the parents of Captain George Schmitt of Cambridge, lying in a Maryland hospital, assuring them that "your son was severely, but not mortally, wounded," was "cheerful, and doing well, and is expected soon to recover."[13] The loss on the field alarmed Congress, who set up a committee to investigate the conduct of the war as well as the issue of civilian control over the nation's armies. For his part, Andrew did not shy away from the truth. "Massachusetts will never know, unless through the exertions of Gov. Andrew the story of the Battle of Balls Bluff and its results," wrote Charles Fox of the Thirteenth Massachusetts. "Somebody blundered 700 souls into eternity. . . . May such experience teach us well."[14]

Andrew found himself unable to contain the raw emotions that arose from the loss of these young soldiers. In such moments, he often went to pray at Reverend Grimes's church. Whatever gains he had made in the wisdom of the world were less significant than the power of his faith, and to his friend Peleg Chandler "[he] spoke emphatically of the childlike simplicity of the early Christians in asking and expecting certain specific results from supplication to God. I want to tell the story in my own way, although I know it is impossible for me to give any information to the Almighty."[15] Andrew wrote to John D. Andrews about the pain of loss but also his hope: "O God! for a Cameronian battle-cry, for a grand, inspiring, electric shout, coming from the high priests themselves, from the very Jerusalem of our course. I wait to hear it, and believe it will yet burst forth, and ring in all our ears."[16]

More than anything, Andrew struggled to justify the personal sacrifice of these fallen soldiers. Though he continued to labor to replenish the ranks and add new regiments, he was weary of Lincoln's limited, conciliatory war aims and his approach to military command. Governors had worked hard to meet Lincoln's quotas; and as the armies expanded, so had their assignments, reaching ever deeper into the South, into its communities and camps. Andrew, who had created the regiments, who had commissioned field, staff, and line officers, wanted to maintain his right to show his citizens that the war was more than a military contest. He wanted them, and Lincoln, to see it as a contest to conquer the South and reshape society. Yet Lincoln's independent commands, meaning those raised by commanders instead of governors, had the potential to ruin federal-state relations. Such irregular commands seemed to be at cross purposes with the regular practice whereby governors raised soldiers to fill the existing ranks. Recruiting for these independent commands complicated and delayed the recruiting for regiments that were either suffering from losses or had been newly assigned from state quotas.[17]

Andrew's relationship with Butler exemplified such federal-state friction. Though he celebrated the commander's contraband policy, he objected to his request for a brigade of Democrats. Yet Butler continued to recruit for it, forming two regiments and encamping them in Pittsfield. Soldiers elected officers for the regiments, but Andrew refused to commission them, and Butler was frustrated. In Washington, Lincoln and Cameron were anxious to steer clear of the feud. They believed it was a personal issue between the men, stemming from their competition in the governor's race. But the dispute created such a voluminous paper trail that the administration could not avoid interfering. Secretary of State William Seward, hoping for a compromise, advised Butler to write directly to Andrew, explaining his case in order to gain the governor's support. Butler did so, but Andrew remained unmoved: "I mean to do just what I have from the first persistently done, and that is to hold with an iron hand and unswerving purpose all the powers which, by the laws pertain to me officially."[18] Butler wired Blair for help: "Governor Andrew goes to Washington today to upset me; do not let him do it. . . . This little piece of secession must be stopped or we shall have a rebellion at home."[19]

Even as he sparred with Butler, Andrew respected the commander but he was absorbed in concerns about soldier welfare. Massachusetts men had been captured after the Battle of Ball's Bluff, and sources had told him that conditions in the Richmond prison were deplorable. He asked Lincoln to develop a system for the immediate exchange of prisoners: "I urge no inhumanity towards even traitors. If we are at war with cannibals, that is no reason why we should eat human flesh ourselves." Andrew deputized Forbes to find funds for the incarcerated men and asked women's aid societies to send blankets, clothing, and other articles to Richmond, where prison authorities allowed Adjutant Charles Pierson of the Twentieth Regiment to distribute them.[20]

Voters responded to the governor's devotion, energy, efficiency, and leadership, and on November 5 he won reelection, defeating Democrat Isaac Davis of Worcester. Given that more than 30,000 Massachusetts soldiers were in the field, only about 97,000 votes were cast, but Andrew won more than 65,000. The *Barre Gazette*, which had supported Davis, reported sourly that Andrew had won every vote cast in Chatham. Yet even his enemies understood why. Butler, still feuding with the governor, admitted to a friend that Andrew had "endeavored faithfully, zealously, and efficiently to put the Commonwealth on the side of the nation and to sustain the Union. I do not say that I would vote for Governor Andrew, but were I at home I would not vote against him."[21]

Andrew's reelection coincided with significant Union command changes. As commander of all the Union forces, McClellan, a limited-war, conservative Democrat, used his new power to appoint like-minded commanders to other departments. Though Andrew hoped that McClellan would be a good leader, he was concerned about his political and military views. Moreover, at about this time, the War Department transferred military procurement responsibilities to the U.S. military quartermaster, sidelining the governors, who had, till now, been providing for their states' soldiers. Andrew had little faith that Cameron or any commander would care for his troops as he did. Thus, he had much on his mind when he and Eliza traveled to Annapolis to visit the U.S. Naval Academy and meet with Seward, Cameron, and other Washington dignitaries. In Virginia, he spent time with the Twenty-third Massachusetts, whose men were stationed in General Ambrose Burnside's camp of instruction and watched an impressive divisional review. After briefly returning to his duties in New England, he returned to Washington to settle the Butler matter, watch the Army of the Potomac's grand review, and visit his Massachusetts soldiers.[22]

Correspondents had been peppering him with complaints about troop conditions, reporting that drunkenness as well as clothing and pay shortages were contributing to low morale. Much of this information came from Count Adam Gurowski, an acid-tongued Polish émigré, now working as a state department translator. He and Andrew had become friendly, and Gurowski admired the governor. "[Andrew] acts promptly, decisively; feels and speaks ardently," he wrote in his diary. In Gurowski's view, he "personified the genuine American people." But the count worried about the administration's handling of the war, telling Andrew that "slowly but uninterruptedly we are drifting to anarchy. The Cabinet is savage [against] McClellan for having allowed Confederates to close the Potomac. Scott stirs up the fire, . . . tr[ying] hard to oust McClellan whom he hates and put in Halleck, whom he considers to be altogether his own . . . man."[23] Such sentiments unnerved Andrew.

He had traveled to Washington with what he dubbed the "ladies' expedition," a party that included Eliza, Samuel and Julia Howe, and Edwin and Charlotte Whipple. The group stayed at bustling Willard's Hotel on Pennsylvania Avenue, described by the novelist Nathaniel Hawthorne as "more justly . . . the centre of Washington and the Union than either the Capitol, the White House, or the State Department." During this trip Andrew may have introduced Lincoln to the Howes, for Julia recalled years later listening to the governor and Lincoln converse and being struck by the president's strong regional accent: "He turned to Andrew, [and said,] 'I once heerd George Sumner tell a story.'"[24]

Reverend Clarke was also in the party, and late one night Andrew asked him to accompany him to the White House. When the two entered the parlor, a porter told them that the president was absent but would return shortly. While they waited, the governor strolled through the first floor, looking into the lighted rooms. Then he went upstairs, with Clarke following behind. They came to a door with two small pairs of shoes beside it. "This is the children's room," Andrew said. "I should like to go in and see them fast asleep." He put his hand on the knob, paused for a moment, and turned away. Clarke never forgot the incident: "In the great palace of the nation, in the midst of the great rebellion, these little children, quietly asleep, took his heart for the moment away from all great affairs of State and of Union."[25]

The great event of the visit was McClellan's grand military review, said to be the largest ever held on the North American continent. The irony of holding it on Virginia's "sacred soil"—a field near Alexandria—was not lost on the press. The November 20 exhibition drew more than 20,000 spectators, including Lincoln and his cabinet. For three hours, 70,000 soldiers paraded, until the Confederates interrupted the ceremony by skirmishing nearby and forcing soldiers and civilians into an abrupt departure. Julia Howe described their escape and their carriage ride back to Washington, when they slowed down and sang marching songs together, concluding with "John Brown's Body." When they came upon a small review of Union soldiers at Upton's Hill, the troops joined in, belting out the chorus: "Glory, glory, hallelujah, his soul is marching on."

Clarke asked, "Mrs. Howe, why do you not write some good words for that stirring tune?" She replied that she had not yet been able to think of new lyrics. On the following morning, however, she sprang out of bed, found the stump of a pen, and drafted a powerful poem about the Day of Jehovah as described in the Old Testament and the Book of Revelation. Eventually, she published the finished version in the *Atlantic Monthly*, and by the following year Union soldiers were singing the words of her poem, "Battle Hymn of the Republic," to the tune of "John Brown's Body."[26]

After the Washington festivities, Andrew and his traveling companions returned to Boston, where he learned that Butler was continuing to raise men, all the while complaining that the governor had stifled his recruitment efforts. While Andrew was absent, Butler had publicly called the governor's rationale a "doctrine of secession," declaring that it "did not seem to me any more sound uttered by a Governor north of the Mason and Dixon's line than if proclaimed by Kentucky Governor Magoffin, south, so that I had paid no heed to it."[27] He went on to disparage the governor's handling of military correspondence, which further deteriorated relations between the two. When Butler transferred his main operations to Washington, the War Department reluctantly stepped in. Though Lincoln and Cameron supported Andrew, they thought it was time for him to sacrifice justice for party harmony and move on. They asked Andrew's aide, Henry Lee, Jr., to tell the governor to commission Butler's officers. Instead, Andrew proposed that the Department of New England be abolished and that the regularly enlisted men be distributed among the volunteer Massachusetts regiments. In the end, Butler could not overcome the governor's principal advantage: that he had the sole power to commission Commonwealth officers. To Sumner, Andrew wrote, "Those who disapprove of my decision must find a remedy in choosing another for Governor."[28]

CHAPTER 14

THE LORD IS MARCHING ON

November 1861–January 1862

All Quiet along the Potomac

Thanksgiving arrived as a welcome reprieve, but it also gave Andrew a public opportunity to forge purpose and prayer. In his holiday proclamation, written on the last day of October 1861, he drew upon the language of the Pilgrims' covenant, made more than 240 years earlier. Late that evening, he pulled out his pocket watch and remarked to his aide Albert Browne, Jr., that he should start writing his proclamation at once. Quickly he filled eight pages, lacing his words with scriptural quotations. When Browne questioned their accuracy, Andrew asked the night watchman to retrieve a copy of the Bible from the library and proved the strength of his memory. A few minutes after midnight, the two men, exhausted, went out for a meal at the Parker House, where, over a bowl of oyster stew, the governor put the final touches on his proclamation. An hour later, Browne took the stew-stained draft to the printer, and the governor walked home to Charles Street, refusing, even at this late hour, to pay for a carriage when money was needed for the nation's defense.[1]

By November the cold had arrived "in earnest," wrote John Greenleaf Whittier to a friend. His letter enclosed a copy of Andrew's proclamation, which the poet acknowledged "was finely written, but it sounds a little too warlike and Old Testamently."[2] Still, its sentiments were powerful, and they reached readers far beyond the Commonwealth. The New York Herald quoted it to show that Massachusetts citizens had "thrown themselves into the contest with an earnestness and a determination which are beyond all precedent."[3] The *Boston Daily Advertiser* saw the proclamation as a way to hearten the people, acknowledging that there was scarcely a home "where some vacant place will not today remind the domestic circle, that on this day of public thanksgiving, civil war, the worst scourge of the earth, is desolating our country."[4] On the Sunday after the proclamation was released, ministers throughout the North borrowed its words as they spoke to their parishioners. "Let us 'seek truth and ensue it,'" Andrew had written, "and prepare our minds for whatever duty shall be manifested hereafter." He showed that the evocation of religion could have a practical application, that it could encourage citizens to stand by their principles. In Dobbs Ferry, New York, Andrew's proclamation was hung on the library door in James Alexander Hamilton's home. Hamilton, a prominent lawyer, and a son of founding father Alexander Hamilton, did not know Andrew personally, but his message resonated. "It was the religious fervor of that proclamation," recalled Hamilton's granddaughter. "The noble poetic ring it had, the *heart* that was in it, that spoke to . . . all of us, and consoled and inspired us through many a dark hour of national reverse and disappointment."[5]

When congressional leaders returned to Washington in early December, radical Republicans planned to focus closely on Lincoln's war management, hoping to inspire him to adjust his conservative aims. One of their first acts was to reject the Crittenden-Johnson resolutions passed months before, which had assured slave states that the Union war effort was not aimed at interfering with slavery but only with preserving the Union. Within a week, House and Senate members formed the Joint Committee on the Conduct of the War to investigate the army's military affairs, including the Ball's Bluff fiasco. Andrew supported the committee, which wanted to hold commanders accountable to civilian authority, eliminate incompetents, and consider the possibility of African American enlistment. The governor, too, was working to counter deficiencies. As Union troops advanced more deeply into the Confederate states, he became more involved in regimental politics around the slave question. Meanwhile, the slave states still in the Union continued to create civil-military dilemmas, particularly Maryland, where slaveowning loyalists were entitled to the return of the property. Andrew became involved in one particular incident involving Commonwealth officers. In Poolesville, two African Americans had come into Camp Benton selling cakes and pies to the Union troops. A German soldier had allowed them to eat breakfast with the men, but later Lieutenant George Macy of the Massachusetts Twentieth saw them peddling their wares among the companies and, under orders from General Charles Stone, had them arrested and returned to their masters.[6]

Andrew protested to Lieutenant Colonel Francis Palfrey, who was under Stone's command, that the men should not be employed in such duty. Palfrey referred his complaint to Stone, who viewed it as a civilian attempt to interfere with military affairs. But Andrew persisted; and on a visit to Washington in early December, he lobbied the Lincoln administration to protect Massachusetts troops from being used as slavecatchers. He asked Sumner to deliver a letter to Secretary of War Cameron to petition Palfrey to remove any officers who had ordered the soldiers to do such work. In a statement to Cameron, he declared that Massachusetts did "not send her citizens forth to become the hunters of men or to engage in the seizure and return to captivity of persons claimed to be fugitive slaves without any recognition or even the forms of law," and he challenged the secretary to make sure that Commonwealth soldiers were not pressed into such dishonorable acts.[7]

Cameron was sympathetic. Since the summer, he had openly supported arming freed slaves, and he had played an important role in advancing Butler's contraband policy. He had also backed other radical generals, including Frémont, as well as Nathaniel Banks, who was commanding troops in Maryland. Early in the war the abolitionist Robert Copeland, a major in the Second Massachusetts and Banks's assistant adjutant general, had advocated for raising African American regiments, as had his close friend, Lieutenant Robert Gould Shaw. Shaw recalled Copeland saying that Banks had agreed with them. Still, employing, or enlisting slaves from loyal states presented Lincoln with serious problems, and Secretary Cameron would not hold his place in the cabinet for long. Nonetheless, his support gave Andrew an opening. He and several other Union governors believed they should have a voice in shaping war policy because they were supplying the manpower and serving as chiefs of their states. In their view, infusing governmental politics into military operations made sense, for the war was as much a political (and racial) battle as it was a military contest.[8]

Andrew's missives to Cameron and Palfrey were an early attempt to insert state leadership into military affairs, and it offended military authorities. The letter made its way up the command chain to Stone and eventually to McClellan, who resented the governor's interference. McClellan retorted that, once volunteer regiments were mustered into federal service, they were entirely removed from the governors' authority. Stone accused Andrew of behaving worse than the secessionists: "It matters little to me whether the usurpation comes from the South or North, Georgia or Massachusetts. I feel it my duty to bring the matter at once to an issue and if possible to arrest the evil before its natural fruits—open rebellion—shall be produced."[9]

This insult did not sit well with the veteran barrister, who was aware of his legal reach over soldiers, regardless of federal military oversight, nor did not deter him from pressing the point. He knew he was responsible for the volunteers whom he handed over to federal service, and he believed this gave him privileges in determining how they would be used. In fact, he maintained, without governors who raised, equipped, officered, and sent forth the soldiers, there would be no volunteer armies. He responded tartly to McClellan:

> The Regiment was *raised* in the State, under my authority in response to a certain requisition, not for *soldiers*, but for ten "Regiments," from the Department of War. I appointed and commissioned its officers, and the regiment was recruited here, on our own soil . . . and marched from here to Washington with every kind of equipment and furniture recognized by the Army Regulations of the United States,—and all of it provided and paid for by this Commonwealth."[10]

Andrew was not about to sever his relationship with his men simply because McClellan wanted to nationalize the army. For him, questions remained: what kind of Union was the administration seeking to preserve, and how could the current conciliatory approach lead to fundamental change? As conservatives worked to check the abolitionist element that was creeping into the conflict, Andrew was pushing for more expansive war aims. The feud had brought his personal political principles into an official forum. He sent the entire Stone-McClellan correspondence to Sumner and asked him to take up the matter on Capitol Hill. The war was marching forward, and so was Andrew.[11]

The governor remained in Washington, working to sort out the situation, and was sitting in Cameron's office when a telegram arrived announcing that Captain Charles Wilkes and his men had captured Confederate envoys James Mason and John Slidell at sea. The secretary read the telegram aloud, and Andrew cheered at the irony that Mason, author of the Fugitive Slave Law, was now in the hands of the government he had sought to destroy. Even better was that Lincoln had the pair imprisoned in Boston's Fort Warren. Back in Massachusetts, Andrew celebrated the capture at a meeting in Faneuil Hall and a private dinner at the Revere House. Mason and Slidell were traitors, and he believed they should be punished accordingly. Compared to them, he said, "Benedict Arnold was a saint," and he praised Wilkes for performing "one of the illustrious services that had made the war memorable."[12] Andrew told Edward Russell, a friend from New York, "I very well remember Mason's insolent overbearing demeanor in that memorable interview between himself and old John Brown," and he rejoiced that his incarceration would send a message to other traitors.[13]

The December weather was severe in Massachusetts, and Andrew had some solace in the fact the Commonwealth soldiers weren't suffering outdoors in New England's arctic temperatures. But other problems were snowballing. Mason's and Slidell's capture had been hailed as a significant naval triumph at a point when the land forces appeared to be stalled on every front. Unfortunately, the facts soon made it clear that Wilkes, acting without instructions, had violated international law by failing to bring the British ship carrying the men into port for adjudication. The matter was handed over to Secretary of State Seward; and some believed, that by releasing the prisoners, he might salve the Union's fraught relations with Great Britain. Andrew was aware of Seward's growing discontent with Britain's neutral stance in the war, which was giving the Confederates an advantage on the high seas. For the governor, the situation was linked to other pressing concerns. If Britain were to recognize the Confederacy as its own nation, another war between the countries might ensue, and Andrew needed to prepare without alarming his citizens. All fall he had badgered the War Department for improved coastal defenses, and the capture of Mason and Sidell had confirmed his arguments. Now, to protect the state's harbors and coasts, he obtained plans and estimates from the Bureau of Engineers to fortify Boston, Provincetown, and Vineyard Sound so that he could present them to the legislature when it convened in January.[14]

As Christmas approached, the governor's office transformed into a charity warehouse for soldiers and their families. Donations poured in from as far away as San Francisco, and Andrew ensured that every contribution found its way into camps and homes. One package particularly drew his attention. It was from the pupils of District No. 4 Grammar and Primary School in Georgetown, Massachusetts, who were sending the proceeds from their harvest to the war effort. In the spring, teachers had asked the students to comply with the governor's request that people on the home front plant an extra hill of corn for cause and country. The students had grown and harvested their corn, sold it, and now were sending the governor $3.02. Their letter read, "Our donation, though small, will show that we are Union boys and girls; and perhaps, when we are older, we'll show you what Union *men* and *women* can do."[15] Such sentiments lifted Andrew's spirits, and he closed out the year with a sense of confidence that Massachusetts had done everything it could to meet Lincoln's expectations.[16]

The governor believed that Lincoln was leaning toward emancipation, and he kept steady pressure on Sumner and Wilson to continue that lobbying work in Washington. The idea of freeing slaves to weaken the Confederacy remained generally unpopular, but the senators were trying to sell the idea that it would be a means of shortening the conflict. In a speech to Congress on December 3, Lincoln had taken a conservative, almost conciliatory tone, yet he had managed to convince members to pass a resolution offering compensation to states that adopted plans for gradual emancipation. In their response, Representative Thaddeus Stevens of Pennsylvania had led the radicals, calling on the president to declare all fugitive slaves free. Senator Wilson had pressed for slavery's abolition in Washington, and Senator Sumner had argued that the administration should no longer require commanders to return fugitive slaves to their masters. In his speech, he referred to Andrew's battle with the military authorities: "The Governor of my State has charged me with a communication to the Secretary of War on this subject, complaining of this outrage, treating it as an indignity to the men, and as an act unworthy of our national flag. I agree with the Governor, and when I call attention to this abuse now, I make myself his representative." He later told Andrew, "Let the doctrine of Emancipation be proclaimed as an essential and happy agency in subduing the wicked rebellion. In this way you will help a majority of the Cabinet, whose opinions on this subject are fixed, and precede the President himself by a few weeks."[17] Lincoln had confided to Sumner that the senator was "ahead of him only a month or six weeks."[18]

Reflecting on the year, the *Daily Advertiser* concluded:

[It] has demonstrated to our whole people the great fact, that in the designs of the Omnipotence the South has been led by its own folly to write the doom of slavery. Heavier and heavier are the blows which descend upon that institution, and more and more significant are the proofs that the South built upon a weak foundation, when within this very year, it announced slavery as the corner-stone of its fabric, political and social.[19]

Andrew must have been pleased by the paper's transformed ideas on the subject.

The New Year

On New Year's Day 1862, a fierce snowstorm blanketed Boston, making it difficult for Commonwealth legislators to convene on their traditional opening day. So Andrew delivered his second inaugural address on January 3. In a speech chronicling the past year's monumental changes, he declared that disunion and war had betrayed the founders' sacred covenant, transforming a peaceable, prosperous republic into a bloody battleground. The year had changed Andrew as well. True, he had matured as a statesman. Since the previous April, he had organized and dispatched more than 30,000 troops and 11,000 sailors. He had procured 2,000 muskets for the loyalists in western Virginia to form a new state, and he had sent supplies and money to Massachusetts prisoners in Richmond. He had studied and reported on coastal defenses, citizen welfare, schools, the Hoosac tunnel, and the probable loss of a congressional seat as a result of the state's decreasing population. He had recommended repealing an amendment aimed at disfranchising Irish-born men, reforming costly criminal procedures, and ending the death penalty.

Now, with this experience behind him, he knew he needed to press the emancipation question. If war was necessary, then securing freedom for slaves must be a precondition for peace. In his inaugural speech, he argued that slavery's extinction was inevitable because its spread had inspired a revolution that had catapulted the nation into war. Though he agreed that he should remain a step behind Lincoln, who was guiding the nation's course, he declared he would always be alongside his soldiers in the field. He ended by quoting from the Book of Ruth: "Where thou goest, I will go; and where thou lodgest, I will lodge; thy people shall be my people, and thy God my God: where thou diest will I die, and there will I be buried."[20]

Andrew's friction with Butler's recruitment practices had carried forward into the New Year, and he and the state legislators were anxious to end it. To set the record straight, Andrew consented to allow the General Court's printer to publish all of the pertinent correspondence on the matter—more than eighty letters and telegrams. He sent copies to Wilson and Sumner and asked them to share their opinions with Lincoln. In response, the president said that he would be "greatly obliged" if Andrew would "arrange somehow with General Butler to officer his two unofficered regiments." Still, Andrew believed Butler's machinations should be exposed. To Frank Howe, he complained, "I *am right*, I know I am, in spite of all that earth and—'t other place can do or say."[21] In the midst of this drama Cameron resigned from his position as secretary of war; but before he left the cabinet, Lincoln sent him to Sumner and asked him to intervene in the Andrew-Butler imbroglio. The senator wired Andrew, saying that if the governor would send his outline for recruiting to Washington, the War Department would adopt it. Andrew replied on January 14 that "the President has my programme written replying to his telegram of last Saturday." He also made it clear that his letters "should directly, and not indirectly, be answered by the President or Department."[22]

By the time Andrew arrived in Washington, his feud with Butler had become fodder for gossip and conversation. Ralph Waldo Emerson, who in January had met the incoming war secretary, Edwin Stanton, noted in his journal that Stanton had heard that the governor had come to the city to deal with the "difficulty." The secretary asked, "Why doesn't he come here? If I could meet Gov. Andrew under an umbrella at the corner of the street, we could settle that matter in five minutes, if he is the man I take him for. But I hear he is sitting on his dignity, & waiting for me to send for him, and, at that rate, for I learn there are 70 letters, I don't know that anything can be done." Sumner and Emerson reassured Stanton that Andrew was a sensible man and wanted to end the impasse.[23] Eventually Sumner summoned Andrew, Forbes, and Emerson to gather in Seward's dingy office, where they expected to meet Stanton. But when they arrived, the new secretary was absent, and the conversation turned away from Butler-Andrew toward other diplomatic matters. Sumner then escorted the party into the library, where they encountered State Department translator Count Gurowski muttering at his desk. Andrew later complained to Emerson that Seward "surpassed all men in the bold attempt at gas—ing other people, & pulling the wool over their eyes," which the governor found "very offensive."[24]

If Andrew did not meet Stanton on this occasion, he came away amused by Gurowski, who had pitched himself into the maelstrom. The translator was known for his contemptuous manner, which the literary critic Edwin Whipple characterized as a "combination of cynic, gossip, philosopher and hero—intrepid, disinterested, with an eye for the weak points of character, enthusiastic in fault-finding, incapable of insincerity . . . furious at incompetency; wishing to hang all dunces in office."[25] But even the hard-to-please Gurowski thought Andrew was a "tip-top" leader, and they shared opinions about the war's progress and its dilatory commanders. "As always," he wrote, "you are the true man because in feelings, comprehension and action you are the man for today and for tomorrow, that is for the great events which overroll us. We want action."[26]

Despite their uncomfortable start, Andrew came to appreciate the new secretary of war. Stanton was no bureaucratic malingerer, as Cameron had been. "If a bombshell had fallen into the Senate Chamber," said the *New York Tribune*, "it would not have produced a greater sensation than did the President's nomination of Mr. Stanton to the office of Secretary of War."[27] Andrew knew that the secretary had a reputation for integrity, and he was glad to share the Andrew-Butler correspondence with him. For his part, Stanton had heard that Andrew was a superior statesman with a splendid legal mind, eminently worthy of respect. He trusted that, after a full explanation, he would be able to redress the governor's grievances. In the meantime, Frank Howe reported to the governor that the cabinet was on his side and that Lincoln, Stanton, and Seward wished to see him in Washington to bring an end to the matter. "The sooner you come the better," Howe told his friend.[28]

But with the General Court in session, Andrew found it difficult to leave Boston. He and legislators had locked horns over a bill that would have provided aid to soldiers who had been illegally recruited into irregular units. In the meantime, Forbes and Samuel Ward, Julia Howe's brother, headed for New York City on the governor's behalf to visit the boys of the Twenty-eighth, who were reportedly freezing and starving at Fort Columbus, thanks to a negligent quartermaster. Not until late January could Andrew extricate himself from executive business and head to Washington. Before he left, he delivered a special message to the Massachusetts legislature, asking the General Court to use its power to "deliver the State and its people" from Butler's recruiting practices; if not, he would veto a bill that would provide aid to those regiments' families. The controversy highlighted the frustrations of waging a state-oriented national war. Though Lincoln and Andrew were pursuing the same goal, civil-military management had impaired federal-state supervision.

Butler, meanwhile, had visited Stanton and outlined a proposal for creating a Department of the Gulf, unaware of the navy's plan to move against New Orleans. In response, the secretary rescinded Butler's orders to Virginia and ordered him to the Gulf Coast; Stanton then called on congressional Radicals and the assistant naval secretary, Gustavus Fox, to persuade McClellan of the plan's merits. With Butler's operations moving forward, the dispute with Andrew fizzled out. The governor took charge of Butler's Massachusetts troops, assigned two regular army officers as regimental colonels, and, with their help, arranged the rosters. Stanton, in turn, terminated irregular approaches to raising regiments and disbanded the Department of New England.

In Washington, Andrew avoided the White House, instead visiting the Massachusetts soldiers stationed around the city. His decision to avoid further discussion of the issue with Lincoln earned him great favor among his friends and political colleagues, who appreciated his steadfast principles. He could not bring himself to attend "Mrs. Lincoln's Ball," asking Frank Howe, "are we not True *Romans?* . . . The more I think of it, the more I feel the improper levity of such a proceeding in the present awful condition of the country. It was on the very brink of ruin, and it is *now*."[29]

Emancipation League

Stanton gave the War Department a new identity in shaping war policy. He understood that the president needed the governors as much as they needed him, so he worked hard to rectify the flaws in civil-military relations. "Of one thing we may, I think be sure," Andrew told him gratefully, "that the slip-shod . . . manner in which the department has been conducted will cease."[30] With Stanton's support, Andrew put the Butler issue to rest, and the commander sailed for Ship Island in Mississippi Sound, where he prepared for an expedition up the river to New Orleans. But the Thirtieth Massachusetts remained unhappy. Its officers' fate had been at stake in the feud; and when the dust settled, the regiment was mustered in without them. "The Governor has carried his point and some of our officers will be forced to go home," wrote one disgruntled soldier from Ship Island, "and he is sending out officers to take the place of Butler's appointments." To the soldier, this seemed unfortunate, "especially after the old officers have recruited and drilled their men." The situation caused "hard feelings" among men and officers who did not like the arrangement. Indeed, several of the officers that Andrew had commissioned, according to Quartermaster Sergeant Henry Warren Howe, "don't know enough to tie up the door of a tent."[31]

Yet when the governor arrived back in Boston, the press praised his professionalism in the victory over Butler. After reading the voluminous correspondence, Theophilus Chandler thanked him for the "best laugh I have enjoyed since the war commenced. You never did anything better. I hope old Lincoln will read it. It is time Cameron was in Russia and Butler in hell."[32] Even more welcome was Stanton's General Order 18, reaffirming that governors were the sole authorities for raising men and commissioning officers.

But Andrew remained dissatisfied. This winter he became ever more convinced that emancipating slaves and using them as soldiers would not only weaken the Confederacy and win the war but also abolish slavery once and for all. He recognized that the conservatives' approach to the war would draw more volunteers than a war against slavery would, but thus far the Union had little to show for its sacrifices. Why had Lincoln built such a massive army if he were going to use it in such a limited way? Like many Union governors, he was frustrated by the conflict's sluggish pace because he knew that conservative commanders and politicians were unwilling to expand the Union's targets and wage a more vigorous war. Seward seemed to be more focused on winning and maintaining friends in the Union than on conquering the nation's enemies. Though radical-minded leaders were frustrated by this approach, the secretary of state's "jaunty optimism" appeared to be ascendant in the administration and was giving shape to Lincoln's border state policy. It did not help that McClellan and the Union commanders in the western theaters of the war, Don Carlos Buell and Henry Halleck, were following this policy religiously.

Yet change was coming. By January's end Lincoln had lost patience with his military commanders, who were determined to sit out the winter instead of campaigning. He moved decisively, issuing Special War Order 1, which called together the Army of the Potomac for an expedition into Virginia, and setting the departure date for February 22. He was anxious to get McClellan's army moving before congressional radicals moved it for him. Andrew took this opportunity to pursue bigger game. Traveling again to Washington, he prodded his friends to push his views in Congress and on the president. "*The South must be conquered*," he barked to Francis Blair, Sr. "The war is *war*. Nobody is to be cheated; but somebody is to be beaten; and Democratic-Republican Liberty is the tremendous stake for which we play. We must fight— fight like warriors, like soldiers, like men of sense, like men in earnest pregnant with victory, [and] . . . give freedom to every slave who follows the flag, or obeys our Generals and aids our cause." Northerners needed to "establish a real government wherever we march" and "fight wherever we go, as if we expected to *meet* somebody, and were not afraid of our own selves." The president "must lead and the people must break down the South, control their ports, command their cotton, and show England and the old world, that the Democracy of the new world is on its native heath, and is inspired by danger and by duty."[33] To Frank Bird, who was stationed in Washington, he said, "The President has never yet seemed quite sure that we were in a war at all. As to Mr. Seward, who has been his mentor, he has always regarded the case about as a police justice would an assault and battery between two loafers in a pot-house,—or else he has worn a well-contrived mask for the last six months."[34] "We must conquer the South," he told Bird, "[and] to do this; we must bring the Northern mind to a comprehension of this necessity":

> The war has gone on *under protest*, as it were, that it was not intended to *conquer* the south but to "restore the Union." I think all that talk twaddle. The people now understand the case twenty times better than they did last July—far better than even three months ago. And, in the stern logic necessity of the logic of the war, they will reach the point of grappling with *Slavery*, and turning the guns of that fortress against the power of Slavery itself. We "black republicans" retard the cause, but we can do little to hasten it—save by swelling the current as it moves.[35]

Many Republicans were still resistant to embracing emancipation as a wartime measure, so George Boutwell joined forces with Bird, Samuel Howe, George Stearns, and other mercantile elites to establish the Emancipation League. Members began planning an extensive lobbying campaign to educate the voters through the press. They intended to push for congressional action in favor of freedom as both a measure of justice and a military strategy to end the war. Organizers arranged a lecture series in Boston focusing on how and why emancipation could end the war and presented evidence that free Black laborers could strengthen the nation's economy. Boutwell's opening talk, "The Justice, Expediency and Necessity of Emancipation," was a long and insightful explanation that set the tone for the series. Andrew sent organizers a copy of his recent letter to Bird, which he asked to be read at the meeting. As much as he wanted to attend in person, he told Boutwell that he thought it would be wise to wait for Lincoln's vanguard.[36]

The Emancipation League was received enthusiastically in Boston, and it expanded into several other northern cities and into Washington. In a winter replete with dismal military news, the league's success was a small triumph. Andrew remained hopeful that it would help people see the war as a conflict with a morally transcendent purpose, yet the conservative press continued to characterize the league's members as "devils" and "miserable demagogues" who were rebelling against heaven in their quest to destroy the Union.[37] Still, Andrew was encouraged when New York's attorney general, Daniel Dickinson, a war Democrat, visited Boston and spoke in support of using slaves to crush the rebellion. Though Dickinson was not focused on advancing African American citizenship but on protecting white citizens, his argument showed that there were cracks in the conservative carapace.

The *Liberator* reprinted Dickinson's speech just above an article reporting on the Boston School Committee's satisfaction at the educational progress of the city's African American children. This must have gratified Andrew. Since 1855, when he and other abolitionists had created an integrated public-school system in the state, Black children had been making gradual but steady advances. "That they are taught without prejudice, and stimulated by a proper competition with the other," reported the committee, "is all cordially welcomed."[38]

As he began his second term as governor, Andrew's popularity had expanded his influence in the Commonwealth. Former governor Edward Everett was among the many who recognized this. In a note complimenting Andrew on his recent legislative address, he lauded the governor's demand for absolute unity behind the Union cause, defined in true Republican fashion as preserving the nation and popular government from the damages of slavery. Everett praised Andrew's "luminous & exhaustive discussion on the subject"—high praise coming from such a distinguished public servant and scholar.[39]

Andrew had been forced to walk a tightrope between Lincoln and the abolitionists, but his reelection was a resounding victory, confirmation that the people supported his cautious moves forward. "We can create a counter current by our own imprudence," he warned Bird, "while we might make the stream now providentially running overwhelming and irresistible."[40] As northern soldiers gained a closer knowledge of slavery, Andrew was confident that they would recognize its evils and begin to see that it must be abolished or, at least, that they should not return fugitives to their masters. The letters he received from the field had convinced him of this. As he told Montgomery Blair, "the slavery question ought not be a foot-ball for debate, to make and unmake parties in this part of our progress. It is a *practical vital* question."[41] For him, the issue extended beyond the borders of the United States. In conversations with Sumner, Fessenden, and others, he endorsed diplomatic recognition of the Black-governed republics of Haiti and Liberia, something that

Lincoln, too, had urged. Yet the president still seemed to believe that the colonization of African Americans could be a permanent solution, whereas Andrew was convinced that assimilation was the answer.[42]

Against fierce opposition, Sumner led the Senate's pro-recognition faction, mostly by advancing pragmatic considerations such as trade to appease his racist colleagues. He shared portions of a bill with Andrew he planned to bring before the Senate in April to authorize the appointment of diplomatic representatives to the republics of Haiti and Liberia. Andrew congratulated the senator on his expectant triumph: "The law when passed, will be a recognition of the *colored man*, not merely of Hayti. It is a jewel in your crown. . . ."[43]

CHAPTER 15

THE CHANGING WAR

January–July 1862

The Roads Will Swarm with the Multitudes

Throughout January 1862, the Union military remained stalled, and northern soldiers hovered close to their camps. Yet in February, as McClellan's army slowly prepared for an offensive on the Virginia peninsula, General Ulysses S. Grant captured two Confederate river forts in Tennessee, forcing the surrender of nearly 12,000 soldiers and the eventual capitulation of Nashville. His spectacular achievement left Confederate leaders scrambling to redeploy their meager western forces. Even more devastating was that the Union army's presence had interrupted slaveowners' control in the region, forcing Confederate leaders into desperate reactionary moves to maintain their grip.

As McClellan prepared to leave Washington. Andrew wrote to Count Gurowski: "How stands the case? Are Stanton & McClellan agreed or not, [and] how stands the Pres[ident]?"[1] Andrew knew that the soldiers' vitality had weakened over the winter, and he worried about Lincoln's next moves. He feared that the longer McClellan and the other commanders continued their conservative approach, the more soldiers would suffer in the field. Creating large armies for limited use, Andrew believed, demoralized soldiers and the citizenry. Meanwhile, what he saw as a pretend conflict focused on the border states while allowing the enemy to maintain its domestic institutions. Surely, he had his critics but many officers on the ground agreed with him. Lieutenant Colonel Horace Sargent wrote to him from the field: "Vindicating the majesty of an insulted Government, by extirpating all rebels, & fumigating their nests with the brimstone of unmitigated Hell, I conceive to be the holy purpose of our further efforts, . . . [and I hope] I shall have a chance to do something . . . in 'the Great Fumigation.'"[2] Andrew also heard from Kansas abolitionists, including one man who pleaded with him to help change the goals of the "proslavery administration": "Delaware, Maryland, Kentucky & Missouri have more influence at Washington than Massachusetts, New York, Pennsylvania, and Ohio, but it is time that the loyal states speak out."[3]

In February, Boston reformers organized a New England branch of the Freedman's Commission and named Andrew president. He asked members to foster the educational, social, and economic improvement of slaves freed in the war. Within weeks, they secured the services of more than thirty teachers, who set sail for Port Royal, South Carolina, taking with them clothes, books, and domestic supplies. There the group met with Edward Pierce, a Boston attorney whom the secretary of the treasury, Salmon Chase, had appointed as his department's special agent for contrabands. By working with Pierce, Andrew ensured, as much as he could, that political differences did not affect the commission's operations.[4]

Andrew also supported Clara Barton's nursing activism. On a visit to Boston to care for her dying father, she asked the governor to open a state agency in Washington, D.C., that would serve as a distribution center for the materials that women were making and collecting for the Commonwealth soldiers stationed in the region. Andrew was taken by the idea and began working to establish one. Soon she petitioned him for permission to join General Ambrose Burnside's troops at Roanoke Island, North Carolina, to care for the Massachusetts wounded, and he wrote a "hearty approval" letter on her behalf. Union forces captured the island on February 8 and Andrew dispatched Dr. Alfred Hitchcock to supervise the Massachusetts wounded. Recently returned to Boston, however, Hitchcock rejected her offer telling the governor that Barton would be in the way. Crushed, she returned to Washington and resumed her efforts there.[5]

As Andrew busily shored up regional defenses, he paid close attention to the naval battle at Hampton Roads, Virginia, between two ironclad warships, the USS *Monitor* and the CSS *Merrimack*. The conflict began on March 7 and ended inconclusively two days later, but it spurred him to ask Commonwealth legislators to contract with the federal government to build an ironclad and enlarge the state's foundry for big guns. The state senate defeated the costly measure, but Andrew was so worried by the situation that he woke up state engineer Henry Eustis in the middle of the night to ask his advice about preparing Boston for such an attack.

Nonetheless, Union victories at Fort Henry, Fort Donelson, and Nashville were encouraging, and in mid-March Secretary of War Stanton summoned Andrew to Washington to discuss expanding ordnance manufacturing in Massachusetts to supply the enlarging field armies. By now Lincoln had removed McClellan as general-in-chief to allow him to focus on the move to Richmond and the commander set sail for Fort Monroe and would soon commence their march up the Virginia peninsula. Changes were also happening in Congress, which had resolved to prohibit fugitives inside Union army lines from being returned to their masters. In addition, representatives had taken up a bill to abolish slavery in Washington, an issue that Andrew had been pressing forward for months. Abolishing slavery in the capital, he told Frank Blair, would "root out the nursery of disloyalty" and, along with recognizing Haiti, would "command with imperative and overwhelming voice the moral and political support of every free state, and would confuse and confound all our enemies." Congress finally passed the measure on April 11.[6]

Sumner was Andrew's voice in Washington, but he was also his ears. By early spring he had confided to his friend that Lincoln had lost confidence in McClellan, even though an attack on Yorktown, Virginia, felt imminent. In turn, Andrew told Sumner of his worry that Lincoln's plan for gradually abolishing slavery had given conservatives and some moderates ammunition against governors such as himself. The radicals had gone too far, their critics alleged, and they must be ousted from power. Meanwhile, supporters doubled down in backing Sumner's and Andrew's course. In Massachusetts, Republicans used Lincoln's proposal and Congress's new resolution against surrendering fugitives to organize for the impending political fray. Despite his critics, Andrew told Sumner, "the Lord is marching on."[7]

As the frosts thawed in Boston, Andrew became ensnarled in political drama. Having already overseen the mustering of German- and Irish-born volunteers into Massachusetts regiments, he now called for the repeal of the Know-Nothing constitutional amendments that had forbidden any male resident of foreign birth to vote until two years after his naturalization. He also vetoed a bill that would have divided the Commonwealth into congressional districts for the purpose of electing representatives, a change that would require voters to limit their choices to inhabitants of a district. Andrew maintained that this was unconstitutional, and Sumner agreed, saying that "Constitutional law was perfect, & so was your mode of stating it." However, state senators overrode his veto.[8]

Even worse, in early April, Stanton halted federal recruiting. Bureaucratic mismanagement had pushed him to find a more effective means of replenishing the ranks before adding new regiments. With several campaigns under way and the ongoing loss of soldiers to sickness, commanders now arranged with state governors to raise volunteers without federal directives. Doubting the plan's wisdom, especially after the two-day Battle of Shiloh in western Tennessee left the Union, even in victory, with more than 13,000 casualties, Andrew opposed it. He sent Bird to the White House with a letter stating his opinion. The missive also included the General Court's resolve to approve the president's call for national cooperation with any state working to abolish slavery. Peleg Chandler traveled with Bird, and he later described how the president received the letter. Sitting in an armchair, with one leg crossed over an elbow, he opened the paper, slowly unfolded it, and then remarked, "Well, it isn't long enough to scare a fellow."[9]

As Union victories increased in the West, congressional Radicals encouraged Stanton to crush the Confederates quickly and emancipate their slaves. Yet victory at the Battle of Shiloh also set the Union back on its heels. As news of the casualties came over wires, Andrew responded quickly, offering to send Massachusetts surgeons to help deal with the wounded. He hoped for better news from McClellan's army in Virginia. By early May, the War Department had permitted Union governors to resume recruiting soldiers, anticipating that commanders would soon requisition them for upcoming campaigns. Anticipating this move, Andrew had already sent agents to various sites in Virginia. He had also worked his way through the prisoner exchange bureaucracy to get officers and medical personnel released and returned to active duty. There was no better reward for his efforts than to see Colonel William Lee, Major Paul Revere, and Dr. Edward Revere return to their comrades in the Twentieth Massachusetts, now camped in Virginia and preparing to advance up the peninsula.[10]

Grant's February victories and the surrender of Nashville in Tennessee had been a shock, but nearly everyone expected great things from McClellan's peninsula campaign against Richmond. If Lincoln lacked confidence in the commander, as Sumner had said, the governor could do nothing but pray for the thousands of Commonwealth troops he had committed to "Little Mac's" army. Yet even though the governor was disheartened, he found a modicum of comfort in an unexpected place. General David Hunter, the abolitionist cousin of Andrew Hunter, who had prosecuted John Brown, issued an order on May 9 declaring that all slaves in the Department of the South were now free, citing military necessity for their liberation. As with Frémont's emancipation edict months earlier, Andrew hailed this as a triumph, and he sent Forbes to Beaufort, South Carolina, to see if Hunter's approach could be a way forward. Would it be possible to work abandoned lands with ex-slaves and perhaps use them in the army? Writing to Sumner, Forbes said that he saw benefits in Hunter's plan and hoped Lincoln would avoid another "Frémont blunder" and not disavow the action. "Whatever may be the case elsewhere," he said, "it is time the Kid glove and Rosewater mode of carrying on the war should be exploded in South Carolina, that *the only loyal men* there should be encouraged to come over to our side!"[11] As expected, however, there was no public consensus on Hunter's decree. In fact, it provoked a national debate. Even Commonwealth soldiers remained divided. As Lieutenant Charles Fox of the Thirteenth Massachusetts wrote in his diary, "The slavery question cannot be made the issue of this war. It would divide the army, the border states, and even New England, and anarchy and ruin cover us all. The institution must and will fail as a result of this rebellion, but it will be as the result, not the cause."[12]

Though Lincoln countermanded Hunter's plan, Andrew was encouraged by the commander's proclamation. When Francis Fletcher, an African American store clerk from Salem, asked if he would soon be able to serve in the Union army, the governor told him the day was not far off. As in Virginia and the Carolinas, the victories at Shiloh and in General Henry Halleck's offensive campaign in northern Mississippi, had loosened the enslavers' grip. The governor was anxious to break the administration's paralysis: the war was advancing, and not just toward Richmond, the Confederate capital. Washington itself was vulnerable. Clearly, more troops were needed, in more places. Confederate general Thomas "Stonewall" Jackson was a particular worry. As his cavalry headed north toward Front Royal in the Shenandoah Valley, their aggressive and deceptive maneuvers befuddled Union commanders and threw northern observers into a panic. Many were sure he would soon drive the Union forces north of the Potomac.[13]

Concerns about Jackson intensified conversations between Stanton and some northern governors. The secretary sent constant telegrams, asking again and again how soon new regiments could be sent to the front. This sudden change in tack caught Andrew off guard, given that Stanton had shut down recruiting a few weeks earlier. Potential volunteers were now cultivating their fields or working at jobs; many lived days away from Boston, and all needed to be equipped. On May 19 he told Stanton that he was confident that he could raise the men in forty days, but he added:

If our people feel that they are going into the South to help fight rebels, who will kill and destroy *them* by all the means known to savages, as well as civilized men; will deceive them by fraudulent flags of truce and lying pretences (as they did the Massachusetts boys at Williamsburg), will use their negro slaves against them, both as laborers and as fighting men, while they themselves must never *"fire at an enemy's magazine,"* I think that they will feel the draft is heavy on their patriotism. But, if the President will sustain General Hunter, recognize *all* men, even black men, as legally capable of that loyalty that blacks are waiting to manifest, and let them fight, with God and human nature on their side, [then] the roads will swarm if need be with the multitudes whom New England would pour out to obey your call.[14]

"The wiley and barbarous horde of traitors"

Andrew wrote a public letter, printed in several New England newspapers, which was designed to attract volunteers by uniting them behind a higher moral cause. Some papers criticized the governor, but many editors agreed with him, declaring in their pages that the sooner the president used the nation's full force, including African Americans, the sooner the war would end. In a note to Andrew, one Boston resident emphasized that such an approach would "save us from a conflict long and bloody, ending only in the bankruptcy and ruin of both North and South. Delays are dangerous, [and] . . . the Government must lead here. The people will acquiesce and even rejoice when the work is . . . done."[15] In his letter, Andrew put Stanton, Lincoln, and the conciliators on notice, declaring that the people were growing tired of the conservative approach. He sent copies to the Massachusetts congressional delegation. Sumner and Wilson praised it, while Congressman John Alley called it "the best letter that this rebellion has called forth."[16]

Meanwhile, Jackson's troops swept north down the Shenandoah Valley in pursuit of Nathaniel Banks's small army. The situation forced Lincoln to recall General Irwin McDowell's force to Washington, a move that infuriated McClellan. Stanton alerted the governors of Pennsylvania, New York, and Massachusetts, warning them to have their militias ready for the onslaught. For two days in May, Washington authorities were in a panic, desperately hastening troops forward to stave off disaster. In Boston, Andrew worked late into the night, desperate to get soldiers into the field as soon as possible. Lieutenant Colonel Francis Parker, thirty-six years old and a former state senator, later recalled the intensity of those days. Summoned by the governor, he found Andrew alone, writing at his desk. Within minutes, other officers and staff appeared, but the governor was the "busiest of the workers, radiant with the joy of one who possesses great powers, and who knows he is wielding them effectually."[17]

Before noon on Sunday, May 25, Stanton wired Andrew that the enemy had completely routed Banks at Winchester and was headed for Harpers Ferry, just sixty miles from Washington. That day, Andrew

FIGURE 7. Governor Andrew in Boston. Print Collection, New York Public Library.

published another public letter, a call to arms to repel the "wiley and barbarous horde of traitors to the People, to the Government, to our Country and to Liberty, menace again the National Capital." In the evening, however, Stanton wired that Banks had crossed the Potomac to safety. The danger had passed; the secretary now ordered that the hastily formed militias be released and that enlistments going forward should be made for three years or the duration of the war. It was a startling reversal, but just as maddening for Andrew.[18]

Andrew's summons had drawn nearly 4,000 men to Boston Common. Now he had to ask them to either enlist for the entire war or return home; most did the latter. Conservatives mocked the governor as a reckless alarmist, and their press hounded him about his public letters. But Sumner stood by him. After Richard Dana, Jr., wrote to him about the uproar in Boston, the senator described Stanton's desperate telegrams and declared that many in Washington had admired Andrew's call to arms, not least because it had challenged Lincoln to expand his war aims. The problem was not Andrew, Sumner maintained, but the Boston press. Still, he saw "no cheerful omens. Victory is possible, but not success—at present. There must be more suffering, debt & bloodshed, to be followed by a famine throughout the slave states."[19] Count Gurowski, agreed, telling Andrew that the *Daily Advertiser*'s editor "deserved the gallows on the Boston Common." "You who have so much pluck," he wrote, "ought [to] stretch your power and finish that infamous traitor."[20]

Andrew's aides implored him to save face by releasing Stanton's official telegrams to the press. "No, sir!" he said, jumping to his feet. "If the people of Massachusetts don't know John A. Andrew well enough without rushing into print with a 'card' to explain his acts every time that somebody is frightened, then let him be misrepresented and misunderstood till the end of time! I will have nothing printed on the subject."[21] He indignantly gathered up the blistering articles and forwarded them to Stanton, who replied that he, too, was not disturbed by the "howling of those who are at your heels and mine."[22] Sumner, however, gave Andrew the full story behind the scare: "The whole trouble is directly traceable to McClellan, who took away to Yorktown an amount of troops beyond what he was authorized to do, *so as to leave Washington defenceless.* When the Pres[ident] became aware of this, he was justly indignant." But Sumner had hope. "We shall begin soon to fire at the magazine," he told the governor. "*Stanton told me this morning that a decree of Emancipation would be issued within two months. If we do not declare Emancipation, we must make up our minds to acknowledge the independence of the rebels. This is fixed.*"[23]

But Andrew's hackles were up. He was infuriated that Lincoln, on Seward's recommendation, had recently appointed former congressman Edward Stanly to be military governor of North Carolina. Stanly had endorsed returning fugitives to their masters, and Andrew found this intolerable. He fumed to Sumner, "Don't they know *whom* they send? Do they wish to drive our N.E. troops out of the field and disgust mankind? The most 'hunker' [politically conservative] officers we have ever sent, cry out, in their private correspondence, that the army is so managed in its relations to Southern men that a positive bribe is held out to whites and blacks both to be disloyal." He lamented that the war looked likely to last for an "indefinite length" and bitterly declared that most politicians "despised the people, think they are foolish and knowing their own personal limitations, believe the people not to be honest."[24]

"Sewardism" was to blame for Lincoln's conservative approach, said Sumner. He assured Andrew that after the war "yr letter on 'firing into the magazine' will be one of the best of yr many claims to public gratitude." He was sorry that Congress had not recognized, as Andrew had, the wisdom of a vigorous war from the beginning. "It must be done," he concluded, "and I regret infinitely that the necessity was not foreseen by our Govt. & prompt preparation made to meet it. *That would have been statesmanship*."[25] Such statesmanship was what Andrew had offered, but all he could do now was to march onward, hoping to convince Stanton to come around to his way of thinking. "This is a dark hour," Sumner wrote to Andrew. "The future is murky. Nobody can see the light on any vista in any direction. Stanton said today that 'Washington is in as much danger as Richmond.' . . . [But he believes] we must meet some great calamity before a proper policy can be adopted." "This is hard," he confided to Andrew, "very hard."[26]

There was no denying that emancipating and enlisting former slaves would injure the Union's volunteer effort. Yet some of the officers were frustrated by Washington's paralysis on the slavery issue. Among them was Major Robert Copeland of the Second Massachusetts, and the governor encouraged him to draft an "Appeal to Arms." In it Copeland blamed Stanton for the problems with Banks's campaign, and his fiery words ultimately got him cashiered from the service. Though many read his complaints about the War Department, and abolitionists agreed with them, conservatives such as Boston's Democratic mayor, Joseph Wightman, repudiated such opinions. He told Lincoln that Andrew was mingling emancipation with the Union's preservation, declared that most viewed his attitude with "the strongest feelings of disapprobation," and predicted that it would damage enlistment.

Corporal John Chase of the First Massachusetts Light Artillery agreed, writing to his brother from Virginia that the "nigger talk of John A. Andrews [*sic*] & Co is not relished very well out here. If he [Andrew] wants to enlist niggers, he had better let the white men come home."[27]

In the North there was much despondency about the progress of the war. Though Union forces had gained access to the James River, McClellan was making only halting progress toward Richmond. Two days of heavy fighting on May 31 and June 1 yielded heavy casualties but little change in position, and troop shortages and low morale deepened the crisis. Weeks before, the president had informed the general that it was "indispensable to *you* that you strike a blow. *I* am powerless to help this. *But you must act.*" Andrew agreed and wrote to the president to remind him of this. But even as Lincoln seemed to be moving toward emancipation as a war measure, McClellan's army on the Virginia peninsula remained stalled.[28]

On June 6, Stanton restored the volunteer recruiting service, and Andrew welcomed the change. By mid-month, however, the tide of volunteers was ebbing. The governor refused to castigate his military-age citizens for avoiding service; instead, he extolled their sacrifice thus far. Yet it had become painfully evident that hollow campaigns and mounting casualties were undermining the president's war management. In Boston, Andrew remained focused on soldier welfare and the return of the dead. He wrote to Major Charles Chandler of the First Massachusetts, stationed near Fair Oaks, Virginia, that he was sending new appointees his way and extending warm wishes to the soldiers. A close family friend, Chandler had been working in Andrew's law office when he became governor. Now, just after sending the letter, Andrew learned that he had likely been killed in action at the Battle of Seven Pines. The governor sent Charles Lowell to Virginia to ascertain the facts. In a letter to General Joseph Hooker, he said, "My love for the major from his boyhood, my intimate relations with his family from my boyhood and my knowledge of the esteem in which you held him induce me to ask of you as a personal favor all aid which you can properly afford to Mr. Lowell in the duty on which he is engaged."[29] When Colonel Powell Wyman fell in Virginia at the Battle of Glendale later in the month, Andrew also made sure that the body was returned to Massachusetts, and he and his staff attended the funeral. In the letter that accompanied the body, Hooker showed his gratitude for Andrew's attention to his soldiers. Andrew responded, "The loss of Wyman falls heavily upon me, but if the gods had willed that his end should be, they could not have chosen a more befitting time and occasion."[30]

As the war escalated into its second year, administrative work at the statehouse became ever more burdensome. Andrew and his staff were awash in correspondence. In the first six months of 1862, they filled five five-hundred-page volumes with orders, letters, and memoranda. Andrew himself personally wrote about fifteen letters a day, many of them hundreds of words long. According to his adjutant general, William Schouler, the governor kept up this "herculean labor of correspondence" until the war's end, an accumulation of letters that was greater than that of all previous Massachusetts governors combined. Not only did he attend to the war's minutiae, but he continued to deal with traditional state and ceremonial business, including invitations to attend commencement exercises at numerous colleges around the Commonwealth. He accepted these invitations, but the war continued to dominate his time and his thoughts.[31]

As the state's newspapers published list after list of the dead and wounded, Andrew could tell that public opinion was turning against Lincoln's conciliatory policy. Stanton again wired governors about pressing troop needs, but their response was gloomy. Count Gurowski's sour assessment of Washington politics was disheartening, and Andrew dispatched Colonel Harrison Ritchie to James River to examine the Commonwealth troops personally. But the count's war-room gossip also suggested that the president was nearing a decision to emancipate the slaves. The Union's western armies were poised to move across the plantation region of the upper South, and Andrew decided to send personal envoys to the White House to convince Lincoln that the time was right for emancipation. Count Gurowski encouraged the governor to speak his mind: "You are stern and inflexible, but, I hesitate to believe that you are wholly correct in not allowing for differences of mental constitution, which must always be taken into account.... There is one *Truth*, but many possible roads to it."[32]

Astor House Ruse

Andrew intended to go to Maine to celebrate Windham's one hundredth anniversary on July 4. As he was preparing for this visit, Seward was carrying a letter from Lincoln to New York City, where he had arranged a meeting at Astor House with Governor Edwin Morgan of New York, Governor Andrew Curtin of Pennsylvania, Governor Charles Olden of New Jersey, the publisher Thurlow Weed, the mayors of New York City and Philadelphia, and members of New York's Union Defense Committee. The topic was how to engineer a call for more troops, and Seward hoped that Morgan would serve as his intermediary with the loyal governors who were not present. Lincoln's plan was to avoid calling for more men himself, which he knew would alarm the citizens. Instead, he wanted the northern governors to petition him for additional men. The ruse would include all loyal governors. Thus, on June 30, before Andrew left Boston, he received a wire from Morgan, explaining the plan. Andrew was suspicious, thinking that it might be a trick to keep the radicals from pressing for emancipation. He replied to Morgan that, as much as he respected his colleagues, he could not sign such a petition. Stanton, however, refused to send it to Lincoln unless Andrew's name appeared, so Seward headed to Boston to convince the governor to sign.

Early on the morning of July 2, Seward appeared at the statehouse with Thurlow Weed, and Adjutant General Catharinus Buckingham. Seward showed Lincoln's letter to Andrew, which convinced him that this was a bona fide ploy. Moreover, it would include $25 in advance pay for every new recruit. Andrew wired Stanton his assent; and by noon, Seward had left for Cleveland and Andrew was heading to Windham. The governor felt he had achieved a small victory as he had long wanted to offer a signing bonus to volunteers. Seward, too, had what he wanted; and two days later, Lincoln used the petition to spur McClellan, calling out 300,000 men for three years in hopes of bringing the war to an end. In his diary Count Gurowski described the backstage maneuvering as "a poor trick," but the governors had proven themselves to be capable of saving Lincoln's public face.[33] Andrew was enroute to Maine when the papers reported Lincoln's call for additional men, which meant 15,000 from Massachusetts.

In Windham, he was able to rest and take pleasure in the familiar surroundings of his native ground. He had been asked to speak at the centennial celebration; and though he had not prepared any formal remarks, his eloquence was never at a loss. Now Andrew spoke about those who were bearing the brunt of the conflict. Yet a great question remained, he told his audience. Did New Englanders have the resolve to decide their fate and change the war's direction, or were they content to let a protracted contest drain them of men and resources? "It remains to you, ye yeomanry of Maine, ye solid *men*," said Andrew, "to see whether this people shall be free and prosperous." He encouraged his listeners "to take this work up, according to the dictates of their own heart. . . . The unwise, yet I think well-intended idea, to fight for freedom and yet to protect the property of rebels in and over the crouching slaves, is depleting our treasury, draining the best blood of our veins, and causing untold misery."[34]

Windham was a refreshment, but in Boston Andrew was immediately hurled back into war realities. On his return to the statehouse, he found several telegrams waiting, all of them detailing the horrific story of the Seven Days Battles, fought near Richmond between June 25 and July 1. Driven back by Confederate general Robert E. Lee, McClellan was forced to pull his army back to Harrison's Landing, where Union gunboats protected it. Morale in the North plummeted, and governors struggled to attract new volunteers. Meanwhile, Andrew wrote his friend Francis Blair, Sr., questioning when those in power would treat the conflict as a war, "not as a picnic or caucus"?[35] He told Blair:

> How dreadful it is, to see our best boys of all the State, slain, bleeding, worn out by ditching, bridging, dirt digging, and wheeling, and by guarding the property of rebels who, with their very slaves, are in the war against us. Now, is not a "nigger" who is good enough to fire grape, cannon and rifle shot into the ranks of a Bunker Hill regiment good enough to fight traitors? That is my only question, [and] . . . before God I believe we are doomed unless we will awake to reason. But I am a follower—not a leader, [and] . . . I will work with the energy of despair even if I am shorn of the buoyancy of Hope.[36]

With McClellan's retreat, Lincoln lost faith in his army's ability to claim victory in Virginia. Despair also gripped the staff in the Massachusetts statehouse. Andrew received yet more disheartening news from John D. Andrews, who was in Washington. "There is a feeling of bitter gloom," he wrote. "If I was a Gov. of a free state I would swear not to give another man until they changed . . . this corrupt & cowardly cabinet."[37] Equally disgusted, Count Gurowski wrote:

> All this evil done by few cursed individuals, Lincoln included, Washington is a cesspool or if you will an arena wherein the destinies of the people are decided by the game of imbecility, ignorance & meanest, lowest intrigue. The fashion here is now to ascribe all the evils to the congress to accuse the people at large of slowness in sacrificing itself to the cause. This accusation is a crime.

He lamented that the sacrifices of the people had been for naught. "Oh for a man! For a man! Not for the 300,000," he wailed.[38]

Gurowski challenged Andrew to be that man, the one who would prod Lincoln forward. In a letter, he confided that Lincoln was about to replace McClellan and that Stanton had agreed to this move. During a visit to Harrison's Landing on the James River, the count wrote to Andrew that the men's morale was low, not only because of setbacks on the peninsula but also because of the severe discipline of martinet officers. He was appalled: Lincoln and McClellan possessed the largest army ever assembled on North American soil, and they could not win battles.[39]

The summer was a mourning season. In Virginia fields, the dead and wounded lay unattended for days. As letters and press reports chronicled the dismal story, Andrew busied himself at home. He tried to localize recruiting as much as possible, showing each city and town the number of men, it had already furnished and the number that would be called in response to Lincoln's new quota. Like many governors, he tried to attract volunteers by offering enlistment in existing regiments that might muster out sooner than the new regiments would. But recruits wanted to serve with their friends in new companies from their hometowns, not with unfriendly companies already at the front. To complicate matters, these new recruits would not accept officers released from existing regiments but wanted to choose their officers from among themselves. "The *local* feeling is so strong," wrote Andrew, "that it seems as if people often would prefer to go to certain death and disgrace under an officer of the bailiwick, rather than to be led to glorious victory under Washington himself."[40]

Andrew abhorred this kind of conditional volunteer patriotism, and he was annoyed that Stanton supported such arguments. When he countered that existing regiments had plenty of officers who could be promoted to lead the new regiments, Stanton questioned how he could move officers "who are [now serving] in the face of the enemy." The governor's hands were tied, but he continued to worry that new recruits were negotiating the terms of their enlistment, unlike those who had gone before. There was no question that Lincoln's "three hundred thousand more" were slow in coming forward and that the eastern armies appeared to be stalled on the front.[41]

Given military setbacks, plummeting morale, and a maddening administration, congressmen decided that it was time to press the president to abandon his conciliatory ways and give him the instruments to charge forth. On July 17 they passed the Militia Act and the Second Confiscation Act. The first was a broad conscription document to be invoked when the president felt that it was necessary to summon able-bodied militiamen (including African Americans) into military service. The second authorized Union armies to confiscate property (including slaves) of persons in rebellion against the United States and provided the basis for placing slaves in the Union armies. The measures delighted Andrew, for they pulled African Americans directly into the war effort. Henry Bowditch congratulated him for his part in influencing Lincoln and Congress to make these moves. "Let the people of the North be told now that they stand before the world *whipped*," Bowditch said, "and the only thing remaining to restore themselves to respectability and honor is to win the game at all hazards—vindicate the freeman over the slave and leave every thing else to be settled after the victory shall be won."[42] Still, Count Gurowski warned Andrew that Seward's influence and the new Confiscation Bill would create a backlash. "Believe me," he told Andrew, "Lincoln, Seward will do all in their might to neutralize . . . the hateful law."[43] John D. Andrews echoed this, also hinting that Halleck was coming to Washington to take command of the eastern army or else serve as Lincoln's chief of staff. The picture remained bleak, and Andrews suggested that the "South will beat us at arming negroes."[44]

CHAPTER 16

EMANCIPATION

July–November 1862

What the Senate Could Not Do

Lincoln was desperate to transform the Union's military fortunes, not only to diffuse public acrimony but also to give Republicans leverage in the fall elections. By July's end, Henry Halleck had arrived in Washington to serve as military chief of staff, Stanton had recalled McClellan from the peninsula, and John Pope had become commander of a reconfigured Army of Virginia. Using his new powers, Lincoln invoked the Militia Act on August 4, giving states just weeks to comply or face a compulsory draft. Andrew reluctantly publicized the mandate; it remained to be seen how citizens would react. Lincoln was now calling for 300,000 volunteers to serve for nine months. On the heels of a similar call the president had made the month before, this new mandate made it appear as if he needed 600,000 soldiers, but in fact the August call was designed to spur volunteers to fill the July call. Still, this meant that Andrew was responsible for immediately raising nearly 20,000 volunteers. To handle the chaos at the statehouse, he appointed a second assistant adjutant general, William Rogers. Though he and his staff were overwhelmed, the governor assured Montgomery Blair that "the work goes bravely on. Stanton is a war minister indeed."[1]

With governors authorized to control the draft, the Union's nation-state alliance was fortified, and Confederates recognized that northerners were in earnest about the war. "They will learn that we are not behind them in determination," wrote an editor for *Harper's Weekly*, "and are far ahead of them in men, money, and resources."[2] Still, the draft was challenging because it localized civilian enrollment. Though Massachusetts was among the wealthier and more industrial states, Andrew feared that both conscription and paying for substitutes would deplete its pool of workers. But Count Gurowski suggested a remedy:

> What the Senate could not do, the *United Governors* may do, if they have the moral courage to shake at the formula. The governors may declare united or separately, to Mr. Lincoln, that the country is in danger, that there is no time to stand upon formulas, that if he Lincoln sees not the imminent danger, the people & the governors see it, that before Congress meets, irreparable disasters may occur. . . . It is the duty of the governors to save the country's cause in spite of the faults & the predilections of the president.[3]

Though Andrew was doing all he could to save the country, he also focused on the suffering on his own doorstep, almost always donating his own money to assist people such as the widow Mary Sherburn, who had appealed to him for aid. In addition, he persisted in the search for his friend Charles Chandler, still missing in Virginia. General Hooker reported that the major's fate was "involved in mystery," as he was rumored to be alive but could not be located.[4]

The governor welcomed federal assistance to attract volunteers but was averse to public conscription, which he saw not only as dishonorable but also as bureaucratic chaos that would delay getting men to the front. He wired Lincoln in early August, emphasizing the need for immediate action: "the iron is hot; strike quick." Andrew assured the president that the people wanted nothing more than "assurance from Washington that [the] enemy shall be conquered and right vindicated at all hazards by all means."[5] Yet three days later, he was complaining that the lack of a federal disbursing officer and a federal paymaster were delaying his ability to get his new regiments off to war. "Everybody here is alive," he told Lincoln. "Men swarm our camps. . . . We will raise regiments until you cry hold! But why not turn over the funds to me, and we will disburse and account for them, and stop delays." In response, Lincoln authorized him to track down the missing federal officials and tell them "that if they do not work quickly I will make quick work with them."[6] This was not the solution he was looking for from the president.

As Andrew cut through the bureaucracy, the state's public squares and commons filled with white military tents, housing for the volunteers who would join the existing three years' regiments as well as recruits for the three new regiments that were readying to join Pope's army. The *Lowell Daily Citizen* reported that 1,000 men were enlisting per day. The governor hoped that these volunteers would be his leverage over Lincoln as he and other abolitionists watched the president move closer and closer to emancipating Confederate slaves. He had never stopped lobbying Lincoln on the matter, doing as much as he could to counter the Seward-McClellan influence, despite the Union's bitter losses.

As he often did, Andrew turned to God during such moments, and on August 10 he delivered a Sunday sermon to the Methodist Camp Meeting Association on Martha's Vineyard. Before 8,000 worshippers, he spoke for more than an hour, delivering the finest oration he ever made. He opened by challenging listeners to decide if their consciences would allow them to believe that God would permit racial prejudice to exist in the afterlife. He emphasized that God made no distinctions between rich and poor, Black and white, because he "made of one blood all nations of men, and he is no respecter of persons" but of souls. Andrew said that he had recently read a speech by an American general who had said say that he disliked and despised African Americans. "Well," said Andrew, "I could not help thinking, my dear fellow, what do you think is going to be done hereafter?"

> Do you know if we have all got to bear one color beyond the grave? Are you certain that God is going to whitewash the colored man and not to color you? Have you any controversy with God, because He painted His complexion black and bleached your own? I never dared, sinner that I am, I never dared—the instructions of my father, the monitions of my mother—I never dared to despise a man because he was humble, or because he was weak, or because he was poor, or because he was black.[7]

When the applause quieted, he repeated what became his most frequently quoted sentiment:

> I know not what record of sin awaits me in the world to come—I cannot tell. But this I do know, that I was never mean enough to despise any man because he was poor, because he was ignorant,—or because he was black. I have never believed it possible that this controversy should end, and Peace resume her sway, until that dreadful iniquity has been trodden beneath our feet. I believe it cannot, and I have noticed, my friends, . . . that, from the day our government turned its back on the proclamation of General Hunter, the blessing of God has been withdrawn from our arms.

Yet he commended his audience for holding fast to faith: "I believe that God rules above, and that he will rule in the hearts of men, and that, either with our aid or against it, he has determined to let the people go. . . . *The appointed hour has nearly come.* . . . I do not believe that this great investment of Providence is to be wasted."[8]

FIGURE 8. The governor of Massachusetts. Courtesy of Special Collections, Fine Arts Library, Harvard University.

Andrew's listeners were enthralled. "The brethren shouted 'glory' and 'amen' to my anti-slavery war views with great unction," he later wrote to Frank Howe. "You electrified us," said Sargent Prentiss. "You electrified me."[9] Spectators would talk of the speech for years to come. Several newspapers printed excerpts, and the *Boston Traveller* characterized it as a "grand and successful effort worthy of the man, the place and the occasion." Years later, Congressman Frederick Gillet quoted it during a debate about racial equality in the House of Representatives: "The most popular governor Massachusetts ever had touched the heart of our people when he said: 'I know not what record of sin awaits me in the world to come—I cannot tell—but this I do know, that I never was never mean enough to despise any man because he was poor, because he was ignorant, because he was poor,—or because he was black.'"[10]

Admirers were quick to send the governor their praise. A resident of South Hadley Falls declared that the people looked to him "to demand that our Brothers and sons shall not be wantonly sacrificed to the dictates of slavery." If Andrew wanted more volunteers, then he must continue to demand that the administration "strike at its cause" and fulfill his "noble declaration."[11] The reformer Harriet Green of Hopedale expressed her gratitude, saying that Andrew's words "electrified my soul":

> [There is] but one hope left for our poor bleeding distracted humanity, that God through his ascended angels will move the hearts of those who have been entrusted with the destinies of the progressive people and inspire them to enact justice. May they listen to the voice of Jehovah, who in thunder times is speaking in this golden hour, 'Let my people go free.'"[12]

The oration went on to have a long life in antislavery lore. But a mere four days later, some of that momentum reappeared in a lecture at the Massachusetts Historical Society given by the merchant George Livermore, an amateur historian and rare book collector. Livermore offered an articulate analysis of the African American connection to American politics and the military, arguing that, because the Founding Fathers had seen Black men as capable of fighting for independence, so should the Union. The press took little notice of the lecture, but listeners, including Edward Everett, were so impressed that they agreed to publish it as a pamphlet. Sumner gave Lincoln a copy, and legend has it that he may have consulted it while drafting his final emancipation proclamation. It is unclear if Andrew attended the lecture or if Sumner sent him a printed copy, but Livermore did inscribe a pamphlet to Andrew and later presented it to him.[13]

Providence and Altoona

Even though the president had concluded to move forward with emancipation and arming the slaves, he feared the political consequences of both measures. That the eastern armies continued to suffer defeat made it all the more worrisome. Too, as much as the president deliberated over the benefits of emancipation and the wisdom of using African Americans as soldiers to aid the war effort, he also understood there could be no retreat from such measures. Andrew surely understood this. His decision might translate into a heroic war effort, but it might not. Then, in mid-August, he hosted a group of African American leaders at the White House to discuss a government-financed colonization project in Central America, intended to be a haven for African Americans freed during the war. The conference was a way to prepare the public for what might lie ahead: emancipation and military service. Lincoln's motives were sincere, yet many radicals ridiculed the idea of colonization. In the *Liberator*, William Garrison called the meeting "a spectacle, as humiliating as it was extraordinary. Did not Mr. Lincoln state a falsehood when he said to the committee of colored men, 'But for the presence of your race in this country, there could have been no war?' Is the *presence* or the *condition* of the black race the cause of the war? Should he not have said, *but for the fact that your race are slaves, there could have been no war?*"[14] Andrew agreed. Undoing racial prejudice was a herculean undertaking that must begin not with relocating or liberating the slaves, but with freeing white minds of prejudice. God had no color line in his Christian army, he maintained, and neither should man.

A few days later Horace Greeley, the editor of the *New York Tribune*, published an open letter to the president titled "The Prayer of Twenty Millions." Arguing that the Union suffered from a "mistaken deference to Rebel Slavery," he called on Lincoln to listen to the 20 million northerners who wanted to crush both the rebellion and slavery. The president responded to Greeley's letter—clear evidence that the topic was on his mind—and explained the political, constitutional, and military courses he had followed. Though he emphasized the limitations of his office, he agreed that he should "correct errors when shown to be errors" and "adopt new views so fast as they shall appear to be true views." He wrote, "What I do about slavery, and the colored race, I do because I believe it helps to save the Union." Andrew would have added that, more than saving the Union, such actions would elevate humankind.[15]

On a practical level, however, the governor was still convinced that emancipating slaves would weaken the enemy and shorten the conflict. The War Department's regulations stipulated that "all able-bodied male citizens of the respective states" were to be enrolled in the militia of the United States. Already, the *Liberator* was arguing that "colored men are citizens of Massachusetts, which no one, I presume, will have the hardihood to deny, in as much as they are tax payers, voters, jurors, and eligible to office, and there is no inequality founded upon distinction of races known to our laws."[16] The racial divide was closing in the Commonwealth, and Andrew had worked hard to make this happen. Now the war was giving him the opportunity to close the divide in more significant ways, He fired off a wire to Stanton: "As the hope rises of vigorous, large, bold and hopeful policy, so rises the enthusiasm of the people."[17] The time had come to act, and the governor summoned Edward Kinsley, a prominent Boston abolitionist and merchant, to the statehouse for an important mission. Kinsley found Andrew standing at a tall desk, shirt sleeves rolled up and signing papers with ink-stained fingers. The governor turned to greet him, placed a hand on Kinsley's shoulder, and said, "I want you to go to Washington." Kinsley demurred, saying he had personal business to attend to and suggesting that Andrew should go instead. The governor retorted, "Never mind about business. If we are not to have a country, business is of no importance. I command you to go. There is something going on. This is a momentous time." He then surprised Kinsley. "Ned, do you believe in prayer?" he asked. "Why, of course," said Kinsley. "Then let us kneel down and pray," said Andrew. The two knelt by a chair, and Andrew began speaking aloud. "I never heard such a prayer in all my life," recalled Kinsley. "I never was so near the throne of God, except when my mother died, as I was then." When they rose, tears were streaming down Andrew's cheeks. He said he wanted Kinsley to talk to the president about emancipation.

Kinsley left for Washington that afternoon. Once there, he met with Sumner and explained his mission, and the senator counseled him to secure an interview with the president. That evening Kinsley visited the White House. He told Lincoln about his conversation with Andrew and assured him that New Englanders were ready for emancipation, a statement that "visibly affected" the president. After a brief silence, Kinsley repeated Andrew's prayer as well as he could. After another pause, Lincoln said, "I do not mind your going back and saying to Governor Andrew, if the Lord God Omnipotent will give us one grand victory, I am persuaded to issue a proclamation of Emancipation; but don't tell Sumner." The president continued: "When we have the Governor of Massachusetts to send us troops in the way he has, and when we have him to utter such prayers for us, I have no doubt that we shall succeed."[18]

According to Kinsley, he then returned to Boston and told Andrew about Lincoln's response, saying that the president was waiting for a decisive victory before announcing emancipation. But the weary governor had trouble dredging up enthusiasm for yet another long wait. Losing had become painfully routine. He spent hours in the "plain three-story brick building where he reside[d]" composing sorrowful letters to the family members of fallen soldiers, devoting "his whole soul" to the task. During fighting at Cedar Mountain, Virginia, that August, the Union army was again defeated, and Andrew wrote a letter to the parents of Captain Edward Abbott of the Second Massachusetts, repeating the mournful words he had so often shared with other bereaved families: "I think you will always have a right to remember, with the pride equaled by parental love, that our inheritance in a Commonwealth is made richer and nobler by the memories of such dear and brave boys of Massachusetts, whose young lives, consecrated even to death, were beautiful testimonies of the preciousness of our birthright and the worth of liberty."[19]

By late August, Andrew's spirit was flagging. Letters poured into the statehouse, most of them despairing. John Emery of Harwich told him that many coastal residents had lost faith in the federal government, despite his inspiring words: "[They] don't believe it is earnest and hardly think it is worth fighting for."[20] Nonetheless, the governor continued to recruit, determined to avoid a draft, and he mandated that businesses close in the afternoon for several days to assist him. On August 27, he spoke at a mass meeting on Boston Common: "Men in other days and times have fought for kingdoms. You fight, each man for himself. Men in other lands may fight for crowns. Each man here fights for the crown of his own honor and the ensign of his own dignity and power." Yet he reminded his listeners that the meeting was not about speeches but about work and said that, even though he had the power to draft men into the state militia, he refused to embarrass the state by relying upon it.[21]

With Pope's defeat at the Second Battle of Bull Run in late August (28–30), rumors began to spread that McClellan would replace him, if for no other reason than to restore the army's shattered morale. This heightened the radicals' acrimony and further demoralized Andrew. The *Newburyport Herald* declared that "certainly we have come to the most serious hour of the whole war."[22] The Union's performance in the field had not equaled the North's sacrifices; change was urgently necessary. Andrew knew that Lincoln had come to see emancipation as a war measure, but he was exasperated by the president's reluctance to announce that decision. As he worked to recruit, the governor employed incentives, appealed to local pride, and used his own funds to assist families. But "unless a new life is breathed into the govt at Washington," he told Count Gurowski, "our efforts will be in vain."[23] Andrew was aware that most northerners cared little about slavery unless Black men could be armed to shorten the war and save white lives. Though he feared that battlefield losses would translate into electoral defeat in the fall, he pressed onward. But, as he told Gurowski, if Lincoln reinstated McClellan as commander, the cause was lost. "I am sadly but firmly trying to help organize some movement, if possible to save the Pres[ident] from the infamy of ruining his country."[24]

Now, with Rhode Island's governor William Sprague, he called a September meeting of New England governors, using Brown University's commencement festivities in Providence as a pretext. At about this time, he also received an invitation from Pennsylvania's governor, Andrew Curtin, to join a September gubernatorial gathering in Altoona. Both meetings would bring northern governors together to consider how to push the federal government forward on emancipation. Andrew planned to attend both gatherings, and other governors were also eager to take part. Maine's governor, Israel Washburn, Jr., declared that it was "time for the states to speak to the federal govt" and asked, "Does any man suppose we can ever live with the South & slavery, after all that has happened?"[25] In the meantime, Charles Gould of New York's National War Committee wrote to Andrew, saying that colleagues on the committee had called on him to petition the governors to meet in council and "point out the remedy" for the problems facing the Lincoln administration.[26]

By September, the press had grown rowdier in its anger over the war, and readers had taken notice. "We are drifting before the storm of revolution," John D. Andrews wrote to Andrew from Washington, "and gradually nearing the shoals of anxiety through treason, ignorance, & imbecility. We are as gloomy as this night."[27] In the days before the Providence meeting, Andrew excoriated the administration. He wired Stanton:

It nearly drives me *mad* when I see the American armies running before a generation of scoundrels, and American liberty almost prostrate before a power which challenges government itself, outrages humanity, and defies God. God only knows whether the President will ever burst his bonds of Border-Stateism and McClellan, but the people somehow are blessed with an instinct of faith, before which, I believe, mountains themselves will move.[28]

Brown University's commencement exercises took place on September 3. After the ceremony, Andrew, Sprague, and Washburn adjourned to the City Hotel, along with Governor William Buckingham of Connecticut and Charles Gould, Prosper Wetmore, and Nehemiah Knight of the National War Committee. The focus of their conversation was slave enlistment, the draft, and current military operations. To foil the press, however, they pretended that the meeting's main objective was to secure quota credit for naval servicemen. Before they adjourned, the governors deputized John Hamilton, John Stevens, Jr., John Williams, and Nehemiah Knight, all of New York, to present the meeting's conclusions about abandoning the Union's conciliatory war aims to Lincoln. The men did so, but their insulting tone angered the president. Nonetheless, like it or not, he now had the governors' views.[29]

Andrew returned to the Massachusetts statehouse to learn that Pope's army had suffered more than 10,000 casualties in its loss at the Second Battle of Bull Run. Even worse, Lincoln had reinstated McClellan, just as General Lee was heading north. As Andrew prepared for the meeting in Altoona on September 24, he also read several dispiriting letters from Washington. "We are rapidly being driven by the storm of events," wrote John D. Andrews. "Stanton is doing his best, but is not sustained. I know not what we are to do. In times of national emergencies, time is fate."[30] Count Gurowski, however, wrote to say that he agreed with Andrew's assessment of Stanton, calling the war secretary "the last true Roman, not in rhetoric, but in the noblest meaning. If the people will be saved, it will not be by Lincoln, Seward, or McClellan."[31]

In the meantime, Andrew traveled to New York City to confer with Thurlow Weed, General Hunter, and others about organizing "loyal blacks" in the South Carolina and Georgia sea islands into a Union regiment. Hunter had begun the enterprise in March 1862 after the Union had captured enough territory in Georgia, Florida, and South Carolina. Stanton had established a new Department of the South with headquarters in Port Royal and dispatched members of the Freedman's

Inquiry Commission to the area. Several Bostonians had taken the lead in establishing humanitarian and educational services. Hunter spent months struggling to raise men, without financial or political support. Finally, in August, he gave up the idea and went on leave. Yet even as he was losing heart, the climate in Washington appeared to be changing in his favor. Declining white enlistment and the recent passage of the militia and confiscation acts had encouraged Lincoln to modify his position on Black soldiers, and by late in the month he quietly permitted the creation of a South Carolina regiment drawn from the sea island region. On August 25, Stanton authorized General Rufus Saxton, a Greenfield native who was serving as the military governor of the Department of the South, to enroll and pay 5,000 Black men to protect settlements occupied by the Union army, though they would be designated as laborers rather than soldiers. Andrew lobbied Saxton to offer his friend Thomas Wentworth Higginson the new command, and Saxton did so in October. Of course, there was backlash about the move, but Andrew hailed it as a signature step in the revolution he was now openly pursuing.[32]

In September, General Lee's Army of Northern Virginia crossed the Potomac River and marched through Maryland toward the Pennsylvania state line, throwing citizens into a panic. In the meantime, the national press was highlighting the growing call for meetings among Union governors. Frank Blair, Sr., wrote to Andrew, saying that he had faith in the army but it needed a decisive battle to "crush the disaffected." The North, he declared, should "proclaim universal emancipation and may *justly* do it as the only guaranty for the maintenance of the Govt. rescued from the conspirators."[33] Governor David Tod of Ohio wired Stanton that Governor Curtin had invited him to the Altoona meeting and asked if he had suggestions for topics. Lincoln and Stanton had already known about the meeting, and were likely apprehensive about it, but the secretary merely replied that he hoped "the counsels may be wise and productive of good." Andrew, however, viewed the Altoona conference as an opportunity to give Washington an ultimatum. He was not alone: most of the governors saw it as an opportunity to convince the president to adopt more vigorous war measures.[34]

A clash loomed in Maryland between Lee's and McClellan's forces, but Lincoln still showed no exterior signs of moving toward emancipation. As Andrew planned for Altoona and anxiously awaited news from the front, he also kept busy with other war matters. He sent train cars loaded with medical supplies to Baltimore in anticipation of a bloodbath. Although the Republican State Convention had convened in Worcester on September 10, Andrew had no time for politics. Yet his name remained at the forefront of the party. The *Daily Advertiser* sang his praises, citing a convention member who compared Andrew's fight for emancipation to "a rifled cannon—as an instrument for accomplishing an end."[35] Republicans renominated Andrew for their gubernatorial candidate and resolved that Sumner should be recommended to the next legislature for reelection. At the same time, however, conservative Republicans and many Democrats were issuing a call for a new People's Party, whose members were expected to pledge unconditional support for the president but not an expansion of war aims. For a few days the movement gained steam and even the support of the *Springfield Republican*. The party's main argument for coming into existence was that Sumner and Andrew had embarrassed the president.[36]

By dawn on September 17, Bostonians were reading early reports of McClellan's glorious victory in Sharpsburg, Maryland. "Happily our soldiers, inspired with hope by the very name of their general, have been led to victory," crowed the *Daily Advertiser*. "The spell of defeat is broken; the chain of misfortune is at an end, and success smiles once more upon our colors."[37] Then telegrams began pouring into the statehouse, describing a "great battle" near Sharpsburg, along meandering Antietam Creek, one with unimaginable carnage. By day's end, premature reports of victory had ceded to tales of slaughter. On the evening of September 18, Lee's army had retreated across the Potomac into Virginia, and McClellan gained the victory. Nonetheless, the horrific battle stunned the North. Thousands of Massachusetts soldiers had fought at Sharpsburg, and the catastrophic losses immediately affected the state's recruiting efforts. Newspapers shied away from printing the gory details and simply listed deaths, thus focusing on local loss rather than national victory. The Battle of Antietam was the single bloodiest day of the war, and the Commonwealth had suffered heavy casualties. Of the six hundred men of the Fifteenth Massachusetts, only a reported 134 were found in the smoldering aftermath. Moreover, despite McClellan's apparent victory, Lee's army had not been destroyed. In fact, Harpers Ferry, an important river and rail nexus, was back in enemy hands.[38]

That McClellan had not lost the battle gave Lincoln the opportunity to justify the emancipation of Confederate slaves. The proclamation had lain in his desk for two months, and now, on September 22, the president made it public. He announced that he was giving the rebellious states one hundred days to return to the Union. Failure to do so would result in the forfeiture of their slaves, who would be declared free. The Emancipation Proclamation had to be couched as a war measure, for, in truth, Union troops occupying Confederate soil had already been emancipating slaves.

When Lincoln made his announcement, Andrew was in Philadelphia waiting for Governor Washburn and Governor Buckingham to arrive so that the three could board a train for Altoona. He immediately wired his secretary with the news:

> The Proclamation of Emancipation is out. It is a poor document, but a mighty act; slow, somewhat halting, wrong in its delay till January, but grand and sublime after all. "Prophets and kings" have waited for this day, but died without the sight. Our Republicans must make it *their* business to sustain this act of Lincoln, and we will drive the "conservatism" of a pro-slavery hunkerism and reactionaries of despotism into the very caves and holes of earth. We can knock the bottom out of the hunker "citizens" movement before ten days are gone. . . . Our cause is bright if we are true.[39]

Finally, he believed, Lincoln, was showing signs of carrying forth John Brown's crusade.

Andrew took great pride in knowing he had been part of the small chorus who had helped push the administration toward this moment. It was not that Lincoln and Andrew were antagonists in this crusade but that each man's temperament and executive position designed a different path toward the mutual goal. Possibly, the governors' upcoming meeting at Altoona had prodded the president into releasing the proclamation, yet Antietam occurred before. After all, with the election approaching, it was better for him to upstage the governors than to have them publicly force his hand. Now they could use the meeting as a way to consolidate their support for this new war measure. Of course, such reasoning would have political consequences in the coming election.

On September 24, the governors gathered in Altoona. They immediately secluded themselves, talking long into the evening and again the next morning. The group discussed an array of war issues, and Andrew and Curtin were asked to prepare resolutions for the president, to be delivered personally. Andrew shared with his colleagues a letter from New York attorney James Hamilton, which had been waiting for him in Altoona. Hamilton wrote that, weeks earlier, Lincoln had asked him to draft a proclamation that would authorize the president to use the army to confiscate and free slaves. Hamilton had been in Washington, prepared to deliver his draft, when Lincoln sent forth his proclamation.

Hamilton was sharing this knowledge now, in hopes that it might be useful to the governors.

According to Governor Curtin, Andrew drafted the group's resolutions that evening, with Curtin by his side, making suggestions. When the task was finished, Andrew "arose and walked the floor nervously. Both of us felt keenly the weight of the tremendous results that would follow our action." The two asked Maryland's governor, William Bradford, to edit the resolutions into an address that could be wired to the president, and he did so, though he would not agree to accompany the pair to Washington. In the end, the governors simply pledged their support for emancipation and for Lincoln. After receiving the telegraph, the president sent a communiqué to Andrew: "The Emancipation Proclamation has been promulgated. Come to Washington for further conference."[40]

Critics of the governors compared them to the Jacobins, the radical group formed in the wake of the French Revolution. Yet several newspapers came to their rescue. The *Daily Advertiser* dryly noted, "The convention of the governors has come and has gone, and still the republic lives."[41] At Lincoln's invitation, perhaps to strengthen nation-state relations, members arrived at the White House in the early afternoon of September 26, and Andrew began reading the address aloud. The president thanked the governors for their support, acknowledging that they had been key to his decision to issue the Emancipation Proclamation. Without aides or reporters present, he explained why he had waited to announce it until after Sharpsburg. The conversation then turned to the ongoing mobilization, and governors made several requests, which Lincoln promised he would consider. Still, he remained reluctant in authorizing Andrew to raise African American regiments. More deliberation and timing were key in advancing this front.[42]

Andrew was disappointed by that restriction, and he was concerned about the future. Reading the news, daily reports, and soldiers' letters had given him a chance to gauge public sentiment about the proclamation. Clearly, many soldiers applauded the new war measures, and Massachusetts continued to be a leading antislavery state. Yet with an election looming, Republican prospects at the federal level were gloomy as many voters and soldiers did not support emancipation. Even Commonwealth voters were disturbed. Timothy Emerton of the Eleventh Massachusetts wrote to his sister and his niece from Alexandria, Virginia: "If ever you write to me and mention niggers. I won't answer your letter. Dam a nigger. I would shoot one as quick as I would eat."[43] "I suppose you feel stronger about the freedom of Negroes than

I do," Captain Henry Russell of the Second Massachusetts wrote to his parents in Cambridge. "I want to use the emancipation to help in whipping the south, but I do not want to whip the south merely for the purpose of freeing the slaves."[44] The measure was intended to weaken the Confederate war effort, even as Andrew considered it a step in lessening white resistance to African Americans. But even though Andrew hoped that oppositionists such as Captain Russell would see Lincoln's move as a way to hasten the end of the war, it was becoming difficult to sell the idea of replenishing the ranks with white soldiers in order to liberate slaves. In the aftermath of the proclamation, Andrew and Sumner faced opposition from Democratic opponents but also from conservatives in their own party. The two were seen as "giants to be slain," punishment for having goaded the president into adopting emancipation.[45]

Every year Massachusetts seemed to undergo what the *New York Tribune* called an "Annual Spasm" for a new political party: "Several hundred gentlemen issue a call, . . . several hundred gentlemen nominate, in convention, a State ticket, [and] . . . upon election day, several hundred men vote for that ticket. And that is the last you hear of the matter!"[46] In October 1862, this spasm took the form of the prowar People's Convention, which lured Democrats and discontented conservative Republicans into a short-lived endorsement of Lincoln's conservative war. The move was a shameless attempt to unseat Sumner and Andrew, not only because the two opposed slavery but also because their policies were now the nation's policies. Members chose Charles Adams, Jr., then Lincoln's minister to the court of Saint James, to run against Sumner and nominated a reluctant Charles Devens, Jr., who owed his brigadier generalship to Andrew, to run for governor. Andrew himself was too busy governing to campaign and had to rely on his war record as proof of his fitness for reelection.[47]

The Emancipation Proclamation became an odd convention platform for the People's Party. Before Lincoln had announced it, members had pledged to support his conciliatory approach, but now they had to back a radical decree. In response to this difficulty, they launched a defamation campaign against Andrew—what Garrison called "Hell from beneath." The conservative *Boston Courier* went so far as to publish libelous allegations against the governor. Yet Andrew remained calm; if his record was not enough to reelect him, then he preferred to be defeated. When delegates at the Republican State Convention nominated him unanimously for another term, he held his ground, declaring in his acceptance speech, "If emancipation is deemed an evil by the rebel states, then let the first day of January find them peaceable, loyal and submissive to their duties." Should they choose to remain at war with the Union, then he would consecrate himself to the task at hand: "[I will] stand in my lot, wherever it may be cast, as a faithful servant of a cause whose service is its own reward."[48]

Still, conservatives continued to spread rumors about underhanded doings at the Altoona conference. In a letter to Daniel Henshaw, a conservative Boston lawyer, Andrew justified his participation: "The meeting was one which, whether as citizens or magistrates, we had a right to hold." Though his enemies claimed that he had interfered in Lincoln's decisions about McClellan, Andrew responded that "I did not either formally or informally, directly or indirectly, at any time, move or suggest that the governors should interfere with the position of Major Genl. McClellan or any other officer of the army or navy."[49] As that letter appeared in the press, Andrew's Bird Club colleague, William Robinson, countered with "A Conspiracy to Defame John A. Andrew," intended to publicly expose the ludicrousness of such rumors. The journalist Warrington believed that Andrew had no need to defend his actions: "If he has been peripatetic, it has been for a useful and noble purpose." In Warrington's view, New York and Boston conservatives and the proslavery press were defaming the governor, and he was determined to expose their plot.[50]

Reelection and Emancipation

On November 4, Andrew was in Washington when voters reelected him governor of Massachusetts. Likewise, the state legislature remained steadfastly behind Sumner and would return him to the Senate. Despite the "malignant hostility" of men who hated Andrew and Sumner because they hated slavery, the victory felt even more significant than it had the previous year.[51] According to the *Saturday Evening Post*, Andrew won by a margin of more than 25,000 votes, essentially ending any serious conservative opposition. Not only was his reelection a testament to his leadership, but it also convinced him that he was doing God's work. He had spent his entire life advancing justice, and voters had repeatedly witnessed his compassion and moral strength. In his mind, the victory belonged to everyone who had come to embrace the mandates of justice—who knew that the war was more than an opportunity to preserve the Union. He was jubilant. As he told Frank Blair, Sr., "We have gained the most splendid political victory known in our history, to which even that of 1860 will not compare in importance."[52]

With the election behind him, Andrew returned his attention to practical matters. He was eager to improve soldier welfare in the field and veteran welfare at home. Given the overwhelming casualties at Antietam, he insisted on reorganizing the state's military surgical department to improve efficiency and care after combat. The need for such changes was crucial, so much so that the supplemental surgeons he had sent to Sharpsburg after the battle had united in a written remonstrance to the War Department. Andrew devoted entire days to researching European methods of triage and battle care so he could adapt them to his regiments' needs. The head of a hospital ward wrote to him from Frederick, Maryland, excoriating the standard treatment of the wounded and the dead:

> As soon as the patient breathes his last, the bunk on which he rests is carried to the dead house and the undertaker . . . comes without delay and the body is taken in the very sheets on which he died and placed in the coffin with all the filth which has accumulated, the sheets thrown over him and the box is nailed up . . . and thrust into the hearse and without even a flag thrown over him to mark that a Union soldier is passing to his long home. He is carried to a ditch and [deposited?] there, and the hearse returns for another victim. This is the end of those brave fellows who have periled all in defense of this Great and Glorious Union.

Such descriptions made Andrew's blood boil. Equally maddening were problems with soldiers' pay, which was routinely late or missing altogether. The matter was so galling that he considered appealing to the state legislature for funds. Indeed, Henry Bowditch used the *Daily Advertiser* to solicit funds for soldiers and their families who had not been paid for several months.[53]

Now that Lincoln had issued his proclamation, it remained to be seen how the transition from slavery to freedom would materialize, especially in the regions unoccupied by Union soldiers. Liberating slaves in the states where secessionists had erected the institution would be problematic, to say the least, and Andrew worried that continuing racial prejudice would damage their freedom. He had been working on a plan with General John Dix regarding temporary asylum for the 2,000 to 3,000 runaway and abandoned "colored men, women, and children" currently encamped at Fort Monroe. Dix wanted to send them north, not only because they were vulnerable to a Confederate attack but also because their wretched condition embarrassed the Lincoln administration. So shameful was their situation, he reported, that some had even returned to their owners. Charles Wilder of the American Missionary Association served as the contraband superintendent at Fort Monroe, and he explained these problems in a meeting with Senator Wilson, Frank Bird, and Andrew. All viewed the relocation program as a humanitarian response to a military crisis, yet some members of the press were framing it as Dix's attempt to promote African American migration north.[54]

While Andrew was in Washington, he appealed for the discharge of the permanently invalided Massachusetts soldiers who were crowding the city's hospitals and discussed Dix's refugee relocation proposal with Stanton. Both men were reluctant to offer asylum to the refugees, chiefly because of concerns about northern prejudice. Despite his humanitarian inclinations, Andrew understood the political and cultural realities of such an enterprise, and he knew that Massachusetts conservatives were anxious. The greatest obstacle to abolition, he had so often argued, were white people's preconceptions about African Americans, and these would be impossible to legislate away. In a letter to Dr. Le Baron Russell, a leading member of the Educational Commission for Freedmen, he suggested that it would be better for the refugees to stay in the South. In the meantime, he asked Dr. Russell to consult with General Rufus Saxton, the Union officer supervising African American laborers in the islands off the South Carolina and Georgia coasts.

After returning to Boston the governor explained to General Dix's envoy, John Bolles, "that the motives of humanity" had persuaded him that the refugees needed to stay where they were:

> For them to come here for encampment or asylum would be to come as paupers and sufferers into a strange land and a climate trying even to its habitués, as a swarm of homeless wanderers, migrating . . . to a busy community where they would be incapable of self help—a course certain to demoralize themselves and endanger others . . . [while giving] a handle to all traitors and to all persons evilly disposed.

Andrew knew that anti-abolitionists would say that emancipation "had failed; that negroes were proved worthless and incapable of taking care of themselves." But he rationalized, "It is precisely because I do not wish the negroes to suffer, precisely because I would save their wives and children from perishing; precisely because I do not wish their new freedom to become license, corruption, and infamy that I respectfully decline to aid or countenance your plan for their transportation North."[55]

Andrew shared these views with Alexander Bullock, the president of the Republican State Convention. He predicted that emancipation would open the South to white laborers and "beckon back to the shores of the Gulf, to their natural climate and its attractions, social and industrial, the poor refugees from slavery now among us." Competition between southern African Americans and laborers "here at home would thus be ended by enabling the "colored man to live as a freeman in his own home." Optimistically, he declared that "the hatreds and prejudices of race will melt away when consciousness of injustice shall cease to engender them, and when the freedom to migrate according to natural attractions, the instincts of race, and the interests of individuals, shall render possible the separation of all those who may be mutually repugnant."[56]

Andrew appeared to be caught between his party's political and moral factions, but he stood by his decision, even as critics charged him with hypocrisy for advocating the use of slaves as soldiers to make up for quota shortages. Yet he remained concerned about the refugees' plight and planned to share those concerns with Congress when it convened in December. For now, public hostility to African American migration continued, and Dix dropped the plan altogether. Still, the question remained: what should states do with former slaves if they should come north? As Andrew and others wrestled with the question, some members of the press alleged that Dr. Russell had pinpointed the true cause of the refugees' suffering: the government owed them more than $60,000 for their labor. Andrew shared this finding with Stanton, who ordered the men to be paid immediately.[57]

Andrew visited Washington frequently in the fall of 1862, and each time he left dispirited. Some of this had to do with the ever-caustic Count Gurowski, who peppered him with depressing gossip. The count had been dismissed from his post as translator shortly after Antietam for, among other things, criticizing the administration, but he continued to assail the governor with his assessment of Lincoln's cabinet. He also pestered Andrew for the names of wealthy contacts who might fund the publication of his diary. Amid such distractions, Andrew kept his focus on the field and news from the officers, and that, too, was dispiriting. Horace Sargent of the First Massachusetts Cavalry wrote to him from camp near Warrenton, Virginia: "This people hate us with a condensed hatred. . . . One of three courses is necessary; either give up the attempt to subjugate them to the law; or, . . . change the population; or, . . . make it safe for them to show fealty & most infernally perilous for them not to do it." Sargent argued that Virginia must be subdued by occupation and devastation because, for every one convert to the Union cause, the federals were creating ten hate-filled enemies.[58]

It was no secret that northern voters were unhappy with the army's lackluster progress; they had made this clear at the polls. Several commanders, including McClellan, had not lived up to expectations, and Andrew welcomed Lincoln's decision to again remove the commander. General Ambrose Burnside now assumed the helm of the demoralized Army of the Potomac. But McClellan's dismissal was a blow to the soldiers, and Burnside proved to be even less capable than his predecessor. At the same time General Nathaniel Banks was appointed commander of the Department of the Gulf in New Orleans, a change that infuriated Benjamin Butler. The Union occupation of New Orleans was popular with radical northerners, who applauded the punitive treatment of southerners, but it enraged Jefferson Davis. Declaring Butler a felon and an outlaw, the Confederate president promised to execute the general if he were ever caught. Moreover, Davis declared that African American soldiers captured in arms against the Confederacy would be returned to their enslavers and the federal officers serving with them would be executed.

In November, Burnside prepared an offensive against Lee's army, which was concentrated along the Rappahannock River, fifty miles north of Richmond. But Andrew remained despondent about the growing casualty lists and the demoralized recruitment. As Thanksgiving approached, so did colder days, and battlefield prospects became gloomier. In Boston, Andrew's old friend Lewis Hayden, now working as a messenger for the secretary of state's office, recognized that the governor was in a melancholy state of mind. So he and his wife invited Andrew to join them for Thanksgiving, along with more than twenty other guests. Heartened by the gesture, the governor accepted and ate his holiday meal in the Haydens' "grim-looking brick house" on Phillips Street, a place he had long known well. As a *Boston Herald* reporter wrote years later, that house had "gathered rich and poor, statesman and philosopher, master and slave. Its old walls ha[d] witnessed the birth of many a plot to strike the shackles from the weak in their unequal struggle against iron-hearted monsters."[59] For Andrew, it was an abolitionist shrine: a safe house along the Underground Railroad, a sanctuary for freedom. It was also a familiar and homey resting place. When asked if it was true that the governor would dine at the Hayden house, a local African American barber replied, "I reckon it's so. Lewis Hayden ain't a mite proud. He'd just as soon set down and eat with a governor as with anybody else."[60]

At dinner that evening, Andrew and Hayden, along with his guests, discussed the enlistment of African American regiments to fight for the Union, an idea that both men had long endorsed and that several Massachusetts officers had been publicly promoting for more than a year. Hayden was convinced that freed African Americans, from both the North and the South, would be willing to fight in a war that had given birth to emancipation. Andrew wholly agreed. William Brown and Robert Morris, both Black abolitionists who were in attendance, thought that such regiments should be officered by African Americans, arguing that men would not enlist without this condition. Andrew applauded the notion but knew that African American officer commissions would be a bridge too far, especially given that the army contained no existing Black officers and had no mandates to provide them. Such a radical proposition would be not only wildly unpopular but also unconstitutional, even though the War Department had made no distinction in color when summoning volunteers for Lincoln's August call. The Militia Act allowed the president to receive persons of African descent into the military. Andrew explained that, for the War Department to authorize the enterprise, it would be best if white officers commanded the men, at least initially; it would be hard enough to find enough white officers willing to take on such a role. Hayden agreed but argued that competent African American soldiers should be promoted when they deserved it. Before Andrew left that evening, he promised Hayden he would seek federal permission to form a regiment as soon as the Emancipation Proclamation went into effect in January.[61]

The friendship between Andrew and Hayden reflected their shared dedication to treating plain people, white or Black, with decency and justice. But the governor knew that African American enlistment depended on Stanton and Lincoln. It was ironic that while the administration considered the venture as a defensive gesture to aid the military, Andrew considered it a measure toward justice and a more perfect Union. As Congress reconvened in Washington that December, eager to find a formula to end the war, the Boston papers raved about the Port Royal community's educational success. Now Andrew was cogitating over possibilities for economic self-sufficiency that could pull slaves out of bondage into freedom. He understood the practical relevance of establishing economic independence before political independence—the precondition to true freedom.[62]

CHAPTER 17

SLAVES NO MORE

December 1862–May 1863

They Must Fight or Be Slaves

As the winter nights lengthened in Boston, the city's African American residents were counting the days until January 1, when Lincoln's proclamation would emancipate all of the slaves in the rebellious states. There was still a month to go; and now, at noon on December 1, as the thirty-seventh Congress's closing session commenced, the legislature prepared to listen to Lincoln's address on emancipation and the path forward. Seventy days had passed since he had issued his ultimatum to the Confederacy. Now he encouraged Americans to "think and act anew," to cast off "the dogmas of the quiet past" that were "inadequate to the stormy present." The Union depended on Americans' ability to weather the storm. The moment had arrived to "nobly save, or meanly lose the last best, hope of earth." To be sure, Lincoln had grown with the movement.[1]

Four days later, the Massachusetts Committee of the Whole Council released the official electoral tally. Andrew had received 79,835 votes, the largest victory in state history and a confirmation of his overwhelming popularity. Even critics of his administration or his abolitionism could not dampen voters' confidence in their governor. Now, as winter settled in and a clash between Burnside's and Lee's troops loomed in Virginia, Andrew still resisted Lincoln's August call for a draft to meet his quota and postponed the mid-December date in order to give his citizens the opportunity to enlist freely. Though the Union troops were making important progress on the western fronts, both Andrew and the president were focused on the threat nearest to Washington. Field reports predicted a titanic battle. Thousands of Massachusetts soldiers were serving in Burnside's ranks, and Confederate soldiers were digging themselves firmly into Virginia soil, resolved to avenge their loss at Antietam.

On December 11, Burnside's army began crossing the foggy Rappahannock River to Fredericksburg, and by mid-morning the Union artillery had positioned itself to open fire on the city. Busy preparing for his upcoming inaugural address, Andrew still found time to read every telegram about the battle. As the day progressed, the dispatches clearly portrayed yet another Union debacle. Over the next few days Burnside's army was soundly thrashed, and initial reports indicated that there were more than 12,000 Union casualties. "It cannot be concealed that we have met with a severe disappointment in the failure of our troops' entrenchments behind Fredericksburg," wrote the editor of the *Daily Advertiser*. "It is a bitter disappointment." Even worse, reported the editor, Burnside had been aware of the impossibility of attacking and taking the enemy's position. A disastrous retreat ensued, and Burnside sent a flag of truce across the river to retrieve the Union wounded.[2]

Two days after the battle ended on December 15, another bombshell exploded in the Washington press. Thirty-two Republican senators were rumored to have colluded to force Lincoln to change his cabinet. Seward's baleful influence on the president was cited as the cause. Certainly, it was no secret that the cabinet members had little affinity for one another. Though the president defused the issue, Andrew found the machinations in Washington hard to bear, given his more pressing problems. His soldiers needed comfort and encouragement. There were wounded to heal, regiments to replenish, and no rest in sight.[3]

In a winter fraught with misery, Andrew committed himself to the unpopular task of meeting his recruitment quota. Yet he had long maintained that the war was larger than the battlefield, and he could not stop worrying about the African American families who would be transitioning from slavery to freedom. Without the ability to sustain themselves economically, they would be vulnerable. He pressed Sumner to spearhead a new venture designed to assist them and suggested that Stanton should assign an assistant to oversee an organization to supervise the transition. These matters may not have been "brilliant things," he told Sumner, but they would be of "immense value, if accomplished."[4] He referred the senator to Dr. Russell, who had already been working with General Dix, suggesting that he be asked to investigate the freed slaves' conditions near Fort Monroe. Other allies were also pressing Sumner on the issue, among them James McKim, a Presbyterian minister and abolitionist from Pennsylvania. The senator brought the idea to Stanton, who favored it, and a few weeks later the Freedman's Inquiry Commission was founded as a federal board under the direction of Samuel Howe, Robert Owen, and James McKaye. Its purpose was to investigate the status of the slaves about to be freed by the Emancipation Proclamation and to ascertain how best to help them become economically independent. This organization would eventually expand to become the Freedman's Bureau.[5]

That Lincoln used emancipation as war measure was not in question for Andrew, but he also believed that enlisting African Americans would lessen northern aversion to their enfranchisement into civil society. It would be a risky but significant step toward racial equality. When Andrew and Sumner pressed Stanton about arming freed slaves, the secretary told them that he and Lincoln both believed that the Union would have 200,000 African Americans under arms before the following June. Stanton's openness to the idea was good news, though election results around the North made Andrew wary. Conservatives had reasserted themselves, and New York State was a particular concern, with the Democrat Horatio Seymour as the incoming governor. Still, Andrew felt the country had reached a tipping point. "We are not living in the same century now in which Pierce and Buchanan reigned," he told Sumner. "No matter how much critics may blow and fume about it, the house will go up, under the hands of mechanics who wield the tools. That is our case. The Hunkers are powerless scolds—nothing more."[6]

Andrew spent the last days of December preparing for his inaugural address to the General Court. He pored over military documents and examined papers related to the state's expansion of higher education. He was delighted to sign the charter that established the new Massachusetts Agricultural College, part of a federal effort to promote the liberal and practical education of the industrial classes. Although he had initially suggested expanding Harvard to include the new college, trustees had convinced him to support a separate university. He had been a guiding hand in the choice of Amherst as the most suitable location.[7]

The Union defeat at the Battle of Fredericksburg had dampened holiday spirits, and Boston was quiet on New Year's Eve. For the city's African Americans, however, the midnight hour was more than the end of another year. For them it signaled the end of "thraldom and ushered in countless years of freedom for their brethren in bondage," as one

Boston reporter wrote. Many gathered at Reverend Grimes's church, waiting for the hour when a new light would shine into the darkness. Two chapels nearby were overflowing with guests expressing thanks. According to a reporter, some attendees were wearing cards on their hats reading "January 1, 1863. No Postage Stamps Received after this date," signifying the beginning of a new era.[8] The reformer William Garrison spent the evening quietly at home, but his children, Willie and Fanny, joined the African American congregants at Bethel Methodist. It is unclear if Andrew and his family were also in attendance. But there is no question that he celebrated the moment in his own way. The nation's moral arc was bending toward justice, and he was surely thanking God.[9]

January 1 was cold, overcast, and gloomy, but one observer recalled that a "feverish unrest and expectation showed itself in the countenances and speech of those who met each other."[10] The morning papers mentioned nothing about the proclamation, so citizens remained on edge, wondering if Lincoln had signed it yet. The conservative Boston Post posited that it would "not be ready for publication until tomorrow" and, in any case, would be "fundamentally in opposition to the welfare of this Government and people."[11] Nonetheless, Andrew waited in the statehouse for the telegram. Midafternoon, word arrived that Lincoln had signed the document, and the celebrations commenced. According to some newspaper editors, the day was as important as the Fourth of July 1776. Throughout Boston, people rejoiced over the long-awaited moment. More than 3,000 gathered at an event at Tremont Temple, organized by local African American residents, to listen to speeches of resolution and hope and raise donations for the work of the Educational Commission for the Freedmen. William Nell, Charles Remond, Lewis Hayden, James Clarke, Frederick Douglass, Samuel May, Jr., and a multitude of other abolitionists came together to consecrate the day. "Hats, muffs, cushions, overcoats and umbrellas even were thrown heavenward, and dancing and stamping became general all over the hall," recorded the Daily Advertiser, and Douglass led attendees in singing "This is the day of jubilee."[12] The editor of the Daily Advertiser wrote, "No instrument of more momentous import, has ever been published since the Declaration of American Independence challenged the attention of the world."[13]

It was a grand, once-in-a-lifetime moment, the culmination of Andrew's life's work. Like Garrison, he declined Nell's invitation to speak at Tremont Temple but sent the crowd "my hearty sympathy, and highest hopes of a great . . . future for our country." Neither man wanted to distract from the celebration by attracting attention to himself, but the audience recognized their vital importance and erupted in "three cheers" when their names were mentioned. That evening Andrew may have joined other abolitionists for a gathering at the home of George and Mary Stearns. Later he might have walked to the Twelfth Baptist Church, where Reverend Grimes was overseeing an all-night celebration.[14]

As joyous as he was for the African Americans of Boston, Andrew was most cognizant of the feelings of the soldiers in the field, especially the former slaves of the First South Carolina Volunteers, who were celebrating "Negro Independence," at Hilton Island under Colonel Higginson. The war had now become a crusade to liberate the slaves, whether that goal was masked as a war measure. A correspondent for the *Liberator* who was traveling with the regiment reported that January 1 was a "pleasant June-like day," and that Massachusetts was well represented in the effort to arm freed slaves against the Confederacy. Indeed, General Saxton declared that "it takes a *Massachusetts man* to rule South Carolina" when he presented Colonel Higginson with the regimental colors.[15] Andrew had worked behind the scenes to ensure that Massachusetts officers would lead these troops and was grateful that Higginson had risen to the challenge, even if he worried about his combat leadership. The First South Carolina Volunteers was the first authorized regiment recruited from freedmen for Union military service, and Higginson was preparing them for an upcoming foray into Florida along the St. Mary's River. "They must fight," he told Andrew, "or be slaves."[16] Andrew had supplied the colonel with printed copies of the Emancipation Proclamation, which Higginson told his men to carry with them to spread the word among the slaves of the region, in hopes that they would self-emancipate. Camped in Newbern, North Carolina, Private Charles Woodwell of the Fifth Massachusetts Infantry recorded that "in the evening the colored people of Newbern assembled in the churches, where they were addressed by Agents of the government, who informed them that they were now free, and that all slaves in North Carolina who could escape from their masters would be free also."[17]

Andrew believed that the Emancipation Proclamation had opened a "new era of national life," one that would give everyone "the inalienable rights of liberty and pursuit of happiness advanced by our Founders." He declared, "We, their children . . . gratefully welcome an immortal act of civil justice and military necessity, which guarantees these sacred rights to millions in our country from whom they have been hitherto withheld."[18] To celebrate the occasion, the governor ordered a hundred-gun salute to be fired on Boston Common, and he readied himself to welcome an influx of volunteers from California. Soon the Second Regiment of Cavalry, known as the "California Hundred," began training at Camp Meigs at Readville. Organized and commanded by Charles Lowell, these men were all Massachusetts natives who had been living in California and now offered their services to Andrew. They would be needed at the front soon, as the casualty reports from Fredericksburg were staggering. One Massachusetts officer wrote to Andrew that the "news of the fearfull and apparently worse than unnecessary slaughter at Fredericksburg has just come to our sad hearts and I am so sick. I do not wish to live to see my country once so great and glorious, vanquished in such a disgracefull rebellion."[19]

Even amid his joy about the proclamation, Andrew remained concerned not only about the casualties on the front lines but also the freed slaves' welfare behind the lines. He feared that land speculators and stock companies would encroach on abandoned southern plantations, including those under military occupation, and use them for their own purposes. The freed slaves, many of them women and children whose husbands and fathers were still in bondage, scores of them aged or infirm, would suffer under such mercenaries. Moreover, such circumstances would embarrass the government. Already there were issues at Port Royal. Andrew had received several communiqués from General Saxton, who had assigned military superintendents to monitor the plantations. In December 1862, Saxton had given land allotments to the freed people so that they could grow their own food and cotton. He had arranged that they would be paid for fieldwork, but the pay had never materialized. Andrew worried that these lands, sold for taxes in February 1863, would undermine the free labor experiment in the South. He advised that public lands sales be postponed until proper legislation could provide for and protect the inhabitants. "The social questions involved are, obviously, of grave importance," he wrote to Treasury Secretary Chase, "and no action hastily or inconsiderably adopted *now*, should stand in the way of the best plan of reorganization which a little longer time may and undoubtedly will develop."[20]

The Massachusetts General Court convened on January 7, and two days later Andrew delivered his third inaugural address. With verve and eloquence, he praised the state's wartime accomplishments. Though several regimental flags had become so tattered that they were unfit for use, not a single Commonwealth banner had been surrendered to the enemy. He reminded his listeners that the war had impoverished many families and encouraged legislators to create a state charity board to relieve their suffering. Shifting away from war topics, he likewise argued that penal reform and sanitary institutions should be centralized under state boards. Primarily, however, his speech emphasized that, by winning the war, "the people of America will have saved the Union, saved Democratic-Republican Liberty, . . . will have perpetuated the Government, magnified the Constitution and made it honorable, and will have crowned a great career of glory with an act of expedient Justice unequalled for its grandeur in all the history of mankind."[21]

Yet if the people were to save the Union, Andrew believed they needed a clearer purpose from Washington. Writing to Frank Bird, he discussed politicians' recent attempts to shake up Lincoln's cabinet but said that he would not rely on Washington's machinery to bring about victory. Rather, the states, the soldiers, and civilian society would be the ones to win the war and advance justice. "We can be saved," Andrew told Bird, "only by a revival of the religion of patriotism, and the power of a resurrection getting its hold on our own friends who are set for the defence of the people and the truth, which is their salvation. Floundering along, without clear purpose, wise, united and practical statesmanship, without any real *head*, how can we be victorious?" Too many members of Lincoln's cabinet, he said, lacked the guiding impulses of leadership and were merely reacting to present conditions. With accruing losses on the field and at the polls, they needed to wake up and recognize that liberating (and arming) the slaves was only the beginning of the nation's journey toward social and civil change.[22]

Congress had given the president the authority to organize "persons of African descent" for military or naval service, but Lincoln was not moving as quickly as Andrew had expected on the matter, even though he had come around to authorizing the First South Carolina regiment. But whether intentionally or not, the Emancipation Proclamation was providing a path toward arming African Americans, and Andrew meant to take advantage of this. Already, several commanders had experimented with using African American soldiers, and the War Department had accepted some units into federal service. Now, hampered by draft resistance and pressed for men, despite the Union's recent victory at the Battle of Stones River in Tennessee, Andrew began asking his friends to promote military recruitment in the African American churches. He remained undeterred by overt racism among the existing troops, though he was aware that officers such as Captain Charles Devereux of the Nineteenth Massachusetts had said that he would not fight for the "good of a negro," that it would discourage enlistment if the army was to fight for African Americans, and that "he hoped to God that every man in the army of the Potomac would come home if they were to fight for the negroes."[23]

As winter blanketed the state, Andrew worked to console his citizenry. The Union appeared to be losing the war, and the loss of Commonwealth men affected him deeply. Even before the war, the state's population had been decreasing, and Andrew believed that this diminishment, along with the state's small land area, was affecting its political prominence. For now, though, it retained its intellectual, academic, and cultural ascendency. Andrew liked to say that the Yankees were the nation's "seed-corn." So when a lawmaker from Indiana told him that his state legislature had created a committee to study why Massachusetts had sent comparatively few troops to the front, Andrew was ready with a rebuttal. In what became known as the "Wetmore" letter, Andrew filled nine pages with pertinent statistics and declared, "We hold that in the moral welfare, the material wealth, the industrial development and intellectual power of all states and people we share ourselves; striving to be unlike the spider, who sucks poison from the sweetest flower, but like the bee, which draws nurture even from the humblest."[24]

African American Troops

On January 26, Lincoln replaced Burnside with General Joseph Hooker. Andrew was pleased with the change. In his congratulatory letter to Hooker, he asked the general to tell the Massachusetts soldiers "that *all* have a country; *all* will hereafter have a history; and that, a hundred years hence, the children by the firesides will be charmed by the stories their mothers will tell them of the valor and manliness of the humblest private who served well or died bravely."[25]

Meanwhile, after a fortnight of unforgiving weather, skies cleared enough for Andrew to travel to Washington, where he and several wealthy philanthropists petitioned the administration to authorize the Commonwealth's African American regiments. From Washington, John Forbes told Andrew that federal officials finally seemed "open to the necessity of using the *negro* for our own salvation first and secondly for his own."[26] On the same day that Hooker was appointed, Stanton gave the governor one hundred days to fill the ranks with Black volunteers but offered no governmental assistance. Andrew, however, proceeded with care. He knew that African American activists would demand clarity about the terms of service before they would enlist. In addition, there were not enough African American military-age males in Massachusetts to form a complete regiment, so he had to petition Stanton again, who reluctantly allowed him to recruit outside the Commonwealth. To fulfill his mission, the governor formed a citizens' committee that would undertake to raise $50,000, to be used to recruit the regiment. The thirty-eight committee members included Forbes, Stearns, Bowditch, and Brigadier General Lorenzo Thomas, an adjutant general in the Union army who had established recruiting stations across the North. Andrew relied on African American leaders, especially Hayden, Grimes, and Nell, to mobilize volunteers. Although Andrew pressed Stanton to allow African Americans to hold lower-grade officer commissions, the secretary refused. This dampened the zeal among some of the state's Black residents, who vowed to protest against enlistment until Stanton changed his mind. That did not happen, however, even though Andrew asked Sumner to press the administration to commission African Americans as chaplains, surgeons, and second lieutenants.[27]

Andrew turned to the press, where he trumpeted news about the recruitment effort. He made it clear that Stanton had pledged that Black and white soldiers would receive pay equal and equal bounties, and the state's conservatives were reluctantly forced to accept the fact that African Americans had been added to the Commonwealth's military quota. Yet as James Bowen of North Adams, a soldier in the Thirty-seventh Massachusetts, later noted in his history *Massachusetts in the War*, "many good and patriotic people had a great reluctance to see the colored man in any way brought actively into the struggle for the preservation of the nation. They felt that in doing this the government was losing sight of the prime object—the restoration of the national authority in the seceded states—and diverting the war to the secondary object of an anti-slavery crusade."[28] Andrew understood that the idea of arming African Americans would continue to rankle. There was work to be done in dispelling discrimination in the North, and neither emancipation nor Union service would automatically erase racial distinctions.

The Commonwealth's new African American regiment, the Fifty-fourth, was numbered in the regular order of the state's volunteer infantry. For leaders, Andrew had in mind Robert Gould Shaw, currently of the Second Massachusetts, and Edward Hallowell, currently of the Twentieth. Both belonged to abolitionist families and would be prepared for the difficulties ahead. The governor explained the undertaking to Shaw's father, Francis, calling the regiment "perhaps the most important corps to be organized during the whole war," which he was anxious to "organize . . . judiciously in order that it be a model for all future Colored Regiments":

> I am desirous to have for its officers, particularly its field officers, young men of military experience, of firm Anti-Slavery principles, ambitious, superior to a vulgar contempt of color, and having faith in the capacity of Colored men for military service. Such officers must be necessarily gentlemen of the highest tone and honor, and I shall look for them in those circles of educated Anti-Slavery Society, which next to the colored race itself have the greatest interest in the success of this experiment.

Andrew was convinced that the undertaking's success or failure would affect the estimation "in which the character of the Colored Americans will be held throughout the World," and he told the elder Shaw that such an opportunity should be "a high object of ambition for any officer."[29] John Forbes also wrote to Francis Shaw, encouraging him to see the venture as "the great movement of the war, and of the age, and opening out a great field for ambition."[30]

Andrew was drawn to Robert Shaw for several reasons, but among the most important was his ability to attract supporters beyond his immediate family. He told the young man's father, "The more ardent, faithful, true Republicans and friends of Liberty would recognize in him a Scion of a tree whose fruits and leaves have alike contributed to the strength and healing of our generation." The same was true of Hallowell, whose father "was a Quaker gentleman of Philadelphia, two of whose sons are officers in our regiments and another is a Merchant in Boston." He told Francis Shaw, "Their home in Philadelphia is a hospital almost for Mass. Officers, and the family are full of good works, Mr. H. being my constant advisor in the interest of our Soldiers, when sick or in distress in that city. I need not add that young Capt. H. is a gallant and fine fellow, true as steel to the cause of Human Nature, as well as to the flag of the Country."[31]

Hallowell accepted the commission immediately and reported to Boston within the week, but Shaw doubted that he was equal to the task. His vacillation caused his mother "the bitterest disappointment I have ever experienced." She told Andrew, "In your description of what you desired in the officers for the new regiment, flattering as it was, I recognized the portrait of my son. You said you should wish him to have 'the assent, support and sympathy of his family.' It would have been the proudest moment of my life, and I could have died satisfied that I had not lived in vain." Andrew was grateful for the letter and told her so. His response no doubt prompted Shaw's father to travel to Virginia in early February, to visit his son and explain the governor's offer in person.[32]

As a result, Shaw eventually accepted the commission, and he and Hallowell struck up a close friendship. Andrew took great care in supporting the young officers, and he worried about placing them in charge of unproven soldiers. Shaw recognized Andrew's genuine concern for the soldiers' welfare. "I took a long drive with the Governor," he told his father, "and liked him very much. His views about the regiment are just what I should wish. We have decided to go into camp at Readville: as we think it best to plunge in without regard to outsiders." He told his mother, "I like the Governor more and more every day. He is not only a liberal minded philanthropist, but a man of good practical sense, I think, and as kind-hearted as he can be." To his wife, Shaw wrote, "Governor Andrew's ideas please me extremely, for he takes the most common-sense view of the thing. He seems inclined to have me do just what I please."[33] Charles Russell Lowell, III, who had served as McClellan's aide-de-camp during the peninsula campaign, was recruiting in Boston as Andrew was working with Shaw and Hallowell. He recognized that the governor needed "men of such character and education as to place them above a prejudice of color," and he took a liking to Shaw, telling him that "it was worth while to come home, if it were only to get acquainted with him."[34]

To help organize the Fifty-fourth, Andrew turned to Colonel Edward Wild of the Thirty-fifth Massachusetts, who was recuperating from a wound he had received at the Battle of South Mountain. Wild was an abolitionist, and his African American connections were immensely helpful to Andrew, who wanted to attract more southern freedmen to the Fifty-fourth and influence northern public sentiment in favor of the experiment. Wild was given authority to select and appoint officers, with the aid of Heinrich Müller, a Baptist preacher and regimental chaplain. Letters from prospective officers poured into Andrew's office. Alonzo Draper, a labor leader and abolitionist from Lynn, was among those who offered himself for a position. Twenty-seven years old, he had served for two years on garrison duty and was anxious to assist "in ameliorating the condition of the colored race, and in their enfranchisement from local social depression to which ignorant popular prejudice has consigned them. This sentiment is not a novel one to me, but is consistent with the whole course of my life."[35]

As Andrew saw it, the Union's greatest challenge lay not at the front lines against the southern enemy but behind the lines against northern conservatism. Garrison buoyed the cause by using the *Liberator* to emphasize the African American volunteers' fitness for combat. He published letters from South Carolina about the progress that New England teachers had made with former slaves and spent days observing drills at the Readville training camp. Several Boston newspaper editors were now promoting the use of slave contrabands in the South to relieve "our troops," an indication of how many were coming to view the use of African American soldiers in the federal army. As the *Daily Advertiser* editor argued, we "must . . . look about for a soldier of any color to save us from the necessity of keeping our white soldier in the field."[36] Still, many citizens were dismayed. Edwin Wentworth of the Thirty-seventh Massachusetts told his brother that he feared the "army of negroes" would "amount to nothing, for white men will not fight beside them; and even if they would, not enough can be raised to do any good."[37]

Though integration of the military collided with constitutional, conservative, and traditional principles, African Americans had fought alongside white soldiers in the Revolutionary War and had served in the U.S. Navy since its inception. Livermore's pamphlet had made this brilliantly clear to Lincoln. Andrew believed that the only way to break barriers was to convince naysayers of integration's merits, yet problems kept arising at the most basic level. Stanton refused to appoint African Americans as line officers, assistant surgeons, or chaplains, as the law simply did not permit it. Worse, his promise to pay African American troops $13 per month, the salary that white soldiers received, had hit a legal snag. William Whiting, a solicitor for the War Department, had ruled that, because these soldiers had mustered in under the Militia Act of 1862, they could only be paid $10, with $3 withheld for clothing. He told Andrew that the decision was final, even though Higginson's soldiers of the First South Carolina had been receiving $13 per month as standard army pay. The governor turned to friends to raise the funds necessary to outfit the regiment and to press the issue of equal pay in Washington. As he often did, he leaned on Frank Bird and George Stearns. Stearns's son recalled a conversation between Andrew and his father during those days. When Andrew asked, "What is to be done?" Stearns replied, "If you will obtain funds from the Legislature for their transportation, I will recruit you a regiment among the black men of Ohio and Canada West. There are a great many runaways in Canada, those are the ones who will go back and fight." "Very good," said the governor, "go as soon as you can, and our friend Bird will take care of the appropriation bill."[38]

Andrew gave Stearns extensive freedom in recruiting, and together they reached out to reformers and philanthropists in Boston, New York, and Philadelphia for assistance. Stearns headed to western New York to enroll African Americans from the Midwest and Canada, and by early March he dispatched an examining physician to look over his volunteers. Andrew, meanwhile, worked the wires between Boston and Washington to ensure that governors opposed to African American regiments in their states would allow Stearns's agents to recruit them for the Massachusetts regiment. Still, his aggressive moves ran the risk of offending both the governors and Stanton, and in late March he warned Stearns, "We may be shut down . . . at any moment."[39]

Stearns had his hands full, not only in assembling the new regiment but also in establishing the training centers that were opened in Boston, Readville, Springfield, and New Bedford. The work he was doing in bringing in out-of-state recruits was crucial. According to the 1860 census, 9,602 African Americans lived in Massachusetts, and many were employed in jobs related to the war effort and were reluctant to leave them for the army. There were only 1,973 African American males of military age, of which only 394 were eligible for service. Massachusetts had lost population due to western emigration and employed a greater percentage of its population in manufacturing than any other state did. African American recruits would help keep white military-age males working at their machines: this was an argument that resonated with conservatives.

Stearns swiftly organized hundreds of African American volunteers. He told Andrew that his efforts were initially "secret and confined to the Blacks"; but as he expanded his efforts, white citizens increasingly came forward to assist, including many governors, who permitted his agents to enlist in their states. Encouraged, Andrew decided to raise an additional African American regiment, and he transferred Colonel Hallowell from the Fifty-fourth to the new Fifty-fifth. News from the Union-occupied Carolinas suggested that more recruits for the Massachusetts regiments could be drawn from the freed slaves in Virginia and North Carolina. Alternatively, they might be formed into a separate "African Brigade," for service in that region.[40]

Still, pay inequities, recruiting delays, wretched field reports, casualty lists, and Confederate reprisals weighed heavily on potential recruits. Andrew was especially sensitive to the pay issue and railed against the notoriously slow paymasters. Many African American families lived in poverty, and losing their fathers and husbands to the army forced them to endure significant hardship. Andrew understood that timely pay would do more to improve enlistment than anything else. He also recognized that regimental cohesion was paramount to success and that soldiers needed African American officers to boast morale. He continued to pester Stanton for an African American chaplain and to use his influence to garner equal pay. He also demanded that the government protect the recruits against Confederate officials who had vowed to kill former slaves who had enlisted. In a letter to the African American abolitionist George Downing, Andrew said he was confident that Stanton and Lincoln would keep their promises:

> When I was in Washington, [Stanton] . . . stated, in the most emphatic manner that he would never consent that free colored men should be accepted into the service to serve as soldiers in the South, until he could be assured that the Government of the United States was prepared to guarantee and defend, to the last dollar, and the last man, [for] all these men, all the rights, privileges and immunities that are given, by the laws of civilized warfare, to other soldiers.[41]

Washington had taken note of Andrew's recruitment success as well as his insights about the difficulty of attracting African Americans to join white soldiers. The governor had proposed to Stanton in early April that it would easier to raise Black troops in areas of the South where there already were African American units. Massachusetts, he argued, could take the lead in providing and positioning such regiments in ways that would attract freedmen to the ranks. Stanton was so impressed that in May he agreed to establish a federal Bureau for Colored Troops, which would centralize and organize African American mobilization. The secretary commissioned Major Charles Foster, a Massachusetts native who entered the military from New Hampshire, to raise troops and administer the bureau, which would serve as a clearinghouse for anything concerning African American soldiers. The existence of a federal bureau made it clear that these troops were no longer fighting for their states but for the United States. Significant problems remained, however, and stories circulated that some African Americans assigned to regimental commands had been captured and sold back into slavery.[42]

National Conscription

Massachusetts legislators had allocated Andrew $1 million to be spent at his discretion for coastal defense, and that spring he sent his secretary, Albert Browne, Jr., to Washington to speak to Lincoln about the state's shoreline vulnerabilities. "*We can't* do much ourselves about the forts, about guns for the forts, nor about an iron-clad," Andrew told Lincoln, "but . . . by offering our *help*, cap in hand, we compel an active zeal and efficient prosecution of the proper work of the U.S. Govt., through its own agents and officers."[43] Sumner also called on the president about the matter, but Lincoln saw it as needless alarm.[44]

By now the volunteer wellspring had nearly run dry. To continue the war, Lincoln needed the means and the authority to undertake federal conscription as a way of coercing civilians into service. According to Stanton's records, more than 100,000 soldiers were absent from the army for a variety of reasons, ranging from AWOL to sickness. The time had come to federalize the volunteer system and distribute the war's burden among all military-age males regardless of the political fallout. Senator Wilson led the way in Congress by gathering support for a conscription act, which would make all male citizens between the ages of twenty and forty-five liable to enrollment while, among other exemptions, releasing those who were physically and mentally unfit for service. The act empowered the president to set draft quotas apportioned along congressional districts within the states but did not offer occupational deferments. Exemptions could be obtained if draftees could hire a substitute or if they could pay $300 to purchase their way out of conscription. As Andrew explained the draft to his citizenry, Congress passed the measure, and Lincoln signed it. Since April 1861, the responsibility for distributing the burden of war among the citizens had belonged to Lincoln and the governors; now they would work with federal provost marshals in handling recruitment and desertions.[45]

Like emancipation, conscription awakened northerners to the war's realities. Andrew exhausted himself attempting to replenish the ranks and prepare his new African American regiments, though some conservatives were still hoping his experiment would fail. As Adjutant General William Schouler wrote, "it was a new thing. . . . Few men in the State had ever seen a colored man in uniform."[46] As the regiments readied for the front, Andrew prodded Stanton to order the Fifty-fourth to a suitable field of operations, preferably South Carolina under Hunter's command. The governor had corresponded with the commander about this possibility, and Hunter had encouraged it. "The Governor is very anxious to get us away in a month," Shaw wrote to his mother, telling her that Andrew wanted the regiment to pass through New York City, not only to display the men but also to test their reception.[47]

Massachusetts abolitionists feared that the state legislature was not taking the Emancipation Proclamation seriously, and Garrison worried that pro-slavery Democrats were undermining the decree by ignoring it. When he pressed Andrew to have legislators endorse the proclamation before adjourning, the governor explained that the body's Committee on Federal Relations had agreed to do so but needed to wait until the other standing committees had finished their work. But he, too, was concerned. "The truth is," he told Garrison, "I really think slavery at this moment is about as unpopular in New England and in the North generally as it ever was in the most anti-slavery community either here or in England." Northerners were distressed by the lack of military progress, and many citizens believed that "the blood and treasure of the free white North is spending not for the good of the nation but simply for the deliverance of black men, whom they do not much like and for whom they would willingly make no sacrifices." Still, he remained optimistic: "The slavery of the colored race, though for a little time it may yet have a 'name to live' on American soil, and may protract for a time a galvanic existence, I am thankful to believe is nevertheless as dead as the kingdom of Belshazzar."[48] Andrew could see the arc of the moral universe bending toward justice.

In late April, Hooker's and Lee's armies clashed near Chancellorsville, Virginia, and a bloody battle unfolded over several days. Lee's army thoroughly thrashed Hooker's, deflating troop morale and demoralizing Washington. The inglorious federal retreat left northerners searching for answers. Stanton publicly refuted claims that the battle had been a disaster, but he privately called it "the darkest day of the whole war."[49] In a telegram, Andrew said that he understood Stanton's attempts at damage control but went straight to the situation on the field: "May I ask if the storm and rise of the Rappahannock determined Hooker's recrossing?" he queried.[50] Yet Julia Howe recalled that the Chancellorsville defeat left Andrew severely depressed: "[He] thought that the bottom had dropped out of everything."[51]

For the governor, the only bright spot that spring was the Fifty-fourth Regiment, which he still clung to as evidence that a new Union was emerging. By mid-May, the soldiers had been outfitted, trained, and mustered into federal service. Thanks to Stearns and his brigade of recruiters, white and Black, the regiments included soldiers from fifteen northern states, five Confederate states, the border states, the West Indies, and Canada. Although the troops carried the Massachusetts regimental flag, they were truly a national achievement, a new coalition, transcending class, and cultural lines. Frederick Douglass's sons, Lewis and Charles, were among the first to enlist from New York, and they stood proudly in the ranks. The regiments' very existence seemed emblematic of the words that their father had delivered months earlier, before a crowd at Cooper Institute: "Away with prejudice, away with folly, and in this death struggle for liberty, country, and permanent security, let the black iron hand of the colored man fall heavily on the head of the slaveholding traitors and rebels and lay them low."[52]

On May 18, thousands of spectators poured into Readville, Massachusetts, to watch the governor present the regimental colors to the Fifty-fourth. Extra trains carried massive crowds to Camp Meigs from Boston. Eliza Andrew accompanied her husband to the ceremony, as she had been part of a ladies' committee that had raised money for the regiment and had often visited the camp. Newspaper correspondents from across the United States were on hand to record the moment. Afterward, the *Milwaukee Sentinel* applauded Andrew as the first governor to "place a full, reliable and well-organized colored battalion in the field, bearing the flag of the Old Bay State to further triumphs."[53]

Colonel Shaw had drawn the men into ranks to listen to the governor speak. As always, Andrew's words were apt and moving. He reminded them that the whole world was watching and said he was confident they would vindicate their race and thus undermine the proslavery argument that had convinced many Americans of their inferiority. "I know not, Mr. Commander," said Andrew, his voice trembling, "where, in all human history, to any given thousand men in arms there has been committed a work at once so proud, so precious, so full of hope and glory as the work committed to you. I stand or fall, as a man and a magistrate, with the rise or fall in history of the Fifty-fourth Massachusetts Regiment."[54]

The regiment was scheduled to leave Massachusetts on May 28, and in the days before its departure the governor went about his executive business. He dealt with routine military commitments; attended municipal, educational, and benevolent board meetings; and made his annual visit to the Hoosac Tunnel. But the most important event on his weekly calendar was the sendoff ceremony for the Fifty-fourth Massachusetts. Every morning, some Boston papers would publish a paean to Andrew's experiment while others would mock it. Some editors suggested that, given the poverty of most African Americans, serving in the military would be more of a "luxury than a privation." Others would claim that Black soldiers were naturally suited to the hardships of the front. The *Daily Advertiser* focused on the dangers at stake for this regiment and its officers, particularly from the Confederate government, and this was what worried Andrew most.[55] A parade and a ceremony were planned, and the governor received so much correspondence opposing the idea that he created a scrapbook of the letters to mark the occasion.

On May 28, the Fifty-fourth paraded through the streets of Boston. Never before had several hundred African American men, all in military uniform, marched through an American city in service to the United States. William Nell was watching on State Street, at the very spot where Crispus Attucks had fallen in the Boston Massacre. It was a spectacular scene. Citizens crowded the route, cheering and waving flags. Nell recalled a "thousand armed colored Americans soldiers *en route* for the land of slavery, marching down State Street, the band playing, and the soldiers singing 'John Brown,' all indicating the free, the happy future, as within a seeming hailing distance,—I could not help mentally exclaiming, 'Glory enough for one day; aye, indeed, for a life-time.'"[56] Henry Wadsworth Longfellow was also watching. "An imposing sight," he called it, "with something wild and strange about it, like a dream."

Garrison attended the ceremony and wrote about the experience in the *Liberator*. He reminded readers that only nine years earlier the entire military force of Boston had escorted one runaway slave named Anthony Burns to a ship that would take him back to his owner in the South. Now an entire African American regiment was marching through the same streets on their way to defeat these same enslavers. A reporter for the *Daily Advertiser* observed that, "notwithstanding the prejudice which it is useless to deny still exists in Boston against the colored race, people in all cases seemed disposed to look with favor on the soldiers and to offer nothing but good wishes for their success."[57]

But not everyone was enthusiastic. On Franklin Street, the regiment passed the office of the *Boston Pilot*, an Irish-run newspaper. In coverage of the event, its editor predicted:

> The blacks will neither bring up the rear with decency, nor lead at the front with honor, nor hold the middle with respectable firmness. They are not yet fit to lead for such a great nation as this the noble career of arms. They are as fit to be the soldiers of this country, as their abettors are to be its statesmen. . . . *Twenty thousand negroes on the march would be smelled ten miles distant.* No scouts need ever be sent out to discover such warriors.[58]

Father Hilary Tucker, a native of Missouri and a staunch conservative, was now serving as rector of Boston's Cathedral of the Holy Cross. He ridiculed the regiment, writing in his diary that its attempt at military formation was laughable: "They will be invincible in battle, at least as much as skunks are, especially if [the] time be hot."[59]

Time would tell how Americans would react once the regiment reached the field.[60] For now the pageantry was over, and the sober journey had begun. Yet as Adjutant General Schouler remarked, "it was a splendid sight to see the large vessel, with its precious freight, vanish in the distance as it proceeded on its way to South Carolina."[61]

Andrew closely tracked the Fifty-fourth's journey to South Carolina, but he had tens of thousands of soldiers to tend; and as military operations heated up, casualty numbers climbed. He arranged to have lemons and oranges sent to the wounded convalescing in Washington hospitals, and he remained concerned about individual cases as well—for instance, writing to the state's military agent in Washington to suggest furloughing Private George Evans of the Nineteenth Massachusetts, who was said to be "much broken down in health."[62]

Yet the African American regiments remained in the forefront of his mind. He was deeply impressed by their determination and sacrifice and hoped the world would finally recognize that they were entitled to the rights and privileges of every soldier. Washington was also impressed, so much so that Stanton assigned Stearns to lead recruiting for the United States Colored Troops, with Philadelphia as his headquarters.

Two days after the Fifty-fourth's regimental review on Boston Common, Andrew wrote to William Clapp, the editor of the Boston *Saturday Evening Gazette*, who had sent him an article about the African American soldiers that was scheduled to appear on May 31. The governor approved the piece and arranged to purchase one hundred copies, to be sent to the White House, various department heads in Washington, and the principal army generals. "What I want," he told Clapp, "is to strengthen their faith in the possibility of making the colored people useful as military instruments, by exhibiting to them the printed proof that it has been successfully done here, since they cannot see it with their own eyes."[63]

CHAPTER 18

OPENING EYES OF NORTH AND SOUTH

May–December 1863

General Harriet Tubman

By late spring Andrew was feeling more encouraged about the war, primarily in the western theater, where General Grant was besieging Vicksburg, the Gibraltar of the Mississippi River. Given such distractions, the Boston papers paid little heed to the clash at Port Hudson, Louisiana, where, on May 27, African Americans of the First and Third Infantry of the New Orleans Corps d'Afrique "lent luster" to combat for the first time and distinguished themselves even in defeat. *"The question is settled,"* reported the New York *Independent*. *"[The] negroes will fight."* But the First Regiment's commander, Captain Andre Cailloux, was killed during the assault, and rebels hanged an African American Union sentry. Atrocity was met with atrocity, when Union soldiers hanged a rebel picket "in full sight of their murdered companion."[1]

Conditions on the eastern front remained worrisome. After the Confederates bludgeoned the Union troops at Chancellorsville, Andrew knew that a victory was crucial if he were to convince his constituents that their sacrifices were not in vain. He followed the news about Hunter's department, where the Fifty-fourth was headed, and was particularly grateful for the *Liberator*, which paid close attention to the regiment. But Hunter's days in the department were numbered. Though the commander had tried to conform with the president's wishes, Lincoln decided to reassign him. In early June, Hunter sailed north, replaced by Brigadier General Quincy Gillmore, a gifted artillerist and engineer.[2] According to press reports, Lincoln removed Hunter because he had threatened to retaliate against Jefferson Davis's execution orders, had protested sending troops to Hooker in Virginia, and could not get along with Charles Foster, who was managing the Bureau of Colored Troops. Francis Merriam, who had been with Brown at Harpers Ferry, had escaped capture, and was now serving as captain of the newly organized Third South Carolina Colored Infantry stationed at Hilton Head, wrote to Andrew about the situation. He had been impressed by Hunter—known to the troops as "Black Dave"—and saw his departure as one of the worst defeats of the war. In Merriam's view, the commander had "conquered the prejudices of his countrymen, . . . [in the] face of the most bitter and malignant opposition." He had strongly supported his African American soldiers; and when some refused to accept their pay, a protest for being paid less than white soldiers were, he had contributed his own funds to fill the gap. Merriam recalled a notable moment when Hunter stood with a pitcher of water, "waiting with it in his hands while a black woman drank." That woman was Harriet Tubman.[3]

Earlier in the war, Andrew had arranged for Tubman to accompany General Butler to Fort Monroe, where she had helped African American refugees obtain food, clothing, and shelter. Tubman had come to see herself as God's instrument, and for years this "medium-sized, partially deaf, illiterate [woman], without the slightest knowledge of letters or geography," had served as the "Moses of her people."[4] An escaped slave herself, she had labored for the Underground Railroad and had recruited supporters for Brown's Harpers Ferry raid. After the start of the war, she would haunt the edges of Union camps in Virginia, retrieving fugitives and piloting them to Union lines and freedom. She became such a nuisance to the Confederacy that Maryland slaveowners placed a $40,000 bounty on her head.

Andrew admired Tubman's work and saw how valuable she might be to the Massachusetts forces serving in South Carolina. Earlier in the war, perhaps on the recommendation of Ednah Cheney, a Beacon Hill abolitionist, he had given Tubman military passage on the *Atlantic* and sent her to Union-occupied Hilton Head, where she worked as a nurse, a laundress, a scout, and a Union spy. Hunter was so impressed with Tubman that he had allowed her free passage everywhere and inscribed on her military pass, "Harriet was sent to me from Boston by Gov. Andrew of Mass., and is a valuable woman."[5]

Tubman operated a dual existence in South Carolina. By day she assisted freed women in the refugee camps and helped them adapt to working for wages, primarily in a newly constructed washhouse. By night, she used funds from Hunter to pay spies and orderlies to assist in clandestine military operations. Eventually, to maintain her cover, she stopped accepting government pay and instead sold pies and root beer, which she made at night, "when not engaged in important service for the Gov't."[6]

The Emancipation Proclamation encouraged Tubman to assume a more active military role in recruiting former slaves to the ranks, and she sought any opportunity to make herself available to commanders. The abolitionist officers Thomas Higginson and James Montgomery were aware of "the general's" capabilities, and in June they enlisted her into a covert campaign. Montgomery, who had had already mobilized several hundred slaves into the Second South Carolina Regiment, was now attached to the United States Colored Troops. He asked Tubman to lead a secret mission near the Combahee River to free hundreds of slaves, destroy Confederate rice plantations, and recruit Black men into the Union army. Tubman procured vital information about rebel torpedoes planted in the river and the whereabouts of freedmen, and in the early morning of June 2 she guided "Lincoln's gun boats" upriver. They carried 150 soldiers from the Second South Carolina Infantry, who came ashore, destroyed several plantations, and rescued more than 750 slaves. It was one of the war's "most brilliant raids," according to the *New York Tribune*, and Colonel Montgomery did not lose a single man. Several southern newspapers reported that the Combahee Raid resulted in the loss of roughly 1,000 slaves and more than $1 million worth of property. The *Savannah Daily News and Herald* called it a "disastrous and mortifying affair—disastrous in the loss of property destroyed and mortifying in the fact that it was accomplished with complete success."[7]

The Combahee Raid was a stupendous achievement, for it not only augmented the Union force in the region but also supplied almost an entire new regiment of men. "What contributed most to my mortification," wrote one planter, "was, that in my whole gang of slaves . . . not one remained loyal to the rebel. This is the complaint of hundreds and thousands of other sufferers. The most petted, trusted and seemingly devoted slaves are found wanting in the hour of trial."[8] Tubman clearly was the expedition's architect, the only African American woman known to have served with such distinction in a military operation during the war. When word reached Andrew, he was euphoric. Hunter told him that Montgomery and Tubman had compelled slaveowners to withdraw further into the interior, and Tubman would later receive a pension as an army major, in gratitude for her work. For now, however, she had a raft of freed slaves on her hands. So she suspended her scouting duties, resumed her relief agent duties, and avoided fame.[9]

As news of the raid made its way north, the Fifty-fourth landed in Beaufort, South Carolina. Colonel Shaw wrote to Andrew, assuring him that the men had been kindly received. A week later, however, the governor was disappointed to learn that Montgomery had ordered them to raze the small coastal town of Darien, Georgia, leaving "nothing but the chimneys standing." Hunter had not ordered the raid but in fact had reminded the colonel to adhere to the rules of war to avoid having atrocities charged to the Union.[10] Nevertheless, though the action was unsavory, Shaw's soldiers had met the enemy, capturing eighty-five cotton bales and no doubt inciting residents' wrath. Shaw was embarrassed by the incident and feared it would discredit his men. Andrew's aide-de-camp Colonel Henry Lee, Jr., worried to Andrew that the Confederates might retaliate by executing captured African American soldiers or their officers. Andrew expected such retribution, and he hoped that Sumner would continue to press congressional leaders on the importance of protecting African American soldiers from vindictive rebels. In a telegram to Lincoln, the governor asked for clarification on the government's policies regarding Black soldiers, especially the inequity in pay. In the meantime, a *Boston Traveller* correspondent dryly declared, "If we *must burn* the South, so be it."[11]

From what Andrew could gather, the African American soldiers in his regiment were proving themselves worthy of the uniform, despite the shameful Darien assignment. Hunter agreed, praising them before he left as "hardy, generous, temperate, patient, strictly obedient, possessing great natural aptitude for arms, and deeply imbued with . . . . religious sentiment." Their work ethic, he said, "went a long way toward reducing the prejudices against them." "With a brigade of liberated slaves already in the field," Hunter told Andrew, "a few more regiments of intelligent colored men from the North would soon place this force in the condition to make extensive excursions upon the mainland."[12] Judge A. D. Smith, a federal tax commissioner in Beaufort, put it more poignantly. "You have opened the eyes of the North and the South," he told Andrew.[13]

By summer all eyes were focused on Lee's army as it swiftly pushed north. The draft had become a reality; Stearns told Andrew that Governor Curtin of Pennsylvania was pressing Stanton for 100,000 troops to defend his state and begging "New England to crush the rebellion by fighting her battle on Penna. Soil."[14] Lincoln called for 100,000 six-month militia commitments from Maryland, Pennsylvania, Ohio, and West Virginia, and Andrew's aide, Albert Browne, Jr., warned the governor that there was little effective organized militia left in

Massachusetts. Nonetheless, James Fry, the U.S. provost marshal, notified the Commonwealth that several congressional districts would be subject to a draft, and Andrew prepared for potential violence at anti-draft demonstrations around the state.[15]

By early July, as Grant closed in on Vicksburg, the War Department telegraphed news of fighting near the small town of Gettysburg, Pennsylvania. The ghastly three-day battle involved a total of more than 165,000 soldiers, with North and South bloodying one another in repeated assaults. The battle ended on July 3, when Lee's army withdrew into Virginia. General George Meade claimed victory, but the conflict had cost his army a staggering 23,000 casualties. Despite the win, Andrew was hard-pressed to explain what had been accomplished through so much loss. His primary task after Meade's so-called success was to rush additional surgeons to the wounded. But news from the West cheered him: Grant had not only captured Vicksburg and nearly 30,000 rebel soldiers but also had conquered more slave soil and freed more slaves. For Andrew this was a far greater victory than Meade's.[16]

By mid-July, several Massachusetts townships had peacefully executed the draft; but as Andrew had feared, several enclaves were threatening violence. On July 15, while he was attending Harvard's commencement exercises, he received an urgent message about a disturbance in Boston's North End. The governor promptly left the platform and headed to the statehouse, as the audience buzzed. By evening he had mobilized some three hundred soldiers to strengthen local police and the militia stationed at the Cooper Street arsenal. The rioters were mostly Irish, angered by the draft's inequities toward the poor. When they burst through the arsenal's doors, soldiers inside fired a cannon, killing several men and sending a message to the public that Andrew would not tolerate violent unrest.[17]

To expedite the draft, a federal provost marshal enrolled military-aged males, making public those who were granted exemptions or procured substitutes and those who paid for commutation. As the governor worked with the marshal to figure out state draft ratios, he discovered that Massachusetts had a deficiency of more than 6,000 soldiers. This was a blow to state pride, but Andrew also saw the reckoning as an injustice. After all, when war fever was at its height in 1861, he could easily have furnished six more regiments, but Cameron had refused them. Now, as he pored over the numbers, he realized that the current estimates took no account of the men who had enlisted as volunteers in 1863 before the draft, a number that was large enough to cancel the deficiency.[18]

Quiet returned to Boston's streets. Then, on July 18, the governor traveled to Readville to present the colors to the Fifty-fifth Massachusetts, the state's second African American regiment. But when he returned to the statehouse that evening, a wire from South Carolina was waiting for him. The Fifty-fourth had taken part in a suicidal offensive at the Battle of Fort Wagner, on Morris Island in South Carolina, which had resulted in 1,500 Union casualties. The men, exhausted and hungry, had stormed across a sand dune against the Confederate batteries, taking the fort's parapet until forced back. Of the six hundred members of the Fifty-fourth, 270 were killed, wounded, or captured. Frederick Douglass's son Lewis was among those who stormed the fort, waving his sword and shouting, "Come on, boys, and fight for God and Governor Andrew." He survived the fight, having already written his parents, "If I die tonight I will not die a coward."[19]

Colonel Shaw was not as fortunate. Shouting, "Onward! Boys," he was struck down and killed. After the battle Confederates desecrated his body and buried him in a pit with his men, face down. When the federals sought to reclaim his body under a flag of truce, one rebel smugly reported, "We have buried him with the niggers!" That burial was his martyrdom, and the acclaimed Philadelphia poet and playwright George Boker used it as inspiration for the ballad "Buried with his Niggers."

Years later, Harriet Tubman said that she had prepared and eaten breakfast with Shaw's men on the day of the battle. According to the story, Shaw had invited her to join him: "Come, sister Harriet and get some breakfast."[20] For several days it was rumored in the North that Shaw had survived and was being held captive. Edward Pierce, who worked for the educational commission in Beaufort, wrote to Andrew to dispel that rumor. He said that, before the battle, Shaw had given him his private letters to be delivered to his father and reminisced about that day in Readville when "you told the regiment that your reputation was to be identified with its fame." Pierce mused, "It was a day of festivity and cheer. I walk now in these hospitals, and see mutilated forms with every variety of wound, and it seems all a dream. But well has the regiment sustained the hope which you indulged and justified the identity of fame you trusted to it."[21]

Comrades without County

On the same day that saw the deaths of so many men in the Fifty-fourth, the African American soldiers of the Fifty-fifth marched through Boston in the drizzling rain, bound for New Bern, North Carolina, or perhaps New Orleans, where Stanton told Andrew they might be sent. Though African American soldiers had proven themselves in the field, many Massachusetts citizens continued to resist or ridicule the Black regiments, even though these soldiers were helping to fill the state's quota and thereby allowing some white men to avoid service. William Garrison's entire family came out to bid farewell to his eldest child, George, who had mustered in as a second lieutenant and now saluted them as he paraded by. He, like other white officers in the regiment, had refused to accept any pay until Congress ended the pay discrepancy. Andrew remained hopeful that the administration would take measures to honor its original pledge, but neither Stanton nor Lincoln showed any inclination to reverse Whiting's opinion.[22]

Yet the Fifty-fourth's debacle had shaken him. "I feel deeply about my most beloved friend Col. Shaw and his brave fellows," Andrew wrote to Reverend Clarke. "When we have taken Charleston—we need to put a monument there to his honor."[23] When Shaw's father learned that the government was attempting to secure his son's remains, he demurred, requesting instead that his son's body lie with those of his men: "We hold that a soldier's most appropriate burial-place is on the field where he has fallen."[24] But without Shaw to protect them, the regiment was vulnerable. One soldier wrote to Andrew from Beaufort, telling him that, since Shaw's death, the men had been treated like "dogs or cattle." He wanted the governor to bring them home. The prisoners were a particular concern, and Andrew asked Lincoln to issue orders to ensure they would be treated properly. Soon after, the president issued General Orders 252, which protected all soldiers in governmental service, no matter their class, color, or condition. Moreover, he stipulated that for every Union soldier killed in violation of the laws of war, a rebel soldier would be executed; for every one enslaved by an enemy, a rebel soldier would be placed at hard labor.[25]

At midsummer, the stream of volunteers was turning sluggish. Andrew likened the task of recruitment to that of a man "with a jug of molasses to empty."[26] By August, the national draft had produced a scant number of troops, but the $325 incentive for each draftee, as well as additional claims from cooperating family members, was a heavy burden for the state. Equally frustrating was the Lincoln administration's delay in solving the issue of commissioning African American officers. The White House had deferred the issue to Congress, which considered it a secondary matter. Nevertheless, with Stanton's permission, Andrew and Forbes moved forward and organized an African American cavalry unit designed to match white cavalry regiments. In Stanton's opinion, Andrew's infantry regiments had settled "the question of the colored man's fitness," and he saw no argument against expanding.[27] Andrew assured Forbes that the men would be known by their numbers and arm of service, "not by their color," and enlisted recruiters to search for suitable horsemen. They became the state's Fifth Massachusetts Cavalry, which Forbes quickly dubbed "Andrew's Black Horse Cavalry." The governor tried to persuade Stanton to let him commission the regiment, pay the soldiers bounties, and receive quota credit, but for the moment the secretary would not budge. So Andrew asked a group of financiers to raise $50,000 for recruiting purposes and circulated public notices requesting volunteers. Still, numbers were low, and Andrew was forced to look outside the Commonwealth for recruits.[28]

Andrew was constantly worried about the sacrifices of his citizens, and even small consolations did much to ease his mind. Years after the war, Reverend J. Vila Blake of Chicago related an incident that took place just after the Battle of Fort Wagner. A friend of General Edward Wild, who was visiting New Bern, was about to leave for Boston on the steamer when "a poor colored woman" asked to see him. She handed him a parcel and said, "There is some money which we have raised to-day, and we will thank you to get a flag for the 'First Norf' [the first Black regiment] same as Governor Andrew gives the Massachusetts men." The soldiers who witnessed the scene were overcome by the woman's earnestness and by the large sum of money she and the poor people around her had raised. "My good woman," the man responded, "your wishes shall be faithfully carried out, and this parcel shall not be opened by any one but Governor Andrew." In Boston, the man visited the governor and presented him with the parcel, which contained "old-fashioned cents, 3, 5, and 10 cent pieces, silver quarter, and all different styles of currency the government ever printed." As Andrew counted the money, "great, honest tears" rolled down his cheeks. "One hundred and eighty dollars," he said. He then took $50 from his wallet, added it to the pile, and told the man, "Go and get a beautiful flag and I will be at the consecration ceremonies." The man returned Andrew's money to him, saying, "Governor, you cannot afford to give anything; the balance necessary for a good flag can easily be got. I can not permit you to give anything." He proceeded to procure a beautiful flag, and the moment remained etched in Andrew's mind.[29]

As Andrew continued to pester Washington for equal pay for all soldiers, he turned to Hayden for help in recruiting African American foot soldiers and cavalrymen. Meanwhile, Lincoln, Stanton, and Congress seemed to be distancing themselves from the pay issue, aware that it could be ruinous at the polls. Though Andrew and Stanton shared a mutual respect, the governor was disappointed at Stanton's reluctance to solve the pay problem. He also feared that any movement toward equality that had developed in wartime would not be carried into peacetime if such issues remained unsolved. Stanton seemed to be unable to convince Lincoln to issue a decree concerning equal pay, perhaps because he himself was not disturbed by it. As far as the War Department and administration were concerned, when volunteers enlisted, they accepted the existing terms of payment. Besides, the problem was producing controversy in the Republican Party, thus delaying legislative action. Establishment of the Bureau of Colored Troops had not changed those discrepancies or the legislative lethargy.[30]

But many African American soldiers had died at Fort Wagner without having received any pay at all. They had refused it as protest against the unequal system, and now their families were suffering. Numerous soldiers had written to Andrew about the issue. Hayden, Grimes, and Nell had also received letters, all of them showing that the regiment felt betrayed by the federal government. The governor worked all angles, but the soldiers refused his personal entreaties until the federal government made good on its pledge. His exasperation boiled over, and in an August 18 letter to his aide, Henry Lee, Jr., when he asked, "Do all these gentlemen think that God will work miracles for us?"[31] A

FIGURE 9. Slave collar sent to John Andrew. Courtesy of the Massachusetts Historical Society.

week later, he was calmer, assuring the soldier Frederick Johnson that he would not "rest until you have secured all of your rights, and that I have no doubt whatever of ultimate success."[32]

That summer Andrew received a letter from Samuel Read, a captain in the Massachusetts Third Cavalry operating near New Orleans, which told a story unlike anything the governor had ever heard. In 1862, with federal soldiers occupying the city, Read led a detachment of troops downriver, where they came upon the plantation of Madame Coutrell. While searching the grounds, he noticed a tiny locked-up house. He demanded the keys and, upon opening the double doors, found himself in the "entrance of a dark and loathsome dungeon, alive with the most disgusting and sickening stench that can be imagined." "In Heaven's name," he asked Madame Coutrell, "what have you here." "Oh, only-a 'ittle girl—she runned away." The captain peered into the darkness and glimpsed, sitting on a low stool, a girl about eighteen years old. "She had this iron torture riveted about her neck," said Read, "where it had rusted through the skin, and lay corroding apparently upon her flesh." Her head was bowed in her hands, and she was nearly insensible from emaciation and foul air. She, along with two other young women, had been shut up for thirteen days for attempting to escape. Read rescued the girl, took her to New Orleans, and had a blacksmith remove the iron collar from her neck. She was made free by military authority.

In the summer of 1863, he mailed the collar to Andrew, along with his explanatory letter. Horrified, the governor sent it to Williams and Everett Gallery in Boston, where it was exhibited for a few weeks, in hopes of shaping public opinion about slavery. In his letter to the gallery, Andrew explained, "Your rooms are visited every day by the multitudes of cultivated and refined Massachusetts women, [and] . . . the sight of [the collar] . . . and the story of the poor child who wore it may remind mothers, wives, and daughters, under whose eyes it may fall, of some of the good done by those whom they have sent from their firesides to encounter the hardships of war."[33]

In mid-September, with such images fresh in his mind, Andrew traveled to Washington, intending to clear up the pay discrepancy once and for all. A few weeks earlier Frederick Douglass had also visited the capital, where he had lobbied for both pay equity and protection of Black prisoners of war. Douglass was engaged in recruiting African Americans, and Stearns had encouraged him to meet with the president. This was their first meeting, and Douglass was quick to bring up the topic of the pay discrepancy. Lincoln agreed that the discrepancy was evident but argued that the "employment of colored troops at all was a great gain to the colored people . . . [and] that they ought to be willing to enter the service upon any condition." In his view, inferior pay "seemed a necessary concession to smooth the way to their employment at all as soldiers." Still, he promised to redress the pay inequity, and Douglass believed him. For his part, Stanton told Douglass that he supported equal pay and had even drafted a bill with such a recommendation but that it had failed in Congress. The idea that Douglass, Lincoln, and Stanton were even discussing pay equity for African American soldiers was extraordinary, and Andrew hoped to build on that conversation during his own visit.[34]

Lincoln had told Douglass that members of Congress were waiting for greater public backing of African American soldiers in uniform before they could move forward with pay reforms. So in his own meeting with the president, Andrew suggested that he ask the attorney general, Edward Bates, for his opinion. He also pressed Stanton to work for congressional legislation. Waiting for Congress meant delay, but Andrew thought it might produce some justice. In addition, Lincoln and Stanton were distracted by concerns about a potential conflict near Chickamauga, Georgia, and Andrew believed he had now pushed the issue as far as he could. He returned to Boston determined to influence the Commonwealth's congressional representatives to sponsor pertinent legislation when they convened in December, and he summoned the General Court to assemble on November 11 with the intention of asking the state to make good on the pay difference.[35]

Still Waters Run Deep

As the early autumn political conventions opened in Massachusetts, major military campaigns were underway in Tennessee, South Carolina, and Virginia. The Democrats gathered in Worcester on September 3 and pounced on the issue of Andrew's African American regiments. Declaring that the national government's interference in local affairs was a diabolical usurpation of power, they nominated Henry Paine for governor. He was a former Whig whose name had appeared last year on the People's Party ticket. "All is chaos," reported the *Daily Advertiser*'s correspondent from Worcester.[36] When Republicans convened later in the month, they agreed that it was the nation's duty to quell the rebellion by whatever means necessary, including emancipation and African American enlistments. Leaders touted recent military victories and Andrew's steady governance and vision and worked to refashion themselves as a Union party. Peace was not possible, they maintained, unless slavery was abolished. They renominated Andrew by acclamation. He was not present but in Norfolk, Virginia, visiting soldiers and freed slaves, perhaps also overseeing the distribution of supplies, and then returning via New York to visit the Commonwealth soldiers who were temporarily stationed there.[37]

The war was taking a financial toll on the governor and his family. By October, he had depleted his bank account on nearly every charitable case that had come to his door. His funds were so tight that Forbes wrote to Cyrus Woodman, telling him that an effort was afoot to raise $50,000 for the governor's family and that Andrew had rejected the proposition. The governor adamantly refused to receive charity, especially given how many African American families were going without military pay. He was also concerned about how his foes would perceive such a gift: "It would not in the least affect his action as towards those who contributed, but it would make him . . . the mark for the shafts of all his enemies." Woodman worried that Andrew might not be able to resume his legal career once he left office, but Forbes disagreed. In the future, there might be an occasion when Andrew's friends could again make an offer to raise funds. For now, Forbes applauded the governor for adhering to his little house, his simple habits, and his refusal of assistance.[38]

The upcoming election was critical to the future progress of the war. Abolitionist voters in New York State, which currently had a Democratic governor, were especially concerned. As a result, its state Republican committee invited Andrew to rally voters to the party, and he strove to focus them on winning the war at all costs. Back in the Commonwealth, he closely followed the wires from Washington, which relayed news of the Union's defeat at Chickamauga, another round of massive casualties, and anxieties about further troop requests. Union armies were pressing the enemy at Charleston, South Carolina; on the Rapidan River in Virginia; and at Chattanooga, Tennessee: the time had come to build on the summer's advances and announce new levies. So on October 17, Andrew received word that Lincoln was calling for 300,000 more men. The federal-state alliance had attempted to decrease the number of drafted men by enrolling African Americans, foreigners, members of the invalid (that is, disabled) corps, and border state slaves. Now, however, Lincoln was returning recruitment to the governors. The Massachusetts quota was 15,903, a severe demand, given that the state's deficit already stood at 22,204 after the summer campaigns. The Commonwealth had suffered some of the highest casualties in the war, and recruitment was difficult, not least because of the wide gap between civilian wages and meager military pay.[39]

The national elections in November would be a referendum on how voters wanted to end the war: by vigorous fighting or peaceful negotiation. Founded in 1863, the Union Club of Boston, which supported Andrew, worked to shape election rhetoric around continuing the battle. Republican colleagues relied on Andrew's popularity with voters as proof that Massachusetts was "sound to the core" in backing the president's agenda. Describing the state's patriotism, the *Daily Advertiser* declared, "Still waters run deep."[40]

Election results confirmed that the Commonwealth was continuing to embrace Lincoln's approach to the war. On November 3, voters gave Andrew his largest victory margin ever; he received 70,483 votes, far outstripping Paine's 29,207. The citizens of Massachusetts were deeply grateful for his leadership—among them, a Siasconset voter who had lost his son in the Battle of Ball's Bluff. He loaned his only horse to transport several voters to the polls to support the governor. Yet he himself walked, determined to cast his vote *"for the soldiers' friend."*[41]

Andrew was encouraged by the election results, as were many of the soldiers. John Parsons, a soldier in the Twenty-third Massachusetts Volunteer Infantry, who was home on furlough during the election, noted in his diary that Andrew had been "reelected by an increased majority. He is very popular and has made a good governor."[42] Major John Mahan of the Ninth Massachusetts Volunteer Infantry learned the news in a camp near Bealeton, Virginia. To his surprise, he noted that conservative voters seemed to be shifting their stance; now they, too, were advocating a fight to the end and the abolition of slavery. In a letter to William Schouler, adjutant general of Massachusetts, he wrote, "*Slavery is doomed.* The Union must and shall be preserved as a sacred legacy to be bequeathed from generation to generation, but *slavery never!*" Mahan applauded Andrew's role in creating this change of perspective, saying that the governor's "worth, patriotism, and integrity" had been responsible for his reelection.[43]

With the election behind him, Andrew again turned to the issue of recruitment. A draft was necessary, but Andrew did everything he could to postpone it. When legislators assembled in November for a week-long special session, they voted to advance him the power to expand aid to soldiers' families and to compensate for the $6 difference between Black and white soldiers' wages. They increased the state bounty for new recruits and for soldiers already in the field who had agreed to reenlist for three years or until the war's end. Around the nation observers took notice of Andrew's leadership. The editor of the *Cincinnati Daily Enquirer* remarked that Massachusetts had become the "bellwether in the Republican flock"; where "she leads . . . Republicans in other states follow."[44]

The governor appointed two special agents to visit the Fifty-fourth and Fifty-fifth regiments and pay the men. He also sent several people to attend Lincoln's speech at Gettysburg, scheduled for November 19. Though he had been invited to attend, he preferred to remain at work in Boston. Surely, however, he read the address in the paper; he may have even knelt with his aides, as was his custom, and conducted a prayer at the statehouse. Andrew spent Thanksgiving Day at the Haydens' home, along with twenty-five African American guests who had gathered to celebrate the year's accomplishments. The *Springfield Republican* reported that there was "no reason why he should not dine with Hayden, or invite him to his own table"—a sign that people were still grappling with the meaning and demonstration of racial equality. As always, Andrew remained at the forefront of change.[45]

The Union army was victorious in clashes at Chattanooga; and as federal troops moved increasingly deeper into the South, congressmen returned to Washington to open the Thirty-eighth Congress on December 7. Now that the tide of war seemed to be turning in the Union's favor, they were beginning to discuss postwar reconstruction. Two factions emerged in this debate: the radicals, who had made emancipation and African American equality a war aim, and the conservatives, who had rallied in defense of the Constitution and states' rights. On December 8, Lincoln issued the Proclamation of Amnesty and Reconstruction: whenever one-tenth of the voters took an oath of allegiance and established a "republican" government, that government "shall be recognized as the true government of the 'State'" and would therefore receive federal protection.

That month Andrew sent a note to General Gillmore at Folly Island, South Carolina, to announce that he was sending Major James Sturgis to pay the Fifty-fourth and Fifty-fifth regiments, as recently authorized by Massachusetts legislators. He asked the commander to remind the soldiers of the "very high appreciation in which their services are held in Massachusetts and to assure them of my own desire to render them any aid and to promote their welfare."[46] But the soldiers rejected the legislature's offer, preferring to wait until the federal government recognized them as citizen-soldiers. Theodore Tilton, writing to the *Boston Journal*, captured the spirit of their protest:

Imagine our surprise and disappointment on the receipt by the last mail of the Governor's address to the General Court, to find him making a proposition to . . . pay this regiment the difference between what the United States Government offers us and what they are legally bound to pay us, which in effect, advertises us to the world as holding out for *money* and not from *principle*,—that we sink our manhood in consideration of a few more dollars.[47]

One corporal wrote:

[We are] not surprised at the solicitude of the Governor to have us paid what we have so dearly earned, nor would we be surprised if the State would cheerfully assume the burden; but the Governor's recommendation clearly shows that the General Government don't *mean* to pay us, so long as there is a loophole to get out of it, and that is what surprises us, a government that recognizes the difference between volunteers in good faith, and a class thrown upon it by the necessities of war. What if they do say that colored troops were raised in the Northern States merely by sufferance. A man who can go on the field counts, whether he be white or black, brown or grey. . . . But, we as soldiers, cannot call in question the policy of the government, but as men who have families to feed, and clothe, and keep warm, we must say, that the *ten* dollars by the greatest government in the world is an unjust distinction to men who have only black skin to merit it.[48]

As much as it pained Andrew to see African American soldiers and their families go without pay, he applauded their unified protest. In the meantime, he dispatched several people to visit camps and hospitals, not only to urge reenlistment but also to share his own good wishes with them. He spent long days catching up on his correspondence, ensuring that every communiqué received an answer. Among them, one note caught his attention. Five young girls had sent him $50, explaining that they had earned it during a Thanksgiving week fair and were donating it to his soldier welfare fund. Such gestures pleased and humbled him. Indeed, he was embarrassed about how little he could now give from his own funds. "I am too poor to give much money nowadays," he wrote to Reverend Clarke, who had asked for a contribution to church causes. "With no earnings but my salary and that worth much less now then in ordinary times and with so many calls on me it would be a mere pretext to try to seem generous. However, I will pledge $50." He hoped that his executive office would allow him to use charity money at his discretion.[49]

Andrew's charity had left him nearly destitute, yet he was never poor in spirit. In late 1863, he presided over a meeting at Boston's Old

South Church to raise funds on behalf of freed slaves in the Mississippi Valley. "Every part of the church was filled," noted a reporter. "The aisles were crowded and around the doors the crowd was almost suffocating; a hundred unable to gain entrance, were turned away." Andrew described the ex-slaves' disgraceful living conditions, part of the larger humanitarian crisis that was keeping more than 50,000 African Americans in poverty. He introduced congregants to the sanitary commissioners who had been working with this population and could attest to the people's desperate need. As citizen after citizen pledged their financial support that evening, Andrew was again winning battles, not as governor but as a long-standing, hardworking advocate of the poor. John Bigelow, a former mayor of Boston, was so impressed by Andrew's leadership that he sent him the seal of the Commonwealth, a token of gratitude for his citizenship. The seal's Latin motto translates as "by the sword we seek peace, but peace under liberty."[50]

By year's end, the war had transformed the national landscape. At Andrew's request, Hayden took a leave from his job in the statehouse and spent months recruiting across the northern states. He carried the governor's name and credibility as he went from town to town sharing stories of the African American soldiers' bravery. Though Andrew was still disturbed by the pay inequities, he lauded Hayden's work:

> Every race has fought for Liberty and its own progress. The colored race will create its own future by its own brains, hearts, and hands. If Southern slavery should fall by the crushing of the Rebellion, and colored men should have no hand and play no conspicuous part in the task, the result would leave the colored man a mere helot; the freedmen, a poor, despised, subordinated body of human beings, neither strangers, nor citizens, but "contrabands," who had lost their master but not found a country.[51]

CHAPTER 19

THE PROMISE OF A NEW YEAR
January–June 1864

A Demand for Right and Justice

Winter weather was exacerbating the nation's war weariness, but an editor at *Harper's Weekly* saw promise was on the horizon in the New Year. The best sign, he believed, was African American enlistment:

> Every citizen ought to insist that they shall have exactly the treatment, chance, and pay as other soldiers. . . . [They] have proved themselves as heroic and docile and patient as soldiers can be, and they simply decline any thing less than bare justice. They do not mutiny, they make no trouble whatever, [but] say simply that the United States Government pledged its honor, and they will wait the fulfillment of the pledge.[1]

As he continued to work for pay equity, Andrew welcomed Senator Sumner's assistance in correcting the administration's "blunder."[2] He also enlisted the American Anti-Slavery Society's aid, and Garrison and Sumner urged its members to press for a constitutional solution. In addition, Garrison reached out to women activists such as Elizabeth Cady Stanton, who had founded the Women's National Loyal League as a complement to the existing Union League. That move paid off as more and more people responded to his efforts. Government officials were also involved. Stanton, for instance, obtained 100,000 signatures asking for the emancipation "of all persons of African descent," which would include border state slaves, and sent the petition to Sumner, who presented it to Congress. For thirty years, abolitionists had been crusading against slavery. Now it was time for Congress to finish what the radical Republicans had started.[3]

By early January, Andrew was laid low with another round of debilitating headaches. They forced him to shorten his long workdays, and friends worried he would not be able to keep up his intense schedule much longer. He often walked down to Samuel Howe's home in the afternoons, where he lay on a chaise lounge in the parlor and dictated his correspondence to an aide. But despite his health problems, he remained deeply engaged in war governance, and he continued to worry that the Emancipation Proclamation would not abolish slavery until after the war. In his mind, it needed to be abolished immediately. Otherwise, Congress might be content to celebrate the Union's preservation without committing to permanently upending the institution and establishing pay and other kinds of equity for all citizens, including African Americans. In a letter to his friend and colleague Charles Hale, Andrew celebrated the moral strength of the Black soldiers: "Poor as they were they [could] afford to wait for their pay until the Union could recognize their position and manhood. I think in this they were inspired by a very honorable feeling—one that I cannot but respect."[4]

The *Daily Advertiser* also applauded the soldiers' boycott. Could not the Massachusetts legislature "do something less gross," it queried, "than make a tender of money to prove the public sense of appreciation of the disinterested gallantry of these citizens?" Andrew thought one appropriate response might be to appoint an African American pastor to be the state's legislative chaplain, and he reached out to Hale and state senator George Williams about the issue. He had Reverend Grimes in mind for the position and thought they would support him. The *Daily Advertiser* did, assuring readers that Grimes was "universally respected as a good citizen, a pious minister, and a faithful and sensible man. Massachusetts will do honor to herself, and in some measure do justice to her colored regiments, by electing him."[5]

But recruiting African Americans had suddenly become more difficult. Andrew received a letter from Reuben Mussey, Jr., who had spent more than a year helping George Stearns recruit Black volunteers. Mussey informed the governor that Stearns, then in Nashville, had resigned from the position. He was no longer able to tolerate Stanton's haughty manner and Lincoln's recalcitrance on the pay issue. Andrew was disappointed but not disheartened. He encouraged Lewis Hayden, who was continuing to recruit, to keep the faith and to remind African Americans who were now thinking of enlisting in other state units that Massachusetts had taken these soldiers when everyone spurned them. "*We* raised colored troops, when it was unpopular," he told Hayden, and the implications were far greater than meeting draft quotas: "human rights and equal liberty."[6] "I do not want either to speculate out of blood or courage of colored men," he wrote days later, "but I rejoice in having been instrumental in giving them a chance to vindicate their manhood, and to strike a telling blow for their own race and the freedom of all their posterity." Andrew wanted them to have a part in the war and in their own manumission otherwise the result "would leave the colored man a mere helot; the freedmen a poor, despised, subordinated body of human beings, neither strangers nor citizens, but 'contrabands,' who lost their masters, but not found a country." "All the prejudices, jealousies, and political wishes, of narrow, ignorant men and demagogues would have full force," he maintained, "and the black man would be the helpless victim of a policy which would give him no peace short of banishment." In his letter to Hayden, he wrote, "The day that made a colored man a soldier of the Union, made him a power in the land. It admitted him to all the future of glory . . . [and] no one can ever deny the rights of citizenship in a country to those who have helped to create it or to *save it*."[7]

The state legislature assembled on January 6, and shortly before two o'clock Andrew accompanied his staff and representatives to the Old South Church, where Reverend William Stearns, the president of Amherst College, led their annual religious service. Stearns, who had lost his son at Fredericksburg, drove home two points: the rebellion must be put down, and Americans in both the North and the South must take a higher view of the nation. His short, profound message resonated with representatives, who had spent the past three years trying to manage an incalculable undertaking. At that evening's annual state dinner at the Parker House, Andrew capitalized on these sentiments. Addressing the attendees, he reminded them of what the Commonwealth had endured. In scattered hamlets throughout Massachusetts, the war had detached thousands of citizens from their homes, knitting military-aged males into the largest nationalized undertaking the republic had ever known. The state's volunteers had understood that the Union's significance was measured by their interdependency, whether fighting in the field or doing support work at home.[8]

On January 8, Andrew delivered his inaugural address to the legislature. He made little mention of war aims but offered a comprehensive report on the state's wartime activities, particularly as regards troop welfare. The Commonwealth had spent nearly $6.7 million, of which more than $5 million had gone to Massachusetts soldiers, either as bounties or family aid. After expressing his hope that the United States would build a military hospital in Massachusetts, he ended his speech with an emotional recitation, listing the names of the state's fallen soldiers. He declared they had not died in vain but to preserve a Union in quest of both liberty and liberation. Though work remained, both on the battlefield and in Congress, "the bell which rang out the Declaration of Independence has found at last a voice articulate to 'Proclaim Liberty throughout all the Land and to all inhabitants thereof.'" The Union's final act of redemption would be universal emancipation.[9] The governor used the occasion to quote from Lord Byron's *Marino Faliero, Doge of Venice*: "We must forget our feelings save the one, we must resign all passions save our purpose, we must behold no object save our Country, and look on death as beautiful, so that the sacrifice ascend to Heaven, and draw down Freedom on her Evermore."[10]

Eliza Quincy, who listened to the speech, agreed with the governor, saying that the "ship of state has again embarked under the pilot who has weathered the storm so successfully." She trusted that Andrew would guide the Commonwealth "through the breakers until she is again moored in a peaceful harbor."[11]

As legislators went to work, Andrew gave himself a few minor reprieves, attending lectures, receptions for returned soldiers, and dinner parties with the Howes, the Clarkes, and other friends. He had recently become closer to former governor Edward Everett, who invited Andrew to join his Thursday Evening Club. Just five years before, Everett had been focused on erecting Daniel Webster's statue on the statehouse grounds as Andrew was petitioning members to enact a law that prohibited racial discrimination in public places of amusement. Yet Everett's mind had changed over time, and he now endorsed Andrew's leadership as the Union's champion.[12]

In February, Lincoln summoned 500,000 men to serve for three years or until the war ended, setting March 10 as the draft deadline. He had recently decided to bring General Ulysses S. Grant east to command all the armies, and he hoped this change in leadership might inspire volunteers to rise to the challenge. By this time some 70,000 African Americans were serving in the army. Now, to compensate for sluggish volunteering, Stanton asked Congress to authorize the recruitment of border state slaves, including those of loyal slaveowners. The move was controversial, not only because border state critics opposed the measure but also because African Americans had little incentive to sign up if the federal government would not promise them equal pay. Andrew had lobbied Wilson and Sumner to sponsor legislation to equalize all soldier pay, and by the second week of February senators took up the measure. Wilson presented a resolution ensuring that all persons of color who had mustered into military service would be treated as equal to their white peers. Sumner amended the bill to make the pay retroactive to soldiers' enlistment. But after several days of contentious debate, conservative opponents stalled it. Though the Senate's finance committee chair, William Fessenden, and other colleagues supported pay equity, many were reluctant to fund retroactive pay for African American soldiers at this critical time. Still, the senator made it clear that there should be no unfair distinction: if soldiers of color served in the same army as white men, they should receive the same pay. In a letter to Bird, Sumner was irate about Fessenden's recalcitrance, calling the debate "discreditable" to New England.[13]

It was a sad commentary that, as political leaders debated pay equity, African American families suffered, and soldiers grew increasingly indignant over the blatant discrimination. Andrew shared their anger; and when he learned that Sergeant William Walker of the Third South Carolina Colored Infantry had been sentenced to be executed at the end of the month for alleged mutiny, he was irate. The previous August, Walker, who had received no pay for several months, had grown irritable and insubordinate. The twenty-three-year-old former slave decided that, because the federal government was not fulfilling its enlistment agreement, he no longer had to perform his soldierly duties. He led company members to Colonel Augustus Bennett's tent, and they stacked their arms. Authorities arrested Walker, tried, and convicted him of mutiny, and sentenced him to execution by firing squad. Andrew was beside himself.[14]

Andrew grew restive at remaining a prisoner to these issues, and in response, embarked on a new humanitarian crusade sending Oliver Gibbs to meet with Lincoln about it. Gibbs was the postmaster of Wareham, Massachusetts, and the governor had often detailed him to serve as a messenger of charity and relief at camps and hospitals. During those visits, Gibbs had told Andrew that some freed slaves and refugees in Washington wanted to head north but were not allowed to leave. So Andrew entrusted him with a letter to the president chronicling his state's commitment to the war effort. In it, the governor said that Massachusetts needed all the laborers it could get because of the continued demand for soldiers, and he asked Lincoln to allow the former slaves to come to the Commonwealth. The president, however, accused Andrew of trying to take recruits from Virginia, through Washington, to Massachusetts, while the loyal Virginia governor was attempting to raise troops to fight in his own state. The president confessed that he had to do for loyal Virginians what he was doing for Massachusetts. After Gibbs left him, Lincoln put these sentiments in writing. Yet in his statement he noted that, if Massachusetts could provide a permanent home for African Americans, he would like to know that, for it would "give relief in a very difficult point." As he sometimes did after writing letters, he placed it in his desk and never sent it. A week later he reread Andrew's letter, "carefully folded it, as for filing, and wrote upon the back: I understand from the within that there are a few hundred colored men in Alexandria who desire to go to Massachusetts and enlist in the United States service. *Let them go!* A. Lincoln." Andrew had his way, and the men came to Massachusetts.[15]

Now that most state legislatures were in session, Unionist majorities took steps to ensure Lincoln's renomination. Although many Massachusetts representatives saw this as a foregone conclusion, Andrew was not convinced. In a letter, Charles Ingersoll had described the Washington political climate as "seething." The Republican Party was breaking into factions, and this division threatened to upend the president's second term. Andrew knew that Salmon Chase and partisans such as senators Benjamin Wade and Henry Davis distrusted Lincoln and the radicals, and they were bitter against the influence of the Blair family. It was not a harmonious party culture; and in a letter to Andrew, Chase shared the disheartening news that he was withdrawing from the cabinet.[16]

Andrew made time that February to attend a reception in Boston for the British abolitionist and activist George Thompson, whom he had last heard speak years before at Bowdoin. In the packed hall, reporters sat "blooming in the midst" of the crowd, eager to record every word. In his speech, Thompson declared that abolition had grown in the United States thanks to a small but fiery group of reformers, and he praised the Commonwealth for doing its part: "Massachusetts has to-day her Sumner and her Wilson in Washington, her Garrison and her Phillips in Boston, and her John A. Andrew in the State House, supported by the moral and political power, combined with the utmost material resources of the Commonwealth." He quoted Andrew's words, spoken the year before when presenting the regimental colors to the Fifty-fourth Massachusetts, because they "are emphatic, because they are historical, because they are prophetic; because, also, they reflect honor . . . upon your Chief Magistrate." Identifying himself with Colonel Shaw's honor in leading these men, Andrew declared that "I stand or fall as a man and a magistrate with the rise or fall in the history of the 54th Massachusetts":

In Christian America, the land of the Sabbath schools, of religious privileges, of temperance societies and revivals, there exists the worst institution in the world. There is not an institution which the sun in the heaven shines upon so fraught with woe to man as American slavery. But now, thank God, I have lived to see the day when the sun in the heavens shines no longer on American slavery.[17]

In March, Andrew addressed graduates at Harvard Medical College's commencement, reminding them that a citizen must regard himself "as made for his country, not regard his country as made for him. If he will but subordinate his own selfhood and ambition enough to perceive how great is his country and how indefinitely less is he, he presently becomes a sharer in her glory and partaker of her greatness." As an example, he mentioned the several hundred surgeons, assistant surgeons, and nurses whom he had dispatched to the war, who had obeyed that summons and served with distinction. He spoke of Luther Bell, a physician who had come out of retirement and hurried to the front: "In camp, on the march, in hospital and on the field, he was like a model of earnest fidelity, of accomplished ability, of modest patience, and of subordination of self to duty which renders a great man entirely great." Andrew's speech was a paean to the possibilities that science was providing to humanity and a celebration of those who shaped its contours.[18]

Nonetheless, recruitment lagged, so the governor's war council convinced him, against his better judgment, to transport and enlist Europeans to fill the Massachusetts quota. With the help of bounties and brokers, the governor attracted nearly 1,000 recruits from Prussia and Switzerland, all of whom received the same pay as white American soldiers did. Andrew made a point of placing these German speakers in German American regiments. Yet what began as a productive enterprise soon spiraled out of control with fraud, and the venture attracted criticism at home and in the ranks. The soldier John Gray, Jr., wrote from camp, "If Governor Andrew has really only imported a few thousand negroes and Dutchmen, it merely shows that he has disgraced himself for nothing." Though he had only reluctantly agreed to undertake European enlistment, critics blamed him entirely, lambasting it as a desperate search for manpower.[19]

Meanwhile, African American troops continued their financial boycott, and a soldier in the Fifty-fourth reported to Andrew that their families were "suffering for want of support, or taken to the Poor Houses."[20] An officer said that he believed his fellow officers were intent "to raise the black man, as far as we can, *in* the army, and *through* it," but that "sometimes we almost despair about our men in the matter of pay and proper recognition":

> We cannot but think that it needs only to be thoroughly understood,—this case of ours,—to have justice done us. Is there no great mind who will gain the blessings of a race by winning over, through the forum or the press, the rulers of the country to this simple act of justice desired by us? . . . Think of their starving families.[21]

Andrew was that "great mind," but he had little control over individual behavior issues in the troops. His correspondence revealed that many white officers, even those from Massachusetts, mistreated African American soldiers. Pistol whippings and beatings with the flat of a sword were common. Joseph Holloway, a soldier in the Fifty-fourth, complained to his "Dear Friend" Andrew that a "parcel of coper head orfices [Copperhead officers; i.e., Confederate sympathizers] . . . drive us worse than ever the secash [corruption of secessionists] did." A former Mississippi slave, he said that he would rather be "back home with my boss than to be in any such a mess as this."[22]

Such experiences disheartened Andrew and he often took reprieves from the statehouse to visit the troops camped around Boston, and in early March he dedicated a new chapel at Fort Meigs in Readville, hoping that it would help soldiers find spiritual guidance. As he worked to make financial arrangements for the troops, he continued to contend with legislators bent on limiting his power, so he often relied on a small confidential group for advice. That month he was particularly annoyed by battles regarding the bounty loan, and he declared that he would not prorogue the legislature until members had passed a loan bill that would meet the coming year's exigencies. He vetoed a bill that forbade violators of the law prohibiting alcohol to serve on juries, and he rebuffed legislators who voted themselves a $100 bonus at the session's end. In response, they bullied him by threatening to override his veto. Frank Bird recalled Andrew's attitude at the session's end. "It was a Saturday," he reported, and "the members were impatient to leave for their homes, and those from a distance commenced drawing their pay from the Treasury." Because legislators had not approved the appropriation bill, Andrew instructed the treasurer not to pay them, which "brought matters to a deadlock." Bird asked the governor what he was going to do. "Do?" said Andrew:

> I am going to let those fellows know that *we* run this machine! They have had their way all winter abusing us, and now I am going to have mine. We have got to carry on this government, and they must pass a loan-bill

that will enable us to do it. Not a man of them shall get his pay, nor will I prorogue them, until they have passed a loan-bill such as we have agreed is necessary.

Members complied, and the finance chair amended the bill to the governor's satisfaction.[23]

Andrew was a tenacious opponent, no matter the issue, but when it came to equalizing soldier pay, he was relentless. Besides sending field complaints to Stanton and the *Liberator*, he used the Union victory at the Battle of Olustee in northern Florida to embarrass the administration into admitting that African American soldiers were hardly mere laborers. Andrew reminded Lincoln that these men were "bearing honorable wounds." By spring, congressional debate was centering on making pay retroactive only to the beginning of the year, not to muster date, which infuriated the governor. He solicited Sumner to carry his appeal to Lincoln, read it aloud, and wait for an answer. As his exemplar, he chose the case of Samuel Harrison, the Fifty-fourth's chaplain, who had been denied the regular $100 a month chaplain's pay as stipulated by an 1862 act of Congress. Andrew protested the government's color distinction, saying that no such line had ever been drawn by the Christian church. He drew Lincoln's attention to the fact that a "refusal by an officer of the Executive department to recognize the capacity and the rights of this chaplain is alike in violation of the rights of the Christian church and of the laws of Congress."[24]

Daylight for the Ages

On a blustery April evening, Andrew attended a reception at the Parker House hosted by Reverend Clarke and other prominent abolitionists in honor of two visiting African American residents of New Orleans. Arnold Bertonneau, a prominent wine merchant and captain of the First Regiment of the Louisiana Native Guards, had initially been in a volunteer African American regiment under the Confederacy, but after the Union occupation of New Orleans he was recommissioned to serve in the Union's reinforcement troops. He had recently resigned in protest, however, due to mistreatment and misuse of his men. Jean Baptiste Roudanez was a machinist and engineer who, with his brother, Dr. Louis Charles Roudanez, had founded *L'Union*, a bilingual French-English newspaper that was widely circulated in Louisiana and inside the Union army. Both men had been instrumental in assisting slaves to freedom, and Andrew was anxious to applaud their efforts in and to hear their views about Reconstruction in Louisiana. In his speech he recalled the shot at Fort Sumter that had exploded into war. "Three years ago," he said, "such a spectacle as this would have been improbable. We have lived many ages during the past three years. What enemies without and what foes within have we had to contend."[25]

That same evening, news came over the statehouse wires reporting the battle and massacre at Fort Pillow, a small Mississippi River stronghold in Henning, Tennessee, forty miles north of Memphis. Initial communiqués reported that Confederate forces had stormed the fort, overwhelmed Union forces, and slaughtered those who surrendered, including more than three hundred African American soldiers. Soon the Boston press was publishing firsthand accounts claiming that, out of the four hundred African American soldiers involved in the incident, only about twenty had survived. Field reports alleged that the fort was torched, Black soldiers in hospitals shot, and African American women and children slaughtered like sheep. The atrocity confirmed Andrew's worst fears about Confederate retaliation. His only comfort was that Congress's Joint Committee on the Conduct of the War immediately launched an investigation into the incident and later confirmed most of the reports. Andrew wrote to his friend Wendell Phillips's son-in-law, George Smalley, a *New York Tribune* correspondent, and encouraged him to publicize the massacre, including the complicity of leading Confederate officers such as General Nathan Bedford Forrest, a former slave dealer. In the meantime, he despaired over the government's response: "The President and the Department of War have in the matter of colored troops and colored people exhibited an ingenuity of fatal, foolish and criminal stupidity. It is even more discouraging to suppose they *mean* right than to declare them willfully wrong."[26]

By mid-April, Andrew was pressing Lincoln again to ask Attorney General Edward Bates for his legal opinion on the issue of pay equity. In a letter to Sumner, Andrew fumed that the War Department's views and Congress's neglect were "more stupid than wicked." He did not know that Lincoln had taken him up on his suggestion to consult Bates, but one evening, as Stanton and Sumner were having dinner together, Lincoln appeared and handed the senator the dispatch from Bates. The attorney general had ruled that the Second Confiscation Act of 1862 authorized the president to employ and pay volunteers, including African Americans, in whatever way he liked. The next day, Sumner sent it to Andrew as a memento, along with a note that began, "At last we see day-light."[27]

Bates's ruling delighted Andrew, not only as regards the pay discrepancy but also because it allowed an opening for African American officer commissions. Lincoln, however, did not make the next move himself, instead leaving Congress to settle the matter. The problem was that many citizens saw pay equality as an unjust measure that would lower white soldiers to the level of Black soldiers. After all, as critics pointed out, African Americans had accepted the terms of the pay agreement when they enlisted, even if it was manifestly unjust. Yet these soldiers countered that the federal government had violated the contractual enlistment terms that Andrew had secured with the authorization to raise regiments. Andrew fumed over Congress's slow progress in solving the problem. He told Edward Kinsley, a Boston merchant and abolitionist friend, who had helped him raise the Fifty-fourth, "I trust the black man will vindicate his own rights so plainly during this war, that the blood of these martyrs shall be the seed of their unquestioned enjoyment of all the rights of Humanity in the years to come."[28]

Still, there was a growing sense that liberation was a part of the new path forward. The Emancipation Proclamation, African American enlistments, the creation of the Bureau of Colored Soldiers, and the founding of the Freedman's Inquiry Commission confirmed that the administration was embracing racial progress. Andrew believed that that Harriet Tubman's work was a large part of this shift; he certainly acknowledged her influence on his own thinking. On April 8, the Senate, by an overwhelming majority, voted to pass the Thirteenth Amendment, which would abolish slavery everywhere in the United States. The governor hoped the House would do the same. In the meantime, he reiterated his earlier advice to Sumner that members should consider establishing a freedman's bureau to help slaves make the transition out of bondage. Still, it was frustrating that the government continued to disgrace African Americans by refusing to equalize soldier pay—for fear, Andrew believed, that the uniform might dignify slaves or make freed Blacks appear worthy of citizenship.

In late April, Andrew received a letter from the Englishman Thomas Barker, thanking him for his hospitality to George Thompson. Barker wanted the governor to know that millions of English citizens stood shoulder to shoulder with him as the governor worked to restore the Union and liberate the slaves. He "hailed the coming day when England and America,—both in peace—viewing each other in offices of mutual good will, shall pursue in concord their grand careers of benevolence and glory, their peoples both happy, prosperous, free, and honored of all nations."[29] Andrew allowed Garrison to reprint the letter in the *Liberator*. Perhaps readers would take courage from the support of so many others around the world.

By May, Andrew was struggling to balance home-front draft troubles with battlefront defeats. Nonetheless, he continued to receive painful letters from his constituents. "I am unwilling to add to your many cares," wrote Daniel Ricketson of New Bedford, "but as you are the Father of the Commonwealth, I suppose you expect that your children should cry to you for bread." Ricketson's brother Joseph was a devoted abolitionist who now needed help, and Andrew obliged.[30] He was less obliging when Stanton asked him to forward a battalion of heavy artillery and all unattached companies currently employed in garrison duty. Behind in his quotas and pressed by the African American soldiers' discontent, he lashed out to Sumner, "For God's sake, how long is the injustice of the Government to be continued towards these men? *If mutiny shall occur, and blood be shed, the responsibility will rest, before God, on the Government at Washington.*" He implored the senator to visit the president and "beg him, for the sake of justice and of the country, to prevent the shedding of innocent blood, and to cause these men to be paid *instantly*."[31] In the meantime, soldiers flooded African American newspapers with letters and petitions, declaring that the issue was not about money but about "liberty, justice, and equality." Andrew asked Hayden to reassure the men that he was doing everything in his power, and he sent a bundle of War Department letters to regimental commanders, along with a cover letter from Hayden that described the governor's labors on their behalf.[32]

By the time the General Court adjourned in mid-May, Andrew had learned that some radicals, led by Wendell Phillips, were working to organize a national political convention, to be held in Cleveland, where they intended to nominate John Frémont for president—a week before the Republican National Convention would take place in Baltimore. The organizers complained that Lincoln was not moving fast enough to advance pay equity for African American soldiers or to abolish slavery entirely. Andrew understood their frustration, remarking to Forbes that the administration lacked "coherence, method, purpose, and consistency."[33] Nonetheless, he saw Lincoln's leadership as better than the alternatives, and he refused to take part in the radicals' plan. Besides, he had other pressing matters—not least the ever-expanding soldier welfare network. Officers entreated him to convince citizens to reenlist, but horrifying field reports from the Battle of the Wilderness, fought in early May in Virginia, intensified recruitment difficulties. Andrew's correspondence was filled with laments about congressional delays and wailing letters from poverty-stricken families. There were reports that African American soldiers were on the verge of mutiny. Andrew forwarded some of these letters to Sumner, demanding that the "wages earned by their valor, their endurance and their blood, be no longer withheld. They have already endured enough."[34]

Though the Union's military fortunes seemed to be improving under Grant, Andrew was losing patience. His "fighting blood was up," recalled his secretary, and he blamed Lincoln. On May 18 he sent the president a communiqué demanding that he settle the equal pay problem once and for all. Soldiers were worn out by their service, and many were dependent on public charity, not to mention humiliated and depressed. Lincoln needed to make good on his Gettysburg pledge to envision the war as a new birth of freedom. In his letter, Andrew invoked the irony of Sergeant Walker's death penalty for mutiny:

> The Government which found no law to pay him except as a nondescript and a contraband nevertheless found law enough to shoot him as a soldier. In behalf of the sufferings of the poor and needy; of the rights of brave men in arms for their country; of the statutes of Congress; and the honor of the nation, I pray your Excellency to interpose the rightful power of the Chief Executive Magistrate of the United States, who is bound by his oath "to take care that that the laws be faithfully executed"; and by its immediate exercise, to right these wrongs.[35]

As Andrew saw it, the federal government had accepted these men into service and established a contractual relationship that conferred citizenship on them. Unequal pay, however, invalidated those terms and made them appear to be second-class citizens. In a letter to Pennsylvania representative Thaddeus Stevens, he pleaded for Congress to act:

> I will never give up my demand for right and justice to these soldiers. I will pursue it before every tribunal [and] . . . will present it in every forum where any power resides to assert their rights and avenge their wrongs. If I should leave this world with this work undone, and there should be any hearing for such as I elsewhere in the Universe, I will carry the appeal before the tribunal of Infinite Justice.

Yet it was humiliating to combat "this contemptible higgling over the price which a great and powerful people are to pay brave men," he told Stevens. The discussion needed to end.[36] Count Gurowski echoed Andrew's sentiments. "The truth is," he told the governor, "that a man is wanting with that terrible patriotic earnestness which is necessary to say truth & open the eyes of the people."[37]

In late May, Andrew drafted a legal brief advocating equal pay—perhaps the greatest brief he ever wrote—and placed it in the hands of George Hale, president of Boston's common council. It was Hale's task to visit Lincoln and hand him the letter. The brief referred to indisputable evidence as displayed in statutes by former Attorney General

William Wirt related to the War of 1812. They confirmed that African American soldiers were entitled to and should receive the same treatment as white soldiers. Andrew appealed to the president "not only by reason of the suffering condition of the men of these regiments and of their families, but also from my conviction of their rights under the laws, and of the justice of their claim":

> It appears . . . that under the law for recruiting the regular Army, [that] . . . colored men were enlisted, paid and enjoyed the bounties accorded to men of the white race [a half-century ago]. . . . Neither Congress nor the Executive Department, nor the People saw cause to deny wages of a soldier to any men who wore the uniform, took the oaths and performed the duties of a soldier—not even though he was black. . . . Their moral claims to consideration and regard, I am sure I need not repeat nor urge anew.[38]

Hale told Andrew that Lincoln lauded the governor's attempt to bend justice toward the African American soldiers. Unfortunately, he added, the president was pressed from all sides and "there was no probability of varying his action at present."[39] Nonetheless, by the time Hale's report reached the statehouse, Sumner had already informed Andrew that the Senate had granted African American soldiers full pay beginning in January 1, 1864. Sumner knew that the governor would be disappointed that the bill had not provided for retroactive pay starting from the time of muster, and he denounced this arrangement as a "conclusion in which nothing is concluded."[40] Moreover, even though the bill would become law on June 15 and African American soldiers were to be given full pay retroactive to January 1, 1864, the administration would not implement it until August 1. Sumner told Andrew that Attorney General Bates had been amiable in his dealings over the issue, though he had equivocated about legal details. Stanton, however, had been his usual recalcitrant, disagreeable self. "I thought his conduct on the occasion very reprehensible," Sumner told Andrew. "This long controversy has embittered him towards our State and those who have persistently pressed the claim of colored troops."[41]

No matter: Andrew and Sumner had pulled off another triumph for justice. Even though it fell short of expectations, Andrew refused to squabble with Stanton and allowed Sumner to mend fences. "I beg you," he told Sumner, "to avail yourself of some early and proper occasion to express to Mr. Stanton my great surprise at hearing as I do from various sources that he is displeased and incensed at me and all those who press this claim." It is unlikely that Andrew had misunderstood Stanton's original declaration that African American soldiers would be paid as much as white soldiers, but the governor was willing to be charitable: "He preferred only that Congress should act upon it, rather than to assume to do anything about it himself." Andrew encouraged Sumner to show Stanton his letter to make it clear that the governor was acting on principle, not from spite. "I grind no man's axes," he told Sumner: "I ask for nothing but for the public good, [but] . . . as one of the sworn servants of the public, I will ask for nothing which is not right, I will neither willingly submit to anything wrong. I will have no controversy until compelled, unless I am in the right and then I will not surrender." Sumner, however, recommended against sharing the letter with Stanton: "I doubt if it will be advisable to approach Mr. Stanton on the contents of your letter. He is very sore, and behaves badly."[42]

Rank-and-file soldiers were not surprised to learn, once again, that their governor was dauntless in his pursuit of justice. "John Andrew works hard & to the purpose & he will get accomplished what he is to work for," wrote Kinsley.[43] Sergeant William Logan of the Fifty-fifth, stationed at Folly Island, South Carolina, said that Andrew was a man "who I would gladly die for," promising that he and his men would yet "show the world what the Gov's colored volunteers can do."[44] Charles Lenox of the Fifty-fourth wrote to Andrew from Morris Island to assure him that there was "at least one member" of the regiment "who knows that Mass has done more for his race, than all the States, and that your Excellency has done more than all Governors put together for their benefit."[45]

Andrew took solace in knowing he had won justice for these troops. He also held out hope that Stanton, Lincoln, and Congress might see their way to removing the prohibitions on African American officer commissions. But given the Union's staggering losses in May and June, the war secretary had no time for such trifles, even if he had been in a better mood about Andrew. Then Andrew received news from Colonel Edward Hallowell that Major General John Foster, commander of the Department of the South, had refused to discharge Sergeant Stephen Swails, an African American soldier, from his regiment so that he could take up a lieutenant's commission in the Fifty-fourth Massachusetts. Swails was a New Yorker who, in answer to Frederick Douglass's call, had enlisted in the Fifty-fourth, where he was soon promoted to first sergeant and eventually to sergeant major. After the Battle of Fort Wagner in Morris Island, South Carolina, Hallowell had assumed command of the regiment, and it became part of General Truman Seymour's Florida expedition. Swails performed valiantly and was wounded at

Olustee. When Hallowell recommended that Andrew promote him to second lieutenant, the governor agreed and began pressing the issue with Lincoln. Assuming that he would be promoted, Swails received an officer's uniform and performed a lieutenant's duties for several weeks. In May, however, the War Department refused Andrew's request, citing Swails's African descent. Colonel William Gurney, the post commander, ordered Swails to remove his officer's uniform and resume his duties as an enlisted man. Yet even though the Swails's case was now slowly cycling through bureaucracy, Andrew had, according to a letter in the *Liberator,* "dealt a sturdy blow to colorphobia."[46] He held on to hope that Lincoln, too, would see the light.

By early June, the governor was eager for battlefield victories, but news from the eastern front did little to buoy Commonwealth spirits as reports from Grant's overland campaign indicated high casualties. The Union war effort had already suffered a political setback when radical Republicans nominated Frémont for president. Now, as the Battle of Cold Harbor raged in Virginia, Republicans and War Democrats assembled in Baltimore, refashioned themselves into the National Union Party, and nominated Lincoln for president and Andrew Johnson of Tennessee for vice president. Initially, Lincoln had intended to offer the vice presidency to Benjamin Butler, but Butler refused to leave the army, to the disgust of many radical Republicans. "Lincoln drifts," said Wendell Phillips. "Butler steers."[47] Yet as none of the major party bosses moved to endorse Frémont, some radicals realigned themselves with Lincoln, while others stayed with the Pathfinder for the time being, though he would eventually withdraw his candidacy in September. Andrew saw Lincoln's nomination as a foregone conclusion, unless he, too, could be induced to withdraw.[48]

As he often did during times of trouble, Andrew turned to the Twelfth Baptist Church for solace. Serendipitously, on the evening of June 20, he was at the church, when William Wells Brown, a celebrated African American abolitionist and novelist, announced that a historic event was about to take place. Reverend Grimes asked the unsuspecting Andrew to accompany him down the aisle to the chancel, and he seated the governor in the pulpit. Hundreds had gathered to witness a remarkable tribute; and as a solemn quiet came over the crowd, William Nell launched into a summary of Andrew's contributions to the African American community. His mission had begun in the winter of 1846, Nell recalled, when he had delivered an address before the Adelphic Union Library Association, "dispensing to us the dewdrops of knowledge."

This, Nell told Andrew, "was but one among many preceding evidences of your heartfelt interest in the improvement of those who then could not, as is our happy privilege now to boast, bask in the sunlight of literary advantages." Nell went on to memorialize Andrew's "brilliant career," characterized by his "heroic and eloquent service for the removal of Judge Loring—protesting against the word *white* on the Statute Book, and against the Dred Scott decision—having already been most zealous in promoting the equal school rights of colored children in Boston." He celebrated Andrew's call to the governorship and confirmed that African American citizens appreciated the sagacity and foresight that had marked his administration early in the war, "augmented by that sense of justice which recognizes man as man, irrespective of accidental differences." He reminded listeners that it was Andrew's "bugle-blast which first summoned colored American soldiers into the field."[49]

Boston's humble servant leader, risen to greatness because of his work for those whom others saw as beneath contempt, blushed before the crowd. Few public servants had ever deserved such accolades; Andrew was surely one of a kind. He had spent his life seeking justice for every man and woman, regardless of color, and he and his African American constituents had become kindred. Nell declared, "Whether as a citizen, a professional man, a legislator, a philanthropist, or a Christian magistrate, yours has ever been the heart to conceive, the head to organize, and the hand to execute the ways and means for the public recognition of the colored man as equal before the law." After these splendid words, Nell presented the governor with a portrait of himself, painted by Jacob Andrews and William Simpson in acknowledgment of his "valuable services in Humanity's cause, and as a medium for the grateful homage of our hearts." Nearly in tears, Andrew responded with a brief impromptu speech highlighting the African American soldiers' heroism, bravery, and conduct, which, he argued, had earned them a place in the annals of history. He was so moved by the tribute he had received that he hung the portrait in his home rather than at the statehouse. It was personal.[50]

CHAPTER 20

THIS JUSTICE

July–December 1864

Years Crowded into an Hour

In early July, Andrew traveled to Washington to ensure that federal paymasters would be delivering the African American soldiers their full pay. Before he left Boston, he wrote to John Langston, an Ohio abolitionist attorney who was recruiting African American troops, to assure him that his victory in the pay equity dispute would affirm citizenship of native-born Americans, regardless of color. "Right will take place" he told Langston, "and justice will be done." Still, he hastened his efforts onward. "The opportunity of years, now crowded into an hour, visits you," he told Langston:

> [It] beckons, entreats, commands, you to come, come *now*, come *instantly*, come with a shout, and receive the baptism which is to admit you into the glorious company of the peoples . . . who, by their own blood, have vindicated their right to all the blessings and all the powers of liberty, and to whose own right arms, the Lord of hosts has given the victory.[1]

Salmon Chase had followed the pay issue and applauded Andrew's efforts in resolving the disparity. "This justice," he penned in his diary, "has been too long & too cruelly withheld."[2]

Accompanied by his secretary, Henry Ware, Andrew called on Stanton and Lincoln at the White House on July 3. In a letter to his mother, Ware said that he and the governor sat with Lincoln for nearly an hour. Although Ware dismissed the White House as a "shiftless looking place," he was excited to be witnessing this "great jubilee" day for African Americans, "such as never was known here." In meeting Lincoln, he described him as "unusually tall and thin with a loose old Bogana coat on such as old ministers wear." The height difference between president and governor was amusing: "The top of the govs head just came under the Prest's chin. . . . The Gov. is round as an orange, and the other excellency looming up like a staff." Although Lincoln had a *"very* pleasant face and voice," his countenance was *"very sad,* except when relaxing for a little fun without which I am sure he could not live a year. I forgive him every story he has told or heard."[3]

Before Congress adjourned that July, representatives authorized seamen who had mustered in during the war to receive credit for military service. This was another victory for Andrew, as the seafaring towns had contributed heavily to the war effort. The ongoing need for sailors had burdened seaside hamlets, and clerks in the Massachusetts adjutant general's office now worked day and night to credit some 16,000 names to state's war effort. Still, manpower needs kept growing as the pool of military-age men shrank. To account for the shortage, Andrew continued to transport foreign-born volunteers into the ranks, but in their haste to muster them, bounty brokers often misled these recruits about their enlistment terms. Congress now also allowed state governors to send agents into the Confederate states (except for Arkansas, Louisiana, and Tennessee) to recruit freedmen. Andrew cautiously dispatched agents into the South, but they soon drew hostile reactions from Union field commanders and soldiers. Critics of the practice alleged that agents were inflating recruitment estimates, and many commanders had a more practical vision for freedmen, believing they should attend to their families and homes instead of joining the army. General Sherman was among the most outspoken critics of the plan. He had a righteous hatred of overzealous brokers and banned them from camp. "It will never do to let the *sharks* go down to the Rebel States," Forbes reported to Andrew. "Such men . . . would discredit our whole plan."[4]

Still, freedmen slowly made their way into the ranks; and though a small coterie supported the endeavor, critics continued to complain about Andrew's efforts. The editor of the *New York World Express* was especially caustic. In an article titled "We Want Darkies Too," he wrote, "The people who are conducting this war think negroes make as good soldiers as white men, and as they are responsible for the war not we, let them have their darkies, so that as many white men as possible may be retained at home."[5] The editor of the *National Intelligencer* asked how Andrew would "like to see Massachusetts invaded for a like purpose by recruiting officers from other States."[6] Even soldiers who supported the enterprise remained skeptical about Black volunteers' combat abilities.

From a camp near Petersburg, Virginia, the surgeon Isaac Stearns of the Twenty-second Massachusetts Volunteer Infantry wrote to his sister, telling her that he supported Andrew but that she should not be taken aback by his attitudes toward African American soldiers:

> When I say that they will not fight unless cornered up, I do not say it to their disparagement. It would be better for all the world if they were universally so. Negroes are superior to white men in their faithfulness, as you will find in the doctrine of the church. Fanatics argue that the negro is equal to the white, intellectually, which is not so—nor is it desirable, if we saw things as they are, I should prefer to be good, rather than wise, in our own estimation.[7]

The war moved at a lethargic pace that summer, but casualties remained high. Meanwhile, in Washington, the administration was wrestling with upheaval. Salmon Chase's retirement left Lincoln at the mercy of political factions, and many in Congress were opposed to the president's lenient 10 percent Reconstruction plan. Andrew, perhaps more than Lincoln, was concerned about African American economic independence and equality before the law than about control of Southern governments, but both knew these issues were intertwined. As an alternative to the president's plan, Senator Benjamin Wade of Ohio and Representative Henry Davis of Maryland co-sponsored a plan to reestablish loyal governments in the Confederacy that would make Congress, not the president, the arbiter of Reconstruction, though it failed to enfranchise Blacks. According to the plan, readmittance into the United States would require most white male citizens to formally swear that they had never supported the Confederacy. Congress passed the bill on July 2, but Lincoln continued to believe that lenient terms were the path to peaceful and productive reconciliation. Andrew agreed. In his view, punitive and humiliating measures would, among other things, result in violence toward freed slaves. Thus, as the congressional season moved toward its end, the president, to the dismay of many, pocket-vetoed the bill.

Congress adjourned on July 4, and that evening Chase invited Sumner, Andrew, and Massachusetts congressman Samuel Hooper to dine with him at his Washington home. The conversation centered on Lincoln's veto. Sumner noted that it had created indignation among the radicals, and his listeners agreed. But even though Andrew preferred Lincoln's lenient approach to Reconstruction, he knew that freed slaves could not expect to receive equitable treatment from Lincoln loyalists; after all, African American soldiers had not received it from the U.S. government, a fact that southern journalists already used as evidence of northern racial prejudice. As much as Andrew advocated expanding war aims to win the conflict, he wanted to avoid pressing too hard against the South and instigating retribution against African Americans. The situation would become even more dangerous if Lincoln were to lose the election.[8]

Battle updates from Petersburg, Virginia, were depressing, and news of heavy fighting there followed Andrew back to Boston. Confederate troops under General Jubal Early crossed the Potomac at Shepherdstown, West Virginia, on July 5 and headed for Washington, throwing residents into a panic, and threatening not only the capital but also Lincoln's candidacy. Back home in Boston, Andrew sifted through his mail at the statehouse and prepared his remarks for Harvard's upcoming commencement, which was held on July 20, a beautiful sunny day. He enjoyed such ceremonies, reminders that the life of the mind continued on, even during war. Edward Everett gave the keynote speech, with a preamble honoring Josiah Quincy, and then Andrew took the podium. He sympathized with the emotions of the occasion, for seventy alumni had already died in the war, most recently Henry Abbott, who had perished at the Battle of the Wilderness. But as much as Andrew craved the intellectual surroundings of a place like Harvard, he knew he had to return to his war duties.[9]

In the late days of July, wires from Petersburg brought more sorrowful news to the statehouse. On July 30, the stenographer transcribed the tale of the Union disaster at the Battle of the Crater, which Grant characterized to Halleck as the "saddest affair I have witnessed in this war."[10] A correspondent for the *New York Times* wrote, "I am called to the fulfillment of an ungracious task tonight. Instead of success and victory which the morning fairly promised, I have to write of disaster and defeat."[11] The casualty numbers were shocking, with the African American regiments suffering the most. Democrats used the episode to criticize Grant's leadership and spread rumors about the hypocrisy of using African Americans to lead an assault. Columnists turned their wrath on Andrew for elevating African Americans to the Union ranks. "Niggers are not fit for soldiers," declared the *New York Herald*. "They can dig, and drive mules, [but] . . . they cannot and will not fight."[12] Some white soldiers called Andrew an enemy of the country. "Many of your beloved brethren in color,—I mean the niggers, for I believe you are half nigger your self—have seriously died [at the Crater] before Petersburg," wrote an anonymous critic, who signed the letter "Not a

Nager." He added a postscript: "John Brown is dead. Glory Halla-he [ruined us.]"[13] Such sentiments confirmed for Andrew that he and the African American soldiers were waging a dual war, and he had difficulty telling if Union prospects were improving on either front.[14]

The Crater hollowed out the North's war spirit that summer, but Andrew took some comfort in knowing that his vision for freedom was marching forth. The Senate passed universal emancipation through constitutional amendment and repealed the Fugitive Slave Law. Congress had even adopted Sumner's bill to compel railway authorities in Washington, D.C., to allow African Americans to travel on streetcars. Despite the cruelty of the press, Andrew was buoyed by the fidelity of his supporters. Appreciative tokens frequently arrived at the statehouse, and one notable memento was a basket boat woven from reeds cut in a South Carolina swamp, caulked with field cotton, and smeared with pine pitch. It had belonged to the slave Jack Flowers, who had used it to escape. Determined to head to the Union camps, he had hidden in the rice fields before slipping through the forest to a creek, where he floated his tiny craft three miles downstream to freedom. General Saxton, headquartered in Beaufort, South Carolina, decided that Flowers's homemade freedom vessel would make a compelling exhibit at Philadelphia's Sanitary Fair, and he shipped it north with the following inscription: "A Freeman's Gift to the Great Central Fair held at Philadelphia, being all that he possessed." Afterward, at Flowers's direction, Saxton had the boat sent to Andrew, a fitting souvenir for his abolitionist work.[15]

By August, the summer military campaigns had beaten down Andrew's hope that the war might soon be over. Lincoln's call in July for 500,000 men was a dispiriting sign. Battleground prospects remained fraught, and critics were launching vitriolic attacks on Andrew and the president, accusing them of hijacking the conflict and transforming it into an abolition war. For many, dying for abolition seemed less noble than dying for the Union's preservation. Horatio Woodman, the editor of the *Boston Evening Transcript* and the younger brother of Andrew's friend Cyrus, told the governor not to raise any new regiments but to let the draft square things fairly. "*Massachusetts has no right to think of a new regiment,*" he declared, "*until every regiment she has in the field is full.*"[16]

In mid-August, a small but powerful Republican committee composed of New York and Massachusetts leaders corresponded with Horatio Seymour, the governor of New York, about emancipation and the Union's future, should the Democrats prevail in the fall elections. They delegated Andrew to take the lead in communicating the need to unite and asked him to arrange a meeting for that purpose. In an August 11 letter, Andrew invited Seymour to find common ground with him regarding the process forward. Both were prominent Union governors, and Andrew thought it would be wise to meet and find mutual solutions "to strengthen the arms of our national power."[17] The war had demoralized the citizenry, and Andrew wanted to reinvigorate the populace via a gesture of gubernatorial solidarity. He offered to meet Seymour in New York during the following weekend, but Seymour preempted him and instead walked into the Boston statehouse on August 19. Andrew told Henry Lee, Jr., "We had a two hours' most interesting conversation, and it seemed to me as if he had been carried away by the subtlety of his own intellect. I believe he is quite sincere, although he and I differed on every point."[18]

In the third week of August, Republican committee members in New York, fearing that Lincoln would lose the election, sent out a circular calling for a new convention to be held in Cincinnati on September 28. Members rallied party leaders in several states, who directed their ire not so much against Lincoln but against Seward and his conservative influence. In Massachusetts, there were conservative rumblings against Andrew's candidacy, but no other Republican could garner nearly so much support. Nonetheless, a number of Commonwealth voters were unhappy with Lincoln; so on August 18, Republican committee members invited Salmon Chase to dinner at Boston's Union Club. Since resigning from the treasury in June, Chase had been touring New England, exploring the possibility of replacing Lincoln. Andrew attended the dinner, along with numerous well-known politicians, journalists, and activists. After discussions, attendees decided to consult state governors and other select leaders to determine the feasibility of a Chase candidacy, and they agreed to meet in New York City after the Democratic National Convention, set for August 29 and 30 in Chicago.[19]

The group, along with members of New York's journalistic intelligentsia, reconvened on August 30 at the home of David Field. Sumner declined to attend, though he told Andrew that the Republican's June convention had seemed "ill-considered & unreasonable" and that he saw no way of meeting the difficulties of Lincoln's candidacy "*unless he withdraws patriotically & kindly, so as to leave no breach in the party.*"[20] After a long discussion, attendees decided on the questions to send state leaders and adjourned to await responses. The journalists asked if Lincoln's reelection was probable, if he would carry their state, or if the interests of the country and National Union Party would be better served by another candidate. Abolitionists had been emboldened by emancipation and the arming Black troops, and they now thought they could influence the coming election.

Respondents expressed discouragement about Lincoln but nonetheless supported him. In the meantime, Forbes, writing from Washington, told Andrew that Frank Howe and William Cullen Bryant, the editor of the *New York Evening Post*, were in favor of supporting Lincoln. They believed that it was too late for a change of leadership. Forbes suggested that Andrew reach out to influential leaders in the West and Pennsylvania to enlist their views and press Lincoln to avoid acquiescing to rumored peace talks. Andrew gave the matter serious reflection. Like Forbes, he thought it was too late to find another candidate. Yet "[since] we must have Lincoln, then the men of motive and ideas must get in the lead, must elect him, get hold of 'the machine' and run it themselves." He encouraged Forbes to speak with Lincoln and convince him to reconstitute his cabinet, should he win reelection.[21] Andrew wrote to Horace Greeley on the same day, laying out the president's shortcomings and bemoaning the Republicans' blunder in hosting a June convention, but concluded that Massachusetts would vote for the "Union Cause at all events" and would thus support Lincoln.[22]

Andrew was eager to help Lincoln and the radicals come to an understanding. He told Edwin Morgan, a senator from New York, that he wanted to meet with Henry Raymond, chair of the Republican National Committee and editor of the *New York Times*, to discuss how to convince Lincoln to steer his policies in the right direction and without fear of consequence. He also wrote to Governor Richard Yates of Illinois, asking to meet him in Washington and to help enlist the western governors in rescuing the president "from the influences which threaten him." Andrew was opposed to any idea of proposing a peaceful ceasefire: "I would spurn the bare *suggestion* of ceasing hostilities *now*, and the very thought of dealing with the rebel chiefs with peace, but I would seize the occasion for an appeal to all *people*, both South and North, against the assassins of liberty, and the enemies of this our Government."[23]

On September 3, General Sherman declared victory in his Atlanta campaign, and Andrew celebrated with a hundred-gun salute on Boston Common. He knew, however, that casualties would be heavy, so he stayed close to the statehouse stenographer, waiting for updates. Despite the bloodshed, he hoped to channel this military victory into a political victory in November, so he arranged a September 6 meeting at Faneuil Hall, where he gave an inspiring address before an enormous crowd. He also briefly stepped aside from his war duties and visited several agricultural fairs around the state. He gave an address at Hampden Park in Springfield, reminding listeners that the war was revolutionizing the ways in which they lived and adapted to economic changes. He boasted of New England's contributions in technology, industry, and agriculture and reassured his audience that the region would emerge from the war more economically vital than ever. He emphasized the importance of education in "the highest development and cultivation of the faculties of *men*, . . . [in] the production and diffusion of *Ideas*."[24] In a letter to his wife, he wrote that the address was a great success: "I think I have never done better, and never got into magnetic relations with an audience more perfectly, for all which, I am very thankful."[25] His former Bowdoin professor, Alpheus Packard, was in attendance and confirmed the speech's effect on listeners: "The views which it advances give authority to the important doctrine in our country, that the material interests should not engross attention at the expense of the aesthetical."[26]

On September 10, the day after his Springfield address, Andrew and Frank Howe set out for Washington. The governor was delighted to have his friend with him at the nation's capital, which he considered "a lonesome place." He had "worked like a beaver these last few days and nights," and it was his "purpose in visiting Washington to help keep the Government up to the tone of our Faneuil Hall meeting of last Tuesday night. . . . I have decided, in company with men in politics whom I believe in, that in order to prevent the catastrophe of Liberty, we *must* take hold, put Lincoln through, guard and protect him if we can, lash ourselves to the mast, and confront the gale."[27]

As Andrew and Howe passed through New York City, they visited with the journalists George Curtis and Sydney Gay and revealed that they were headed to Washington to dissuade the president from undertaking a negotiated peace. In the capital, they met Forbes at the White House, and the three spoke with Lincoln. Andrew showed the president letters from Governor Yates and Governor John Brough of Ohio, who agreed with Andrew that negotiated peace should not be an option. He spent ten days in Washington and afterward said, "I have worked very hard here, on many matters, state, national, civil, political, and philanthropic; and have done some good."[28]

As Andrew read the news of Sherman's campaign, he was impressed by the general's treatment of African Americans. He told Frank Bird:

[Sherman] does not make any difference between white and black people. He sends all noncombatants away from Atlanta, allowing them to choose whether they will go South or North. . . . Those whose loyalty prefers North he sends to the rear & provides for all as well as he can. The colored men able to give efficient labor are all said to be employed by him, thus enabling them to help their families."[29]

Andrew remained concerned about pay issues because many African American soldiers did not yet know that Congress had acted to give them back pay. For the moment their families continued to suffer, and they let the governor know it. "Sir," wrote Rachel Wicker, the sister of Robert Wicker of the Fifty-fifth, "I write to you to know the reason why our husbands and sons who enlisted in the 55th Massachusetts regiment have not bin paid off I speak for my self and mother and I know of a great many others as well as ourselves are suffering for the wont of mony to live on. . . . I think it a piece of injustice to have those soldiers there 15 months with out a cent of mony for my part." Letters such as these helped explain why Andrew gave so much of his salary to suffering families.[30]

The Mandate of Victory

Even in Washington, Andrew rode a high tide of political influence. The Republican National Committee invited him to speak in New York City and across the Empire State in October. In preparation, he labored over his address while in the nation's capital, writing it out in full, complete with inspirational quotations, platform details, and military examples of the importance of Union victory. Like Lincoln, Andrew had learned that public opinion could be a great strength in political life, so long as it favored your candidacy. As leaders in other states pulled Andrew into the national canvass, Massachusetts Republicans gathered in Worcester in mid-September, where more than 1,000 members renominated him by acclamation, with only three dissensions. Party leaders called it one of the largest and most enthusiastic conventions ever held in the state. The Commonwealth's attorney general, Dwight Foster, believed that Andrew's governance ability was unparalleled: "What he has done for Massachusetts outweighs all that Massachusetts has done for him."[31] Convention attendees endorsed the National Union Party platform, spoke strongly in favor of the prosecution of the war, congratulated the country on ending slavery, applauded recent military victories, and called for a prompt prisoner exchange.[32]

By the time Andrew left Washington on September 20, a full-scale war had broken open in the Shenandoah Valley. The day before, General

Philip Sheridan's 40,000 federals had waged an all-out assault against General Jubal Early's rebels near Winchester, Virginia and won the day. "We have just received news of a brilliant victory by Sheridan," Andrew wired Henry Ware.[33] Union casualties again were high, but victory gave the Union the upper hand in the valley. This triumph, combined with Sherman's Atlanta victory, seemed to guarantee Lincoln's and Andrew's reelection, but work remained. In mid-October, Andrew sent his adjutant general, William Schouler, south on a two-week furlough to visit soldiers in the field. The pair had worked exhaustively that summer, and it was time, Andrew believed, for Schouler to see the war with his own eyes. He traveled from camp to camp, visiting the Massachusetts soldiers and compiling notes and regimental rolls. In letters to Andrew, he described the soldiers' daily lives and travails, keeping the governor closely attuned to their needs.

Back in Boston, Andrew searched for ways to inspire the men, and he turned to Scripture and to great speeches of the past, among them Edward Everett's. "It might hardly seem becoming in me," he told Everett, "to attempt to declare how deeply I feel the weight and value of the repeated contributions of your voice and pen, during the present struggle, for the instruction and encouragement of the people."[34] He was still facing criticism of his African American troops, and he was now worried that African American recruiting in the southern states was showing sign of corruption. Conservatives were eager to mock him. According to a correspondent for the *Springfield Republican*, "[a Democrat] of the genteel stamp lately told me that in a few years hence Gov. Andrew will be more detested than Jeff. Davis. I might have replied with truth that his class detest the Governor now much more than they do Jeff. Davis."[35] Meanwhile, Albert Browne, Jr., confirmed Andrew's fears about conditions in the South. "The poor negroes are hunted like wild beasts, and besides, there are few sound, able-bodied men among them," he wrote from Beaufort, South Carolina:

There is a perfect panic throughout all these islands. Old men and invalids have taken to the brush through fear of the conscription; one poor fellow jumped overboard at St. Helena last week and was drowned. I have been among the families of these poor creatures, and I can conceive of no greater terror and distress on the coast of Africa after a slave hunt than I have seen. They have been pursued and fired at by cavalry. I was informed that a d—d black-hearted, black-coated pseudo Chaplain, now turned negro broker, tried to procure bloodhounds wherewith to hunt contrabands.

Browne lamented the heinous acts and closed with "I have read the above hasty words to Genl. Saxton, *and he confirms all I have said about negro hunting.*"[36]

Such letters left Andrew seething, and he unloaded his feelings on Reverend Clarke. He told Clarke about a recent conversation with Secretary of State Seward, which had confirmed why he could never have supported him for president. According to Andrew, Seward had said:

> Governor Andrew, we have been contending for three principles: First, to put down the rebellion by force; secondly, the abolition of slavery, and thirdly, to restore the Union. Now, I think we shall fail in the two first. We shall not be able to put down the rebellion by force. We shall not be able to abolish slavery. But by means of some compromise with the southern leaders we may be able to restore the Union.

The governor was not altogether shocked by the secretary's point of view, but he could not understand why Lincoln had retained him for so long. When Clarke asked Andrew what he had said in reply, the governor responded, "There was nothing to be said to a man that was in that state of mind, and I took my hat and came away."[37]

Accompanied by Frank Howe, Andrew stumped in upstate New York for the National Union ticket in October, though he was uneasy about Andrew Johnson's racist predilections. As Maine supreme court justice Woodbury Davis noted, Johnson may have opposed slavery, but "he was for a government of *White men.*"[38] Andrew had hoped to attend the national convention of African American leaders in Syracuse on October 4 but had been delayed in leaving from Boston. But he did have time to respond to a letter from the African American abolitionist lawyer John Rock, who had praised the governor's dedication to ensuring "equal opportunities for usefulness and success in all the occupations and duties of life to men of equal intelligence, industry, and integrity, whether that be white or black."[39]

While speaking in Rochester, Andrew escaped serious injury when a "democratic stone hurled at a Union transparency" crashed through a window and missed his head by inches. By the time he reached Lockport, just north of Buffalo, he was suffering with severe migraines and nosebleeds, which detained him for days. He was unable to travel to New Hampshire, where he was scheduled to speak at a Union meeting. The bout was so alarming that a doctor ordered complete rest for a day or two, no speech making, and a slow journey back to Boston. Along the way Andrew reconsidered his decision to accept the Republican nomination for the governorship. Explaining his relapse to Eliza, he said, "I have attended most immense meetings, spoke with great earnestness, in the open air, and what with the labor of travelling and the physical effort and brain-work involved in speaking I suppose I sent the blood too freely to my head."[40] Yet he knew the administrative machine better than anyone else, and he decided to remain a candidate. He wanted to be in office to see the war end, the Union preserved, and slavery abolished.[41]

On November 7 Schouler returned to Boston after his 1,800-mile sojourn into the South. Within days he held a conference with the still ailing governor. The adjutant general had been on statehouse duty for more than two and a half years, but till now he had only known the soldiers via muster rolls and correspondence. Andrew had dispatched him to study the soldiers' lives and conditions, encouraging him to look beyond bureaucratic accounting, and Schouler had reveled in the assignment. During his travels, he had come to recognize that Andrew's African American regiments were not only challenging racial norms but also dispelling color prejudice. "Colored Regiments can now march down Broadway," he reported, "not only without insult, but amid the ringing of enthusiastic cheers." They had "become nationalized. Thus far in the march of an enlightened civilization, we have advanced during the last two years." In his view, any true history of the war must recount Andrew's commitment to the "formation and payment of the colored regiments." Everywhere Schouler went, soldiers were celebrating the governor's work. Yet he also saw terrible scenes, and one in particular had shaken him deeply. Near the Maryland Navy Yard, along the Potomac River's East Branch, he had come upon a soldier on horseback pulling a twenty-foot rope attached to two handcuffed Black women, both running to avoid being dragged by the fast-moving horse. No other observers seemed to be outraged, so he concluded that this must be a routine occurrence. When he inquired what the women had done, an officer replied that "they had been loafing around the camp for two or three days." Schouler reported the incident to the regimental colonel, but his complaint went nowhere. Still, whatever the soldiers' racist proclivities, their universal plea, Schouler recalled, was that they wished to see their governor.[42] His report confirmed what Andrew had suspected: even as the army was marching forth to consummate justice, racial prejudice remained in the ranks.

The clangorous bells that had marked Atlanta's fall two months earlier had silenced. The political war still raged at the ballot box. On November 8, voters went to the polls, and both Andrew and Lincoln won overwhelmingly. The Commonwealth vote was the largest ever recorded, with 126,742 tallied for president and 125,281 for governor. Andrew beat the Democrat Henry Paine by 76,091 votes. "We have knocked down and stamped out the last Copperhead ghost in Massachusetts," he wrote to Frank Howe.[43] For him, this political victory was greater than any battlefield triumph. A "weight seems lifted from my heart," he wrote to Frank Blair, Sr. "I seem now to myself to *see through*. The vote is an earnest of virtue and intelligence of the People, and a proof that the country is and must hereafter remain true to Liberty, to Democratic ideas, constitutional, Republican government, to its own honor and renown." Andrew hoped that Lincoln, too, would be inspired by the election:

[The] work of the next four years is a great one. It involves the restoration of order, government, society in all the rebel states, and their reconstruction on the basis of Liberty as opposed to Slavery. How much patience, faith, courage, manhood, intelligence, practical sagacity wedded to the inspiration of high ideas, how much of the spirit of genuine leadership is demanded by this great occasion.[44]

On election evening, Andrew's friends gathered at the Cornhill Street and, with a marching band at their head, paraded to Faneuil Hall, where a host of distinguished politicians gave speeches in celebration.[45]

Andrew and his staff, along with their wives and daughters and members of the executive council, spent the days after the election focusing on citizen issues. They visited the Connecticut Asylum for the Education and Instruction of Deaf and Dumb Persons in Hartford, the Connecticut State Reform School in Meriden, and the Commonwealth's state almshouse at Monson. Admirers were coming to believe that Andrew was destined for horizons beyond the state, perhaps in Lincoln's new cabinet or as Wilson's replacement in the Senate. Andrew himself did not have such aspirations. As governor, he relied on his judicial mind and compassionate heart, and the position gave him considerable power to advance the reform dearest to his heart—advancement of African Americans' civil rights. Still, radicals had hopes that Lincoln might consider him for a position in the reshuffled cabinet. Both Postmaster-General Montgomery Blair and Treasury Secretary Salmon Chase had already stepped down. There was pressure on Seward to leave the secretary of state position, and Gideon Welles, secretary of the navy, seemed likely to retire. In a letter to Forbes, Garrison said that he hoped Andrew would be considered for a cabinet post and promised he would lobby on his behalf. The editor believed that the governor's "rare fitness and eminent services commandingly justify" such an honor.[46]

When Andrew returned from his charity circuit, he found a letter from Frank Blair, Sr., telling him that Maryland had constitutionally abolished slavery. The governor spent his Sunday evening responding to this gratifying news: "I rejoice with you and all good people, 'with joy unspeakable' at the deliverance of Maryland by the adoption of her *free* constitution. I watched the whole progress of the emancipation movement there in all its stages with, sometimes trembling, but still with constant, hope." The national election results seemed be a sign that slavery was doomed, but Andrew knew that the freed slaves' struggles were just beginning, and he hoped that Lincoln would work to assuage them by surrounding himself with men of "faithful hearts, iron wills, clear heads, and untiring hands."[47] For now, Andrew turned his own focus to the freedmen and African American soldiers who had been imprisoned for violating Maryland's defunct slave laws. He asked the Baltimore merchant Worthington Snethen to help secure the release of Massachusetts men who were being held in the Maryland penitentiary for violating the slave code. A week later Snethen was able to report that all persons confined for offenses against the code had been released.[48]

Andrew was one of the most popular governors among the Washington political elite, and Forbes encouraged them to propose his name for a cabinet vacancy. Andrew, however, vetoed this plan. He knew his own limitations and told Forbes the only position he was suited for was attorney general. Others thought differently. The *Rochester Democrat* suggested that Andrew could replace Attorney General Bates or even Senator Sumner, who was rumored to be in the running for secretary of state. Andrew refused to consider any such nomination, at least until receiving White House confirmation that Sumner would replace Seward.

For his part, Sumner was faced with friends who were urging Lincoln to consider Andrew as Seward's replacement. This made the senator uneasy about his own cabinet prospects, and he began telling colleagues that the governor would be content to be senator. Others thought Lincoln might appoint Andrew to direct the Freedman's Bureau or to serve as a U.S. district judge. The commotion over Andrew probably threatened Sumner's ego, for neither Frank Howe nor Bird could convince him to come out publicly for Andrew, and this annoyed them. The point became moot in any case. The governor's chance to be attorney general was never a serious option once Lincoln appointed James Speed to the position.[49]

Although Andrew had favored waging war from the beginning, he was increasingly distressed by its human cost, a consequence, he believed, of conservative influence that lengthened the contest. Now Lincoln asked the governors to submit reports on state election results, recruiting numbers, and casualties, and the figures were astounding. Even as the war had strengthened the Union and the nation-state partnership, it had scarred the populace. On Thanksgiving, Andrew made a point to express publicly his appreciation and sorrow and then headed to Washington to visit the Commonwealth soldiers stationed in the region. Writing to Reverend Clarke, he argued that the federal government ought to provide rations for freed slaves and the war-torn poor and emphasized there was much need for private charity:

> Labor disorganized, fields wasted, crops unmade, planters impover-ished and demoralized, the freedmen uncertain, half protected, they and their old masters mutually doubtful of each other, the poor white hostile in great measure, and all the victims more of their ignorance and of antecedent circumstances than of present bad intentions. This is the picture a large part of the South now exhibits. We in the North are in comfort and prosperity, [and] . . . we must intervene for the immedi-ate preservation of the colored people of the South, powerless for the moment to save themselves, and, by wise and prudent generosity, help to float them over, until a new crop can be made.

Andrew believed that, once the Union prevailed, it should extend goodwill to the vanquished. Instead of usurping power from civil gov-ernments and forcing acknowledgment of defeat, he advocated send-ing money to rebuild the economy and establish a new Zion for the freed slaves.[50]

In November, Schouler asked Andrew to reach out to Lincoln and ask him to write a condolence letter to Lydia Bixby, a Boston widow who claimed to have lost five sons in the war. The governor, in turn, told Lincoln that her case was "so remarkable that I really wish a let-ter might be written her by the President of the United States, taking notice of a noble mother of five dead heroes so well deserved." Lincoln honored the request (though some allege that Lincoln's secretary, John Hay, drafted the letter), and the widow received an official White House acknowledgment of her loss. In truth, Bixby had lost two sons, not five, but that did not diminish her grief.[51]

By early December, Union and Confederate armies had clashed south of Nashville. Union troops remained entrenched around Peters-burg, and Sherman's army was marching toward Savannah. As northern congressmen reconvened in the nation's capital, Reconstruction was taking on new meaning for the freed slaves. On December 6, Lincoln delivered his State of the Union address, and his words gave radicals reason to be optimistic, especially now that Maryland had abolished slavery. In Andrew's view, God was watching voters undo the diabolical institution that humanity had made. That month Lincoln nominated Salmon Chase to become chief justice of the Supreme Court, and the Senate confirmed him. This was perhaps the most dramatic change to the Court since its formation, as Chase, unlike his predecessor, represented the radical antislavery path to justice. In Boston, as Andrew was preparing his annual legislative address, he learned about this welcome appointment along with favorable military updates, and he directed Browne to pay the new chief justice a visit to express his delight. Yet even as he celebrated the good news, he was undergoing another round of ill-health and had to cancel appearances.[52]

Andrew closed the year at home, convalescing as he pored over legislative documents, congressional proceedings from Sumner, and Washington gossip from Browne and Frank Howe. One letter especially caught his interest. John Motley, a Dorchester native and a close friend of Sumner's, was serving as American minister to Austria, and he had written approvingly about Andrew's wartime governance and his recent address in Springfield. "Believe me," said Motley, "it is most refreshing to read such a calm, thoughtful and truly eloquent discourse as this of yours before the farmers of N. England, and to reflect that it is pronounced in the midst of the excitement, the tumult and the sufferings of the most gigantic war of principles ever known." He congratulated Andrew on his recent election and for using the conflict to promote the diffusion of ideas and the importance of science in securing the democratic ideals of the founders. Motley deplored the attitudes of southern leaders, not only for their commitment to slavery but also because they refused to cultivate the "higher interests of humanity and [work] towards the stability and improvement of those democratic institutions on which our progress in civilization and in true liberty depend."[53]

With the year winding down, Andrew sent his old friend Hayden a note and a package:

> I send you with this note, for presentation to the [Masons of] Prince Hall Grand Lodge, a gavel, made from a piece of the whipping-post at Hampton, Va. The gentleman who sent it forth [said that the] . . . post stood directly in the rear of the old court-house and in front of the jail: while I was cutting it, about twenty colored men and women bore testimony to me, that it was the identical post or tree that they had been tied to, and had their backs lacerated with the whip.

This gift, he hoped, would join the "rude boat of straw" that Jack Flowers had forwarded to him earlier that year. Andrew told Hayden that he knew of no place more fitting for the preservation of such "memorials of the barbarous institution that is now tottering with its rapidly approaching fall, than the [Masonic] association of free colored citizens of Massachusetts over which you preside." Such relics would remind lodge members of the "difference between obedience wrung from an oppressed race by power and might, with thumb-screws, whipping-posts, branding-irons, and the lash, and that obedience so willingly rendered by us as freemen to those in authority, where the rights of the poor and most humble citizen are sacred and protected by law."[54]

Ever since his carefree youth in Windham, Andrew had relished the holiday season. The cold air and snowy landscape invigorated him, and this year he needed such physical restoration. As Christmas approached, Boston was filled with festivities. The holiday fell on a Sunday, and two days later the state prison in Charlestown held its customary celebration. As was his annual tradition, Andrew joined the prisoners at their Christmas feast. There was no pomp; he simply came as he was—as a reformer and servant leader. After a religious service, the warden Gideon Haynes announced several pardons. Festivities followed, and prisoners were allowed to leave their cells and visit with the governor. Andrew spoke with every prisoner individually before he departed. His manner made it clear that he believed that all were equal in God's eyes.

When he returned to the statehouse, he learned that Sherman had taken Savannah and was sending Union troops into South Carolina. The day of jubilee was nearing, but provisions were necessary to relieve the suffering of Savannah's freed slaves. Andrew's health was improving, and he spent last few days of December pulling together supplies to be sent south.[55]

CHAPTER 21

THIRTEENTH AMENDMENT
January–June 1865

The Scripture Is Fulfilled

By the New Year, the Confederacy was perishing, yet Andrew's work continued. He spent the first week of January assembling paperwork for newly mustered recruits, calculating state financial projections, and revising his legislative address. He was entering his fifth year as governor, all of them served during an unimaginably brutal war. As he had redefined the executive office, he had also mapped a path forward for the nation's African Americans. His friends were so thankful for his guidance that they presented him with an antique clock, dating back to the Battle of Lexington, birthplace of the future republic. It was an appropriate gift for someone who relished history and understood that he was tied to the leaders who had gone before.

Throughout his tenure as governor, Andrew had remained devoted to his duties and his principles. He had attended commencement exercises and lectures; he had visited reform schools, asylums, prisons, and county fairs. He made regular appearances at the Saturday Club and the Thursday Club; he went to church services, Sunday school classes, and evening Bible studies. "No magistrate," said Bird, "[has applied] himself more carefully, laboriously and conscientiously."[1] Yet Andrew was always impatient with legislative bureaucracy. Democracy was in peril, and he had no time to trifle with those who opposed his solutions for saving it. His years as a lawyer had equipped him to handle critics and prejudice. Rarely did he walk into a meeting or assembly without someone carping against his leadership style. Conservatives continued to scorn and ridicule his influence on Lincoln—releasing the Emancipation Proclamation, expanding the state government, promoting African American enlistment, and supporting a constitutional amendment to abolish slavery. Yet he knew he was on the side of justice, and friends such as James Hamilton of New York agreed with him, declaring that abolishing slavery by constitutional amendment was the path forward and descrying a sense of urgency about the matter in Congress.[2]

The General Court assembled on January 4, and two days later Andrew gave his fifth address to its members, which colleagues described as an encyclopedic review of Massachusetts wartime contributions. Cyrus Woodman was present for the speech and wrote afterward to praise it:

> When, under the difficulties which surrounded you, you first entered upon your duties as Chief Magistrate of the Commonwealth, I trembled lest the difficulties might be overwhelming. I rejoice that my fears were groundless, and have now an abiding faith that you will go on successfully to the end, and leave a record of which all your friends may be proud.[3]

In his address, Andrew reviewed the state's educational, financial, agricultural, and industrial progress over the past year. Though Lincoln had already called for more volunteers, the Commonwealth no longer had manpower shortages; instead, it had to deal with the ever-increasing burden of supporting veterans behind the lines and at home. "The statesmanship of the future," he predicted, "gives cause for more anxiety than any military concern for the present." He acknowledged that his work as war governor was coming to an end: under Grant's and Sherman's generalship, the Union's final triumph was not far off. Now he counseled forgiveness, reminding his listeners that the poor people of the South were their brethren. "We fight," he told legislators, "to carry the schoolhouse, the free press, the free ballot, and all the independent manhood of our own New England liberty to the people of the slave-ridden South."

Andrew celebrated Maryland's decision to abolish slavery, and asked attendees to keep working for national abolition: "[The] color of African extraction, so long the badge of slavery, [must] cease to be the badge of exclusion from any of the privileges of citizenship." Only then, he maintained, could the nation "restore government, order and society" and reconstruct the rebellious states on principles and faith.[4] He recommended that a bureau of military employment be established for disabled veterans and closed his speech by memorializing the soldiers' service: "In the vestibule of the Capitol, you pass . . . beneath a hundred battle-flags, war-worn, begrimed, and bloody. They are sad but proud memorials of the transcendent crime of the Rebellion, the curse of slavery, the elastic energy of a free Commonwealth, the glory and the grief of war." According to the *Daily Advertiser*, "no Governor of Massachusetts, ever approached the close of his official career . . . with stronger claims upon the respect of his fellow-citizens, for whatever fidelity, patriotism and ability can deserve."[5]

During the legislature's opening days, Andrew continued to press the representatives about crucial issues of equity. He was particularly concerned about the status of women in the state. Presenting facts about their employment, he declared that "it cannot be pretended that women have the same opportunity now or the same freedom [as] . . . men." Andrew pointed out, "Any shipmaster . . . knows that the steerage passage for a passenger ship—wholly fit for a man's passage, [is] . . . wholly unfit for a woman, however she may be protected. Any man who has sisters would rather die than see one of them go alone on such a passage, where he might gladly go himself." While women were needed "in the dairy, in the school-room and in all other forms of industry," they were discouraged from going out to work because of unfit conditions. *Frank Leslie's Illustrated* said that Andrew's vision combined "more of practical philosophy, with propagandist zeal than [that of] any [other] statesman of the day."[6] Although the legislature took no practical action on the matter, several Boston philanthropists did join forces with authorities in Washington Territory to provide suitable transportation for women heading west.

The governor also retained his focus on racial inequality. When he learned that Missouri had abolished slavery, he wrote to congratulate Governor Thomas Fletcher: "Massachusetts salutes Missouri with grateful joy, commending her to the highest rewards of Happiness and Honor as a Commonwealth of Freemen."[7] Yet even though African Americans had gained much ground during the war years, Andrew worried that the Thirteenth Amendment, already passed in the Senate, might fail in the House and deny them freedom everywhere in the United States.[8]

With his friend Edward Everett and all the other New England governors, Andrew had recently established the New England Refugees' Aid Society to assist freed slaves in the South. Now, on January 16, Andrew and many around the region mourned Everett's death. He had dedicated his life to shaping a more perfect Union, and Andrew would miss his intellect, his rhetoric, and his philanthropic spirit. From Washington, Secretary of War Stanton ordered all military posts to display their flags at half-mast and draped all government buildings in black for thirty days. Boston, too, was draped in black, and Andrew arranged a formal burial ceremony and appeared alongside his executive staff during the processional.[9]

By month's end, Lincoln believed he had secured the votes to pass the Thirteenth Amendment in the House. On January 31, before a packed gallery, the representatives came to a final decision on the most important issue of the nineteenth century. When the speaker announced victory, the celebration was historic. "The great feature of the existing rebellion," noted the *New York Times*, "was the passage to-day by the House of Representatives of the resolutions submitting to the Legislatures of the several States an amendment to the Constitution abolishing slavery. No attempt was made to suppress the applause which came from all sides."[10]

Andrew had asked Lincoln to send him a telegram at the very moment he signed the resolution amending the constitution. It was a banner day, and the governor could hardly contain himself. That evening he received the president's wire and forwarded it to the *Daily Advertiser*. A few days later, on the evening of February 3, he wired Lincoln that Massachusetts "has today ratified the Constitutional Amendment abolishing slavery by a unanimous yea vote."[11] Organizers elaborately decorated Boston's Faneuil Hall for a massive celebration. Still, the euphoria that pervaded the statehouse was broken momentarily by a pressing deadline: in the coming days, Hugh Riley of the Eleventh Massachusetts Volunteers was sentenced to be shot for desertion. The governor dashed off a wire to Lincoln requesting that he suspend the execution, telling the president that, although Riley was an "old soldier," he was "only a boy." Lincoln spared Riley's life.[12]

As clamor over the amendment quieted, the war returned to the front pages. Meanwhile, Andrew's friends continued to press Lincoln to bring the governor into the cabinet. Noah Brooks, a young California journalist, wrote that "a strong pressure, with a fair show of success, is being made upon the President to place Governor Andrew of Massachusetts in his Cabinet, as a representative of the 'radical' element. Strange to say, the Blairs and [Thurlow] Weed support the movement, which is designed to place Andrew in the Navy Department."[13] Stearns also pressed Vice-President Johnson to influence Lincoln on Andrew's behalf, noting that the governor had "always been true and efficient in this direction, his name is before the country, and needs neither eulogy or apology."[14] For his part, Andrew had already hinted to William Claflin, chair of the Massachusetts Republican Committee, that he would not seek reelection, and Forbes, concerned, told Sumner that they could not afford to lose Andrew from public life. Forbes saw him as a rare leader among the radicals; he was imminently qualified, and Forbes knew no one who could inspire more general confidence. He implored Sumner to use his influence to bring about a cabinet appointment.[15]

The *Daily Advertiser* cited numerous other newspapers that had published articles about Andrew's possible future in the cabinet. These papers claimed that New York and Massachusetts political insiders had gone to Washington to push Andrew's name forward and that Senator Edwin Morgan of New York had presented a petition on the matter from several prominent merchants. Andrew's former law partner, William Burt, telegraphed him that a position in the War Department "can be had if desirable."[16] Still, the governor disliked the idea of accepting any position other than attorney general: "My legal training and tastes would help me to master its duties, while the functions and the opportunities for usefulness in that office are such as peculiarly to tempt me to risk a failure for the sake of the chance of doing good." Besides, Andrew believed himself too "obstinate and insusceptible to external influences" to get on well in Washington."[17] As for Stanton, Andrew told Burt that he hoped to God that someone would take his place. It had taken some time, but Andrew had come to see Stanton as an impediment on the pay equity issue, even though he was an improvement over Simon Cameron.[18] Forbes sympathized with his friend, agreeing that his name and reputation would "be most surely promoted by giving back to your profession for the next three years." Nonetheless, he assured the governor that he could be of great service even in a non-legal capacity, and he warned Andrew that friends might be pushing harder for him than he wanted.[19]

Forbes encouraged Andrew to consider a smaller cabinet post or an appointment at the Freedman's Bureau. At all events he should commit to returning to his law practice after his governorship. He was aware that Andrew's talents would be useful after the war, especially regarding economic issues. Forbes and his friend Edward Atkinson, who owned a textile mill, were eager to push Lincoln to restart the South's cotton economy after the war. They understood the connections between conservative money and political leadership and hoped Andrew could be a leading voice in bringing a solid economic plan to Washington. Writing to Atkinson, Forbes said, "I think all radical men like *you*, [and] . . . all conservative ones like me, ought to push hard to have him in the Cabinet as the Representative man of the North."[20] In their view, Congress should consider Andrew's ideas on economic reconstruction, whether or not he was in the cabinet.

But the governor remained more interested in advancing African Americans than in advancing himself in Washington. In mid-February, he celebrated the War Department's telegram that ordered Stephen Swails to muster in as a second lieutenant in the Fifty-fourth's Company D, ending an almost year-long battle on his behalf. Swails resumed his duties as a line officer and participated in numerous actions, and Andrew quietly reveled in yet another milestone.[21]

By early March, the Union armies were moving closer to final triumph, and eighteen states had ratified the Thirteenth Amendment. The news encouraged Lincoln as he drafted his second inaugural address. "With malice toward none," he challenged Americans to "bind up the nation's wounds"—words that resonated with Andrew when they came over the wires. Yet new problems were surfacing in Washington, many of them swirling around the behavior of the vice-president. On the night before the inauguration, Johnson had allegedly gotten drunk with old friends at the Metropolitan Hotel. Hung over the next morning, he walked into the Senate and asked Senate clerk John Forney for whiskey, then gulped down two shots of bourbon before the ceremony.[22]

Updates from the Virginia front were more uplifting. With Lee's surrender imminent, Andrew requested prisoner exchanges. He encouraged Lincoln to sign a proclamation of amnesty and to pardon deserters who would voluntarily return to duty. Such a gesture, he argued, would be a "crowning act of kindness and would endear not only the Commander-in-Chief, but the Government itself, to the soldiers and their relatives, many of whom have been alienated by what seems to them the unjustifiable severity of the punishment of their fathers, brothers, and relatives. I trust . . . [that] you will frame and promulgate a general pardon and amnesty to all."[23]

In this heady atmosphere, Andrew declared March 28 a day of "fasting, humiliation, and prayer" in honor of the Commonwealth's citizenry, the nation's "unselfish and patriotic rulers," and even for the "authors of the terrible strife which has drenched the land with blood, and made desolate the homes of thousands." He hoped that the "bitterness of war may subdue in them the unhallowed ambition which seek selfish supremacy at the cost of common good."[24] As the war neared its end, Andrew turned inward, depending on faith and his own strength as he worked to keep the state steady and prepare for peace. That spring, Massachusetts legislators were mired in debates over the state's usury law, which forbade interest rates of more than 6 percent. For years, bankers, businessmen, and several legislators had been advocating for change. Andrew backed revisions to the law, arguing that money was being sent out of state to places where the legal interest rate was higher; and bank commissioners and the U.S. Board of Trade agreed. In the session's final days, the General Court wrangled over whether to increase the rate, which would violate the obsolete state law, or repeal the existing law to allow more rate flexibility and allow national banks to prosper in Massachusetts. Many senate businessmen favored repeal; and knowing that Andrew agreed, the legislature yielded to his wish. But members who had lost the battle retaliated by conducting a survey of the salaries of the military men whose pay had been fixed by the governor as well as of men in similar positions whose salaries had been fixed by the legislature. The survey revealed excessively high salaries among Andrew's appointees, and he was forced to reduce them.[25]

Andrew spent the last evening of March attending the Grand Military and Civic Ball at the Soldiers' Rest in Worcester. During the war, the city had become a transfer point for soldiers and other weary travelers who were awaiting rail or stage connections. In response, the women of the city had collaborated with the local soldiers' relief society and opened the Soldiers' Rest, a respite for the exhausted soldiers who were passing through. The weather on the night of the ball was grim. "A more dismal, gloomy evening could not have been selected," reported a correspondent, yet Andrew and his guests raised more than $1,200 for a soldiers' welfare fund.

Rumors still swirled about a place for Andrew in Lincoln's cabinet, and Forbes was beginning to hate the idea of the governor working in Washington "among the vultures brought here by the public spoils." He told his friend, "I would like to see you heading the bar of Mass.," coming to Washington "only when you have special cases." He encouraged Andrew to return to his legal practice, and their conversation left the governor with much to think about as he rode back to Boston— choices that would tug at his heart and his vocation.[26]

Lincoln, meanwhile, started for army headquarters in City Point, Virginia, to confer with Grant and Sherman. "Can you believe it?" Browne wrote to Andrew from Washington. "Is it not one of the absurdities of history? That at this moment of all moments, when half a million men are facing one another in arms in Virginia and North Carolina, and the fighting has actually begun, *the object of the President's visit to his Lieutenant General is to settle with him Singleton's Fredericksburg tobacco, and Thurlow Weed's Norfolk Cotton matters.*" Browne may have believed this, but Lincoln had more important reasons for the visit.[27] He spent April 1 aboard the *River Queen*, docked at City Point at the confluence of the James and Appomattox rivers, waiting in the chilly wind for reports from the field. Lee, it seemed, had abandoned Petersburg and was directing his dwindling legions to Five Forks, a series of crossroads to the southwest of that city; and the Confederate government had retreated hastily to Danville. In Boston, Andrew learned that Union forces had closed around Richmond, and two days later General Godrey Weitzel wired Stanton, "I took Richmond at 8:15 a.m." After Weitzel established his headquarters in Jefferson Davis's home, Lincoln and a small military entourage traveled to Richmond. As federal troops entered the city, Stanton wired all the northern governors that the war was nearing an end. Andrew was delighted. "I give you joy on these triumphant victories," he wrote to Stanton. Noting that Weitzel's division of the Twenty-fifth Corps, an African American unit, had reportedly been the first to enter Richmond, he said, "The colored man, received last, got in first and thus the Scripture is fulfilled."[28]

The Negro Is Coming Up

With the "colored man" as political leverage, the Republican party had to finish the war by forcing the Confederates to surrender. Months earlier Andrew had alluded to this imperative in a speech to the New England Agricultural Society: "The duty of suppressing the rebellion involves that of restoring and reconstructing order, society, civilization, where treason and slavery have subverted them." Thus, Richmond's capitulation signaled more than military success; with the surrender of the slaveowners who had triggered the war, it also symbolized slavery's demise. Andrew wanted this defeat to extend far beyond the battlefield. He believed that slavery's abolition would forever reshape the United States, forcing southerners and northerners to think and act in new ways. In a letter to Andrew, Colonel Charles Francis Adams, Jr., of the Fifth Massachusetts Cavalry, an African American regiment, pondered the irony of marching "amid the wildest enthusiasm into the Capital of the State of Virginia." John Brown's dream had become truth on Virginia soil.[29]

Northerners were expecting Lee's surrender. When Andrew received the news on April 9, he immediately alerted the legislature. Excitement was intense, and reporters struggled to describe it. The state senate adjourned, and the senators rushed into the house, where a great cheer greeted them, and the crowd began singing "John Brown's Body." When Andrew entered the chambers, legislators erupted in joyous shouts and reprised the song in his honor as he joined them in the chorus: "Glory,

glory, hallelujah." It was a moment for the ages. Demonstrations spread throughout Boston, and that afternoon citizens held a "Great Jubilee" meeting in Faneuil Hall, where Senator Wilson proclaimed that the "long and dreary night of this civil war is ended forever."[30] With tears flowing down his cheeks, Frederick Douglass managed to deliver an emotional impromptu speech. "I tell you, the negro is coming up," he shouted. By the force of the Massachusetts example, "he is rising—rising."[31]

Andrew was jubilant. The arc of the moral universe was bending toward justice. God, he believed, had broken the shackles of bondage. After emancipation, African American enlistment, Black officer commissions, equal pay for all soldiers, and the abolition of slavery, the march of African American soldiers into Richmond could only have been omnipotent design. Andrew did not go so far as to call himself God's instrument in bringing forth this more perfect Union, but many thought otherwise. James Hamilton wrote to him encouragingly. Now the second act was beginning, and it would require people like Andrew, people of "wisdom and statesmanship," who could reconstruct the "moral, intellectual, and physical condition of about 3 million of a . . . child-like race."[32]

Andrew missed the Faneuil Hall festivities to attend the Unitarians' first national convention in New York City, where delegates named him president. "New duties were opening before them," Andrew told the attendees. "It became them to carry forward the banner of Christ as fast as Providence revealed its way." He had endured his tenure as a war leader by leaning on God. He would continue to rely on that devotion as he turned his attention to veterans' welfare and other postwar responsibilities. By the time Lee's surrender was official, he had already instructed the state's surgeon general to forward surplus money and supplies to Frank Howe, who would distribute it among the New England soldiers who were passing through New York City on their way home.[33]

In these exhilarating April days, Lincoln and Andrew also offered up gratitude for an enduring nation-state partnership. The war had been a story of secession, but it had also been a story of cooperation. As the southern states had drifted out to sea, the loyal states had worked with Lincoln to tug them back to shore. As the president pondered the future, he turned his thoughts to Charleston Harbor and Fort Sumter. He wanted General Robert Anderson to return to the fort and raise the same American flag that he had been forced to lower four years earlier. Andrew was invited to attend the ceremony but declined, preferring to focus on the details of transitioning to peacetime. But many other dignitaries, including Garrison, were present as, on April 14, exactly four years later, the American flag flew again over Fort Sumter. For Garrison, however, the most striking moment of his southern visit had happened in Savannah, days before—a city whose Confederate officials had offered a $5,000 reward for him, dead or alive. Driving through the streets with Henry Smith, he came upon "a very old colored man feebly resting in the sun." Smith stopped and called out, "Uncle, did you ever hear tell of William Lloyd Garrison?" The man's face lit up and he replied, "Oh, bress the Lord, Massa, yis, yis." "Well, uncle," said Smith, "this is William Lloyd Garrison." The gentleman sprang to his feet, stumbled to the carriage, seized Garrison's hand, and, covering it with tears and kisses, called down "blessings upon the New Englander."[34] The image of the broken and careworn slave etched in Garrison's abolitionist mind had become flesh, a confirmation of his life's work.

Since Lee's surrender, Boston had been bustling with activity. Crowds filled the Boston Theatre to witness Edwin Booth's stunning performance as Sir Edward Mortimer in *The Iron Chest*. Little did they know that his brother, John Wilkes Booth, was also plotting a performance. On April 14, the same day as the ceremony at Fort Sumter, terrible news came over the wires. "A shock from Heaven," wrote the *Daily Advertiser*'s Washington correspondent at 11:15 p.m. "Laying half the city in instant ruins would not have startled us as did the word that started out from Ford's Theatre half an hour ago, that the President had been shot." Forty-five minutes later came the news that Andrew was dreading. "The President is reported dead," inscribed the stenographer. "God save the Republic."[35]

Horrified, Andrew remained at the statehouse, trying to gather himself for a legislative statement. But speech was difficult. As Frank Howe said, "I have no heart to write."[36] When the sun rose the next morning, pedestrians wandered the Boston streets in silence. Mourners gathered on State Street, where workers were draping the public buildings in black crepe. Three days later, Andrew rose before the General Court and paid tribute to Lincoln, a man who was "not by nature a leader . . . [or] a follower" yet who had managed to guide the nation through a terrible storm:

> Educated wholly as a civilian, his fame will forever be associated with his administration of public affairs in a civil war, unexampled in its proportions, and conducted on his own side with such success as to command his own reelection by the free will of a free people. Few men have ever written or spoken with greater effect or to better purpose in appealing

over the passions of the hour, to the sober judgment of men. . . . He [knew] how to reach the understanding of the plain and honest men who compose the intelligent masses of the American people.

Lincoln had not wanted war, but he had been unwilling to forfeit government property to insurgent states. He had not proposed to interfere with slavery, but he had "proclaimed liberty to three millions of American slaves, and prepared the way for universal emancipation."[37] In death, Lincoln had mingled his blood with that of the many soldiers and civilians who had given their lives for the nation. Now the survivors, Andrew said, must carry forth his determination to create a more perfect Union, to build "a country . . . [that is] the home of liberty and civilization."[38]

As law enforcement hunted for Lincoln's assassins, Andrew's friends became anxious, fearing that the governor might be the next target. They urged him to remain in Boston instead of traveling to Washington. In fact, Andrew did receive a frightening letter, allegedly from John Wilkes Booth: "Governor Andrew: You will be a dead man this time next week if I had my way and I am sure i will Beware of your life yours, J. Wilkes Booth now in Boston I killed Mr. Lincoln and I will kill you to I am sure of it."[39] Nonetheless, Andrew refused to stay in the statehouse. With his staff and several members of Boston's city government, including Reverend Grimes and Samuel Hooper, he attended Lincoln's funeral on April 19. Church bells rang across the North as the president was laid to rest. "Never was King or Emperor honored with such obsequies as those with which our Republic has laid to rest its greatest hero," noted a correspondent for *Harper's Weekly*, "it was not the pomp of the procession, not the splendor of the funeral rites, that gave character to the touching ceremony, but the infinite tenderness and love of a great people."[40] The next day the Massachusetts delegation met with Andrew Johnson, and the governor assured the new president that he would stand firmly by him. Johnson replied that Andrew's past record would be an indicator of his future policy, and Andrew hoped this meant that his own accomplishments would be secure in Johnson's hands.[41]

The General Court was still in session when Andrew returned to Boston, and he quickly derailed a legislative attempt to prohibit criminals from serving on juries. He pressed legislators to establish public accommodations laws for the Commonwealth that would prohibit discrimination in "any licensed inn, in any public place of amusement, public conveyance, or public meeting," and on May 16 representatives passed that statute, one of the nation's first. Senators then seized upon new sumptuary legislation as an attempt to regulate the sale and consumption of alcohol. Know Nothings had enacted such laws ten years before, but they had rarely been enforced in Boston, primarily because violators were seldom convicted. Andrew opposed the sumptuary movement and was prepared to veto the measure but instead returned a message that outlined his rationale against the resolve in its present form and advised members to revise the legislation or risk veto. Supporters dropped the matter. In the meantime, senators passed a bill to establish a special police force in Boston. Although Andrew opposed it, he endorsed a compromise measure whereby a state constabulary would be created, to be used at the governor's discretion to enforce Commonwealth laws.[42]

Perhaps the most troublesome issue in this session was a death penalty case that attracted considerable community and legislative wrath against Andrew when he refused to sign the warrant. Edward Green was a twenty-eight-year-old postmaster who, in an attempt to rob the Malden Bank, in December 1863, had shot and killed a teller, Frank Converse. Green had been prosecuted in Lowell in April 1864. Pleading guilty to first-degree murder, he was sentenced to be hanged. Green's case subsequently came before the executive council's committee on pardons, whose members, including Frank Bird, agreed with Green's defense counsel that he was not of sound mind. But medical examiners determined otherwise. In the meantime, Green's wife appealed directly to Andrew, declaring that her husband could not been in his right mind when he committed the crime.[43] Andrew appealed to the Massachusetts Supreme Court to review the case and reduce Green's sentence to imprisonment for life. Green had confessed to the murder and had been sentenced on that plea. Thus, in Andrew's view, there had been no legal trial and should be no legal execution. But this rationale was a stretch; and the longer Green remained in prison, the louder his critics railed against him. In the meantime, the justices argued that they had indeed followed proper constitutional and legal procedures and that Green's guilty plea had removed the necessity for a jury trial. The death warrant came before Andrew, but he delayed his signature; and, by May, some senators were so outraged that they threatened to investigate all of Andrew's pardons.[44]

As legislators were demanding an explanation from Andrew, orthodox Unitarians were also demanding explanations about the delay, claiming that the governor was behaving heretically by refusing to sign the warrant. The rigid Unitarian publication *Congregationalist* had long regarded his opposition to capital punishment as well as his push to permit women to remarry after divorcing adulterous husbands as abridgments of conventional social doctrines. The editor was so adamantly opposed to these policies that he had refused to endorse Andrew for a Lincoln cabinet post, arguing that his refusal to execute Green made him unfit for higher office. Though most Unitarian delegates continued to overwhelmingly support Andrew, evangelical critics charged him with undoing orthodox religious practices for practical expediency. Andrew held firm to his convictions—hate the sin but not the sinner, even if that sinner was a murderer. Yet he told Bird that the Green situation was wearing him out. "I work as hard as I can," he confided, "so hard that I am getting sleepless from over-work. *I can't even get time to write out my points. But, when I can I will.*"[45]

As Andrew wrestled such legislative uproars, he stayed true to his routine, continuing to visit various almshouses, reform schools, and prisons, where he spent many evenings with prisoners and the poor. He was particularly disturbed by the children, treated callously and identified by number rather than name. In his view, the state pauper system was contrary to God's law. The poor should remain within society, he maintained, not be segregated into pens. His secretary, Henry Ware, wrote that long after Andrew had left the governorship, many poor children recalled his affection and devotion. Gideon Haynes, the warden of Charlestown Prison, said that no governor was ever more interested in the inmates, including the young ones at Westborough Reform School. The governor often spent a half-hour alone in a dark cell, trying to experience solitary confinement for himself. Along with Samuel Howe and Frank Sanborn, he took a special interest in Boston's incarcerated girls, who had been publicly tarred as depraved, and he also visited the state's industrial school for girls in Lancaster. Learning from these visits, he worked to shift philanthropic regulation from the local to the state level and increased government involvement in supervising public welfare institutions. This resulted in the establishment of the Board of State Charities of Massachusetts, the first of its kind in the country.[46]

In the weeks following Lincoln's assassination, Andrew received numerous mementos from soldiers, an expression of thanks for seeing them through the fiery trial. Brigadier General Charles Russell, who had commanded a brigade in the Twenty-fifth Corps comprised of African Americans, sent him the original copy of General Lee's farewell address to the Army of Northern Virginia after his surrender to General Grant. Andrew responded, "I prize it highly, and shall cause it to be framed, and hung in my library."[47] Augustus Clark, a Boston native and now a clerk in the War Department's Ordnance Office, sent the governor scraps of the towel used to soak up Lincoln's blood at the Peterson House, the boardinghouse where Lincoln had died. Clark had lived in the very room.[48]

Such items were memorials of the war and of the loss of Lincoln, but they were also reminders that work remained to be done. The nation was beginning to accept the realities of a new world made by the war. Though the guns were silent, antagonism against African Americans had not ended. Indeed, the color line was as powerful outside the shackles as it had been inside them. Andrew understood that, without citizenship, freed slaves would continue to face severe prejudice, and he wanted them to have time to establish economic stability before being thrust back into a battle for their rights. Emancipation had been a watershed moment, but it remained to be seen what would become of the people, now that they were legally free. In Andrew's mind, the economics of freedom would help determine the terms of that freedom, but it would not diffuse racial prejudice or violence, especially if the former slaves demonstrated their fitness for such challenges. The governor knew that his African American regiments had suffered from enemies in the front and in the rear. The fight over equal pay was a galling indication of how little the government had cared about African Americans' equal standing in the military, though their service had offered observers a vision of agency, respectability, and self-worth. Andrew was convinced that free labor was superior to slave labor; yet unlike many of his Republican colleagues, he also insisted that the marketplace and the social world be made equitable to both races.[49]

Now, as the nation mourned Lincoln's loss, there was also the matter of formally celebrating the Union victory, and President Johnson declared that the time had come to honor the triumphant Union soldiers in Washington. He invited nearby troops to participate in a two-day celebration on May 23 and 24 that came to be known as the Grand Review. Andrew attended the ceremony and arranged a viewing stand for Commonwealth dignitaries, with a banner read that read, "Massachusetts Greets the Country's Defenders." Forbes vividly remembered the day. Always indifferent to appearances, Andrew was his usual accommodating self. Washington streets were thronged, and when he arrived, he could only find a seat for his wife in an omnibus. So instead, he hired a cart, deposited their baggage in it, and appeared at Forbes's residence "perched on the top of it." Forbes remembered that, on the second day of the review, "when Sherman's bronzed regiments were approaching the grand stand, Gov. Andrew, wearied by the well drilled monotony of the previous day, when no shouting was permitted, slipped down from his seat, and ... obtained permission for Sherman's veterans to give a touch of their quality by their ringing cheers when passing the official headquarters."[50]

Once the days of pageantry ended, Washington entered an unaccustomed peaceful summer. Senator Sumner, however, refused to relax. He had spent nearly every day since Lincoln's assassination with Andrew Johnson, grooming him to take up the gauntlet for civil justice. At first the senator believed that Johnson would not only punish the southern traitors but also extend suffrage to African American men. Sumner hoped that, with Congress's adjournment, the president would take steps to ensure equal rights. But Andrew was skeptical. Making treason odious and punishing and impoverishing traitors, he feared, might do more harm than good to the freed slaves struggling for economic independence. It might be better to allow the southern landscape and its citizens to heal before politicizing readmission to the Union. Though conferring citizenship before advancing suffrage might diffuse the backlash against radicals, that, too, would cause problems. While Andrew understood that a large-scale relief program would benefit the freed slaves, he also promoted the idea that they should demonstrate their fitness in the marketplace, just as they had on the battlefield—a way to display their fitness for citizenship. By demonstrating their willingness to work and thereby acquire some self-sufficiency, they might temper southern anger. Even as traitors might be punished, states' rights would prevail. Johnson, like Lincoln, believed that the states had never legally seceded. Thus, he also declared that the federal government could not advance political suffrage for African Americans without state consent.[51]

Reconstruction

Andrew spent several days after the Grand Review at the Blair family's home in Silver Spring, Maryland. There was much to talk about. Johnson released his Reconstruction plan in late May, disguising it as proclamations conferring amnesty and pardon, including restoration of all property, upon former Confederates who pledged loyalty to the Union and the Thirteenth Amendment. He excluded, however, fourteen groups of southerners, who could apply for individual presidential pardons. At first, he seemed to be declaring that he wanted to overturn the planter slaveocracy and support the ascendency of Unionist yeomen, but soon his approach to pardoning routinely offered clemency to southern wealthy elites, with the idea that they would govern best.

Besides, Johnson believed that the franchise was a state matter, not a federal one. Given reports from the South in the spring, Andrew worried that African Americans remained vulnerable without citizenship protections, and they needed those protections if they were to acquire land and wage-paying jobs. Realities were setting in.

If many conservatives approved of Johnson's initial approach to Reconstruction, Republicans, anxious for retribution, came to view the president's terms for amnesty and pardon as far too lenient. In protest, Boston radicals organized a June 21 meeting in Faneuil Hall to consider the reorganization of the rebellious states. Theophilus Parsons's opening salvo addressed the issue head-on: "As we are victorious in war, we have a right to impose upon the defeated party any terms necessary for our security. If the question of freedman suffrage is left open, persistent and widespread agitation is inevitable." Richard Henry Dana, Jr., and Henry Ward Beecher both expounded on Parsons's argument, challenging the audience to recognize that the freed slaves needed political rights. "We are in a state of war," said Dana. "We hold each State in the grasp of war until the State does what we have a right to require of her."[52]

Andrew had been traveling to New York and Washington, and he was tired and ill. Unable to speak at the Faneuil Hall meeting, he sent a letter instead. His thoughts on Reconstruction were evolving, and he understood that some Commonwealth citizens supported the president's conservative approach because it promised to stabilize the economy, even if it denied suffrage to freed slaves. Though Andrew felt that his letter to the Faneuil Hall attendees was unworthy of the occasion, a contemporaneous letter to Stearns reveals a great deal of his thoughts about the postwar world and the plight of the freed slaves. He was not convinced that the secessionist states could be safely entrusted with governmental restoration:

> Whether the white man only votes or whether the colored man also votes, I regard the movement at the present moment with inexpressible concern. It has taken us four years to conquer the rebels in all of them. I would not run any risk—great or small—of allowing the same class of men to beat us by an appeal to *fraud*. They appealed to *force* and were conquered.

Andrew believed the Union victory was a mandate for rebuilding the southern states in a new image but worried more over the plight of the freed slaves in that process. As much as he had protested Lincoln's slowness in instituting emancipation, African American enlistment, and abolition, he had come to appreciate the president's use of "parental kindness" and "conciliation" to achieve in war what he hoped to gain in peace. After the iron fist of victory, it was time to wield the velvet glove of compassion—an approach, Andrew thought, that Lincoln would have appreciated.

The news coming into the statehouse confirmed for the governor that "the loyalty of the South needs *time for concentration*." If the South were pressed too hard, he feared, Reconstruction might turn violent. He did not believe that African American suffrage "would prevent the failure which seems most likely to result from these experiments, and we may be glad not to have them involved in the catastrophe. They will vote by and by, [and] . . . their *votes* will be wanted just as their *arms* were wanted. All people will yet see that poor and ignorant as they are, they are on the right side, and that they can neither be cheated nor bullied into its betrayal or desertion." In the meantime, freed slaves would gain knowledge about citizenship and its functions, privileges, and protections. The governor longed for an era of "calm, wise and yet brave and hopeful counsels," yet he was naïve to expect that the "freedmen might have the opportunity of a brief future unprejudiced by becoming immediately the subject of political controversy." He did not expect to find the president's decisions at odds with the judgments of Massachusetts. Weeks earlier, in the presence of the state delegation, Johnson had declared that his sole purpose was to make the country "permanently free," which had convinced Andrew (and Sumner) that the freed slaves' future was secure. In his letter to the Faneuil Hall listeners, he reminded them that freedoms had been constantly accruing, and he encouraged them to remain patient, judicious but cautious.[53]

After returning to Boston, Andrew attended a monument dedication in Lowell, memorializing Luther Ladd and Addison Whitney, two of the four Sixth Massachusetts soldiers who had been killed while passing through Baltimore in 1861. Andrew used the opportunity to talk about unity between Maryland and Massachusetts and how history had brought these two states back together. The monument "shall speak to your children, not of death, but of immortality," he said, and "shall stand here, a mute, expressive witness of the beauty and the dignity of youth and manly prime consecrated in unselfish obedience to duty." His inspiration had come from a letter written by Charles Devens, which had included a note from the journal of James Litchfield, a first lieutenant in the Fortieth Massachusetts. "These men have been true and valiant soldiers," Devens told Andrew, "but war is not their trade; they have been soldiers only because the Republic has called on them to draw a sword and they gladly exchanged it for the implements which are the agencies of art and peace."[54] Francis Lieber, the German emigrant and political philosopher who had written the pamphlet on military law that governed the Union Army, told Andrew that his address in Lowell, with its emphasis on the regimental communities that went to war, was truly "the beginning of the history of the Civil War."[55]

Communities were on the governor's mind that summer as he prepared to speak at Harvard's commencement. In a letter to Frank Blair, Sr., Andrew explained that Harvard was unlike any other institution in the world. He used his position on the college's board of overseers to invite President Johnson to the commencement: "Here the President will meet a body of men representing all the opinions and see the varieties of thought, skill, learning and intelligence of Massachusetts and of her most devoted patriotism. No where can so many men of liberal culture and liberal feelings and of that generous and catholic spirit be found together in America." Andrew praised the college as the "most ancient and worthy of American institutions of learning."[56] Such a visit, he told Blair, could serve "a thousand advantages of a public nature. . . . I am sure that at no moment in the history of the Union has any occurrence of circumstances yet happened where more good could be done by any such means." But Johnson did not accept the invitation.[57]

Speaking in Lowell and at Harvard gave Andrew the chance to expound on his views about the path forward. Writing to John Motley, he said he understood that the war had been a version of politics and that reconciling northerners and southerners and securing the rights of the freed slaves would be a daunting task. With the war had ended, peace would require an altogether different approach. Andrew had never doubted "our bravery in the field":

> [I] dreaded the temptations of peace, and the opportunities given by the cessation of arms to the schemers of every side who trade politics, sometimes bargaining away the rights of black men, and sometimes trading upon a freshly discovered zeal in their behalf, substituting the heartless of the mere spectacular in public concerns for the wisdom and fidelity of thoughtful patriotism. But on this field, as well as on that of war, I feel sure at the last we shall win. The work of Divine Goodness will be done. We of the North cannot be allowed, even if we would, to suffer it, or spoil it, or abuse it utterly.[58]

As much as Andrew longed for peace and the Union's preservation, he feared that another, longer war was unfolding.

CHAPTER 22

LAST MONTHS IN THE STATEHOUSE
July–December 1865

Yankees Are a Singular People

Andrew spent the early summer attending celebrations for soldiers returning to the Commonwealth. Though he had hoped to be in Hingham in July, the return of headaches and nosebleeds forced him to cancel his visit. He also missed the celebration in Boston commemorating the anniversary of American independence. In his regrets, Andrew penned a story to be read at the festivities, the retelling of an incident that had occurred when he was in Washington on July 4, 1859. He thought it exemplified the notion of Yankee ingenuity that was so central to Boston's standing as the "Cradle of Liberty." When a southern member of President Buchanan's cabinet had disparaged Andrew by calling "Yankees" a "singular people," Andrew had replied, "Indeed we are, sir. I hope to see the day when something of our *singularity* may strike as high as the city of Washington." His hopes had certainly been fulfilled.[1]

Andrew did muster enough strength to speak at the unveiling of a statue of Horace Mann in Boston. Mann had been instrumental in establishing the Massachusetts Board of Education, the model for common-school administration across the United States.[2] It was ironic, Andrew wrote to Frank Blair, Sr., that the Mann statue was erected so near Daniel Webster's. Webster had endorsed the 1850 Compromise and the Fugitive Slave Law in his impassioned "Seventh of March Speech." In contrast, Mann, though neither an abolitionist nor an integrationist, had opposed slavery and had spoken against its expansion into the territories, once calling Webster a "Lucifer descending from Heaven!"[3] Though Andrew, too, was disturbed by Webster's legacy, he took a conciliatory approach in his speech:

> On the one hand is the statue of Daniel Webster, the great Jurist, the great Statesman, the great American. On the other hand is the statue of Horace Mann, the teacher of Philosophy in its application both to politics and to popular learning, whose constituency was Mankind. . . . The rising sun of morning will turn from the purple East to salute his brow; and when his golden orb ascends the zenith, shining down from on high in Heaven, he will wrap and warm them both with generous embrace, in his lambent love and glory; and when at last the God of Day is descending beneath the horizon, his expiring ray will linger upon the brow of Webster.

A reporter noted that, as Andrew spoke these words, the light of the rising sun, having already enveloped Mann's statue, was just beginning to play on Webster's carven head. "The setting sun," he said, "would reverse this picture."[4]

In the nation's capital, the sun was also rising on a new epoch. In his article "Celebrating the Fourth with the Negroes," a *Daily Advertiser* correspondent described the Fourth of July scene. Though more than 4,000 African Americans and 500 white citizens had gathered on the mall, at least one policeman reported that the city had never seen "such an orderly" holiday. Still convalescing, Andrew had declined his invitation to this celebration and instead sent a letter to be read, as did Douglass, Greeley, Reverend Channing, and others. The letter emphasized Andrew's conviction that that equal rights and unprejudiced liberties must now be bestowed on all Americans, regardless of color. The governor was confident that the day would soon come when freed slaves would be able to exercise the privileges the war had given them. Indeed, he thought it was remarkable that they continued to exercise restraint against their former masters. In response, the crowd erupted in extended applause.[5]

In mid-July, Boston hosted a convention of adjutant generals who were presenting their final reports about the war. After concluding their formal business, they retired to the governor's chambers, where Schouler introduced them to Andrew, now recuperated from his illness. Maryland's Governor Bradford had sent a silk flag as a peace offering to Massachusetts, and Andrew took note of the gift. Nathaniel Baker, an attendee from Iowa, was impressed by the gathering. He was honored to "pay our respects" and acknowledge Andrew's service during the war. For his part, Andrew was thrilled that the adjutant generals had chosen Boston for their convention, and he thanked them for honoring his state's war effort. Although weakened by secession, the Union had not fallen because the loyal states had held it up; and Andrew trusted that "the arch of the Union would stand as long as the sun and moon shine."[6]

Andrew attended several ceremonies commemorating the war's end, toured the Massachusetts coast with government engineers, and found time to entertain General Meade at the Revere House. Since his war-related duties had diminished, he was able to accept more invitations. He spoke to the thirteen graduates of Bradford Academy in Haverhill, Massachusetts, one of New England's earliest educational institutions for women, now celebrating its sixty-first anniversary. On July 21, he was among the more than 1,000 guests walking among Cambridge's elms toward Harvard's commencement ceremonies. Speakers celebrated not only the graduates but also those alumni who had given labor and life to the Union cause. Andrew was joined on stage by numerous local luminaries, and in his speech to the graduates the governor said that the work of sending Harvard students off to war had made the college especially dear to him:

> If there were words of human speech fit to portray their history, they spring not from human lips; they are not born from oral speech, but there are testimonies more potent, more impressive, more electric than the human voice, and they are here today, in that cloud of living witnesses, who have come back with glory from the fields where their comrades fell.

He singled out several alumni, including Chaplain Arthur Fuller of the Sixteenth Massachusetts, "who, musket in hand, fell in front of Fredericksburgh":

> The memory of mankind shall preserve their names when all monumental structures shall have sunk beneath the dust that cover us. You can make a monument that shall keep in remembrance not only your brethren, but yourselves, by making mankind your debtors by the fidelity with which you adhere to the truth and the doctrines for which they died.

When he finished, the crowd erupted with applause and a standing ovation.[7]

Even as demobilization consumed Andrew's attention, he found respite in this first summer of peace, even though the war would not officially end until months later. Still plagued by fatigue, headaches, and nosebleeds, he told Sumner that he would be happy to relinquish his political duties and refused to "tempt providence" by thinking of higher office. He longed to spend time with his family, and he was tired of depending on voters for his livelihood. Yet his war work was far from over, and he remained especially concerned about African Americans serving in the South. Andrew's correspondents kept him apprised of their situation. "In 4 years of warfare," Colonel Edward Wild wrote from Georgia, "I thought I had learned something of the abominations of slavery. But I confess that I am staggered by the daily reports of awful outrages that come into this city. Slavery exists every where except under the immediate shadow of our flag." Wild believed that it would take months to convince rural residents of the region that the U.S. government had abolished slavery in February.[8] A soldier in the Fifth Cavalry complained to Andrew that the men were "treated worse than dogs and slaves." Some soldiers, he said, had been "noced [noosed] and draged about, . . . dying like sheep." "For God's sake and ours," he pleaded, "do something for us."[9]

Late in the month, Andrew made a brief trip to New York City to visit Frank Howe but returned to Boston to meet General Grant at the Revere House on the evening of July 29. The following day, Andrew, Grant, Sumner, Wilson, and several other dignitaries attended services at the Old South Church and afterward spent time exchanging war stories. On Monday morning, Andrew and his guests toured the city, the naval yard, and the monument grounds. When they returned to Faneuil Hall, thousands of citizens had gathered to greet the commander. In the afternoon, the group paid a short visit to Harvard, to Mount Auburn Cemetery in Cambridge, to the Watertown arsenal, and finally to Boston's Union Club, where the governor had arranged a private dinner. Both Andrew and Grant later recorded their admiration for one another.[10]

The summer's slower pace allowed Andrew to focus on several matters that were near to his heart. One was his vision for helping single women safely emigrate west—a plan that the Daily Advertiser called a "novel and noteworthy scheme." The idea was making headway within philanthropic circles and territorial governments, and by August some three hundred women had boarded the steamer De Molay bound for Washington Territory, at no cost to themselves. They would be transported to Aspinwall, Panama (today known as Colón), then taken across the isthmus by rail and up the west coast to Washington by water. Andrew also kept his eye on education issues, attending a three-day convention of the American Institute of Instruction in New Haven. His speech before a packed house reminded listeners that Americans needed to be as vigilant in supporting their institutions of learning as they had been in preserving the Union: "New England has a work to do, which is an aggressive missionary work in this country, or else she fails utterly of her high vocation. New England is the most powerful three and a quarter millions of people under the sun, and our country demands the utmost of the peculiar power which it is the gift of New England to wield."[11]

In mid-August, Andrew traveled to Washington, where he met with treasury officials to settle the remaining war funds owed to the state. His visit was longer than anticipated as President Johnson subsequently invited him to the White House to discuss Reconstruction, though Andrew mentioned nothing of the meeting his correspondence. Perhaps his silence was indicative of his growing disappointment in the president. While he was in the city, Andrew read in the press that the trustees of Antioch College in Ohio, which was affiliated with the Unitarians, would be offering him the presidency. Horace Mann had been the institution's first president, but the college had closed during the war and was now struggling to find leadership and adequate funding. After General James Garfield of Ohio declined the position, board members turned to Andrew. He was interested, and rumors abounded that he would accept it after his term as governor had ended.[12]

Just as the governor was about to leave Washington, he learned that the Fifty-fourth Massachusetts would be arriving in Boston within the next few days. Quickly he wrapped up his business and headed home. After mustering out of service on August 20, the soldiers were discharged in Boston on September 1. On the following day, just as he had done two years before, Andrew stood at the top of the statehouse steps as the soldiers marched past, offering a salute as they made their way to Boston Common. There, the men formed a square, and Andrew poured out his thanks for their support. His eyes filled and his voice cracked as he dismissed the men for a final time, watched as they stacked their arms, and wished them well as they scattered to civilian life. The tattered regimental colors were carried to the statehouse and displayed alongside those of the many other Massachusetts regiments, with no sign of a color line. A *Daily Advertiser* reporter noted the occasion's significance: "This regiment was the leader" of the war's "most important movement."[13]

In early September, Andrew went to Providence to address graduates at Brown College's commencement. He returned to Boston in time to join Anson Burlingame's dinner party for Sir Frederick Bruce, Great Britain's minister to the United States, held at the Parker House.[14] At this time, Andrew advised party leaders that he would not seek reelection, which allowed Republicans to nominate Alexander Bullock for governor. Bullock was a wealthy lawyer, politician, and businessman; importantly, he was also a Bird Club member. Yet some voters wanted Andrew to remain in politics. "We can't afford to lose you," wrote a Worcester resident. "We need you. We cannot fulfill our destiny without you. We look upon you as our prophet and high Priest of freedom." Andrew was still considering the possibility of accepting the presidency of Antioch College, and Elizabeth Peabody, a celebrated educational activist, told him that she understood why he was drawn to the position. But others cogitated about ways to redirect him back into politics. The editor of the *New York Independent* proposed that Representative Samuel Hooper of Massachusetts should resign his seat in Congress to make room for Andrew, though he did admit that the college president position might be a relief after politics. Andrew wavered for weeks, but in the end declined Antioch's offer. He felt that he and his family were Yankees through and through and would find it difficult to leave New England. Moreover, his sister Sarah was sick with typhoid in Gorham, Maine, and this may also have influenced his decision.[15]

During two cloudless days in late September Andrew attended the Hingham Agricultural Fair. Visiting such exhibitions was among his favorite tasks as governor. Though he was a man of letters and culture, he thoroughly enjoyed fair events such as ox pulls and local band performances. Andrew wandered the grounds, basking in this foretaste of life as a private citizen. He made no speeches, though he did accept Josiah Quincy's heartfelt toast. It was not Andrew's time to shine; he wanted the event to remain a celebration of New England and her people.[16]

By the end of the month, Andrew was in New York City again, negotiating with Barings Bank of London for a short-term loan to cover Commonwealth shortages until the federal government paid its war debts to the state. He used the opportunity to travel upstate to Ithaca to meet Ezra Cornell, the founder of Western Union and an educational philanthropist. Cornell was planning a new university and wanted to discuss Andrew's interest in the presidency. Andrew White, a college professor, and a New York state senator had been working with Cornell on the project and had suggested Andrew as a candidate. In the end, they did not offer him the position. But if they had, the governor would have declined it. He was ready to leave politics but not ready to leave home.[17]

Andrew returned to Boston to chair a meeting about the establishment of a state association to promote social science, a discipline that had long intrigued him. With his political career coming to a close, he wanted to extend his influence on the projects that meant the most to him. He was able to escape from his duties in early October when he and Eliza joined Julia Ward Howe on Cape Cod for Barnstable's annual agricultural festival and ball. Andrew and his guests, including Schouler and General Daniel Sickles, arrived on the second day and spent a chilly evening enjoying dinner and awarding fair premiums. The grand ball was held in the agricultural hall. Howe's daughter recalled her mother's description of the evening. Apparently, the band leader stopped the music two hours earlier than scheduled, much to the chagrin of the guests: "The townspeople thought [this was] because the pretty girls were all engaged beforehand for the dance." Howe commemorated the event in her poem "The Barnstable Ball," in which she quipped that Andrew wouldn't "hang for homicide," a reference to his delay in signing the death warrant for Edward Green.[18]

As the curtain slowly descended on Andrew's political career, his thoughts turned often to the freed slaves in the South. Captain William How, who operated the Freedman's Bureau's Sixth District in Virginia, sent news from his Winchester headquarters. He had just returned from Harpers Ferry and Charles Town and told Andrew that he was impressed with the work being done in establishing schools. Horace Mann's sister was teaching more than sixty children and leading them in worship, and How had volunteered to assist. He asked Andrew to erect a school "on the site of the gallows from which John Brown was hung. . . . The colored people are very anxious for an opportunity to send their children to school." Yet local white citizens protested such advances, so How had to arrange for troops to protect the students. Andrew responded generously, giving freely from his own funds; and as the president of the New England Freedman's Aid Society, he rallied members to support the endeavor.[19]

Just as he believed that northerners must invest in education for the former slaves, Andrew was convinced that the South's economy could only be regenerated with an infusion of Yankee reformers and investors, who in turn would open opportunities for them. Thus, it was important for businessmen to reshape that economy with African American labor before the government imposed harsh measures that would undermine cooperation. Andrew did not believe that the business of Reconstruction needed to rely solely on federal coercion but rather other civic philanthropic support. Beyond building schools, getting people back to work was paramount.[20] He took this message to Harwich, Massachusetts, in a speech he gave at the opening of the new Cape Cod Central Railroad that October: "Let me repeat what I may have said on former occasions, that liberality is the economy of the States, that liberality is the economy of communities."[21] With the war over, it was time to work toward prosperity for everyone. Andrew aimed to establish confidence between North and South, whites and African Americans. With Stearns, he had already launched a new brokerage business, the American Land Company and Agency. Northern capitalists backed the venture, which was designed to bring southern planters into cooperation with northern financiers, farmers, and mechanics in order to revitalize the southern economy. Unlike the many corrupt attempts to swindle southern land, Andrew's enterprise was altruistic, an endeavor to make emancipation an early, visible success through economic self-sufficiency. Board members named Andrew president and Frank Howe vice-president and general agent in the North, and Cyrus Woodman became secretary. Yet not all Commonwealth citizens were comfortable with the venture. Some thought it was eminently patriotic, but conservatives feared that it would lure farmers away from New England and further weaken local communities. "What will a Yankee gain by going South?" lamented the editor of the *Vermont Chronicle*. "The white and colored races are in constant collision, churches, schools, and colleges, have been chiefly suspended or ruined . . . [and] society is composed of discontented aristocrats, poor white trash and equally poor black trash."[22]

Andrew, however, remained confident in his venture. The approaching winter would give people time to purchase land and find a labor source for spring planting, and even a small investment might yield substantial gains quickly. In a letter to Reverend Thomas Conway, a commissary officer for the Louisiana Freedman's Bureau, he said:

> The waste of war has left land-owners poor in all save their lands. Floating capital has disappeared in the South. And, just now, when they need credit more than ever, to replace them, they are without bankers, factors, lenders. . . . Without money or credit, the planter can neither buy mules, corn, bacon, small stores, cloth for the support of the freedmen, nor can he pay them their needful wages, while making the crop. . . . For the purchase of lands in large lots or to be cut up into small freeholds and resold to the freedmen, poor whites, immigrants, our company could act for them I think, with efficiency and success.

By bringing "capable, ambitious and right-minded men into the South," Andrew's enterprise could "confirm Peace for us all, and practical freedom and happiness to the Colored race."[23]

If many southern whites assumed that former slaves would mistake idleness for freedom, Andrew believed otherwise. He argued that the Union's military management of plantations had shown that freed slaves were willing to work hard. In his opinion, political leaders should use both the marketplace and the federal government to reestablish a relationship between people and place in free society. Yet white southern defiance was an obstacle to African American landownership, and his enterprise needed support in the South because a corporation chartered in one state did not have the right to own property in another. More importantly, Andrew had failed to appreciate that southern whites and conservative northerners would not accept freed slaves as landowners.[24] As a result, the new land company struggled to gain a footing, but Andrew held out hope, and his associates and investors continued to praise the venture as admirable and missionary-like. In the meantime, he concentrated on matters close to home, including a memorial for Colonel Robert Gould Shaw, killed in action while commanding the Fifty-fourth. Joshua Smith, a prominent African American businessman, had proposed erecting a monument to Shaw, and in early October he met with Andrew, Sumner, Colonel Henry Lee, and Samuel Howe to plan the project. Shaw and the African American regiments "have a hold upon my memory and my heart which must be perpetual," Andrew wrote.[25]

Though the governor prayed that white Americans would soon learn to accept color difference, he understood that segregation still controlled attitudes everywhere. He hoped to combat this via the new American Association for the Promotion of the Social Science. The association was devoted to using social science to guide practical improvements in education, public safety, public morality, sanitation, and regulation and to diffuse sound economic, finance, and trade principles. Its leadership included several of his close friends, among them George Boutwell and Frank Sanborn. Through conversations with these and other colleagues, Andrew came to understand that Reconstruction would be far more complicated and violent than he had initially imagined.[26]

In early November, Massachusetts voters elected Alexander Bullock to be their next governor. After the polls closed, Andrew dispatched Schouler to congratulate the new chief and invite him to the statehouse to prepare for the transition. Then he turned his attention to his own future, arranging to return to his law practice and, as much as possible, remove himself from the public arena. Although he had never lived a secluded life, the past five years had been unprecedented, and Andrew wanted to open his next chapter in peace. Yet even as he was preparing to step back from the fray, the nation's divisions were growing ever more bitter. The president's actions had encouraged some white southern elites to view him as an ally in their quest for self-governance. For their part, Radical Republican leaders objected to Johnson's easy pardons and to his appointment of military governors with broad administrative powers. In November, elections in the South swept anti-secessionists and former Whigs to victory. This was the bar for readmission to the Union, but it remained to be seen what lay ahead. [27]

Johnson's contradictory positions not only fractured the Massachusetts electorate but also weakened the long friendship between Sumner and Andrew. After the war, Andrew had tried to work with Johnson and southern planters to establish a peaceful economy in which freed slaves could thrive without punitive federal coercion. Perhaps he had fallen under the spell of thinkers such as Reverend Henry Ward Beecher, whose sermon, "Conditions of a Restored Union," argued that northerners needed to trust southerners so as to allow them some self-respect and Christian charity. Sumner, however, had alarming information about the freed slaves' condition and their vulnerability as non-citizens. He rejected Johnson's and Beecher's lenient approach, demanding more aggressive governmental measures that would deny former Confederates a place in their own governance. Carl Schurz, a German revolutionary who became an American general, had traveled in the South on Johnson's orders and had returned with an embarrassing report on southern conditions. Perhaps to garner support, he had prematurely leaked his findings to the Boston press. Then he invited Sumner and Andrew to meet him in New York City, hoping that they might rally support to resist the president's course. In response, Sumner said that Andrew would attend the meeting but that he could not; matters were far too pressing. "My own convictions," he said, "are now stronger than ever with regard to our duty. *The rebel states must not be allowed at once to participate in our govt.*"[28]

Late that fall, on the heels of Schurz's report, came Lewis Parsons, whom Johnson had appointed as Alabama's provisional governor. He arrived in Boston to solicit capitalist support for his state. Parsons was a moderate who had combated the move to subjugate freed slaves, opposed Johnson's pardons, and urged voters to ratify the Thirteenth Amendment. Stanton, who was desperately laboring for the Union's restoration, encouraged Parson to meet with the Boston elite. So at a November 7 gathering at the Union Club, the Alabama governor, flanked by Andrew and Reverend Beecher, asked members to purchase state bonds to help restore his state's destroyed economy. With winter fast approaching, he said, both freed slaves and whites would suffer. The Boston-based publisher James Fields attended the gathering and afterward wrote in his diary about Parsons's "sad stories . . . of the suffering and destitution of the South, especially of his own State." Beecher, too, was moved and told Parsons that several New York capitalists would subscribe to a $1.5 million loan at 8 percent interest. But then Sumner, who was also in attendance, rose and suggested that what "the gentleman from Alabama needed was *candor*, as well as cash." He remarked that he did not believe that New Englanders would invest one dollar in Alabama bonds so long as that state denied civil and political rights to nearly one-half of its population.[29]

Before Andrew could respond, Beecher interrupted Sumner, saying that if the Alabama bonds were not good, then neither were the bonds of any state that denied suffrage to African Americans, including Ohio, Indiana, and New York. Andrew agreed. In the absence of an apology, Sumner nonetheless outlined his terms for Confederates' readmission to the Union. "Alabama was a very bogus state," he said, "not more than half converted from disloyalty, and though perhaps not intending to take up arms again, yet fully intending to re[e]stablish institutions as nearly as possible on the old basis of injustice and slavery to the black race." While Andrew might have agreed with Sumner's assessment, this was not the time or place to be indignant. Angry, he sprang to Parsons's defense. "Until this moment," he declared, he "had hoped Gov. Parsons would be treated by gentlemen as a gentleman." The governor had long been smoldering over Sumner's lack of support for his cabinet appointment, and he now proceeded "in a very personal and offensive strain to reply to Mr. Sumner, concluding with an appeal for cooperation with, rather than antagonism to, the South."[30]

Sumner did not budge. In reporting the affair to Stanton, he took offense at Parsons's comment "that rather than allow negroes to vote he would emigrate," which, to the senator's mind, set "a bad example."[31] Andrew, too, had found Parsons's comment insulting, but his reaction to Sumner arose from a larger disagreement with the radical Republicans: when it came to Reconstruction, he preferred the olive branch to the sword. For his part, Sumner was angry—not at Andrew, whom he respected, but with Johnson and his minions. After all, he still bore the physical scars of that beating in Congress; he knew what southerners were capable of. It was obvious to him that there was little hope of a judicious way forward in the South. He told the president that unless he stopped giving power to Confederates and asserting that all men should have a say in self-governance, the "house will continue divided against itself."[32]

As Sumner and some Republicans pushed a more radical approach to Reconstruction, Andrew continued to believe that there could be an alternative path to a mutual goal. He, too, was frustrated with Johnson; he knew the former enslaver was no friend to African Americans. Still, it was easier for Andrew to mask his feelings about the president in Boston than for Sumner to hide them in Washington. Even as maddening as Lincoln's conciliatory approach to war had been, it had borne fruit. If he had lived, perhaps a lenient approach would have worked, but his assassination should have shown the governor that southerners would not take defeat easily. Andrew's peacetime moderation appeared at odds with his wartime attitude but not with his spiritual beliefs and his hope for peaceful and redemptive reconciliation. He hated the sin of slavery more than he hated the enslaver, who could be redeemed if he changed his ways. At the same time, he feared for the freed slaves' safety and contemplated how to navigate divergent paths forward to a common goal. It was not that he was Johnson's advocate but that he dreaded the depredations of former Confederates. The more the freed slaves advanced, Andrew believed, the more they invited the prejudice that came with difference, and he feared punitive measures would aggravate hostility toward them. Thus, protecting their civil rights was paramount.[33]

A few weeks after their public dispute, Sumner sent Andrew a note along with a letter from an Alabama resident that described what the senator characterized as "the actual condition of society there."[34] Andrew was not surprised by the deplorable conditions but held out hope for the rule of law. In response, he told Sumner:

> There are unhappily thousands of men and brutal minds who hate, despise and dread the negro. The master used to be a protection. Now the law must supply that protection, or he is a necessary victim. But the law also must have moral support, or it too is powerless. The presence of Northern men, of the influences and motives of free civilization, *must be had*. Without them there will be a long failure.

To accomplish this task, he wrote, the administration needed to cultivate "the possible good" in southerners, especially the educated and most enlightened, who had "a strong tendency *now* towards the right side." The war had taught them that they must cooperate with northerners, must conform to a new social order, and they needed encouragement, not chastisement. Moreover, "as to the Freedman's Bureau, . . . [it] ought to control and command the local military, and not be subordinate to the military." Its leader should be a "first class, clear, strong, self-reliant, bold man, with *power* in his brain, *power* in his heart and *power at hand* and *in* his hand, which he can wield for the protection of his wards, and the assertion of his own official rights."[35]

As Andrew lost confidence in Johnson, he still hoped for the success of the Freedman's Bureau, especially as winter approached. If the bureau failed, he told Sumner, "all would fail." As to the reception of southern senators and representatives in Congress, "the position for *New England* is one of friendliness, not of antagonism":

> In taking the latter we are defeated,—in the former we shall win. And we shall carry our own doctrines into the South. We can get the southern people, by popular vote, to adopt the necessary amendments to their Constitutions, and meanwhile they will wait outside of Congress. During this time Congress should pass laws to *carry into effect* the Great Amendment of Freedom, to assure the freedmen in their rights, get President Johnson's signature, and *then* the freedmen will have their real chance for safety and progress.

Andrew believed it was better to work with those southerners who were willing to avoid political and racial friction rather than exclude them altogether. Taking this approach was courageous, perhaps naïve, but, more than anything, a grand gesture of reconciliation: "We have dealt the death-blow to one barbarism by the arm of another. Now we have Civilization, Reason, Religion,—all these to work with."[36]

There was a deep moralism in Andrew's rationale, and Sumner appreciated his views, even while challenging them. As for apologizing to Andrew about his outburst in Boston, he simply replied in the third person:

> Mr. S hopes that the Governor will not cease that watchfulness which has done him so much honor. He ventures to suggest that first & foremost "among the arts and methods of peace," which the Govr now wishes to cultivate, is justice to the oppressed, & he entreats the Govr. not to allow any negro-hater, with his sympathizers, to believe him, at this crisis, indifferent to the guarantees of Human Rights or disposed to postpone his efforts in their behalf.[37]

There was no doubt that Andrew would continue to watch over his African American brethren. He made this topic the subject of his Sunday School lesson at the Twelfth Baptist Church, where the New England Convention of Colored People would shortly convene to appoint a delegation to attend upcoming congressional sessions in Washington. As inspiration, he chose Luke 4:16–20, verses that emphasize the apostle's evangelism among the poor, celebrating the release of the captive, sight for the blind, and freedom for the oppressed. He referred to the portrait of slavery in *Uncle Tom's Cabin* and argued that God had called all people to a higher purpose in securing freedom's fundamental rights for everyone, regardless of color: "We have been taught to feel, to our innermost being that there is something worth more than life, many things worth infinitely more than peace—duty, destiny, hope, love, immortality." As he looked out over the crowd that Sunday, he reminded the congregants that "you are, in a certain sense, a city set upon a hill; and there has never been a time hitherto, where there has been such an opportunity and such responsibilities as there now are laid upon this very hill. I tell you, there is not a man with black skin from the Atlantic to the Rio Grande who would not suffer in consequence if it."[38]

As his governorship drew to a close, Andrew issued his final Thanksgiving Proclamation, which echoed Lincoln's second inaugural address. "In a spirit of forgiveness and charity toward all," he said, "let us adore the Goodness which has given such victory and such honor to the right; has restored peace to our land and the promise of liberty and unity for all the inhabitants thereof forever."[39] So popular was the address that the *National Intelligencer* printed the message of charity for its Washington readers, and even the *Arkansas Gazette* published portions for its Little Rock subscribers.[40]

Even as he chose to move outside of politics, Andrew retained his sway within the African American community and the state's Republican Party. Thus, he knew he needed to mend fences with Sumner. The senator's conceit irritated him, but their division had been his own fault. In truth, they were simply arguing for different means to the same end, securing safety and progress for the freed slaves. Not long after their exchange of letters, the governor reiterated his views on Reconstruction to Hermann Bokum of the Bureau of Immigration. Bokum was a German native, who had immigrated to Pennsylvania, living there for nearly three decades before moving to eastern Tennessee in 1861. As hostilities began, he had refused to pledge his loyalty to the Confederacy; and after receiving death threats, he had moved to Philadelphia, where he became a hospital chaplain. Writing to Bokum, the governor said, "A rebel vote is the best of all, if it is only cast in the right way." If southerners were not prepared to vote to accept the Union's necessary measures, "then they are not prepared in their minds for *reconstruction*." In his view, the path forward belonged in their hands, provided they did they did the honorable thing by accepting congressional demands.[41]

Andrew's thoughts on Reconstruction had been maturing for some time and for good reason. South Carolina and Mississippi legislators had disappointed him by enacting a series of state laws known as the Black Codes, intended to limit freed slaves' rights and responsibilities. Combined with Johnson's swift power transfer, they undermined the opportunities that Andrew and the radical Republicans had hoped to establish, instead bringing labor regulations, land ownership, and criminal laws under white control. Without civil rights protections, soon to follow, Andrew feared, would be public and school segregation, which he had fought so hard against in the Commonwealth. He had naïvely imagined that southerners would embrace the Christian charity extended by the federal government's lenient terms of repatriation, as evidenced to some degree by wartime reconstruction. Now he had to reckon with the fact that the South's "natural leaders" had again relegated African Americans to subservience by reasserting their belief in white superiority.[42]

Andrew's gubernatorial career was closing at a discouraging time. For him, the departure was bittersweet. No other Massachusetts governor could lay claim to having fundamentally reshaped the United States. Other than his health and a desire for peace, he had no compelling reason to retire. Yet he was looking forward to returning to private life, where he would continue battling injustice in the courts. He had advanced the arc of the moral universe in revolutionary ways during the war. As successful as he had been as a political leader, he was more comfortable before judge and jury, and he knew that a new and difficult day was dawning in Washington. Quietly, he knew his health was no match for the storm ahead; words, vision, and prayers were all he could offer.

In a meeting with President Johnson on December 2, Sumner noted a remarkable contrast between his present views and those of the previous summer. Instead of the "kindly sympathetic disposition he then saw," he found the president "harsh, petulant and unreasonable. His heart was with the ex-rebels. . . . For the Unionist, white or black, who had borne the burden of war, he had little feeling." Sumner told Peleg Chandler that the president was "impenetrable, . . . stolid, & without any sympathy for the freedmen."[43] Thus, when the Thirty-ninth Congress convened on December 4, radical Republican congressmen immediately went on the attack, quickly aligning to use their constitutional powers to seize control of the South. Within hours, even before receiving the president's message to Congress, Representative Thaddeus Stevens of Pennsylvania proposed the creation of a joint committee on Reconstruction. Members seized upon the Black Codes, presidential pardons, and other discriminatory measures as justification for their swift action, turning the tables on their recalcitrant southern colleagues, some of whom had been high-ranking Confederates just months before.[44]

Andrew followed these proceedings closely, hoping to glean some insights from them to use in the valedictory address he would present to Commonwealth legislators in the coming weeks. He and Sumner were still not entirely reconciled, largely because Sumner was angry that Johnson had made use of the governor's views, prominence, and credibility in justifying his southern policy. The senator was also chagrined that the president's annual message to Congress in December had been well received by many Republicans. This was not Andrew's fault, but it chafed Sumner. Now, as the governor watched events unfold in Congress, he informed a member of Congress privately that the South "must clearly and completely cede to the freedman *the same civil rights enjoyed by the whites.*" Johnson had made a grievous mistake, Andrew believed, by allowing the southern states to form governments while neglecting Black suffrage. He went so far as to propose to a friend an amendment that would enfranchise Black men on the same basis as white men throughout the United States. To encourage harmony, however, he suggested that the law take effect after a twenty-five-year delay. There was some merit to the idea. John Binney, a New York Republican, had suggested the same idea to Senator Stevens and President Johnson, promoting it as a concession that might secure the president's approval. Andrew would rather advance the freed slaves' civil rights than destroy the southern aristocrats' political rights. Yet he had learned that doing the former required the latter.[45]

To say that Andrew had acquired national credibility was an understatement. He had stepped out of political obscurity into the state's highest office, winning unprecedented public acclaim and commanding great influence. A Kentucky soldier said, "There is only one governor whose whole name I know; and that is John A. Andrew of Massachusetts."[46] If he had wanted a congressional seat at any time during the past four years, Massachusetts voters would have rewarded him. Andrew had been the consummate war governor and was perhaps more popular than Sumner and Wilson among the state's businessmen, capitalists, and soldiers. They appreciated both his morality and his moderation. Andrew was "a radical believer in the *suffrage* for all men of competent capacity, irrespective of color or natural origins"; but unlike Sumner, he had drawn the line at raising the "general question of the suffrage for colored men in the South, as yet." In his view, suffrage was a privilege, to be granted "according to capacity and desert." Before receiving it, freed slaves needed to demonstrate their ability to grow "in knowledge and in admitted capacity for exercising the political functions of citizenship." Without education, he believed, they would be political pawns.[47]

Andrew spent weeks poring over documents in preparation for his final legislative address, behaving as if he were priming himself for a sermon at the Twelfth Baptist Church or the Bethel Chapel. He invited friends and colleagues to his chambers to listen to his numerous drafts. As he reflected on those consuming years of mobilization and anxiety, memories of surrender, of Lincoln's assassination, of the Grand Review filtered through his mind. But always the Commonwealth soldiers and their families remained foremost in his thoughts. As a student of history, Andrew knew how quickly memories could fade, and he wanted to remind citizens that the struggle to "think and act anew" was ongoing. He decided that Boston would play host to its own Grand Review before his term ended, and he began organizing a regimental ceremony for war veterans. The occasion would be known as the Return of the Flags, a reference to the Union's regimental flags, which the War Department had ordered to be deposited with U.S. mustering officers and then transferred to their respective governors. This had often taken place without fanfare, but Andrew wanted to honor their return in proper ceremonial fashion, officially receiving them into the Commonwealth's archives. The event would take place on Forefathers' Day, December 22, the 245th anniversary of the Pilgrims' landing at Plymouth—a way to commemorate the state's past and present.[48]

To mark the occasion, merchants suspended business, thousands of spectators lined the sidewalks of Boston, and banners hung across many streets. The uniformed veterans marched through the snowy streets; and as each regiment reached the statehouse and paused, its color bearer mounted the steps to where Andrew stood. When the tattered flags were gathered, he accepted them on behalf of Massachusetts citizens. Then he addressed the veterans for the last time:

> Borne, one by one, out of this capitol during more than four years of civil war as the symbols of the nation and the Commonwealth, [the flags] . . . come back again, borne hither by surviving representatives of the same heroic regiments and companies to which they were entrusted. . . . [They were] proud memories of many a field; sweet memories alike of valor and friendship.

He thanked God that those lost had not died in vain and dismissed the regiments. Afterward, the flags were carried into Doric Hall to become archives of war. They would be placed side by side without a color line to distinguish white and Black regiments. In the words of an observer who attended the affair, Andrew had "ordered the overcoats." Now he had "received the flags."[49]

As Andrew labored over his valedictory speech, he reflected on how he had grown into his office and his duties as war governor. Others reflected as well. Years later Thomas Higginson recalled that many citizens had feared that Andrew might not be up to the challenge, yet his natural abilities were "so superior and his capacity for labor so great that he rose at once to an equality with the demands of the time." Importantly, he "read character very acutely and truly" and never wavered from his instincts.[50] Charles Francis Adams wrote from London, "My nation state has, during the period of trial that has passed, been so fortunate as to possess a chief magistrate who has fully sustained her ancient reputation, and has placed himself, to say the least, on the highest level attained by the most worthy of a long line of worthy predecessors."[51] George Curtis, a political editor for *Harper's Weekly*, declared, "[If Andrew's accomplishments were] only in Literature—you might be content—but they are in history, and in all our hearts—in your state and in the nation."[52] Writing in the *Congregationalist*, Reverend Alonzo Quint said, "The public can never forget what Governor Andrew has done in these years of war. He took office when the clouds were lowering and the storm about to burst. He leaves it with the tempest over and the air clean. His thrilling appeals went to the heart of the people."[53] General Schouler, who knew the governor intimately, called him the "greatest, the wisest, and noblest of Massachusetts governors," possessing a "transcendent genius as an executive officer."[54] Forbes assured Andrew that "the best law business in the city is open to you if you return to it, *'pure and simple.'*"[55]

According to Reverend Clarke, the governor had seldom wavered in his decisions. He was the "pilot who weathered the storm." Yet even in the darkest days, he had been calm and patient, always ready with a joke or a funny story.[56] He had cared for every constituent: man or woman, rich or poor, Black or white, Protestant or Catholic, civilian or soldier. After the war the *Boston Herald* printed a story illuminating Andrew's indiscriminate compassion. Late one afternoon, when the governor was about to leave the statehouse for home, a messenger announced that a poor elderly Irish woman was waiting to speak to him, hoping that Andrew could release her husband from prison. "I'll get rid of her for you," said the messenger. "No, you won't," said Andrew. "I am here to see just such people, and the poorer they are the more necessary it is that they should see me." The woman told the governor that her husband had been injured on the railway. Now disabled, he had begun to support himself by selling a little rum out of his shanty. In consequence, he had been arrested and jailed. "Don't worry, my good woman," said Andrew. "I'll pardon your husband tomorrow." After she left, he told the messenger, "I'll pardon out every such case as long as I'm governor of this state and they confine to prison poor men for doing what rich hotel-keepers do every day unmolested. There shall not be one sort of justice for the poor and another for the rich."[57] Such stories abounded, so many that Harriet Beecher Stowe decided to include a portrait of Andrew among the sketches of America's leading political men that she published in the Boston-based *Christian Watchman and Reflector.*[58]

In a striking coincidence, Andrew's departure from office paralleled another notable retirement. On December 29, William Lloyd Garrison bid his readers farewell, and the *Liberator* ceased publication. Founded thirty-five years earlier, it had accomplished its noble goal: voters had abolished slavery by constitutional amendment. The *Liberator* had become the nation's premier abolitionist newspaper, a voice for the slaves, a friend when they had no other friends. Risking his own life and the lives of his family, even with a southern bounty on his head, Garrison had never hesitated. He had carved a path through treacherous political and cultural terrain and bloodied himself in the cause, and now he lay down his work with the knowledge that he had championed righteousness. "Better to be always in a minority of one with God, in defence of RIGHT," he reminded his readers, "than like Herod, having the shouts of a multitude, crying, 'It is the voice of a god, and not of a man.'"[59] Though Andrew and Garrison had often disagreed about methods and had taken divergent paths, both had been crucial in the abolition of slavery, and they respected one another deeply. Even those who found fault with the editor's harsh refusal to "equivocate" acknowledged that he had "be[en] heard." Unlike many humanitarians, Garrison had lived to see the accomplishment of his life's work.

In late December, Andrew received a letter from Republican John Binney of New York, which included a copy of a letter from a congressman referring to a constitutional amendment that would "enfranchise[e] the colored people." Binney wrote, "This is the cornerstone of the work of Reconstruction. To neglect this work would be a stupid blunder in statesmanship & a great national crime. Every vestige of slavery ought, by a grand & comprehensive scheme, to be swept off territories of the Union." He implored Andrew to use his influence with New Englanders who were the "brain & soul of the nation to rouse their patriotic enthusiasm in support of such a scheme," suggesting that he should "seize the platform & the press & have them kindled into an electric flame." With such a goal before him, Andrew ended his term in office.[60]

CHAPTER 23

WORKING FOR THE AGES

January–April 1866

Valedictory

Wind and arctic temperatures made walking through Boston's streets treacherous on New Year's Day, but Andrew managed to make his way to Tremont Temple to celebrate Emancipation Day. Lewis Hayden, who presided over the glorious affair, thanked the governor and the state's congressional representatives for fighting so bravely for freedom. Andrew reveled in the moment, yet he could not help pondering the strangeness of his position. Here he was in peacetime, after so many years of war, preparing to deliver his valedictory address. Yet even now the state's conservatives and radicals struggled to find a way forward. The task was not finished; indeed, it was just beginning anew.[1]

In preparation for the governor's address, the *Daily Advertiser* devoted several columns to chronicling his career, concluding that Massachusetts was deeply fortunate to have had him as its navigator through the treacherous shoals of war.[2] Andrew planned to deliver the speech on January 4, his last day in office, and he invited his staff and close friends to accompany him to the legislative chambers. He had worked hard on his words, and they were the finest he would ever deliver, one of the century's most profound analyses of Reconstruction, his contemporaries later claimed. His thoughts had evolved throughout Johnson's presidency, his trips to Washington and his correspondence with political and business leaders had broadened his knowledge, and now the chamber was crowded with men and women, white and Black, eager to hear their remarkable chief executive deliver his final words.

Side by side sat abolitionists, conservatives, traditionalists, and radicals, many of whom had never met before. In dramatic fashion, the man and the hour had come together one last time. Just before 1:00, he began his valedictory that poured forth for nearly ninety minutes.[3]

Andrew saw the address not only as the transfer of his executive duties, honors, and responsibilities to the next governor but also as a doctrine, a path forward for the nation. In doing so, he drew on prewar arguments against slavery and on Congress's mandate to maintain a "republican form of government." He pointed out that the Confederates had controlled the states, had given their allegiance to another government, had made war against the Union, and had been conquered. These vanquished states had not reverted into territories, nor had they committed suicide; rather, they had functioned as states in rebellion. The federal alliance between nation and state, as the founders had conceived it, was an attempt to create a more perfect Union: *more perfect* because the partners had mutual interests that were perpetually binding. The rebellious people may have imagined they would have more rights outside of the Union, but the war had determined otherwise: "It seems to me that the stream of life flows through both State and Nation from a double source, which is a distinguishing element of its vital power. Eccentricity of motion is not death; nor is abnormal action organic change."[4] But the Constitution, the laws, and the rights of war had fixed the position of the Confederate states. The only thing they had accomplished by rebellion was their own conquest. They had forfeited their membership in the Union and had lost their political representatives in the process. Because the federal constitution provided no means for their departure, Andrew argued, it likewise provided no means for their return. No such venture could be constitutionally sanctioned. Federal membership was a privilege afforded to faithful representatives, who now must work with the government to guarantee that southern states would live under the same republican form of government.

State governments must be restored; as Andrew saw it, this was not in question. But he believed that restoration would best be achieved not by federally controlled reorganization but by a reliance on republican measures that would enable the people to see the error of their ways. They must learn to embrace democracy's—and Christianity's—design or suffer federal intervention. Lincoln's olive branch–style republicanism was not a new concept, but it would need to gain ascendency among the rebellious people. If it did, loyal citizens would be able to assert, maintain, and conduct state government in true republican form. If not,

Andrew declared, then war must continue until the Union's goals were accomplished. Echoing Lincoln's words from his inaugural address, Andrew placed the momentous issue of Reconstruction in the hands of southerners, former Confederates, to decide their future. For now, as the victors, the Union had the right to govern belligerent states until republican principles were guaranteed for all southerners. Regarding states that had already been restored under Lincoln and Johnson, the federal government ought to require that they reform their constitutions immediately to annul secession, disaffirm Confederate debt, ratify the Thirteenth Amendment, guarantee African Americans the same civil rights as whites, and regulate the elective franchise according to universal laws, not by arbitrary, capricious, and personal rules. To consecrate this covenant, Andrew suggested that the people, not the legislatures, should decide their own fate. If they declined these conditions, they were not ready to be restored to the United States.

Andrew disagreed with President Johnson's decision to exempt powerful, wealthy southerners from punishment. He quarreled with the assumption that such powerbrokers had influenced the rebellion more than the common people had. He cautioned his listeners not to be deceived. Had not the "poorer and less significant men" fought just as hard against the Yankees? Had they not hated the abolitionists and the "colored man" as much as they had loved the Confederacy? Johnson's pardon of high-ranking rebels suggested that the South's natural leaders could not be discarded in the process of repairing the Union. They had been instrumental in leading the people into secession and war and could also lead them through governmental reorganization: "The capacity of leadership is a gift, not a device. They whose courage, talents and will entitle them to lead, will lead."[5] The vast reorganization necessary demanded men to show great moral courage. They must renounce their own past opinions and do so boldly, publicly, and humanely. In this way, they would inspire the people to follow them in recognizing that slavery had been buried beyond hope of resurrection.

Had it not occurred to all Americans, asked Andrew, that "we are now proposing the most wonderful and unprecedented of human transactions"?[6] He assumed that the freed slaves would agree with the measures he had outlined because it afforded them civil rights protections. Therefore, their votes on the matter would be unnecessary, sparing them the wrath of former enslavers. If white voters refused to guarantee readmission on the Union's republican terms, then Andrew argued for "holding on—just where we are now." In a struggle between a white minority, aided by freed slaves, against a purely white majority, he was not in favor of surrendering the Union's rights. Nor was he willing simply to allow the conquered rebel states to collapse into chaos. In his view, African American enfranchisement was not a prerequisite to reorganizing the rebel states, and he rejected the idea of allotting congressmen based on the number of legal or qualified voters, an idea that Sumner had proposed:

> By diminishing the representative power of the southern states, in favor of the other states, you will not increase southern love for the Union. Nor, while Connecticut and Wisconsin refuse the suffrage to men of color, will you be able to convince the South that your amendment was dictated by political principles, and not by political cupidity. You will not diminish any honest apprehension at extending the suffrage, but you will enflame every prejudice, and aggravate discontent. Meanwhile, the disfranchised freedmen, hated by some because he is black, condemned by some because he has been a slave, feared by some because of the antagonisms of society, is condemned to the condition of a hopeless pariah of a merciless civilization. In the community he is not it. He neither belongs to a master nor to society.

In an indirect response to Sumner, Andrew declared that the senator's policy "would inflame animosity and aggravate oppression, for at least the lifetime of a generation, before it would open the door to the disenfranchised."[7]

Because southern whites remained angry about military defeat and slave liberation, Andrew thought it was important to protect the freed slaves' civil rights before advancing their political rights. After all, it had taken decades for abolitionists to achieve a common goal of freeing slaves. Moreover, southern bitterness and mistrust would result in challenges related to color, suffrage, and citizenship, which would also pose constitutional challenges. Andrew understood that racial prejudice was endemic in both the North and the South. Though voting rights were an indispensable precondition for readmission to the Union, achieving them would have a high and violent cost.

Andrew declared that educated suffrage was essential for both whites and African Americans. In his opinion, demanding the qualification of intelligence was consistent with rights for all. Suffrage was an instrument of protection for the people against the deceptions of demagogues and their own prejudices. The rebellion, he said, showed how firebrands could sweep through the masses. Remedies for such disaster included free compulsory education, which would preserve public liberty. He believed that even the wisest southerners would stand up for liberty against the jealousy of ignorance and the traditions of prejudice. But if the rebel states' educational measures seemed unreasonable or impractical, then Congress had the right to refuse them readmission to the Union.[8]

Andrew pleaded for cooperation between northerners and southerners as they worked to resolve the problems of Reconstruction. Southerners had vigorously sought war, and now they should vigorously pursue peace. Northerners had fought to preserve the Union, and now they should preserve liberty, bringing the freed slaves under the nation's protection, never to desert them. The war had been an opportunity to recalibrate America and advance African Americans' civil rights as a first step toward reconciliation. Forgiveness, the governor maintained, was a righteous act. Like many moderates, he believed that the white South must be judged according to "present loyal purpose" rather than "past disloyalty." The war had expanded federal power but not at the expense of nation-state federalism.[9]

If radicals questioned Andrew's moderate Reconstruction policies they needed only to review his life's work to confirm that he had not and would not abandon the freed slaves. Years later, Warrington reminded readers that no white person had ever been seen more often in African American churches, had ever championed the African American cause or advanced racial justice more vehemently. In the *Springfield Republican*, the reporter wrote, "If the prejudice against color was alien to any Caucasian, it was alien to [Andrew]." No man was more revered for his work in advancing African Americans civil rights, whether as private citizen, abolitionist, friend and defender of fugitive slaves, or hater of the gallows. Not even Sumner had done so much, according to some contemporaries.[10] As for suffrage education, it was true that Andrew had once opposed the Know Nothings' desire for an educational test, calling it discriminatory. When it came to employing such measures in the South, however, he saw education as a device to strengthen the popular vote against racial prejudice.[11]

Private Citizen

Andrew stepped away from the podium to deafening applause, and the ceremony concluded. Afterward, he walked through the council chamber with the new governor, Alexander Bullock, and the department heads, where he presented Bullock with the trappings of the office: "Hereafter, your Excellency, you will regard me as a private citizen of Massachusetts, faithfully devoted to her cause as represented in your person and your official power." He bade adieu and walked into the hallway, which was lined on both sides with the clerks, messengers, and staff members who had been with him throughout the war. Andrew looked down, eyes welling with tears, as each came forward to shake his hand one last time. Without fanfare, a historic chapter closed.

Moments later, Andrew descended the statehouse steps and returned to Boston's rank and file. Frank Bird, who had preferred not to witness Bullock's imminent induction, walked beside his friend. He was struck that a man would leave such high office to return to a legal practice that served Boston's lowliest citizens, a vocation offering little money but utter exhaustion. Andrew's expression that day was worn, pouchy, and absent, a look Bird had seen often, one that meant he needed to be alone. Bird was worried. "Governor," he said, "there is but one course which, in my judgment, will prolong your life beyond a very few years—perhaps beyond a few months. You must put at least six months—it ought to be a year or more—between this hour and a single hour of work. Leave the country, hide yourself in the mountains of Switzerland where American politics and American newspapers cannot reach you." Andrew replied, "I dare say you are right, but I must work for bread and butter for my wife and children." As Bird recalled, "this he did, a martyr to his services for the grand old commonwealth he so loved and honored."[12]

That evening, staff members and close friends gathered with Andrew for a farewell dinner, marking the occasion with stories, photographs, and souvenirs that chronicled the nightmare war. Bird had accurately diagnosed the governor's precarious health; within a few days his nosebleeds returned and forced him into another prolonged convalescence. He missed a scheduled appearance at the National Bazaar held in Faneuil Hall and spent several bedridden days reading letters from admirers. These included a note from his secretary, Henry Ware:

> Those of us whose great privilege it has been to serve in close personal relations to yourself, know how richly deserved are the commendations of your public service that are heard every day from every part of the Commonwealth, but . . . those who have been so near to you as I, have occasion chiefly to thank you for the high example that your daily life has set before us.[13]

Henry Dawes, a Republican friend, wrote admiringly of Andrew's ability to work productively with both conservatives and radicals: "Permit me to congratulate myself, condemned for 'conservatism,' when away from Massachusetts, that I find myself at home, in accord with one who has won so distinguished a position in Radicalism."[14] Charles Eliot Norton, an author and social critic, wrote:

To you more than to any other man is due the fact that throughout these years of trial Massachusetts has kept her old place of leadership. Through you she has given proof of her constancy to those principles to which she was from the beginning devoted. You have helped her to be true to her own ideal. You have represented all that is best in her spirit and her aims. There are no better years in her history than those with which your name will be forever associated in honor. The cares, the anxieties, the responsibilities and the trials of your position during these years must be amply compensated by the happiness of knowing that your services are universally recognized and will always be held in grateful remembrance.[15]

Annie Fields, the wife of the publisher James Fields, wrote to say that she and her husband were "really disappointed" not to be in Boston to hear the farewell address and to tell Andrew that his New York friends had been deeply impressed by it.[16]

Many newspaper editors were equally generous. According to the *Boston Transcript*, "there is a kind of epic completeness in his official career, rare in the experience of American governors. . . . As the future historian of Massachusetts goes over the long roll of her governors, no name will more surely arrest his attention . . . than that of John A. Andrew."[17] The *Daily Advertiser* made note of his wartime accomplishments, arguing that the conflict's magnitude "would have crushed a man of less rooted convictions, of less tenacity of purpose, or of inferior executive powers." His was a record, said the editor, "to which our children's children will point with just pride and admiration."[18] Several papers simply printed the eloquent tributes of other papers. The *Lowell Daily Citizen* found the *Independent*'s tribute especially worthy: "There was needed a man of great executive talent, familiarity with affairs, fervent patriotism, profound insight, and withal, able to make himself trusted and listened to by an administration at the capital that was always far behind him."[19]

The farewell address drew many accolades. The governor had conceptualized a formula for peace and reconciliation that one Boston editor believed would "attract attention far beyond the borders of this Commonwealth."[20] The New York Republican John Binney valued it so highly that he sent copies to friends in Congress, calling special attention to it as a "wise noble, considerate, Statesmanlike oration, eminently worthy of the glorious state of Massachusetts."[21] "No broader or better view of the whole subject has been presented by any one man," remarked the editor of the *Springfield Republican*, "and through the success of his recommendations, both of spirit and form, do we believe that peace and justice and restoration will be soonest and most completely achieved by and for the Union."[22] Thomas Upham, Andrew's professor at Bowdoin, told him that "it is a great personal gratification to me that your name has become intimately associated with a great & trying crisis in history; and that it will pass onward most honorably to future generations."[23]

If Andrew had remained in politics, the address might have been treated as one of the nineteenth century's greatest state papers. Likewise, if Americans had embraced his approach to Reconstruction, they might have pursued a Lincoln-style "malice toward none" policy toward the South. Whatever "God Hath Wrought" through the war, he believed, it belonged to mortals to engineer a more perfect Union that advanced justice and protection for the freedmen.[24] The *Harper's Weekly* editor evidently thought so, calling the speech "a most sagacious paper. Moderate in tone and temperate in style, it discusses the question of reorganization with remarkable clearness, catholicity, and sagacity [and] . . . is plainly the work of a sound political thinker and wise statesman."[25]

Charles Norton greatly admired the governor's thoughts about Reconstruction and universal suffrage. Otherwise, "the late slaves will be practically held as serfs & will hardly fare even as well as the blacks in Jamaica." He argued that ignorance, not color, would be used to maintain their place in society and questioned congressional debates about such issues, and he queried Andrew about precisely what constituted a proper interpretation of a "republican form of government" and how Americans had interpreted it over past decades.[26]

The speech did have its critics. As always, the *Boston Post* led the way, reprinting words from the *Worcester Palladium*, whose editor could not "readily comprehend what metamorphosis Gov. Andrew's intellectual and moral nature has passed through in the short period of five years;—commencing his gubernatorial period what is sometimes called a 'fiery radical,' and coming out dressed in 'imperial purple,' of a huge that would please even the hard fancy of a Louis Napoleon, or a Charles X." Yet even the *Post* admitted that the *Palladium*'s convulsion was in "consequence" of Andrew using the words "natural leaders of the people," noting that the *Palladium* "is ridiculously crotchety."[27]

To be sure the address had shortcomings, primarily in that it revealed a gap between Andrew's optimism and southern realities. At the time, even Forbes, one of his closest friends, disagreed with his views. Along with several northern wealthy entrepreneurs, Forbes viewed Black suffrage as the only condition that would foster a political culture that protected civil rights and attracted northern investment in the South. Twenty years later Forbes recalled that, after having been one of the "strongest advocates of using every weapon to put down the rebellion . . . [Andrew] took the ground that in reconstruction we were bound to forget and forgive, and that the education, intelligence, and brains of that portion of the Southern people which had led them out ought to be used to bring them back again." Yet Forbes admitted:

Many of us, myself among the number, received this far-sighted advice with coolness or opposition, but the history of reconstruction now seems to prove conclusively that his views were statesman-like and prophetic. After trying first military rule, and then the effect of Federal patronage to bolster up carpet-bag misrule at the South, without any degree ameliorating the disordered state of things there, we are now finding that prosperity and good government are returning under the lead of the reconstructed rebels. From one of the most advanced radicals of the time, . . . [we received] a legacy carefully studied and treasured up. It was in advance of public opinion, and did not at the time have the weight it deserved, but, in my judgment, it will stand in the future alongside the farewell address of George Washington.[28]

Writing from Beaufort, South Carolina, General Rufus Saxton, the former military governor of the Department of the South and a current assistant commissioner of the Freedman's Bureau, thanked Andrew for his address and hoped that the Confederates would indeed meet the Yankees halfway and that "we shall have to wait only part of a generation for antagonisms to pass away." But as Saxton explained, for now, the southerners were not disguising their hatred of former slaves and Union sympathizers: "There is no remedy here but the equal suffrage for which you plead so ably."[29]

In Washington, Congress seemed to be "afflicted with a mania for amending the Constitution," as a correspondent for the *Daily Advertiser* dryly noted.[30] Andrew understood that adding a Fourteenth Amendment to the Constitution to shore up the inalienable rights of freedmen by defining citizenship would be necessary. Sumner, along with congressmen John Bingham of Ohio and Thaddeus Stevens of Pennsylvania and Senator Jacob Howard of Michigan, was in the vanguard of this effort. As the debate over the new amendment unfolded that February, "the finest audience" of the session gathered to hear Sumner's two-day speech regarding the joint committee's proposed draft, which he maintained had not gone far enough in securing equal rights for all. In his "Equal Rights for All" oration, however, Sumner maintained that no state government could be considered "republican" if it excluded any class from the franchise. Critics pointed out that by Sumner's logic, no state, including Massachusetts, had ever been republican since women were denied the franchise. Andrew knew as much and might have saved Sumner from himself had they been communicating about the issue. The heart of the matter, Andrew believed, was that securing fundamental and constitutional guarantees about citizenship, and thus civil rights, would serve to protect freedmen from hostility and violence more than determining suffrage rights. In his mind, defining the former would achieve the later. As the session continued, the first draft of the Fourteenth Amendment targeting the right to vote went down in defeat. For all his rhetoric, Sumner had not moved the needle in his direction. Although the Senate voted 25 to 22 in favor of the draft, it was short of the two-thirds majority required by the Constitution. Sumner himself, as well as several other Republicans, voted against it. Moving forward, senators would make civil rights the focus of the next draft, in attempt to provide African Americans full citizenship rights. In the end, Andrew agreed with Sumner's vote and the new direction representatives had chosen aimed at protection of freedmen by defining citizenship, thus securing their civil rights. Writing to Andrew's friend Horatio Woodman, Sumner was glad the former governor had agreed with him in opposing the amendment. "I know that I am right," said Sumner. "People will sometime or other thank me for having resisted it. Many will think it the best thing of my life."[31]

Regardless of Sumner's political currency in Massachusetts and the posturing over amendments, Andrew remained intensely concerned about the freed slaves. As winter passed, northern businessmen lost confidence in southern investments, and his own company suffered as well. In March 1866, Andrew reminded Frank Howe that those who had "contemplated the early enjoyment of political rights by the colored freedmen [now] resist the bare idea of the protection of the civil or human rights of the same freedmen by national legislation." These men, Andrew said, had concluded that the government would receive the rebel senators and congressmen, withdraw all troops, end the Freedman's Bureau, and leave the freed slaves, northern emigrants, and few loyal southern whites to the subjugation of the "reconstructed" rebels. "With this idea prevailing, there is little hope of our procuring investments to be made in the South,—certainly not for the present."[32]

The Good Fight

During these disheartening days, Cyrus Woodman sent Andrew a heartwarming letter about fighting the "good fight" of Reconstruction. In it, Woodman recalled his friend's election as governor:

> I congratulated you, but it was with fear and trembling. Now that you have finished your course, I congratulate you upon having fought the good fight and upon having won, honor for yourself and the good old Commonwealth. High as you stood in the estimation of your friends and the people before you were elected Governor, you stand much higher now."

Even as Andrew followed the congressional debates on the Fourteenth Amendment, there was considerable work to be done. Although he was attempting to refocus himself on his private life and law practice, he remained agitated about the depressing news emanating from the South. Thus, when Francis Child, a distinguished folklorist and professor, implored Andrew to use his power as president of the Freedmen's Aid Society to expand the membership, with a focus on attracting funders who would support teachers in southern schools for African American students, Andrew agreed to speak.[33]

Other friends tried to keep him engaged in politics. Knowing that Andrew had once endorsed Johnson's approach to Reconstruction, Montgomery Blair now asked him to spearhead New England support for the president. Blair believed that the governor's economic ideas about reuniting northern textile manufacturers and southern cotton producers had merit, at least on paper. Meanwhile, Blair's father Frank had been lobbying Johnson to appoint Andrew to the cabinet, arguing that he might be a useful counter to Sumner and the radical Thaddeus Stevens. Montgomery told Andrew that he would be visiting Boston to address a Faneuil Hall meeting of the president's friends, surely to denounce Stevens and Sumner. He asked Andrew to preside, but the former governor declined. He was no longer interested in supporting Johnson. Southerners, he believed, could not return to the United States without specific arrangements that the war had made necessary. Anything less would create antagonism, not patriotism. He preferred to wait until New Englanders could join the Blair family and other "large minded men at the South, in working through the agencies, which political economy, business enterprise, etc., etc., easily suggest to promote a practical Reconstruction." Andrew anticipated that southerners would soon accept citizenship and, in his mind the protection of the civil rights and enfranchisement for the freed slaves that came with it. He hoped that the former rebels would support those who championed the extension of suffrage to all men without respect to condition, color, or descent. In a lengthy letter to Blair, Andrew said that he had come to a brutal conclusion: "I see no hope for real peace, on other conditions. The black man must be treated as a citizen, or he must be exterminated."[34]

In this postwar climate, Andrew understood that southern whites continued to wrestle against three fundamental realities. First, the slaves were free. Second, the freed slaves demonstrated every day that they were more than capable of civic responsibility. Three, they were not biologically inferior, as Confederate vice-president Alexander Stephens had portrayed them in his "Cornerstone of the Confederacy" speech in March 1861. Yet he maintained that every man's reconstruction began with improving his educational and economic life to provide opportunities for advancement and independence and that such progress could be maintained only by legal protections. His land agency's dismal struggles illustrated that southerners were resistant to forgiving their conquerors. Even worse, the southern crop harvest failed in 1865, crippling the next year's projections. The situation had become so bad that Andrew had suspended the agency's business. He wrote dolefully to Frank Blair, Sr.:

> Every Northern man engaged in planting has lost his entire investment, many their entire fortunes. We do not report one instance of success amongst those who went through our agency, and from whom commissions are due. Not one has escaped without the loss of his entire capital invested, and nearly all have returned North and abandoned everything, while the two or three who remain promise no better. These purchasers are now suffering without exception, from the peculiar trials of their new position, but more than all from the terrible and ruinous seasons of the past two years.[35]

In the wake of this loss, Andrew felt compelled to travel to Maryland and Washington, where he spent several weeks in the Blair home, discussing Reconstruction and trying to convince Frank the elder to help him coax southern financiers into investing in economic recovery. Andrew hoped to purchase land in the cotton belt and sell it to northerners or to others who promoted free labor; he thought the plan might lure midwestern African Americans to move south for work. Andrew was not presently interested in debating the suffrage issue; he felt that urgent circumstances required immediate remedies. It was necessary to put the freed slaves to work, both for their own sake and for the sake of the southern economy. Such a plan, he said, would allay "jealousy and dissension," and extend to the negro proper and natural field for employment and education." Moreover, it would gather freed slaves into a region where they could take the lead in developing that economy. But after meeting with numerous influential people from around the South and discussing matters with his field agents, he admitted to Frank Howe that current conditions seemed to "render any present success of our Company as a Land Agency practically impossible." Though he had imagined that freed slaves would remain in the South and extend their growing prosperity to the New Englanders who invested in their enterprises, he had come to see that the very business leaders who had professed support for the freed slaves now "resist[ed] and resent[ed]" the idea of protecting their rights.[36]

In mid-March, William Stewart, a Republican from Nevada, provided a new compromise measure on the question of Reconstruction, which caught Andrew's attention. He brought a resolution before the Senate that authorized Congress to offer southerners universal amnesty if they amended their constitutions to eliminate civil rights discriminations, renounce all claims of compensation for emancipated slaves, and propose suffrage without reference to color or previous condition of servitude. This could be achieved, Stewart maintained, as an immediate congressional settlement rather than a constitutional amendment. Andrew hoped it would pass. "It seems plain to me," he told the senator, "that the colored men must be invested with the rights, both political and civil, which pertain to citizenship . . . or else they must be exterminated." Defining citizenship as a legal status, he believed, would secure all fundamental rights derived from the constitution, including suffrage. Yet, he still maintained that the leaders and voters who had carried states out of the Union must be the same ones to bring them back to loyalty: "Any other 'reconstruction' is dangerous and delusive."[37] This letter to Stewart became public. The *Lowell Daily Citizen* called it "bold and brilliant," and it was printed in the *Washington Chronicle* and several other papers.[38]

Stewart and several New York–based editors urged Andrew to come to Washington to offer his direct support for the bill, but he demurred—at first for health reasons, though he later admitted that he did not feel it was proper to go without an invitation from the Massachusetts delegation. Yet when Governor Bullock invited him to act as counsel for Massachusetts in her claim for federal reimbursement for wartime coastal defense, he also declined. Perhaps Andrew surmised, as did Stewart and many others, that the "growing bitterness between Congress and the Executive darkened counsel, and precluded the possibility of favorable consideration of so just and mild a plan."[39]

The war had aged Andrew and had significantly damaged his health. His close friends knew of his decline but had little success in convincing him to reduce his workload. According to Forbes, Andrew at one point told Bird that he needed a long vacation to repair his health, and Bird had encouraged him to do so, but Andrew did not have enough money: the war had depleted his savings. Behind the scenes, Forbes pulled together resources to help, and colleagues agreed to purchase a $50,000 life insurance policy, to be sent anonymously to his family. In reaching out for aid, Forbes had written, "I know that every liberal man has for five years given nobly to the soldiers and the sick and the poor, but this is an exceptional case. We only have one John A. Andrew, and we shall never have as appropriate a time as now to express ourselves toward him."[40]

Andrew continued to stay busy. During the war, he had become interested in extending New England's rail network through Maine into New Brunswick, terminating at an ice-free port in Novia Scotia, where railcars would connect with transatlantic shipping from Europe. He saw this as an opportunity to strengthen relations between New England and Canada's Atlantic provinces. The undertaking would be expensive, but many agreed that it had merit. Thus, in early 1866, he presented the idea to committees in Congress and the Massachusetts legislature, asking them to support the creation of the European and North American Railway. Yet the plan stalled when Congress refused to renew the Canadian American Reciprocity Treaty that spring.[41]

Perhaps the saddest event in Andrew's life that spring was the execution of Edward Green, whose case had drawn nationwide attention as the first armed bank robbery in the United States that resulted in death. Green had been in jail for more than two years for the murder of a bank teller, and in the last week of Andrew's term, the governor had asked the legislature to commute his sentence to imprisonment for life. The General Council had overruled that request by a vote of six to three, and now Governor Bullock was tasked with carrying out the sentence. In late March, Andrew appealed the decision before the Supreme Judicial Court and lost. Many saw his actions as grandstanding, and they infuriated his opponents, some of whom were Unitarian colleagues.[42]

Andrew was not alone in his mission to fight Green's death penalty. For the past two years, numerous ministers and journalists had been railing against the execution, and the acclaimed journalist James Redpath's 1864 exposé, "Shall We Suffocate Ed. Green," had been particularly vitriolic. These advocates were not arguing for Green per se but for their own principled opposition to capital punishment, yet Green wrote several letters thanking them for their exertions on his behalf, and he asked Andrew to be present at his hanging.

On the evening of April 12, Green briefly fell asleep in his Cambridge jail cell until the jailer awakened him for visitors. An open Bible lay on his cot, and he could hear a carpenter pounding a hammer on his scaffold. With every blow, he became more and more unnerved. His visitors included Redpath and the Methodist minister Gilbert Haven. They prayed together, and Green apologized for staining his family's reputation. The jailer remained with the men throughout the night, and during those hours Green wrote a final letter to Andrew.

The early morning was cloudy, and a light shower dampened the gallows. Green ascended the steps under the gaze of three hundred other prisoners. At 11 a.m., just as the sun broke through the clouds, a jailer removed Green's cap and placed a hemp noose around his neck. The sheriff said, "May God have mercy on his soul," and Green's foot touched a hidden spring. A trap door dropped, and the condemned man plunged to his death. Nineteen minutes later, surgeons verified that he was gone. Viewers dispersed, and the prison yard "resumed its wonted quiet." Andrew was not present for the hanging, but he received Green's letter later that day. It began with "My Dear Friend," and ended by declaring that God would reward Andrew for his work on behalf of the condemned.[43]

CHAPTER 24

POSTWAR YANKEE

May 1866–May 1867

Summer Vacation

"Everybody knew the lofty Christian sacrifice made by Governor Andrew in refusing to sign the death warrant of Edward W. Green" said the *Daily Advertiser*, but in doing so "he substantially signed the death of his own political prospects."[1] Perhaps so, but that mattered little to the former governor. Writing to Reverend Clarke, he said, "If I did this it would seem as though I were placing myself in opposition to the courts, which would be an evil. I prefer to bear the misrepresentation myself. My back is broad enough for that."[2]

Anxious to distance himself from the political rancor, Andrew focused on expanding his practice. In the spring of 1866, at the urging of some colleagues, he considered relocating to Washington and securing work as a solicitor before the Supreme Court or the Court of Federal Claims. Yet even though he was clearly suited for the position, it seemed out of character for the "poor man's lawyer." George Stearns encouraged him to move to New York City, where he would likely earn a good living, but Andrew found the idea oppressive. John Forbes, however, understood his friend's attachment to New England, and he convinced Andrew that his name and experience would serve him better in Boston than elsewhere. Andrew submitted to his friend's opinion. "I have *one* benefit of being here," he told Forbes, "viz: that I keep on my feet and move about in the air among the departments,—which is useful to my weak and half worn out head, relieving me of much of the pain in my head and back I have suffered from these last three months."[3]

Andrew's health continued to decline, forcing him to refuse several lucrative positions, including an invitation from Governor Bullock to sit on the Massachusetts Supreme Court after Charles Allen announced his resignation. The shift from administering a vast executive office to coping with the cerebral pressure of a law practice was draining his energy. Yet he always found time to listen to the people who sought his counsel. According to Clarke, an African American woman appeared at Andrew's chambers seeking help to reclaim damages for articles she had lost on a vessel shipwrecked at sea. She had been returning from Port Royal, South Carolina, where she had been teaching the children of freed slaves. When she entered the office, Andrew was busy, consulting first with a man, then with a woman, both seeking jobs. After they left, the waiting woman identified herself. Andrew shook her hand and laughed when she remarked, "I thought a teacher required some patience, but I believe a lawyer needs the most." He then listened to her story as if her business were the most important on his schedule. As she handed him the notes she had made about the wreck, she told Andrew that she had heard an officer complain that "there are niggers and nigger-teachers enough on board to damn any boat." A pained look came over Andrew's face, and he assured her that he would investigate the matter, sending her off with a comforting "God-speed in our work."[4]

Andrew's empathy also continued to endear him to both veterans and those who were beginning to recount the history of the war. James Pierce, who was compiling a memorial for the fallen officer, Charles Lowell, Jr., wrote to Andrew to confirm a story he had heard from his friend. Lowell had told Pierce that, in April 1863, he had returned to Boston and gone to the statehouse. Saluting Andrew, he had announced that, in the discharge of his military duties, he had "shot a man." Then he had quietly withdrawn. According to statehouse gossip, Andrew had said to a bystander, "I need nothing more. Col. Lowell is as humane as he is brave."[5]

Even as he focused on his law practice, Andrew remained involved with his struggling land agency and did not give up hope on plans for a European and North American Railway. These pursuits required him to be in Washington frequently. Andrew's son Forrester had come of age during his father's governorship, and now, at age sixteen, he became a traveling companion, often accompanying his father on such journeys.[6] Andrew was close to all of his children, and his secretary, Albert Browne, Jr., recalled his joviality with them: "[Andrew] had as quick and lively perception of the ludicrous as President Lincoln himself, and his anecdote was free from coarseness. Of the Yankee dialect he was a master; . . . [he] had studied it analytically, just as he studied the intricacies of the typical Yankee character." What he loved most, however, was the "every-day life of the country villages of New England, of their shops, farm-yards, stage-coaches, taverns, sewing circles, and household firesides." These details were "familiar to him, . . . and served him constantly for illustrations of stories which he told with a hearty enjoyment it excites a smile to remember." Andrew often used such humor to diffuse the "little mishaps and annoyances" that would have "vexed and perplexed any man of less animal vigor and buoyant spirit."[7]

Both politically and socially, Boston was a club-oriented city, and Andrew moved easily among classes, comfortable in the poorer wards yet remaining connected to Boston's elite. He and Eliza regularly spent time with Samuel and Julia Howe, James and Annie Fields, and William and Emma Rogers, all of them associated with the city's intellectuals. Conservatives and anti-Johnsonites welcomed him into their Friday Club (perhaps to keep an eye on him), and he continued his long association with Frank Bird's Saturday Club. He had been a charter member of the Union Club, founded in 1863, and later joined the Examiner Club, a dining association for ministers and the editors of Christian periodicals. He seldom made a trip to Washington without spending a night in New York, Dobbs Ferry, or Philadelphia and was a frequent visitor to his friends' seaside retreats.[8]

Despite his sociability, Andrew appreciated the simple pleasures that came from living a modest life. Harriet Beecher Stowe came to know the governor through personal and mutual acquaintances and recorded several noteworthy moments confirming this. According to one of her essays, someone suggested to Andrew during the war that he ought to have the funds to appear in public with more pomp, but he repelled the idea sternly. She wrote, "Never, while the country was struggling under such burdens, and her brave men bearing such privations in the field, would he accept of anything more than the plain average comforts of a citizen." She recalled that one of his secretaries often told a story about Andrew's ceremonial governor's coat, adorned with lace and buttons. After wearing it on two occasions, he "pulled it off and threw it impatiently into a corner [of his executive chamber], saying, 'Lie there old coat—you won't find me wearing you again soon.'"[9]

Andrew's name retained an almost celebrity status, and his legal practice became lucrative, with other lawyers routinely making use of his wide-ranging expertise. In one notable instance, Forbes enlisted him to serve as co-counsel with the New York–based lawyers William Evarts and Joseph Choate on a case involving the steamship *Meteor*.

The ship had been prevented from leaving port under suspicion that it was laden with war materials bound for Chile, which was at war with Spain. Forbes was personally involved in the case: he and his brother Robert, along with a group of New York and Boston investors, had originally built the ship so that the U.S. government could pursue Confederate privateers. After the war, the *Meteor* transported troops from New Orleans to New York City. Now Forbes told Andrew that the ship had been bound for Panama, not Chile, and he denied any knowledge of war materials.

In New York, Andrew joined Evarts and Choate, and the three applied, via the usual channels, to have the vessel delivered to them. However, the U.S. district attorney protested, and the judge refused to release the ship. So Andrew traveled to Washington, hoping to convince Secretary of State Seward to intervene and drop the case. While Seward responded pleasantly, he was anxious to stop the war between Spain and Chile, and he declined to interfere. In a furious letter to Forbes, Andrew called the secretary "as diplomatic as the arch enemy of mankind. He evidently knows nothing but to adhere to his policy of using and abusing every power of the Government to reach his purpose." Andrew disliked Seward, later calling him the "falsest and most hollow of mortal men. If I am right in the opinion, and he proves unwilling to do anything to gratify his own vanity and love of power, I think I shall at last win the right to denounce him some time, and treat him accordingly."[10]

Eventually, in mid-July 1866, Judge Samuel Betts of New York's Southern District Court allowed the vessel to be bonded and delivered to the owners, whereupon Forbes brought it to Boston for repairs. When the ship set sail shortly afterward, the government again seized it, and the case was tied up in the courts for more than two years. Finally, on November 6, 1868, the Supreme Court decided in favor of the owners. Congress issued a joint resolution that the U.S. government had wrongfully seized and detained the *Meteor* and ordered that government compensate the owners for the damages it had incurred in New York Harbor. The case consumed Andrew for months, and he never lived to see its conclusion.[11]

Andrew was well paid for his part in the case. This may have been Forbes's intent, knowing that his friend would never take charity. In the summer of 1866, this and other cases funded family trips to Washington, the White Mountains, and Canada. Andrew spent much of June at Willard's Hotel in the nation's capital, though his wife pressed him to come north with the family. While he was there, local ladies' associations solicited his photograph, hoping to auction it off to raise money for the orphans of Union soldiers. Andrew returned to Boston briefly that summer before finally setting out with Forrester for New Hampshire and Quebec. The vacation was good for his health and spirits, and he enjoyed his son's growing curiosity and knowledge about the world outside of Massachusetts.[12]

In late July Andrew and Forrester returned to Boston for a day or two. Then, within a week, Andrew was off again, this time to visit Frank Howe in New York City, a dreadfully depressing place, he wrote to Eliza. Howe was hoping to discuss Andrew's political and legal future and to share his belief that the land enterprise could not be revived. But Andrew was eager to return to New England and spent time in the city drafting an address to be delivered at Vermont's Brattleboro Agricultural Fair in September.[13]

Even as Andrew focused on his own concerns, he stayed attuned to the plight of the freed slaves. Interestingly, however, his correspondence makes no mention of his soured relations with Sumner. The divide did bother the senator, who told Bird privately that he was disappointed in the gossips who had misrepresented his feelings about Andrew: "I have often said that whenever Andrew desires my place I shall not be in his way." Bird, hoping for a rapprochement, invited Andrew to dine with him. He clearly wanted to talk about the former governor's congressional prospects and how Sumner might help. If they convened, however, Andrew made no mention of their conversation.[14]

Andrew continued to receive, and decline, invitations to stump for Republicans across the Northeast, citing his poor health and his local pursuits. But he worried about current events, confessing to a friend that recent race riots in Memphis and New Orleans had greatly disturbed him. He feared that southerners were plotting a new rebellion and believed that northerners needed to institute firmer Reconstruction measures to protect African Americans and keep down recalcitrant rebel leaders. Though his distaste for Johnson's Reconstruction plan had grown intense, there was speculation that he might endorse the National Union Convention, a conservative-backed assembly, held in mid-August in Philadelphia and intended to showcase moderate Republican and northern Democratic support for the president. However, he published a public letter in the press dispelling that rumor: "The revolted States cannot and ought not to be allowed to fix the conditions upon which they shall resume their forfeited rights."[15]

Despite Andrew's reluctance to reengage with politics, many friends and colleagues remained convinced that he should campaign for Congress, perhaps to replace Congressman Samuel Hooper. Edward Atkinson, an old Vigilance Committee colleague, urged him to seek a seat. An unnamed delegate to the National Union Convention told him that his name had often come up in conversation, mentioned as a "leader of the reasonable men who while they will not sacrifice a single principle, would yet not be governed by an impracticable animosity."[16] Yet Andrew's closest friends feared for his health, his finances, and his newly restful family life. Andrew agreed; public service, he said, was for wealthy bachelors and the elite. Instead, he recommended that Congressman Thomas Dawes Eliot stand for reelection, telling him in a September letter that this would comfort all Massachusetts citizens, especially the African American population: "I want to say earnestly to you that I think *the country* has a claim *on you*."[17]

On September 3, Andrew attended the Southern Loyalist Convention in Philadelphia, which the *New York Herald* dubbed "The Nigger-Worshippers Convention." The gathering was designed to upstage Johnson's advocates; and even as a spectator, Andrew drew spirited applause when introduced by the convention's leaders.[18] Yet he was delighted to return to New England and speak at the Brattleboro Agricultural Fair, where an enormous crowd had gathered to celebrate the harvest. His theme was industrial diversification and its relationship to American farmers, and the speech enumerated numerous encouraging statistics about the region's agricultural and industrial production, arguing that both were driven by the science of innovation. Diversification was at the heart of ingenuity, Andrew argued, creating a political economy that united workers and farmers and dignified their labor. "By patience, industry, and frugal manners," he said, "[New Englanders had] turned rocks and ice and wasting waters into thrift and comfort. . . . Here trade is free, commerce is unrestricted and unconstrained. The lands are freely sold to all purchasers. Institutions, social and political are free." He challenged his listeners to "continue to invite and to welcome recruits from all the world, who come to join the conquering army of a more perfect liberty." The *Daily Advertiser* suggested that the oration had furnished "a model which agricultural fair speakers everywhere would do well to imitate, in its silence upon political topics."[19] Though Andrew had just returned from a political assembly, he had preferred to focus on other topics. He knew that listeners were not interested in hearing yet another recitation about

Johnson's Reconstruction policy. Instead, he spoke to them about their own world.[20]

Andrew's favorite agricultural fair was the small two-day community gathering in Hingham in late September. That year, "the misty clouds hugged the earth all day, enveloping everybody and everything in their disagreeable moisture."[21] Andrew was not deterred, sloshing through the exhibits, and watching the ox teams compete in the mud. He had intended to remain a private citizen, but rain did not keep the crowds from demanding to hear from their beloved son. Fair leaders succumbed to pressure, spoiling Andrew's privacy by introducing him as a speaker. Though he had done nothing to encourage rumors, the press suggested that he was quietly canvassing for Congress. In a letter to Stearns, he again denied this: "At a time when there is no more danger of a republican defeat than there is of an invasion by the Turks, I perceive no reason for my leaving the retirement in which your letter finds me. . . . [If there were] any danger to our cause, and there was a forlorn hope anywhere, I would return to politics and lead it." He simply wanted to remain "wholly aside, out of every one's way," and devote his days to regaining his health and practicing law.[22]

That fall, Andrew accepted several nonpolitical invitations. He consented to serve as a government director for the Union Pacific Railroad and became a trustee of the Massachusetts Institute of Technology. He joined the executive committee of the American Unitarian Association, which allowed him to get involved with southern projects for freed slaves and with emigrant aid societies. He was also named president of the New England Historic-Genealogical Society. Always a student of history, he had become increasingly interested in its importance in shaping the national narrative. "History touches all human life on every side," he said. "It instructs the individual. It gives a new tone to a community. It elevates a nation. It enlivens a generation. It inspires the human race."[23]

At this time, Samuel Howe was spearheading an effort to support Cretan rebels who were attempting to overthrow the "incubus imposed upon them by the despotic and barbarous Turkish government."[24] He enlisted several close friends, including Andrew and wealthy abolitionist colleagues, to assist him in the endeavor. The scene was reminiscent of the old days, when the friends had met in Andrew's law office to raise funds for fugitive slaves.[25]

In October, Andrew traveled to New York to deliver lectures in Manhattan and Brooklyn on the Cretans and Reconstruction. In part, the venture was a way to leave Boston during the tail end of the political season. Thus, he missed the National Conference of the Unitarian Churches, which was meeting in Syracuse. His presidential term had expired, and now the torch was passed to Thomas Dawes Eliot. In his absence, however, members elected him to the executive committee. Andrew returned to Boston in November and attended the Republican rally in Williams Hall, where, according to one journalist, guests expected a "stirring time." Andrew supported Charles Mitchell, an African American candidate, for the state's third district, the wealthiest in the state. Mitchell had served as a lieutenant in the Fifty-fifth Massachusetts, and Andrew had come to know him through Hayden and Garrison.

Andrew made good use of his time that autumn as president of the New England branch of the Freedman's Union Commission. Collaborating with Garrison, Beecher, Father Taylor, Reverend Grimes, and other prominent Bostonians, he worked to raise awareness about educating the freed slaves. He presided over a late November meeting at Tremont Temple, where he had the pleasure of introducing the British abolitionist George Thompson and his close friend Edward Pierce, who managed the schools for freed slaves in South Carolina. In his speech, Andrew declared that the freed slaves had been largely abandoned, meaning that their lives now depended on the work of northern benevolent organizations. Most public rhetoric had been about the franchise, he said, but the first urgency was their livelihood. Massachusetts, he said, must do this work, raising them upward in a "brotherly spirit": "We cannot think of separating the blacks and the whites. The dream of ultimate separation will never be realized. They have got to live together until there is no more land, no more sea, and no more cotton crops. They must live together, love each other, and pull together, or they must fight together as no men ever fought before." He read testimonials from teachers confirming that the freed slaves were "thirsting for education." If their claims upon Bostonians were great, Andrew reminded his audience, this was because Massachusetts had great possessions and thus the responsibility to help.[26]

Steadfast in His Work

By late summer the election season had consumed the nation. Johnson had embarked on a calamitous speaking campaign, aptly dubbed the "swing around the circle," in an attempt to gain election support for his mild Reconstruction policies and preferred candidates. Hoping to reach constituents as far away as Chicago and St. Louis, he undertook the massive tour despite vehement opposition to his policies, and it became a political disaster as crowds gathered to heckle him.

Meanwhile, as the president's star was falling, Andrew's was on the rise. This would not have been the case for most people who had done what he had done: that is, decline several high-profile legal cases, a seat on the Massachusetts Supreme Court, and a college presidency. He had instead chosen to continue routine legal work for his needy clients and to take his seat every Sunday in the Twelfth Baptist Church. He had become a pit player in the political orchestra, yet, if anything, his popularity had increased. So had his critics' ire. Though Andrew had always been a thorough radical on issues related to African American civil rights, his patience and moderation about suffrage tempted some, such as Wendell Phillips, to declare that the former governor had "gone over to the enemy." Forbes would have none of this, countering that Andrew was "nearer right than any other man of his day, in public life."[27]

Part of Phillips's distrust arose from Andrew's willingness to work alongside moderates and conservatives to advance freed slaves' educational and economic opportunities. For instance, to support educational initiatives among the freed slaves in the South, Andrew aligned with Robert Winthrop, a long-time political opponent, to raise money. As war governor, Andrew had impressed Winthrop. Now, despite their divergent politics, he believed that the former governor would make an excellent senator, and many others in Massachusetts shared this feeling. But no matter how much Andrew may have a wanted a Senate seat, he would not disavow Sumner.[28]

In December, the Thirty-ninth Congress convened, and representatives were ready to diminish Johnson's power. They had seen enough of his Reconstruction plan, which had done no more than ignite race battles. Election results showed that Johnson had lost influence, and congressmen had become more sympathetic to the concerns of the freed slaves and less interested in placating southerners. Many were determined to use their federal powers to secure universal suffrage. For his part, Andrew remained steadfast in his work on the ground, continually focusing on advancing freed slaves' economic independence. He knew Reconstruction was failing; his own land company had given him ample evidence. Edward Atkinson had advised him that anyone who sold land to African Americans in the cotton states was likely to be murdered and advised against offering money without guarantees that "mean white" southerners could be kept under control.[29]

By mid-December, the Boston press was reporting that Treasury Secretary Hugh McCulloch, a Maine native, had appointed Andrew to go to England to look after the pecuniary interests of the U.S. government "arising from the wreck of the rebel confederacy." The *New Hampshire Statesman*, which had promoted Montgomery Blair for the post, noted sarcastically that "it will be a point gained to be rid of so restless a spirit." But Andrew quickly denied the rumor. He preferred to remain in Boston and attend to his legal and philanthropic work.[30] Likewise, he declined Secretary of State Seward's invitation to represent U.S. legal claims in England, though Seward and William Chandler, first assistant secretary of the treasury, had promoted him as the "best man" to take charge of those cases.[31]

In Boston, the New Year opened with cold and snow squalls. Amid whispers of Johnson's potential impeachment, Andrew entered his second term as president of the New England Historic-Genealogical Society and, on January 2, presided over its twenty-second annual meeting. He had collected material for two essays. One focused on the history of the spinet, which interested him because it had been the first musical instrument he had ever heard; the other was a study of the 1758 Siege of Louisburg, a pivotal operation of the Seven Years' War, which ended the French colonial era in Atlantic Canada and led to the British campaign to capture Quebec. John Quincy Adams, Jr., admired Andrew's commitment to intellectual exploration, which Adams saw as a prototypically New England value: "[He] was thoroughly in-grain a New England man. He believed absolutely in our principles, our methods, training, and ideas. He had a wholesome smack of the soil of the region in his strong and shrewd talk, vivid sense of humor, and his liking, once in a while. For the anecdotes and peculiar wit, which, in their best form, are sometimes found scattered freely in New-England."[32]

In early January, Andrew assembled his old gubernatorial staff for dinner at the Parker House, a celebration and also a remembrance. The nation had been at peace for twenty months, and all were glad to be private citizens again. He also made time for several public appearances, including a lecture at the state prison and an address to a crowd at the Union Club on whether the legislature should pass measures that would allow the Parker House to stay open on Sundays. Andrew proposed that the hotel should be open with restrictions: only a few rooms and no liquor. James Fields recalled that he "made an excellent speech, full of his fine humanity, which is to be sure to carry the majority over to his side."[33]

News from Washington chronicled the nation's ongoing governance struggle over Reconstruction. Political instability, violence, and schemes of rebellion were sinking Andrew's hopes for peaceful reconciliation. He lamented to Montgomery Blair:

It is easier to sell an imaginary copper mine in Jupiter than it is to hire ten per cent on the best lands in the South, on the northern market. I hope time and good conduct will root out those apprehensions, but constant reports from sojourners in those States, and the return of men ruined in the effort to live as neighbors to the "Secesh," are daily received, and universally believed.

Andrew's only desire in launching his land enterprise had been "to do some good." He had believed that that war had erased the "old, political questions." But "if I was wrong," he told Blair, "I am glad that it was my heart which erred, and not my head."[34] So he was delighted when Congress overturned Johnson's veto on African American suffrage in Washington, D.C. Change was in the air; it would be only a matter of time before Congress seized the reins of Reconstruction.[35]

That winter Andrew joined Salem's Essex Institute, a literary and scientific society that maintained a library and museum, arranged educational programs, and produced scholarly publications. He was reading widely, devouring not only the daily news but also classical and contemporary histories and works on political economy. His book purchases reflected his interests: Arthur Perry's *Principles of Political Economy*, Frank Moore's *Rebellion Record*, and the 1866 *Report of the Capital Punishment*, published by the British Royal Commission on Capital Punishment. Recognizing his expertise, colleagues in several states sought his legal advice on death-penalty issues; and in Massachusetts, legislators were systematically agitating to abolish capital punishment. He ignored rumors that Sumner intended to retire at the end of his term, with Andrew replacing him. He was content with his private life.[36]

In early March, Anna Lowell reached out to Andrew, asking for financial assistance to establish an industrial school for African American girls and women, who had moved from the South to Massachusetts. The goal was to teach them practical housekeeping skills so that they could be gainfully employed in the North. In her letter, she drew on New England's reformist history:

> Our institutions, generally, if not always, are to reform criminals or vagrants—we want to take the good, and teach them to "use" their hands well—and also to a certain degree their heads, and I think too we owe it to the freed people, because it is enough to send money and teachers, but to take them in amongst us, and teach them a little N. England thrift and independence is much harder.

Lowell had served as a Union nurse, and her brother, Andrew's friend Charles Lowell, had been killed at the Battle of Cedar Creek. Andrew agreed to help, and he and Henry Bowditch championed the endeavor against conservative opposition. They drew up articles of incorporation for what became the Howard Industrial School for Colored Persons, funded by the Freedman's Bureau, named in honor of General Charles Howard, a commissioner at the bureau. Lowell hoped Andrew could also use his influence with the Massachusetts philanthropist George Peabody, who had a penchant for promoting industrial education in the destitute regions of the South. When Andrew replied that he had no connection with Peabody, Lowell was embarrassed. She had believed that everybody in the state knew the governor. She nonetheless expressed gratitude, and local reporters were "glad to see connected with this enterprise the name of ex-Governor Andrew whose willing aid was always to be obtained for those who are 'poor or ignorant or black.'"[37]

During these winter weeks Andrew was engaged in a legal case involving state liquor prohibition, its current lack of enforcement under the law, and whether the legislature should license or suppress the state's liquor shops. This was not his first experience with the law. As governor, he had twice vetoed measures to repeal the law, though legislators had argued that it could not be enforced. Now, as the General Court convened in January 1867, citizens presented petitions to repeal prohibition and replace it with a stringent license law. Innkeepers claimed that, in its present form, the law prevented them from selling wine and spirits to guests, and the Massachusetts College of Pharmacy said that it was legally impossible for apothecaries to conduct their medicinal business. But many citizens remained opposed to any amendment to the existing law.

Representing the prohibitionists, Asahel Huntington, Reverend Alonzo Miner, and William Spooner appeared before the legislature, armed with the Bible and a time-worn argument about the evils of liquor. Innkeepers, businessmen, and the college asked Andrew and Linus Child to argue their side of the case. As he weighed the possible outcome, Reverend William Thayer, secretary of the Massachusetts State Temperance Alliance, agreed that the license advocates had acquired, in Andrew, "the strongest man they could find for counsel" but predicted their defeat, which would prove "disastrous to the rum selling interest, and all the more encouraging and hopeful to our righteous cause."[38]

The proceedings commenced on February 19, and the parties met four days a week until April 3, attracting a vast amount of public attention. Andrew threw himself into the work. New England's established liquor laws were deeply engrained, and he knew that change would displease many of the citizens who had endorsed him as governor. Andrew himself was a wine drinker, and he despised the prevailing hypocrisy about its use, though he also recognized the evils of intemperance. For witnesses, he called on professors, lawyers, political leaders, scientists, clergy, and other professionals. According to Albert Browne, Jr., "there was not a single act which afforded him more internal satisfaction than this attack."[39]

More than a hundred witnesses from across the Commonwealth appeared during the hearings. When Andrew was scheduled to speak, the audience swelled to such a size that it became necessary to hold sessions in the representatives' chamber and admit people by ticket. The prohibitionists' arguments were familiar: alcohol was poison and indulging in spirits was immoral. Andrew devoted himself to overthrowing both points; and on April 3, he spent four hours driving the prohibitionists to the wall. He presented facts about alcohol from wide-ranging sources, including the celebrated German chemist Justus von Liebig, who categorized alcohol as an "alimentary substance" and "Respiratory Food," not a poison. He asked physicians to testify that they had prescribed small doses of alcohol for medicinal purposes. He noted that saltpeter "kills a man in doses of one ounce or upward. Eight ounces dissolved in a pint of water killed a horse. . . . [Yet it] is used without fear of evil consequence in the curing of hams and other meats. Shall we say that a sandwich is poisonous and should be prohibited by law?"[40]

In arguing against alcohol's immorality, Andrew attacked the cumulative arguments that prohibitionists had used for decades: "The evils of this world are too great to render exaggeration any more consistent with wisdom than with truth. What we need is courage, not cowardice, for the controversy against them. . . . [The] moral dangers are within ourselves, not in the objects of nature." Drunkenness accompanied poverty and other miseries, he said, but was not the cause of degradation and crime. He considered the drinking patterns among Europeans, citing travelers who commented on the habitual temperance of the people—among them, William Cullen Bryant, whose letters from Spain described sobriety and moderation. "Disease, filth, ignorance, licentious manners, neglect of human want and woe, judicial cruelty, and pauperism," said Andrew, "It only needs drunkenness to complete the picture." Yet he insisted that alcohol *"was not the cause of all this but . . . a necessary concomitant; a part of the natural expression of an almost infinite inward evil."*[41]

Andrew knew he was unraveling century-old puritanical assumptions, but changing public opinion proved more difficult than he had imagined. Just as advancing racial arguments against public injustice had both added to and detracted from his reputation, his arguments during these hearings both intensified his popularity and increased ire against him. Bishop Gilbert Haven was among the listeners who, though spellbound by Andrew's oratory, was aware that the lawyer's words were lacerating his own public face.

The case was closely followed in the national press, and out-of-state colleagues asked Andrew for expert advice in their own fights against punitive liquor laws. In Massachusetts, though the anti-prohibitionists lost the legislative battle, political change via the ballot box won them the war later that year: pro-license candidates were overwhelmingly victorious and were able to repeal the statute themselves. They replaced it with the law that Andrew had favored, one that endorsed public sales by licensed taverns, apothecaries, and reputable grocers; with restrictions as to time and place; and with inspections by authorized personnel.

Days after his closing argument, Andrew left for Washington to attend a meeting of the Lincoln Memorial Association, thus avoiding much of the immediate criticism that rained down. After opponents claimed that Andrew was promoting drunkenness, a *Harper's Weekly* reporter wrote wryly:

> The ferocity with which Governor Andrew has been assailed by some persons as a reprobate and lost leader because he differed with them as to the best method of promoting temperance is amusing. It is the comical side of what was so tragical in the Southern States in the good old times, when slavery, which Mr. Charles O'Conner described as so blessed and beautiful, had full swing, and any man who questioned its divinity was mobbed, ridden on a rail, hung or burned amidst the applause of the "great Democratic party," which has so wholesome a contempt for "moral ideas."[42]

Though Andrew suffered unrelenting abuse after the hearings, he knew he had taken a practical approach to the issue. Many of his friends agreed. "Even if I were wholly opposed to him in opinion in this question of Prohibition and License," wrote Reverend Clarke to the editor of *Zion's Herald,* "I could not join with those who slander and abuse a wise and good man simply because . . . he differs in respect to the remedy."[43] The editor of the *Daily Advertiser* declared that Andrew's proposition for licensing the sale of wines and spirits "would be the most effective measure for the promotion of real temperance that has ever been brought forward in this Commonwealth."[44]

Later that year, the novelist Charles Dickens, who was staying with James and Annie Fields, read Andrew's speech and confirmed the editor's assessment. He told Fields that it was "very moving. I could not put it down till I had finished it. That man must always hold a high position in your country."[45]

CHILDREN WILL CALL YOU BLESSED
April 1866–October 1897

Illustrious Class of '37

Andrew went to Charlestown in early April to attend Fast Day at the state prison.[1] A few days later he was stunned to learn that his close friend George Stearns had died in New York City. The funeral was held in Medford, Massachusetts; and although Andrew was unable to attend, Emerson, Garrison, and George Thompson were all present. John Greenleaf Whittier dedicated a poem to Stearns, which appeared in the May issue of the *Atlantic Monthly*: "Ah, well!—the world is discreet, there are plenty to pause and wait; / But here was a man who set his feet / Sometimes in advance of his fate."[2]

Stearns would have rejoiced to know that Andrew was continuing to carry freedom's torch. In early June, Andrew met with Forbes, Frederic Lincoln, Jr., and George Hale at his Washington Street office to discuss ways of expanding aid to former slaves. Yet he still could not evade the call of politics. That spring Secretary of State Seward asked him to serve as the U.S. government's counsel against John Wilkes Booth's co-conspirator, John H. Surratt, who had fled the country but was later arrested in Egypt. Two years earlier Andrew had attended his mother Mary Surratt's trial; the *Daily Advertiser* had identified him as the "most noticeable spectator." Now, however, he declined to "help the Government put a rope around the neck of a fellow-man." "In truth," he wrote to General Schouler, "if I had the power, I would find a way to avoid a further prosecution of this poor wretch, leaving him, if in fact he is a murderer, to the divine curse of Cain, and relieving the public sensibilities and the pages of our current history from the shocking recital of a thrice-told tale of horror, with a fresh execution on the gallows to lighten its intensity."[3] Instead of taking on that prominent case, Andrew chose to defend a Boston woman, Belinda Ellms, who was suing for breach of matrimonial promise. Andrew won the case and convinced the jury to award Ellms $7,000 in damages.[4]

In late May, Andrew spoke at the Unitarian Festival, held at the Music Hall in Boston, where he was introduced as the "tailor who put two thousand boys in blue." In his address, Andrew declared that Americans were standing at a "parting of the ways," and he called on Unitarians to embrace the opportunity to assist the freed slaves. Otherwise, their shame would obliterate the glory of the war. Andrew urged them to be "morally, religiously, and educationally reconstructed. . . . We of the North [are] to be the Apostles" in this work. He quoted a teacher in Beaufort, North Carolina, who had written to him about an African American man who had never seen the alphabet until coming to her school. He shared anecdotes that illustrated the former slaves' inborn faith and piety: "[they] still possessed the divine love which had given them that elasticity of spirit which carried them through their long night of darkness."[5]

In mid-June, working behind the scenes, Andrew focused on bringing together the Union Leagues of Boston, Philadelphia, and New York to resolve the Republican Party quarrel between unionists and conservatives in Virginia over congressional reconstruction proposals, a dispute that threatened to disturb party unity throughout the South. "The trouble in Virginia and all over the South has been that was no Union party and no Union sentiment apparent," reported the *Philadelphia American and Gazette*. "The great body of the rebels prefer to wear their distinction as rebels, and to separate themselves from the southern Union men."[6] The clubs sent delegations to Richmond, and Senator Wilson agreed to lead the Massachusetts group. At the Virginia governor's mansion, Wilson played a leading role in getting the delegations to agree on a joint call for a party convention to be held in August.[7]

After two years in private practice, Andrew's finances had rebounded, and he and family were able to enjoy a summer tour through New England and Canada. He was temporarily detained when President Johnson visited to dedicate Boston's new Masonic Temple in late June. Despite the mayor's enthusiasm, Andrew remained unimpressed. He mentioned to friends, however, that the president had had an "immense time" in Boston and that his son Forrester had shaken Johnson's hand. After his family set off for Gorham, New Hampshire, in the White Mountains, Andrew joined Cyrus Woodman for a month-long trip through British Canada.

They returned through Maine, staying with Peleg Chandler in Brunswick and strolling through their Bowdoin stomping grounds. It was a restful trip, one that Woodman said "will be long remembered by me."[8]

Back in Boston, Andrew found a stack of social and academic invitations, legal inquiries, and several personal letters. One was from Elbridge Dudley, a Boston lawyer who shared Andrew's commitment to emancipation and equal rights for African Americans. Dudley had purchased a plantation in Beaufort, South Carolina, and he was updating Andrew about the condition of the freed slaves, especially given the political developments in South Carolina. In July, citizens had organized a state Republican Party, one of the radical changes wrought by the war. Most delegates to the convention were African Americans who had been recently enfranchised by Congress. Dudley had attended the convention, and "the proportion of colored to that of white delegates was about three to one," though "it was very difficult drawing the line as to where the white race began, & the colored race ended. Four delegates, whose names I could give you, passed for *colored men*, whom if you should meet them on Washington St. today at broad noon, you would never suspect of having a drop of African blood in their veins." All had stories to tell about their slave days, and Dudley was "astonished at the amount of intelligence & ability shown by the colored men of the Convention." He said their speeches could rival anything spoken in Faneuil Hall. Clearly, by numbers alone, they would take control of the party.

Dudley knew that Massachusetts men worried about African Americans' fitness for leadership and feared that southern whites would succumb to demagogues intent on confiscating and redistributing land. Yet African Americans in South Carolina, despite violence and death threats, remained dedicated to building the party's membership. This was the only path forward, Dudley believed. Andrew agreed. His letter was a testimonial to the intelligence, ability, and courage of the state's first Black Republican leaders, some of whom had purchased their own freedom. Dudley hoped that Andrew would support this work, but he also wanted the former governor to know how much the people had valued his leadership during the war: "Allow me, my dear Sir, in behalf of the colored people here, to most heartily thank you, for the great work you have done in the elevation of a race from the most abject and cruel bondage the world ever knew, to that of free citizens of a free Republic. Their children's children will rise up to call you blessed."[9] Such sentiments confirmed that the righteous cause Andrew had enlisted in as a young reformer was advancing justice far from Boston.

Equally confirming was the letter Andrew received from the writer and activist Lydia Maria Child, who was lamenting the plight of freed slaves in Tennessee. They were struggling to find work and felt they were being punished for their loyalty to the United States. "The *moral* influence of sustaining them by our sympathy," she wrote, "would be of more worth than the temporary relief of their physical wants." Child wielded great influence among her fellow abolitionists. According to John Greenleaf Whittier, "men like Charles Sumner, Henry Wilson, Salmon P. Chase, and Governor Andrew availed themselves of her fore-thought and sound judgment of men and measures." Indeed, Andrew had been so impressed by her *Appeal in Favor of that Class of Americans Called Africans* (1833) that he had presented a copy to his sisters.[10]

For him, letters such as Dudley's and Child's confirmed that African Americans were both eager and able to assert themselves in the political culture, even as whites remained bent on keeping them impoverished. He was deeply worried that white ascendency in the South would rechain them, and his correspondence with Elizabeth Van Lew confirmed those fears. Born in Richmond to prosperous slave-owning parents, Van Lew had followed a remarkable path to abolitionism. After education at a Friends' school in Philadelphia, she had returned to Virginia; and when her father died in 1843, she and her mother freed the family slaves. The pair, along with her brother John, spent the next several years purchasing their former slaves' relatives so that they, too, could be granted freedom. When the Civil War broke out, Elizabeth and her mother worked on behalf of Union soldiers imprisoned in Richmond and soon developed an elaborate spy ring, smuggling messages from the Confederate capital to Union commanders. Allegedly, to accomplish this task, Van Lew feigned lunacy, which earned her the posthumous nickname "Crazy Bet." Union commanders, including Grant, greatly valued her assistance, so much so that he later appointed her to serve as Richmond's postmaster.[11]

Andrew had long been aware of Van Lew's work, and for two years they had been corresponding about postwar conditions in Richmond. In her view, he was "one of the most devoted, hearty, intelligent friends of the Union," and she had hung his portrait in her home. Now she told him she had written a book about Reconstruction. "I am not a writer," she said, "but this book is only facts," and she urged him to travel south and see for himself "what Union people are forced to submit to."[12] Freed slaves were being treated dreadfully, she said, and they needed his assistance. She described the treasonous behavior of white residents in Richmond and shared her despair over race riots in Memphis and New Orleans. In response, Andrew sent her $500 to distribute among the freed slaves in her city.[13]

Andrew applauded Van Lew's work for the freed slaves just as he had applauded her efforts, years before, in attending to the Massachusetts soldiers in Richmond who had been taken prisoner at Ball's Bluff. She had risked her life with such work. Van Lew, in turn, admired the governor. So several months later, when she traveled to New York to give her manuscript to a friend for revision, she made plans to visit Andrew in Boston. He was in Vermont, however, so he asked a few of his friends, including Colonel William Lee, to review it. Lee later wrote to Andrew thanking him for his note, which had enclosed a photograph of "our friend, that noble Virginia woman, Miss Van Lew, who I shall proudly place among my treasured ones." Lee planned to be in Richmond in the summer of 1867, and "by jingo, excuse me, I'll not desert that woman if I have to challenge and fight every man in Congress." "She is too [true], too good & too loyal a woman, to be forgotten and neglected."[14]

It was unclear if Van Lew ever met Andrew when she was in Boston, but she was unable to interest a publisher in her book. Disappointed, she nonetheless wrote to thank him for his support and told him she had used his money to help hospitalized women and children. In the meantime, Lee told Andrew that he had embarked on a fundraising campaign to help her publish the manuscript and had raised $500 from five people, one of whom was Andrew. By the end of January 1867, Lee asked Van Lew to send him the manuscript, with the understanding that it would surely need revision. She was thrilled, but the state of Reconstruction quickly doused her excitement. "I am worn out with a life time fight," she told Andrew. "My heart and my strength fail me," she said, writing that she was "despondent of success." Still, she was buoyed by Andrew's unwavering support for her family, her efforts and was grateful he had enlisted Colonel Lee and John Forbes to work on her behalf. Yet by the end of July 1867, Andrew had heard nothing more and he turned his sights to other matters.[15]

That summer Andrew's Bowdoin classmates asked him to give an address at the "illustrious class of '37" reunion in early August. "Pray come if possible," wrote Reverend John Fiske. "If the dates forbid, send us 'showers of blessings' in the form of a letter."[16] Andrew was pleased by the invitation and agreed to return to Brunswick for the ceremony, where he joined distinguished alumni and Maine natives Joshua Chamberlain, made famous at the Battle of Gettysburg and now serving as governor of Maine, and James Bradbury, an editor, lawyer, and former Maine senator. Afterward he traveled to Gorham and Windham, where he spent time with his family. He had never stopped loving his childhood home, and on this visit, he tore a shingle from his old house as a keepsake. The place had changed in certain ways: the old schoolhouse that his father had built was gone, burned in 1864. Yet much remained familiar. As he walked the roads, he came upon a family friend, who invited him to tea and the two had a long conversation that strengthened his "attachment to old places and old friends." When his childhood acquaintances referred to him as "governor," he implored them to call him Albion. He was "so glad to feel that he could throw off the restraints and conventionalities that were so frequented about him and indulge in a familiarity which revived the memory of early days and cherished friends, and which made him feel like a boy again."[17]

Andrew returned to Boston in late August to find his legal calendar overflowing and to learn that Harvard had reappointed him to its board of overseers. He also learned that President Johnson was considering him for secretary of the War Department. In September, the Republicans of Boston's Sixth Ward elected him as a delegate to the state convention, and Forbes took this opportunity to invite his friend to spend a few days with him. He asked Andrew to bring his family to Forbes's summer home on Naushon Island, off Massachusetts's southeastern coast. Andrew, who disliked sailing, demurred:

I have two or three matters *hot*, and must stand by the anvil, or near enough if need be. All the children are absent, and Mrs. Andrew is living in her trunk. I command the whole army from this base; and the scattered condition of the forces is another reason which requires me to be within reach of rail and wire. We have had Ch[ief] Jus[tice] Chase and Gerrit Smith here this week, [and] . . . Grant keeps between the wind and all of them, and makes ten-strikes, every time, in the popular estimation.[18]

Andrew declined an invitation to Antietam that September to commemorate the battlefield anniversary that had triggered Lincoln's preliminary Emancipation Proclamation. He preferred to stay focused on helping African Americans navigate Reconstruction and helping veterans adjust to peace. Theologians as well as national and state politicians continued to consult him about his views on Reconstruction, and some pressed him to reenter politics. According to New Yorker John Binney, Andrew should "stir up the Republican party to exert their energy" in the fall elections. "There is at present too great apathy in the Republican party, and you should lead your whole energy to sweep the whole field." But Andrew remained firm in his decision to stay "quiet in politics": "Now the *Law* is a jealous mistress. You must be faithful, or you are discarded." Certainly, he was not "an indifferent observer"; in fact, he was always "*constantly* doing *something*," and political meetings were frequently held in his office. But he told Binney that Grant should take the party's lead as the presidential nominee. "I believe fully in the patriotic fidelity of *Gen. Grant*. He is pure gold, no political trickster nor self-seeker, and he has entirely learned the wisdom and truth of our essential creed."[19]

Andrew remained committed to elevating the freed slaves via economic and constitutional change. He declared to Binney that, in his focus on freedom, he was "always *radical*" but, in respect to measures, was "always conservative."

> Principles are of God are founded in the Eternal fitness, harmony and reality of the Universe, over which he presides. Measures on the other hand, are human devices by which men attempt to actualize in human affairs the principles they perceive and believe in. We can safely trust a principle, and go [to] its very roots, because it is—when true at all— radically true. . . . The rebel states were for a time, before actual war began, *in* the Union, but not *of* it. They were machinating inside of it how to weaken and injure it, as a preparation for war against it.

Andrew continued to believe that the nation's first task was to create a "*general economic prosperity*—which can come only of industry and good crops." Otherwise, southerners would keep refusing to cooperate with the federal government. "Therefore, I do not lament the disappointment of our hopes of an earlier reconstruction," he said. "Indeed—I wish never to worry about results. I regret any failure, honestly to try, boldly and faithfully to *endeavor*."[20]

Andrew feared that the Republican Party had not understood the magnitude of this transformational undertaking: "We are working for the ages, not merely for an election campaign. If we show ourselves broadminded, true hearted, patient, hopeful, and statesmanlike, the people will not allow the Election to go against us. The ark of Israel is entrusted to our shoulders. We can be beaten only by ourselves."[21]

If Andrew had held a national office, he may have been able to put forward these convictions more effectively. In fact, President Johnson later admitted that he "may have erred in not carrying out Mr. [Montgomery] Blair's request by putting into my Cabinet, Morton, Andrew, and Greeley. . . . Morton would have been a tower of strength . . . and so would Andrew."[22] But the former governor did not seem to regret this. He continued to stay busy, accepting invitations to deliver formal addresses at various institutions and shorter speeches at regional fairs. He accepted invitations to give an address at the dedication of Everett's statue in Boston's Public Garden and to speak to the renowned Philoclean Literary Society at Rutgers and chaired a committee to raise money for a tribute to Garrison. He never missed an opportunity to talk to released prisoners in the Commonwealth. Still, by mid-October, his name was being routinely mentioned as Grant's possible vice-presidential choice for the 1868 election. Albert Browne, Jr., confided that he had dined recently at Houghton's in Cambridge with Charles Dana and Samuel Bowles, who reported that the party would be looking for a New Englander, and Bowles mentioned Andrew as a strong candidate.[23]

In mid-October, Andrew dealt again with a round of headaches, and he declined several invitations, even refusing to attend gatherings of local freed-slave organizations, a true indication of his suffering. Dining with Bird Club members at Young's Hotel, he was chatty but clearly weaker than he had been. Nonetheless, he regaled the men with war stories and kept his thoughts on the nation's political future and the Republican Party. In a letter to Browne, he denied rumors that he would be replacing Stanton as Johnson's war secretary. The political "tendency of the hour is towards Grant," he said, "and that is best."

> It is not the ideal good. It is bad for the country that he must leave his present post,—bad for him, the soldier, to try and to endure the hard fate which awaits him, in civil life. But it is the apparently *best practical good* the country can have. And Grant is so square and honest a man that I believe he is bound to be *right* in the main, *anywhere*.[24]

Andrew was in court on Monday, October 28, and the following day was away from Boston on legal business. He returned to his Charles Street home early on Tuesday evening and was in the library with his children at about 9 p.m. Walking across the room to give a paper to one of his daughters, he tripped on the carpet, stumbled forward, but caught himself. Although he recovered, his breath grew short, and he went to the front door for air, where he met an associate counsel in a case he was preparing. Andrew invited his colleague in, escorted him to the library, made light conversation, and prepared tea. Still breathing heavily, he suddenly complained again that he needed air and staggered toward the window, where he fell over. He then struggled to the sofa and asked his visitor to call Dr. George Derby. Eliza and the children were upstairs and, on hearing the commotion, rushed down to his side. Eliza grasped his hand, and Andrew placed his other hand on her cheek, tried to speak, and made signs for writing materials. She gave him a pencil, which he vainly tried to use with his right hand, then with his left, then with his teeth. To no avail: the pencil dropped from his mouth, and he fell unconscious. By this time, several doctors had arrived, and they remained watching over him throughout the night. Later that night his brother Isaac arrived. Under the moonlight, a crowd of African Americans had gathered outside the house. Crooning "Battle Hymn of the Republic," they prayed that Andrew would pull through. He lingered, unconscious, until 6 a.m. on October 30, when he died in Isaac's arms. *The Medical and Surgical Journal* reported that he had suffered a massive apoplectic effusion—that is, a stroke. He was forty-nine years old.[25]

William Burt, Andrew's long-time legal associate and wartime judge advocate general, telegraphed Grant: "Gov. Andrew died at his house . . . at six (6) oclock. He was unconscious from the time of the attack the evening before. His family were all with him."[26] The news passed swiftly through Boston. "Governor Andrew lies dead," wrote James Fields in his diary. "Since the death of President Lincoln no man can be so great a loss to the country. To us . . . the loss is doubled, for he failed in none of the hospitalities of daily life. He was benevolent and accessible always, and as charitable a man, in the largest sense of the word, as ever walked the earth."[27] James Russell Lowell wrote to Fields the next day:

> What a loss we all have in Governor Andrew. So good a man is rare anywhere, so upright a politician especially rare. His jolly courage and good humored firmness made a combination we shall not see again, and let them say what they would of the rhetoric of his speeches, you felt a heart beating all through them. . . . Where shall we find another unselfish public man?[28]

FIGURE 10. John Andrew's library. Courtesy of the Boston Public Library.

Bishop Gilbert Haven wrote in his diary, "Governor Andrew died . . . sad, sudden, terrible. Great in many gifts."[29]

Commonwealth citizens were devastated, especially the state's African American residents, many of whom flocked to Andrew's home to express their sorrow to Eliza. Heavy-hearted Bostonians draped the city in black, in memory of their beloved governor; and Mayor Otis Norcross began planning a memorial ceremony. The funeral took place on the morning of November 2 at the Unitarian church on the corner of Boylston and Arlington streets. Fields recalled, "The sun shone through a veil of autumnal mist, as we walked across the Public Garden to the church, and the trees shook their last gold leaves pensively in the blue air. It was a lovely season, and tempered like the nature of the friend we had lost." All the city's businesses were closed, and mourners crowded into the galleries and side pews. Poor residents, many of them African Americans, packed the vestibule and stood outside the building.[30]

Many people lined the streets and walked in the long procession that, after the service, escorted the hearse to beautiful Mount Auburn Cemetery in Cambridge. "Perhaps the most touching sight of all," wrote Reverend Clarke, "were the colored women who ran by the side of the coffin the whole five miles from Boston to Mount Auburn, to take one last look at the face of their friend."[31] The *Springfield Republican* reported that "such a crowd has not been seen at a funeral of public or private individual in Boston for years." Walking before the coffin were Reverend Clarke, Father Taylor, and Reverend Grimes, the religious triumvirate that had shaped the governor's spiritual life. "In him," said Clarke, "was illustrated the original and central sense of the word integrity." He saw Andrew's entire life as a lesson in "the power of character."[32] "He was a leader among men," said former governor Nathaniel Banks, "a representative of principles, and those who believe in those principles had confidence in him and followed him with the utmost faith."[33]

In the days that followed, eulogies poured forth. In the *Springfield Republican*, Warrington" likened Andrew's death to "that chapter in Carlyle's French Revolution which describes the death of Mirabeau. One little sentence sticks to the memory, and when a great man dies, it always recurs to me. In the restaurateur's [sic] of the Palais Royal the waiter remarks, 'Fine weather, monsieur.' 'Yes, my friend,' answers the ancient man of letters, 'very fine; Mirabeau is dead.'" Warrington recalled moments during the war when Andrew's friends thought the governor might break down:

He had a worn, absent, "flabby" look, and had to go off for a few days to recover himself. I saw that same look on him, I thought,—an uncertainty of gait, as it seemed to me,—the last time I met him, perhaps ten days ago, on Tremont street. . . . He was chatty and cheery, . . . but hardly so strong and muscular and vital as he used to be. He told stories with the old flavor, and I heard him repeat with feeling a poem by Henry Timrod, a southerner of literary pretensions, who has lately died. No man, with the exception of [death penalty reformer] Robert Rantoul, was more honorably connected with the reform which seeks to root up that abominable monument of barbarism.[34]

John Andrew, Warrington said, was everything: "the private citizen, the abolitionist, the friend and defender of the fugitive slave, the hater of the gallows."[35]

John Jay, Jr., of New York, a physician who had served the Union cause during the war, wrote that "we recognize in Governor Andrew all that is most excellent in the traits usually attributed to New-England, blended with a breath of thought, a largeness of aim, and an absence of anything like provincial or sectarian prejudice, that raised him to the full height of the American ideal."[36] Peleg Chandler believed that Andrew "was fortunate in living at a time when his peculiar talents could be used to such vast advantage in public affairs. In great emergencies the man finally appears who is fitted to take the lead, and, under Providence, conduct affairs to a successful result."[37] Andrew would always be associated with the Civil War, said Chandler, but he was so much more. The Congregationalist minister Elias Nason agreed:

To my mind, he most resembled in his taste and temper, life and deeds, the incorruptible patriot Samuel Adams, the war leader of Massachusetts through the old Revolution. Like Mr. Adams, he was simple in his style of living, and averse to personal display. . . . He loved to study the manners and the customs of the old colonial days; like him, he had a pleasant humor and a sparkling wit; like him, cultivated vocal music, and made the word of God his law. . . . Both great men were earnest friends of popular education; both liberal in their benefactions to the poor.[38]

The distinguished antislavery journalist Parke Godwin recalled Andrew's endearing qualities: "Simple as a child in his manners; gentle as a woman in his affections; earnest as the enthusiast in his persuasions of truth; and steadfast as the martyr to his own inferior faith; he was yet prudent, moderate, and wise, as the statesmen in his action."[39]

In a letter to Eliza, Charles Whipple, the superintendent of the Office of the Massachusetts Society for Aiding Discharged Convicts, called Andrew "a far-sighted statesman and as an ardent patriot, we will testify to the Christian charity with which he regarded the outcasts of society and the violators of law. He was not only a faithful worker in aid of discharged convicts, he was a pioneer in the cause. His mercy for wrongdoers never failed. In John A. Andrew, every prisoner has lost a friend."[40] George Hilliard, Sumner's law partner, who was then serving as a U.S. district attorney for Massachusetts, said that he had never known "a man who left this world with less of the stain of sin." Richard Henry Dana, Jr., wrote that Andrew "could not be deflected from the course of duty by any of the temptations which address themselves to the weaknesses of public men."[41] William Evarts, Andrew's co-counsel on the *Meteor* case, believed that his name "would go down in history with the complete heroic fame of Samuel Adams and James Otis of the Revolution."[42]

Cyrus Woodman, who was deeply distressed by his friend's death, sent Eliza a long, heartfelt letter: "Albion's death has overwhelmed me, yet I feel that I must say a few words over his grave, however cold and unfitting they may seem to you to be. . . . Our friendship, beginning when he was fourteen years old, was never interrupted. It grew with our growth and strengthened with our strength, and was, I fondly trust, a comfort and a blessing to him as well as to me." Without Andrew, he said, "my great affection overshadows me and darkens all my future," and Woodman prayed he would "meet him on the other side."[43]

Our acquaintance, which began at Gorham, was continued in college and afterwards in Boston, where we studied law. From the first we were friends and our friendship knew no variableness or shadow of turning. No man seemed destined to do so much good as he in the councils of the nation. The country by his death seems poorer and weaker. People were beginning to be aware that he was the foremost statesman in the country, . . . [but] this great, courageous, manly soul has left us and the whole state mourns as Massachusetts never before mourned the death of any of her citizens. He was great in heart as well as in intellect, and in a simple, natural, unpretending way followed Christ more nearly than any man I have ever known.[44]

Andrew's unbending goal of justice and civil rights for all was a reflection of American democracy's finest virtues. "Not since the news came of *Abraham Lincoln's* death were so many hearts truly smitten," wrote a correspondent for *Harper's Weekly*. "Every morning, he passed across the Common, swinging his lawyer's bag, as if he were sixteen and were on his way to Latin school with his satchel."[45] John Van Lew wrote to Eliza from Richmond, telling her that, when he was in Andrew's company, he felt he was in the "presence of an exalted character." Andrew was a "noble, charitable" soul; he "lived outside himself," and "his comprehensive and powerful mind was ever subjected to the utmost tension with untiring and unceasing efforts for the moral and practical preferment of the human race and of the nation. I very much fear we have no such man remaining so honorable so able and so pure."[46]

Shortly, after Andrew's death, Harriet Beecher Stowe wrote to Annie Fields asking for some "anecdote" that would "show how good & generous Andrew was."[47] Annie shared several stories, prompting Stowe to ask for a copy of his valedictory address, which she had often heard mentioned in conversation. In 1871, she included a sketch of Andrew in *The Lives and Deeds of Our Self-Made Men*. In it she recounted the story of a poor woman, the wife of a soldier, who had come to Andrew's office about an issue related to her sister's pension. The governor told her that she would need to submit her application in another office in the statehouse. Then, noticing her exhaustion, he asked where she lived. She was not from Boston and had no friends or relatives in the city. So he offered her his sofa to rest on and "from his own frugal stores a glass of wine and a cracker for refreshment.[48] In her final analysis, Stowe recalled that it had been said of Lincoln that he embodied a pure Christian statesmanship. "In the same manner," she said, "it may be said of John A. Andrew that he presented a type of consistently Christian State governor."[49]

Associates of the Suffolk County bar and current and former state legislators drafted tributes to the former governor. Chandler and Dana spoke of his high incorruptibility, his earnest convictions, his industry, and his modest character. "Few public men in Massachusetts," wrote a reporter for the *New York Times*, "are more highly esteemed and respected by the people of the entire Commonwealth than he has been since he first became prominently identified with the political affairs of the State."[50] According to the *Boston Investigator*, "no public man has ever died in New England who had so many Christian, benevolent, and philanthropic institutions to mourn his loss, as Governor Andrew."[51] Even the conservative *Boston Post* noted that the governor "possessed an extraordinary power of winning a man's heart, because his heart was honest, and he could look every man in the face with true feelings of a 'brother man.'"[52]

In the week after Andrew's death, members of Boston's Zion Church, led by Reverend Grimes and William Nell, celebrated the life of the friend who had assisted fugitives to freedom and abolished segregation in the public schools and in public accommodations, who had succored orphans, widows, and prisoners. On November 26, city officials held a morning memorial service at the Music Hall. Boston, still cloaked in black, again closed that day. The service featured a marble bust of Andrew flanked by another of John Brown and by John Rogers's statue *Uncle Ned's School*, representing a freed slave receiving instruction from a young girl. Edwin Whipple presided and offered a eulogy: "If Massachusetts ever produced a man who was thoroughly incorruptible, who was insensible to bribes presented to vanity, prejudice, and ambition as well as to interest, and whom all the powers of the world could not push or persuade into a dishonest action, that man was John A. Andrew." Whipple recalled the visit of British minister Sir Frederic Bruce, who had found Andrew's statehouse chambers crowded with African American women waiting for news about the fathers, brothers, and sons in the Fifty-fourth and Fifty-fifth. Bruce was awed by Andrew's warm manner and afterward remarked that, whatever might be the advantages of a republican government, he had never believed it could be paternal until he had witnessed Andrew's compassion.

The service was led by the transcendentalist professor Reverend Frederic Hedge, who characterized the death of so young a statesman as "a national calamity."[53] Father Taylor offered the benediction, and John Knowles Paine, the first American-born composer to achieve fame for large-scale orchestral composition, performed John Sullivan Dwight's transcription of "Wir setzen un smit Tränen nieder," the final chorus from Bach's *St. Matthew Passion*. The service closed with a Bach chorale that opened with the words "What God does surely is well done."[54]

Julia Ward Howe had long respected Andrew's dedication to abolition and his deep humanitarianism. She and her husband were among his closest friends; and during the war the governor and Sumner had often taken refuge at their home. "I seemed to live in and along with the war while it was in progress," she recalled, "and to follow all its ups and downs, its good and ill fortune with these two brave men."[55] In her view, both Andrew and Lincoln had been war victims, and she blamed his death on an overtaxed brain. Physicians had repeatedly warned him against exhausting himself, but he had remained steadfast in his duties.[56]

Howe was in Europe at the time of Andrew's death, so she composed a poem to be read at his memorial service:

I STOOD BEFORE HIS SILENT GRAVE

I stood before his silent grave,
And heard a record long and low,
How he was merciful and brave,
How his swift help sped to and fro.

Great deeds of heart were told of him,
And musing whispered at the fire,
Whose burden stirred in thought and limb
The energies of high desire

The honors of the State were his,
The better crownings of esteem;
Faith yielded him her mysteries,
And charity was not a dream.

And Hope her steadfast anchor threw
To match God's promise in the storm:
When billows roared and tempests blew,
He left us that consoling form.

No snare was in his ringing speech,
Nor malice in his sunny smile;
No passion, hidden out of reach,
Drugged his poor manhood with its guile.

A champion in our hour of need,
A prophet armed with forethought wise,
He flung our banner on the lead,
He gave our watchword to the skies.

Poorly our blended efforts try
To set his image in his room;
We lift the Poet's laurel high
To lay it on the Patriot's tomb.

And this I said when, laid in earth,
His funeral song was asked of me:
"The world has few to match his worth,
And none to praise it perfectly."[57]

It was no secret that Andrew had left office financially poorer than he had been when he entered and that he had strained himself to restart his lucrative legal practice. Soon after his death, friends and colleagues proposed to raise $100,000 for his family. According to the *National Intelligencer*, the plan was "being successfully carried out," and citizens quickly raised more than $73,000. A board of trustees was established to oversee the family's welfare, and within weeks more

FIGURE 11. John Andrew's statue, Hingham, Massachusetts. Courtesy of the Boston Public Library.

than four hundred friends donated $86,000, to be spent at the family's discretion. James and Annie Fields subscribed $1,000 under the name of James's publishing business, Ticknor and Fields. Individual subscriptions to the fund ranged from 10 cents to $1,000, and among the donors were many African Americans who had "justly regarded him as their friend."[58]

In 1869, on the anniversary of his death, Andrew's body was disinterred and transferred from Mount Auburn to a cemetery in Hingham. In December 1871, at the annual reunion of the officers of the Thirty-second Massachusetts Volunteers, the regiment's commander, Luther Stephenson, Jr., noted that "a little flag, planted by some tender hand in the graveyard at Hingham, is all that marks the burial-place of that loyal Governor, who covered the State with a mantle of glory. It is well that until now he should have slept in the stillness of nature which he loved, without a sound of the hammer or the chisel to disturb his grand repose." But Andrew's family had since consented to a memorial statue, and organizers now formed the John A. Andrew Monument Association to collect funds to erect one. Stephenson headed the drive, considering it essential that veterans " testify their gratitude to the Executive, who in the great struggle for the nation's life, had been their constant friend and supporter, who had sent them forward with words of cheer and inspiration, and received them on their return with welcome and congratulations such as could emanate only from a heart inspired by the truest friendship, and an earnest conviction of the justice and glory of the cause for which they had fought."[59]

In 1873, the Hingham Cemetery Commission contracted with Thomas Gould to design a statue of Andrew to be placed near his gravesite. Gould was a well-known sculptor from Boston, now living in Florence, Italy, who had been acquainted with Andrew. As material, he selected Carrara marble, which could endure New England weather. Though he estimated that the job would cost $10,000, he agreed to limit his fee to the $6,500 raised by the association. Because Andrew had not been tall, he recommended that the statue be kept under seven feet high and promised to study the grounds and the surrounding landscape as he planned the monument's aesthetics. Gould sculpted the statue in Italy, and in October 1875 he brought it to Hingham himself so that he could supervise its transport and placement. Commission members chose to site the statue beneath the town's soldiers' and sailors' monument overlooking the town harbor. Lead cases containing twenty-five documents relating to Andrew's time as governor were deposited in a cavity within the statue. To symbolize the promise of a new era, his carved face was turned toward the rising sun. Stephenson predicted that "the people of this land shall come here to revive the fires of patriotism, to reflect upon their duties to God and their country, to learn that the noblest impulses of life demand sacrifice." Perhaps most significantly, "the soldier of the Union will come, and beside this marble form, live over again the deeds of the past. . . . The dark-skinned child of Ethiopia shall come, and kneeling at the feet of him whose philanthropy and love was limited by no distinction of race or color, class or condition, shall drop a tear of gratitude and affection."[60]

The unveiling was a moment "of rare beauty," noted one observer. Thousands of veterans came to pay their respects to the war governor and reflect on his role in preserving the Union.[61] According to a correspondent for *Appleton's Journal*:

> The statue . . . represents the governor standing, dressed in a double-breasted frock-coat, and with a long military-cloak hanging from his shoulders, and fastened across his chest by a cord and tassels. Upon the collar is carved the star of the Commonwealth's escutcheon. Governor Andrew, as all will recollect him, was a short stout man with a firm, broad-shouldered figure, well knitted and determined, but his beauty lay in his fine and well-poised head. No subject could be better adapted for the sculptor than his clean-cut Roman nose, with nostrils flexible and energetic, his well-marked handsome mouth, with full lips and rounded chin, dimpled in the middle, and his large eyes, and forehead crowned by closely-curling hair.[62]

While many Boston residents regretted that Andrew's statue was not situated in their city, they appreciated that Andrew would have approved of its placement in the old Hingham graveyard.[63] The sculpture was adorned with a single word, "Andrew," a name that encapsulated a lifetime's pursuit of justice. The town was proud to have it. Years later, at the turn of the twentieth century, Arthur Beale, an adjutant of Hingham's Grand Army of the Republic Hall, wrote that Hingham was "particularly pleased with the fact that not only did Governor Andrew spend many of his living years here, but in death the town has custody of his body."[64]

As he worked on the statue, Gould believed that it would speak to later generations, who would remember and appreciate Andrew's contributions and chronicle his deeds. So did most of his contemporaries. As a writer observed in the *New York Times*, "probably no Governor of Massachusetts ever better embodied the spirit of his people and of the people of New England stock throughout the North than did Andrew or possessed in fuller measure the qualities that made that stock so potent in the affairs of the Nation."[65]

The Grand Army of the Republic halls were the primary posts for gatherings of Union veterans. Immediately after the war, membership was mostly limited to white men. In August 1887, however, more than three hundred African Americans gathered in an independent reunion at Boston's Tremont Temple to commemorate their service and to honor their beloved governor. Attendees listened to speeches, paraded through the streets, and capped off the meeting with a boat trip to Hingham to visit Andrew's grave. Although the gathering was primarily a Massachusetts affair, it reflected the national climate of race relations. The Civil War had been over for decades, but they were still fighting their own war. Now they called on white comrades and citizens to recognize the "patriotic Negro soldier and his kin." It was time to embrace the change that the war had wrought, they maintained.[66]

In 1897, on Memorial Day, thousands poured into rainy Boston and stood at the statehouse steps to witness the unveiling of the Robert Gould Shaw Memorial on Boston Common. The ornate statue, the work of the eminent sculptor Augustus Saint-Gaudens, was a singular testimonial to African American freedom. If John Brown's raid and execution had brought on the war, it had been Andrew who had "seen the glory of the coming of the Lord," who had spent his life "trampling out the vintage where the grapes of wrath are stored," and who had identified Shaw as a man who could guide this work to fruition. Among the speakers at the unveiling was Booker T. Washington. As he took the stage, his eyes filled. He gazed into the crowd, "tears glisten[ing] in the eyes of the soldiers and civilians on the platform," and spoke of those courageous leaders who had lifted "humanity out of wretchedness and bondage." In his words, Shaw, Andrew, and Stearns became a great humanitarian triumvirate, striving to make the unfathomable possible. Andrew's "prophetic vision and strong arm," alongside Stearns's "hidden generosity and a great sweet heart," had helped to "turn the darkest hour into day."[67] Andrew would have appreciated that sentiment.

NOTES

PREFACE

1. *BDA*, July 27, 1887; *BrT*, July 22, 1897; Pearson, *Andrew*, 1:20–21; *Lib*, Oct. 11, Nov. 1, 14, 1834, Mar. 4, 1864; "Bowdoin College," *Scribner's Monthly*, 47–59; Hatch, *History of Bowdoin College*, 290–92; Mayer, *All on Fire*, 190–94.

2. Parker, *Ten Sermons of Religion*, 84–85; Parker, "Some Thoughts on the Progress of America, and the Influence of Her Diverse Institutions, May 31, 1854," in Cobbe, ed., *The Collected Works of Theodore Parker*, 2:3, 4, 5, 14, also 6:1–43; Stange, *Patterns of Antislavery Among American Unitarians*, 162–63; Siebert, *The Vigilance Committee of Boston*, 1–23; *MLR*, Aug. 1854; May 1855, 1–17; *Lib*, May 9, 1856; *BA*, July 7, 1852; Robboy and Robboy, "Lewis Hayden," 606–10; Bowditch, *Life and Correspondence of Henry Ingersoll Bowditch*, 1:263–72.

3. Taken from Lincoln's Second Inaugural Address, Abraham Lincoln Papers, Series 3, General Correspondence, 1837–1897, LC; Donald, *Lincoln*, 398.

4. *TD*, May 16, 1904; *OL*, July 23, 1904.

5. Deval Patrick, address on the state of the Commonwealth of Massachusetts, Jan. 17, 2013, *BDG*, Jan. 13, 2017; *HJ*, May 13, 2010; Sargent, *Memorial Address delivered before the John Albion Andrew Monument Association*.

6. *WR*, 2 Jan. 2, 1868; *BDA*, Nov. 27, 1867; *LDC*, Nov. 29, 1867; Trent, *The Manliest Man*, 233; *DJM*, Dec. 7, 1867.

7. To date, only one published account of Andrew's life exists: Pearson, *Andrew*. Also see, however, Hamrogue, "John A. Andrew."

CHAPTER 1: WINDHAM ORIGINS

1. Traub, *John Quincy Adams*, 466–483, 520–21; *American Academy of Arts and Science Proceedings*, 310–17; Putnam, *Memoirs of the War of '61*, xi; *Lib*, Sept. 18, Oct., 1846; *TI*, May 29, 1873, carried an article from Wilson, *Rise and Fall of Slave Power in America*, 2:54–58; *BA*, Sept. 24, 25, 26, 1846; Richards, *Letters and Journals of Samuel Gridley Howe*, 2:239–48.

2. *American Academy of Arts and Science Proceedings*, 310–17; Putnam, *Memoirs of the War of '61*, xi; *EFA*, Oct. 7, 1846; *BI*, Sept. 30, 1846; *BA*, Sept. 24, 25, 26, Oct. 1, 1846; *Lib*, Oct. 23, Nov. 6, 1846; Richards, *Letters and Journals of Samuel Gridley Howe*, 2:239–48; Peterson, *The City-State of Boston*, 609–10; Masur, *Until Justice Be Done*, 132–34; Hall, *The Story of the Battle Hymn of the Republic*, 11–13.

3. *BET*, Sept. 23, 1846; *EFA*, Sept. 23, Oct. 7, 1846; *ZHWJ*, Sept. 23, 1846; *Lib*, Oct. 23, Nov. 6, 1846; *CR*, Sept. 17, 1846; *BA*, Sept. 24, 25, 26, Oct. 1, 24, 1846; *BI*, Sept. 30, 1856; Richards, *Letters and Journals of Samuel Gridley Howe*, 2:239-48; *Lib*, Oct. 23, Nov. 6, 1846; *TI*, May 29, 1873; Wilson, *Slave Power in America*, 2:54-58.

4. Boston Vigilance Committee Record Book and Papers of the Anti-Man Hunting League, MHS; Andrew, *Address of the Committee Appointed by a Public Meeting Held at Faneuil Hall*, 31; Putnam, *Memoirs of the War of '61*, xi; Sinha, *The Slave's Cause*, 392-93; Olsavsky, "Fire and Sword Will Affect More Good: Runaways"; Richards, *Letters and Journals of Samuel Gridley Howe*, 2: 239-48.

5. *Address of the Committee Appointed by a Public Meeting Held at Faneuil Hall, Sept. 24, 1846*; Traub, *Adams*, 520-527; *BWJ*, Sep. 16, 1856; Boston Vigilance Record Book and Boston Anti-Man Hunting League Papers, MHS; Richards, *Letters and Journals of Samuel Gridley Howe*, 2: 239-48.

6. Andrew, *Address of the Committee Appointed by a Public Meeting Held at Faneuil Hall*; *CR*, Oct. 17, 1846; Andrew to Sumner, Sept. 24, Oct. 30, 1846, Charles Sumner Papers, HU; BVC Record Book, and Boston Anti-Man Hunting League Papers, MHS; Richards, *Letters and Journals of Samuel Gridley Howe*, 2:239-48.

7. *BDA*, Aug. 11, 1891. Sanborn recalled that Andrew made the motion to appoint a forty-man vigilance committee; *BWJ*, Sept. 16, 1846; Pearson, *Andrew*, 1:4-43; McDougall, *Fugitive Slaves*, 40-41; Wilson, *Slave Power in America*, 2:54-57; Schwartz, *Samuel Gridley Howe*, 160-61; Andrew, *Address of the Committee Appointed by a Public Meeting Held at Faneuil Hall*; Siebert, "The Vigilance Committee of Boston," 1-45.

8. Stowe, *The Lives and Deeds of Our Self-Made Men*, 2:328; *WR*, Jan. 2, 1868; *BDA*, Nov. 27, 1867, Jan. 3, 1871; *LDC*, Nov. 29, 1867; *DJM*, Dec. 7, 1867.

9. *TI*, Feb. 23, 1871; *BDA*, Aug. 23, 1867.

10. *LLA*, Dec. 7, 1867; Chandler, *Memoir*, 11-13.

11. Alumni Biographical Files, BowC; *MF*, July 12, 1888, May 5, Aug. 25, 1892; Browne, "Governor Andrew," 249-77; *Private and Special Statues of the Commonwealth of Massachusetts from the Year 1780*, 1:323-25.

12. Whipple, *Eulogy*, 3; Chandler, *Memoir*, 11-14; Pearson, *Andrew*, 1-5; Browne, "Governor Andrew," 249-77; *HW*, June 23, 1888; *TCR*, May 9, 1918; Nason, *Discourse*, 14-21, 63-65; Alumni Biographical Files, BowC; Burnham, "Hon. John Albion Andrew," 1-12.

13. Whipple, *Eulogy*, 3; Browne, "Governor Andrew," 249-77; *HW*, June 23, 1888; Chandler, *Memoir*, 11-13; *TCR*, May 9, 1918; Nason, *Discourse*, 15-18, 63-65; Alumni Biographical Files, BowC; Burnham, "Hon. John Albion Andrew," 1-12.

14. Chandler, *Memoir*, 12-14; Pearson, *Andrew*, 1-5; Browne, "Governor Andrew," 249-77; *HW*, June 23, 1888; *TCR*, May 9, 1918; Nason, *Discourse*, 17-18, 63-65; Alumni Biographical Files, BowC; Burnham, "Hon. John Albion Andrew," 1-12.

15. Stone, "Sketch of John Albion Andrew," 1-30; Nason, *Discourse*, 16-18; Pearson, *Andrew*, 1:2-3, 12, 34.

16. Stowe, *Lives and Deeds*, 328; Pearson, *Andrew*, 3-5.

17. *BrAx*, Sept. 3, 1898; *TI*, Feb. 23, 1871; *LLA*, Dec. 7, 1867; *TYC*, Oct. 7, 1880. Still, only a few inches out of place, was "entirely out of place." Pearson, *Andrew*, 1:5; *BrAx*, Sept. 3, 1898.

18. *BrAx*, Sept. 3, 1898; *TI*, Feb 23, 1871; *CE*, July 30, 1898; Chandler, *Memoir*, 12-14; Nason, *Discourse*, 19; Alumni Biographical Files, BowC; *BET*, Aug. 6, 1892; Pearson, *Andrew*, 1:6-7.

19. Nason, *Discourse*, 17-18.

20. Alumni Biographical Files, BowC; *BET*, Aug. 6, 1892; Nason, *Discourse*, 17-19.

21. Alumni Biographical Files, BowC; *BET*, Aug. 6, 1892; Nason, *Discourse*, 17-19; Lewis, ed., *History of Gorham*, 283; Pierce, *A History of the Town of Gorham, Maine*, 97.

22. Chandler, *Memoir*, 116-19; Nason, *Discourse*, 20-22; Alumni Biographical Files, BowC; Pearson, *Andrew*, 1:13; Eliot, *Heralds of a Liberal Faith*, 3:358-62; Morison, *A Sermon*

Preached at the Installation of Rev. George W. Briggs, 59; *BR,* Sept. 11, 1840; *BDA,* June 1, 1893; "Education and Literary Institutions," 273; *MF,* Nov. 14, 1867; Packard, *History of Bowdoin College,* 355.

23. Pearson, *Andrew,* 1:3-8; Chandler, *Memoir,* 12-14; Nason, *Discourse,* 18-20; "Education and Literary Institutions," 273-78; Mellen, "The Marty's Triumph, the Buried, and Other Poems," 194-98; *MF,* Aug. 28, 1856, Nov. 14, 1867; Lewis, *History of Gorham,* 283; *Annual Report of the Maine Temperance Society, January 23, 1833,* 22; *BR,* Sept. 11, 1840.

24. Nason, *Discourse,* 20-22; Pearson, *Andrew,* 1:7-10; *LLA,* Dec. 7, 1867; Alumni Biographi. cal Files, BowC; John Andrew Scrapbook 10, Andrew Papers, MHS.

25. Pearson, *Andrew,* 1:12-13; Wilentz, *The Rise of American Democracy,* 254-33; Traub, *John Quincy Adams,* 315-27.

26. Griffin, *History of the Press of Maine,* 64-65; *Minutes of the General Conference of Maine at Their Annual Meeting in Gorham, June 1828; American Congregational Year-Book, for the Year 1858,* 5: xix; Chandler, *Memoir,* 24-25; Hamrogue, "John A. Andrew," 4; Pearson, *Andrew,* 1:10-14; *TCM,* Nov. 16, 1869, Sept. 2, 1873, Apr. 22, 1876; Merrill and Ruchames, *The Letters of William Lloyd Garrison,* 2:148, 516; *Lib,* June 22, 1833; Mayer, *All on Fire,* 106-13; Neal, *Portland Illustrated,* 86-87; *Maine Minutes,* 111-12.

27. Pearson, *Andrew,* 1:10-14; *TCM,* Nov. 16, 1869, Sept. 2, 1873, Apr. 22, 1876; Merrill and Ruchames, *Letters of William Lloyd Garrison,* 2:148, 516; *Lib,* June 22, 1833; Mayer, *All on Fire,* 106-13; Brooke, "There Is a North," 30-39.

28. Chandler, *Memoir,* 24-25; Hamrogue, "John A. Andrew," 4; Pearson, *Andrew,* 1:10-14; *TCM,* Nov. 16, 1869, Sept. 2, 1873, Apr. 22, 1876; Merrill and Ruchames, *Letters of William Lloyd Garrison,* 2:148, 516; *Lib,* June 22, 1833; Mayer, *All on Fire,* 106-113; Brooke, "There Is a North," 30-39.

29. Lewis, *History of Gorham,* 227-44; Hawley, *The Olden Time,* 22; Pearson, *Andrew,* 1:14-17; *MF,* Apr. 11, Aug. 1, 1840.

30. Lewis, *History of Gorham,* 227-44; Hawley, *The Olden Time,* 22; Pearson, *Andrew,* 1:14-17; *MF,* Apr. 11, Aug. 1, 1840.

31. Nason, *Discourse,* 22; *MF,* Apr. 11, 1840; "Education and Literary Institutions," 273-78; Lewis, *History of Gorham,* 698-99; Pierce, *An Address Delivered on the Twenty-sixth of May;* Beatley, "Memorial Day and the John A. Andrew Centenary"; Gara, "Cyrus Woodman," 9; *TCR,* Feb. 21, 1835; *MF,* Apr. 11, 1840; *EA,* Apr. 15, 1833; *TI,* Feb. 23, 1871; *Celebration of the One Hundred and Fiftieth Anniversary of Gorham,* 76; Emery, "Cyrus Woodman," 113-24.

32. Pearson, *Andrew,* 1:9-13; Andrew Scrapbook 10, Andrew Papers, MHS; Nason, *Discourse,* 20-22; Lewis, *History of Gorham,* 698-99; Pierce, *An Address Delivered on the Twenty-sixth of May;* Beatley, "Memorial Day and the John A. Andrew Centenary," 450; Gara, "Cyrus Woodman," 9; *TCR,* Feb. 21, 1835; *MF,* Apr. 11, 1840; *EA,* Apr. 15, 1833; *TI,* Feb. 23, 1871; *Celebration of the One Hundred and Fiftieth Anniversary of Gorham,* 76; Emery, "Cyrus Woodman," 113-24.

33. Pearson, *Andrew,* 1:10-13; *TCR,* June 13, 1912, May 9, 1918; Chandler, *Memoir,* 24-25; Alumni Biological Files, BowC; *BR,* Sept. 11, 1840; *BDA,* June 1, 1893; "Education and Literary Institutions," 273; *MF,* Nov. 14, 1867; *BDA,* July 10, 1868.

34. Beatley, "Memorial Day and the John A. Andrew Centenary," 450.

35. Andrew to Woodman, Oct. 13, 1833, Cyrus Woodman Papers, SHSW; Pearson, *Andrew,* 1:14-15; Usher, "Cyrus Woodman," 393-412; *Catalogue of the Officers and Students of Bowdoin College and the Medical School of Maine, 1836,* and *Catalogue of the Officers and Students of Bowdoin College and the Medical School of Maine, 1837,* 14; Woodman to Mrs. Andrew, Nov. 10, 1867, Andrew Papers, MHS; Deane, "Memoir of Cyrus Woodman," 345; Gara, "Cyrus Woodman," 9-10; *Celebration of the One Hundred and Fiftieth Anniversary of Gorham,* 76; Gara, *Westernized Yankee,* 6-7.

CHAPTER 2: THE BOWDOIN COLLEGE YEARS

1. NWR, July 19, 1834; BR, July 26, 1834; Lib, July 26, 1834; Mayer, All on Fire, 150–167; Wilentz, The Rise of American Democracy, 330–403.
2. The Opinion of Judge Story in the Case of William Allen vs. Joseph McKeen; Pearson, Andrew, 1:15–18; Packard, History of Bowdoin College, 11; Hatch, History of Bowdoin College, 47–84; Gara, "Cyrus Woodman," 8–9; Catalogue of the Officers and Students of Bowdoin College and the Medical School of Maine, 1834; Andrew to Cyrus Woodman, Feb. 5, 1834, Woodman Papers, SHSW; Students Admitted into Bowdoin College, 1802–67, Logbook, 1802–1867, Office of Student Records/Registrar: Matriculation Books, vol. 1, BowC. Founded in 1794, before Maine was a state, Bowdoin had been chartered as a private corporation by Massachusetts but when Maine became a state in 1820, the Democratic legislature passed an act that gave the governor the power to appoint Bowdoin's trustees and overseers.
3. Basbanes, Cross of Snow, 19–40; Underwood, Henry Wadsworth Longfellow, 43–66; "Bowdoin College," TAMUEK; "Bowdoin College," Scribner's Monthly, 47–59.
4. Hatch, History of Bowdoin College, 47–84; Catalogue of the Officers and Students of Bowdoin College and the Medical School of Maine, 1834, 17–20; "Bowdoin College," TAMUEK; Abbott, New England and Her Institutions, 151–63.
5. Newspaper clippings, Andrew File, BowC; Catalogue of the Officers and Students of Bowdoin College and the Medical School of Maine, 1834, 23.
6. "Bowdoin College," TAMUEK; Longfellow, Life of Henry Wadsworth Longfellow, 1:178–202; Abbott, New England and Her Institutions, 151–55; BDWC, Feb. 6, 1888; TYC, Oct. 7, 1880; Pearson, Andrew, 1:5; Gara, "Cyrus Woodman," 12; Records of the Praying Circle, 1832–1847, 64–68, BowC; Hatch, History of Bowdoin College, 34, 278; Catalogue of the Officers and Students of Bowdoin College and the Medical School of Maine, 1834, 10; "Bowdoin College," Scribner's Monthly, 47–59; Chandler, Memoir, 15; Smyth, Three Discourses Upon the Religious History of Bowdoin College, 77; BDA, Oct. 11, 1886.
7. TYC, Oct. 7, 1880; Pearson, Andrew, 1:5; Gara, "Cyrus Woodman," 12; Records of the Praying Circle, 1832–1847, 64–68, BowC; Hatch, History of Bowdoin College, 34, 278; Catalogue of the Officers and Students of Bowdoin College and the Medical School of Maine, 1834, 10; "Bowdoin College," TAMUEK; "Bowdoin College," Scribner's Monthly, 47–59; Chandler, Memoir, 15; Smyth, Three Discourses Upon the Religious History of Bowdoin College, 77; BDA, Oct. 11, 1866.
8. BDA, Oct. 11, 1886; Andrew Scrapbook 10, Andrew Papers, MHS; MDS, June 28, 1875; BDG, Oct. 12, 1886.
9. Gara, "Cyrus Woodman," 14–16; Nason, Discourse, 23; Autograph Album of Jordan G. Ferguson, BowC; Catalogue of the Officers and Students of Bowdoin College and the Medical School of Maine, 1834, 7; BDA, Oct. 11, 1886; MDS, June 28, 1875; Hatch, History of Bowdoin College, 324; Andrew Scrapbook 10, Andrew Papers, MHS; "Bowdoin College," TAMUEK; "Bowdoin College," Scribner's Monthly, 47–59; Gara, "Cyrus Woodman," 10–11.
10. Nason, Discourse, 23; Alumni Biographical Files, BowC; MDS, June 28, 1875; Mitchell, Elijah Kellogg, 27–40; Michener, "Rivals and Partners," 214–30.
11. Pearson, Andrew, 1:15–18; Michener, "Rivals and Partners," 214–30; Gara, "Woodman," 9–15; Nason, Discourse, 22–23; newspaper clippings in the Andrew Files, see this file for the poem: Alumni Biographical Files, BowC; Hatch, History of Bowdoin College, 290–92; Catalogue of the Officers and Students of Bowdoin College and the Medical School of Maine, 1834, 3; "Bowdoin College," TAMUEK; "Bowdoin College," Scribner's Monthly, 47–59; NYT, Oct. 17, 1886; MDS, June 25, 1875; VC, Aug. 30, 1837.
12. "Bowdoin College," Scribner's Monthly, 47–59; NYT, Oct. 17, 1886; MDS, June 25, 1875; VC, Aug. 30, 1837; BDA, Oct. 11, 1886; MDS, June 28, 1875; Hatch, History of Bowdoin College, 278.
13. BDA, July 27, 1887, taken from the BrT, July 22, 1887; BDA, Oct. 11, 1886; Lib, Oct. 11, Nov. 1, 14, 1834, Mar. 4, 1864; Pearson, Andrew, 1:19–20; E. Bond to Cyrus Woodman in

the Andrew Scrapbooks, MHS; Browne, "Governor Andrew," 249–76; *Catalogue of the Officers and Students of Bowdoin College and the Medical School of Maine, 1834,* 19–21; MDS, June 28, 1875; "Bowdoin College," *Scribner's Monthly,* 47–59; Hatch, *History of Bowdoin College,* 290–92; Mayer, *All on Fire,* 190–94.

14. BDA, July 27, 1887; BrT, July 22, 1897; Pearson, *Andrew,* 1:20–21; Lib, Oct. 11, Nov. 1, 14, 1834, Mar. 4, 1864; "Bowdoin College," *Scribner's Monthly,* 47–59; Hatch, *History of Bowdoin College,* 290–92; Mayer, *All on Fire,* 190–94.

15. Pearson, *Andrew,* 1:20–21; Lib, Nov. 1, 14, 1834, Mar. 4, 1864.

16. Newspaper clippings, Andrew File, BowC; BDA, July 27, 1887; MDS, June 28, 1875; Andrew Scrapbook 10, Andrew Papers, MHS; Lib, Nov. 1, 14, 1834; Pearson, *Andrew,* 1:19–20; BrT, July 22, 1887; Browne, "Governor Andrew," 249–76; *Catalogue of the Officers and Students of Bowdoin College, and the Medical School of Maine 1836,* 19–21; BDA, Oct. 11, 1886; MDS, June 28, 1875; "Bowdoin College," *Scribner's Monthly,* 47–59.

17. TCM, Nov. 16, 1869; Clarke, *Memorial and Biographical Sketches,* 7; newspaper clippings in the Andrew File, BowC; BDA, Jan. 3, 1871.

18. Pearson, *Andrew,* 1:16–17; newspaper clippings in the Andrew File, BowC; Alumni Biographical Files, BowC; BC, Feb. 22, 1836; NYS, Feb. 25, 1836; NHS, Feb. 27, 1836.

19. Andrew to Cyrus Woodman, May 17, Nov. 25, 1836, Apr. 21, Aug. 1, 1837, Woodman Papers, SHSW; Gara, "Cyrus Woodman," 16–21; Nason, *Discourse,* 2–25; Deane, "Memoir of Cyrus Woodman," 345; BP, Nov. 12, 1839.

20. *Catalogue of the Officers and Students of Bowdoin College and the Medical School of Maine, 1836,* 19–21.

21. Hatch, *History of Bowdoin College,* 278–79, 292; "Bowdoin College," TAMUEK; "Bowdoin College," *Scribner's Monthly,* 47–59; Dole, *Sketches of the History of Windham,* 117; Pearson, *Andrew,* 1:17–19; Shrady, *Medical Record,* 626; Packard, *History of Bowdoin College,* 497–98.

22. Hatch, *History of Bowdoin College,* 278–79; Records of the Praying Circle, Apr. 1837, BowC; "Bowdoin College," TAMUEK; "Bowdoin College," *Scribner's Monthly,* 47–59; Dole, *Sketches of the History of Windham,,* 117; Pearson, *Andrew,* 1:17–19; Shrady, *Medical Record,* 626; Packard, *History of Bowdoin College,* 497–98; Hatch, *History of Bowdoin College,* 278–79, 292.

23. NYT, June 23, 1875; MDS, June 28, 1875; BDA, Oct. 11,1886; BR, Sept. 8, 1837; BC, Aug. 10, 1837.

24. *Ceremonials at the Unveiling of the Statute of Gov. John A. Andrew,* 28; Governor William Claflin gave this quote that appears in Pearson, *Andrew,* 1:21–22; Chandler, *Memoir,* 16; Nason, *Discourse,* 23–25.

25. *Ceremonials at the Unveiling of the Statute of Gov. John A. Andrew,* 28; Pearson, *Andrew,* 1:21–22; Chandler, *Memoir,* 16; Nason, *Discourse,* 23–25; Ammi R. Bradbury Papers, Biographical Information, AAS; *Catalogue of the Officers and Students of Bowdoin College and the Medical School of Maine,,* 1834, 7; *History of Penobscot County, Maine,* 729; *General Catalogue of Bowdoin College,* 99.

26. Pearson, *Andrew,* 1:21–25; BR, Sept. 8, 1837; ZHWJ, Sept. 20, 1837; NYT, June 23, 1875; MDS, June 28, 1875; BDA, Oct. 11, 1866.

27. Gara, "Cyrus Woodman," 22–23; NYT, June 23, 1875.

CHAPTER 3: THE POOR MAN'S LAWYER

1. Andrew to Woodman, Aug. 1, 1837, Woodman Papers, SHSW; Pearson, *Andrew,* 1:23–24; BR, Dec. 30, 1847; Deane, "Memoir of Cyrus Woodman," 345; Gara, "Cyrus Woodman," 21–23; Emery, "Cyrus Woodman," 113–25; Wheelwright, "Hon. John Forrester Andrew," 351–52; Perley, *History of Boxford,* 29, 74; Reno, *Memoirs of the Judiciary,* 3:377–80.

2. BA, June 22, 1837; BC, June 22, July 17, 1837; Mayer, *All on Fire,* 200–222; Wilentz, *The Rise of American Democracy,* 403–83; O'Conner, *Boston Irish,* 49; Cullen, *The Story of the*

Irish in Boston, 71-73. In her work, *Force and Freedom*, Kellie Carter Jackson charts the rise of African American radicals who led protest movements, which often led to violence through resistance against the law.

3. *BA*, June 22, 1837; *BC*, June 22, July 17, 1837; Mayer, *All on Fire*, 200-222; Wilentz, *The Rise of American Democracy*, 403-83; O'Conner, *Boston Irish*, 49; Cullen, *The Story of the Irish in Boston*, 71-73. In her work, *Force and Freedom*, Kellie Carter Jackson charts the rise of African American radicals who led protest movements, which often led to violence through resistance against the law.

4. Reynolds, *John Brown Abolitionist*, 64-65; *BC*, Nov. 30, 1837; *BA*, Dec. 6, 1837; *Lib*, Dec. 8, 1837; *VC*, Dec. 4, 6, 1837; Howe, *The Political Culture of the American Whigs*, 65-67; Wilentz, *The Rise of American Democracy*, 466-69.

5. Nason, *Discourse*, 16; Stearns, *Cambridge Sketches*, 242; Cyrus Woodman to Mrs. Andrew, Nov. 10, 1867, Andrew Papers, MHS; Whipple, *Eulogy*, 5; *BDG*, Oct. 12, 1886; Pearson, *Andrew*, 1:24-25; Winsor, *The Memorial History of Boston*, 4:69-235.

6. *Memorial Biographies of the New England Historic Genealogical Society*, 1:410-422; "Obituary Notice for Henry Holton Fuller," 354-60; Nason, *Discourse*, 26; "Historical Notices of Thomas Fuller and his Descendants," 351-60; Clarke, *Memorial and Biographical Sketches*, 7; Livingston, *Biographical Sketches of Distinguished Americans*, 121-33; *EOS*, May 23, 1885; *BA*, Aug. 9, 1836, Feb. 27, 1838.

7. Chandler, *Memoir*, 16-17, 75-80, 125-26; Pearson, *Andrew*, 1:24-25; Deane, "Memoir of Cyrus Woodman," 345-50; Gara, "Cyrus Woodman," 21-27; Emery, "Cyrus Woodman," 113-25; "Obituary Notice for Henry Holton Fuller," 351-60; Clarke, *Memorial and Biographical Sketches*, 7; Nason, *Discourse*, 27; *Memorial Biographies of the New England Historic Genealogical Society*, 1:410-422; Stearns, *Cambridge Sketches*, 242-43; Woodman to Mrs. Andrew, Nov. 10, 1867, Andrew Papers, MHS; Andrew to Cyrus Woodman, Apr. 5, 1841, Woodman Papers, SHSW; Gara, *Westernized Yankee*, 13-14.

8. Cumbler, *From Abolition to Rights for All*, 6-7, 52-55; Andrew to Cyrus Woodman, Jan. 30, 1842, Woodman Papers, SHSW; *BDG*, Oct. 12, 1888.

9. Lerner, *The Grimké Sisters from South Carolina*, 3-11; Dalton, Wirkkala, and Thomas, *Leading the Way*, 131-33; Channing, *Memoir of William Ellery Channing*, 3:199-200; *BDA*, Dec. 2, 1837; *Lib*, Feb. 25, 1837, Jan. 19, 26, Mar. 2, June 21, 1838; Mayer, *All on Fire*, 220-55.

10. Mayer, *All on Fire*, 220-55; *Lib*, Oct. 22, Feb. 25, June 16, 1837, Feb. 16, 1838; Lerner, *The Grimké Sisters from South Carolina*, 3-11, 85-155.

11. Chandler, *Memoir*, 18; *EOS*, May 23, 1885; *BC*, May 25, 1840; "Historical Notices of Thomas Fuller and his Descendants," 354-60; "Obituary Notice for Henry Holton Fuller," 351-60; Nason, *Discourse*, 29-31, 48; *BDA*, Oct. 31, 1867, Oct. 11, 1886; *BT*, Oct. 31, 1867; Stearns, *Cambridge Sketches*, 243; Andrew to Woodman, Jan. 30, May 27, Sept. 7, 1842, Woodman Papers, SHSW; *Memorial Biographies of the New England Historic Genealogical Society*, 1:410-422; Whipple, *Eulogy*, 5; *BP*, May 25, Sept. 7, 1842; Dickerson, *Margaret Fuller*, 223; Bailey, Viens, and Wright, *Margaret Fuller and Her Circles*, 128-47.

12. Stearns, *Cambridge Sketches*, 244-45, 256; Chandler, *Memoir*, 16-18; Pearson, *Andrew*, 1:25-26; "Obituary Notice for Henry Holton Fuller," 354-60; Nason, *Discourse*, 29-31; *BDA*, Oct. 31, 1867, Oct. 11, 1886; *BT*, Oct. 31, 1867.

13. Chandler, *Memoir*, 18; *EOS*, May 23, 1885; *BC*, May 25, 1840; Stearns, *Cambridge Sketches*, 244-45, 256; Pearson, *Andrew*, 1:25-26; "Obituary Notice for Henry Holton Fuller," 354-60; Nason, *Discourse*, 29-31; *BDA*, Oct. 31, 1867, Oct. 11, 1886; *BT*, Oct. 31, 1867; Andrew to Cyrus Woodman, Jan. 19, May 20, 1840, Woodman Papers, SHSW.

14. *EOS*, May 23, 1885; Pearson, *Andrew*, 1:27; Andrew to Cyrus Woodman, Jan. 30, 1842, Woodman Papers, SHSW.

15. Andrew to Woodman, Nov. 26, 1844, Woodman Papers, SHSW; Pearson, *Andrew*, 1:27.

16. Chandler, *Memoir*, 83-84; Pearson, *Andrew*, 1:27-28; Clarke, *Memorial Sketches*, 7; *BC*, Mar. 30, 1843; *The Senate of the Commonwealth of Massachusetts*, "Public Officers

Section," 14. In March 1843, the governor appointed him a Suffolk County Justice of the Peace.

17. John Andrew Personal Account Book, 1842–1845, Andrew Papers, MHS; Chandler, *Memoir*, 19, 82–83; Pearson, *Andrew*, 1:28–30; *EOS*, May 23, 1885; *BDG*, Oct. 12, 1886.

18. Clarke, *Memorial Sketches*, 7; Hale, *James Freeman Clarke*, 167–244; *BDA*, Jan. 3, 1871.

19. Andrew to Cyrus Woodman, Jan. 30, 1842, Andrew Papers, HU; Pearson, *Andrew*, 1:31–32; Hale, *James Freeman Clarke*, 313; Stange, *Patterns of Antislavery Among American Unitarians*, 110; Hale, *James Freeman Clarke*, 167–244; Chandler, *Memoir*, 21; *EOS*, May 23, 1885.

20. Andrew to Cyrus Woodman, Jan. 30, 1842, Andrew Papers, HU; Pearson, *Andrew*, 1:32–33, Andrew joined this church in September 1841. Hartman and Wells, "John Albion Andrew of Massachusetts," 324–28; Hale, *James Freeman Clarke*, 167–244; Knickerbocker, *Bard of the Bethel*, 153–54; 191–92.

21. *BH*, Dec. 16, 1919; Hartman and Wells, "John Albion Andrew of Massachusetts," 324–28; Clarke, *Memorial and Biographical Sketches*, 8–9; Andrew to Clarke, Jan. 30, 1842, James Freeman Clarke Papers, HU; Mendelsohn, *Channing, the Reluctant Rebel*, 203–22; Pearson, *Andrew*, 1:34; Hamrogue, "John A. Andrew," 6.

22. *BDA*, Jan. 15, 1868; *LGL*, Mar. 14, 1840; *AG*, Mar. 17, 1840; Mott, "The Eloquence of Father Taylor," 102–13; Dana, *Two Years before the Mast*, 82, 117, 128; Stange, *Patterns of Antislavery Among American Unitarians*, 110; Hartman and Wells, "John Albion Andrew of Massachusetts," 324–28; Haven and Russell, *Father Taylor*, 108–73; *SR*, July 26, 1906; *Twentieth Annual Report of the Boston Port Society*; see also various *Annual Reports of the Boston Port Society, 1846–1864*, in the MHS; *TUM*, Jan. 21 1843; *ZHWJ*, Apr. 20, 1871; Clarke, *Memorial and Biographical Sketches*, 9–10; Knickerbocker, *Bard of Bethel*, 153–93; Mendelsohn, *Channing, the Reluctant Rebel*, 248–75; Cooke, *Unitarianism in America*, 449; "Intelligence," 125; Woodson, *The History of the Negro Church*, 178–82; Spurgeon, *Broad Churchism*, 1–24; *TCR*, Oct. 30, 1847; *BA*, Jan. 10, 1843.

23. Mott, "The Eloquence of Father Taylor," 102–13; Dana, *Two Years Before the Mast*, 117; Stange, *Patterns of Antislavery Among American Unitarians*, 110; Hartman and Wells, "John Albion Andrew of Massachusetts," 324–28; Haven and Russell, *Father Taylor*, 108–73; *SR*, July 26, 1906; *Twentieth Annual Report of the Boston Port Society, Boston*, 1849; *Annual Reports of the Boston Port Society, 1846–1864*, in the MHS; *TUM* Jan. 21, 1843; *ZHWJ*, Apr. 20, 1871; Clarke, *Memorial and Biographical Sketches*, 9–10; Knickerbocker, *Bard of Bethel*, 153–93; Mendelsohn, *Channing, the Reluctant Rebel*, 248–75; Cooke, *Unitarianism in America*, 449; "Intelligence," 125; Woodson, *The History of the Negro Church*, 178–82; Spurgeon, *Broad Churchism*, 1–24; *TCR*, Oct. 30, 1847; *BA*, Jan. 10, 1843.

24. Kantrowitz, *More Than Freedom*, 74; *Lib*, Oct. 28, Nov. 4, 11, 25, Dec. 16, 1842, Feb. 3, 1843; *EFA*, Nov. 3, 17, Dec. 1, 1842; *NYOC*, Nov. 26, 1842; *Acts and Resolves Passed by the Legislature of Massachusetts*, 1843, chap. 69, 33; *BC*, Nov. 7, 1842; *BA*, Nov. 22, 1842; Mayer, *All on Fire*, 316–20; Archer, *Jim Crow North*, 119.

25. *EFA*, Nov. 3, 17, Dec. 1, 1842; *Lib*, Nov. 4, 11, 1842; *BC*, Nov. 7, 1842; *BA*, Nov. 22, 1842.

26. Chandler, *Memoir*, 145–90; *NA*, Sept. 13, 1844; *BA*, Sept. 11, 1844; *EFA*, Dec. 1, 1842; *EOS*, May 23, 1885; Kantrowitz, *More Than Freedom*, 75–83; Archer, *Jim Crow North*, 112–19.

27. *EOS*, May 23, 1885; Andrew to Cyrus Woodman, Apr. 5, 1841, and an undated letter, 1841, Woodman Papers, SHSW.

28. *BH*, Dec. 16, 1919; Browne, *Sketch of the Official Life of John A. Andrew*, 19–21; Clarke, *Memorial and Biographical Sketches*, 10–12; Stearns, *Cambridge Sketches*, 259–260; *BDA*, June 9, 1888; *BH*, Dec. 16, 1919; Howe, *Reminiscences*, 261–62; Pearson, *Andrew*, 1:36–37; Parker, "A Discourse on the Transient and Permanent in Christianity," *TCR*, July 31, 1841; *BO*, July 31, 1841; *TBQR*, 4 (Oct. 1841): 436–45; Peabody, *Memoir of James Freeman Clarke*, 10; Chadwick, *Theodore Parker*, 144–45; "James Freeman Clarke to Mr. Shippen, July 13, 1886"; Capper and Wright, *Transient and Permanent*, 81.

29. *Trial of Orrin De Wolf for the Murder of Wm. Stiles*, 1–16; *MF*, June 26, 1845; *WS*, June 25, 1845; Rogers, *Murder and the Death Penalty in Massachusetts*, 80–84.

30. Chandler, *Memoir*, 81–82; Hamilton, *Memoirs, Speeches, and Writings of Robert Rantoul, Jr.*, 2–50; Pearson, *Andrew*, 1:30–31; Court of Common Pleas, Suffolk County, Oct. 1841–Oct. 1851, MJA, these records contain several citations for Andrew appearing before the court either with Chandler and Rantoul or by himself. The spelling of his name however was listed as John A. Andrews. Also see Boston City directory for 1841 that lists his name correctly and lists him as counsellor, 19 Court. See also the Suffolk Civil and Criminal Dockets, and the Boston Municipal Court, Criminal Court; Dray, *There Is Power in a Union*, 50–55; PF, Aug. 13, 1845; John Andrew to Francis Jackson, Dec. 2, 1845, Anti-Slavery Collection, BPL; Hamrogue, "John A. Andrew," 5; *TUM*, Sept. 6, 1845; EOS, May 23, 1885; Formisano, *Transformation of Political Culture*, 320.

31. Pearson, *Andrew*, 1:26–27; EOS, May 23, 1885; *Lib*, Jan. 31, 1845; PF, Jan. 22, 1845, Feb. 25, 1846, Feb. 3, 1847, Feb. 1, 1850; BA, Oct. 10, 1842; BP, Feb. 2, 1846; Emerson, Channing, and Clarke, *Memoirs of Margaret Fuller Ossoli*, 1:370–71; Fuller, *Recollections of Richard Frederick Fuller*, 33–77, 81–84; Hamilton, *Memoirs, Speeches, and Writings of Robert Rantoul, Jr.*, 27–30; McKivigan, *Forgotten Firebrand*, 94; Greenwood and Harris, *An Introduction to the Unitarian and Universalist Traditions*, 77; PF, Apr. 2, 1845, Mar. 18, 1846, Sept. 1, 1848. Charles Spear was the proprietor and editor, and his brother John Murray Spear was the associate editor. It was issued initially on January 1, 1845, under the radical masthead *The Hangman*, which violated public sensibilities, so they changed the name at the end of the year to the *Prisoner's Friend*. The *New York Tribune* applauded their decision to discard the "uncouth and barbarous name," to one that better accorded the paper's spirit; Rogers, *Murder and the Death Penalty in Massachusetts*, 80–102.

32. Taylor, *Legendary Locals of Beacon Hill Massachusetts*, 37–52; Whipple, *Eulogy*, 6–8; NYT, Aug. 14, 1904; Davis, *Bench and Bar of the Commonwealth of Massachusetts*, 1:346–47; Stackpole, "The Early Days of Charles Sumner," 405–18; Pearson, *Andrew*, 1:26–27; SEP, Oct. 20, 1877.

33. *Lib*, May 9, 23, 30, June 20, 1845; BA, Mar. 8, 1845; Mayer, *All on Fire*, 334–75; Blight, *Frederick Douglass*, 110–39; Wilentz, *The Rise of American Democracy*, 570–81; Howe, *What Hath God Wrought*, 699; Adams, *Memoirs of John Quincy Adams*, 12:171; Traub, *John Quincy Adams*, 498–99.

34. Palmer, *The Selected Letters of Charles Sumner*, 1-154-77; Donald, *Charles Sumner and the Coming of the Civil War*, 140–42; Richards, *Letters and Journals of Samuel Gridley Howe*, 2:191–92; Holt, *The Rise and Fall of the American Whig Party*, 226–27, 340–41; Howe, *The Political Culture of the American Whigs*, 65–95; For a great work on what it meant to be conservative in the North prior to the Civil War, see Smith, *The Stormy Present*; Mayer, *All on Fire*, 334–43; Sinha, *The Slave's Cause*, 392–93; Wilentz, *The Rise of American Democracy*, 488–89; ER, Nov. 8, 1848; BA, Jan. 13, 1844, June 23, 1847, June 12, 1849. Andrew served as the treasurer for the society; *Report of the Boston Society for Aiding Discharged Convicts*, 1–15; *Second Annual Report of the Boston Society for Aiding Discharged Convicts*, 5–32; PF, May 13, 1846, Mar. 10, 24, 1847; *Lib*, July 31, 1846; EFA, May 26, June 2, 1847.

CHAPTER 4: THE EMERGING POLITICIAN

1. *Congressional Globe*, 29th Congress, 1st session, 1213–1217, 30th Congress, 1st session, 304; CC, Aug. 20, 1846; NA, Aug. 17, 1846; Nevins, *Ordeal of the Union*, 1:9; Wilentz, *The Rise of American Democracy*, 594–97; Potter, *The Impending Crisis*, 20–21.

2. BP, Sept. 10, Oct. 29, 1846; NWR, Nov. 21, 1846; BA, Sep. 9, 12, 19, Oct. 31, Nov. 4, 6, 1846; EFA, Oct. 14, 1846; Mayer, *All on Fire*, 348–49; 314–16.

3. Pierce, *Memoir and Letters of Charles Sumner*, 3:135–36; CC, Oct. 12, 1848; BP, Sept. 10, Oct. 29, 1846; NWR, Nov. 21, 1846; BA, Sep. 9, 12, 19, Oct. 31, Nov. 4, 6, 1846; EFA, Oct. 14, 1846; BP, Oct. 29, 1846; Pearson, *Andrew*, 1:43–44; TI, May 2, 1872; *Lib*, Nov. 6, 1846; Minutes of the Rally of Independent Whigs at the Tremont Temple, November 5, 1846, Andrew Papers, MHS; BDA, July 27, 1846, Oct. 30, 1846, Sept. 14, 1848; BDW, July 16, 22 1846, Nov. 2, 1846; Cumbler, *From Abolition to Rights for All*, 64–65; BA, Apr. 18, 1844,

Jan. 29, 1845; Palmer, *Selected Letters of Sumner*, 1:169–79; Donald, *Charles Sumner and the Coming of the Civil War*, 144–51; Holt, *Rise and Fall of the American Whig Party*, 226–27, 340–41.

4. Andrew to Sumner, Oct. 30, 1846, Sumner Papers, HU; Pearson, *Andrew*, 1:44, Pierce, *Memoir and Letters of Charles Sumner*, 3:136; Cumbler, *From Abolition to Rights for All*, 65.

5. *BChr*, Oct. 6, 1847; *CWHP*, Oct. 7, 1847; Palmer, *Selected Letters of Sumner*, 1:177–79; *BDA*, Oct. 28, 30, 1846; *BA*, Oct. 28, 30, 1846; *BDW*, 2 Nov. 1846; Minutes of the Rally of Independent Whigs at the Tremont Temple," Nov. 5, 1846, Andrew Papers, MHS; Hamrogue, "John A. Andrew," 18; Pierce, *Memoir and Letters of Charles Sumner*, 3:130–32, 136–37; Pearson, *Andrew*, 1:39–43; *NYE*, Oct. 1, 1846; *Lib*, Oct. 23, 1846, Nov. 1, 1850; *TCR*, Sept. 17, 1846; *NYTrib*, Nov. 1, 1850; Siebert, *The Vigilance Committee of Boston*, 1–23; *BWJ*, Sept. 16, 1846; Trent, *The Manliest Man*, 158.

6. *NYE*, Oct. 1, 1846; *Lib*, Oct. 23, 1846, Nov. 1, 1850; *TCR*, Sept. 17, 1846; Pierce, *Memoir and Letters of Charles Sumner*, 3:130–32; Siebert, *The Vigilance Committee of Boston*, 1–23; *BWJ*, Sept. 16, 1846; Trent, *The Manliest Man*, 158; Pearson, *Andrew*, 1:39–43

7. *NYE*, Oct. 1, 1846; *Lib*, Oct. 23, 1846, Nov. 1, 1850; *TCR*, Sept. 17, 1846; Pierce, *Memoir and Letters of Charles Sumner*, 3:130–32; Siebert, *The Vigilance Committee of Boston*, 1–23; *BWJ*, Sept. 16, 1846; Trent, *The Manliest Man*, 158; Pearson, *Andrew*, 1:39–43.

8. *EFA*, May 12, 1847; *TF*, Dec. 19, 1896; Clarke, *Memorial and Biographical Sketches*, 15–17; Robboy and Robboy, "Lewis Hayden," 591–613; *BDG*, Apr. 7, 8, 1889; Apr. 11, Sept. 24, 1890, Feb. 11, 1973; *BP*, Apr. 13, 1889; Pearson, *Andrew*, 1:42–43; Mayer, *All on Fire*, 364–70; *DIO*, Apr. 8, 1889; Kantrowitz, *More Than Freedom*, 106; *Lib*, Oct. 24, 1845; John Andrew to Francis Jackson, Dec. 2, 1845, Anti-Slavery Collection, BPL; Prentice, *The Life of Gilbert Haven*, 308–10.

9. Andrew to Woodman, Sept. 14, 1846, Dec. 2, 1846; Woodman Papers, SHSW; Andrew to Sumner, Oct. 30, 1846, Sumner Papers, HU; Donald, *Charles Sumner and the Coming of the Civil War*, 147–51; Pearson, *Andrew*, 1:36.

10. Andrew to Cyrus Woodman, Sept. 14, 1846, Woodman Papers; Chandler, *Memoir*, 30–87; Hamrogue, "John A. Andrew," 6; *BA*, Nov. 21, 1846; Cumbler, *From Abolition to Rights for All*, 64–65.

11. Andrew to Cyrus Woodman, Sept. 14, 1846, Woodman Papers, SHSW; Chandler, *Memoir*, 30–87; Hamrogue, "John A. Andrew," 6; *BA*, Nov. 21, 1846.

12. *BA*, Nov. 9, 1846; Donald, *Charles Sumner and the Coming of the Civil War*, 154–55; Andrew to NA, perhaps Woodman, Feb. 8, 1847, John Andrew Papers, HU; *BA*, May 28, 1846; Pierce, *Memoir and Letters of Charles Sumner*, 1:161; Rayback, *Free Soil*, 81–93; Richards, *Letters and Journals of Samuel Gridley Howe*, 2:122; Tharp, *Three Saints and a Sinner*, 80; Donald, *Charles Sumner and the Coming of the Civil War*, 63–64.

13. Donald, *Charles Sumner and the Coming of the Civil War*, 63–64, 154–55; Andrew to N.A, perhaps Woodman, Feb. 8, 1847, John A. Andrew Papers, HU; *BA*, May 28, 1846; Pierce, *Memoir and Letters of Charles Sumner*, 1:161; Rayback, *Free Soil*, 81–93; Richards, *Letters and Journals of Samuel Gridley Howe*, 2:122; Tharp, *Three Saints and a Sinner*, 80.

14. Schwartz, *Samuel Gridley Howe*, 160–65; Pearson, *Andrew*, 1:44–45; *TI*, May 2, 1872; Julian, "Political Recollections and Notes," 321; Luthin, "Abraham Lincoln and the Massachusetts Whigs in 1848," 619–32; *BDA*, Oct. 30, Nov. 2, 1846; Donald, *Charles Sumner and the Coming of the Civil War*, 149–51; Rayback, *Free Soil*, 80–89; Harrold, *American Abolitionism*, 128–29; Sewell, *Ballots for Freedom*, 140; Remini, *Daniel Webster*, 600–609; Davis, "Liberty Before Union," 15–20.

15. Andrew to Clarke, Aug. 3, Sept. 9, 1847, James Freeman Clarke, Additional Correspondence, HU; Kantrowitz, *More Than Freedom*, 106–110.

16. Randolph, *From Slave Cabin to the Pulpit*, 28–34; *Lib*, Sept. 24, Oct. 15, 1847, May 18, 1855; Jones, *No Right to an Honest Living*, 28–31, 43–44, 130–33, 371–72. Jones notes that Andrew initially had an unfavorable impression of the new arrivals. She quotes from the *Christian Register* from June 1, 1867, in which Andrew remarked that he thought

"most of them looked to be a very crooked sort of old men. And those who didn't claim to be more than 50, had a way of lifting up their feet in the morning and putting then down in the afternoon; every one was crooked in the back except Peter." By using the word "crooked" Jones admits that Andrew might not have been referring to them negatively as characters but rather as physically disabled from working in the field. Andrew and Randolph became good friends, assisted Randolph legally, and kept up with the Edloe group. Yet, in May 1867, Andrew allowed to some Unitarian clergymen at a Boston meeting that he was not initially impressed by their appearance but over the years witnessed their adjustment to urban industrial life and that not only were they hard workers but also that many of them owned their own homes.

17. Trent, *The Manliest Man*, 174; *TCR*, July 19, 1900; Chadwick, *Theodore Parker*, 237–55; Thomas, *James Freeman Clarke*, 98–99; Thomas, "The Conversational Club," 296–98; *Lib*, Sept. 28, 1860; *BI*, June 23, 1869.

18. Traub, *John Quincy Adams*, 525–29; Sumner, *The Works of Charles Sumner*, 2:53; Holt, *The Rise and Fall of the American Whig Party*, 340–82; Wilentz, *The Rise of American Democracy*, 601–20; *NYH*, July 1, 1848; *Lib*, June 23, July 7, 1848; *ER*, Sept. 20, 1848; Davis, "Liberty Before Union," 15–22.

19. Sumner, *The Works of Charles Sumner*, 2:53; *BP*, June 29, 1848; *Reunion of the Free-Soilers of 1848*, 15–17, 54–56; Holt, *The Rise and Fall of the American Whig Party*, 340–82; Rayback, *Free Soil*, 205; Wilentz, *The Rise of American Democracy*, 601–20; *NYH*, July 1, 1848; *Lib*, June 23, July 7, 1848; *ER*, Sept. 20, 1848; Wall, *Reminiscences of Worcester*, 286–87; Gatell, "Conscience and Judgment," 18–45; Brooke, *"There Is a North,"* 48–54.

20. Howe, *Reminiscences*, 260–61; *BA*, Sept. 8, 1854; Trent, *The Manliest Man*, 166; Richards, *Letters and Journals of Samuel Gridley Howe*, 2:232–33, this episode must have happened in 1854, or 1855; Donald, *Charles Sumner and the Coming of the Civil War*, 160–75; *TCR*, Feb. 19, 1848; Sumner, *The Works of Charles Sumner*, 2:53; *BP*, June 29, 1848; *Reunion of the Free-Soilers of 1848*, 15–17, 54–56; Holt, *The Rise and Fall of the American Whig Party*, 340–82; Rayback, *Free-Soil*, 205; Wilentz, *The Rise of American Democracy*, 601–20; *NYH*, July 1, 1848; *Lib*, June 23, July 7, 1848; *ER*, Sept. 20, 1848; Wall, *Reminiscences of Worcester*, 286–87; Gatell, "Conscience and Judgment," 18–45. To be sure Andrew had a flare for theatrics, and many years into their friendship, she remembered when she was arranging some tableaux for one of her children's parties and had chosen the subjects from British novelist William M. Thackeray's fairy tale *The Rose and the Ring*. Julia came to Andrew in some perplexity and said, "Dear Mr. Andrew, in the tableaux this evening Dr. Howe is to personate Kutasoff Hedzoff; would you be willing to pose as Prince Bulbo?" "By all means," was his response. Julia bought the book and Andrew "studied and imitated the costume of the prince, even to the necktie and the rose in his buttonhole."

21. Robinson, "William S. Robinson," 313–23; Donald, *Charles Sumner and the Coming of the Civil War*, 160–75; *TCR*, Feb. 19, 1848; Sumner, *The Works of Charles Sumner*, 2:53; *BP*, June 29, 1848; *Reunion of the Free-Soilers of 1848*, 15–17, 54–56; Holt, *The Rise and Fall of the American Whig Party*, 340–82; Rayback, *Free-Soil*, 205; Wilentz, *The Rise of American Democracy*, 601–25; *NYH*, July 1, 1848; *Lib*, June 23, July 7, 1848; *ER*, Sept. 20, 1848; Wall, *Reminiscences of Worcester*, 286–87; Gatell, "Conscience and Judgment," 18–45.

22. Congdon, *Reminiscences of a Journalist*, 154–58; Robinson, "William S. Robinson," 313–23; Bird, *Francis William Bird*, 5–30; *BA*, Oct. 3, Nov. 10, 1845, Nov. 1, 1848; *BP*, Nov. 15, 1848; Wilentz, *The Rise of American Democracy*, 629; *Lib*, Aug. 11, Oct. 23, 1848.

23. As quoted in Donald, *Charles Sumner and Coming of the Civil War*, 166–69; Lucid, *The Journal of Richard Henry Dana, Jr.*, 1:348–56; Schwartz, *Samuel Gridley Howe*, 166–67; Howe, *Reminiscences*, 258–59; *BA*, June 7, 1848; *TBS*, June 23, 1849; Nov. 15, 1851; Andrew to James Freeman Clarke, Feb. 26, 1848, Clarke Papers, Additional Correspondence, HU; Baum, *Civil War Party System*, 23–25; Harrold, *American Abolitionism*, 128–29; Wilentz, *The Rise of American Democracy*, 620–29; Mayer, *All on Fire*, 380–381; *Lib*, Aug.

11, Oct. 23, 1848; Congdon, *Reminiscences of a Journalist*, 155–58; *BP*, Nov. 15, 1848; Blue, *The Free Soilers*, 133.

24. "The Free Soil Party and the Late Election," 105–27.

25. Donald, *Charles Sumner and the Coming of the Civil War*, 180–87; see also Andrew's Notes on Free Soil Convention in Massachusetts, Andrew Papers, MHS; Wilentz, *The Rise of American Democracy*, 625–32; Potter, *Impending Crisis*, 90–91; *BA*, Nov. 7, 24, 1849; *NE*, Dec. 20, 1849; Sweeny, "Rum, Romanism Representation, and Reform," 116–37; Richards, *Great in Goodness*, 185–238; Formisano, *Transformation of Political Culture*, 317–40; Brooks, *Liberty Power*, 143–60; *A Memorial of the Hon. Charles Allen from His Children*, 55–57; Cumbler, *From Abolition to Rights for All*, 64–65

26. Chandler, *Memoir*, 80; *American Quarterly Register and Magazine* 3 (Dec. 1849): 309–26; *BA*, Dec. 11, 1848; Wilentz, *The Rise of American Democracy*, 636–50; Potter, *Impending Crisis*, 94–120; Donald, *Charles Sumner and the Coming of the Civil War*, 180–87; see also Andrew's Notes on Free Soil Convention in Massachusetts, Andrew Papers, MHS; Potter, *Impending Crisis*, 90–91; *BA*, Nov. 7, 24, 1849; *NE*, Dec. 20, 1849; Sweeny, "Rum, Romanism Representation, and Reform," 116–37; Richards, *Great in Goodness*, 185–238; Formisiano, *Transformation of Political Culture*, 317–40.

27. Pearson, *Andrew*, 1:48–49; Chandler, *Memoir*, 133–34; *TCU*, Oct. 17, 1889; *BA*, Sept. 11, 1844; Andrew to Woodman, Aug. 9, 1844, Woodman Papers, SHSW.

28. Andrew to Isaac Andrew, May 10, 1843, May 4, 17, Dec. 14, 1847, Andrew Papers, PEM; Andrew to "Dear Sir," Oct. 4, 1853, John A. Andrew Papers, AAS.

29. *BP*, Dec. 27, 1848, Sept. 9, 1923, Pearson, *Andrew*, 1:50–54; Reno, *Memoirs of the Judiciary and the Bar of New England for the Nineteenth Century*, 3:377–80; Hamrogue, "John A. Andrew," 6; Chandler, *Memoir*, 71–72; Andrew Scrapbook 10, Andrew Papers, MHS; Long, *After-Dinner and Other Speeches*, 191; Lincoln and Burr, *The Town of Hingham in the Late Civil War*, 317–18; Brown, *Yarmouth, Nova Scotia*, 46.

30. Andrew to Cyrus Woodman, Nov. 26, 1844, Woodman Papers, SHSW; Long, *After-Dinner and Other Speeches*, 191.

31. Nason, *Discourse*, 32; *BP*, 9 Sept. 1923; Chandler, *Memoir*, 71–72; Marriage Certificate of John Albion Andrew and Eliza Hersey, Dec. 24, 1848, Andrew Papers, MHS; Pearson, *Andrew*, 1:50–54; *TCR*, June 13, 1912; *BA*, Dec. 27, 1848; *BP*, Dec. 27, 1848; Adams, ed., *Memorial Biographies of the New-England Historic Genealogical Society*, 6: 247.

32. Pearson, *Andrew*, 1:54–55; Andrew to Isaac Andrew, July 3, 1850, James Freeman Clarke to Andrew, June 11, 1850, Andrew Papers, PEM; Reno, *Memoirs of the Judiciary and the Bar of New England for the Nineteenth Century*, 3:377–80; Chandler, *Memoir*, 15, 71–72; *TCR*, June 13, 1912; Adams, *Memorial Biographies of the New-England Historic Genealogical Society*, 6: 247.

33. Andrew to James Freeman Clarke, Nov. 21, 1850, Clarke Papers, Additional Correspondence, HU; Pearson, *Andrew*, 1:50–54; Andrew to Isaac Andrew, July 3, 1850, Andrew Papers, PEM; Chandler, *Memoir*, 71–72; *TCR*, June 13, 1912. Charles Albion died September 28, 1850.

34. Long, *After-Dinner and Other Speeches*, 191; *BA*, Mar. 17, 1851, Jan. 17, 1852, Feb. 1, 1854; Seguin, *Idiocy and Its Treatment by the Physiological Method*, 250–52; Rose, *No Right to Be Idle*, 19–20.

35. Levesque, *Black Boston*, 216–27; *PF*, Apr. 1, 1849; 366–69; *Lib*, Mar. 30, Apr. 13, May 4, 1849; *BoPil*, June 2, 1849; *BP*, June 2, 1849; *TUM*, Aug. 10, 1849; *CR*, Aug. 7, 1849; *BA*, Jan. 5, Mar. 23, Apr. 10, 12, May 26, 1849; *BC*, May 21, 1849, Feb. 19, 1851; *BET*, May 25, 1849; Buescher, *The Remarkable Life of John Murray Spear*, 49–52; Rogers, *Murder and the Death Penalty in Massachusetts*, 90–105.

36. *PF*, Apr. 1, June 1, 1849; Hall, "Coverage of the Prohibition Issue in Selected Massachusetts Newspapers, 1851–1855," 19–77; *NS*, Apr. 20, 1849; *Lib*, Jan. 26, Mar. 30, Apr. 13, May 4, June 1, 1849; *CWR*, May 31, 1849; *PR*, May 24, 1849; Andrew to James Freeman Clarke, Dec. 18, 1848, Clarke Papers, Additional Correspondence, HU; *BET*, May 25,

1849; *Trial and Execution of Washington Goode; BA*, Jan. 16, 1849, May 26, 1849; *BT*, May 25, 1849; *BoPil*, June 2, 1849; Buescher, *Life of John Murray Spear*, 49-52; Rogers, *Murder and the Death Penalty in Massachusetts*, 90-105.

CHAPTER 5: ON THE RIGHT SIDE OF GOD

1. Donald, *Charles Sumner and the Coming of the Civil War*, 180-87; Baum, *Civil War Party System*, 24-25; Wilentz, *The Rise of American Democracy*, 632-45; Dalton, Wirkkala, and Thomas, *Leading the Way*, 134; Potter, *Impending Crisis*, 90-120.

2. Mayer, *All on Fire*, 398-99; Wiltse and Birkner, *The Papers of Daniel Webster*, 7:144; Donald, *Charles Sumner and the Coming of the Civil War*, 180-87; Baum, *Civil War Party System*, 24-25; Wilentz, *The Rise of American Democracy*, 632-45; Dalton, Wirkkala, and Thomas, *Leading the Way*, 134; Potter, *Impending Crisis*, 90-120; Brooke, "There Is a North," 65-99.

3. *NE*, May 8, 1851; *TH*, May 24, June 7, 1851; *Lib*, Jan. 24, May 9, 1851, June 29, 1855; *FR*, Aug. 11, 1849; Wilentz, *The Rise of American Democracy*, 646-47.

4. Quotes come from the *Lib*, Oct. 18, 1850; Harrold, *American Abolitionism*, 125-26; Dalton, Wirkkala, and Thomas, *Leading the Way*, 134; Donald, *Charles Sumner and the Coming of the Civil War*, 183-99; see Andrew's thoughts in a undated letter or draft of a letter written shortly after the enactment, Andrew Papers, MHS; Stange, *Patterns of Antislavery Among American Unitarians*, 118; Siebert, *The Vigilance Committee of Boston*, 1-23; Account Book, Jackson Papers, MHS; Blackett, *The Captive's Quest*, 397-440 Robboy and Robboy, "Lewis Hayden," 600-604; Wilentz, *The Rise of American Democracy*, 645-47.

5. Trent, *The Manliest Man*, 184; Stearns, *Cambridge Sketches*, 162-79; Mulkern, *The Know-Nothing Party in Massachusetts*, 150; Zebley, "God and Liberty," 38-39; Howe, *Boston*, 242-49; Emerson, *The Early Years of the Saturday Club, 1855-1870*; Emerson Scrapbook and Notes on the Saturday Club, Edward Waldo Emerson Papers, MHS; Robinson, "William S. Robinson," 313-23; Robinson, *"Warrington" Pen Portraits*, 60; Cumbler, *From Abolition to Rights for All*, 52-53; Pearson, *Andrew*, 1:39; Lucid, *The Journal of Richard Henry Dana, Jr.*, 2:397-402; McKay, "Henry Wilson and the Coalition of 1851," 338-57; Grodzins, "'Slave Law' versus 'Lynch Law' in Boston," 1-33; Donald, *Charles Sumner and the Rights of Man*, 74; Stearns, *The Life and Public Services of George Luther Stearns*, 74; Hack, *Reaping Something New*, 25.

6. Howe, *Boston*, 242-49; Emerson, *The Early Years of the Saturday Club, 1855-1870*; Ralph Waldo Emerson Scrapbook and Notes on the Saturday Club, Edward Waldo Emerson Papers, MHS; Robinson, *"Warrington" Pen Portraits*, 60; Cumbler, *From Abolition to Rights for All*, 52-53; Pearson, *Andrew*, 1:39; Lucid, *The Journal of Richard Henry Dana, Jr.*, 2:397-402; McKay, "Henry Wilson and the Coalition of 1851," 338-57; Grodzins, "'Slave Law' versus 'Lynch Law' in Boston," 1-33; Donald, *Charles Sumner and the Rights of Man*, 74; Stearns, *The Life and Public Services of George Luther Stearns*, 74; Hack, *Reaping Something New*, 25. Initially, members gathered at Young's Hotel on Court Street, a favorite of Boston businessmen. A few years later they would establish the *Atlantic Monthly* to promote New England authors and provide a broader platform for reformers and abolitionists.

7. Howe, *Boston*, 242-49; Emerson, *The Early Years of the Saturday Club, 1855-1870*; Ralph Waldo Emerson Scrapbook and Notes on the Saturday Club, Edward Waldo Emerson Papers, MHS; Robinson, *"Warrington" Pen Portraits*, 60; Cumbler, *From Abolition to Rights for All*, 52-53; Pearson, *Andrew*, 1:39; Lucid, *The Journal of Richard Henry Dana, Jr.*, 2:397-402; McKay, "Henry Wilson and the Coalition of 1851," 338-57; Grodzins, "'Slave Law' versus 'Lynch Law' in Boston," 1-33; Donald, *Charles Sumner and the Rights of Man*, 74; Stearns, *The Life and Public Service of George Luther Stearns*, 74; Hack, *Reaping Something New*, 2017, 25.

8. Collison, *Shadrach Minkins*, 60–70; Horton and Horton, *Black Bostonians*, 4; Jackson, *Force and Freedom*, 70–71; Anbinder, *Nativism & Slavery*, 8–14.

9. Andrew to Clarke, Mar. 5, 1851, Clarke Papers, Additional Correspondence, HU; Clarke, *Memorial and Biographical Sketches*, 17–18; Blackett, *The Captive's Quest*, 409–40; BA, Feb. 24, 28, Mar. 4, 5, 31, Apr. 2, June 7, 12, 14, 16, 18, Aug. 21, 1851; Adams, *Richard Henry Dana*, 1:82; Robboy and Robboy, "Lewis Hayden," 600–606; Andrew to John M. Niles, Mar. 31, 1851, Andrew Papers, CHS. Andrew invited John Milton Niles, former Free-Soil Connecticut Senator to address a convention of people in Massachusetts opposed to the Fugitive Slave Law; Collison, *Shadrach Minkins*, 63–100; Jonathan Blanchard to Stephen C. Phillips, Mar. 30, 1851, Andrew Papers, MHS; Harrold, *American Abolitionism*, 124–27; Sinha, *The Slave's Cause*, 505–8; *Lib*, Feb. 21, 28, Mar. 7, 14, June 20, Nov. 7, 1851; Wilentz, *The Rise of American Democracy*, 646–47; Jackson, *Force and Freedom*, 70–71; Wells, *Blind No More*, 99.

10. *Lib*, Apr. 11, May 2, 1851; "The Case of Thomas Sims," 1–16; *NE*, Apr. 10, 1851; *BSWA*, Apr. 9, 12, 16, 1851; *BP*, Feb. 18, 1851; Blackett, *The Captive's Quest*, 413–20; *Trial of Thomas Sims on an Issue of Personal Liberty*; Cumbler, *From Abolition to Rights for All*, 75, 125–27; Robboy and Robboy, "Lewis Hayden," 602–6; Francis Jackson to Andrew, Sept. 12, 1860, Andrew Papers, MHS. Andrew's thoughts on the case in drafts of letter to invite people in Massachusetts about reacting to the Fugitive Slave Law, Mar. 31, 1851, Andrew Papers, MHS; Mayer, *All on Fire*, 410–12; Jackson, *Force and Freedom*, 72–73.

11. *BSWA*, Apr., 9, 11, 12, 16, 1851; *Lib*, May 2, 1851; *BP*, Feb. 18, 1851; Blackett, *The Captive's Quest*, 413–20; *Trial of Thomas Sims on an Issue of Personal Liberty*; Cumbler, *From Abolition to Rights for All*, 75; Robboy and Robboy, "Lewis Hayden," 602–6; Francis Jackson to Andrew, Sept. 12, 1860, Andrew Papers, MHS, see also draft of letter inviting people in Massachusetts about reacting to the Fugitive Slave law, Mar. 31, 1851, Andrew Papers, MHS; Harrold, *American Abolitionism*, 125–27; Mayer, *All on Fire*, 410–12; Jackson, *Force and Freedom*, 73–73.

12. Parker, *The Boston Kidnapping*, 36–53; Siebert, *The Vigilance Committee of Boston*, 1–23; *NYH*, Apr. 4, 1851; *BSWA*, Apr. 5, 9, 1851; *BH*, Apr. 12, 1851; Blackett, *The Captive's Quest*, 397–440; Kantrowitz, *More Than Freedom*, 196–97.

13. Mayer, *All on Fire*, 411; *Lib*, Apr. 25, 1851, quote taken from the *BH*, Apr. 25, 1851.

14. Geldard, *God in Concord*, 147; Strangis, *Lewis Hayden and the War Against Slavery*, 38–63; *BSWA*, Apr. 16, 18, 30, 1851; Blackett, *The Captive's Quest*, 417–19; Robboy and Robboy, "Lewis Hayden," 600–10; Donald, *Charles Sumner and the Coming of the Civil War*, 190–212; *BDC*, Mar. 21, 1851.

15. Andrew to Sumner, Jan. 22, 1852, Sumner Papers, HU; Johnson, "Charles Sumner," 146–47; Collison, *Shadrach Minkins*, 63–100, 158, he might have even been Andrew's barber; *Lib*, May 2, 1851; Andrew to Clarke, Mar. 5, 1851, Clarke Papers, Additional Correspondence, HU; Handlin, *Boston's Immigrants*, 192–98; O'Conner, *Lords of the Loom*, 87–92; Hamrogue, "John A. Andrew," 20–21; Pearson, *Andrew*, 1:40–58; McKay, "Wilson and the Coalition of 1851," 338–57; Collison, "'The Flagitious Offense,'" 609–25; McCaskill, "Ellen Craft: The Fugitive who Fled as a Planter," in *Georgia Women: Their Lives and Times*, ed. Chirhart and Wood, 85; Craft and Craft, *Running a Thousand Miles for Freedom*; NASS, Jan. 30, 1851; Lucid, *The Journal of Richard Henry Dana, Jr.*, 2:412–32; *BDC*, Mar. 29, 1851; Donald, *Charles Sumner and the Coming of the Civil War*, 196–212; BA, June 14, 16, 18, 1851.

16. Lucid, *The Journal of Richard Henry Dana, Jr.*, 2:487; *BSWA*, Apr. 16, 1851; Amestoy, *Slavish Shore*, 163; *Lib*, Apr. 9, 1852; Wilentz, *The Rise of American Democracy*, 655–56; Hendrick, *Harriet Beecher Stowe*, 206–32; Brooke, *"There Is a North,"* 116–201.

17. Wilentz, *The Rise of American Democracy*, 655–56; Brooke, *"There Is a North,"* 116–201.

18. Andrew to Sumner, May 17, June 2, 1852, Sumner Papers, HU.

19. Chandler, *Memoir*, 71–72; Donald, *Charles Sumner and the Coming of the Civil War*, 228–34; Mayer, *All on Fire*, 333–431.

20. Andrew to Robert Carter, Aug. 28, 1852, Carter Papers, HU; *TLW*, Feb. 15, 1879. Joseph Lyman was chief editor at the time and John G. Palfrey was contributing editor. When Palfrey accepted the Free-Soil nomination for governor, he stepped down as editor in October. Lyman stepped down at the same time; Wilentz, *The Rise of American Democracy*, 662–64; *United States Magazine and Democratic Review*, 29 (July 1851): 72; *Lib*, Apr. 11, 18, 1851; Peck, "John Van Buren," 328.

21. *Lib*, Sept. 10, Dec. 24, 1852; *NE*, Aug. 26, 1852; Donald, *Charles Sumner and the Coming of the Civil War*, 218–29; Wilentz, *The Rise of American Democracy*, 661–64.

22. Donald, *Charles Sumner and the Coming of the Civil War*, 218–29; Wilentz, *The Rise of American Democracy*, 661–64; *Lib*, Sept. 10, 1852, Dec. 24, 1852; *NE*, Aug. 26, 1852.

23. Andrew to Emerson, Oct. 18, Nov. 6, 1853, Sept. 23, Nov. 27, 1854, Emerson Papers, HU; Rusk, *The Letters of Ralph Waldo Emerson*, 8:361; Andrew to Governor John Clifford, Apr. 14, 1853, Andrew Papers, MHS; *MLR* 15 (1853): 354–60; *BA*, Oct. 29, Nov. 2, 1853, Jan. 9, 10, 1854, Jan. 6, Oct. 12, 1853, Jan. 9, 1854; *SR*, Nov. 14, 1853; Andrew to Isaac Andrew, May 23, 1854, Andrew Papers, PEM; Reno, *Memoirs of the Judiciary and the Bar of New England for the Nineteenth Century*, 3:377–89; Chandler, *Memoir*, 71–72; *BH*, Nov. 14, 1853.

24. Hurd, *History of Plymouth, Massachusetts*, 3; Andrew to Ralph Waldo Emerson, Oct. 18, Nov. 6, 1853, Sept. 23, Nov. 27, 1854, Emerson Papers, HU; Andrew to Governor John Clifford, Apr. 14, 1853, Andrew Papers, MHS. Andrew sent him copies of a report and that he read to the council; *BA*, Sept. 20, 1852, Jan. 6, Oct. 12, 29, Nov. 2, 1853, Jan. 9, 10, 1854. His name was on the ballot in 1850, 1851, and 1853. Returns of Votes for State Senators, 1842–1885 and Abstract of Votes for Plymouth District, 1850, SC1/series 198X, MSA; Returns of Votes for State Senators, 1842–1885 and Abstract of Votes for Plymouth District, 1851, SC1/series 198X, MSA; Returns of Votes for State Senators, 1842–1885 and Abstract of Votes for Plymouth District, 1853, SC1/series 198X, MSA; In a close primary race, Andrew drew 4,124 votes, *SR*, Nov. 14, 1853; Andrew to Isaac Andrew, May 23, 1854, Andrew Papers, PEM; Reno, *Memoirs of the Judiciary and the Bar of New England for the Nineteenth Century*, 3:377–89; Chandler, *Memoir*, 71–72; *BH*, Nov. 14, 1853.

25. Andrew to Emerson, Oct. 18, Nov. 6, 1853, Sept. 23, Nov. 27, 1854, Emerson Papers, HU; Andrew to Governor John Clifford, Apr. 14, 1853, Andrew Papers; *MLR* 15 (1853): 354–60; *BA*, Jan. 6, Oct. 12, 29, Nov. 2, 1853, Jan. 9, 10, 1854; *SR*, Nov. 14, 1853; Andrew to Isaac Andrew, May 23, 1854, Andrew Papers, PEM; Reno, *Memoirs of the Judiciary and the Bar of New England for the Nineteenth Century*, 3:377–89; Chandler, *Memoir*, 71–72; *BH*, Nov. 14, 1853; Brooke, "There Is a North," 202–94.

26. *Lib*, Mar. 24, 1854, *CI*, Mar. 24, 1854; *Congressional Globe*, 33rd Congress, 1st session, 221–22; Wilentz, *The Rise of American Democracy*, 670–75; Brooke, "There Is a North," 202–94; Davis, "Liberty Before Union," 20–33.

27. Richard H. Dana, Jr., Diary, Feb. 9, 1854, Dana Family Papers, MHS; *Lib*, Feb. 24, Mar. 3, 1854.

28. Lucid, *The Journal of Richard Henry Dana, Jr.*, 2:617; Adams, *Richard Henry Dana*, 1:258; *Lib*, Mar. 3, 1854; Brooke, "There Is a North," 202–94.

29. *Lib*, May 26, 1854; Wilentz, *The Rise of American Democracy*; Potter, *Impending Crisis*, 166–67; Nichols, *Blueprints for Leviathan*, 117–18.

30. *BSWA*, June 7, 1854; Donald, *Charles Sumner and the Coming of the Civil War*, 260–61; Wilentz, *The Rise of American Democracy*, 670–75; Brooke, "There Is a North," 202–94.

31. Bowditch, *Life and Correspondence of Henry Ingersoll Bowditch*, 1:263–72; "The Case of Anthony Burns," 181–211.

32. Mary Blanchard to Father (Benjamin Seaver), May 28, June 4, 18, 1854, Seaver Papers, MHS; Blackett, *The Captive's Quest*, 421–40; *BDA*, June 5, 1854; *Lib*, June 2, 1854; Bowditch, *Life and Correspondence of Henry Ingersoll Bowditch*, 1:263–72; Robboy and Robboy, "Lewis Hayden," 605–8; Donald, *Charles Sumner and the Coming of the Civil*

War, 260–62; Shapiro, "The Rendition of Anthony Burns," 34–51; Harrold, *American Abolitionism*, 122–27; Sinha, *The Slave's Cause*, 515–20.

33. Parker, *Ten Sermons of Religion*, 84–85; Parker, "Some Thoughts on the Progress of America, and the Influence of her Diverse Institutions, May 31, 1854," in Cobbe, ed., *The Collected Works of Theodore Parker*, 2:3, 4, 5, 14, also 6:1–43; Stange, *Patterns of Antislavery Among American Unitarians*, 162–63; Siebert, *The Vigilance Committee of Boston*, 1–23; "The Case of Anthony Burns," and "The Removal of Judge Loring"; *Lib*, May 9, 1856; *BA*, July 7, 1852; Robboy and Robboy, "Lewis Hayden," 606–10; Bowditch, *Life and Correspondence of Henry Ingersoll Bowditch*, 1:263–72.

34. *BP*, June 3, 1854, *NYT*, June 5, 1854; "The Case of Anthony Burns," 181–211.

35. *BP*, June 3, 1854; *NYT*, June 5, 1854; *TI*, June 8, 1854; Stange, *Patterns of Anti-Slavery Among American Unitarians*, 220–21; Grodzins, "'Slave Law' versus 'Lynch Law' in Boston," 1–33; Lucid, *The Journal of Richard Henry Dana, Jr.*, 2:632–34; Robboy and Robboy, "Lewis Hayden," 606–10; Blackett, *The Captive's Quest*, 425–40.

36. Clarke, *Anti-Slavery Days*, 172–73; Hartman and Wells, "John Albion Andrew of Massachusetts," 324–27.

37. Clarke, *Anti-Slavery Days*, 172–73; Hartman and Wells, "John Albion Andrew of Massachusetts," 324–27; *NYT*, June 5, 1854.

38. Clarke, *Memorial and Biographical Sketches*, 38–39; *NYT*, June 5, 1854.

39. Mary Blanchard to Father, Benjamin Seaver, June 4, 1854, Seaver Papers, MHS; *NYT*, June 5, 1854; *BA*, May 30, 1854.

40. "The Case of Anthony Burns," 50–60; Grodzins, "'Slave Law' versus 'Lynch Law' in Boston," 1–33; Wilson, *History of the Rise and Fall of Slave Power in America*, 2:435–46; *Lib*, May 9, 1856; "The Case of Anthony Burns."

41. Grodzins, "'Slave Law' versus 'Lynch Law' in Boston," 1–33; Lucid, *The Journal of Richard Henry Dana, Jr.*, 2:672–73; *TI*, June 8, 1854; *Lib*, Apr. 6, 1855; *BDC*, June 3, 1854; *BDA*, Apr. 4–14, 1854; June 3, 5, 1854; Weiss, *Life and Correspondence of Theodore Parker*, 2:146–47; *BA*, Apr. 4, 5, 1855; Blackett, *The Captive's Quest*, 434–40; Mayer, *All on Fire*, 440–44; Maltz, *Fugitive Slave on Trial*, 108–9, 140–41.

42. *Lib*, June 16, 1854; Russell and Nason, *Life and Public Services of Hon. Henry Wilson*, 118; Mann, *Life of Henry Wilson*, 44; Gienapp, *Origins of the Republican Party*, 135; Donald, *Charles Sumner and the Coming of the Civil War*, 250–65; *BA*, June 1, 1854; *Lib*, June 2, 1854; *NE*, June 8, 1854.

43. Andrew to Sumner, Aug. 28, 1854, Sumner Papers, HU; Pearson, *Andrew*, 1:63–64; *Lib*, July 28, Sept. 14, 19, 1854; *SR*, July 21–25, 1854; *BA*, July 14, 24, Sept. 8, 1854; Schwartz, *Samuel Gridley Howe*, 173–77; Flower, *History of the Republican Party*, 337; Donald, *Charles Sumner and the Coming of the Civil War*, 265–68; Russell and Nason, *Life and Public Services of Hon. Henry Wilson*, 118; Mann, *Life of Henry Wilson*, 44; Gienapp, *Origins of the Republican Party*, 135.

44. Andrew to Sumner, Aug. 28, 1854, Sumner Papers, HU; Pearson, *Andrew*, 1:63–64; *Lib*, July 28, Sept. 14, 19, 1854; *BA*, July 24, Sept. 8, 1854; Schwartz, *Samuel Gridley Howe*, 173–77; Donald, *Charles Sumner and the Coming of the Civil War*, 265–68; Russell and Nason, *Life and Public Services of Hon. Henry Wilson*, 118; Mann, *Life of Henry Wilson*, 44; Gienapp, *Origins of the Republican Party*, 135.

45. Greeley to Andrew, Sept. 1, 1854, Andrew Papers, MHS.

46. *Lib*, Sept. 15, 1854; *BA*, Sept. 8, 1854; Donald, *Charles Sumner and the Coming of the Civil War*, 266–67.

47. *Lib*, Sept. 15, 1854; *BT*, Sept. 8, 1854; *SR*, Sept. 8, 1854; *BA*, Sept. 15, 1854; Anbinder, *Nativism & Slavery*, 95; Baum, *Civil War Party System*, 25–30; Mulkern, *The Know-Nothing Party in Massachusetts*, 73–74; Wilentz, *The Rise of American Democracy*, 685; Davis, "Liberty Before Union," 20–35.

CHAPTER 6: THE REPUBLICAN TIDE

1. McMaster, "The Riotous Career of the Know Nothings," 524-37; Mulkern, *The Know-Nothing Party in Massachusetts*, 67-79, 125-45; Amestoy, *Slavish Shore*, 213-35; Donald, *Charles Sumner and the Coming of the Civil War*, 267-72; Baum, *Civil War Party System*, 28-34; *Lib*, Dec. 1, 1854; *BDA*, Dec. 1, 1854, June 29, 1888; *BI*, Nov. 22, 1854; *BA*, Nov. 14, 15, 1854; Kantrowitz, *More Than Freedom*, 166-67; Gienapp, *Origins of the Republican Party*, 136; Anbinder, *Nativism & Slavery*, 90-92.

2. Mulkern, *The Know-Nothing Party in Massachusetts*, 67-79; 125-45; Amestoy, *Slavish Shore*, 21-35; Donald, *Charles Sumner and the Coming of the Civil War*, 267-72; Baum, *Civil War Party System*, 28-34; *Lib*, Dec. 1, 1854; *BDA*, Dec. 1, 1854, June 29, 1888; *BA*, Nov. 13, 14, 15, 1854; *BI*, Nov. 22, 1854; Kantrowitz, *More Than Freedom*, 166-67; Gienapp, *Origins of the Republican Party*, 136; Anbinder, *Nativism & Slavery*, 90-92; Pearson, *Andrew*, 1:65-66.

3. Taylor, "Progressive Nativism," 167-84; Mulkern, *The Know-Nothing Party in Massachusetts*, 67-79; Dalton, Wirkkala, and Thomas, *Leading the Way*, 127-42.

4. *Lib*, Feb. 12, 1847, Mar. 10, 1848, quote Apr. 6, 1855; Pearson, *Andrew*, 1;70-71; *PF*, Apr. 1, 1855; *BDA*, Nov. 27, 1867; *BA*, Feb. 19, 1851; Bovee, *Reasons for Abolishing Capital Punishment*, 232.

5. Folsom, "Henry Ingersoll Bowditch," 310-32; Benjamin Danforth to Andrew, Sept. 13, 1853, Collamore Papers, MHS; Boston Anti-Man Hunting League Papers, and the Boston Vigilance Committee Record Book, MHS; newspaper clippings, Andrew File, BowC; Cumbler, *From Abolition to Rights for All*, 72-80; *Lib*, Feb. 18, 1860; Bowditch, *Life and Correspondence of Henry Ingersoll Bowditch*, 1:271-82; DeLombard, *Slavery on Trial*, 66-67; Andrew even took on a case (and won) in defense of an Episcopalian parishioner Ebenezer Garron for fighting with fellow parishioner John T. Wooley over a church dispute, *BI*, Apr. 25, 1855.

6. *Lib*, July 14, 1854; Mayer, *All on Fire*, 443-46; Kritzberg, "Thoreau, Slavery, and Resistance to Civil Government," 535-65; DeLombard, *Slavery on Trial*, 66-67; Benjamin Danforth to Andrew, Sept. 13, 1853, Collamore Papers; Boston Anti-Man Hunting League Papers, and the BVC Record Book, MHS; newspaper clippings, Andrew File, BowC; *Lib*, Feb. 18, 1860; *BDG*, Oct. 12, 1886; Bowditch, *Life and Correspondence of Henry Ingersoll Bowditch*, 1:271-82; *BI*, Apr. 25, 1855; Cumbler, *From Abolition to Rights for All*, 72-80; DeLombard, *Slavery on Trial*, 66-67; Brock, *The Road to Dawn*.

7. Cramer, "I to Myself,"103; *Lib*, July 14, 1854; Mayer, *All on Fire*, 443-46; Andrew to Sumner, Jan. 22, 1852, Sumner Papers, HU; Johnson, "Charles Sumner," 146-47; Collison, *Shadrach Minkins*, 63-100, 158; Morgan-Owens, *Girl in Black and White*, 70-75; Morgan-Owens, "The Enslaved Girl Who Became America's First Poster Child," 8; Mitchell, "The Real Ida May," 54-88; In her article, Mitchell refers to Botts master as James Tolson, but Morgan-Owens refers to him as James Folson. Mitchell argues in her article on page 83, that in 1860 slave schedules, Tolson is incorrectly listed as Folson.

8. Andrew to Sumner, Jan. 22, 1852, Sumner to Andrew, Feb. 4, Andrew to Sumner, Aug. 3, 12, 1852, Sumner Papers, HU, also in MHS; Wilson, *Rise and Fall of the Slave Power in America*, 2:440-43; Morgan-Owens, *Girl in Black and White*, 70-75; Johnson, "Charles Sumner," 143-55; Mitchell, "The Real Ida May," 83.

9. Morgan-Owens, *Girl in Black and White*, 70-85; Andrew to Sumner, Jan. 22, Aug. 4, 12, 1852, Dec. 16, 26, 1853, Jan. 18, Mar. 11, 1854, Sumner Papers, HU; Johnson, "Charles Sumner," 143-55; Mitchell, "The Real Ida May," 56-66; Deed manumitting Botts, dated Jan. 12, 1852, signed July 28, 1854, Andrew Papers, MHS; the Deed manumitting Seth Botts, Jan. 13, 1852, Andrew Papers, MHS; Andrew explained the transaction in a letter he published in a Broadside as S.P.H., "History of Ida May" Andrew Papers, MHS; Mitchell, "The Real Ida May," 84.

10. Andrew to Sumner, Feb. 2, 1855, Sumner Papers, HU; Mitchell, "The Real Ida May," 67.

11. Andrew to Sumner, Aug. 3, 1852, Jan. 22, 24, Feb. 2, 16, 23, Mar. 10, 1855, Sumner Papers, HU; *NYT*, Mar. 9, 1855; Pierce, *Memoirs and Letters of Charles Sumner*, 3:413-14; *Lib*,

Mar. 30, 1855; Johnson, "Charles Sumner," 143-55; Morgan-Owens, *Girl in Black and White*, 70-85. Mitchell, "The Real Ida May," 60-72; *BC*, Mar. 12, 1855, *BR*, Mar. 15, 1855; *NYDT*, Mar. 9, 16, 1855; Johnson, "Charles Sumner," 143-55; Morgan-Owens, *Girl in Black and White*, 182-86; Tewell, *A Self-Evident Lie*. Although the wealthiest resident in Alexandria, Neale demanded to be paid for his expenses in retrieving the family and requested an additional $47.25, so not until Andrew arranged to send more money did the family start on their journey.

12. Mitchell, "The Real Ida May," 69-72; Andrew to Sumner, Feb. 16, 23, 1855; Sumner Papers, HU; Morgan-Owens, *Girl in Black and White*, 182-86; Tewell, *A Self-Evident Lie*.

13. *Lib*, Mar. 30, 1855, although he sent another letter to Andrew, this letter published in the paper was addressed to "Dear Doctor," presumably to Dr. James W. Stone; *NYDT*, Mar. 1, 1855; *BA*, Feb. 28, 1855; Mitchell, "The Real Ida May," 55-58, 73.

14. Andrew to Longfellow, Mar. 9, 1855, Longfellow Papers, HU; Morgan-Owens, *Girl in Black and White*, 2-4, 102-4, 200-219; *NYTD*, Mar. 1, 1855; *BA*, Feb. 28, 1855; Andrew, *History of Ida May*, Broadside; Andrew to Christopher Neale, Apr. 14, 1854, Andrew Papers, TPML; *Lib*, Mar. 30, 1855; Andrew to Sumner, Aug. 4, 12, 1852, July 11, 22, 1854, Jan. 22, 24, 31, Feb. 2, 16, 19, 23, 26, Mar. 3, 10, 1855, May 3, 1856, Sumner Papers, HU; Mitchell, "The Real Ida May," 55-58. In the novel *Ida May* by Mary Hayden Green Pike, published in 1854, Ida May, a white child from Pennsylvania is stolen, beaten unconscious, stained brown, and sold across state lines, and is raised a slave in South Carolina until her identity is recovered eight years later. Donald, *Charles Sumner and the Coming of the Civil War*, 154.

15. Andrew to Sumner, Jan. 24, Mar. 10, 1855, Sumner Papers, HU; *BC*, Mar. 12, 1855, *BR*, Mar. 15, 1855; *NYDT*, Mar. 9, 16, 1855; Johnson, "Charles Sumner," 143-55; Mitchell, "The Real Ida May," 68.

16. Andrew, "History of Ida May"; Donald, *Charles Sumner and the Coming of the Civil War*, 180; Kantrowitz, *More Than Freedom*, 168.

17. *WS*, Mar. 12, 1855; Morgan-Owens, *Girl in Black and White*, 2-4, 102-4, 200-219; *NYTD*, Mar. 1, 1855; *BA*, Feb. 28, 1855; Andrew, *History of Ida May*; Andrew to Christopher Neale, Apr. 14, 1854, Andrew Papers, TPML; *Lib*, Mar. 30, 1855; Andrew to Sumner, Aug. 4, 12, 1852, July 11, 22, 1854, Jan. 22, 24, 31, Feb. 2, 16, 19, 23, 26, Mar. 3, 10, 1855, May 3, 1856, Sumner Papers, HU; Mitchell, "The Real Ida May," 55-58; Donald, *Charles Sumner and the Coming of the Civil War*, 154.

18. Andrew to Sumner, Feb. 2, 1855, Sumner Papers, HU; *Lib*, Apr. 6, 1855; Palmer, *Selected Letters of Sumner*, 1:428-29; Mitchell, "The Real Ida May," 56-67, 83-84.

19. *Lib*, Nov. 13, Dec. 18, 1857, May 7, 1858; Pearson, *Andrew*, 1:57-58; Browne, "Governor Andrew," 249-76; Andrew Scrapbooks, 11, 12, Andrew Papers, MHS; *BA*, Feb. 20, 27, Mar. 6, 1855; Schouler, *A History of Massachusetts in the Civil War*, 12; Wirzbicki, "Black Transcendentalism," 269-90; Hancock, "The Elusive Boundaries of Blackness," 115-29.

20. *Index to the Executive Documents Printed by Order of the Senate of the United States, First and Second Sessions, Thirty-Fourth Congress, 1855-56*, 1-67-98; MLR 8 (Sept. 1855): 254-63; *NI*, July 20, 24, 1855; *Lib*, Nov. 30, 1855; *BDA*, Mar. 26, Apr. 7, July 18, 1855; *NA*, July 20, 1855; *BA*, Feb. 20, 27, Mar. 6, June 30, July 18, 20, 27, 1855; *NYDT*, Apr. 26, July 18, 1855; Burnham, *Genealogical Records of Henry and Ulalia Burt*, 233.

21. *FDP*, Mar. 2, 1855; *TI*, Jan. 3, 1856; *NE*, Apr. 19, 1855; *Lib*, Jan. 19, Feb. 9, 1855; Maltz, *Fugitive Slave on Trial*, 104-7; *Journal of the House of Representatives of the Commonwealth of Massachusetts*, 3-14, 287-89, 390-98, see House Bill #167 (Mar. 17, 1855); Thomas W. Higginson to Andrew, June 9, 1854, Anti-Slavery Collection, BPL; *The Trial of Theodore Parker*; Sinha, *The Slave's Cause*, 518-19; Gosse, *The First Reconstruction*, 284-85.

22. *BT*, Apr. 20, 1855; *NS*, Apr. 20, Sept. 7, 1855; *BR*, Aug. 13, 1846; *Lib*, Apr. 4, 1851, Aug. 18, 1854, Mar. 30, Aug. 17, 31, Sept. 24, Dec. 28, 1855; *NYT*, May 13, 1856; White, "Antebellum School Reform in Boston," 203-17; *Acts and Resolves Passed by the General Court of Massachusetts, 1854-66*, Chapter 256, 674-75; *Massachusetts House of Representatives, House*

Report, No. 167; Wirzbicki, "Black Transcendentalism," 269-90; Hancock, "The Elusive Boundaries of Blackness," 115-129; Levesque, "White Bureaucracy, Black Community," 140-55; Finkelman, *Race and Law Before Emancipation,* 278.

23. *NS,* Sept. 7, 1855; *BR,* Aug. 13, 1846; *Lib,* Apr. 4, 1851, Aug. 18, 1854; Mar. 30, Aug. 17, 31, Sept. 24, Dec. 28, 1855; *NYT,* May 13, 1956; White, "Antebellum School Reform in Boston," 203-217; *Acts and Resolves Passed by the Genral Court, 1854-66,* Chapter 256, 674-75; *Massachusetts House of Representatives, House Report, No. 167;* Wirzbicki, "Black Transcendentalism," 269-290; Hancock, "The Elusive Boundaries of Blackness," 115-29; ·Levesque, "White Bureaucracy, Black Community," 140-155; Finkelman, *Race and Law Before Emancipation,* 278; For an excellent discussion of this decision impacted white and Black schools going forward see a report of the Special Meeting of the School Committee, *Lib,* Jan. 29, 1858; Wesley and Uzelac, *William Cooper Nell,* 33; Laurie, *Beyond Garrison,* 280; Kantrowitz, *More Than Freedom,* 168-69.

24. *Lib,* July 27, 1855; *NE,* June 14, 1855; Angell, "The Recall of Ministers," 486-97; *Lib,* May 4, June 1, 15, 1855; *NS,* June 8, 1855.

25 *BDA,* Nov. 8, 1855, Sept. 4, 1854; Palmer, *Selected Letters of Charles Sumner,* 1:433; Wesley and Uzelac, *William Cooper Nell,* 438; Dalton, Wirkkala, and Thomas *Leading the Way,* 130; Cumbler, *From Abolition to Rights for All,* 90; Amestoy, *Slavish Shore,* 174-225; *BA,* Sept. 21, Oct. 31, 1855; Baum, *Civil War Party System,* 29-40; Duberman, "Some Notes on the Beginnings of the Republican Party in Massachusetts," 364-70; *NYTrib,* Oct. 29, 1855; Hollandsworth, *Pretense of Glory,* 22-32; Gienapp, "Nativism and the Creation of a Republican Majority in the North before the Civil War," 529-59; Stearns, *Cambridge Sketches,* 244; *BDA,* Sept. 8, 1854; *BA,* Aug. 2, Oct. 23, 1855; Bushman, et al., *Uprooted Americans,* 161-208.

26. *Lib,* Dec. 14, 21, 28, 1855, Jan. 4, 18, 1856; *BA,* Jan. 11, 1856, *BT,* Jan. 11, 1856

27. Palmer, *Selected Letters of Charles Sumner,* 1:436.

28. *BA,* Feb. 29, Sept. 26, 1856; Chandler, "Two Letters from Kansas," 77-79; Ropes, *Six Months in Kansas,* 153-231; *NYOC,* Feb. 14, 1856; *Lib,* Feb. 8, 15, Sept. 12, 1856; Pearson, *Andrew,* 1:66-67; Wilentz, *The Rise of American Democracy,* 687-88. It was also in this year that Andrew argued a petition for a writ of habeas corpus to test the legality of the imprisonment of the Free State officers of Kansas at Topeka.

29. Chandler, "Two Letters from Kansas," 77-79; Ropes, *Six Months in Kansas,* 153-231; *NYOC,* Feb. 14, 1856; *BA,* Sept. 26, 1855; *Lib,* Feb. 8, 15, 1856; Pearson, *Andrew,* 1:66-67; Wilentz, *The Rise of American Democracy,* 687-88.

30. *Lib,* June 6, 1856; *BDA,* May 24, 1856; *NHS,* June 7, 1856; *NYT,* June 4, 1856; *SEP,* June 7, 1856; *NE,* May 29, 1856; Donald, *Charles Sumner and the Coming of the Civil War,* 278-84; Palmer, *Selected Letters of Charles Sumner,* 1:437-56; Freeman, *Field of Blood,* 215-16; Wilentz, *The Rise of American Democracy,* 689-93; *Annual Announcement of Lectures in the Atlanta Medical College,* 103-5.

31. *BA,* May 26, 1856; Ropes, *Six Months in Kansas,* 229; *Lib,* June 27, 1856; *BDA,* May 26, 27, 1856; *BC,* May 24, 26, 1856; Wilson, *Rise and Fall of the Slave Power in America,* 2: 486; Gienapp, "The Crime Against Sumner," 218-45; Donald, *Charles Sumner and the Coming of the Civil War,* 298-303; Freeman, *Field of Blood,* 215-26; Sinha, "The Caning of Charles Sumner," 233-62; Wilentz, *The Rise of American Democracy,* 690-92.

32. *BA,* May 26, 1856; Ropes, *Six Months in Kansas,* 229; *Lib,* June 27, 1856; *BDA,* May 26, 27, 1856; *BC,* May 24, 26, 1856; Wilson, *Rise and Fall of the Slave Power in America,* 2:486; Gienapp, "The Crime Against Sumner," 218-45; Donald, *Charles Sumner and the Coming of the Civil War,* 298-303; Freeman, *Field of Blood,* 215-26; Sinha, "The Canning of Charles Sumner," 233-62; Wilentz, *Rise of American Democracy,* 690-92.

33. Ropes, *Six Months in Kansas,* 229; *Lib,* June 27, 1856.

34. Wilentz, *The Rise of American Democracy,* 692.

35. *BDA,* May 26, 27, 1856; *BC,* May 24, 26, 1856; Wilson, *Rise and Fall of the Slave Power in America,* 2:486; Donald, *Charles Sumner and the Coming of the Civil War,* 298-303; Freeman,

Field of Blood, 215–26; Sinha, "The Caning of Charles Sumner," 233–62; Wilentz, *The Rise of American Democracy*, 690–92; Brooks, *Liberty Power*, 216–17. Although Blair maintained a residence in Washington on Pennsylvania Avenue, known as the Blair House, he built a spacious summer home he called the Silver Spring in nearby Maryland, which he moved into in 1854. At this mansion on Christmas Day 1855, Sumner, Salmon P. Chase, Nathaniel Banks, Preston King, and Gamaliel Bailey came together to form the Republican Party.

36. *Proceedings of the First Three Republican National Conventions of 1856, 1860 and 1864*, 15; *NYDT*, July 18, 1856; *BDT*, July 17, 1856; *Lib*, July 18, 1856; *BDA*, May 26, 27, July 17, 1856; *BA*, July 17, 1856; *BC*, May 24, 26, 1856; Wilson, *Rise and Fall of the Slave Power in America*, 2:486, Donald, *Charles Sumner and the Coming of the Civil War*, 298–303; Freeman, *Field of Blood*, 215–26; Sinha, "The Caning of Charles Sumner," 233–62; Wilent, *The Rise of American Democracy*, 690–92.

37. *BA*, July 7, 1856; *Lib*, July 18, 25, 1856.

38. *BT*, July 2, 7, 17, 25, 1856; *BDA*, May 26, 27, July 17, 1856; *NYDT*, July 18, 1856; *BDT*, July 17, 1856; *Lib*, July 18, 25, 1856; Donald, *Charles Sumner and the Coming of the Civil War*, 298–303; *BC*, May 24, 26, 1856; Wilson, *Rise and Fall of the Slave Power in America*, 2:486; Freeman, *Field of Blood*, 215–26; Sinha, "The Caning of Charles Sumner," 233–62; Wilentz, *The Rise of American Democracy*, 690–92.

39. *BA*, July 2, 5, 1856; *NYH*, Sept. 17, 1856; *BA*, July 2, 5, 1856; Doherty, "The Republican Party in Massachusetts," 505–15; Lunt, *The Origin of the Late War*, 1:260; Gienapp, *Origins of the Republican Party*, 389; Pearson, *Andrew*, 1:66–67; Donald, *Charles Sumner and the Coming of the Civil War*, 320–21; Baum, *Civil War Party System*, 35–40; Wilentz, *The Rise of American Democracy*, 693–706.

40. *BA*, Sept. 9, 1856; *BDA*, Sept. 9, Nov. 3, 6, 1856; *NYH*, Sept. 17, 1856; *BA*, July 2, 5, Sept. 9, 19, 1856; McCaughy, *Josiah Quincy*, 210–12; Doherty, "The Republican Party in Massachusetts," 505–15; Lunt, *The Origin of the Late War*, 1:260; Gienapp, *Origins of the Republican Party*, 388–89; Pearson, *Andrew*, 1:66–67; Donald, *Charles Sumner and the Coming of the Civil War*, 320–21; Baum, *Civil War Party System*, 35–40; Wilentz, *The Rise of American Democracy*, 693–706.

41. Andrew to Sumner, Dec. 18, 1856, Sumner Papers, HU; Pierce, *Memoirs and Letters of Charles Sumner*, 3:518.

42. Andrew's thoughts were taken from his Bowdoin Athenaean Society address, Chandler, *Memoir*, 186–89; Andrew Scrapbook 10, 12, 13, Andrew Papers, MHS.

CHAPTER 7: THE RADICAL CHAMPION

1. Mayer, *All on Fire*, 469–470; *BA*, Feb. 7, 1867; Donald, *Charles Sumner and the Coming of the Civil War*, 298–345; Wilentz, *The Rise of American Democracy*, 700–706.

2. *Speeches of John A. Andrew at Hingham and Boston*, 13; *Lib*, Mar. 13, 20, 1857; *BDA*, Mar. 12, 1857; Wilentz, *The Rise of American Democracy*, 706–7; Mayer, *All on Fire*, 470–74; Potter, *Impending Crisis*, 267–303; Taylor, *Fighting for Citizenship*, 32–37.

3. *BDA*, Mar. 12, 1857; *Lib*, Mar. 13, 20, 1857; *Speeches of John A. Andrew at Hingham and Boston*, 13; Wilentz, *The Rise of American Democracy*, 706–7; Mayer, *All on Fire*, 470–74; Potter, *Impending Crisis*, 267–303.

4. *McCrea v. Marsh*, 78 Massachusetts 211 (1858), Plaintiff's Exceptions," *McCrea v. Marsh*, Sept. 1, 1857, and "Judgment," Suffolk County Superior Court Judicial Court Records, MSA; Pattee, *Illustrative Cases in Reality*, 482–83; *AG*, Oct. 22, 1857; *MLR* 21 (Jan. 1859): 557;*BA*, Dec. 27, 1856; Pearson, *Andrew*, 1:58–59; Wilentz, *The Rise of American Democracy*, 706–7; William L. Burt assisted him; Bergeson-Lockwood, "We Do Not Care Particularly about the Skating Rinks" 254–88; "Recent Decisions," 561–62; "Notes. Rights under a Theatre Ticket," 455–56; Donald, *Charles Sumner and the Coming of the Civil War*, 298–345; Palmer, *Selected Letters of Charles Sumner*, 1:474–75; Mayer, *All on Fire*, 472–75. It remains unclear why McCrea sued Marsh instead of the theater manager, though it

could have been that the exhibition manager made this a contractual condition when agreeing to do the show.

5. *Acts and Resolves Passed by the General Court of Massachusetts, 1858,* 169, 182, 183, 189, 190; Baum, *Civil War Party System,* 10–45; Pearson, *Andrew,* 1:68–75; Hollandsworth, *Pretense of Glory,* 12–32; Schouler, *Massachusetts in the Civil War,* 12–13; *Lib,* Nov. 6, 20, 1857; Pearson, *Andrew,* 1:66; Mayer, *All on Fire,* 474–76.

6. *Acts and Resolves Passed by the General Court of Massachusetts, 1858,* 169, 182, 183, 189, 190; Baum, *Civil War Party System,* 10–45; Pearson, *Andrew,* 1:68–75; Hollandsworth, *Pretense of Glory,* 12–32; Schouler, *Massachusetts in the Civil War,* 12–13; *Lib,* Nov. 6, 20, 1857; Mayer, *All on Fire,* 474–76; Hughes, *Letters (Supplementary) of John Murray Forbes,* 2:62–63.

7. *Lib,* Feb. 6, 1857.

8. Schouler, *Massachusetts in the Civil War,* 12–13; *BDA,* June 12, Sept. 4, 1857; *LDC,* Aug. 28, 1857; *Lib,* Nov. 6, 20, 1857; Baum, *Civil War Party System,* 10–45; Pearson, *Andrew,* 1:68–75; Hollandsworth, *Pretense of Glory,* 12–32; Mayer, *All on Fire,* 474–76.

9. *Lib,* Nov. 13, Dec. 18, 1857; *BDA,* Nov. 12, 1857; *BET,* Nov. 13, 1857; *BB,* Nov. 20, 1857; *PDJ,* Nov. 20, 1857; *LS,* Nov. 27, 1857.

10. *Lib,* Nov. 13, 27, Dec. 18, 1857, May 7, 1858; *RR,* Nov. 18, 1857; Pearson, *Andrew,* 1:57–58; Browne, "Governor Andrew," 249–76; Schouler, *Massachusetts in the Civil War,* 12; Wirzbicki, "Black Transcendentalism," 269–90; Hancock, "The Elusive Boundaries of Blackness," 115–29; *BDA,* Nov. 12, 1857; *BET,* Nov. 13, 1857; *BB,* Nov. 20, 1857, *PDJ,* Nov. 20, 1857; *LS,* Nov. 27, 1857.

11. *Lib,* Nov. 10, 13, 1857; *NYH,* Nov. 9, 1857.

12. *Lib,* Oct. 23, 1857.

13. Strangis, *Lewis Hayden,* 115; *BSWA,* Nov. 4, 1857; *BWJ,* Oct. 31, 1 Nov. 1867; Hollandsworth, *Pretense of Glory,* 15–32; Wilentz, *The Rise of American Democracy,* 720–23.

14. Sumner to Andrew, Dec. 12, 1857, Andrew Papers, MHS.

15. *Lib,* Jan. 15, Feb. 5, 12, 26, Mar. 26, 1858; *TN,* Apr. 7, 1892; Gilbert, "The Ordeal of Edward Greeley Loring," 300–301; Pearson, *Andrew,* 1:78–79; Andrew to Wendell Phillips, Feb. 4, 1858, Phillips Papers, HU. Fuess, *The Life of Caleb Cushing,* 2:211–17.

16. Andrew to Sumner, Feb. 4, 1858, Sumner Papers, Andrew to Wendell Phillips, Feb. 4, 1858, Phillips Papers, HU; Pearson, *Andrew,* 1:74–79; Palmer, *Selected Letters of Charles Sumner,* 1:492–97; *Lib,* Feb. 26, Mar. 5, 26, 1858, *TN,* Apr. 7, 1892.

17. *Lib,* Jan. 15, Mar. 5, 1858; *BB,* Feb. 1, 1858; Fuess, *The Life of Caleb Cushing,* 2:211–17; *SR,* Jan. 8, 1858; Gilbert, "The Ordeal of Edward Greeley Loring," 300–302.

18. *Lib,* Feb. 5, 12, 19, 26, Mar. 5, 1858; *NYTrib,* quoted in *Lib,* Feb. 26, 1858; George Prentiss to Caleb Cushing, Feb. 1, 1858, Cushing Papers, LC; Fuess, *The Life of Caleb Cushing,* 2:211–17; Stewart, *Wendell Phillips,* 183.

19. Stone, "Sketch of John Albion Andrew," 1–30; *ART,* May 7, 1857, Mar. 12, 1859.

20. *Lib,* Feb. 26, Mar. 26, 1858; *BSWA,* Mar. 6, 1858; *BP,* Mar. 5, 6, 1858; *BDA,* Mar. 6, 1858; *BP,* Mar. 3, 1858; *SR,* Mar. 4, 1858; Wesley and Uzelac, *William Cooper Nell,* 497–98; *BWJ,* Nov. 4, 1867; Gilbert, "The Ordeal of Edward Greeley Loring," 305–13.

21. *Lib,* Mar. 26, 1858; *BP,* Mar. 3, 1858; *SR,* Mar. 4, 1858; Belohlavek, *Broken Glass,* 290–93; Gilbert, "The Ordeal of Edward Greeley Loring," 305–13.

22. *Lib,* Mar. 26, 1858; *BP,* Mar. 5, 6, 1858; *BDA,* Mar. 6, 1858; *BP,* Mar. 3, 1858; *SR,* Mar. 4, 1858; newspaper clippings, Andrew Papers, BowC; Pearson, *Andrew,* 1:78; Gilbert, "The Ordeal of Edward Greeley Loring," 305–13; *TN,* Apr. 7, 1892.

23. *TN,* Apr. 7, 1892, reviewing Hampton L. Carson's book titled *The Supreme Court of the United States: Its History* (Philadelphia: John Y. Huber Co. 1891), 268–70; *Lib,* Mar. 26, 1858; *BP,* Mar. 5, 6, 1858; *BDA,* Mar. 6, 1858; *BP,* Mar. 3, 1858; *SR,* Mar. 4, 1858; newspaper clippings, Andrew Papers, BowC; Pearson, *Andrew,* 1:78; Gilbert, "The Ordeal of Edward Greeley Loring," 305–13.

24. Palmer, *Selected Letters of Charles Sumner*, 1:493–97; Stone, "Sketch of John Albion Andrew," 1–30; *ART*, May 7, 1857, Mar. 12, 1859.

25. Andrew to Sumner, Mar. 6, 1858, Sumner Papers, HU; Pearson, *Andrew*, 1:77; *BDA*, Mar. 17, 1858.

26. *BP*, Mar. 5, 11, 19, 1858; *Lib*, Jan. 15, Feb. 5, 12, 26, 1858; *TN*, Apr. 7, 1892, 269; *BB*, Jan. 29, 30, 1858; *SR*, Jan. 12, 30, 1858; Pearson, *Andrew*, 1:78–79; Andrew to Wendell Phillips, Feb. 4, 1858, Phillips Papers, HU; Fuess, *The Life of Caleb Cushing*, 2:211–213.

27. Pearson, *Andrew*, 1:81; Chandler to Sumner, Mar. 10, 1858, Sumner Papers, HU; Gilbert, "The Ordeal of Edward Greeley Loring," 305–13; Stone, "Sketch of John Albion Andrew," 6.

28. Pearson, *Andrew*, 1:81; Bird to Sumner, Mar. 8, 1858, Sumner Papers, HU; Stone, "Sketch of John Albion Andrew," 4–5; Hollandsworth, *Pretense of Glory*, 32–36; Stearns, *Cambridge Sketches*, 167.

29. *Lib*, Mar. 26, 1858; *BP*, Mar. 19, 20, 1858; Fuess, *The Life of Caleb Cushing*, 2:215–16; Stone, "Sketch of John Albion Andrew," 4–19; Pearson, *Andrew*, 1:85–87; Blackett, *The Captive's Quest*, 438.

30. Stone, "Sketch of John Albion Andrew," 4–5; *Lib*, Mar. 26, 1858; *BDA*, Mar. 18, 1858; *BP*, Mar. 19, 20, 1858.

31. *Lib*, Mar. 26, 1858; *BP*, Mar. 19, 20, 1858; Stone, "Sketch of John Albion Andrew," 4–19; Pearson, *Andrew*, 1:85–87; Blackett, *The Captive's Quest*, 438.

32. *BDA*, Mar. 20, 1858; *BB*, Mar. 24, 1858; Pearson, *Andrew*, 1:88–89; Stone, "Sketch of John Albion Andrew, 4–19; Fuess, *The Life of Caleb Cushing*, 2:215–16; Hamrogue, "John A. Andrew," 27–30.

33. *BDA*, Mar. 20, 1858; *BB*, Mar. 24, 1858; Pearson, *Andrew*, 1:88–89; Stone, "Sketch of John Albion Andrew," 4–19; Fuess, *The Life of Caleb Cushing*, 2:215–16; Hamrogue, "John A. Andrew," 27–30.

34. *BDA*, Aug. 11, 1891; Fuess, *The Life of Caleb Cushing*, 2:211–19, *NYT*, Mar. 24, Apr. 2, 1858.

35. *BP*, Mar. 22, 1858.

36. *NYT*, Mar. 24, 1858.

37. Hall, *The Story of the Battle Hymn of the Republic*, 30–31.

38. *NYT*, Mar. 15, 1858; *BDA*, Mar. 20, 1858; Maltz, *Fugitive Slave on Trial*, 140–55; Gilbert, "The Ordeal of Edward Greeley Loring," 315–23. The last line is from Shakespeare's *Hamlet*.

39. *Lib*, Feb. 26, Mar. 26, 1858; *BSWA*, Mar. 6, 1858; Wesley and Uzelac, *William Cooper Nell*, 497–98.

40. *BH*, Mar. 19, 29, 1858, *Lib*, Jan. 15, Mar. 12, 26, 1858, *NYT*, Mar. 25, 1858; Andrew to Sumner, Mar. 6, 1858, Sumner Papers, HU; *BP*, Mar. 18, 26, 1858; *BDA*, Mar. 11, 1858; *BWJ*, Mar. 11, 1858; *BSWA*, Mar. 3, 6, 9, 10, 20, 1858; Blackett, *The Captive's Quest*, 438; Stone, "Sketch of John Albion Andrew," 25; Blackett, *The Captive's Quest*, 438; Hollandsworth, *Pretense of Glory*, 12–32; Maltz, *Fugitive Slave on Trial*, 140–42; Chandler, *Memoir*, 92–93; Mayer, *All on Fire*, 441.

41. Stone, "Sketch of John Albion Andrew," 11–12.

42. Fuess, *The Life of Caleb Cushing*, 217; Hollandsworth, *Pretense of Glory*, 35, 36; *NYTrib*, Mar. 25, Apr. 29, 1858; *BDJ*, Mar. 19, 20, 1858; *BP*, Mar. 24, 1858; Pearson, *Andrew*, 1:76, 81–92; Stone, "Sketch of John Albion Andrew," 10–17; Hollandsworth, *Pretense of Glory*, 35; Merrill and Ruchames, *Letters of Garrison*, 4:513.

43. Harrison, *Biographical Sketches of Preeminent Americans*, 4: see chapter on John Andrew.

44. Sumner to Andrew, Mar. 24, 1858, Andrew Papers, MHS; Palmer, *Selected Letters of Charles Sumner*, 1:495–96.

45. *BSWA*, Mar. 31, 1858; *Lib*, Apr. 2, 1858; *PJI*, Apr. 2, 1858; *FDP*, Mar. 11, 1859; Maltz, *Fugitive Slave on Trial*, 140–55; *Bulletins for the Constitutional Convention*, 1917–1918, 2:573–74; *NYT*, Mar. 25, 1858; *BP*, May 12, 1858.

46. *LDC*, May 24, 26, July 10, 1858; Donald, *Charles Sumner and the Coming of the Civil War*, 342–43; Palmer, *Selected Letters of Charles Sumner*, 1:510–22.

CHAPTER 8: REPUBLICAN STAR RISING

1. *NYT*, Sept 9, 10, 1858; *LDC*, Sept. 7, 8, 1858; *BP*, Aug. 26, Oct. 20, 1858; Wilentz, *The Rise of American Democracy*, 734–44.
2. *Lib*, Sept. 10, 1858; *NYT*, Sept. 10, 1858.
3. Stone, "Sketch of John Albion Andrew," 19; *Lib*, Sept. 10, 1858; *NYT*, Sept. 9, 1858, Jan. 14, 1874; Pearson, *Andrew*, 1:92–95; Chandler, *Memoir*, 71–72, 94–95.
4. *NHS*, Nov. 6, 1858; *BP*, Oct. 14, 1858; *LDC*, Oct. 19, 1858; *NYH*, Nov. 1, 1858; *NI*, Nov. 4, 1858; *Lib*, Nov. 5, 12, 1858; Mayer, *All on Fire*, 488–93.
5. Andrew to William Chamberlain, Oct. 8, 1858, Andrew to Benjamin R. Curtis, Oct. 5, 1858, Chamberlin Collection of Autographs, BPL; Deane, "Memoir of Cyrus Woodman," 345; *NHS*, Nov. 6, 1858; *BP*, Oct. 14, 1858; *LDC*, Oct. 19, 1858; *NYH*, Nov. 1, 1858; *NI*, Nov. 4, 1858; *Lib*, Nov. 5, 12, 1858; Mayer, *All on Fire*, 488–93.
6. *BDA*, Jan. 26, 1859; *Lib*, Feb. 18, Mar. 18, 1857; *Acts and Resolves Passed by the General Court of Massachusetts*, 1858.
7. *CI*, Mar. 26, 1859; *BDA*, Mar. 3, 5, 7, 8, 10, 17 Apr. 14, 1859; *LDC*, Mar. 3, 1859; *BDWC*, Apr. 6, 9, 1859; *BDJ*, Apr. 6, 1859; *Eleventh Annual Report of the Massachusetts School for the Idiotic and Feeble-Minded Youth*, 31; *Acts and Resolves Passed by the General Court of Massachusetts in the Year 1859*, 1:440–41, 447; *Proceedings of the Twenty-Second Annual Meeting of the Association for the Support of the Warren Street Chapel*, 1859, 3–25. Andrew was appointed chairman of the association in 1859.
8. *LDC*, May 14, 1859; *BDWC*, May 21, 1859; *BDA*, May 25, 1859.
9. Woodman to Andrew, June 3, 1858, Woodman Papers, SHSW; Pearson, *Andrew*, 1:95–96; *BDA*, May 13, 1859, Mar. 8, 1860; *LDC*, May 13, 14, 18, 1860.
10. *BDA*, July 7, 20, 1859; *LDC*, July 7, 9, 1859; *NBES*, July 7, 1859; *BB*, July 8, 1859; *BDJ*, June 23, 24, 25, 30, 1859; *BC*, Nov. 10, 27, 1858; *NHS*, July 16, 1859; *Reports of Cases Determined in the Circuit Court of the United States for the First Circuit*, 3:1–71; *NYT*, Aug. 26, 1858, July 9, 24, 1859; *BT*, June 21, 1859; *CIS Index to Presidential Executive Orders & Proclamations, Part 1*, 139; Harris, "Mutiny on Junior," 110–29; *NYTrib*, July 3, 1859; *BP*, Apr. 22, July 8, 1859; *PP*, July 8, 1859.
11. *Lib*, July 14, 1865; *BDA*, July 6, 1865; Andrew to F. W. Lincoln, Jr., June 30, 1865, Andrew Papers, MHS.
12. Chandler, *Memoir*, 199–235; *TC*, June 10, 1859; *BP*, July 13, 18, 20, 1859; *PPH*, July 9, 1859.
13. *LDC*, July 20, 1859; *BDA*, July 20, 1859; *Twenty-eighth Annual Report of the American Anti-Slavery Society 1861*, 46; Siebert, *The Vigilance Committee of Boston*, 1–23; Siebert, "The Underground Railroad in Massachusetts," 86; *Lib*, July 22, Aug. 19, 1859; *BDJ*, July 18, 1859; *BG*, July 22, 1859; *NYT*, July 20, 21, 1859; *NYH*, July 20, 1859, Aug. 10, 1860; *PlyR*, July 21, 1859.
14. *LDC*, July 20, 1859; *BDA*, July 20, 1859; *Twenty-eighth Annual Report of the American Anti-Slavery Society 1861*, 46; Siebert, *The Vigilance Committee of Boston*, 1–23; Siebert, "The Underground Railroad in Massachusetts," 86; *Lib*, July 22, Aug. 19, 1859; *BDJ*, July 18, 1859; *BG*, July 22, 1859; *NYT*, July 20, 21, 1859; *NYH*, July 20, 1859, Aug. 10, 1860; *PlyR*, July 21, 1859.
15. *Lib*, July 29, Aug. 12, 1859.
16. Richards, *Letters and Journals of Samuel Gridley Howe*, 2:472–74.
17. Boteler, "Recollections of the John Brown Raid," 399–416; Sanborn, "Comment by a Radical," 416–18.
18. *Report of the Select Committee of the Senate Appointed to Inquire into the Late Invasion and Seizure of the Public Property at Harper's Ferry*, 32–33, 186–95; *Acts and Resolves Passed by the General Court of Massachusetts*, 1858; Baum, *Civil War Party System*, 10–45; Pearson, *Andrew*, 1:66–75; Hollandsworth, *Pretense of Glory*, 12–32; Schouler, *A History of*

Massachusetts in the Civil War, 12–13; *Lib*, Nov. 6, 20, 25, 1857; Mayer, *All on Fire*, 474–76, 495–98; Schwartz, *Samuel Gridley Howe*, 233; Hughes, *Reminiscences of John Murray Forbes*, 2:62–63; Oates, *To Purge This Land with Blood*, 254–92; Reynolds, *John Brown Abolitionist*, 292–333; Harrold, *American Abolitionism*, 152–54; Sinha, *The Slave's Cause*, 550–66; Wilentz, *The Rise of American Democracy*, 744–753; Blight, *Frederick Douglass*, 290–305; Hudson, *The Making of "Mammy Pleasant,"* 24–44; Jackson, *Force and Freedom*, 112–14.

19. Stearns, *The Life and Public Services of George Luther Stearns*, 188; Andrew, "Legal Opinion for Franklin Sanborn," Oct. 21, 1859, Sanborn Papers, BPL; Heller, *Portrait of an Abolitionist*, 83–85, 106–7; Blight, *Frederick Douglass*, 305–15; Renehan, *The Secret Six*, 206–9; Keith, *When It Was Grand*, 104–5; Harrold, *American Abolitionism*, 152–54; speech delivered on Oct. 22, 1859, Andrew Papers, MHS; *Report of the Select Committee of the Senate Appointed to Inquire into the Late Invasion and Seizure of the Public Property at Harper's Ferry*, 186–95; Hughes, *Reminiscences of John Murray Forbes*, 2:62–63; *Lib*, Nov. 25, 1859; Oates, *To Purge This Land with Blood*, 271–358; Reynolds, *John Brown Abolitionist*, 292–333; Mayer, *All on Fire*, 495–98; Sinha, *The Slave's Cause*, 550–66.

20. Andrew to Montgomery Blair, Oct. 26, 1859, Blair to Andrew, Oct. 28, 29, 1859, see also George Hoyt to John LeBarnes, Oct. n.d., 1859, and Thomas Chilton to Andrew, Nov. 3, 1859, Andrew Papers, MHS; Heller, *Portrait of an Abolitionist*, 106–7; Reynold, *John Brown Abolitionist*, 292–337; *Speeches of John A. Andrew at Hingham and Boston*, 9; Villard, *John Brown*, 646; *NYH*, Oct. 28, Nov. 1, 1859.

21. Andrew to Hoyt, Oct. 26, 1859, Circular, Nov. 2, 1859 inviting colleagues to contribute money for John Brown's defense, Andrew to Blair, Oct. 31, Blair to Andrew, Nov. 3, 1859, Andrew Papers, MHS; Schwartz, *Samuel Gridley Howe*, 234–35; Shackelford, "From the Society's Collections," 97–114; *Report of the Select Committee of the Senate Appointed to Inquire into the Late Invasion and Seizure of the Public Property at Harper's Ferry*, 186–95; Smith, *The Francis Preston Blair Family in Politics*, 1:451; Oates, *To Purge This Land with Blood*, 271–358; Renehan, *The Secret Six*, 208–11; Reynolds, *John Brown Abolitionist*, 334–41; *LDC*, Feb. 13, 1860.

22. Reynolds, *John Brown Abolitionist*, 354; Oates, *To Purge This Land with Blood*, 327.

23. *Lib*, Nov. 4, 1859; Oates, *To Purge This Land with Blood*, 327–29; Renehan, *The Secret Six*, 213–15; Reynolds, *John Brown Abolitionist*, 292–355.

24. *Report of the Select Committee of the Senate Appointed to Inquire into the Late Invasion and Seizure of the Public Property at Harper's Ferry*, 186–95; Shackelford, "From the Society's Collections," 97; Oates, *To Purge This Land with Blood*, 327–58; BP, Oct. 11, Nov. 2, 7, 1859; BC, Oct. 20, 22, 1859; Davis, "Liberty Before Union," 37–52.

25. Stearns to Andrew, Nov. 5, 1859, Andrew to Blair, Nov. 5, 1859, Blair to Andrew, Nov. 6, 16, 1859, Andrew Papers, MHS.

26. Renehan, *The Secret Six*, 224–27; Sanborn to Higginson, Nov. 13, 1859, Higginson Papers, BPL; Trent, *The Manliest Man*, 214–18.

27. Shackelford, "From the Society's Collections," 99–14; Andrew to Green, Jan. 16, 1860, Brown Manuscripts, CU; Andrew to Higginson, Dec. 23, 1859, MS E5.1, BPL; Stearns to Andrew, Nov. 5, 1859, Andrew to Blair, Nov. 5, 1859, Blair to Andrew, Nov. 6, 16, 1859, Andrew Papers, MHS. The act says nothing about precluding habeas corpus, *U.S. Statutes at Large*, IX, 29th Congress, 1st session, chapter 98, section 7; Palmer, *Selected Letters of Charles Sumner*, 2:6–9; Oates, *To Purge This Land with Blood*, 320–58; Reynolds, *John Brown Abolitionist*; LDC, Feb. 14, 1871; Renehan, *The Secret Six*, 206–9, 220–28; Trent, *The Manliest Man*, 214–18; Andrew came into possession of incriminating letters and advised him to come by the office to retrieve them. Sanborn, *Recollections of Seventy Years*, 1:189–91; Sanborn to Higginson, Dec. 20, 1859, Andrew to Higginson, Dec. 23, 1859, Higginson Papers, BPL.

28. "Letter from Gov. Andrew," 211–13; Pearson, *Andrew*, 1:104–6; Schwartz, *Samuel Gridley Howe*, 236–38; Shackelford, "From the Society's Collections," 99–114.

29. Renehan, *The Secret Six*, 214–15; Hollandsworth, *Pretense of Glory*, 37–39; Heller, *Portrait of an Abolitionist*, 107–11; Howe to Andrew, Dec. 30, 1859, Frank Sanborn to Andrew, Feb. 24, 1860, Andrew Papers, MHS. Hoyt wrote Andrew that he believed there was a *"systematic* effort on the part of abolitionists of the *Garrison School* to thwart our efforts to a achieve anything out of our theory of his [Brown's] insanity." He argued that Blair was pleased with the affadavits and that whether Brown was insane or not, they ought to try it, Hoyt to Andrew, Nov. 22, 1859, Andrew Papers, MHS. Blair responded to Andrew's Nov. 21 note two days later with a long letter, Blair to Andrew, Nov. 23, 1859, Andrew Papers, MHS; *BDA*, Sept. 21, Nov. 30, 1859; *NYH*, Nov. 10, 1859.

30. Chandler, *Memoir*, 86–87; Harrold, *American Abolitionism*, 152–54; Clark, *History of the Temperance Reform in Massachusetts*, 97–98; *MLR* 22 (Nov. 1859): 440–44; Gray, *Reports of Cases Argued and Determined in the Supreme Judicial Court of Massachusetts*, 14:226–41; *LDC*, Nov. 8, 1859; *BDA*, Nov. 1, Dec. 22, 1859. In one instance in November, a most curious precedent established the General Court's Lower House as a body for executive oversight, with judicial authority. George P. Burnham, commissioner of the State Liquor Agency having charge of the statewide distribution of liquors for medicinal purposes was arraigned at the bar of the House. Burnham had refused to cooperate with the legislator's special committee investigating charges of adulteration of agency liquor. The House responded by ordering him to court. He hired Andrew to represent him and refused to produce the documents pertaining to his agency's work which were demanded by the House Speaker. His refusal led to his being declared in contempt by the House, whereby the sergeant-at-arms escorted him to the Suffolk County jail, where he served out a sentence of twenty-five days. Judge Hoar of the Supreme Court ruled in *George P. Burnham vs. John Morrissey* that his incarceration was both legal and proper for charges of contempt. Although for adulteration of liquor was later brought against Burnham by the Suffolk County district attorney, the charges were dropped, and the case never went to trial. There were rumors that Andrew considered hiring Ben Butler to defend Brown but the barrister had injured his ankle and was unable to travel. *SR*, Nov. 8, 1859; *WTran*, Nov. 1, 1859; Davis, "Liberty Before Union," 54–55.

31. *Speeches of John A. Andrew at Hingham and Boston*, 8–9; Villard, *John Brown*, 646; Andrew Scrapbook 13, Adams to Andrew, Nov. 6, 1859, Andrew Papers, MHS; Pearson, *Andrew*, 1:100–101; *Lib*. Nov. 25,1859, 21 Sept. 1860; *Outlook*, Nov. 21, 1896; Keith, *When It was Grand*, 107–108; Palmer, *Selected Letters of Charles Sumner*, 2:6–7; *Lib*, Nov. 25, 1859; *NYH*, Nov. 20, 21, 1859.

32. *BC*, Sept. 7, 1860; *Lib*, Nov. 25, Sept. 7, 1860; Sanborn, *Dr. S. G. Howe*, 270; *Speeches of John A. Andrew at Hingham and Boston*, 8–10; James Freeman Clarke to Andrew, Nov. 8, 1859, on contributing money, Blair to Andrew, Nov. 8, 12, 1859, Samuel Bowles to Andrew, Nov. 16, 1859, Andrew Papers, MHS; Pearson, *Andrew*, 1:98–100.

33. Stearns, *Cambridge Sketches*, 246.

34. Oates, *To Purge This Land with Blood*, 351; *LDC*, Dec. 20, 1859; *NYH*, Dec. 16, 24, 1859; *Lib*, Sept. 7, 1860; *BC*, Sept. 7,1860.

35. Oates, *To Purge This Land with Blood*, 351; this note was printed in several papers including the *LDC*, Dec. 20, 1859; *NYH*, Dec. 16, 24, 1859; *Lib*, Sept. 7, 1860; *BC*, Sept. 7, 1860.

36. Oates, *To Purge This Land with Blood*, 351; *HW*, Dec. 3, 10, 1859.

37. Lepore, "How Longfellow Woke the Dead," 33–46; Reynolds *John Brown Abolitionist*, 354–438.

38. *SR*, Dec. 2, 1860; Merriam, *The Life and Times of Samuel Bowles*, 1:253.

39. Renehan, *The Secret Six*, 23–40; Pearson, *Andrew*, 1:104–5; Reynolds, *John Brown Abolitionist*, 354–438; *NYT*, Dec. 3, 1859; *NYH*, Dec. 2, 1859; Prentice, *The Life of Gilbert Haven*, 308–10; *NA*, Dec. 1, 1859. Commonwealth Senators voted 11 to 8 against adjournment. *BP*, Dec. 3, 1859; *BET*, Dec. 2, 1859.

40. Shackelford, "From the Society's Collections," 97–114; newspaper clippings in Andrew

Papers, BowC; Green to Andrew, Nov. 23,1859, Allan B. Magruder to Andrew, Nov. 23, Dec. 2, 1859, William Green to Andrew, Dec. 30, 1859, Andrew Papers, MHS.

41. Sumner to Andrew, Dec. 8, 9, 10, 12, 15, 1859, Sumner Papers, HU; Palmer, *Selected Letters of Charles Sumner*, 2:6–14; Langsdorf, "Thaddeus Hyatt," 225–39; *NYTrib*, July 18, 1860; Knickerbocker, *Bard of Bethel*, 372; Finkelman, *His Soul Goes Marching On*, 7–9; Renehan, *The Secret Six*, 207–9; 236–40; Reynolds, *John Brown Abolitionist*, 329–429; Trent, *The Manliest Man*, 214–18; NYT, Apr. 5, 1860; BDA, Dec. 3, 1859; LDC, Dec. 5, 1859; NI, Dec. 6, 1859.

42. Andrew to William Pitt Fessenden, Nov. 16, Dec. 12, 1859, Fessenden to Andrew, Dec. 15, 1859, Brown Manuscripts, CU; Blair to Andrew, Dec. 7, 1859; Andrew to Blair, Dec. 1, 1859, Blair to Andrew, Dec.[3?] 7, 1859, James M. Mason to Andrew, Feb. 2, 1860, Henry Wilson to Andrew, Dec. 17, 1859, Andrew Papers, MHS; Palmer, *Selected Letters of Charles Sumner*, 2:9–10; Andrew to Sumner, Dec. 6, 9, 1859, and Feb. 18, Mar. 3, 1860, Sumner to Andrew, Feb. 4, 7, 1860, Sumner Papers, HU.

43. Andrew to Blair, Dec. 31, 1859, Howe to Andrew, Jan. 11, 1860, Woodman to Andrew, Dec. 25, 1859, Andrew Papers, MHS.

44. Howe to Andrew, Jan. 31, and two undated letters in February to Andrew, Sanborn to Andrew, Jan. 19, 18, 1860, Andrew Papers, MHS; *Report of the Select Committee of the Senate Appointed to Inquire into the Late Invasion and Seizure of the Public Property at Harper's Ferry*, 159, 166–67, 186–95; James Jackson had also been summoned to Washington and Wendell Phillips wrote Andrew seeking advice regarding whether he should appear. He ended up going to Washington and appeared but testified that he had only sent money to Francis J. Meriam, one of Brown's men, but had no knowledge it was to be used in the raid on Harpers Ferry. See Phillips to Andrew, Feb. n.d., 1860, Andrew Papers, MHS; BDA, Dec. 3, 1859. Henry Wilson asked Andrew to call on Lysander Spooner, an outspoken abolitionist who endorsed Brown's plan, to not publish a letter Seward had written five years before to Gerrit Smith complimenting Spooner's book, *The Unconstitutionality of Slavery* written in 1845. Spooner had apparently asked Seward for permission to make it public, and Seward had responded that he wished that the letter was not made public. Wilson allowed that Seward was suffering under "terrible fire of abuse," and he wanted Andrew's help to diffuse the issue, especially as the fallout from the Brown conspiracy continued. Always the loyal friend, Andrew complied. Wilson to Andrew, Jan. 27, 1860, Andrew Papers, MHS.

45. *Report of the Select Committee of the Senate Appointed to Inquire into the Late Invasion and Seizure of the Public Property at Harper's Ferry*, 186–95 Andrew to Sumner, Feb. 4, 1860, Sumner to Andrew, Feb. 7, 1860, and an additional letter without date, 1860, Andrew Papers, MHS; Palmer, *Selected Letters of Charles Sumner*, 2:16–17; BDA, Aug. 8, 1860; LDC, Feb. 8. 1860.

46. Pearson, *Andrew*, 1:104–7; *Report of the Select Committee of the Senate Appointed to Inquire into the Late Invasion and Seizure of the Public Property at Harper's Ferry*, 192; Blair to Andrew, Jan. 6, 21, 1860, *Letters Received by Samuel Gridley Howe*, MHS; Sumner to Andrew, Jan. 12, 1860, Sumner Papers, HU; Schwartz, *Samuel Gridley Howe*, 244–45; *NYTrib*, Feb. 17, 1860; *Lib*, Feb. 17, 1860; Samuel Chilton to Andrew, Dec. 22, 1859, Andrew Papers, MHS; BDA, Aug. 8, 1860.

47. Pearson, *Andrew*, 1:107–8; *Report of the Select Committee of the Senate Appointed to Inquire into the Late Invasion and Seizure of the Public Property at Harper's Ferry*, 192; *Speeches of John A. Andrew at Hingham and Boston*, 9–13; BDA, Aug. 8, 1860.

48. *Report of the Select Committee of the Senate Appointed to Inquire into the Late Invasion and Seizure of the Public Property at Harper's Ferry*, 192–93; Pearson, *Andrew*, 1:109; Hamrogue, "John A. Andrew," 13–16.

49. LDC, Feb. 11, 13, 1860.

50. Howe, *Reminiscences*, 261; Thoreau quote taken from his public address at North Elba,

July 4, 1860, in Dircks, *Essays and Other Writings of Henry Thoreau*, 131–32; Andrew Scrapbook 11, Andrew Papers, MHS.

CHAPTER 9: THE GOVERNORSHIP

1. Howe, *Reminiscences*, 263; Home for the Aged Colored Women, Records and Annual Reports of the Proceedings, Jan. 8, 1861, see also First Annual Report of the Board of Managers of the [Boston] Home for Aged Colored Women, Jan. 8, 1861, MHS; Mac-Carthy, "The Home for Aged Colored Women," 55–73; Hale, *James Freeman Clarke*, 6; Glymph, *The Women's Fight*, 160–61.

2. NYT, June 5, 1883; MacCarthy, "The Home for the Aged Colored Women," 55–73; Hale, *James Freeman Clarke*, 6; BP, Jan. 16, 1860.

3. Andrew to Cyrus Woodman, Apr. 2, 1860, Woodman Papers, SHSW; *LDC*, Mar. 8, 1860; J. P. Sanderson to Andrew, Mar. 8, 1860, Shrady to Andrew, Mar. 11, 1860, Stevens to Andrew, Apr. 16, Russell Errett to Andrew, Apr. 17, 1860, Andrew Papers, MHS; *BDA*, Mar. 8, 1860, Aug. 11, 1891; *BP*, Feb. 28, Mar. 8, 1860. BDA, Feb. 24, 1860; Pearson, *Andrew*, 1:112; Harrington, *Fighting Politician*, 48; Donald, *Charles Sumner and the Coming of the Civil War*, 363–65; Hamrogue, "John A. Andrew," 31–32; Davis, "Liberty Before Union," 99–105.

4. *TCU*, July 17, 1884; *Lib*, Apr. 13, 1860; "Sanborn's Case," 7–20; *EOS*, June 21, 1884; *LDC*, Feb. 24, 1860; Hyatt to Andrew, Mar. 17, 1860, Andrew to P. W. Chandler, Feb. 20, 1860, Andrew Papers, MHS; Andrew to Sumner, Mar. 3, 14, 21, and Sumner to Andrew, Mar. 18,1860, Sumner Papers, HU; Palmer, *Selected Letters of Charles Sumner*, 2:20–21; Samuel E. Sewall and John A. Andrew, Argument on Behalf of Thaddeus Hyatt, LV; Andrew to Thaddeus Hyatt, Mar. 1860, Brown Manuscripts, CU; Langsdorf, "Thaddeus Hyatt," 225–39; Andrew defended Thaddeus Hyatt. A New York member of the National Kansas Aid Committee, Hyatt had been summoned because his name was found in Brown's papers. He went to Washington, but refused to testify before the Senate, whereby the deputy sergeant at arms had him arrested. The New Yorker chose the martyrdom path and spent several months in jail, even while Andrew came to his defense, urged him to testify, and enlisted Sumner's assistance. From prison, Hyatt thanked Andrew for his letters and advice, and that as much as he was imprisoned, confessed that "stone walls do not a prison make. . . ."

5. Mayer, *All on Fire*, 506; R. H. Fuller to Andrew, Apr. 4, 1860, Andrew Papers, MHS; Pearson, *Andrew*, 1:108–10; Hughes, *Reminiscences of John Murray Forbes*, 2:62; *Lib*, Apr. 13, 1860; NYT, Apr. 5, 1860; Circular, Sept. 27, 1860, Andrew Papers, MHS; *TPF*, Nov. 15, 1860; Sumner to Andrew, Jan. 12, 1860, Sumner Papers, HU; Palmer, *Selected Letters of Charles Sumner*, 2:21–22; "Sanborn's Case," 7–37; Chandler, *Every Other Saturday*, 1:197; Stearns, *The Life and Public Services of George Luther Stearns*, 188; Reynolds, *John Brown Abolitionist*, 430–31.

6. Pearson, *Andrew*, 1:113; BDA, May 10, 12, 1860.

7. Halstead, *Caucuses of 1860*, 140.

8. *Proceedings of the First Three Republican National Conventions of 1856, 1860 and 1864*, 155–56; BDA, May 16, 19, 25, 1860; LDC, May 28, 1860; Tarbell, *The Life of Abraham Lincoln*, 1:360; Halstead, *Caucuses of 1860*, 122–54, for Coffin comments see newspaper clipping entitled War Reminiscences in the Edward Waldo Emerson Papers, MHS; Griffis, *Charles Carleton Coffin*, 71–74; *BP*, May 16, 18, 19, 20, 1860; Burlingame, *Abraham Lincoln*, 1:613–19; Autobiography of Honorable John S. Keyes, 177, Keyes Papers, CFPL; NYT, May 19, 1860; McClure, *Abraham Lincoln and Men of War-Times*, 39; Taber, Hawk, & Co. to Andrew, Mar. 23, 1860, Andrew's Speech and Notes on the 1860 Chicago Convention, Miscellaneous Papers, Andrew Papers, MHS; Carpenter, "How Lincoln Was Nominated," 853–59; Wilentz, *The Rise of American Democracy*, 758–59. There is a little legend associated with the convention and Andrew's influence. According to Nevins, *The Emergence of Lincoln*, 2:258, Andrew steered the Massachusetts delegation to meet with the New Jersey delegation and reported that if Seward could not be elected, they

would support anyone else who could. Andrew maintained that opposition was divided between Lincoln, Cameron, and Dayton, and that unless Pennsylvania, New Jersey, Indiana, and Illinois decided on one of these, the Massachusetts delegates would cast their votes for Seward. Later that evening the New Jersey, Illinois, and Pennsylvania representatives visited Andrew and said they could not vote for Seward. After several hours long into the night, representatives finally agreed to see which of the candidates had the greatest strength and Lincoln appeared on everyone's list.

9. Pearson, *Andrew*, 1:112–13; Brockett, *The Life and Times of Abraham Lincoln*, 165–70; *Proceedings of the First Three Republican National Conventions of 1856, 1860 and 1864*, 155–56; Tarbell, *The Life of Abraham Lincoln*, 1:360; Halstead, *Caucuses of 1860*, 122–54, newspaper clipping entitled *War Reminiscences* in the Edward Waldo Emerson Papers, MHS; Griffis, *Charles Carleton Coffin*, 71–74; BP, May 16, 18, 19, 20, 1860; Burlingame, *Abraham Lincoln*, 1:613–19; Autobiography of Honorable John S. Keyes, 177, Keyes Papers, CFPL; NYT, May 19, 1860; BDA, May 16, 19, 25, 1860; McClure, *Abraham Lincoln and Men of War-Times*, 39; Taber, Hawk, & Co. to Andrew, Mar. 23, 1860, Andrew's Speech and Notes on the 1860 Chicago Convention, Miscellaneous Papers, Andrew Papers, MHS; LDC, May 22, 1860; Carpenter, "How Lincoln Was Nominated," 853–59; Wilentz, *The Rise of American Democracy*, 758–59.

10. Bartlett, *The Life and Public Services of Hon. Abraham Lincoln*, 143.

11. LDC, May 25, 1860; BDA, May 19, 25, 26, 1860; Pearson, *Andrew*, 1:115–16; FC, June 9, 1860; Ware, *Political Opinion in Massachusetts*, 22–28.

12. BDA, May 19, 25, 26, 1860; Pearson, *Andrew*, 1:115–116; FC, June 9, 1860; Ware, *Political Opinion in Massachusetts*, 22–28.

13 Andrew to Garrison, July 31, 1860, *Speeches of John A. Andrew at Hingham and Boston*, 13; Hamrogue, "John A. Andrew," 16; Chandler, *Memoir*, 86–87; Mayer, *All on Fire*, 508–509.

14. Pearson, *Andrew*, 1:117.

15. *Lib*, Aug. 10, 1860; *Speeches of John A. Andrew at Hingham and Boston*, 13.

16. WS, Aug. 25, 1860; LDC, Aug. 27, 1860.

17. *Lib*, Sept. 7, 21, 1860; Sumner to Andrew, Aug. 11, 1861, Sumner Papers, HU; Hollandsworth, *Pretense of Glory*, 38–42; Mayer, *All on Fire*, 510–17; Harrington, "Nathaniel Prentiss Banks," 626–54; NYH, Sept. 27, 1860; Foner, *Free Soil, Free Labor, Free Men*, 3–9.

18. SR, July 14, 1860; Heller, *Portrait of an Abolitionist*, 128–29; BDC, Jan. 11, 1868; NYH, Sept. 27, 1860; Pearson, *Andrew*, 1:118–19.

19. NYOC, May 17, 1860; "The Yacht Wanderer, G. B. Lamar," 139–50; *Decisions of Hon. Peleg Sprague in Admiralty and Maritime Causes*, 515–21; BT, Jan. 23, 1860; NYT, June 12, 15, Oct. 24, 1858, Dec. 17, 22, 31, 1858, Jan. 1, Mar. 22, Apr. 1, 1859; FLIN, Jan. 21, 1860; *Lib*, Dec. 24, 1858; NYH, Jan. 7, Apr. 24, May 25, June 2, 16, 22, 1860; BDJ, June 21, 1860; J. B. Lamar to Andrew, Apr. 30, 1860, Caleb Cushing to Andrew, Oct. 30, 1860, Andrew Papers, MHS; Chandler, *Memoir*, 85–86; Jordan, "Charles Augustus Lafayette Lamar and the Movements to Reopen the African Slave Trade," 247–90; Wells, *The Slave Ship Wanderer*, 10–11; Calonius, *The Wanderer*, 75–78; Finkelman, *Slavery in the Courtroom*, 246–48.

20. Donald, *Charles Sumner and the Coming of the Civil War*, 363–65; SR, Aug. 29, 30, 1860; Stone, "Sketch of John Albion Andrew," 9–20; BDJ, Jan. 11, 1868, Andrew Papers, BowC; Hollandsworth, *Pretense of Glory*, 39–42; Ware, *Political Opinion in Massachusetts during the Civil War*, 28–32; NYTrib, Aug. 24; SR, Aug. 27, 1860; LDC, Aug. 25, 1860; Pearson, *Andrew*, 1:120–21; Davis, "Liberty Before Union," 109–12.

21. SR, Aug. 29, 30, Sept. 1, 1860; Pearson, *Andrew*, 1:121–22; BDA, Aug. 24, 1860; Hamrogue, "John A. Andrew," 35; Hollandsworth, *Pretense of Glory*, 39–42; Stone, "Sketch of John Albion Andrew," 10–20; BDJ, Jan. 11, 1868, Andrew Papers, BowC; Donald, *Charles Sumner and the Coming of the Civil War*, 363–66; George W. McLellan to Andrew, Aug. 21, Andrew to Gentlemen, Sept. 5, 1860, Correspondence and Speech Preparations, Andrew to George Boutwell, Sept. 15, 1860, Andrew Papers, MHS; NYT, Sept. 6, 1860.

22. BDA, Aug. 11, 1891, Aug. 30, 1860; SR, Aug. 29, 30, Sept. 7, 1860; NYH, Aug. 30, Sept. 6, 1860; TLW, Sept. 1, 1877; Robinson, "Warrington" Pen-Portraits, 92–93; Lib, Aug. 31, 1860; NHS, Sept. 1, 1860; LDC, Aug. 27, 1860.

23. Speeches of John A. Andrew at Hingham and Boston, 2–5, 13–15; NYT, Sept. 6, 1860; LDC, Sept. 5, 6, 1860; NDH, Sept. 1, 4, 5, 1860; BP, Sept. 3, 6, 1860; Lib, Sept. 7, 1860; Galluzzo, Looking Back at South Shore History, 55–57.

24. BDA, Sept. 6, 1860; Speeches of John A. Andrew at Hingham and Boston, 5–8; Hamrogue, "John A. Andrew," 37; See also, a copy of Andrew's speech accepting the nomination Sept. 1860, in the miscellaneous papers of the Andrew Papers, MHS.

25. Charles Frederick Winslow Diary, Sept. 4, 6, 1860, Winslow Papers, MHS.

26. James A. Dix to Charles Frederick Winslow, Sept. 5, 1860, Andrew to Winslow, Sept. 7, 1860, Winslow Diary, Sept. 4, 6, 1860, Winslow Papers, MHS.

27. BP, Sept. 12, 1860.

28. Merriam, The Life and Times of Samuel Bowles, 1:318.

29. SR, Aug. 30, 1860; Merriam, The Life and Times of Samuel Bowles, 1:266–67; NYH, Aug. 31, 1860; Lib, Sept. 7, 1860; Pearson, Andrew, 1:123–24; Donald, Charles Sumner and the Coming of the Civil War, 363–65.

30. BP, Sept. 13, 1860; BC, Oct. 1, 1860; Hamrogue, "John A. Andrew," 30–40; Lib, Sept. 7, 1860. Andrew refused to deny that he had fought for African Americans, but he sought redress for Lunt's sloppiness by providing copies of what he said to the editor. Lunt apologized, but continued his transgressions against Andrew, who threatened to sue him for libel, which forced the editor into retreat.

31. Bird, "Recollections of Andrew," BDJ, Jan. 11, 1868, Andrew Papers, BowC; Lib, Sept. 7, 1860; "Wet Blanket" quote, taken from LDC, Sept. 26, 1860. The Constitutional Union Party polled well in the wealthier side of the Sixth Ward.

32. Lib, Sept. 7, 1860.

33. BP, Sept. 17, 1860.

34. BDA, Sept. 8, 1860; Speeches by John A. Andrew at Hingham and Boston, 16; NYH, Sept. 7, 1860; LDC, Sept. 11, 1860.

35. Winslow Diary, Sept. 26, 27, 29, 1860, Winslow Papers, MHS; Pearson, Andrew, 1:125; Speech of Hon. Robert C. Winthrop; Winthrop, A Memoir of Robert C. Winthrop, 213–14; LDC, Oct. 2, 1860.

36. Rogers, Life and Letters of William Barton Rogers, 2:41.

37. NHS, Sept. 1, 1860; BDA, Oct. 4, 5, 1860; PBCE, Oct. 19, 1860.

38. LDC, Oct. 20, 1860.

39. LDC, Nov. 7, 9, 1860; Pearson, Andrew, 1:56; Lib, Feb. 18, 1860; Pickard, Life and Letters of John Greenleaf Whittier, 2:434; BDA, Sept. 11, Oct. 11, 1860; Bowen, Massachusetts in the War, 1; Trefousse, Ben Butler, 58–62; Schouler, A History of Massachusetts in the Civil War, 2–3; BDA, Sept. 4, Nov. 9, 1860; Miller, States at War, 1:252–53 Leonard, Benjamin Franklin Butler, 48–49.

40. NYT, Nov. 2, 1860; Davis, "Liberty Before Union," 119.

41. LDC, Nov. 9, 1860; BDA, Nov. 9, 10, 1860; Davis, "Liberty Before Union," 53–55.

42. Richard S. Faye to Banks, Dec. 6, 1860, Banks Papers, LC; Baum, Civil War Party System, 48–52; G. B. Lamar to Andrew, Nov. 15, Dec. 1, 7, 1860, Andrew Papers, MHS; NYT, Nov. 2, 1860; SR, Nov. 9, 1860; Hamrogue, "John A. Andrew," 39.

43. Baum, Civil War Party System, 55–56; BDJ, Jan. 11, 1868, Andrew Papers, BowC; Stearns, Cambridge Sketches, 168–74; SR, Apr. 28, 1901.

44. NYT, Oct. 17, 1886; BDA, Oct. 11, 1886.

45. Winslow Diary, Nov. 30, 1860, Winslow Papers, MHS; Pearson, Andrew, 1:131; NYTrib, Dec. 5, 1860, BET, Dec. 3, 1860, BDJ, Dec. 5, 1860; Lib, Nov. 23, 30, 1860; BDA, Dec. 4, 1860; LDC, Dec. 4, 1860; Baum, Civil War Party System, 48–49; Miller, States at War, 1:253; SR, Dec. 4, 14, 1860; Holzer, Lincoln, President Elect, 51. Andrew wrote a letter to Moses Kimball, the Republican owner of the Boston Museum about the affair and

to congratulate him on his nomination for mayor even though he lost to Democrat Joseph Wightman. Andrew was ill and could not attend the Boston Republican Convention that nominated Kimball and he praised the owner for being on the right side of free speech and the meeting should never have been broken up. "Rich or poor, white or black, great or small, wise or foolish, in season or out of season, in the right or in the wrong, whosoever will speak, let him speak, and whosoever will hear, let him hear." *Lib*, Dec. 14, 1860. In the meantime, Andrew wrote Lincoln a letter on behalf of Amos Nouse of Bath, Maine, as a recommendation for him in the position of Special Agent for the Treasury Department for Inspecting the Custom Houses of New England. Andrew to Lincoln, Dec. 13, 1860, RG 56 Records of the Division of Appointments, Records relating to Special Agents and Inspectors and Custom House Appointments, NARA.

46. *Lib*, Dec. 14, 1860; *SR*, Dec. 4, 14, 1860; *BI*, Dec. 19, 1860; Whipple, *Eulogy*, 16.

47. Merriam, *The Life and Times of Samuel Bowles*, 1:259.

48. Andrew to Sumner, Dec. 5, 1860, Sumner Papers, HU.

49. Andrew to Banks, Dec. 14, 1860, Banks Papers, LC; Andrew to Sumner, Dec. 5, 1860, Sumner Papers, HU; Andrew to Forbes, Jan. 3, 1861, Andrew Papers, MHS; *BP*, Dec. 13, 1860; Andrew Papers, MHS; Donald, *Charles Sumner and the Coming of the Civil War*, 365–73; Stearns, *The Life and Public Services of George Luther Stearns*, 236–37; Heller, *Portrait of an Abolitionist*, 130–32; Hamrogue, "John A. Andrew," 41.

50. Andrew to Montgomery Blair, Nov. 24, 1860, Blair-Lee Family Papers, PU; also quoted in Green, *Freedom, Union, and Power*, 65; Pearson, *Andrew*, 1:133–34; Andrew to Sumner, Dec. 14, 1860, Sumner to Andrew, Dec. 19, 1860, Sumner Papers, HU; Winslow Diary, Nov. 30, 1860, Winslow Papers, MHS; Donald, *Charles Sumner and the Coming of the Civil War*, 365–73.

51. *LDC*, Nov. 18, 1867.

52. Stearns, *Cambridge Sketches*, 249; Pearson, *Andrew*, 1:135, Andrew to Jonathan Bourne, Jr., Sept. 6, 1860, Andrew Papers, MHS; Helper, *Impending Crisis of the South*; Rhodes, *History of the United States*, 2:419–20; Heller, *Portrait of an Abolitionist*, 131–32; *BP*, Dec. 22, 24, 1860.

53. Pearson, *Andrew*, 1:135–36; Pearson mentions that these comments came from an October 17, 1864, speech, see *BDA*, Oct. 18, 24, 1864; *BP*, Oct. 18, 1860; Meyer, *Colonel of the Black Regiment*, 177; Hamrogue, "John A. Andrew," 42; *BP*, Dec. 24, 1860.

54. Winslow to Andrew, Dec. 23, 1860, Andrew to Winslow, Dec. 23, 1860, Andrew Papers, MHS.

55. Curtis reproduced his letter for the Philadelphia *Times* in 1883 for publication in Buchanan, *The Messages of President Buchanan*, 312–15; Moore, *The Works of James Buchanan*, 11:49; biblical references from the Book of Isaiah.

CHAPTER 10: MAN FOR THE HOUR

1. *BDA*, Jan. 2, 1861; Dalton, Wirkkala, and Thomas, *Leading the Way*, 145; Reynolds, "Benevolence on the Home Front in Massachusetts during the Civil War," 14–16.

2. Sumner to Andrew, Dec. 27, 1861, two letters on Jan. 3, 1862, Sumner Papers, HU; Baum, *Civil War Party System*, 56–57, 75; Bowen, *Massachusetts in the War*, 10–22; Harrington, "Nathaniel Prentiss Banks," 650–54; Moore, *Works of James Buchanan*, 11:49; Pearson, *An American Railroad Builder*, 113–14; Pearson, *Andrew*, 1:137

3. Andrew to Forbes, Jan. 3, 1861, Andrew Papers, MHS

4. Chandler, *Memoir*, 30, 84–85; *NYTrib*, Nov. 21, 1880.

5. Schouler, *A History of Massachusetts Massachusetts in the Civil War*, 8.

6. *BDA*, Jan. 7, 1861.

7. Miller, *States at War*, 1:242–53; Schouler, *A History of Massachusetts in the Civil War*, 8–16; Andrew to John Murray Forbes, Jan. 3, 1861, Andrew Papers, MHS; Richard Miller makes the point that for a state that had the nation's highest population density,

Massachusetts had a significant imbalance of females to males by roughly 37,000, which meant that supplying military-age males for future enlistment would prove problematic, because enlistment quotas were based on an assumption of gender equivalence in the state population. Moreover, many of the females were foreign-born. It did not help that many younger males departed for the perceived riches of the West. All of these factors would burden the state when it came to meeting state quotas for military-age males. Pearson, *Andrew*, 1:137-39; Browne, *Sketch of the Official Life of John A. Andrew*, 28; Robinson, *"Warrington" Pen Portraits*, 406, 413; *Massachusetts Senate Documents, 1861*, 1-43; Bowen, *Massachusetts in the War*, 2-3; Chandler, *Memoir*, 28-29, 41.

8. *NYT*, Jan. 5, 1861; Depew, *The Library of Oratory: Ancient and Modern*, 9:295-303; *Massachusetts Senate Documents, 1861*, 1-43; Schouler, *A History of Massachusetts in the Civil War*, 8-12; *BDA*, Jan. 7, 1861; Pearson, *Andrew*, 1:138-40.

9. *MF*, Jan. 10, 1861; *CI*, Jan. 5, 1861; *BC*, Jan. 14, 1861; Lepore, "How Longfellow Woke the Dead," 33-46; *BDA*, Jan. 7, 1861; *LDC*, Jan. 2, 1861; *BDWC*, Dec. 26, 1860; Hamrogue, "John A. Andrew," 46.

10. *LDC*, Jan. 14, 1868, contains Bird's letter of the conversation; Adams to Andrew, Jan. 4, 8, 1861, Erastus Fairbanks to Andrew, Jan. 7, 19, 1861, William Schouler to Andrew, Jan. 8, 1861, William Sprague to Andrew, Jan. 8, 1861, Andrew Papers, MHS; Hamrogue, "John A. Andrew," 49; Bowen, *Massachusetts in the War*, 4-5; Schouler, *A History of Massachusetts in the Civil War*, 16-; *BDA*, Jan. 7, 1861, Aug. 23, 1883; Pearson, *Andrew*, 1:142-43: Engle, *Gathering to Save a Nation*, 21-38; Engle, "Under Full Sail," 43-81.

11. Palmer, *Selected Letters of Charles Sumner*, 2:40-41.

12. Sumner to Andrew, Jan. 8, 1861, Andrew Papers, MHS; Palmer, *Selected Letters of Charles Sumner*, 2:41-43; Donald, *Charles Sumner and the Coming of the Civil War*, 366-88.

13. Palmer, *Selected Letters of Charles Sumner*, 2:45-46; see also Sumner to Andrew, Jan. 21, 23, 24, 1861, Sumner Papers, HU; Donald, *Charles Sumner and the Coming of the Civil War*, 377-88.

14. Smith to Andrew, Jan. 7, 1861, George Stevens to Andrew, Jan. 7, Charles Beecher to Andrew, Jan. 31, 1861, Andrew Papers, MHS.

15. Pierce to Andrew, Jan. 8, 1861, Dow to Andrew, Jan. 19, 1861, Andrew Papers, MHS.

16. Emily Howland to Andrew, Jan. 1, 1861, Andrew Papers, MHS, see also an undated letter to Lincoln in January 1861, in which she scribbled on the letter "please destroy after reading." There are several pages and involves her desire to have Lincoln speak in New York about the current state of affairs; *NYT*, Nov. 20, 1927, June 30, 1929; Myers, *Miss Emily*, 15-47; Breault, *The World of Emily Howland*, 5-50.

17. Sargent to Andrew, Jan. 11, 1861, R. J. Burbank to Andrew, Jan. 12, 1861, James Freeman Clarke to Andrew, Jan. n.d., and Jan. 14, 1861, Andrew to Albert G. Browne, Jr., Jan. 9, 1861, Henry Lee, Jr., to Andrew, Jan. 15, Wendell Phillips to Andrew, Jan. n.d., 1861, Andrew Papers, MHS; Horace B. Sargent to John Wetherell, Jan. 12, 1861, Wetherell Papers, AAS; Chandler, *Memoir*, 95-96; *BDA*, Jan. 14, 1861; *LDC*, Apr. 20, 1861; Pearson, *Andrew*, 1:145-46; Schouler, *Massachusetts in the War*, 13-21.

18. Sumner to Andrew, Jan. 21, 24, 26, 1861, Sumner Papers, HU; *BDA*, 17, 29, Jan. 1861; Miller, "Brahmin Janissaries," 212-34; Bowen, *Massachusetts in the War*, 5; Schouler, *A History of Massachusetts in the Civil War*, 18-21; Pearson, *Andrew*, 1:148.

19. Palmer, *Selected Letters of Charles Sumner*, 2:43-46; *Congressional Globe*, 36th Congress, 2nd session, 362, 364-65, 378; Davis, "Liberty Before Union," 215-22.

20. *Lib*, Feb. 1, 1861; Phillips, *Disunion*; *NYT*, Jan. 21, 22, 1861; Phillips to Andrew, Jan. n.d., 1861, Sargent to Andrew, Jan. 21, 1861, Andrew Papers, MHS; Pearson, *Andrew*, 1:148; Karcher, *The First Woman in the Republic*, 440; Clarke, *Memorial and Biographical Sketches*, 30-33; Andrew to Edmund Quincy, Jan. 24, 1861, Andrew Papers, PEM; Garrison and Garrison, *William Lloyd Garrison*, 4:3-10; Mayer, *All on Fire*, 516-17; *BDA*, Jan. 25, 1861; *BA*, Jan. 25, 1861; *BET*, Jan. 24, 1861.

21. Winslow Diary, June 18, 1861, Winslow Papers, MHS; Francis Jackson to Andrew, Jan. 28,

1861, Andrew Papers, MHS; Pearson, *Andrew*, 1:149; Garrison and Garrison, *William Lloyd Garrison*, 4:3–7; Smalley, "Memoirs of Wendell Phillips," 137–45; Ware, *Political Opinion in Massachusetts during the Civil War*, 89–90; *Lib*, Feb. 1, 1861, *BP*, Jan. 25, 1861; *BDA*, Jan. 26, 1861. Boston transcendentalist reformer and Andrew family friend Caroline Healey Dall attended the meeting and rode home with several of the rioters and penned in her diary "that all they knew was, that they had turned 'Gov. Andrew out of his hall' & that the Mayor, 'wasn't the man to stand insult.'" Deese, *Daughter of Boston*, 302.

22. Clarke, *Memorial and Biographical Sketches*, 30–32; Sumner to Andrew, Jan. 17, 1861, C. H. Ray to Andrew, Jan. 17, 1861, James Freeman Clarke to Andrew, Jan. 17, 1861, George Bigelow to Andrew, Jan. 17, 1861, Andrew Papers, MHS.

23. Morse, *Memoir of Colonel Henry Lee*, 57–58; Pearson, *Andrew*, 1:152–53; Howe, *Reminiscences*, 263; *BDA*, Jan. 28, 1860; Stone, "Sketch of John Albion Andrew," 17; Andrew to Col. Lee, Jan. 25, 1861, Lee Family Papers, MHS; *ESJ*, Feb. 1, 1861; *BET*, Jan. 23, 1861; *BA*, Jan. 28, 1861.

24. Adams to Andrew, Jan. 28, 1861, Alfred B. [Ely] to Andrew, Jan. 31, 1861, George Morey to Andrew, Feb. 3, 1861, Andrew Papers, MHS; Duberman, *Charles Francis Adams*, 250–54; Blair to Andrew, Jan. 31, 1861, Andrew to Montgomery Blair, Feb. 3, 1861, Blair Family Papers, LC; Sumner to Andrew, Jan. 21, 24, 26, 28, 1861, Sumner Papers, HU; Palmer, *Selected Letters of Charles Sumner*, 2:47–48; Donald, *Charles Sumner and the Coming of the Civil War*, 377–88; Bowen, *Massachusetts in the War*, 2–4; McClintock, *Lincoln and the Decision for War*, 178–80.

25. Adams to Andrew, Jan. 28, 1861, Alfred B. [Ely] to Andrew, Jan. 31, 1861, George Morey to Andrew, Feb. 3, 1861, Andrew Papers, MHS; Duberman, *Charles Francis Adams*, 250–54; Blair to Andrew, Jan. 31, 1861, Andrew to Montgomery Blair, Feb. 3, 1861, Blair Family Papers, LC; Sumner to Andrew, Jan. 21, 24, 26, 28, 1861, Sumner Papers, HU; Palmer, *Selected Letters of Charles Sumner*, 2:47–48; Donald, *Charles Sumner and the Coming of the Civil War*, 377–88; Bowen, *Massachusetts in the War*, 2–4; McClintock, *Lincoln and the Decision for War*, 178–80.

26. Chandler to Andrew, Jan. 22, 1861, Andrew Papers, MHS; Bundy, *The Nature of Sacrifice*, 164.

27. Ford, "Sumner's Letters to Governor Andrew, 1861," 223–33; Hughes, *Reminiscences of John Murray Forbes*, 2:102–4; Forbes to Montgomery Blair, Mar. 13, 1861, Blair Family Papers, LC; Albert G. Browne, Jr., to Charles Frederick Winslow, Jan. 22, 1861, Winslow Papers, MHS; Bowen, *Massachusetts in the War*, 3–5; William F. Slocum to Andrew, Feb. 5, 1861, P. W. Chandler to Andrew, Feb. 6, 1861, Sumner to Andrew, Jan. 26, 1861; Henry Wilson to Andrew, Jan. 29, 1861, Edward Everett to Andrew, Feb. 1, 1861, Andrew Papers, MHS; Pearson, *Andrew*, 1:156; Donald, *Charles Sumner and the Coming of the Civil War*, 375–88; Ware, *Political Opinion in Massachusetts during the Civil War*, 52–53.

28. Bird, *Francis William Bird*, 40; Pearson, *Andrew*, 1:157; Ware, *Political Opinion in Massachusetts during the Civil War*, 56–59; Donald, *Charles Sumner and the Coming of the Civil War*, 376–88; Sumner to Andrew, Jan. 26, 1861, Charles C. Chaffee to Andrew, Feb. 4, 1861, Andrew Papers, MHS; Ford, ed., *Letters of Henry Adams*, 85–86; Engle, *Gathering to Save a Nation*, 27; Montgomery, *Beyond Equality*, 121.

29. Bird to Andrew, Jan. 31, 1861, Bird Papers, HU.

30. Sumner to Andrew, Feb. 3, 1861, Andrew to Sumner, Jan. 30, 1861, Andrew Papers, MHS; Palmer, *Selected Letters of Charles Sumner*, 2:50–51; Donald, *Charles Sumner and the Coming of the Civil War*, 377–88.

31. Palmer, *Selected Letters of Charles Sumner*, 2:55–56; Sumer to Andrew, Feb. 5, 20, 1861, Sumner Papers, HU; Henry Moore to Andrew, Feb. 4, 1861, Andrew Papers, MHS.

32. Thomas and Hyman, *Stanton*, 111.

33. Thomas and Hyman, *Stanton*, 111; Sumner to Andrew, Jan. 21, 23, 26 quote, 28 quote, 1861, Andrew Papers, MHS; U.S. War Department, *War of Rebellion*, hereinafter cited as OR; Palmer, *Selected Letters of Charles Sumner*, 2:47–48; Pearson, *Andrew*, 1:159.

34. Forbes to Andrew, Feb. 2, 1861, two letters with same date, Andrew to Gen. Scott, Jan. 12, 1861, Andrew Papers, MHS; Pearson, *Andrew*, 1:159–62; *List of the Executive and Legislative Departments of the Government of the Commonwealth of Massachusetts, 1862*; Schouler, *A History of Massachusetts in the Civil War*, 34–36; Donald, *Charles Sumner and the Coming of the Civil War*, 376–79; Palmer, *Selected Letters of Charles Sumner*, 2:47–48.

35. Andrew to Lincoln, Jan. 20, 1861, Andrew to Lincoln, Feb. 2, 1861, Lincoln to Andrew, Feb. 7, 1861, Hamlin to Lincoln, Dec. 14, 1860, Lincoln Papers, LC; Baum, *Civil War Party System*, 57; Holzer, *Lincoln, President Elect*, 143; Andrew also supported Montgomery Blair for the cabinet, Andrew to Blair, Jan. 20, 1861, and Blair to Andrew, Jan. 23, 1861, Andrew Papers, MHS; Schouler, *A History of Massachusetts in the Civil War*, 36.

36. Andrew to Lincoln, Jan. 20, Feb. 2, 1861, Lincoln to Andrew, Feb. 7, 1861, Hamlin to Lincoln, Dec. 14, 1860, Lincoln Papers, LC; Baum, *Civil War Party System*, 57; Holzer, *Lincoln, President Elect*, 143; Andrew to Blair, Jan. 20, 1861, and Blair to Andrew, Jan. 23, 1861, Andrew Papers, MHS; Schouler, *A History of Massachusetts in the Civil War*, 36.

37. Schouler, *A History of Massachusetts in the Civil War*, 35–39; Pearson, *Andrew*, 1:162; Miller, *States at War*, 1:254–55.

38. Pearson, *Andrew*, 1:163.

39. Adams to Andrew, Feb. 8, 1861, Andrew Papers, MHS; Pearson, *Andrew*, 1:163; Schouler, *A History of Massachusetts in the Civil War*, 36–43.

40. Nason, *Discourse*, 56; Stone, "Sketch of John Albion Andrew," 24–25.

41. Nason, *Discourse*, 45–48, 55. Clarke's daughter Lillian kept a diary and chronicled Andrew's many visits he paid on her family; Lillian Clarke Diaries, Feb. 16, 1861, Perry-Clarke Collection, James Freeman Clarke Papers, MHS.

42. Pickard, *The Letters of John Greenleaf Whittier*, 3:6; Engle, "Under Full Sail," 43–82; Engle, "Shaping the Contours of Federalism," 83–108.

43. Whipple, *Eulogy*, 13.

44. Miller, "Brahmin Janissaries," 204–34; Binney to Andrew, Jan. 11, 1861, Ritchie to Andrew, Jan. 12, 1861, and Andrew Scrapbook 13, Andrew Papers, MHS; Morse, *Memoir of Colonel Henry Lee*, 55–56; Schouler, *A History of Massachusetts in the Civil War*, 30–46.

45. Howe, "The Great Agitation," 285.

46. Andrew to Blair, Feb. 23, 1861, Blair Family Papers, LC; Howe to Bird quote is in Pearson, *Andrew*, 1:167–69, Andrew to Bird, Dec. 14, 1861, Theophilus Chandler, Jan. 6, 1861, Goodrich to Andrew, Feb. 2, 1861, Andrew Papers, MHS; Schouler, *A History of Massachusetts in the Civil War*, 28–29; Merriam, *Life and Times of Samuel Bowles*, 1:318; Hamrogue, "John A. Andrew," 36; Schouler, *A History of Massachusetts in the Civil War*, 29–31.

47. Adams to Andrew, Feb. 8, 1861, Andrew Papers, MHS; Pearson, *Andrew*, 1:169–70.

48. Andrew to Sumner, Mar. 11, 26, 1861, Sumner Papers, HU; Andrew to Sumner, Mar. 11, 26, 1861, Andrew Papers, MHS; Duberman, *Charles Francis Adams*, 244–45; Andrew to Blair, Mar. 4, 1861, Blair Family Papers, LC; Stahr, *Seward*, 222; Pearson, *Andrew*, 1:170–71. Andrew appointed his brother Issac to a position in the Boston Custom House, which he held until advancing age forced him to resign in 1888.

49. Goodrich to Andrew, Mar. 4, 1861, Linus B. Comins to Andrew, Mar. 6, 1861, Andrew Papers, MHS.

50. Pearson, *Andrew*, 1:173–75; Hale, *The Story of Massachusetts*, 327–30; Stowe, *Lives and Deeds*, 333; Horace Binney Sargeant would later compose a ceremonial poem about this entitled "The Return of the Standards." See this in MHS; Nolan, *Benjamin Franklin Butler*, 60–66; Marshall, *Private & Official Correspondence of Gen. Benjamin F. Butler*, 1:6–13; "Benjamin F. Butler," 39–42; Trefousse, *Ben Butler*, 62; Schouler, *A History of Massachusetts in the Civil War*, 32–34; L. L. Doty of Governor Edwin Morgan's staff to Andrew, Mar. 8, 1861, William L. Garrison to Andrew, Mar. 8, 1861, John Murray Forbes to Andrew, Mar. 8, 1861, Browne to Andrew, Mar. 28, 1861, and Andrew to Lucius Slade, Mar. 30, 1861, Andrew Papers, MHS; Mayer, *All on Fire*, 515–17; Leonard, *Benjamin Franklin Butler*, 54–55.

51. Strangis, *Lewis Hayden*, 115-18; Robboy and Robboy, "Lewis Hayden," 608-10; *NYT*, Apr. 8, 1889; *Acts and Resolves Passed by the General Court of Massachusetts in the Year 1861*, 1249; Stephens and Yacovone, *A Voice of Thunder*, 237; Kantrowitz, *More Than Freedom*, 233-34. In the meantime, his lieutenant governor John Zacheus Goodrich desired an appointment as the Collector of Customs for Boston and Andrew consented to the appointment, and Goodrich resigned from the executive office, took over the Customs Office, and served in that capacity throughout the war. Andrew served without a lieutenant governor until John Nesmith, an antislavery Windham, New Hampshire, native was elected the following November and took office in January 1862. Bowen, *Massachusetts in the War*, 4-7.

CHAPTER 11: A GRAND ERA HAS DAWNED

1. Howe to Andrew, Apr. 13, 1861, Andrew Papers, MHS; Richards, *Letters and Journals of Samuel Gridley Howe*, 2:480.
2. Andrews to Andrew, Apr. 14, 1861, Cyrus Woodman to Andrew, Apr. 15, 1861, Andrew Papers, MHS; Pearson, *Andrew*, 1:166-67, 176; Robinson, *"Warrington" Pen Portraits*, 100; Baum, *Civil War Party System*, 57-59; Bowen, *Massachusetts in the War*, 7-8; Trent, *The Manliest Man*, 219.
3. Richards, *Letters and Journals of Samuel Gridley Howe*, 2:480.
4. Newspaper clippings, Andrew Papers, BowC; Prentice, *The Life of Gilbert Haven*, 310-11; *NYTrib*, Feb. 22, 1880; Pearson, *Andrew*, 1:176; DIO, Jan. 15, 1894.
5. Bowen, *Massachusetts in the War*, 7; Schouler, *A History of Massachusetts in the Civil War*, 48-51; BDA, Apr. 16, 19, 1861.
6. OR, 3:1, 66, 70-75; Schouler, *A History of Massachusetts in the Civil War*, 5-57; Andrew to Cameron, Apr. 17, 1861, Massachusetts Governor, Letters Official, 1861-1925, RG GO1, MSA; Pearson, *Andrew*, 1:178-79; Sargent, *The Return of the Standards*, was a poem written in tribute to Andrew for having the foresight to being prepared for the war; Bowen, *Massachusetts in the War*, 1:7-9; BDA, Apr. 19, 1861.
7. Pearson, *Andrew*, 1:179-84; Butler, *Butler's Book*, 173; McGraw, "Minutemen of '61," 101-15; Nolan, *Benjamin Franklin Butler*, 64-66; Trefousse, *Ben Butler*, 62-63; Stearns, *Cambridge Sketches*, 250; Hughes, *Letters (Supplementary) of John Murray Forbes*, 1:206; Hughes, *Reminiscences of John Murray Forbes*, 2:107-10; BDA, Apr. 16, 17, 18, 1861; Leonard, *Benjamin Franklin Butler*, 56-57.
8. BDA, Apr. 18, 1861.
9. BDA, Apr. 18, 19, 1861; Pearson, *Andrew*, 1:185-87; McGraw, "Minutemen of '61," 101-15.
10. Schouler, *A History of Massachusetts in the Civil War*, 76; Pearson, *Andrew*, 1:189; McGraw, "Minutemen of '61," 101-15; Trefousse, *Ben Butler*, 63-67.
11. Howe, *Passages from the Life of Henry Warren Howe*, 85; Pearson, *Andrew*, 1:189; McGraw, "Minutemen Militia," 101-15; Trefousse, *Ben Butler*, 63-67.
12. BDA, Apr. 19, 1861, see also official communications in Andrew's letters official, MSA; Pearson, *Andrew*, 1:190-92; Schouler, *A History of Massachusetts in the Civil War*, 99-103; *Annual Report of the Adjutant-General of the Commonwealth of Massachusetts*, 1861, 72-74; Marshall, *Private & Official Correspondence of Gen. Benjamin F. Butler*, 1:17-21; BDA, Apr. 20, 1861; SR, Apr. 20, 1861; Trefousse, *Ben Butler*, 66-67; Butler, *Butler's Book*, 202; OR, series 1, 2:596-602.
13. Schouler, *A History of Massachusetts in the Civil War*, 99-103; *Annual Report of the Adjutant-General of the Commonwealth of Massachusetts*, 1861, 72-74; Marshall, *Private & Official Correspondence of Gen. Benjamin F. Butler*, 1:17-21; BDA, Apr. 20, 1861; SR, Apr. 20, 1861; Trefousse, *Ben Butler*, 66-67; Butler, *Butler's Book*, 202; OR, series 1, 2:596-602; Pearson, *Andrew*, 1:190-92
14. Francis B. Crowninshield to Andrew, June 6, 17, 1861, Lee Family Papers, MHS; Morse, *Memoir of Colonel Henry Lee*, 244; Miller, "Brahmin Janissaries," 212-34; Bowen, *Massachusetts in the War*, 1:22; Schouler, *A History of Massachusetts in the Civil War*, 57-108,

218–20; Pearson, *Andrew*, 1:192–93; *BDA*, Apr. 22, 1861; Miller, *States at War*, 1:256; Hale, *The Story of Massachusetts*, 330.

15. *SR*, Apr. 17, 1861; *BDA*, Apr. 19, 22, 23, 1861; Pearson, *Andrew*, 1:194–95.

16. Andrew to Lincoln, May 3, 1861, as quoted in Schouler, *A History of Massachusetts in the Civil War*, 1:130–31; *BDA*, Apr. 22, May 15, 1861.

17. Andrew to Francis Wright, Apr. 19, 1861, Massachusetts Governor, Letters Official, MSA.

18. Pearson, *Andrew*, 1:196; Nash, *Stormy Petrel*, 73.

19. Mason, *Apostle of Union*, 284; Miller, *States at War*, 1:256.

20. Cushing to Andrew, Apr. 25, 1861, Andrew to Cushing, Apr. 27, 1861, Chamberlain Collection of Autographs, BPL; Pearson, *Andrew*, 1:197–98; Mason, *Apostle of Union*, 282; Belohlavek, *Broken Glass*, 318–19; Chandler, *Memoir*, 102–3; *BDWC*, Jan. 17, 1874.

21. *BDA*, Oct. 11, 1886.

22. Fuess, *The Life of Caleb Cushing*, 2:278; Pearson, *Andrew*, 1:199; Hughes, *Reminiscences of John Murray Forbes*, 1:218–24; *NYTrib*, May 6, 16, 1861; *VS*, May 17, 1861.

23. Stone, "Sketch of John Albion Andrew," 10–20; Andrew to Isaac Andrew, Apr. 29, 1861, Andrew Papers, PEM; *NYTrib*, Feb. 22, 1880; *BDJ*, Jan. 11, 1868; Browne, "Governor Andrew," 249–76; Charles R. Lowell to Andrew, May 20, 1861, and Charles H. Dalton to Andrew, May 29, 30, 31, 1861, Charles Russell Lowell and Charles Henry Dalton Papers, DU; Andrew Scrapbook 11, Andrew Papers, MHS.

24. Schouler, *A History of Massachusetts in the Civil War*, 131; Pearson, *Andrew*, 1:200; F. B. Crownshield to Andrew, May 8, 1861, Schouler Papers, MHS; Browne, "Governor Andrew," 249–77; Stone, "Sketch of John Albion Andrew," 10–24; Andrew to Mrs. Anna H. Clarke, Apr. 18, 1861, James Freeman Clarke, Additional Correspondence, HU; Reynolds, "Benevolence on the Home Front in Massachusetts during the Civil War," 27–28; *BP*, Apr. 19, 1861.

25. Andrew to William Grey, Apr. 19, 1861, Andrew Letterbooks, MHS; *BDA*, Apr. 25, 27, 29, 1861; *BET*, Apr. 24, 1861; *BP*, Apr. 25, 1861; Pearson, *Andrew*, 1:200; Hamrogue, "John A. Andrew," 111; Massachusetts Soldiers' Fund: Rules Adopted at the Meeting of the Committee of One Hundred, in the Senate Chamber of Massachusetts, Saturday, Apr. 27, 1861, Boston, 1861, *Massachusetts Senate Documents, 1861*, no. 1, 19; Reynolds, "Benevolence on the Home Front in Massachusetts," 217–20.

26. *OR*, series 3, 1:120; Pearson, *Andrew*, 1:202–4; Andrew to Boutwell, Apr. 25, 1861, Andrew Papers, MHS; Boutwell, *Reminiscences of Sixty Years in Public Affairs*, 1:285; Marshall, *Private & Official Correspondence of Gen. Benjamin F. Butler*, 1:17–77.

27. Andrew to Blair, May 6, 1861, Blair Family Papers, LC; Montgomery Blair to Andrew, Apr. 18, 1861, Andrew Papers, MHS.

28. Winslow to Andrew, Apr. 19, 1861, Andrew Papers, MHS.

29. Albert G. Browne, Jr., to A. W. Campbell, May 24, 1861, Andrew to John Carlisle, June 22, 1861, Massachusetts Governor, Letters Official, MSA; William H. Clark to Andrew, June 3, 1861, John Murray Forbes to Andrew, June 3, 9, 1861, Andrew Papers, MHS; Miller, *Harvard's Civil War*, 21; Bowen, *Massachusetts in the War*, 10–30; Hamrogue, "John A. Andrew," 114; Pearson, *Andrew*, 1:206–8.

30. Marshall, *Private & Official Correspondence of Gen. Benjamin F. Butler*, 1:30–77; Albert G. Browne, Jr., to Butler, May 13, 1861, Massachusetts Governor, Letters Official, MSA; Nolan, *Benjamin Franklin Butler*, 80–83; Hamrogue, "John A. Andrew,"121–22; Bowen, *Massachusetts in the War*, 39; Trefousse, *Ben Butler*, 67–72; Schouler, *A History of Massachusetts in the Civil War*, 156–57; Witt, *Lincoln's Code*, 203; Reidy, *Illusions of Emancipation*, 195; Marshall, *Private & Official Correspondence of Gen. Benjamin F. Butler*, 1:37–41; *BDA*, May 24, 1861; Boutwell, *Reminiscences of Sixty Years in Public Affairs*, 1:289–90; Leonard, *Benjamin Franklin Butler*, 59–60.

CHAPTER 12: COMMUNITIES AT WAR

1. Morse, *Memoir of Colonel Henry Lee*, 62, 219, 233; Sargent, *Memorial Address Delivered before the John Albion Andrew Monument Association*, 25–34; Pearson, *Andrew*, 1:211–12,
2. Andrew to Lincoln, May 10, 1861, Lee Family Papers, MHS.
3. Sargent, *Memorial Address Delivered before the John Albion Andrew Monument Association*, 33.
4. Sargent, *Memorial Address Delivered before the John Albion Andrew Monument Association*, 25–34; BDA, Apr. 19, 1861; Pearson, *Andrew*, 1:212–13.
5. Bowen, *Massachusetts in the War*, 9.
6. Felton to Andrew, Apr. 21, 1861, Packard to Andrew, June 11, 1861, Andrew Papers, MHS.
7. Rogers, *Life and Letters of William Barton Rogers*, 2:86.
8. Charles Bowers to Lydia, Apr. 28, 1861, and Charles to his son Charles E. Bowers, May 8, 1861, Charles Bowers Papers, MHS; Andrew to Philadelphia Major George Brown, Apr. 20, 1861, Andrew Papers, MHS; Howe, *Reminiscences*, 261; Pearson, *Andrew*, 1:213; Andrew, *Address on the Occasion of Dedicating the Monument to Ladd and Whitney*; Miller, *States at War*, 1:258; NYT, June 18, 1865.
9. Chandler, *Memoir*, 53–54.
10. Andrew to Col. Robert Cowdin, May 11, 1861, Massachusetts Governor, Letters Official, MSA; Hamrogue, "John A. Andrew," 106.
11. Ebenezer R. Hoar to Charles A. Lowell, May 15, 1861, Albert G. Browne, Jr., to Dalton, June 1, 1861, Dalton Papers, MHS; Howe to Andrew, May 7, 1861, Andrew to Lincoln, May 18, 1861, Andrew Papers, MHS; Andrew to Cameron, May 7, 1861, Amory Family Papers, MHS; Forbes to Andrew, May 2, 1861, Charles Sumner to Andrew, May 25, 1861, Lee Family Papers, MHS; BDA, May 17, 31, 1861; Trent, *The Manliest Man*, 220–21; Richards, *Letters and Journals of Samuel Gridley Howe*, 2:481–82; Schouler, *A History of Massachusetts in the Civil War*, 132–53, 177; Pearson, *Andrew*, 1:214–18; Bowen, *Massachusetts in the War*, 10–29; Wesley and Uzelac, *William Cooper Nell*, 602; Bundy, *The Nature of Sacrifice*, 179–81.
12. Schouler, *A History of Massachusetts in the Civil War*, 154; Andrew to Howe, May 2, 1861, Massachusetts Governor, Official Letters, MSA; Howe to Andrew, May 7, 1861, Wilson to Andrew, May 8, 1861, Andrew Papers, MHS; Pearson, *Andrew*, 1:219–21; Dalton to Andrew, May 29, 1861, Andrew to Dalton, June 11, 1861, Henry Lee, Jr., to Charles H. Dalton, May 27, 1861, Dalton to Andrew, May 30, 1861, Dalton Papers, MHS; Hamrogue, "John A. Andrew," 119; BDA, May 31, 1861; Reynolds, "Benevolence on the Home Front in Massachusetts during the Civil War," 314–15; NYH, June 12, 1861; Miller, *States at War*, 1:256–57. It was during this time, that Andrew carried out the execution of Alexander Desmarteau on April 26 to the surprise of the press and his friends who thought he would grant a reprieve. As much as he had been sympathetic to favor the oppressed and the criminal, had gone out of his way to assist them, and was an opponent of capital punishment, he ordered the execution of Desmarteau, a twenty-two-year-old white man who was arrested for the abduction, rape, and murder of an eight-year-old orphan girl named Augustina Lucas. He took her to a remote area along the banks of the Connecticut River, where he choked the little girl into submission, raped repeatedly, and then bludgeoned her with a rock. Then went home and proceeded to get drunk. Witnesses testified that he was the last person seen with the little girl, and he soon confessed to the murder. Banks had actually prepared the warrant for execution in his last days as governor. Chandler, *Memoir*, 107; Hearn, *Legal Executions in New England*, 237; LDC, Jan. 10, 1861; BI, Nov. 28, 1860.
13. Bowen, *Massachusetts in the War*, 1–30; *Massachusetts Senate Documents*, 1861, Extra Session, 3–5; Blair to Andrew, May 11, 1861, Blair Family Papers, LC; BDA, May 16, 17, 1861; Schouler, *A History of Massachusetts in the Civil War*, 143–77, 181–83; Pearson, *Andrew*, 1:222–24, 249; Hamrogue, "John A. Andrew," 92.

14. Bowen, *Massachusetts in the War*, 1–30; *Massachusetts Senate Documents*, 1861, Extra Session, 3–5; Blair to Andrew, May 11, 1861, Blair Family Papers, LC; *BDA*, May 16, 17, 1861; Schouler, *A History of Massachusetts in the Civil War*, 143–77, 181–83; Pearson, *Andrew*, 1:222–24, 249; Hamrogue, "John A. Andrew," 92.

15. *NYH*, May 15, 1861; Schouler, *A History of Massachusetts in the Civil War*, 170–73; *Massachusetts Senate Documents*, 1861, Extra Session, no. 2, 4–5; *BDA*, May 14, 15, 1861; Bowen, *Massachusetts in the War*, 1–30; *Massachusetts Senate Documents*, 1861, Extra Session, 3–5; Blair to Andrew, May 11, 1861, Blair Family Papers, LC; *BDA*, May 16, 17, 1861; Schouler, *A History of Massachusetts in the Civil War*, 143–77, 181–83; Pearson, *Andrew*, 1:222–24, 249; Hamrogue, "John A. Andrew," 92.

16. *Massachusetts Senate Documents*, 1861, Extra Session, 3–5; Blair to Andrew, May 11, 1861, Blair Family Papers, LC; *BDA*, May 16, 17, 1861; Schouler, *A History of Massachusetts in the Civil War*, 143–77, 181–83; Pearson, *Andrew*, 1:249; Hamrogue, "John A. Andrew," 92; Bowen, *Massachusetts in the War*, 15.

17. Schouler, *A History of Massachusetts in the Civil War*, 148, 165; Pearson, *Andrew*, 224–25; Miller, *States at War*, 1:257.

18. Andrew to Walbridge, June 23, 1861, Massachusetts Governor, Letters Official, MSA; Pearson, *Andrew*, 1:227–28; *OR*, series 3, 1:169, 203; Schouler, *A History of Massachusetts in the Civil War*, 132; Bowen, *Massachusetts in the War*, 27–28; *NYH*, June 3, 1861.

19. Andrew to Walbridge, June 23, 1861, Massachusetts Governor, Letters Official, MSA; Pearson, *Andrew*, 1:227–28; *OR*, series 3, 1:169, 203; Schouler, *A History of Massachusetts in the Civil War*, 132; Bowen, *Massachusetts in the War*, 27–28; *NYH*, June 3, 1861.

20. Pearson, *Andrew*, 1:228; *LDC*, June 5, 1861.

21. Hughes, *Reminiscences of John Murray Forbes*, 1:226.

22. Bowen, *Massachusetts in the War*, 33; *BDA*, Oct. 16, 1861.

23. Chandler, *Memoir*, 111; Pearson, *Andrew*, 1;233; Peleg W. Chandler to Andrew, June 17, 1861, Lee Family Papers, MHS; Carl Schurz to Andrew, Apr. 21, 1861, Andrew to Peleg W. Chandler, June 29, 1861, Andrew Papers, MHS; Butler, *Butler's Book*, 307–8.

24. Chandler to Andrew, May 18, 1861, Andrew Papers, MHS; Miller, "Brahmin Janissaries," 210–13; Schouler, *A History of Massachusetts in the Civil War*, 222–23; Pearson, *Andrew*, 1:252–54; Miller, *States at War*, 1:259; *BDA*, June 1, 1861.

25. Pearson, *Andrew*, 1:236–38; Ford, *The Story of the Fifteenth Regiment Massachusetts Volunteer Infantry*, 29; McNamara, *The History of the Ninth Regiment*, 20; Andrew to Peleg Chandler, June 29, 1861, James Stone to Andrew, June 17, 1861, Edward A. Wild to Andrew, June 17, 1861, Andrew Papers, MHS; Andrew to Israel Washburn, May 28, 1861, Massachusetts Governor, Letters Official, MSA; Hamrogue, "John A. Andrew," 110.

26. Pearson, *Andrew*, 1:242; *BDA*, June 25, 1861; *LDC*, Aug. 24, 1861.

27. Pearson, *Andrew*, 1:235, 243–44; Browne, *Sketch of the Official Life of John A. Andrew*, 65; Miller, "The Trouble with Brahmins," 38–72; Bowen, *Massachusetts in the War*, 30–31.

28. *BDA*, July 4, 1861.

29. Albert Gallatin Browne, Jr., to Messrs. Brown and Alger, July 3, 1861, and to Brig. Gen. Bullock, July 3, 1861, and to Frank E. Howe, July 3, 1861, Andrew Papers, MHS; *BDA*, July 13,1861; *OR*, series 3, 1:327; Hughes, *Reminiscences of John Murray Forbes*, 1:227; Miller, *Harvard's Civil War*, 33.

30. Palmer, *Selected Letters of Sumner*, 2:68; *BDA*, May 27, 28, June 1, 2, 8,1861; Eicher, *The Longest Night*, 71–81.

31. Deese, *Daughter of Boston*, 312; *BDA*, July 18, 1861; *BP*, July 17, 18, 1861; *BDWC*, July 22, 1861; *LDC*, July 18, 1861; Weeden, *War Government*, 93.

32. Andrew to Adams, July 18, 1861, Adams Family Papers, LC; Hamrogue, "John A. Andrew," 91; Andrew to Lt. Col. George D. Wells, July 23, 1861, Massachusetts Governor, Letters Official, 1861, MSA; *OR*, series 3, 1:455; *NYT*, Aug. 17, 1876; *BDA*, June 15, July 22, 23, 24, 28, 1861; *Lib*, Oct. 24, 1862; Eicher, *The Longest Night*, 87–109; Oakes, *Freedom National*, 100–29; Leonard, *Benjamin Franklin Butler*, 67–74.

33. *TC*, May 17, 1894.
34. "War Letters of Charles P. Bowditch," 415–16.
35. *OR*, series 3:1, 38–84; 348–49, 413–14, 444–45, 374; Sears, *The Civil War Papers of George B. McClellan*, 90; Upton, *The Military Policy of the United States*, 235–36; Sears, *George B. McClellan*, 113; Sumner to Andrew, July 9, Aug. 11, 1861, Sumner Papers, HU; Sumner to Andrew, Aug. 11, 1861, George D. Wells to Andrew, July 22, 1861, Albert G. Browne, Jr., to Andrew, July 9, Aug. 13, 1861, Andrew Papers, MHS; Miller, *Harvard's Civil War*, 44; BDA, July 24, 1861; LDC, July 25, 1861; VC, Aug. 13, 1861.
36. *OR*, series 3, 1:406–7, 413–14; Pearson, *Andrew*, 1:244–45; Dalton to Andrew, July 22, 24, 1861, Dalton Papers, MHS; Hughes, *Reminiscences of John Murray Forbes*, 2:60–61; Miller, "Brahmin Janissaries," 210–34; Howe to Andrew, May 9, 1861, Ebenezer Rockwood Hoar to Andrew, May 7, 1861, Henry Wilson to Andrew, May 8, 1861, Andrew Papers, MHS; Shannon, *The Organization and Administration of the Union Army*, 1:259; BDA, July 24, 30, 1861; Kahan, *Amiable Scoundrel*, 186.
37. Boutwell to Andrew, Aug. 17, 1861, Andrew Papers, MHS; Cabot, *Letter to the Governor of Massachusetts*; Hamrogue, "John A. Andrew," 109–10; BDA, Aug. 20, 1861.
38. Miller, *States at War*, 1:258, 334; Sanger, *Statutes at Large*, 331; BDA, Aug. 7, 1861; Pearson, *Andrew*, 1:246–48; Bowen, *Massachusetts in the War*, 34–39; Andrew to Joseph McKeen, Bowdoin College, July 30, 1861, Andrew Papers, MHS; Andrew to Frank Howe, May 22, 1861, in NYT, May 22, 1861.
39. *Massachusetts Senate Documents, 1861*, Extra Session, no. 2, 4–5; Pearson, *Andrew*, 1:249; Harris, *Lincoln and the Union Governors*, 6; Eicher, *The Longest Night*, 109–10; Oakes, *Freedom National*, 151–56; Thomas, *Abraham Lincoln*, 278.
40. As quoted in Miller, *Harvard's Civil War*, 44; OR, series 3, 1:419–20, 456, 459, 812–15; BDA, Aug. 29, Sept. 7, 1861; LDC, Aug. 29, 1861; NI, Aug. 31, Sept. 10, 1861; Lib, Sept. 13, 1861.
41. Moore, *The Rebellion Record*, 3:65–67; BDA, Sept. 7, 1861; Pearson, *Andrew*, 1:250–51, 265–76; Miller, *Harvard's Civil War*, 45–46; Hamrogue, "John A. Andrew," 133–35; NYT, Sept. 6, 1861; BDJ, Jan. 18, 1868; Clarke, *Memorial and Biographical Sketches*, 20–28; newspaper clippings, Andrew Papers, BowC; Chandler, *Memoir*, 100–101.
42. Basler, *Collected Works of Abraham Lincoln*, 4:506, 517–18; Weeden, *War Government*, 191–94; NYT, Sept. 6, 1861; BDA, Aug. 29, Sept. 7, 1861; LDC, Aug. 29, 1861; NI, Aug. 31, Sept. 10, 1861; Lib, Sept. 13, 1861; Escot, *The Worst Passions of Human Nature*, 18–20; Manning, *Troubled Refuge*, 31–62; Leonard, *Benjamin Franklin Butler*, 65–77; Goodheart, *1861*, 293–348.

CHAPTER 13: THE POLITICS OF COMMAND

1. Nagel, *Descent from Glory*, 239–40; "Reminiscences of Julia Ward Howe," 701–12; Howe, *Reminiscences*, 265–69; "Frank E. Howe," 1:124; NYT, May 24, 1883.
2. Stearns, *Cambridge Sketches*, 257; Moore, *The Rebellion Record*, 3:66–67; BDJ, Jan. 18, 1868; Clarke, *Memorial and Biographical Sketches*, 20–28; newspaper clippings, Andrew Papers, BowC; Chandler, *Memoir*, 100–101; Holloran, *Boston's Wayward Children*, 113; Allen, *Westboro' State Reform School Reminiscences*, 6; *Address of His Excellency John A. Andrew to the Two Branches of the Legislature of Massachusetts, Jan. 3, 1862*, 35–36; "The Massachusetts Board of State Charities, and the Westborough Reform School," 118; Putnam, "Massachusetts State Care of Children," 360–61; Johnson, *The Professional Convict's Tale*, 50; TWJ, Feb. 2, 1878; Hamrogue, "John A. Andrew," 133–34; Pearson, *Andrew*, 1:265–76;
3. Marshall, *Private & Official Correspondence of Gen. Benjamin F. Butler*, 1:219–20; Schouler, *A History of Massachusetts in the Civil War*, 226–27, 254–56; Pearson, *Andrew*, 1:286–87; OR, series 3, 1:498–99, 563–63, 810–12, 815–16, series 2, 2:81; Basler, *Collected Works of Abraham Lincoln*, 4:263, 438–39, 515; Bowen, *Massachusetts in the War*, 1:38–45; Trefousse, *Ben Butler*, 88–89; Luskey, *Men Is Cheap*, 80–81; Miller, *States at War*, 1:262; *Congressional Globe*, 37th Congress, 1st session, 222–23, 258–622; Oakes, *Freedom National*, 127–40.

4. Marshall, *Private & Official Correspondence of Gen. Benjamin F. Butler*, 1:219–20; Schouler, *A History of Massachusetts in the Civil War*, 226–27, 254–56; Pearson, *Andrew*, 1:286–87; OR, series 3, 1:498–99, 563–63, 810–12, 815–16, 819–34, Series 2, 2:81; Basler, *Collected Works of Abraham Lincoln*, 4:515; Bowen, *Massachusetts in the War*, 1:38–45; Trefousse, *Ben Butler*, 88–89; Luskey, *Men Is Cheap*, 80–81; Miller, *States at War*, 1:262; Miller, *States of War*, 1:264–66; Andrew to Cameron, Aug. 22, 1861, Massachusetts Governor, Letters Official, MSA; Hamrogue, "John A. Andrew," 122–30; Leonard, *Benjamin Franklin Butler*, 76–79.

5. *BDA*, Apr. 10, July 22, Oct. 19, Sept. 26, 1861, Apr. 24, 1862, Mar. 1, 1866, Mar. 6, 1868; *LDC*, Apr. 24, 1862; *BP*, July 17, 1861; Andrew to Charles Stevenson, Jan. 14, 19, 1861, Herman Haupt to Andrew, Jan. 18, 1861, Thomas Drew of Andrew's staff to Frank Bird, May 17, 1862, Andrew Papers, MHS; Baum, *Civil War Party System*, 65–66; Weber, *The Northern Railroads in the Civil War*, 138–40; *The Hoosac Tunnel and Troy Greenfield Railroad, 1862-1863*, 1–194; *Report on the Hoosac Tunnel and Troy and Greenfield Railroad by the Joint Standing Committee of 1866*, 71–96.

6. Howe, *Reminiscences*, 266; Pearson, *Andrew*, 1:270–71; newspaper clippings, Andrew Papers, BowC; Baum, *Civil War Party System*, 65–66; *BSEG*, June 30, 1895.

7. *LDC*, Sept. 7, 1861; *NI*, Sept. 10, 1861; *Lib*, Sept. 13, 1861; Pearson, *Andrew*, 1:273–74; Bushman et al., *Uprooted Americans*, 163–202; Formisano, *For the People*, 78–220.

8. Pearson, *Andrew*, 1:276–77; *BDC*, Jan. 18, 1868.

9. *TI*, Oct. 3, 1861; *PS*, Oct. 10, 1861; Bowen, *Massachusetts in the War*, 44; *BDA*, Oct. 2, 4, 1861; *Lib*, Oct. 4, 18, 1861.

10. *BDA*, Sept. 28, 30, Oct. 1, 2, 1862; *Lib*, Oct. 18, 1861; *BG*, Nov. 8, 1861; *NYT*, Nov. 6, 1861; *PS*, Oct.10, 1861; Bowen, *Massachusetts in the War*, 43–44; *BP*, Sept. 19, 1861; *BC*, Oct. 22, 18, Nov. 6, 1861; Pearson *Andrew*, 1:276–77; Hamrogue, "John A. Andrew:," 135–38; Saunders, "The People's Party in Massachusetts during the Civil War," 174–87.

11. *BDA*, Oct. 28, 1861; *BB*, Oct. 31, 1861; Shannon, *The Organization and Administration of the Union Army*, 1:186–87; Miller, *Harvard's Civil War*, 7–90; *BDA*, Oct. 23, 24, 25, 26, 1861; Eicher, *The Longest Night*, 125–128; *BDJ*, Oct. 28, 1861; Marshall, *Private & Official Correspondence of Gen. Benjamin F. Butler*, 1:250, 266–67, 308; OR, series 3, 1:823–32; W. Raymond Lee to Andrew, Jan. 21, 1864, Andrew Papers, MHS.

12. Chadwick, *A Life for Liberty*, 208; Howe, *Justice Oliver Wendell Holmes*, 104; *NYT*, Oct. 29, 1861; *BDA*, Oct. 26, Oct. 31, 1861; Pearson, *Andrew*, 1:278; Miller, *Harvard's Civil War*, 66–67; Underwood, *James Russell Lowell*, 8; Grant, *Oliver Wendell Holmes, Jr.*, 49.

13. Schouler, *A History of Massachusetts in the Civil War*, 235–36; Moore, *The Rebellion Record*, 3:99; Miller, *Harvard's Civil War*, 70–71.

14. Charles Barnard Fox Diary, Oct. 29, 1862, Fox Papers, MHS; Andrew to Gen. Nathaniel Banks, Oct. 25, 1861, Lee Family Papers, MHS; Tap, *Over Lincoln's Shoulder*, 63; Sumner to Andrew, Jan. 3, 1862, Sumner Papers, HU; *Congressional Globe*, 37th Congress, 2nd session, 189–91.

15. Chandler, *Memoir*, 120; Pearson, *Andrew*, 1:279.

16. Schouler, *A History of Massachusetts in the Civil War*, 234–35; *BDA*, Oct. 31, Nov. 6, 1861; *Lib*, Nov. 1, 1861.

17. OR, series 3, 1:813–14; Pearson, *Andrew*, 1:280–81; Andrew to Charles Amory, Oct. 3, 1861, Amory Family Papers, MHS; Schouler, *A History of Massachusetts in the Civil War*, 254; Weeden, *War Government*, 199–206, 212–13; Engle, *Gathering to Save a Nation*, 100–118.

18. Marshall, *Private & Official Correspondence of Gen. Benjamin F. Butler*, 1:254–63, 280–81; Pearson, *Andrew*, 1:284–85, 290–91; Henry Lee, Jr., to Wife, Nov. 2, 1861, Andrew to Henry Lee, Jr., Nov. 4, 6, 1861, Col. Ritchie to Henry Lee, Jr., Nov. 14, 1861, Lee Family Papers, MHS; Ritchie to John Wetherell, Nov. 15, 1861, Wetherell Papers, AAS; Leonard, *Benjamin Franklin Butler*, 77–80; Nolan, *Benjamin Franklin Butler*, 114–16; Trefousse, *Ben Butler*, 89–91; OR, series 1:2, 593–94; 3, 1:632–33, 817, 835–36; Hamrogue, "John A. Andrew," 123–30; Butler, *Butler's Book*, 307; Weeden, *War Government*, 200–205.

19. Marshall, *Private & Official Correspondence of Gen. Benjamin F. Butler*, 1:253-77; *OR*, series 3:1, 637.
20. Andrew to Lincoln, Dec. 16, 1861, Lincoln Papers, LC; Forbes to Andrew, Nov. 25, 1861, Massachusetts Governor, Letters Official, MSA; Hughes, *Reminiscences of John Murray Forbes*, 1:259; Miller, *Harvard's Civil War*, 94-95; Bowen, *Massachusetts in the War*, 43-45; *OR*, series 2, 2:81, 164-65, Series 2, 3:51, 53; Ely, *Journal of Alfred Ely*, 200; Harris, *Prison Life in the Tobacco Warehouse at Richmond*, 158; *LDC*, Oct. 7, 1861; *NYH*, Oct. 9, 19, 21, 1861; *BDA*, Oct. 17, 1861.
21. *NI*, Sept. 9, 1861; *BDA*, Nov. 2, 6, 8, 1861; Saunders, "The People's Party in Massachusetts," 174-87; Bowen, *Massachusetts in the War*, 1:43-45; Schouler, *A History of Massachusetts in the Civil War*, 244-50; *BG*, Nov. 8, 1861; Charles F. Winslow to Andrew, Dec. 14, 1861, Andrew Papers, MHS; *LDC*, Nov. 6, 7, 1861; *Lib*, Nov. 8, 1861; Hamrogue, "John A. Andrew," 137.
22. *PBCE*, Nov. 21, 1861; *HP*, Nov. 20, 1861; *BDA*, Nov. 14, 1861; *NYH*, Nov. 13, 18, 1861; Engle, *Gathering to Save the Nation*, 125-28.
23. Gurowski to Andrew, Oct. 24, 1861, C. R. Chauncey to Andrew, Oct. 21, 1861, Horace B. Sargent to Andrew, Oct. 22, 1861, Henry Sith to Andrew, Oct. 26, 1861, Henry Lee to Andrew, Oct. 31, Nov. 2, 1861, Andrew Papers, MHS; Gurowski, *Diary from March 4, 1861, to November 12, 1862*, 42; *BDA*, Nov. 14, 1861; *NYH*, Nov. 13, 18, 23, 1861.
24. "Reminiscences of Julia Ward Howe," 701-12; Andrew to Clarke, Nov. 7, 1861, Clarke Papers, HU; Furgurson, *Freedom Rising*, 142-43; Gamble, *A Fiery Gospel*, 30-31.
25. Newspaper clippings, Andrew Papers, BowC; *LDC*, Jan. 6, 1871; Andrew to Clarke, Nov. 7, 1861, Clarke Papers, HU; Gamble, *A Fiery Gospel*, 30-33; *NRep*, Nov. 21, 1861; *HW*, Dec. 7, 1861.
26. Trent, *The Manliest Man*, 223; *BDA*, Nov. 21, 1861; *LDC*, Mar. 3, 1871; Pearson, *Andrew*, 1:269; Showalter, *The Civil Wars of Julia Ward Howe*, 162-65; Aamodt, *Righteous Armies, Holy Cause*, 81-82; Howe, "What Life Means to Me," 285-89; "Reminiscences of Julia War Howe," 701-12; Holzer, Symonds, and Williams, *Exploring Lincoln*, 123-45; Gamble, *A Fiery Gospel*, 30-33; White, *Midnight in America*, xi-xii.
27. *OR*, series 3, 1:652-57; *BDA*, Nov. 26, 1861; Horatio Woodman to Andrew, Nov. 15, 1861, Woodman Papers, MHS. Woodman was a lawyer, editor of the *Boston Evening Transcript*, and the younger brother of Andrew's close friend Cyrus Woodman. He proposed to Andrew that he use his influence in Washington to have the Union army occupy Texas as a way to prevent the rebellion from spreading.
28. Andrew to Sumner, Dec. 29, 1861, see also Dec. 17, 26, 28, 29, 30, 1861, Sumner Papers, HU; *OR*, series 3, 1:840-44, 852; Pearson, *Andrew*, 1:298-300; Andrew to Montgomery Blair, Oct. 13, 1861, Blair Family Papers, LC; Henry Lee, Jr., to Wife, Nov. 2, 1861, Andrew to Henry Lee, Jr., Nov. 4, 6, 1861, Col. Ritchie to Henry Lee, Jr., Nov. 14, 1861, Lee Family Papers, MHS; Trefousse, *Ben Butler*, 92-95; Basler, *Collected Works of Abraham Lincoln*, 4:556-57; Nolan, *Benjamin Franklin Butler*, 116-18; Hamrogue, "John A. Andrew," 128; Meneely, *The War Department*, 200-218; Trefousse, *Ben Butler*, 90.

CHAPTER 14: THE LORD IS MARCHING ON

1. *NYH*, Nov. 8, 1861; *LDC*, Nov. 7, 11, 1861; *BP*, Feb. 13, 1888; *BDA*, Nov. 21, 1861; *BET*, Nov. 23, 1867; newspaper clippings, Andrew Papers, BowC; *TCir*, Nov. 21, 1861; *MPNEJA*, Nov. 26, 1887; *TYC*, Nov. 25, 1915; Pearson, *Andrew*, 1:322; Bacon and Howland, *Letters of a Family during the War for the Union*, 1:215-16.
2. Pickard, *The Letters of John Greenleaf Whittier*, 3:25.
3. *NYH*, Nov. 8, 1861; *LDC*, Nov. 7, 11, 1861; *BDA*, Nov. 21, 1861; Bacon and Howland, *Letters of a Family during the War for the Union*, 1:215-16; *BET*, Nov. 23, 1867; newspaper clippings, Andrew Papers, BowC; *TCir*, Nov. 21, 1861; *MPNEJA*, Nov. 26, 1887; *TYC*, Nov. 25, 1915; Pearson, *Andrew*, 1:322
4. *BDA*, Nov. 21, 1861; Bacon and Howland, *Letters of a Family during the War for the Union*,

1:215–16; *BET*, Nov. 23, 1867; newspaper clippings, Andrew Papers, BowC; *TCir*, Nov. 21, 1861; *MPNEJA*, Nov. 26, 1887; *TYC*, Nov. 25, 1915; Pearson, *Andrew*, 1:322.

5. Pearson, *Andrew*, 1:322; Bacon and Howland, *Letters of a Family during the War for the Union*, 1:215–16; *BET*, Nov. 23, 1867; newspaper clippings, Andrew Papers, BowC; *TCir*, Nov. 21, 1861; *MPNEJA*, Nov. 26, 1887; *TYC*, Nov. 25, 1915.

6. Miller, *Harvard's Civil War*, 84–106; *OR*, series 2, 1:784–93.

7. *OR*, series 2, 1:784–88, 791–93; Sampson Urbino to Andrew, Dec. 10, 1861, Thomas Drew to Sumner, Dec. 7, 1861, Andrew to Cameron, Dec. 7, 1861, Massachusetts Governor, Letters Official, MSA; Hughes, *Reminiscences of John Murray Forbes*, 2:151–53; Miller, *Harvard's Civil War*, 89–104; Miller, "The Trouble with Brahmins," 46–51; Milano, "The Copperhead Regiment," 31–63; Hamrogue, "John A. Andrew," 141; Bowen, *Massachusetts in the War*, 35; Schouler, *A History of Massachusetts in the Civil War*, 238–39; *BDA*, Dec. 17, 1861; *VC*, Dec. 17, 1861; Copeland, *Statement of R. Morris Copeland*, 8; Duncan, *Blue-Eyed Child of Fortune*, 23–24, 125, 162, 202; Kahan, *Amiable Scoundrel*, 200–201.

8. *OR*, series 2, 1:784–88, 791–93; Sampson Urbino to Andrew, Dec. 10, 1861, Thomas Drew to Sumner, Dec. 7, 1861, Andrew to Cameron, Dec. 7, 1861, Massachusetts Governor, Letters Official, MSA; Hughes, *Reminiscences of John Murray Forbes*, 2:151–53; Miller, *Harvard's Civil War*, 89–104; Miller, "The Trouble with Brahmins," 46–51; Milano, "The Copperhead Regiment," 31–63; Hamrogue, "John A. Andrew," 141; Bowen, *Massachusetts in the War*, 35; Schouler, *A History of Massachusetts in the Civil War*, 238–39; *BDA*, Dec. 17, 1861; *VC*, Dec. 17, 1861; Copeland, *Statement of R. Morris Copeland*, 8; Duncan, *Blue-Eyed Child of Fortune*, 23–24, 125, 162, 202; Kahan, *Amiable Scoundrel*, 200–201.

9. *OR*, series 2, 1:786–87, 790–93; Miller, "The Trouble with Brahmins," 45–51; Sears, *The Civil War Papers of George B. McClellan*, 146; Pearson, *Andrew*, 1:314; Engle, *Gathering to Save a Nation*, 136–37; Kahan, *Amiable Scoundrel*, 157–214.

10. Andrew to McClellan, Dec. 30, 1861, Andrew Papers, MHS; Pearson, *Andrew*, 1:315–16; Browne., *Sketch of the Official Life of John A. Andrew*, 93; *OR*, series 2, 1:784–97; Bowen, *Massachusetts in the War*, 35.

11. *OR*, series 2, 1:793; *BDA*, Dec. 16, 19, 1861; *NYH*, Nov. 28, Dec. 6, 1861; Engle, *Gathering to Save a Nation*, 136–37.

12. *BDA*, Dec. 16, 19, 1861; "Selections from Charles Francis Adams Correspondence," 94; Fair-Play, *The True State of the American Question*, 26; Rhodes, *History of the Civil War from the Compromise of 1850*, 71; Pearson, *Andrew*, 1:317–19; Warren, *Fountain of Discontent*, 35; Welles, *Lincoln and Seward*, 187; Harris, *The Trent Affair*, 120; *NYT*, Nov. 17, 19, 23, 27, 1861; Gray, ed., *Letters of Asa Gray*, 2:476; *BDJ*, Nov. 27, 1861; Chalfant, *Both Sides of the Ocean*, 351; Miller, *President Lincoln*, 194; *LDC*, Nov. 28, 1861; W. A. Hall to Andrew, Dec. 14, Frank Howe to Andrew, Dec. 20, 1861, Andrew Papers.

13. *BDA*, Dec. 16, 1861; "Selections from Charles Francis Adams Correspondence," 94.

14. Andrew to Lincoln, Jan. 13, 1862, Lincoln Papers, LC.

15. *TPF*, Nov. 21, 1861.

16. Schouler, *A History of Massachusetts in the Civil War*, 241–42, 283–85; *BDA*, Jan. 2, 1862.

17. Pierce, *Memoirs and Letters of Charles Sumner*, 4:42–64; *Charles Sumner, His Complete Works*, 8:3–11; *Congressional Globe*, 37th Congress, 2nd session, 130; Abbott, *Cobbler in Congress*, 143–45.

18. Palmer, *Selected Letters of Charles Sumner*, 2:76, 85; *Charles Sumner, His Complete Works*, 6:152; *BDA*, Dec. 12, 1861; Sumner to Andrew, Dec. 27, 1861, Jan. 7, 1861, Andrew Papers, MHS.

19. *BDA*, Dec. 31, 1861.

20. Schouler, *A History of Massachusetts in the Civil War*, 284–87; *BDA*, Jan. 2, 4, 1862; Pearson, *Andrew*, 1:323–24; Sumner to Andrew, Jan. 3, 7, 1862, Sumner Papers, HU; Bowen, *Massachusetts in the War*, 1:45; *OR*, series 3, 1:698–708; Andrew to Frank Bird, Dec. 14, Andrew to Frank Blair, Sr., Dec. 18, 1861, Andrew Papers, MHS; Rogers, *Life and Letters of William Barton Rogers*, 2:142–43;

21. Pearson, *Andrew*, 1:304; Hamrogue, "John A. Andrew," 131–32; OR, series 3, 1:754–55, 864–65; Sumner to Andrew, Jan. 3, 7, 10, Feb. 9, 1862, Sumner Papers, HU; Andrew to Sumner and Wilson, Jan. 13, 1862, Andrew Papers, MHS; Marshall, *Private & Official Correspondence of Gen. Benjamin F. Butler*, 1:300–33; Trefousse, *Ben Butler*, 94–97; BDA, Jan. 21, 22, 23, 24, 1862.

22. OR, series 3, 1:862–65; Palmer, *Selected Letters of Charles Sumner*, 2:95; Weeden, *War Government*, 206; Marshall, *Private & Official Correspondence of Gen. Benjamin F. Butler Correspondence*, 1:296–344; Schouler, *A History of Massachusetts in the Civil War*, 252–82; Robinson, "*Warrington*" *Pen Portraits*, 410.

23. Emerson and Forbes, *Journals of Ralph Waldo Emerson*, 15:188–89, 197; Ralph Waldo Emerson Diary, Feb. 3, 1862, Ralph Waldo Emerson Papers, MHS; Nolan, *Benjamin Franklin Butler*, 114–20; Schouler, *A History of Massachusetts in the Civil War*, 321–22; BDA, Jan. 14, 1862.

24. Emerson and Forbes, *Journals of Ralph Waldo Emerson*, 15:188–89, 197.

25. Pearson, *Andrew*, 2:25; Gurowski to Andrew, Jan. 8, 1862, Andrew Papers, MHS; *Massachusetts Senate Documents*, 1862, 1–70; Hamrogue, "John A. Andrew," 144–53; Fischer, *Lincoln's Gadfly*; Bowen, *Massachusetts in the War*, 1:45–46; Schouler, *A History of Massachusetts in the Civil War*, 285–87.

26. Gurowski to Andrew, Jan. 8, 1862 (and Dec. 21, 1861) Andrew Papers, MHS; Gurowski, *Diary from March 4, 1861, to November 12, 1862*, 121; Bowen, *Massachusetts in the War*, 1:45–46; Schouler, *A History of Massachusetts in the Civil War*, 284–87.

27. *NYTrib*, Jan. 14, 1862.

28. Frank Howe to Andrew, Jan. 21, 23, 1862, Andrew to Wilson, Dec. 31, 1861, Andrew Paper, MHS; Marshall, *Private & Official Correspondence of Gen. Benjamin F. Butler Correspondence*, 1:300–44; BDA, Jan. 14, 25, 1862; Trefousse, *Ben Butler*, 95–97; OR, series 3, 1:810–67; Pearson, *Andrew*, 1:307–9; Andrew to Francis P. Blair, Sr., Jan. 13, 1862, Blair Lee Family Papers, PU; Andrew to Lincoln, Jan. 11, 1862, Lincoln Papers, LC; *Lib*, Jan. 17, 1862; *NYTrib*, Jan 14, 15, 1862; Marvel, *Lincoln's Autocrat*, 153–57.

29. Frank Howe to Andrew, Jan. 21, 23, 1862, Andrew Papers, MHS; Butler, *Butler's Book*, 323–34; Marshall, *Private & Official Correspondence of Gen. Benjamin F. Butler*, 1:330–34; Trefousse, *Ben Butler*, 96–97; Pearson, *Andrew*, 1:306–9; OR, series 16:677–78; 53:506, series 3, 1:896–97; BDA, Jan. 17, 18, 22, 23, 24, 25, 1862, Aug. 13, 1888; Leonard, *Benjamin Franklin Butler*, 79–80.

30. Andrew to Stanton, Jan. 14, 1862, Stanton Papers, LC; Andrew to [?], Jan. 16, 1862, Andrew Papers, MHS; Leonard, *Benjamin Franklin Butler*, 81–82.

31. Coddington, *Faces of the Civil War*, 17; Howe, *Passages From the Life of Henry Warren Howe*, 114–16; Marshall, *Private & Official Correspondence of Gen. Benjamin F. Butler*, 1:300–344; Trefousse, *Ben Butler*, 97; Andrew to Frank E. Howe, Jan. 13, 28, 1862, Andrew to Frank P. Blair, Sr, Jan. 13, 1862, Andrew to Sumner and Wilson, Jan. 13, 1862, Andrew to S. G. Howe, Jan. 29, Feb. 9, 1862, Andrew Papers, MHS; Engle, *Gathering to Save a Nation*, 146–48.

32. Pearson, *Andrew*, 1:274–75, 307–9; Trefousse, *Ben Butler*, 96–97; Andrew to Horace Binney Sargent, Jan. 8, 1862, MS 6000, Andrew Papers, BPL; Andrew to John D. Andrews, Jan. 24, 27, 1862, Andrew Papers, MHS; Schouler, *A History of Massachusetts in the Civil War*, 322; BDA, Jan. 17, 22, 24, 25, 26, 1862.

33. Andrew to Francis P. Blair, Sr., Dec. 18, 1861, Andrew Papers, MHS; Pearson, *Andrew*, 2:2–3; *NYT*, Dec. 6, 1881; Palmer, *Selected Letters of Charles Sumner*, 2:103; OR, series 3, 1:898; Burlingame, *Abraham Lincoln*, 2:285–302.

34. Pearson, *Andrew*, 2:2–3; Andrew to Bird, Dec. 14, 1861, Andrew Papers, MHS; *NYT*, 6 Dec. 1861; newspaper clippings, Andrew Papers, BowC.

35. Andrew to Bird, Dec. 14, 1861, Andrew Papers, MHS; *NYT*, Dec. 6, 1881; newspaper clippings, Andrew Papers, BowC.

36. *NYT*, Dec. 6, 1881; *Lib*, Dec. 20, 1861; Garrison and Garrison, *William Lloyd Garrison*,

4:48; Richards, *Letters and Journals of Samuel Gridley Howe*, 2:499–502; Ware, *Political Opinion of Massachusetts during the Civil War*, 93–94; *Lib*, Dec. 20, 27, 1861, Jan. 24, Mar., 14, 1862; *NYE*, Jan. 9, 1862; *LDC*, Jan. 27, 1862; Mayer, *All on Fire*, 529–33; Emancipation League, *Facts Concerning the Freedmen*; Heller, *Portrait of an Abolitionist*, 139–13; Reidy, *Illusions of Emancipation*, 423; Link and Broomall, *Rethinking American Emancipation*, 221; Boutwell, *Emancipation*.

37. *Lib*, Dec. 27, 1861, quoting the *Boston Herald*; Mayer, *All on Fire*, 525–32.

38. *Lib*, Dec. 13, 1861; *BDA*, Dec. 10, 11, 1861.

39. Mason, *Apostle of Union*, 285; Pearson, *Andrew*, 2:4; *Address of His Excellency John A. Andrew to the Two Branches of the Legislature of Massachusetts, Jan. 3, 1862*.

40. Bird, *Francis William Bird*, 57–58; newspaper clippings, Andrew Papers, BowC.

41. Andrew to Francis P. Blair, Sr., Mar. 6, 1862, Andrew Papers, MHS; Cook, *Civil War Senator*, 144.

42. Burlingame, *Abraham Lincoln*, 2:351–54; Sumner to Andrew, Mar. 30, 1862, Sumner Papers, HU; Andrew to Fessenden, Mar. 6, 1862, Andrew Papers, MHS; also Cook, *Civil War Senator*, 144; Dubois, *Haiti*, 178–79; Pearson, *Andrew*, 2:8.

43. *Charles Sumner, His Complete Works*, 8:322–33; Pearson, *Andrew*, 2:8; Sumner to Andrew, Mar. 30, 1862, Sumner Papers, HU; Andrew to Fessenden, Mar. 6, 1862, Andrew Papers, MHS; Cook, *Civil War Senator*, 144; Dubois, *Haiti*, 178–79. Eventually, the United States recognized the republic of Haiti in July 1862, when Lincoln commissioned Benjamin Whidden as diplomatic representative.

CHAPTER 15: THE CHANGING WAR

1. Andrew to Gurowski, Feb. 29, 1862, Andrew Papers, MHS; Eicher, *The Longest Night*, 170–80.

2. Horace Binney Sargent to Andrew, Mar. 3, 1861, Andrew to Col. George D. Well, Mar. 7, 1862, Andrew to Frank Howe, Mar. 26, 1862, Andrew Papers, MHS; Randall, *Lincoln the President*, 2:206.

3. John Wood to Andrew, Feb. 18, 1862, Andrew Papers, MHS.

4. *LDC*, Mar. 12, 1862; *Lib*, Mar. 7, 14, May 2, 1862; Andrew to Lincoln, Feb. 12, 1862, Andrew Papers, MHS; *BDA*, Mar. 14, 1862; Macleod, *Good Words for 1864*, 117; Alvord, *Third Semi-Annual Report on Schools for Freedmen*, 69; Pearson, *Andrew*, 2:8; Voegeli, "A Rejected Alternative," 771; Eicher, *The Longest Night*, 190–200.

5. Oates, *A Woman of Valor*, 38–42, 120; Barton to Andrew, Mar. 20, 1862, Clara Barton Papers, LC; Barton, *The Life of Clara Barton*, 1:156, 61–63; Pryor, *Clara Barton*, 84; Pearson, *Andrew*, 2:126; Schouler, *A History of Massachusetts in the Civil War*, 294–95; Miller, *States at War*, 1:277.

6. Andrew to Frank B. Blair, Sr., Mar. 6, 1862, Andrew Papers, MHS; *OR*, series 3, 1:926–27; Palmer, *Selected Letters of Charles Sumner*, 2:109–10; *BDA*, Mar. 17, 1862; *LDC*, Mar. 15, 1862; Abbott, *Cobbler in Congress*, 144–45; *Congressional Globe*, 37th Congress., 2nd sess., 1861–1862, 1050–53.

7. *Charles Sumner: His Complete Works*, 8:201; Sumner to Andrew, Mar. 30, 1862, Sumner to Andrew, Apr. 22, 1862, Andrew to Sumner, Apr. 27, 1862, Sumner Papers, HU; Andrew to Fessenden, Mar. 6, 1862, Andrew to Gurowski, Apr. 8, 1862, Andrew Papers, MHS; Palmer, *Selected Letters of Charles Sumner*, 2:104–13; Charles M. Storey to Wilson, Apr. 26, 1862, Wilson Papers, LC; Baum, *Civil War Party System*, 62–63; Donald, *Charles Sumner and the Rights of Man*, 74–83; *BDA*, Apr. 8, 1862; Chandler, *Memoir*, 48–49; *SR*, Oct. 24, 1862; Pearson, *Andrew*, 2:8; Cook, *Civil War Senator*, 144; Dubois, *Haiti*, 178–79.

8. Palmer, *Selected Letters of Charles Sumner*, 2:112; *BDA*, Mar. 3, 4, 17, Apr. 8, 1862; Pearson, *Andrew*, 2:209; *Acts and Resolves Passed by the General Court of the Commonwealth of Massachusetts, 1862*, 244–45, 254, 318, 324, 362; *Reports of Controverted Elections in the Senate and House of Representatives of the Commonwealth of Massachusetts from 1853–1885*, 495–96.

9. *BDJ*, Jan. 11, 1868; Bird, *Francis William Bird*, 60; Pearson, *Andrew*, 2:8; Sandburg,

Abraham Lincoln: The Prairie Years and the War Years, 468; Voegeli "A Rejected Alternative," 771; Eicher, *The Longest Night*, 190-200; LDC, Mar. 12, 1862; *Lib*, Mar. 14, 21, 1862; Bowen, *Massachusetts in the War*, 47; Schouler, *A History of Massachusetts in the Civil War*, 326-29; Andrew to Bird, Apr. 8, 1862, Andrew Papers, MHS; Thomas and Hyman, *Stanton*, 200-201; Engle, *Gathering to Save a Nation*, 162.

10. Schouler, *A History of Massachusetts in the Civil War*, 329-32; OR, series 3, 2:28; Miller, *Harvard's Civil War*, 115-18.

11. Forbes to Sumner, May 16, 1862, Sumner Papers, HU; Hughes, *Reminiscences of John Murray Forbes*, 2:184-87; Basler, *Collected Works of Abraham Lincoln*, 5:222-23; OR, series 3, 2:43, 45; Weeden, *War Government*, 116-17; Palmer, *Selected Letters of Charles Sumner*, 2:109-12; Miller, *Lincoln's Abolitionist General*, 96-104; BDA, May 6, 1862; Pearson, *Andrew*, 2:9; Bundy, *The Nature of Sacrifice*, 253-55; Burlingame, *Abraham Lincoln*, 2:347.

12. Charles Barnard Fox Diary, Feb. 5, 1862, Fox Papers, MHS.

13. Schouler, *A History of Massachusetts in the Civil War*, 329-33; McClellan, *McClellan's Own Story*, 345-46; Thomas and Hyman, *Stanton*, 195; Eicher, *The Longest Night*, 241-73; Basler, *Collected Works of Abraham Lincoln*, 5:203, 210; Burlingame, *Abraham Lincoln*, 2:310-15, 347-50.

14. Andrew to Stanton, May 19, 1862, Hooper to Andrew, May 28, 1862, Horace Binney Sargent to Andrew, Apr. 13, Seward to Andrew, May 23, 1862, Andrew Papers, MHS; is slightly different than the OR, series 3, 2:2, 44-45, 68-72, 85-114; Schouler, *A History of Massachusetts in Civil the War*, 333; Andrew to Stanton, May 23, 1862, Edwin M. Stanton Papers, LC; BDA, May 25, 26, 27, 30, 31, 1862; Thomas and Hyman, *Stanton*, 200; Paludan, *Presidency of Lincoln*, 130-31; Pearson, *Andrew*, 2:12-13; Andrew to Montgomery Blair, Apr. 12, 1862, Blair Family Papers, LC; NYTrib, May 24, 1862; Bowen, *Massachusetts in the War*, 1:47; Engle, *Gathering to Save a Nation*, 170-71; Hamrogue, "John A. Andrew," 147-48; NI, Aug. 2, 1864; FC, June 7, 1862.

15. N. H. Whiting to Andrew, June 15, 1862, Andrew Papers, MHS; Schouler, *A History of Massachusetts in the Civil War*, 333; BDA, May 27, 30, 1862.

16. Pearson, *Andrew*, 2:13-14; BDA, May 24, 25, 27, 1862; OR, series 2, 2:42, 3:652; Andrew to Bird, May 11, 1862, Andrew Papers, MHS. In the meantime, Andrew sent Frank Bird to visit Annapolis on his way to Washington to meet the Maryland Treasurer's office to receive the $7,000 designated for the families of the soldiers killed the year before in the streets of Baltimore.

17. Parker, *Story of the Thirty-Second Regiment Massachusetts Infantry*, 25-26; BDA, May 26, 27, 30, 1862; OR, series 3, 2:64, 68; LDC, May 26, 1862; Pearson, *Andrew*, 2:16; Cozzens, *Shenandoah 1862*, 380-83.

18. LDC, May 26, 1862; see the OR, series 3, 2:42-84; Schouler, *A History of Massachusetts in the Civil War*, 333-34; Pearson, *Andrew*, 2:18; BDA, May 26, 27, 30, 1862; NYT, May 25, 26, 1862; NA, May 26, 1862; Stahr, *Stanton*, 207-210.

19. Palmer, *Selected Letters of Charles Sumner*, 2:116-17; Schouler, *A History of Massachusetts in the Civil War*, 333-34; Pearson, *Andrew*, 2:19-21; NYTrib, June 4, 1862; BDA, May 25, 26, 27, 1862; NYT, May 25, 26, 1862; SR, May 30, 1862.

20. Gurowki to Andrew, May 29, 1862, Andrew to Gurowski, Feb. 9, Apr. 18, 1862, see also Gurowski to Andrew, Apr. 21, May 7, 1862, Andrew Papers, MHS; Fischer, *Lincoln's Gadfly*, 89; Pearson, *Andrew*, 2:25; Stahr, *Stanton*, 208-10.

21. BDC, Nov. 9, 1867; OR, series 3, 2:85; Thomas and Hyman, *Stanton*, 199-201; Pearson, *Andrew*, 2:21; Stahr, *Stanton*, 208-10.

22. OR, series 3, 2:93-94.

23. Palmer, *Selected Letters of Charles Sumner*, 2:114-15; Sumner to Andrew, June 7, 11, 1862, Sumner Papers, HU; Sumner to Andrew, May 28, 1862, Andrew to Gurowski, May 9, 27, 1862, Andrew to Sumner, May 27, 1862, Andrew to Katherine Chase, May 27, 1862, John D. Andrews, May 27, 1862, Andrew to Charles Ingersoll, May 27, 1862, Andrew Papers, MHS. What added to Andrew's frustration was that Stanton refused to allow him to

continue the practice of offering recruits a month's advance pay for their families. He wrote the governor and expounded on the political machinations in the cabinet and lamented West Point clique of generals who caused problems, and yet worse was civil members of Lincoln's cabinet who continually disagreed with one another. He allowed that Blair hated Stanton and so did Seward, but that Blair had considerable influence over Lincoln in war and political matters. Gurowski to Andrew, May 30, 1862, Andrew Papers, MHS; OR, series 3, 2:97–98.

24. Palmer, *Selected Letters of Charles Sumner*, 2:114–15; OR, series 1, 9:396, series 3, 2:43, 106, 595–96; Pearson, *Andrew*, 2:22–23; Andrew to Sumner, June 4, 1862, Andrew to Gurowski, May 9, 1862, Andrew Papers, MHS.

25. Palmer, *Selected Letters of Charles Sumner*, 2:118–19; Sumner to Andrew, June 5, 1862, Andrew Papers, MHS.

26. Sumner to Andrew, June 21, 30, 1862, Sumner Papers, HU.

27. Collier and Collier, *Yours for the Union*, 104, 111; Wightman to Lincoln, May 23, 1862; Lincoln Papers, LC; Weeden, *War Government*, 168, 326; Hamrogue, "John A. Andrew," 147–48; Schouler, *A History of Massachusetts in the Civil War*, 333; G. Thorne to Andrew, May 26, 1862, O. W. Albee, to Andrew, May 24, 1862, Andrew Papers, MHS; Copeland, *Statement of R. Morris Copeland*, 14–16.

28. Basler, *Collected Works of Abraham Lincoln*, 5:184–85; George D. Andrews to Col. Henry Lee, Jr., June 25, 1862, Lee Papers, MHS; Eicher, *The Longest Night*, 275–80.

29. Andrew to Maj. Charles P. Chandler, June 18, 1862, Andrew to Gen. Joseph Hooker, Aug. 4, 1862, Andrew to Stanton, Aug. 4, 1862, Chandler Family Papers, BowC; Cudworth, *History of the First Regiment Massachusetts Infantry*, 34, 49, 154, 199, 236, 246, 374; Schouler, *A History of Massachusetts in the Civil War*, 304–8; OR, series 3, 2:109–15, 142–43.

30. Joseph Hooker to Andrew, July 15, 1862, Brown Family Papers, MHS; William Schouler to Henry Lee, Jr., July 21, 1862, Lee Family Papers, MHS; BDA, June 3, 4, 1862; LDC, July 21, 1862.

31. Weeden, *War Government*, 93; William Schouler to Henry Lee, Jr., July 7, 10, 21, Aug. 12, 1862, Lee Family Papers, MHS; Schouler, *A History of Massachusetts in the Civil War*, 335.

32. Gurowski to Andrew, June 20, 1862, Andrew to Gurowski, June 25, 1862, Andrew Papers, MHS; Schouler, *A History of Massachusetts in the Civil War*, 308–11; Pearson, *Andrew*, 2:26

33. Gurowski, *Diary from March 4, 1861, to November 12, 1862*, 234; Pearson, *Andrew*, 2:30; Stahr, *Seward*, 333; OR, series 3, 2:162–64, 175–209; BDA, June 26, July 2, 3, 7, 1862; LDC, July 2, 1862; NI, July 2, 1862; VC, July 8, 1862; HMT, July 2, 3, 1862; Engle, *Gathering to Save a Nation*, 185–87; OR, series 3, 2:181–82, 186–88; Stahr, *Stanton*, 215–17.

34. BDA, July 2, 3, 4, 7, 1862; OR, 3:2, 180–209; Basler, *Collected Works of Abraham Lincoln*, 5:296–97; Bowen, *Massachusetts in the War*, 48; Schouler, *A History of Massachusetts in the Civil War*, 338–39; Albert Browne, Jr., to Andrew, July 3, 1862, Browne to Charles Amory, July 3, 1862, Massachusetts Governor, Letters Official, MSA; Pearson, *Andrew*, 2:33; Stahr, *Stanton*, 215–17.

35. Andrew to Frank P. Blair, Sr., July 5, 1862, Andrew Papers, MHS; Schouler, *A History of Massachusetts in the Civil War*, 338–39; Dwight Foster and Albert G. Browne, Jr., to Andrew, July 3, 1862, Massachusetts Governor, Letters Official, MSA; Pearson, *Andrew*, 2:34–35.

36. Andrew to Frank P. Blair, Sr., July 5, 1862, Andrew Papers, MHS; Pearson, *Andrew*, 2:24.

37. John D. Andrews to Andrew, July 3, 4, 1862, Frank Howe to Andrew, July 3, 1862 (two letters), Andrew Papers. MHS; Basler, *Collected Works of Abraham Lincoln*, 5:298; Donald, *Lincoln*, 354–65.

38. Gurowski to Andrew, July 3, 4, 1862, John C. Fremont to Andrew, July 5, 1862, Andrew Papers, MHS.

39. Gurowski to Andrew, July 3, 4, 12, 17, 1862, Andrew Papers, MHS; Schouler, *A History of*

Massachusetts in the Civil War, 338–341; Bowen, *Massachusetts in the War*, 48–49; Pearson, *Andrew*, 2:36; Sumner to Andrew, July 15, 1862, Andrew Papers, MHS.

40. Pearson, *Andrew*, 2:36–37; Bowen, *Massachusetts in the War*, 48–49; BDA, July 17, 18, 1862; Schouler, *A History of Massachusetts in the Civil War*, 338–39.

41. Pearson, *Andrew*, 2:38–39.

42. Henry Ingersoll Bowditch to Andrew, July 20, 1862, Andrew Papers, MHS; *Congressional Globe*, 37th Congress, 2nd session, 3267–3268, 3276.

43. Gurowski to Andrew, July 24, 26, 1862, Andrew Papers, MHS.

44. John D. Andrews to Andrew, July 11, 1862, Andrew Papers, MHS.

CHAPTER 16: EMANCIPATION

1. Andrew to Blair, July 22, 28, 1862, Blair Lee Family Papers, PU; Andrew to Lincoln, July 28, 1862, Lincoln Papers, LC; Andrew to Washburn, Aug. 27, 1862, Washburn and Andrew to Lincoln, Aug. 27, 1862, Massachusetts Governor, Letters Official, MSA; Schouler, *A History of Massachusetts in the Civil War*, 354–55; OR, series 3, 2:291–96; Pearson, *Andrew*, 2:39.

2. HW, Sept. 6, 1862.

3. Gurowski to Andrew, Aug. 2, 5, 1862, Andrew Papers, MHS; BDA, July 18, 22, 1862; LDC, July 23, 1862.

4. Schouler, *A History of Massachusetts in the Civil War*, 352; Mary Sherburn to Andrew, Aug. 4, 1862, Andrew Papers, MHS; Moore, *The Rebellion Record*, 5:261.

5. OR, series 3, 2:327; Schouler, *A History of Massachusetts in the Civil War*, 355–57; Andrew to B. E. Bates and others, July 22, 1862, Clapp Papers, HU; Hamrogue, "John A. Andrew," 183; NDH, Aug. 5, 1862.

6. OR, series 3, 2:327, 353, 363–64; Schouler, *A History of Massachusetts in the Civil War*, 357–58; Pearson, *Andrew*, 2:40–42.

7. NYH, May 27, 29, 1860, June 2, 1861; NYE, Aug. 28, 1862; NYT, Aug. 10, 1862; OR, NYH Series 3, 2:642–43; LLA, Dec. 7, 1867; BDA, Feb. 19, Aug. 5, 9, 1862; LDC, Aug. 11, 21, 1865; Yerrinton, *Report of the Case of George C. Hersey*, 2–263; Pearson, *Andrew*, 2:43. In an odd twist of executive fate, the day before he left for the island, the peace loving, anti-death penalty governor, ordered the execution of Hingham shoemaker George C. Hersey, who had been convicted of seduction, abortion, and murder by poison of his wife Betsy Frances Tirrell two years before. The accused had been properly tried, and duly convicted, and the lifelong advocate against the death penalty succumbed to the judicial pressure.

8. Browne, "Governor Andrew," 262–63; DPG, Aug. 19, 1862; Chandler, *Memoir*, 55–56; Browne, *Sketch of the Official Life of John A. Andrew*, 71–72; Lib, Aug. 22, 1862; BI, Sept. 10, 1862; Headley, *Massachusetts in the Rebellion*, 27–28; Pearson, *Andrew*, 2:45.

9. TI, Mar. 2, 1871; Pearson, *Andrew*, 2:47.

10. *Congressional Record—House, Fifty-Seventh Congress, First Session*, 35:4494; *Forty-Second Annual Report of the Executive Committee of the Children's Mission*, 17; Lib, Aug. 22, 1862, LDC, Aug. 13, 1862, BT, Aug. 12, 1862; NBM, Aug. 12, 1862; NRep, Aug. 26, 1862; DPG, Aug. 19, 1862.

11. [F. Judd] to Andrew, Aug. 11, 1862, R. C. Waterson to Andrew, Aug. 12, 1862, Andrew Papers, MHS.

12. Harriet N. Green to Andrew, Sept. 29, 1862, Andrew Papers, MHS. She edited or co-edited the *Radical Spiritualist* (1858–60), *Progressive Age* (1862), *Spiritual Reformer* (1860–62), and *Modern Age* (1862–66); Okker, *Our Sisters*, 189; Carroll, *Spiritualism in Antebellum America*, 90; Brock, *Pacifism in the United States*, 440–44. Green, and her husband Brian J. Butts, were part of the Hopedale community experiment organized by Adin Ballou in 1841 as a utopian regenerative reformer community that practiced Christian socialism.

13. Livermore, *An Historical Research Respecting the Opinions of the Founders of the Republic*

on Negroes as Slaves, as Citizens, and as Soldiers; he delivered the lecture on August 17, 1862, in Boston. Pierce, *Memoirs and Letters of Charles Sumner*, 3:113; Masur, *Lincoln's Hundred Days*, 114; Burlingame, *Abraham Lincoln*, 2:469; *BT*, Jan.23, 1863; *Lib*, Jan. 23, Nov. 21, 1863.

14. *Lib*, Aug. 22, 29, 1862; BDA, Aug. 26, 1862; Mayer, *All on Fire*, 538–39; Foner, *Fiery Trial*, 223–24; Burlingame, *Abraham Lincoln*, 2:395–402, 463–67; OR series 3, 2:433–34; VC, Aug. 19, 1862

15. Basler, *Collected Works of Abraham Lincoln*, 5:388–89.

16. *Lib*, Aug. 22, 1862,

17. Pearson, *Andrew*, 2:48.

18. Dean, "Undercurrents of the Great Rebellion," 7:2–21; Chandler, *Memoir*, 34–36; Ordered to Washington by Governor Andrew, copy of Edward Kinsley's personal account, Kinsley Papers, UMass; Doherty, "The Republican Party in Massachusetts," 21–24, 33–35; TCR, May 27, 1909; BDA, Dec. 31, 1891; Pearson, *Andrew*, 2:46–47, 51.

19. Schouler, *A History of Massachusetts in the Civil War*, 361–62; NYEP, Aug. 26, 1862; Eicher, *The Longest Night*, 320–22; BDA, Aug. 20, 1862; Basler, *Collected Works of Abraham Lincoln*, 5:370–75; NYTrib, Aug. 20, 1862; Ordered to Washington by Governor Andrew, a copy of Edward Kinsley's personal account, Kinsley Papers, UMass; Masur, "African American Delegation to Abraham Lincoln," 117–44.

20. John W. Emery to Andrew, Aug. 23, 1862, Gurowski to Andrew, Aug. 10, 23, 24, 1862, Andrew Papers, MHS.

21. Andrew, *Addresses of His Excellency Governor John A. Andrew, Hon. Edward Everett, Hon. B. F. Thomas and Hon. Robert C. Winthrop*; Andrew to Col. Edward A. Wild, Aug. 23, 1862, Andrew Papers, BA; *BDA*, 25 Aug. 1862.

22. NDH, Sept. 5, 1862; Murray and Hsieh, *A Savage War*, 192–204; Donald, *Lincoln*, 371.

23. Andrew to Gurowski, Aug. 30, 1862, Gurowski to Andew, Aug. 28, 1862, Andrew Papers, MHS; Hamrogue, "John A. Andrew," 155.

24. Andrew to Gurowski, July 17, Aug. 7, 8, 10, 23, 30, Sept. 6, 1862, Gurowski to Andrew, Aug. 8, 23, 24, 30, 1862, Andrew Papers, MHS; Pearson, *Andrew*, 2:48–49.

25. Washburn to Andrew, Sept. 6, 1862, Gurowski to Andrew, Sept. 2, 1862, Curtin to Andrew, Sept. 6, 1862 Andrew Papers, MHS; Curtin to Andrew, Sept. 6, 1862, Andrew to Sprague, Aug. 30, 1862, Andrew to Curtin, Sept. 6, Sept. 15, 1862, Andrew to Rev. B. Sears of Brown, Aug. 29, 1862, Andrew to Sprague, Aug. 30, 1862, Andrew to Washburn, Berry, Holbrook, Buckingham, Aug. 30, 1862, Massachusetts Governor, Letters Official, MSA; BDA, Sept. 4, 1862; Schouler, *A History of Massachusetts in the Civil War*, 366–67.

26. Gould to Andrew, Sept. 6, 1861, John D. Andrews to Andrew, Sept. 7, 11, 1862, Gurowski to Andrew, Sept. 6, 1862, Andrew Papers, MHS; BDA, Oct. 2, 1862.

27. John D. Andrews to Andrew, Sept. 2, 1862, Andrew Papers, MHS.

28. Andrew to Stanton, Aug. 30, 1862, Massachusetts Governors, Letters Official, MSA.

29. BDA, Sept. 4, Oct. 2, 1862; NI, Sept. 8, 1862; Engle, *Gathering to Save a Nation*, 214–17.

30. John D. Andrews to Andrew, Sept. 7, 11, 1862, John Murray Forbes to Andrew, Sept. 11, Andrew Papers, MHS; Eicher, *The Longest Night*, 326–36. Andrews told Andrew on Sept. 11 that if the governors meet, he offered to be secretary of the meeting without pay.

31. Gurowski to Andrew, Sept. 2, 6, 7, 1862, Andrew Papers, MHS; Eicher, *The Longest Night*, 326–36.

32. BDA, Sept. 11, 17, 18, 1862; Joseph B. Spears to Andrew, Sept. 10, 1862, Alexander H. Bullock to Andrew, Sept. 12, 1862, Frank Howe to Andrew, Sept. 17, 19, 1862, John D. Andrews to Andrew, Sept. 18, 1862, Andrew Papers, MHS; *Lib*, Sept., 12, 24, Oct. 4, 17, 1862; Miller, *Lincoln's Abolitionist General*, 112–46; Higginson, *Army Life in a Black Regiment*, 1–41; OR, series 1, 14:102–94; McPherson, *The Struggle for Equality*, 197; Howard C. Westwood, "Generals David Hunter and Rufus Saxton and Black Soldiers," 165–81

33. Frank Blair, Sr., to Andrew, Sept. 1, 10, 1862, Curtin to Andrew, Sept. 14, 1862, Andrew

to Howe, Sept. 19, John D. Andrews to Andrew, Sept. 11, 1862, Gould to Andrew, Sept. 6, 1862 Andrew Papers, MHS; Andrew to Lincoln, Aug. 20, 1862, Lincoln Papers, LC; Pearson, *Andrew*, 2:48-50; *Addresses of His Excellency Governor John A. Andrew, Hon. Edward Everett, Hon. B. F. Thomas and Hon. Robert C. Winthrop*, 6; *PDJ*, Sept. 5, 6, 8, 1862; *PEN*, Sept. 4, 1862; *BDA*, Sept. 4, 1862; *NI*, Aug. 18, 1862; Andrew to Gideon Welles, Aug. 30, 1862, Andrew to Lincoln, Sept. 13, 1862, Andrew to Curtin, Sept. 6, 1862, Washburn to Andrew, Sept. 8, 1862, Massachusetts Governor, Letters Official, MSA; McClure, *Lincoln and Men of War-Times*, 251; Eicher, *The Longest War*, 334-39.

34. *OR*, series 3, 2:543-44.

35. *BDA*, Sept. 11, 17, 18, 1862; Joseph B. Spears to Andrew, Sept. 10, 1862, Alexander H. Bullock to Andrew, Sept. 12, 1862, Frank Howe to Andrew, Sept. 17, 19, 1862, John D. Andrews to Andrew, Sept. 18, 1862, Andrew Papers, MHS; *Lib*, Sept., 12,Oct. 24, 1862; Browne, "Governor Andrew," 264; Robinson, *A Conspiracy to Defame John A. Andrew*, also in Andrew Papers, MHS; Saunders, "The People's Party in Massachusetts during the Civil War"; Donald, *Charles Sumner and the Rights of Man*, 28-29, 74-85; Schouler, *A History of Massachusetts in the Civil War*, 371-73; *SR*, Oct. 24, 1862; Hamrogue, "John A. Andrew," 169; Pearson, *Andrew*, 2:54-55.

36. *BDA*, Sept. 11, 17, 18, 1862; Joseph B. Spears to Andrew, Sept. 10, 1862, Alexander H. Bullock to Andrew, Sept. 12, 1862, Frank Howe to Andrew, Sept. 17, 19, 1862, John D. Andrews to Andrew, Sept. 18, 1862, Andrew Papers, MHS; *Lib*, Sept., 12,Oct. 24, 1862; Browne, "Governor Andrew," 264; Warrington, *A Conspiracy to Defame John A. Andrew*, also in Andrew Papers, MHS; Saunders, "The People's Party in Massachusetts during the Civil War"; Donald, *Charles Sumner and the Rights of Man*, 28-29, 74-85; Schouler, *A History of Massachusetts in the Civil War*, 371-73; *SR*, Oct. 24, 1862; Hamrogue, "John A. Andrew," 169; Pearson, *Andrew*, 2:54-55.

37. *BDA*, Sept. 17, 1862

38. Williamson and Hsieh, *A Savage War*, 228-41; Eicher, *The Longest Night*, 336-65; *BDA*, Sept. 13, 16, 17, 20, 1862.

39. Browne, "Governor Andrew," 263-64; *LDC*, Jan. 13, 1868; Browne, *Sketch of the Official Life of John A. Andrew*, 74; Schouler, *A History of Massachusetts in the Civil War*, 354-57; Pearson, *Andrew*, 2:55-56; *BDA*, Sept. 11, 20, 22, 23, 24, 1862; Eicher, *The Longest Night*, 360-66.

40. Shoemaker, *The Last of the War Governors*, 56; Engle, *Gathering to Save a Nation*, 230; McClure, *Lincoln and Men of War-Times*, 269-70; Egle, *Andrew Gregg Curtin*, 305-30; McClure, *Recollections of Half a Century*, 360, Nicolay and Hay, *Complete Works of Abraham Lincoln*, 4:164-167; *BDA*, Sept. 26, 27, 1862; James A. Hamilton to Andrew, Sept. 22, 1862, Frank Howe to Andrew, Sept. 19, 23, 25, 1862, Altoona Address, Sept. 25, 1862, Andrew Papers, MHS; Burlingame, *Abraham Lincoln*, 2:405, 469-70; Hamilton, *Reminiscences of James A. Hamilton*, 532-33.

41. *BDA*, Sept. 29, 1862.

42. Gienapp and Gienapp, *The Civil War Diary of Gideon Welles*, 69; Niven, ed, *The Salmon P. Chase Papers*, 1:403-4; Andrew to Chase, Sept. 25, 29, 1862, Holbrook to Andrew, Oct. 2, 1862, Morgan to Andrew, Oct. 2, 1862, Washburne to Andrew Sept. 26, 1862, Andrew Papers, MHS; *BDA*, Sept. 27, 29, 30, Oct. 3, 4, 1862; Engle, *Gathering to Save a Nation*, 227-31; When he heard that the *New York Herald* had depicted the Altoona meeting as a secretive assembly intent on removing McClellan and making Fremont the "great man," Andrew laughed. The governor was vexed how this report could have surfaced given it was closed off to reporters. Some governors were disturbed by a *New York Herald* account of the meeting and decided to write a rebuttal offering the facts of what transpired; Pearson, *Andrew*, 2:51-53.

43. Timothy O. Emerton to Niece, Oct. 17, 1862, Emerton Papers, MHS.

44. Henry Sturgis Russell to Parents, Oct. 26, 1862, Henry Sturgis Russell Papers, MHS.

45. *Lib*, Oct. 24, 1862.

46. *NYTrib*, Oct. 17, 1862.

47. Schouler, *A History of Massachusetts in the Civil War*, 373–75; Bowen, *Massachusetts in the War*, 50–51; Pearson, *Andrew*, 2:58–61; BDA, Sept. 23, Oct. 8, 22, 1862; *Lib*, Sept. 26, Oct. 24, 1862; *NYTrib*, Oct. 17, 1862; LDC, Oct. 14, 1862; Ware, *Political Opinion in Massachusetts during the Civil War*, 102–3; TI, Oct. 16, 1862.

48. BDA, Oct. 21, 1862; LDC, Oct. 23, 1862; *Lib*, Oct. 24, 1862; manuscript of speech in Andrew Papers, MHS.

49. Andrew to Henshaw, Oct. 22, 1862, Frank Howe to Andrew, Sept. 30, 1862, Andrew Papers, MHS; Pearson, *Andrew*, 2:56–57; *Lib*, Oct. 31, 1862; SR, Oct. 11, 1862; George Francis Train, *Train Extra! Right of Free Speech!*, Oct. 6, 1862, Train Papers, MHS; Robinson, *A Conspiracy to Defame John A. Andrew*, 1–16; BDA, Oct. 1, 24, 1862; *NYTrib*, Oct. 17, 1862; LDC, Oct. 14, 1862; TI, Oct. 16, 1862; BA, Feb. 27, 1862; Egle, *Andrew Gregg Curtin*, 327.

50. Robinson, *A Conspiracy to Defame John A. Andrew*, 1–16; Robinson, *"Warrington" Pen Portraits*, 95. In response to a clipping someone sent him from the *Boston Courier* that reported "our own Governor indeed, can be proved to have declared in New York, a few days ago, that the government should not have a man from Massachusetts, until the change in the command of the army was effected." Andrew admitted that he tried to get the Massachusetts men sent to other campaigns in North Carolina, and away from the Potomac. He confessed that he had conversed with Thurlow Weed when in he was in New York on business and that he blamed the petty jealousies of the generals that resulted in Pope's defeat and that he would not consent to raise soldiers for such a fate. He did allow that if a command change was to occur, he supported Joe Hooker as he "always does his best and is never equaled by any other." Moreover Andrew allowed that "I know my official duties too well to flag or waver a hair's breadth. And I know my moral duties as a man, too well not to avail myself of all proper opportunities to use the personal influence I may have with like Weed and the Pres etc., etc., to aid in curing the terrible evils under which we have been suffering, almost to the destruction of our army and our cause." Pearson, *Andrew*, 2:58–61; Taaffe, *Commanding the Army of the Potomac*, 55.

51. LDC, Nov. 4, 1862; Baum, *Civil War Party System*, 64–67; Burlingame, *At Lincoln's Side*, 214; Hamrogue, "John A. Andrew," 170–71; Bowen, *Massachusetts in the War*, 50–51; SEP, Nov. 15, 1862; BDA, Nov. 5, 1862; Donald, *Charles Sumner and the Rights of Man*, 74–86.

52. Andrew to Blair, Nov. 8, 1862, Andrew to Daniel Henshaw, Oct. 22, 1862, Frank P. Blair, Sr., to Andrew, Oct. 9, 1862, Andrew to Gurowski, Apr. 24, 1864, Andrew to Stanton, Nov. 12, 1863, Andrew Papers, MHS; BC, Sep. 27, 1762; Pearson, *Andrew*, 2:60; *Lib*, Oct. 24, Nov. 7, 1862; Francis L. Lee to Wife, Nov. 4, 1862, and Wife to Francis, Nov. 7, 1862, Francis L. Lee Papers, MHS; Andrew to Wife, Oct. 31, 1862, Lee Family Papers, MHS; Baum, *Civil War Party System*, 64–67; Burlingame, *At Lincoln's Side*, 214; Hamrogue, "John A. Andrew," 170–71; Bowen, *Massachusetts in the War*, 50–51; SEP, Nov. 15, 1862; BDA, Nov. 5, 1862; Donald, *Charles Sumner and the Rights of Man*, 74–86; Williamsburg Industrialist Joel Hayden was elected as his new lieutenant governor and would serve with Andrew until he left office in 1866.

53. Libbies Stetson to Andrew, Oct. 5, 1862, Andrew to Benj. [*sic*] Lincoln, Oct. 1, 1862, Albert G. Browne, Jr., to Andrew, Oct. 5, 1862, Andrew Papers, MHS; Andrew to Col. George H. Gordon, Jan. 6, Nov. 7, 1862, and Gordon to Andrew, Dec. 11, 1862, Gordon Papers, MHS; OR, series 3, 2:737; Schouler, *A History of Massachusetts in the Civil War*, 353–83; LDC, Oct. 11, 1862; BDA, Sept. 23, Oct. 2, 14, Nov. 15, 1862; Pearson, *Andrew*, 2:123–24.

54. Andrew to Bolles, Oct. 16, 1862, Dix to Andrew, Sept. 23, Nov. 5, 1862, John A. Bolles to Andrew, Sept. 30, Oct. 6, 1862, Massachusetts Governor, Letters Official, MSA; Voegeli, "A Rejected Alternative," 765–90; Berlin, et al., *Freedom*, Series 1, 2:85–94; Andrew to Montgomery Blair, Feb. 23, 1861, Blair Family Papers, LC; BDJ, Oct. 6, Nov. 1, 1862; NI, Nov. 5, 1862; SR, Aug. 13, 1862; OR, series 3, 2:663; Andrew to Rufus Saxton, Sept. 26, 1862, Albert G. Browne, Jr., to Andrew, Oct. 5, 1862, Andrew Papers,

MHS. Andrew's funds were dwindling. He had to cut his subscriptions to the several papers he took to keep him informed including the *Brunswick Telegraph*; Andrew to Editor of the *Brunswick Telegraph*, Oct. 6, 1862, Andrew Papers, MHS.

55. Andrew to Bolles, Oct. 16, 1862, Dix to Andrew, Sept. 23, Nov. 5, 1862, John A. Bolles to Andrew, Sept. 30, Oct. 6, 1862, Massachusetts Governor, Letters Official, MSA; Voegeli, "A Rejected Alternative," 765–90; Berlin, et al., *Freedom*, Series 1, 2:85–94; Andrew to Montgomery Blair, Feb. 23, 1861, Blair Family Papers, LC; *BDJ*, Oct. 6, Nov. 1, 1862; *NI*, Nov. 5, 1862; *SR*, Aug. 13, 1862; *OR*, series 3, 2:663; Andrew to Rufus Saxton, Sept. 26, 1862, Albert G. Browne, Jr., to Andrew, Oct. 5, 1862, Andrew Papers, MHS; Andrew to Editor of the *Brunswick Telegraph*, Oct. 6, 1862, Andrew Papers, MHS.

56. *BDA*, Oct. 21, 1862; Bullock to Andrew, Oct. 15, 1862, John A. Poor to Andrew, Oct. 22, 1862, Gurowski to Andrew, Oct. 25, 1862, Andrew Papers, MHS; *BET*, Oct. 21, 1862; Voegeli, "A Rejected Alternative," 765–90.

57. *BDA*, Oct. 18, 25, 31, 1862; Voegeli, "A Rejected Alternative," 765–90; Dix to Andrew, Sept. 23, Nov. 5, 1862, Andrew Papers, MHS; John A. Bolles to Andrew, Sept. 30, Oct. 6, 1862, Massachusetts Governor, Letters Official, MSA; Berlin, et al., *Slaves No More*, 114–15; *OR*, series 3, 2:663, 897–912; Reidy, *Illusions of Emancipation*, 252–53. Six days before the election, the *Boston Post* brought Dix's proposal into the campaign. On the morning of October 30, it reported that correspondence was in progress between Andrew and officials in charge of the contrabands who are multiplying by the thousands on the hands of the government. General Dix had asked Andrew to provide for five hundred negro families as the first installment of this state's quota. Frank Bird shot back an ingenious rebuttal. According to Bird, refugees had earned enough by their work for the army to support the three to four thousand fugitives at and near Fortress Monroe, but the army had refused to pay them much of the wages due them. Bird acknowledged that Major Bolles had informed Andrew the refugees were in danger of re-enslavement in event of rebel attack and urged him to provide temporary asylum. Bird revealed in what became the most frequently quoted part of his statement, the governor "promptly and decidedly declared his disapproval of the whole scheme, mainly on the ground, that whenever the government officials will do the contrabands justice, they have shown they can take care of themselves—that they are not wanted here, and that they are, or they soon will be, wanted there." Bird argued that Dix's scheme was politically motivated, "another form of the attempt to fasten upon the Republican party the odium of bringing black laborers into the free states." The scheme originated with Dix, not with Andrew and Republicans in the state praised Andrew for his position. *BP*, Oct. 30, 1862; *BDJ*, Oct. 30, 1862; *BET*, Oct. 30, 1862.

58. Sargent to Andrew, Nov. 11, Dec. 5, 1862, Gurowski to Andrew, Oct. 28, Nov. 1, 9, 1862, Frank Howe to Andrew, Oct. 29, 1862, Andrew Papers, MHS.

59. *BDWC*, Apr. 11, 1889; Robboy and Robboy, "Lewis Hayden," 591–613; *Lib*, Jan. 23, 1863; *SR*, Jan. 22, 1863; Eicher, *The Longest Night*, 381–86; *BDA*, Nov. 24, 1862; Leonard, *Benjamin Franklin Butler*, 119–29.

60. Strangis, *Lewis Hayden*, 118–20; *TF*, Dec. 19, 1862; *NYA*, Mar. 31, 1888, Apr. 13, 1889; *BDWC*, Apr. 11, 1889; *BP*, Jan. 2, 1863; *Lib*, Jan. 23, 1863; *SR*, Jan 22. 1863.

61. Strangis, *Lewis Hayden*, 118–20; *TF*, Dec. 19, 1862; Scrapbook 13, Andrew Papers, MHS; *BP*, Jan. 2, 1863; *Lib*, Jan. 23, 1863; *DIO*, Jan. 15, 1894; Copeland, *Statement of R. Morris Copeland*, 4, 11–16.

62. Stahr, *Stanton*, 281; Reid, *Freedom for Themselves*, 13; Oakes, *Freedom National*, 376–80.

CHAPTER 17: SLAVES NO MORE

1. Basler, *Collected Works of Abraham Lincoln*, 5:518–37; Donald, *Lincoln*, 396–98; Burlingame, *Abraham Lincoln*, 2:440; *BDA*, Dec. 2, 3, 4, 1862; Mayer, *All on Fire*, 543.

2. *BDA*, Nov. 4, 6, 10, Dec. 18, 1862; *LDC*, Nov. 5, 6, 1862; *NI*, Oct. 16, 1862; Eicher, *The Longest Night*, 395–407.

3. Donald, *Lincoln*, 396–98; Burlingame, *Abraham Lincoln*, 2:440; Eicher, *The Longest Night*, 395–407; Paludan, *Presidency of Abraham Lincoln*, 172; Stahr, *Seward*, 356–59; Goodwin, *Team of Rivals*, 573–96.

4. Andrew to Sumner, Dec. 13, 1862, Sumner Papers, DU; Palmer, *Selected Letters of Charles Sumner*, 2:134–35; Andrew to Sumner, Dec. 10, 1862, Sumner Papers, HU; BDA, Dec. 1, 4, 5, 1862; Pearson, *Andrew*, 2:69.

5. Andrew to Sumner, Dec. 10, 23, 25, 1862, Sumner Papers, HU; Frank Bird to Andrew, Nov. 15, 1862, Andrew Papers, MHS; Schouler, *A History of Massachusetts in the Civil War*, 373–77; Rose, *Rehearsal for Reconstruction*, 208; U.S. War Department, *Preliminary Report Touching the Condition and Management of Emancipated Refugees*; Faulkner, *Women's Radical Reconstruction*, 27–28; OR, series 3, 4:289–322; Pearson, *Andrew*, 2:69; Lowenstein, *Ways and Means*, 210–11; Stahr, *Stanton*, 279–83.

6. Andrew to Sumner, Dec. 26, 1862, Sumner to Andrew, Dec. 2, 28, 1862, Andrew to Sumner, Dec. 13, 1862, Sumner Papers, HU; Sumner to Andrew, Dec. 26, 28, 1862, Andrew Papers, MHS; Pearson, *Andrew*, 2:64–65; Baum, *Civil War Party System*, 59–60; Palmer, *Selected Letters of Charles Sumner*, 2:134–35; Stahr, *Stanton*, 280–82; Belz, "Law, Politics, and Race in the Struggle for Equal Pay During the Civil War," 197–202.

7. "President Eliot and M.I.T.," 430–31; MPNEJA, Nov. 22, 1884, Feb. 8, 1879; "Massachusetts Agricultural College," 836–49; Pearson, *Andrew*, 2:67, 237–38, 295–97; Goodall, "The Massachusetts Agricultural College," 224–31; Stratton and Mannix, *Mind and Hand*, 258; Rogers, *Life and Letters of William Barton Rogers*, 2:75–85; Louis Agassiz to Andrew, Mar. 2, 1861, Andrew Papers, MHS; Browne, *Sketch of the Official Life of John A. Andrew*, 119.

8. BDA, Jan. 2, 1863.

9. Mayer, *All on Fire*, 544–45.

10. Lib, Jan. 9, 1863; Mayer, *All on Fire*, 544–45.

11. BP, Jan. 1, 2, 1863.

12. BDA, Jan. 2, 1863; Mayer, *All on Fire*, 545–47.

13. BDA, Jan. 2, 1863; Mayer, *All on Fire*, 545–47.

14. Wesley and Uzelac, *William Cooper Nell*, 634; Lib, Jan. 9, 1863, CI, Jan. 17, 1863; BG, Nov. 20, 2012; Strangis, *Lewis Hayden*, 118–21; BDA, Jan. 2, 1864; Mayer, *All on Fire*, 546–47; Stearns, *Life and Public Services of George Luther Stearns*, 266–76; Blight, *Frederick Douglass*, 382–84; Reynolds, *John Brown Abolitionist*, 4–5.

15. Lib, Jan. 16, 1863; CI, Jan. 17, 1863.

16. Higginson to Andrew, Jan. 17, 1863, Massachusetts Governor, Letters Official, MSA; Smith, *Blacks Soldiers in Blue*, 314; Higginson, *Army Life in a Black Regiment*, 1–80.

17. Charles H. Woodwell Diary, Jan. 1, 1863, Woodwell Papers, LC; Bowen, *Massachusetts in the War*, 52; BDA, Jan. 2, 3, 1864; Smith, *Lincoln and the U.S. Colored Troops*, 4; Higginson, *Army Life in a Black Regiment*, 71.

18. Lib, Jan. 9, 1863.

19. G. A. Swasy to Andrew, Jan. 2, 1863, Andrew Papers, MHS; Schouler, *A History of Massachusetts in the Civil War*, 392–95; Lib, Jan. 9, 1863; Bundy, *The Nature of Sacrifice*, 250–61.

20. Niven, *The Salmon P. Chase Papers*, 3:355–56; Berlin, et al., *Freedom*, Series 1, 3:98–99, 222–25, 261; Escott, *The Worst Passions of Human Nature*, 77–81.

21. Andrew, *Address of His Excellency John A. Andrew to the Two Branches of the Legislature of Massachusetts, January 9, 1863*; Pearson, *Andrew*, 2:66–67; Richards, *Letters and Journal of Samuel Gridley Howe*, 2:509–13; Cumbler, *From Abolition to Rights for All*, 137; BDA, Jan. 8, 1863.

22. Bird, Recollections of Andrew, BDC, Andrew Papers, BowC.

23. Frank, *With Ballot and Bayonet*, 132–33; J. George Hubbard to Andrew, Jan. 19, 1863, Massachusetts Governor, Letters Official, MSA; Mendez, *A Great Sacrifice*, 29–33; Engle, *Gathering to Save a Nation*, 268–69; Pearson, *Andrew*, 2:70–71; OR, series 3, 2:445, also series 1, 14:377; Berlin, et al., *Slaves No More*, 195–96.

24. John Andrew, "Letter to S. F. Wetmore, Feb. 3, 1863," (Boston, 1863); Pearson, *Andrew*, 2:239–41; Albert G. Browne, Jr., to Edward E. Hale, Jan. 16, 1865, Browne, Jr., to Andrew, Jan. 25, 1865, Oregon Territory Papers, MHS; *NYT*, Feb. 8, 1863; Browne, *Sketch of the Official Life of John A. Andrew*, 66; *NYTrib*, Feb. 12, 1863.

25. Schouler, *A History of Massachusetts in the Civil War*, 404–5.

26. Forbes to Andrew, Jan. 22, 1863, Andrew Papers, MHS; Andrew to Chase, Jan. 3, 1863, Niven, *Salmon P. Chase Papers*, 3:354–55; Niven, *Salmon P. Chase*, 328; Schouler, *A History of Massachusetts in the Civil War*, 426; OR, series 3, 3:20–21, 36, 46; Duncan, *Blue-Eyed Child of Fortune*, 19–21; Browne, *Sketch of the Official Life of John A. Andrew*, 104; Bowen, *Massachusetts in the War*, 52; *Lib*, Jan. 30, 1863; *BT*, Jan. 27, 1863; Stearns, *Life and Public Services of George Luther Stearns*, 277–86; Engle, *Gathering to Save a Nation*, 270–74; Pearson, *Andrew*, 2:73, 97; Reid, *Freedom for Themselves*, 13–14; Reidy, *Illusions of Emancipation*, 52–53; Stahr, *Stanton*, 280–81; Masur, *Until Justice Be Done*, 288–91.

27. Andrew to Chase, Jan. 3, 1863, Niven, *Salmon P. Chase*, 328; Schouler, *A History of Massachusetts in the Civil War*, 426; OR, series 3, 3:20–21, 36, 46; Browne, *Sketch of the Official Life of John A. Andrew*, 104; Bowen, *Massachusetts in the War*, 52; *FDM*, Mar. 1863; *Lib*, Jan. 30, Feb. 20, 27, Mar. 6, 1863; *BT*, Jan. 27, 1863; Stearns, *Life and Public Services of George Luther Stearns*, 277–86; Kantrowitz, *More Than Freedom*, 282–83; Engle, *Gathering to Save a Nation*, 270–74; Pearson, *Andrew*, 2:73, 97; Reid, *Freedom for Themselves*, 13–14; Reidy, *Illusions of Emancipation*, 52–53; Stahr, *Stanton*, 280–81; Masur, *Until Justice Be Done*, 288–91.

28. Bowen, *Massachusetts in the War*, 53–57; Schouler, *A History of Massachusetts in the Civil War*, 405–9; *BDA*, Jan. 29, 1863; In mid-January, Thaddeus Stevens submitted a bill to the House that among other things stipulated that African American soldiers would draw the same pay as white soldiers and not as laborers. Trefousse, *Thaddeus Stevens*, 140; Egerton, *Thunder at the Gates*, 208.

29. Andrew to Francis G. Shaw, Jan. 30, 1863, in Berlin, Reidy, and Rowland, eds., *Military Experience*, 86f; see the letter in Andrew Papers, MHS; Pearson, *Andrew*, 2:74; Strangis, *Lewis Hayden*, 118–20; Hamrogue, "John A. Andrew," 173–74; Bowen, *Massachusetts in the War*, 54; Glatthaar, *Forged in Battle*, 38–39, 136; Duncan, *Blue-Eyed Child of Fortune*, 21–27; O'Conner, *Civil War Boston*, 128.

30. Hughes, *Letters (Supplementary) of John Murray Forbes*, 2:54.

31. Andrew to Francis G. Shaw, Jan. 30, 1863, Andrew Papers, MHS.

32. Andrew to Francis Shaw, Feb. 3, 1863, Letters to Robert G. Shaw, MHS.

33. Duncan, *Blue-Eyed Child of Fortune*, 287–90.

34. Duncan, *Blue-Eyed Child of Fortune*, 296; Charles Russell Lowell to Col. Francis L. Lee, Feb. 18, 19, 1863; and Wife to Francis L. Lee, Mar. 26, 31, 1863, Francis L. Lee Papers, MHS.

35. Bryant, *The 36th Infantry United States Colored Troops in the Civil War*, 63; Pearson, *Andrew*, 2:79–80; Wife to Francis Lee, Apr. 10, 26, May 7, 1863, Francis L. Lee Papers, MHS; Öfele, *German-Speaking Officers in the United States Colored Troops*, 84, 87, 101, 115; Reid, "Raising the African Brigade," 266–97; Glatthaar, *Forged in Battle*, 35–39, 53; Cornish, *The Sable Arm*, 197–204; Bowen, *Massachusetts in the War*, 57–58; Smith, *Black Soldiers in Blue*, 250–55; Reid, *Freedom for Themselves*, 13–14, 43; OR, series 3, 3:109–14, 118–22; Casstevens, *Edward A. Wild and the African Brigade in the Civil War*, 63–66.

36. *BDA*, Feb. 2, 1863; Mayer, *All on Fire*, 549–52

37. Edwin O. Wentworth to Brother John, Feb. 13, 1863, Wentworth Papers, LC.

38. Stearns, *Cambridge Sketches*, 264; Heller, *Portrait of an Abolitionist*, 145–47; OR, series 3, 3:36–37, 252; Pearson, *Andrew*, 2:74; Smith, *Black Soldiers in Blue*, 40–49; Belz, "Law, Politics, and Race in the Struggle for Equal Pay During the Civil War," 197–213.

39. Pearson, *Andrew*, 2: 82–83; Hughes, *Reminiscences of John Murray Forbes*, 2:212–13; Mary Stearns to Andrew, Feb. 20, 1863, George Stearns to Andrew, Feb. 20, Mar. 21, 1863, Andrew to George Stearns, Mar. 6, 1863, Massachusetts Governor, Letters Official,

MSA; Berlin, et al., *Slaves No More*, 199–200; Heller, *Portrait of an Abolitionist*, 147–51; Thomas and Hyman, *Stanton*, 262–63; Mezurek, *For Their Own Cause*, 38–42, 75–76; Blight, *Frederick Douglass*, 391–922.

40. Bryant, *The 36th Infantry*, 31–36; Warner, *Abstract of the Census of Massachusetts*, 1865, 234, 291; OR, series 3, 3:43–45; McPherson, *The Negro's Civil War*, 173; Hughes, *Reminiscences of John Murray Forbes*, 1:298–300; Abbott, "Massachusetts and the Recruitment of Southern Negroes," 197–98; Berlin, et al., *Slaves No More*, 199–200; Heller, *Portrait of an Abolitionist*, 150–51; Blight, *Frederick Douglass*, 391–92.

41. Andrew to Downing, Mar. 23, 1863, in Berlin, et al., eds., *Freedom's Soldiers*, 88–89; Pearson, *Andrew*, 2:85–86; Hughes, *Reminiscences of John Murray Forbes*, 2:211–12; Trudeau, *Voices of the 55th*, 10–11; Smith, *Black Soldiers in Blue*, 338; Taylor, *Fighting for Citizenship*, 88–90; Schouler, *A History of Massachusetts in the Civil War*, 81–87; SR, June 25, 1863; Stearns to Andrew, Mar. 28, 1863, Massachusetts Governor, Letters Official, MSA.

42. Andrew to Lincoln, May 4, 1863, Andrew to Lincoln, Apr. 27, June 24, 1863, Andrew to Sumner, Apr. 28, 1863, Lincoln Papers, LC; OR, series 2, 5:455, 3:100–101, 216, 4:769–70, 484, 8:633–34, 646; series 3, 3:109–10, 118; Mendez, *A Great Sacrifice*, 31; Glatthaar, *Forged in Battle*, 10, 38; Smith, *Black Soldiers in Blue*, 25–28; Reidy, *Illusions of Emancipation*, 52–53; Thomas and Hyman, *Stanton*, 262–65; Schouler, *A History of Massachusetts in the Civil War*, 412–15; Mezurek, *For Their Own Cause*, 37–42; Stahr, *Stanton*, 282–83.

43. Andrew to Lincoln, May 4, 1863, Andrew to Lincoln, Apr. 27, June 24, 1863, Andrew to Sumner, Apr. 28, 1863, Lincoln Papers, LC; OR, series 2, 5:455, 3:100–101, 216, 4:769–70, 484, 8:633–34, 646; Mendez, *A Great Sacrifice*, 31; Glatthaar, *Forged in Battle*, 10, 38; Smith, *Black Soldiers in Blue*, 25–28; Reidy, *Illusions of Emancipation*, 52–53; Thomas and Hyman, *Stanton*, 262–65; Schouler, *A History of Massachusetts in the Civil War*, 412–15; Mezurek, *For Their Own Cause*, 37–42; Stahr, *Stanton*, 282–83.

44. Palmer, *Selected Letters of Charles Sumner*, 2:155; Andrew to Lincoln, May 4, 1863, Ritchie to Andrew, May 11, 1863, Andrew Papers, MHS; Andrew to Montgomery Blair, May 4, 1863, Andrew to Gideon Welles, May 4, 1863, Blair Family Papers, LC; Pearson, *Andrew*, 2:126–32; Mason, *Apostle of Union*, 284–85.

45. OR, series 1, 23, pt. 2, 47, series 3, 3:570–71; Abbott, *Cobbler in Congress*, 130–35; *Congressional Globe*, 37th Cong., 3rd sess., 1863, 7-8-15, 729–37, 976–78; Murdock, *Patriotism Limited*, 73; Engle, *Gathering to Save a Nation*, 277–78; Pearson, *Andrew*, 2:133.

46 Schouler, *A History of Massachusetts in the Civil War*, 408.

47 Duncan, *Blue-Eyed Child of Fortune*, 322–23; OR, series 3, 3:109–11, 190–91, 209; Schouler, *A History of Massachusetts in the Civil War*, 408; Reidy, *Illusions of Emancipation*, 52–53; Schouler to Andrew, Mar. 25, 1863, Andrew Papers, MHS; Hamrogue, "John A. Andrew," 189–90.

48. Andrew to Garrison, Apr. 7, 9, 1863, Anti-Slavery Collection, BPL; Merrill and Ruchames, *The Letters of William Lloyd Garrison*, 5:141–42; Garrison to Andrew, Apr. 6, 1863, Andrew Papers, MHS.

49. Burlingame and Ettlinger, *Inside Lincoln's White House*, 112–13; Thomas and Hyman, *Stanton*, 270–71; Schouler, *A History of Massachusetts in the Civil War*, 442–43; BDA, May 8, 9, 1863.

50. OR, series 1, 25, pt. 2, 451–52; Schouler, *A History of Massachusetts in the Civil War*, 443.

51. Howe, *Reminiscences*, 265–66.

52. LDC, Feb. 16, Mar. 18, 1863; Blight, *Frederick Douglass*, 390–99; NI, Apr. 17, 1863; *Lib*, May 22, 1863; Berlin, et al., *Freedom*, Series 2, 370–71; Mitchell S. Haynes to Andrew, Mar. 27, 1863, Massachusetts Governor, Letters Official, MSA; Taylor, *Fighting for Citizenship*, 88–92.

53. MDS, Mar. 21, 1863; Kantrowitz, *More Than Freedom*, 286–87.

54. Typescript of Andrew's speech, in Andrew Papers, MHS; His speech is misquoted in some places "where for when"; *Lib*, May 22, 1863; BDA, May 19, 1863; NA, July 20, 1863; Hallowell, "The Negro as a Soldier in the War of the Rebellion," 301; Pearson, *Andrew*,

2:87; Emilio, *A Brave Black Regiment*, 20–27; BDJ, June 2, 1863; Hughes, *Reminiscences of John Murray Forbes*, 2:254–55; Blight, *Frederick Douglass*, 388–400; Records of the 54th Regiment, Apr. 21, 30, May 18, 1863, MHS; Stearns to Andrew, Apr. 3, May 6, 8, 26, 1863, Andrew to Stearns, May 6, 28, 1863, Andrew Papers, MHS; OR, series 3, 3:118, 209, 210, :372; Stearns, *Life and Public Services of George Luther Stearns*, 294–95; Andrew to Tod, May 29, 1863, and Chambers Baird to Tod, May 23, 1863, Andrew Papers, DU; Heller, *Portrait of an Abolitionist*, 147–55.

55. *Lib*, May 29, 30, 1863; BDA, May 18, 20, 28, 1863; BDJ, June 2, 1863; Hughes, *Reminiscences of John Murray Forbes*, 2:254–55; Blight, *Frederick Douglass*, 388–400; Records of the 54th Regiment, Apr. 21, 30, May 18, 1863, MHS; Stearns to Andrew, Apr. 3, May 6, 8, 26, 1863, Andrew to Stearns, May 6, 28, 1863, Andrew Papers, MHS; OR, series 3, 3:118, 209, 210, 372; Stearns, *Life and Public Service of George Luther Stearns*, 294–95; Andrew to Tod, May 29, 1863, and Chambers Baird to Tod, May 23, 1863, Andrew Papers, DU; Heller, *Portrait of an Abolitionist*, 147–55.

56. Wesley and Uzelac, *William Cooper Nell*, 641; *Lib*, May 29, 30, 1863; BDA, May 20, 28, 1863; Kantrowitz, "A Place for 'Colored Patriots,'" 96–117.

57. BDA, May 29, 1863; Schouler, *A History of Massachusetts in the Civil War*, 409; Baum, *Civil War Party System*, 61; *Lib*, May 22, June 5, 26, 1863; Thomas, *Abraham Lincoln*, 364; Mayer, *All on Fire*, 550–51; Richardson, *William James*, 54–56.

58. Wesley and Uzelac, *William Cooper Nell*, 641.

59. O'Toole, *Passing for White*, 89–91.

60. Henry to Sister Abbey, May 17, 1863, Wellington Papers, MHS.

61. Schouler, *A History of Massachusetts in the Civil War*, 410; Duncan, *Blue-Eyed Child of Fortune*, 38–40.

62. Andrew to Gardiner Tufts, June 23, 1863, Andrew Papers, PEMPL; Miller, "The Trouble with Brahmins," 38–72; Bruce, *The Twentieth Regiment of Massachusetts Volunteer Infantry*, 263; BDA, June 1, 1863.

63. Andrew to William W. Clapp, May 30, 1863, William Clapp Papers, HU; BDA, June 17, 24, 1863; BSEG, May 31, 1863; Heller, *Portrait of an Abolitionist*, 154–59; LDC, June 17, 1863; Shillaber, "Experiences during Many Years," 628; Berlin, et. al., *Freedom*, Series 2:113–115; Pearson, *Andrew*, 2:90; BC, Sept. 5, 1863; NI, Sept. 5, 1863; NYJC, Sept. 5, 1863.

CHAPTER 18: OPENING EYES OF NORTH AND SOUTH

1. TI, June 11, 18, 1863; NYTrib, June 9, 1863; NYE, July 9, 1863; Eicher, *The Longest Night*, 437–85, 501–65, 471–73; Mayer, *All on Fire*, 554–57; NYT, May 1, June 11, 1863; OR, 1,26, pt. 1:45; *Lib*, Feb. 5, 1864.

2. Eicher, *The Longest Night*, 437–85, 501–65, 471–73; Mayer, *All on Fire*, 554–57; NYT, May 1, June 3, 11, 1863; OR, 1,26, pt. 1:45; NYE, July 9, 1863; TI, June 11, 18, 1863; NYTrib, June 9, 1863.

3. *Plain*, Sept. 9, 1892; TCRec, July 25, 1901; Bradford, *Scenes in the Life of Harriet Tubman*, 6, 55, 69. Merriam implored Andrew to use his influence to have Hunter reinstated including calling on Sumner. When Andrew became aware of the situation, he urged Stanton to appoint Brigadier General Francis C. Barlow, something Shaw suggested. Lawyer and writer Edward L. Pierce, who had been Chase's private secretary before the war, and a strong antislavery advocate, was a correspondent for the *New York Tribune* as a private in the Massachusetts volunteers wrote to Andrew July 3 about the poor conditions in the Department of the South, even under Hunter and advocated that Rufus Saxton, the department's military governor should be in command. So concerned was Andrew that he forwarded his letter to Sumner with the endorsement that he regretted Saxton had not been chosen for commander of that department. Pierce to Andrew, July 3, 1863, Andrew to Sumner, July 10, 1863, Andrew Papers, MHS; Egerton, *Thunder at the Gates*, 100–101, 125; Miller, *Lincoln's Abolitionist General*, 141–46; Clinton, *Harriet Tubman*, 148–74; Larson, *Bound for the Promised Land*, 210–13.

4. *Plain*, Sept. 9, 1892; *TCRec*, July 25, 1901; *SR*, Mar. 19, 1913; Bradford, *Scenes in the Life of Harriet Tubman*, 6, 55, 69; Egerton, *Thunder at the Gates*, 100–101, 125; Miller, *Lincoln's Abolitionist General*, 141–46; Larson, *Bound for the Promised Land*, 210–13; Clinton, *Harriet Tubman*, 148–74.

5. Humez, *Harriet Tubman*, 52; *NaR*, June 12, 1897; *CA*, July 6, 1901; Oertel, *Harriet Tubman*, 59–67; Clinton, *Harriet Tubman*, 148–74; Wickenden, *The Agitators*, 194–99.

6. Bradford, *Scenes in the Life of Harriet Tubman*, 68–69; Humez, *Harriet Tubman*, 55–56; Sernett, *Harriet Tubman*, 59, 86–92; Oertel, *Harriet Tubman*, 59–67; Clinton, *Harriet Tubman*, 148–74.

7. *SDNH*, June 5, 22, 1863; *NYTrib*, June 4, 5, 1863; *BDA*, June 8, 1863; *NA*, June 20, 1863; *BDWC*, June 8, 1863; Bradford, *Scenes in the Life of Harriet Tubman*, 85–86; *HW*, July 4, 1863; Humez, *Harriet Tubman*, 56–57; *OR*, series 1, 14:297–306, 463–64; *VC*, June 9, 1863; *NI*, June 11, 1863; Higginson, *Army Life in a Black Regiment*, 69–78.

8. *NYT*, July 29, 1863.

9. *NYT*, June 23, July 29, 1863; Higginson, *Army Life in a Black Regiment*, 69–78; Bradford, *Scenes in the Life of Harriet Tubman*, 85–86; Petry, *Harriet Tubman*, 221–27; Oertel, *Harriet Tubman*, 59–61; *NA*, June 8, 20, 1863; *BDA*, June 8, 1863; *OR*, series 1, 14:297–306, 463–64; *OL*, July 2, 1898; Wickenden, *The Agitators*, 224–25; Keith, *When It Was Grand*, 176–77.

10. *Lib*, June 26, July 3, 1863; *BET*, June 23, 1863; *BDA*, June 2, 3, 27, 1863; Casstevens, *Edward A. Wild and the African Brigade in the Civil War*, 62; *OR*, series 1, 14:307–18, 462–63; *NYH*, June 23, 1863.

11. Taken from the *LDC*, July 1, 1863; Palmer, *Selected Letters of Charles Sumner*, 2: 178; Egerton, *Thunder at the Gates*, 104–6, 162–65; Duncan, *Blue-Eyed Child of Fortune*, 364; Petition of Henry Lee to Andrew, June 17, 1863, Andrew to Lincoln, June 17, 1863, Andrew to Lincoln, June 17, 1863, Lincoln Papers, LC; Andrew to Sumner, June 18, 1863; Sumner to Andrew, June 20, 1863, Sumner Papers, HU; *HW*, Aug. 15, 1863; Hunter to Andrew, June 3, 1863, Shaw to Andrew, June 5, 14, 1863, Andrew Papers, MHS; Coulter, "Robert Gould Shaw and the Burning of Darien, Georgia," 363–73; Smith, *Blacks Soldiers in Blue*, 322–23; Casstevens, *Edward A. Wild and the African Brigade in the Civil War*, 62; Witt, *Lincoln's Code*, 242–49; *NYTrib*, June 1, 24, 1863; *OR*, series 1, 14:317–319; *BDA*, June 25, 1863.

12. *OR*, series 3, 3:190–91; *BDA*, May 14, 16 1864; Wesley, *Ohio Negroes in the Civil War*, 33; A. D. Smith to Andrew, June 11, 1863, Andrew Papers, MHS; Shaw's mother was so aggrieved by the affair that after her son's death, she pledged funds to rebuild the churches in Darien. See Coulter, "Robert Gould Shaw and the Burning of Darien, Georgia," 363–73; Ochiai, "The Port Royal Experiment Revisited," 94–117.

13. A. D. Smith to Andrew, June 11, 1863, Andrew Papers, MHS.

14. George Stearns to Andrew, July 1, 2, 1863, Andrew Papers, MHS.

15. *OR*, series 1, 27:141, 163, series 3, 3:462–71, series 1, 27, pt. 2:885; Schouler, *A History of Massachusetts in the Civil War*, 476.

16. Williamson and Hsieh, *A Savage War*, 269–90, 309–22; Schouler, *A History of Massachusetts in the Civil War*, 450–58, 476–80, 576–81; *BDA*, July 14, 16, 1863; Pearson, *Andrew*, 2:133–34; Bowen, *Massachusetts in the War*, 66; *NI*, July 15, 16, 18, 23, 1863.

17. Schouler, *A History of Massachusetts in the Civil War*, 450–58, 476–80, 576–81; *BDA*, July 14, 16, 1863; Pearson, *Andrew*, 2:133–34; Trudeau, *Voices of the 55th*, 10–14; Burnham, "Hon. John Albion Andrew," 10–11; O'Toole and Quigley, *Boston's Histories*, 71–76; Richardson, *William James*, 56; *BDA*, July 16, 1863; *SR*, July 26, 1904.

18. Bowen, *Massachusetts in the War*, 65–71; *BDA*, July 16, 1863; *OR*, series 3, 3:537; Miller, *States at War*, 1:298–300; Pearson, *Andrew*, 2:136. Of the 164,178 persons enrolled, 32,079 names were drawn, and of these 6,690 were held to serve and of those only 743 joined the service, 2,325 procured substitutes, 22,343 were exempted, 3,044 failed to report, ad 3,623 paid a commutation which totaled $1,085,800.

19. Blight, *Frederick Douglass*, 401; Egerton, *Thunder at the Gates*, 129; *Lib*, Aug. 28, Sept. 18, 1863; Schouler, *A History of Massachusetts in the Civil War*, 482–83; *NYT*, July 31, 1863; Eicher, *The Longest Night*, 565–73; Emilio, *A Brave Black Regiment*, 74–101; Charles Kline to Sister, July 28, 1863, Charles Kline Papers, LC.

20. *CA*, July 6, 13, 1901; *BDA*, May 7, 1897; *LLA*, Aug. 29, 1863; Emilio, *A Brave Black Regiment*, 102–3; *NYT*, July 31, Aug. 7, 28, 1863; *Lib*, July 31, 1863; *BDA*, July 28, 1863; Eicher, *The Longest Night*, 565–73; Guthrie, *Camp-Fires of the Afro-American*, 466–67; Wilson, *The Black Phalanx*, 237; *WAA*, Nov. 7, 1863; *DIO*, Mar. 19, 1888; Andrew to Stanton, Nov. 9, 1863, Letters Received, 1863–1864, Records of the Adjutant General's Office, 1762–1984, NARA.

21. Edward L. Pierce to Andrew, July 22, 1863, Andrew Papers, MHS; *BDA*, July 29, 1863; *NYT*, July 31, 1863.

22. Schouler, *A History of Massachusetts in the Civil War*, 482; *NA*, July 20, 1863; *Lib*, July 24, 1863; *BDA*, July 20, 22, 1863; *OR*, series 3, 3:473–74, 483, 537, 551, 557, series 2, 6:189; Mayer, *All on Fire*, 553–55; Taylor, *Fighting for Citizenship*, 92–93; Cheek and Cheek, *John Mercer Langston and the Fight for Black Freedom*, 396–98; Langston, *From the Virginia Plantation to the National Capital*; Belz, "Law, Politics, and Race in the Struggle for Equal Pay During the Civil War," 200–204.

23. Andrew to Clarke, Aug. 11, 1863, Clarke Papers, HU; *BDA*, July 24, 27, 30, 1863.

24. Glatthaar, *Forged in Battle*, 136–41; Longley, *For the Union and the Catholic Church*, 210.

25. Andrew to Clarke, Aug. 11, 1863, Clarke Papers, HU; Andrew to Lincoln, July 27, 1863, Lincoln Papers, LC; *BDA*, June 25, July 29, 30, 1863, *OR*, series 2, 6:163; *Lib*, Aug. 7, 1863; Edward L. Pierce to Andrew, July 22, 1863, Andrew Papers, MHS; *NYT*, July 30, 1863; Basler, *Collected Works of Abraham Lincoln*, 6:357; Hamrogue, "John A. Andrew," 196.

26. Pearson, *Andrew*, 2:137; *OR*, series 3, 3:537, 577; Andrew to Stanton, Sept. 5, 1863, Massachusetts Governor, Letters Official, MSA; Hamrogue, "John A. Andrew," 197.

27. Stanton to Andrew, Sept. 10, 1863, Andrew to Stanton, Sept. 5, 1863, Massachusetts Governor, Letters Official, MSA; Schouler, *A History in Massachusetts in the Civil War*, 491; *Lib*, Aug. 7, 1863; LaBarre, *The Fifth Massachusetts Colored Cavalry in the Civil War*, 10–25; *OR*, series 3, 3:537, 577; Hamrogue, "John A. Andrew," 197; Pearson, *Andrew*, 2:137; Miller, *States at War*, 1:296–30.

28. Forbes to Andrew, Nov. 18, 21, 24, 25, 29, 1863, Andrew Papers, MHS; Schouler, *A History of Massachusetts in the Civil War*, 490–91; Pearson, *Andrew*, 2:92; LaBarre, *The Fifth Massachusetts Colored Cavalry*, 10–25.

29. *DIO*, Mar. 19, 1888.

30. Col. M. S. Littlefield to Andrew, July 24, 1863, Letters to Robert G. Shaw, MHS; Shaw to Andrew, July 3, 1863, Andrew Papers, MHS; Pearson, *Andrew*, 2:96–99; *OR*, series 3, 3:420, series 2, 3:252; McPherson, *The Struggle for Equality*, 212–13; Glatthaar, *Forged in Battle*, 165–72; Schouler, *A History of Massachusetts in the Civil War*, 481–87; Blight, *Frederick Douglass*, 401–3; Stahr, *Stanton*, 300–306; Pearson, *Andrew*, 2:99; Alt and Alt, *Black Soldiers, White Wars*, 41–43; Belz, "Law, Politics, and Race in the Struggle for Equal Pay During the Civil War," 200–202.

31. Andrew to Lee, Aug. 18, 1863, Lee Papers, MHS; Mrs. Octavia Grimes to Andrew, Aug. n.d., 1863, Frederic Johnson to Andrew, Aug. 10, 1863, Mark De Mortie to Andrew, Aug. 17, 1863, Executive Department, Letters Received, MSA; Kantrowitz, *More Than Freedom*, 289–91.

32. Redkey, *Grand Army of Black Men*, 232–48; Schouler, *A History of Massachusetts in the Civil War*, 481–87; Reidy, *Illusions of Emancipation*, 52–53.

33. *Lib*, Oct. 9, 1863; in his letter to Andrew on August 28, 1863, he makes no mention that there were two other slaves in the house; Ewer, *The Third Massachusetts Cavalry in the War for the Union*, 283–84; "Letter of John A. Andrew," 2.

34. McKivigan, *The Frederick Douglass Papers*, 272–73; Burlingame, *Abraham Lincoln*, 2:522–23; Blight, *Frederick Douglass*, 407–10; *BDA*, Sep. 19, 1863; Stahr, *Stanton*, 300–305.

35. Niven, *Salmon P. Chase Papers*, 1:441; Schouler, *A History of Massachusetts in the Civil War*, 490–91; BDA, Oct. 31, Nov. 5, 1863; Eicher, *The Longest Night*, 580–93. Andrew returned to Boston and authorized the purchase of artillery for coastal fortifications and ordered Colonel Harrison Ritchie of his staff to sail to England to oversee the manufacture and to take charge of contracts. He wanted someone with engineering experience to accompany this expedition, so he asked the directors of the New Bedford Copper Company to loan him distinguished engineer John Hoadley to accompany the expedition. Andrew appointed Hoadley, who was an engineer (and Herman Melville's brother-in-law) as an assistant quartermaster for the state and sent these gentlemen to England to inspect and study the machinery and the techniques employed to see if they could be manufactured in the United States. Garner, *The Civil War World of Herman Melville*, 270; Schouler, *A History of Massachusetts in the Civil War*, 496–97.

36. BDA, Sept. 3, 4, 1863.

37. The Republicans met September 24. Baum, *Civil War Party System*, 68–71; Bowen, *Massachusetts in the War*, 70; Schouler, *A History of Massachusetts in the Civil War*, 497–501; BDA, Sept. 3, 19, 21, 23, 24, Oct. 9, Nov. 4, 1863.

38. Hughes, *Reminiscences of John Murray Forbes*, 2:265–66; Woodman to Andrew, Aug. 30, 1863, Andrew Papers, MHS; TCR, May 9, 1918.

39. Schouler, *A History of Massachusetts in the Civil War*, 500–503.

40. BDA, Nov. 2, 3, 1863; LDC, Nov. 2, 1863; Bundy, *The Nature of Sacrifice*, 260–61.

41. Lib, Nov. 21, 1863; BDA, Nov. 4, 5, 1863; LDC, Nov. 4, 1863; Fields, *James T. Fields*, 86–87. On November 3, Fields noted that a dinner was held in honor of the beautiful organ in the Boston Music Hall and Andrew "surpassed himself in interesting conversation," which Fields noted in his diary.

42. John D. Parsons Diary, Nov. 3, 1863, Parsons Papers, MHS; Baum, *Civil War PartySystem*, 68–71; Bowen, *Massachusetts in the War*, 70; Schouler, *A History of Massachusetts in the Civil War*, 497–501; BDA, Oct. 9, Nov. 4, 1863.

43. John W. Mahan to William Schouler, Nov. 13, 1863, William Schouler Papers, MHS; George W. Taylor to Cousin Frank, Nov. 2, 1863, Ordway Papers, MHS.

44. CDE, Oct. 1, 1863; Forbes to Andrew, Nov. 18, 21, 1863, Andrew Papers, MHS.

45. Washington, *Sojourner Truth's America*, 305; BDA, Nov. 20, 1863; TCR, May 9, 1918; Burlingame, *Abraham Lincoln*, 2:574; Barton, *The Life of Abraham Lincoln*, 2:203; Wills, *Lincoln at Gettysburg*, 21–42; Carmichael, *Lincoln's Gettysburg Address*, 70–71; "Open Letters," 637; OR, series 3, 3:252; Glatthaar, *Forged in Battle*, 168–72; Pearson, *Andrew*, 2:104; Members of the New York State Union Committee to Andrew, Oct. 9, 1863, Forbes to Andrew, Nov. 18, 21, 1863, Andrew Papers, MHS; Emilio, *A Brave Black Regiment*, 137; BDJ, Dec. 12, 1863; Schouler, *A History of Massachusetts in the Civil War*, 481–87, 501–3; Hughes, *Reminiscences of John Murray Forbes*, 2:264; Bowen, *Massachusetts in the War*, 1:70–71; OR, series 3, 3:1095–96, 252, 939; Glatthaar, *Forged in Battle*, 168–72; Emilio, *A Brave Black Regiment*, 137.

46. Andrew to Gillmore, Dec. 3, 1863, Andrew Papers, DU; Payne and Green, *Time Longer than Rope*, 47; Schouler, *A History of Massachusetts in the Civil War*, 482–85; Basler, *Collected Works of Abraham Lincoln*, 7:53–56; BDA, Dec. 28, 1863; Burlingame, *Abraham Lincoln*, 2:582–610.

47. Emilio, *A Brave Black Regiment*, 137, BDJ, Dec. 12, 1863; OR, series 3, 3:252; Glatthaar, *Forged in Battle*, 168–72; Pearson, *Andrew*, 2:104; Hughes, *Reminiscences of John Murray Forbes*, 2:264; Forbes to Andrew, Nov. 18, 21, 24, 1863, Andrew Papers, MHS; Bowen, *Massachusetts in the War*, 70–71; Schouler, *A History of Massachusetts in the Civil War*, 501–503; OR, series 3, 3:939, 1095–96.

48. Gooding, *On the Altar of Freedom*, 83; Keith, *When It Was Grand*, 233; BDWC, Jan. 9, 1863; BDA, Jan. 9, 1864; Giesberg and Miller, *Women and the American Civil War*, 198–99.

49. Andrew to Clarke, Dec. 11, 1863, Clarke Papers, HU; Comey, *A Legacy of Valor*, 151; Andrew to Isaac Watson Andrew, Nov. 6, 1863, Andrew to Gurowski, Dec. 12, 1863,

Andrew to Stanton, Nov. 12, 1863, Andrew to William L. Burt, Nov. 18, 1863, Andrew to Gurowski, Nov. 18, Dec. 1, 1863, Mary Allen, Abbie Davis, Emma Barnes, Celia Twichell, Sarah Bartlett to Andrew, Dec. 2, 1863, Horace Binney Sargent, Dec. 5, 1863, Andrew Papers, MHS; Bowen, *Massachusetts in the War*, 68-69; *LLA*, Dec. 7, 1867; Andrew to Colonels or Commanding Officers of the Volunteer Regiments of Massachusetts, Dec. 3, 1863, Kinsley Papers, UMass.

50. Andrew to John Bigelow, Dec. 26, 1863, Bigelow Papers, HU; Andrew Scrapbook 12 and 13, Andrew Papers, MHS; *BDA*, Nov. 30, 1863; *NI*, Dec. 2, 1863; *BP*, Dec. 2, 1863.

51. Andrew to Lewis Hayden, Nov. 19, Dec. 4, 1863, Hayden to Andrew, Dec. 24, 1863, Andrew Papers, MHS; Hayden to Andrew, Dec. 17, 1863, Massachusetts Governor, Letters Official, MSA; Pearson, *Andrew*, 2:70; Trudeau, *Voices of the 55th*, 10-11; McPherson, *The Struggle for Equality*, 204; Buehrens, *Conflagration*, 215; Kantrowitz, *More Than Freedom*, 294-97; Taylor, *Fighting for Citizenship*, 89-93; Richards, *Letters and Journals of Samuel Gridley Howe*, 2:505.

CHAPTER 19: THE PROMISE OF A NEW YEAR

1. *HW*, Jan. 9, 1864.

2. Palmer, *Selected Letters of Charles Sumner*, 2:212-213.

3. Mayer, *All on Fire*, 557-558; Palmer, *Selected Letters of Charles Sumner*, 2:229; *Lib*, Mar. 11, 1864.

4. Andrew to Charles Hale, Jan. 3, 1864, Forbes to Andrew, Jan. 26, 1864, Frank Howe to Andrew, Feb. 19, 1864, Andrew Papers, MHS; Pearson, *Andrew*, 2:268; 2:149; Sumner to Andrew, Jan. 23, 1864, Sumner Papers, HU.

5. *BDWC*, Jan. 9, 1864; *BDA*, Jan. 9, 1864; Andrew to George Williams, Jan. 3, 1864, Andrew Papers, MHS; Taylor, *Fighting for Citizenship*, 103-109.

6. Andrew to Hayden, Dec. 19, 1863, Lewis Hayden to Andrew, Dec. 24, 1863, Mussey to Andrew, Jan. 3, 31, 1864, Forbes to Andrew, Feb. 26, 1864, Andrew Papers, MHS; Lewis Hayden to Andrew, Dec. 17, 1863, Massachusetts Governor, Letters Received, MSA; Schouler, *A History of Massachusetts in the Civil War*, 509; Stearns, *Life and Public Services of George Luther Stearns*, 321-27; Heller, *Portrait of an Abolitionist*, 177-79; *OR*, series 3, 4:90; Williams, *A History of the Negro Troops in the War of the Rebellion*, 120; C. Ripley, et al., *The Black Abolitionist Papers*, 5:298.

7. Schouler, *A History of Massachusetts in the Civil War*, 509; Andrew to Hayden, Dec. 19, 1863, Massachusetts Governor, Letters Official, MSA; Andrew to Charles Hale, Jan. 3, 1864, Hayden to Andrew, Jan. 8, 1864, Andrew Papers, MHS; Taylor, *Fighting for Citizenship*, 71-126. Hayden complained to Andrew from Philadelphia that "colored persons going from this city to Boston are kidnapped in New York."

8. *BDA*, Jan. 7, 1864; *Address of His Excellency John A. Andrew to the Two Branches of the Legislature of Massachusetts, January 8, 1864*; Julia Ward Howe to Andrew, Jan. 17, 1864, Andrew Papers, MHS.

9. *Address of His Excellency John A. Andrew to the Two Branches of the Legislature of Massachusetts, January 8, 1864*; Bowen, *Massachusetts in the War*, 71-72; Schouler, *A History of Massachusetts in the Civil War*, 522-26; *BDA*, Jan. 9, May 16, 1864; *OR*, series 3, 4:9-10; Albert G. Browne, Jr., to Andrew, Jan. 17, 1864, Owen Lovejoy to Andrew, Feb. 22, 1864, ndrew Papers, MHS.

10. *Address of His Excellency John A. Andrew to the Two Branches of the Legislature of Massachusetts, January 9, 1863*, 24; *The Poetical Works of Lord Byron, Complete*, 319.

11. Eliza Quincy to Andrew, Jan. 8, 1864, Sumner to Andrew, Jan. 23, 1864, Andrew Papers, MHS.

12. *Lib*, Mar. 18, 1859; Mason, *Apostle of Union*, 285; Rogers, *Life and Letters of Williams Barton Rogers*, 83; Marvel, *Burnside*, 340-41; John D. Parsons Diary, Jan. 21, 1864, Parsons Papers, MHS; Diary of Lillian Clarke, Jan. 13, 14, 17, 1864, James Freeman Clarke Papers, Perry-Clarke Collection, MHS; *BDA*, Jan. 18, 21, Feb. 11, 1864.

13. Palmer, *Selected Letters of Charles Sumner*, 2:227-28; *Congressional Globe*, 38th Congress, 1st session, 562-66, 632-643, 632, 1178-79, 1228-35; *BDC*, Feb. 12, 19, 1864; John Murray Forbes to Andrew, Feb. 26, Gurowski to Andrew, Feb. 1, Mar. 10, 27, Sumner to Andrew, Feb. 1, 1864, Andrew Papers, MHS; Cook, *Civil War Senator*, 164-65; Kinsley to Andrew, Feb. 10, 1864, Wilkinson Papers, DU; *Lib*, Feb. 12, 1864; Burlingame, *Abraham Lincoln*, 2:628-31; Stahr, *Stanton*, 339; McPherson, *The Struggle for Negro Equality*, 215; Bowen, *Massachusetts in the War*, 72; *OR*, series 3, 4:59; Engle, *Gathering to Save a Nation*, 365; Bogue, *The Earnest Men*, 169-72.

14. Hallowell, "The Negro as Soldier," 25-42; Berlin, et. al, *Freedom*, Series 2:394-95; Glatthaar, *Forged in Battle*, 173; Mendez, *A Great Sacrifice*, 46-47; Pearson, *Andrew*, 2:109; Westwood, "The Cause and Consequence of a Union Black Soldier's Mutiny and Execution," 222-36; James A. Dix to Andrew, Apr. 20, 1864, Andrew Papers, MHS.

15. Andrew to Lincoln, Feb. 12, 1864, Lincoln to Andrew, Feb. 18, 1864, Lincoln Papers, LC; Basler, *Collected Works of Abraham Lincoln*, 7:190, 204; John Murray Forbes to Andrew, Feb. 26, 1864, Andrew Papers, MHS.

16. Charles Ingersoll to Andrew, Feb. 23, 1864, Andrew to Chase, May 2, 1864, Andrew Papers, MHS; *SR*, Feb. 4, 1864; Pearson, *Andrew*, 2:151; Andrew to Frank P. Blair, Sr., Jan. 31, 1864, Blair-Lee Family Papers, PU.

17. *BDA*, Feb. 24, 1864; *Lib*, May 22, 1863, Mar. 4, 24, 1864; William S. Andiers to Andrew, Jan. 18, 1864, Garrison to Andrew, Feb. 12, 1864, John H. Stephenson to Andrew, Feb. 12, 1864, Isaac Watson Andrew to Andrew, Mar. 14, 1864, Andrew Papers, MHS.

18. Burnham, "Hon. John Albion Andrew," 1-12; Ruschenberger, "Naval Staff Rank," 356-70; John A. Andrew, *An Address to the Graduating Class of the Medical School in the University at Cambridge*; Clarke, *Memorial and Biographical Sketches*, 18-19; *BDA*, Mar. 5, 10, 1863.

19. Ford, *War Letters*, 449; Sandburg, *Abraham Lincoln: The War Years*, 3:185.

20. Wilson, *Campfires of Freedom*, 178-83; "Anon." to Andrew, Mar. 25, 1864, and Sgt. A. S. Fisher to Andrew, Mar. 14, 1864, Executive Department, Letters Received, MSA; Schouler, *A History of Massachusetts in the Civil War*, 540-49; Taylor, *Fighting for Citizenship*, 106-109.

21. *Lib*, Apr. 8, 1864.

22. Quoted in Wilson, *Campfires of Freedom*, 30-31, 34-36, taken from J. J, Holloway to "Dear Friend" Andrew, Mar. 7, 1864, Executive Department, Letters Received, MSA; J. J. Holloway to Andrew, Mar. 7, 1864, Andrew Papers, MHS; Bryant, *The 36th Infantry United States Colored Troops in the Civil War*, 32-38; Andrew wrote Governor Francis Pierpont of Alexandria, Virginia, of the Restored Government of Virginia, to clarify that he had not authorized anyone to recruit outside Massachusetts for a Massachusetts regiment without the consent of the governor of that state. The Fifth Regiment of Massachusetts Volunteer Cavalry was then organizing in Camp Meigs at Readville and George J. Downing who was in charge of recruiting wired Andrew asking that he reassure Pierpont that recruits obtained in Virginia would receive the Massachusetts bounty. Thus, Andrew was happy to comply and made it clear that the Commonwealth would treat all volunteers alike, "making no distinction whatsoever in respect to race, nativity, or color." Andrew to Pierpont, Mar. 11, 1864, Pierpont Executive Papers, LV; Smith, *Black Soldiers in Blue*, 280; Andrew to Pierpont, May 16, 1864, Andrew Papers, MHS.

23. Luce, *Legislative Problems*, 225; Pearson, *Andrew*, 2:202-4, 207; *BDC*, Feb. 1, 1868; Chandler, *Memoir*, 48-49; *BDA*, Mar. 9, 24, 1864; Moses Kimball to Andrew, May 19, 1864, Andrew Papers, MHS; Miner and Pitman, *Shall Criminals Sit on the Jury*, 69; Clarke, *History of the Temperance Reform in Massachusetts*, 137.

24. *OR*, series 3, 4:276-77; *Lib*, Feb. 26, May 6, 13, 27, 1864; Palmer, *Selected Letters of Charles Sumner*, 2:237; Forbes to Andrew, Mar. 25, 30, Apr. 4, 1864, Andrew to Gurowski, Apr. 24, 1864, Andrew Papers, MHS; Lincoln to Andrew, Feb. 18, 1864, Bates to Lincoln, Apr. 23, 1864, Andrew to Lincoln, May 27, 1864, Lincoln Papers, LC; Basler, *Collected*

Works of Abraham Lincoln, 7:280; Hamrogue, "John A. Andrew," 207; *Annual Report of the Adjutant-General of the Commonwealth of Massachusetts, 1864*, 72–91; Egerton, *Thunder at the Gates*, 236–46; Coles, "Far from Fields of Glory," 141–47.

25. *BDA*, Apr. 13, 1864; *NI*, Apr. 16, 1864.

26. Andrew to George W. Smalley, Apr. 19, 1864, Smalley to Andrew, Mar. 22, 1864, Forbes to Andrew, Apr. 4, 1864, Andrew Papers, MHS; *NYT*, Apr. 16, 18, 19, 24, 26, 1864; Castel, "The Fort Pillow Massacre," 37–50; Cimprich and Mainfort, "Fort Pillow Revisited," 293–306; Pearson, *Andrew*, 2:110; *Lib*, Apr. 22, 29, 1864; Eicher, *The Longest Night*, 655–57; *BDA*, Apr. 12, 1864.

27. Sumner to Andrew, Apr. 30, 1864, Andrew to Sumner, Apr. 23, 1864, Sumner Papers, HU; Palmer, *Selected Letters of Charles Sumner*, 2:237; Andrew to Lincoln, Mar. 24, May 13, 1864, Lincoln to Bates, Apr. 4, 1864, Edward Bates to Lincoln, May 13, 1864, Lincoln Papers, LC; Pearson, *Andrew*, 2:107–8; *NYT*, May 8, 1864; Thomas D. Freeman to Andrew, June 1, 1864. John M. Forbes to Andrew, Apr. 7, 1864. Andrew to Sumner, Apr. 11, 1864, Andrew Papers, MHS; Hamrogue, "John A. Andrew," 207; *OR*, series 3, 4:271–77; *Annual Report of the Adjutant-General of the Commonwealth of Massachusetts, 1864*, 63–91; Basler, *Collected Works of Abraham Lincoln*, 7:280; *Lib*, May 6, 13, 1864; Horton, "Naturally Anti-Slavery: Lincoln, Race, and the Complexity of American Liberty," in Wilentz, ed., *The Best American History Essays on Lincoln*, 77–78; Smith, *Lincoln and the U.S. Colored Troops*, 70–72; Taylor, *Fighting for Citizenship*, 102–7.

28. Andrew to Kinsley, Apr. 28, 1864, Edward Wilkinson Papers, DU.

29. *Lib*, Apr. 29, 1864; Andrew to Sumner, Apr. 4, 11, 1864, Sumner to Andrew, Apr. 30, 1864, Sumner Papers, HU; Palmer, *Selected Letters of Charles Sumner*, 2:237; Andrew to [Edward Kinsley], Apr. 25, 1864, Kinsley Papers, UMass; *Congressional Globe*, 38th Congress, 1st session, 1479–90; Vorenberg, *Final Freedom*, 89–160; Thompson to Andrew, Apr. 6, 1864, Andrew Papers, MHS.

30. Daniel Ricketson to Andrew, Apr. 19, 1864, Andrew Papers, MHS.

31. Schouler, *A History of Massachusetts in the Civil War*, 549; Stephens and Yacavone, *A Voice of Thunder*, 78–79; Kantrowitz, *More Than Freedom*, 292–94.

32. Foner, *The Fiery Trial*, 253.

33. Hughes, *Reminiscences of John Murray Forbes*, 2:122.

34. Andrew to Charles S. Hale, May 31, 1864, Andrew to George S. Hale, May 31, 1864, Forbes to Andrew, Apr. 7, 1864, Andrew Papers *Voice of Thunder*; Pearson, *Andrew*, 2:108; Andrew to Lincoln, May 27, 1864, Lincoln Papers, LC; Andrew to Sumner, Apr. 23, 1864, Sumner Papers, HU; Palmer, *Selected Letters of Charles Sumner*, 2:237; *BDA*, May 16, 1864; Schouler, *A History of Massachusetts in the Civil War*, 520–55; Eicher, *The Longest Night*, 662–71.

35. Andrew to Lincoln, May 18, 1864, Lincoln Papers, LC; *Lib*, May 27, 1864; Taylor, *Fighting for Citizenship*, 97–106.

36. Andrew to Thaddeus Stevens, June 4, 1864, Andrew Papers, MHS; Pearson, *Andrew*, 2:11; Sandburg, *Abraham Lincoln: The War Years*, 3:183; Taylor, *Fighting for Citizenship*, 112–16; Burlingame, *Abraham Lincoln*, 2:634–37.

37. Gurowski to Andrew, Apr. 27, 1864, Andrew Papers, MHS.

38. Sandburg, *Abraham Lincoln: The War Years*, 3:183–85; McPherson, *Marching Toward Freedom*, 95–96; Cox, *Lincoln and Black Freedom*, 23; Ellis, *George S. Hale*, 9–10; Stephens and Yacavone, *A Voice of Thunder*, 77.

39. Sandburg, *Abraham Lincoln: The War Years*, 3:184–85; Pearson, *Andrew*, 2:112.

40. Pearson, *Andrew*, 2:112; Sumner to Andrew, May 29, 1864, see this: *U.S. Statutes at Large, Treaties, and Proclamations of the United States* (Boston: Little, Brown & Co., 1866), 13:126–30.

41. Sumner to Andrew, June 14, 21, 27, 1864, Sumner Papers, HU; *OR*, *Proclamations of the United States* Series 3, 4:564–65; Foster to Andrew, July 12, 1864, Andrew to Salmon P. Chase, May 2, 1864, Samuel Hooper to Andrew, May 1, 31, 1864, Andrew Papers, MHS; Berlin, et al., *Freedom*, Series 2:21; *U.S. Statutes at Large, Treaties, and Proclamations of the*

United States, 13:129-30; Williams, *A History of the Negro Troops in the War*, 153; Pearson, *Andrew*, 2:114.

42. Andrew to Sumner, June 20, 21, 1864, Sumner Papers, HU; Pearson, *Andrew*, 2:117-18; Henry Ware to Little Mamma, July 4, 17, 1864, Ware Family Papers, MHS.

43. Kinsley to Col. Hartwell, June 30, 1864, Kinsley Papers, LC; Trudeau, *Voices of the 55th*, 106-9; *NYT*, June 10, 1880.

44. Trudeau, *Voices of the 55th*, 138-39.

45. Charles W. Lenox to Andrew, June 16, 1864, Executive Department, Letters Received, MSA; Hamrogue, "John A. Andrew," 212.

46. *Lib*, Mar. 4, Apr. 15, May 14, 27, 1864, Jan. 27, 1865; *LDC*, May 2, 24, 1864; Andrew to Lincoln, May 13, 1864, Lincoln Papers, LC; *OR*, series 3, 3:36; Hallowell to Andrew, June 19, 1864, Foster to Andrew, Nov. 18, 1864; Andrew's Endorsement of Sergeant Swails, Nov. 18, 1864, Browne, Jr., to Andrew, Dec. 9, 1864, Executive Department, Letters Received, MSA; Andrew to Gov. Reuben Fenton, Jan. 21, 1864, Andrew Papers, MHS; *BDA*, Mar. 16, 1864; Pearson, *Andrew*, 2:120; Hamrogue, "John A. Andrew," 198-200; Bowen, *Massachusetts in the War*, 57; Glatthaar, *Forged in Battle*, 179; Berlin, et al., *Slaves No More*, 213; Schouler, *A History of Massachusetts in the Civil War*, 583-84; Egerton, *Thunder at the Gates*, 173-74; Emilio, *A Brave Black Regiment*, 179, 367; Taylor, *Fighting for Citizenship*, 109-10; Rhea, *Stephen A. Swails*, 17-85. Hallowell obtained a furlough for Swails and the sergeant sent him along with his paperwork to General Foster. Once there, Swails presented his case, and the soldier secured Foster's endorsement and he returned to the regiment. He was also allowed to travel to Washington to make his case to the War Department and to Congress. In the meantime, he resumed his duties as a soldier. Andrew, however, went to work with his congressional friends and asked Wilson to accompany him to see Stanton about the case. Andrew remained hopeful but recognized that Swails promotion was more important to him than to anyone in the War Department or in Congress.

47. As quoted in Merrill, "General Benjamin F. Butler in the Presidential Campaign of 1864," 547; Williamson and Hsieh, *A Savage War*, 391-96; J. Lathrop Motley to Andrew, Dec. 16, 1864, Andrew Papers, MHS; *Lib*, May 27, 1864; *TCRec*, May 7, 1864; *LDC*, June 6, 7, 1864; *BDA*, June 6, 1864; Taylor, *Fighting for Citizenship*, 106-8; Burlingame, *Abraham Lincoln*, 2:641-45; Leonard, *Benjamin Franklin Butler*, 143-46.

48. Williamson and Hsieh, *A Savage War*, 391-96; J. Lathrop Motley to Andrew, Dec. 16, 1864, Andrew Papers, MHS; *Lib*, May 27, 1864; *TCRec*, May 7, 1864; *LDC*, June 6, 7, 1864; *BDA*, June 6, 1864; *TCRec*, July 23, 1864; Taylor, *Fighting for Citizenship*, 106-8; Burlingame, *Abraham Lincoln*, 2:641-45.

49. Wesley and Uzelac, *William Cooper Nell*, 647-48; *Lib*, June 24, July 1, 1864; *BT*, June 23, 1864.

50. Wesley and Uzelac, *William Cooper Nell*, 647-48; quotes taken from the *Lib*, June 24, July 1, 1864; *BT*, June 23, 1864; *TCRec*, July 23, 1864.

CHAPTER 20: THIS JUSTICE

1. Schouler, *A History of Massachusetts in the Civil War*, 482-83, 568; Niven, *Salmon P. Chase Papers*, 1:475-76; *Annual Report of the Adjutant-General of the Commonwealth of Massachusetts, 1864*, 66; *BDA*, June 6, July 2, 1864; Cheek and Cheek, *John Mercer Langston*, 424-26; Hooper to Andrew, May 31, 1864, Amos Binney to Andrew, June 1, 1864, Julia Ward Howe to Andrew, June 4, 1864, Andrew Papers, MHS.

2. Niven, *Salmon P. Chase Papers*, 1:475-76.

3. Henry Ware to Mamma, July 3, 1864, Ware Family Papers, MHS; Schouler, *A History of Massachusetts in the Civil War*, 560-63.

4. Forbes to Andrew, July 1, 7, 1864, Howe to Andrew, July 6, 1864, Andrew Papers, MHS; Schouler, *A History of Massachusetts in the Civil War*, 570; *Congressional Globe*, 38th Congress, 1st session, 3540-47; *OR*, series 3, 4:484-86; *Lib*, Aug. 12, 1864; *BDA*, July 15, 1864; Simpson and Berlin, *Sherman's Civil War*, 677-80.

5. *Lib*, Aug. 12, 1864.

6. *NI*, July 8, 1864.

7. Stearns to Sister, July 26, 1864, Stearns Family Papers, VT; *Answers of the Governor of Massachusetts to Inquiries Respecting Certain Emigrants Who Arrived in this Country from Europe, and Who are Alleged to be Illegally Enlisted in the Army of the United States and Other Papers on the Same Subject*; Geary, *We Need Men*, 159-61; Pearson, *Andrew*, 2:141-43; Schouler, *A History of Massachusetts in the Civil War*, 560-69.

8. Niven, *Salmon P. Chase*, 368-69; Schouler, *A History of Massachusetts in the Civil War*, 570-71; BDA, July 21, 1864; Foner, *Reconstruction*, 61-64; Burlingame, *Abraham Lincoln*, 2:659-65.

9. Browne, Jr., to Andrew, July 8, 1864, Howe to Andrew, July 9, 1864, Forbes to Andrew, July 22, 1864, Andrew Papers, MHS; Schouler, *A History of Massachusetts in the Civil War*, 569-72; BDA, July 20, 21, 1864; ZHWJ, July 27, 1864; Burlingame, *Abraham Lincoln*, 2:655.

10. Simon, *Papers of Ulysses S. Grant*, 11:361; *Lib*, Aug. 5, 19, 1864; Williamson and Hsieh, *A Savage War*, 401.

11. *NYT*, July 30, 1864.

12. Taken from the *Lib*, Aug. 12, 19, 1864.

13. "Not a Nager" to Andrew, Aug. 2, 1864, Massachusetts Governor, Letters Received, MSA, also cited in Frank, *With Ballot and Bayonet*, 174.

14. *TCRec*, July 30, 1864, Jan. 28, 1886; BDA, Aug. 4, 1864; *NI*, Aug. 3, 13, 1864; *VW*, Aug. 5, 1864.

15. Hayden, *Caste Among Masons*, 70-72; Andrew to Lee, Dec. 3, 1864, Lee Papers, MHS; Andrew to Frank Howe, Dec. 16, 18, 1864, Andrew to Albert G. Browne, Jr., Dec. 18, 1864, Andrew Papers, MHS; Litwack, *Been in the Storm So Long*, 52; *Lib*, Aug. 19, 1864, quoting the *New York Daily News*, Aug. 5, 1864; *LDC*, July 7, 1864; *NA*, June 10, 1864; *BDA*, June 14, 1864; *CDG*, July 15, 1864; Egerton, *The Wars of Reconstruction*, 46; Masur, *An Example for All the Land*, 107-10; Kantrowitz, *More Than Freedom*, 309-11.

16. Horatio Woodman to Andrew, July 30, 1864, Forbes to Andrew, Aug. 3, 5, 1864, Andrew to Frank Howe, Aug. 12, 17, 18, 1864, Andrew to P. W. Chandler, Aug. 13, 19, 1864, Andrew to Seymour, Aug. 17, 1864, Andrew Papers, MHS; Schouler, *A History of Massachusetts in the Civil War*, 571-72; Basler, *Collected Works of Abraham Lincoln*, 7:448-49; BDA, Aug. 9, 22, 1864; Morse, *Memoir of Colonel Henry Lee*, 237; "Locomotive Traction," 4.

17. Schouler, *A History of Massachusetts in the Civil War*, 571-72; Andrew to Frank Howe, Aug. 12, 17, 18, 1864, Andrew to Peleg W. Chandler, Aug. 13, 19, 1864, Seymour to Andrew, Aug. 16, 1864, Andrew to Seymour, Aug. 17, 1864, Ellison to Andrew, July 8, 1864, Andrew Papers, MHS; Basler, *Collected Works of Abraham Lincoln*, 7:448-49; BDA, Aug. 9, 22, 1864; Morse, *Memoir of Colonel Henry Lee*, 237; "Locomotive Traction," 4; Harris, *Lincoln and the Union Governors*, 116.

18. Morse, *Memoir of Colonel Henry Lee*, 237; Pearson, *Andrew*, 2:158-59; Weeden, *War Government*, 302; Nicolay and Hay, *Complete Works of Abraham Lincoln*, 7:10; Seymour to Andrew, Aug. 16, 1864, Andrew Papers, MHS; Schouler, *A History of Massachusetts in the Civil War*, 571-72.

19. Andrew to David D. Field, Aug. 18, 1864, Sumner to Andrew, Aug. 24, 1864, Frank Bird to Andrew, Aug. 26, 1864, Andrew Papers, MHS; Hamrogue, "John A. Andrew," 218-19; Burlingame, *Abraham Lincoln*, 2:665-96.

20. Palmer, *Selected Letters of Charles Sumner*, 2:250-52; Sumner to Andrew, Aug. 24, 1864, Sumner Papers, HU; Pearson, *Andrew*, 2:160; *NYSun*, June 30, 1889; Niven, *Salmon P. Chase Papers*, 1:490; Andrew to Greeley, Godwin, Tilton, Sept. 3, 1864, Andrew Papers, MHS; Green, *Freedom, Union, and Power*, 278-79; Engle, *Gathering to Save a Nation*, 416-21.

21. Hughes, *Reminiscences of John Murray Forbes*, 2:289-96; Andrew to Howe, Sept. 8, 1864, Andrew to Greeley, Godwin, Tilton, Sept. 3, 1864, Andrew Papers, MHS; Green, *Freedom, Union, and Power*, 277-79; Pearson, *Andrew*, 2:162-65; Burlingame, *Abraham Lincoln*, 2:682-96.

22. Andrew to Frank Howe, Sept. 3, 6, 1864, Andrew to Greeley, Godwin, Tilton, Sept. 3, 5, 1864, Andrew Papers, MHS; Hughes, *Reminiscences of John Murray Forbes*, 2:289-96; Green, *Freedom, Union, and Power*, 277-79; Pearson, *Andrew*, 2:162-65.

23. Schouler, *A History of Massachusetts in the Civil War*, 575-76; Hughes, *Reminiscences of John Murray Forbes*, 2:292-98; Pearson, *Andrew*, 2:167; Andrew to Howe, Sept. 6, 1864, Forbes to Andrew, Sept. 3, 1864, John Brough to Andrew, Sept. 3, 1864, Andrew Papers, MHS; Hamrogue, "John A. Andrew," 221; Ford, *A Cycle of Adams Letters*, 2:194-96; Morgan to Stanton, Sept. 15, 1864, Stanton Papers, LC.

24. *BDA*, Sept. 4, 6, 7, 10, 29, Oct. 6, 1864; *LDC*, Sept. 7, 1864; *Lib*, Sept. 8, 1864.

25. Pearson, *Andrew*, 2:170; Andrew to Blair, Nov. 13, 1864, Blair-Lee Family Papers, PU; Andrew, *An Address Delivered before the New England Agricultural Society on Hampden Park, Springfield, Mass., September 9, 1864*; *BDA*, Sept. 10, 1864; *VC*, Sept. 17, 1864.

26. Alpheus S. Packard to Andrew, Nov. 7, 1864, Preston King to Andrew, Nov. 18, 1864, Andrew Papers, MHS.

27. Andrew to Howe, Aug. 10, Sept. 6, 8, 1864, Andrew Papers, MHS; *BDA*, Sept. 14, 1864; Pearson, *Andrew*, 2:169-70.

28. Pearson, *Andrew*, 2:172-74; Browne, Jr., *Sketch of the Official Life of John A. Andrew*, 141; Hamrogue, "John A. Andrew," 213-14.

29. Andrew to Bird, Sept. 19, 1864, Bird to Andrew, Sept. 17, 1864, MS 6003, BPL.

30. Mendez, *A Great Sacrifice*, 65, 69; *OR*, series 3, 4:747-48.

31. Schouler to Andrew, Sept. 16, 1864, Charles Smith to Andrew, Sept. 22, 1864, Andrew to William Claflin, Sept. 23, 1864, Andrew to Alexander Rice, Oct. 1, 1864, Howe to Andrew, Oct. 4, 1864, Andrew to Thurlow Weed, Oct. 14, 1864, Andrew Papers, MHS; Schouler, *A History of Massachusetts in the Civil War*, 588; Bowen, *Massachusetts in the War*, 77-79; *BDA*, Sept. 15, 16, 1864; *LDC*, Sept. 16, 1864; Pearson, *Andrew*, 2:172-74; Browne, *Sketch of the Official Life of John A. Andrew*, 141; Hamrogue, "John A. Andrew," 213-14.

32. Schouler, *A History of Massachusetts in the Civil War*, 586-607; *BDA*, Sept. 15, 16, 1864; Bowen, *Massachusetts in the War*, 77-79; *SR*, Sept. 3, 1864; P. W. Chandler to Andrew, Aug. 22, 1864, Andrew Papers, MHS.

33. Andrew to Henry Ware, Sept. 20, 1864, Andrew Papers, MHS; *BDA*, Sept. 19, 22, 1864; Williamson and Hsieh, *A Savage War*, 408-9; Eicher, *The Longest Night*, 694, 95, 735-48.

34. Schouler, *A History of Massachusetts in the Civil War*, 579, 590-91; *BDA*, Sept. 19, 22, 1864.

35. *BDA*, Oct. 6, 1864.

37. *BDA*, Jan. 3, 1871.

38. Woodbury Davis to Andrew, May 24, 1864, Amos Binney, June 2, 1864, Andrew Papers, MHS.

39. Andrew to John S. Rock, Oct. 4, 1864, Massachusetts Governor, Letters Official, MSA; Andrew to Loring, Oct. 29, 1864, Loring Papers, HU; Pearson, *Andrew*, 2:175; Ripley, et al., *Black Abolitionist Papers*, 5:304-5; *BDA*, Oct. 10, 18, 22, 24, 25, 27, Nov. 2, 1864; *BE*, Oct. 31, 1864; *MDS*, Oct. 31, 1864; Andrew to William Claflin and Albert Wright, Nov. 7, 1864, Andrew Papers, MHS; Hamrogue, "John A. Andrew," 221-22; Cheek and Cheek, *John Mercer Langston and the Fight for Black Freedom*, 425-31; *Proceedings of the National Convention of Colored Men, Held in the City of Syracuse, N.Y., October 4, 5, 6, and 7, 1864*, 35-52; *WAA*, Nov. 5, 12, 19, 1864; *Lib*, Dec. 23, 1864.

40. Pearson, *Andrew*, 2:172-74; Browne, *Sketch of the Official Life of John A. Andrew*, 141; Hamrogue, "John A. Andrew," 213-14; Charles Smith to Andrew, Sept. 22, 1864, Andrew to Thurlow Weed, Oct. 14, 1864, Andrew to Alexander H. Rice, Oct. 1, 1864, Andrew Papers, MHS.

41. Henry J. Raymond to Andrew, Oct. 8, 1864, Robert Carter to Andrew, Oct. 18, 1864, E. C. Sprague to Andrew, Oct. 22, 1864, Andrew to Henry Ware, Oct. 25, 26, 1864, Andrew to H. B. Anthony, Oct. 29, 1864, Andrew to William Claflin and Albert Wright, Nov. 7,

1864, Governor Gilmore to Andrew, Oct. 1, 1864, Forbes to Andrew, Oct. 1, 1864, Browne, Jr., to Andrew, Oct. 1, 1864, Andrew Papers, MHS; Andrew to John S. Rock, Oct. 4, 1864, Massachusetts Governor, Letters Official, MSA; Andrew to Loring, Oct. 29, 1864, Loring Papers, HU; BDA, Oct. 10, 18, 22, 24, 25, 27, Nov. 2, 1864; BE, Oct. 31, 1864; MDS, Oct. 31, 1864; Pearson, *Andrew*, 2:175; Ripley, *Black Abolitionist Papers*, 5:304–5; Hamrogue, "John A. Andrew," 221–22; Cheek and Cheek, *John Mercer Langston and the Fight for Black Freedom*, 425–31; *Proceedings of the National Convention of Colored Men, Held in the City of Syracuse, N.Y., October 4, 5, 6, and 7, 1864,* 35–52; WAA, Nov. 5, 12, 19, 1864; Lib, Dec. 23, 1864.
42. Schouler, *A History of Massachusetts in the Civil War*, 606; BP, Nov. 10, 1864; *Annual Report of the Adjutant-General of the Commonwealth of Massachusetts, 1864,* 32, 63.
43. Andrew to Howe, Nov. 8, 1864, Andrew to Claflin, Nov. 7, 1864, Andrew Papers, MHS; Bowen, *Massachusetts in the War*, 79; Schouler, *A History of Massachusetts in the Civil War*, 590–91; Lib, Jan. 20, 1865; BDA, Nov. 9, 1864, Nov. 8, 1867; BT, Nov. 9, 1864; Lib, Nov. 25, 1864.
44. Andrew to Frank B. Blair, Sr., Nov. 13, 1864, Blair, Sr., to Andrew, Nov. 4, 1864, Andrew Papers, MHS; Pearson, *Andrew*, 2:176–77; Wild to Kinsley, Oct. 27, 1864, Kinsley Papers, LC; Andrew to Lincoln, Nov. 16, 1864, Lincoln Papers, LC; Baum, *Civil War Party System*, 70–71; BDA, Jan. 9, 1865. There is a great story reported to Andrew about Lincoln that on election night, the president was reminded of an incident that occurred in Illinois some years before. A friend of his, passing along a village street, was painfully bitten by an ugly dog. A single blow of a heavy stick, skillfully aimed, was sufficient to kill the dog, but the enraged pedestrian still continued to pummel the corpse, till little vestige of the canine form remained. At length he was accosted with "What are you about? That dog has been dead this ten minutes." "I know it," was the reply, "but I want to give the beast a realizing sense that there is punishment after death."
45. BDA, Nov. 9, 1864.
46. William Lloyd Garrison to John M. Forbes, Jan. 21, 1865, Garrison Papers, BPL; BDJ, Jan. 11, 1868, Andrew Papers, BowC; Andrew to Howe, Nov. 19, 1864, Forbes to Andrew, Nov. 19, 1864, Andrew to Maj. Charles Blake, Nov. 19, 1864, Andrew to Blair, Nov. 13, 1864, Andrew to Frank Howe, Nov. 19, 1864, Forbes to Andrew, Nov. 19, 1864, George B. Baker to Andrew, Jan. 13, 1865, Andrew Papers, MHS; BDA, Nov. 11, 12, 1864. Former Illinois Colonel James F. Jaquess reported a claim before the Committee on Military Affairs in 1870 that after the election he went to Boston and allegedly brought Andrew to New York City, then went to Albany and brought Seymour to New York City, where they met and Andrew convinced Seymour to agree to cease his opposition to the administration and to furnish troops to fill his quota, which he alleges Seymour agreed to do. Jaquess was working secretly for Lincoln at the time. See *Senate Report,* 42nd Congress, 2nd session, Mar. 6, 1873, *Index to the Reports of the Committees of the Senate of the United States,* 1–5; Burnette, *James F. Jaquess,* 92–94.
47. Andrew to Frank P. Blair, Sr., Nov. 13, 1864, Blair-Lee Family Papers, PU; Blair to Andrew, Nov. 4, 1864, Andrew Papers, MHS; Green, *Freedom, Union, and Power,* 127; Lib, Nov. 11, 1864.
48. Schouler, *A History of Massachusetts in the Civil War*, 640–41.
49. Bird to Claflin, Jan. 16, 1865, Forbes to Frank P. Blair, Sr., Jan. 6, 1865, Andrew to W. L. Burt, Feb. 6, 1865, Andrew to Weed, Feb. 6, 1865, Howe to Andrew, Feb. 7, 1865, Forbes to Andrew, Feb. 7, 1865, Andrew to Forbes, Feb. 9, 10, 1865, Forbes to Andrew, Feb. 11, 12, 18, 26, 1865, Bird to Sumner, Feb. 27, 1865, Andrew Papers, MHS; BDA, Dec. 2, 1864; Pearson, *Andrew*, 2:145, 181, 201; OR, series 3, 4:931; BDC, Feb. 8, 1868; Hughes, *Reminiscences of John Murray Forbes,* 3:26–27; Andrew to Forbes in newspaper entitled "War Reminiscences," Edward Waldo Emerson Papers, MHS.
50. Schouler, *A History of Massachusetts in the Civil War*, 641–42; TC, Nov. 26, 1891; BDA, Nov. 29, 1864; William Shreve Bailey to Andrew, Nov. 20, 1864, Andrew Papers, MHS. Bailey

was an Ohio native, who moved to Newport, Kentucky, and published an abolitionist paper called *The Free South*, and he communicated with Andrew about his activities and the governor's reelection.

51. Burlingame, *At Lincoln's Side*, 170-84; Schouler, *A History of Massachusetts in the Civil War*, 578; Burlingame, "New Light on the Bixby Letter," 59-71.

52. Schouler, *A History of Massachusetts in the Civil War*, 584-86; Hayden, *Caste among Masons*, 70-72; Andrew to Lee, Dec. 3, 1864, Lee Papers, MHS; Andrew to Frank Howe, Dec. 16, 18, 1864, Andrew to Albert G. Browne, Jr., Dec. 10, 18, 1864, see also letter to New York Union League Club, Dec. 10, 1864, Andrew Papers, MHS; Litwack, *Been in the Storm So Long*, 52; *Lib*, Aug. 19, 1864; Niven, *Salmon P. Chase*, 373-78 ; Kantrowitz, *More Than Freedom*, 309-11; BDA, Dec. 14, 26, 1864.

53. Motley to Andrew, Dec. 16, 1864, Howe to Andrew, Dec. 17, 1864, Andrew to Frank Howe, Dec. 16, 18, 1864, Andrew to Albert G. Browne, Jr., Dec. 18, 19, 1864, Sumner to Andrew, Dec. 14, 24, 1864, Browne to Andrew, Dec. 16, 1864, Louis Agassiz to Andrew, Dec. 25, 1864, Forbes to Andrew, Dec. 27, 1864, Andrew Papers, MHS; Schouler, *A History of Massachusetts in the Civil War*, 584-86; Hayden, *Caste among Masons*, 70-72; Andrew to Lee, Dec. 3, 1864, Lee Papers, MHS.

54. Schouler, *A History of Massachusetts in the Civil War*, 584-86; Robert Morris, Thomas Dalton, and Francis Clary to Andrew, Jan. 20, 1865, Andrew to Frank Howe, Dec. 16, 18, 1864, Andrew to Albert G. Browne, Jr., Dec. 18, 1864, Sumner to Andrew, Dec. 14, 1864, Browne to Andrew, Dec. 16, 1864, Andrew Papers, MHS; Hayden, *Caste among Masons*, 70-72; Andrew to Lee, Dec. 3, 1864, Lee Papers, MHS; Litwack, *Been in the Storm So Long*, 52; *Lib*, Aug. 19, 1864; Kantrowitz, *More Than Freedom*, 309-11; BDA, Dec. 14, 26, 1864.

55. BDA, Dec. 28, 1864, Jan. 4, 5, 7, 8, 9, 1865; LDC, Jan. 17, 1868; Hartman and Wells, "John Albion Andrew of Massachusetts," 324; Eicher, *The Longest Night*, 762-85.

CHAPTER 21: THIRTEENTH AMENDMENT

1. Browne, *Sketch of the Official Life of John A. Andrew*, 79; BDA, Dec. 26, 1864; Pearson, *Andrew*, 2:194; BDC, Feb. 1, 1868; Ralph Waldo Emerson Scrapbook and Notes on the Saturday Club, Edward Waldo Emerson Papers, MHS.

2. James A. Hamilton to Andrew, Dec. 10, 1864, Horace Binney Sargent, Dec. 10, 1864, Andrew Papers, MHS; SR, May 3, 1862; BDC, Feb. 1, 1868; LDC, Jan. 9, 1865; BDA, Jan. 9, 10, 1865, published the letter from Frank Bird to John S. Eldridge, Jan. 7, 1865; Pearson, *Andrew*, 2:197-202.

3. Woodman to Andrew, Jan. 6, 1865, Andrew Papers, MHS.

4. Schouler, *A History of Massachusetts in the Civil War*, 610-15; Andrew to Clarke, Jan. 4, 1865, Clarke Papers, HU; BDA, Jan. 5, 7, 9, 10, 11, 1865; Pearson, *Andrew*, 2:244; Andrew to Cyrus Woodman, Jan. 5, 1865, Levi Lincoln to Andrew, Jan. 5, 1865, Edward Everett to Andrew, Jan. 4, 1865, Andrew Papers, MHS; Bowen, *Massachusetts in the War*, 77; William L. Garrison to Andrew, Jan. 17, 1865, Lucinda Otis Jameson to Andrew, Jan. 18, 1865, Garrison to Andrew, Jan. 17, 1865, Massachusetts Governor, Letters Official, MSA; Merrill and Ruchames, *Letters of William Lloyd Garrison*, 5:251.

5. BDA, Jan. 7, Feb. 8, 1865; Andrew, *Address of His Excellency John A. Andrew to the Two Branches of the Legislature of Massachusetts, January 6, 1865*; LDC, Jan. 7, 1865; NI, Jan. 9, 1865; *Lib*, Jan. 13, 1865; Chandler to Andrew, Jan. 24, 1865, Andrew Papers, MHS.

6. *Address of His Excellency John A. Andrew to the Two Branches of the Legislature of Massachusetts, January 6, 1865*; BDA, Feb. 20, July 24, 27, 1865; FLIN, Oct. 28, 1865.

7. Andrew to Fletcher, Jan. 13, 1865, Howe to Andrew, Jan. 6, 1865; Andrew Papers, MHS; LDC, Jan. 17, 1865; Schouler, *A History of Massachusetts in the Civil War*, 610-15; BDA, Jan. 17, 18, 1865.

8. Robert Morris, Thomas Dalton, and Francis Clary to Andrew, Jan. 20, 1865, Andrew to Fletcher, Jan. 13, 1865, Howe to Andrew, Jan. 6, 1865, Andrew Papers, MHS; LDC, Jan.

17, 1865; Schouler, *A History of Massachusetts in the Civil War*, 610–15; BDA, Jan. 17, 18, 1865.

9. *NYT*, Feb. 5, 1865, and Jan. 16, 1865; Bowen, *Massachusetts in the War*, 80; Schouler, *A History of Massachusetts in the Civil War*, 614; *Lib*, Jan. 27, 1865; *SR*, Jan. 17, 1865; *BDA*, Jan. 16, 17, 20, 1865; Everett to Andrew, Dec. 22, 1864, William Everett to Andrew, Jan. 20, 1865, Proposed Constitution of the New England Refugees' Aid Society, Andrew Papers, MHS

10. *NYT*, Feb. 1, 1865; *BDA*, Feb. 1, 2, 4, 1865; Remini, *The House*, 186–88; Vorenberg, *Final Freedom*, 176–210.

11. Andrew to Lincoln, Feb. 1, 3, 1865, and Andrew to Massachusetts Legislature, Feb. 8, 1865, Lincoln Papers, LC; *BDA*, Feb. 2, 6, 1865; Bowen, *Massachusetts in the War*, 79–80; Schouler, *A History of Massachusetts in the Civil War*, 617.

12. Andrew to Lincoln, Feb. 9, 1865, John G. Nicolay to Andrew, Feb. 9, 1865, Lincoln Papers, LC; *BDA*, Feb. 6, 10, 14, 1865; Basler, *Collected Works of Abraham Lincoln*, 8:297; *NYT*, Feb. 13, 1865; *NA*, Feb. 13, 1865; *BP*, Sept. 26, 1865.

13. Burlingame, *Lincoln Observed*, 159; Howe to Andrew, Jan. 31, 1865, see also letter dated Jan. 31, 1865, from several citizens advancing Andrew's candidacy for cabinet, Andrew Papers, MHS; James Alexander Hamilton to Andrew, Jan. 14, 1865, Andrew Papers, MHS; Bowen, *Massachusetts in the War*, 80; Schouler, *A History of Massachusetts in the Civil War*, 614; *NYT*, Jan. 16, 1865; *Lib*, Jan. 27, 1865; *SR*, Jan. 17, 1865; *BDA*, Jan. 16, 17, 20, 1865.

14. Graf and Haskins, *The Papers of Andrew Johnson*, 7:414–15; Heller, *Portrait of an Abolitionist*, 187.

15. Hughes, *Letters (Supplementary) of John Murray Forbes*, 3:9–10.

16. William L. Burt to Andrew, Feb. 1, 3, 1865, Frank Howe to Andrew, Jan. 14, Feb. 7, 1865, Thurlow Weed to Andrew, Feb. 1, 20, 1865, Schouler to Andrew, Feb. 22, 1865, Andrew Papers, MHS; *BDA*, Feb. 18, 20, 1865; *BP*, Feb. 17, 1865; *NWCA*, Feb. 20, 1865; Abbott, *Cobbler in Congress*, 153–55; *BET*, Jan. 21, 31, 1865; Hughes, *Reminiscences of John Murray Forbes*, 2:121; *NYT*, Jan. 21, 1865.

17. Andrew to Forbes, Feb. 6, 1865, Forbes to Andrew, Feb. 7, 1865, Andrew to Howe, Feb. 6, 8, 1865, Andrew to Weed, Feb. 6, 1865, Andrew to William Burt, Feb. 6, 1865, Andrew Papers, MHS Howe to Edward Atkinson, Feb. 2, 1865, Atkinson Papers, MHS; Hughes, *Letters (Supplementary) of John Murray Forbes*, 3:13–14; Andrew to William Claflin, Sept. 13, 1865, Claflin Papers, RBHPL; Merrill and Ruchames, *Letters of William Lloyd Garrison*, 5:253–54; Schouler, *A History of Massachusetts in the Civil War*, 645–46; Samuels, *Henry Adams*, 64–66.

18. Pearson, *Andrew*, 2:179; Andrew to William L. Burt, Feb. 6, 1865, Andrew Papers, MHS.

19. Forbes to Andrew, Feb. 7, 11, 12, 13, 14, 16, 1865, Howe to Andrew, Feb. 7, 1865, Wilson and Sumner to Andrew, Mar. 10, 1865, Andrew Papers, MHS.

20. Forbes to Atkinson, Jan. 29, 1865, Atkinson Papers, MHS; Forbes to Andrew, Mar. 12, 1865, Albert G. Browne, Jr., Mar. 16, 1865, Andrew Papers, MHS; Williamson, *Edward Atkinson*, 13–20; Hamrogue, "John A. Andrew," 225.

21. Forbes to Andrew, Feb. 7, Mar. 12, 1865, Andrew to Forbes, Feb. 9, 10, 15, Mar. 2, 1865, Andrew Papers, MHS; Rhea, *Stephen A. Swails*, 17–85.

22. *BDA*, Feb. 22, 23, Mar. 2, 7, 1865, *Lib*, Apr. 7, 1865, *CCom*, Apr. 1, 7, 1865; Washington Letter to the *Cleveland Leader*, Jan. 10, 1885; Palmer, *Selected Letters of Charles Sumner*, 2:272. The letter cited in the *Boston Transcript*, March 2, 1865, might have been from Cyrus Woodman.

23. *OR*, series 3, 4:1250; *BDA*, Feb. 22, 23, 1865; *NYT*, Mar. 10, 1878; To make the case, Andrew used an example of a private in the 3rd Massachusetts Heavy Artillery, Department of Washington, D.C., named Andrew Allen of Boston. *OR*, series 3, 4:1249–51; Andrew to Sumner, Apr. 16, 1865, Sumner Papers, HU; Schouler, *A History of Massachusetts in the Civil War*, 619–21; Andrew to Tufts, May 12, 1865, Andrew Papers, MHS. Andrew's former secretary Browne, whom he had recommended to Chase as Treasury Agent for

the Department of the South, was in Washington shortly after the inauguration. He told Andrew that he had met Frank P. Blair, Sr., on the White House portico, and after a little preliminary conversation, conveyed the governor's delight that the Blairs had "taken Andy Johnson home and has got him in charge, for the same reason and in the same way he did with your man Sumner, some years ago when he had something the matter with his head." Blair responded by saying that the vice president was "all right," that he had not said anything that was "bad sense, only bad taste." Johnson had been sick with typhoid for months, said Blair, and had taken a couple shots of whiskey that morning that left him a "little disordered, by the situation and all the other things." Had Sumner not made such a fuss, Blair professed, it would have passed away as Washington hearsay. Andrew was no Sumner in many respects, but Johnson had shamed himself that day, which reflected poorly on New Englanders, who abandoned one of their own for Johnson at the convention the year prior. Nonetheless, Blair knew he could count on Andrew's support going forward. The Commonwealth executive was not about to engage in trivialities over Johnson's intemperance and allowed his Maryland colleague the victory. That Blair had to mention it all was satisfaction enough. Browne, Jr., to Andrew, Mar. 21, 1865, Andrew Papers, MHS.

24. *BDA*, Mar. 28, 1865; Pearson, *Andrew*, 2:262; Andrew to Chase, Apr. 8, 1865, Andrew Papers, MHS.

25. Pearson, *Andrew*, 2:205–12; *SR*, May 27, 1865; Reno, *Memoirs of the Judiciary and the Bar of New England for the Nineteenth Century*, 3:379; Fairbanks, *The Laws of the Commonwealth of Massachusetts Relating to Marriage and Divorce*, 70; *BDA*, Sept. 10, 1864; Jan. 7, 27, Mar. 4, Apr. 24, May 15, 26, 1865; *BA*, Mar. 12, 1865.

26. Forbes to Andrew, Mar. 27, 1865, Andrew Papers, MHS; *BDA*, Apr. 1, 3, 1865; Hurd, *History of Worcester County, Massachusetts*, 1:196; Schouler, *A History of Massachusetts in the Civil War*, 704; Goodrich, *A Tribute Book*, 121–22.

27. Browne to Andrew, Mar. 24, 1865, Andrew Papers, MHS; Burlingame, *Abraham Lincoln*, 2:695–96, 721, 747, 754, 760–64. Browne is referring to James Washington Singleton, a Quincy, Illinois, Peace Democrat, whom Lincoln supposedly allowed to purchase Southern tobacco and cotton with Greenbacks to help move the commodities through Southern lines to General Grant to encourage cotton trading. Thurlow Weed was among the cotton pirates to whom Lincoln gave trading permits.

28. Weitzel to Stanton, Apr. 3, 1865, Andrew to Stanton, Apr. 3, 1865, Telegrams Received by the Secretary of War, RG 107, NARA; Basler, *Collected Works of Abraham Lincoln*, 8:372–81; *OR*, series 1, 46, pt. 3:96, 392–93; Donald, *Lincoln*, 571–80; Eicher, *The Longest Night*, 804–6; Engle, *Gathering to Save a Nation*, 467–68; Bowen, *Massachusetts in the War*, 80; quote from *BDA*, Apr. 1, 6, 1865; Bowen, *Massachusetts in the War*, 80.

29. *BDA*, Sept. 9, 1865.

30. *Lib*, Apr. 14, 1865; *BDA*, Apr. 9, 1865; Bowen, *Massachusetts in the War*, 81; Schouler, *A History of Massachusetts in the Civil War*, 622–25.

31. *Lib*, Apr. 14, 1865; *BDA*, Apr. 9, 1865; Bowen, *Massachusetts in the War*, 81; Schouler, *A History of Massachusetts in the Civil War*, 622–25.

32. Hamilton to Andrew, Apr. 8, 1865, Andrew Papers, MHS.

33. Andrew to William Dale, Apr. 10, 1865, Schouler Papers, MHS; William Dale to Andrew, Apr. 10, 1865, Lee Papers, MHS; *BDA*, Apr. 6, 7, 8, 11, May 5, 1865.

34. *TC*, June 4, 1879; *NYTrib*, June 13, 1879; *WRC*, June 20, 1879; *NI*, Apr. 12, 1865; Eicher, *The Longest Night*, 834–35; Mayer, *All on Fire*, 580–86; Jordan, "The Occupation of Fort Sumter," 406–26.

35. *BDA*, Apr. 15, 17, 1865.

36. Howe to Andrew, Apr. 15, 1865, Andrew Papers, MHS.

37. *Lib*, Apr. 21, 1865; *BDA*, Apr. 14, 17, 18, 1865; Pearson, *Andrew*, 2:245.

38. *BDA*, Apr. 18, 1865; *Lib*, Apr. 21, 1865; Pearson, *Andrew*, 2:245.

39. John Wilkes Booth to Andrew, Apr. 24, 1865, Andrew Papers, MHS.

40. HW, May 6, 1865; Sumner to Andrew, Apr. 15, 1865, David Thayer to Andrew, Apr. 15, 1865, Browne, Jr., to Andrew, Apr. 15, 1865, Andrew to Charles Loring, Apr. 15, 1865, Horace Binney Sargent to Andrew, Apr. 15, 1865, Andrew Papers, MHS.
41. Andrew to Lincoln, Apr. 11, 1865, Lincoln Papers, LC; Browne, *Sketch of the Official Life of John A. Andrew*, 162; Pearson, *Andrew*, 2:245–46; Bowen, *Massachusetts in the War*, 81; BDA, Apr. 19, 20, 21, 1865; Burnham, "Hon. John A. Andrew," 10.
42. Pearson, *Andrew*, 2:215–18; Dalton, Wirkkala, and Thomas, *Leading the Way*, 127–28; Pittman and Miner, *Shall Criminals Sit on the Jury*; *General Laws and Resolves Passed by the Legislature of Massachusetts During the Session of 1865*, chapter 277, 86; *Acts and Resolves Passed by the General Court of Massachusetts in the Year 1866*, 365–79; McPherson, *The Negro's Civil War*, 274; Johnson, *The Development of State Legislation Concerning the Free Negro*, 28; BDA, Apr. 27, 28, 1865; *Acts and Resolves Passed by the General Court of Massachusetts in the Year 1865*, 650, 660; Guilmette, *The First to Serve*, 17–18; ZHWJ, July 26, 1865.
43. NYT, June 12, 1864; TC, Feb. 3, Mar. 10, Apr. 14, 1865; The Case of Edward W. Green, Andrew Papers, MHS; Muldoon, *You Have No Courts with Any Sure Rule of Law*, 139, 164–65; CAJ, Mar. 10, 1864; NPG, Apr. 21, 1866; MF, Apr. 19, 1866; TI, Feb. 18, 1864; BDA, Jan. 15, Oct. 31, 1867; newspaper clippings, Andrew Papers, BowC; Andrew, *Governor Andrew's Opinion in the Case of Edward W. Green*, 1–17; Chandler, *Memoir*, 107; BDA, Jan. 15, 1867; TN, June 11, 1868; Pearson, *Andrew*, 2:221–23.
44. BDA, Feb. 8, 9, Apr. 20, May 9, June 3, Oct. 17, Nov. 3, 9, 1864, Jan. 4, 13, May 18, 1865; LDC, Feb. 12, Apr. 13, 19, June 16, Nov. 10, 1864, May 18, 1865; Lib, July 8, 1864; TC, Jan. 9, 1873.
45. TC, Feb. 3, Mar. 10, Apr. 14, 1865; The Case of Edward W. Green, Andrew Papers, MHS; Muldoon, *You Have No Courts with Any Sure Rule of Law*, 139, 164–65; CAJ, Mar. 10, 1864; NPG, 21 Apr. 21, 1866; MF, Apr. 19, 1866; TI, Feb. 18, 1864; BDA, Jan. 15, Oct. 31, 1867; newspaper clippings, Andrew Papers, BowC; *Governor Andrew's Opinion in the Case of Edward W. Green*, 1–17; Chandler, *Memoir*, 107; BDA, Jan. 15, 1867; TN, June 11, 1868; Pearson, *Andrew*, 2:221–23.
46. Moore, *The Rebellion Record*, 3:66–67; BDC, Jan. 18, 1868; Clarke, *Memorial and Biographical Sketches*, 20–28; newspaper clippings, Andrew Papers, BowC; Chandler, *Memoir*, 100–101; Browne, *Sketch of the Official Life of John A. Andrew*, 55; *Governor Andrew's Opinion in the Case of Edward W. Green*, 1–17; BDA, Mar. 29, 1866; BP, Nov. 6, 1875; NHS, Mar. 6, 1868; Holloran, *Boston's Wayward Children*, 113; Allen, *Westboro' State Reform School Reminiscences*, 6; *Address of His Excellency John A. Andrew to the Two Branches of the Legislature of Massachusetts, January 3, 1862*, 35–36; "The Massachusetts Board of State Charities, and the Westborough Reform School," 118; NYT, June 5, 1883; Sanborn, *Reports on the Status of Paupers in Massachusetts,*; Sanborn, *The Public Charities of Massachusetts during the Century Ending Jan. 1, 1876*; LDC, May 25, 1865; Putnam, "Massachusetts State Care of Children," 360–61; Johnson, *The Professional Convict's Tale*, 50; TWJ, Feb. 2, 1878; TN, June 11, 1868; Richards, *Letters and Journals of Samuel Gridley Howe*, 2:509–25; Hamrogue, "John A. Andrew," 133–34; Pearson, *Andrew*, 1:265–76, 2:225–28. Secretary Browne recalled that on one Christmas eve, the governor had, on the warden's recommendation, granted a pardon to a convict and he wanted to communicate this to the family before Christmas Day. When he went to the office of the Secretary of the Commonwealth he found it closed half an hour earlier than usual. It was during a severe snow storm that prompted the office closures, and sick though he was, he walked in the driving snow to the home of the State Department clerk, and returned with him to the office, and stood by him while the pardon was drawn up, affixed the state seal, and then dispatched one of his secretaries to deliver the pardon. Browne, *Sketch of the Official Life of John A. Andrew*, 54–55; Pearson, *Andrew*, 2:229.
47. Schouler, *A History of Massachusetts in the Civil War*, 628–29; BDA, May 5, 1865.
48. Abel, *A Finger in Lincoln's Brain*, 180; Augustus Clark to Andrew, May 5, 1865, Andrew Papers, MHS.

49. Andrew, *Valedictory Address of His Excellency John A. Andrew, January 5, 1866;* Andrew to Stearns, June 19, 1865, Slack Papers, KSU.
50. John Murray Forbes told this story in a letter read at the Governor Andrew Memorial Day of the Massachusetts Club in January 1888, see the *NYT,* Feb. 5, 1888; Hughes, *Reminiscences of John Murray Forbes,* 3:2–5; *War Reminiscences* in Edward Waldo Emerson Papers, MHS; Miller, *Harvard's Civil War,* 423; Brooks, *Washington in Lincoln's Time,* 307–23; Pearson, *Andrew,* 2:248–49; *SR,* Jan. 30, 1888. Andrew may have even travelled to Richmond, see Andrew to F. Hoe, May 12, 1865, Andrew to Gillman Collamore, June 7, 1865, Ellen Starbucks to S. G. Howe, June 7, 1865, Howe to Andrew, May 15, 16, 1865, Dick Busteed to Andrew, May 15, 1865, Andrew Papers, MHS; *BDA,* May 23, 24, 1865
51. Foner, *Reconstruction,* 178–85; Pierce, *Memoirs and Letters of Charles Sumner,* 4:421–46; Bancroft and Dunning, *The Reminiscences of Carl Schurz,* 3:219–20; Trefousse, *Andrew Johnson,* 212–13; Donald, *Charles Sumner and the Rights of Man,* 221–23
52. *BDA,* June 22, 1865; *LDC,* June 6, 1865; *Lib,* June 30, 1865; Dana, *Richard Henry Dana, Jr.,* 234–72; Trefousse, *Andrew Johnson,* 218–33.
53. Andrew to George Stearns, June 19, 1865, Slack Papers, KSU; see also notes of Andrew's letter in Andrew Papers; *Lib,* June 30, 1865; Parsons, *Re-organization of the Rebel States, Public Meeting in Faneuil Hall; NYT,* June 22, 1865; Andrew to Frank P. Blair, Sr., June 19, 1865, Blair-Lee Family Papers, PU; Donald, *Charles Sumner and the Rights of Man,* 229–32; Pearson, *Andrew,* 2:263–64.
54. Charles Devens to Andrew, June 17, 1865, MS 24, BPL, also in the Journal of James A. Litchfield, MS 2813, BPL; Schouler, *A History of Massachusetts in the Civil War,* 627–28; Andrew to Frank P. Blair, Sr., June 19, 24, 1864, Blair-Lee Family Papers, PU; *HW,* July 8, 1865; *NYT,* June 18, 1865; Andrew to President Johnson, June 23, 24, John Kennedy to Andrew, June 21, 1865, Andrew Papers, MHS.
55. Francis L. Lieber to Andrew, June 28, 1865, Andrew Papers, MHS.
56. Andrew to Frank P. Blair, Sr., June 19, 24, 1864, Blair-Lee Family Papers, PU; Andrew to Blair, June 23, 1865, Andrew to President Johnson, June 23, 24, 1865, Andrew Papers, MHS; Schouler, *A History of Massachusetts in the Civil War,* 629–36; Dowling, *Charles Eliot Norton,* 37.
57. Andrew to President Johnson, June 23, 24, 1865, Andrew Papers, MHS; *NYT,* July 25, 27, 1865, *BDA,* July 15, 19, 1865; Barrows, *A Memorial of Bradford Academy,* 1–143.
58. Schouler, *A History of Massachusetts in the Civil War,* 633–35; Curtis, *The Correspondence of John Lothrop Motley,* 16–19; Motley to Andrew, Dec. 16, 1864, Andrew Papers, MHS.

CHAPTER 22: LAST MONTHS IN THE STATEHOUSE

1. *Lib,* July 14, 1865; *BDA,* July 6, 8, 1865; *LDC,* July 6, 1865; Andrew to Frederick W. Lincoln, June 30, 1865, Edward Cook to Andrew, June 17, 1865, Frank Howe to Andrew, June 15, 20, 1865, Andrew Papers, MHS.
2. *Lib,* July 14, 1865; *BDA,* July 6, 8, 1865; *LDC,* July 6, 1865; Andrew to Frederick W. Lincoln, Jr., June 30, 1865, Edward Cook to Andrew, June 17, 1865, Frank Howe to Andrew, June 15, 20, 1865, Andrew Papers, MHS.
3. Andrew to Frank P. Blair, Sr., June 23, 1865, Andrew to Sumner, July 18, 31, 1865, Andrew Papers, MHS; *Lib,* July 7, 14, 1865; *BDA,* July 8, 1865; *BDJ,* July 5, 8, 1865; Hubbell, *Horace Mann,* 264–65; Hinsdale, *Horace Mann and the Common School Revival in the United States,* 238–29, 265; Pearson, *Andrew,* 2:253–54.
4. *Lib,* July 14, 1865; *Massachusetts Teacher and Journal of Home and School Education,* 267–74; Pearson, *Andrew,* 2:254; Schwartz, *Samuel Gridley Howe,* 171, Andrew to Frank Howe, Aug. 7, 1865, Andrew Papers, MHS; Pearson, *Andrew,* 2:255; Schwartz, *Samuel Gridley Howe,* 171.
5. *BDA,* July 6, 8, 1865; Andrew to William Syphax and John F. Cook, July 1, 1865, Massachusetts Governor, Letters Official, MSA; *Celebration by the Colored People's Educational Monument Association in Memory of Abraham Lincoln,* 1–33.

6. *BDA*, July 14, 1865.
7. *NYT*, July 25, 1865; *BDA*, July 13, 22, 25, 1865; Graf and Haskins, *The Papers of Andrew Johnson*, 8:278, 333; Miller, *Harvard's Civil War*, 1–6; Pearson, *Andrew*, 2:251; Depew, *The Library of the Oratory*, 9:304–12; Andrew to Frank P. Blair, Sr., June 19, 24, 1861, Blair-Lee Family Papers, PU; Frank P. Blair, Sr., to Andrew, July 10, 1865, Andrew Papers, MHS; Schouler, *A History of Massachusetts in the Civil War*, 629–36; Dowling, *Charles Eliot Norton*, 37; Hall, *The Story of the Battle Hymn of the Republic*, 117–18.
8. Edward Wild to Andrew, July 3, Andrew to Sumner, July 18, 1865, Andrew Papers, MHS.
9. As quoted in Wilson, *Campfires of Freedom*, 72; Anon. to Gov. Andrew, July 22, 1865, Executive Department, Letters Received, MSA.
10. *Lib*, Aug. 4, 1865; *NYT*, Aug. 1, 1865; Schouler, *A History of Massachusetts in the Civil War*, 650–51; *BDA*, July 26, 27, 31, 1865; Cyrus Woodman to Andrew, July 25, 1865, Andrew Papers, MHS.
11. *BDA*, July 24, 27, 1865; Aug. 7, 10, 11 (quote), 1865; *SR*, Aug. 7, 1865; *NDA*, July 28, 1865; *NI*, July 28, 1865; *NA*, Sept. 23, 1865.
12. *BDA*, Aug. 15, 16, 17, 18, 19, 24, 29, Sept. 13, 28, 1865; *TI*, Sept. 27, 1865; Hines, *Illustrated History of the State of Washington*, 829–30; Ronda, *Letters of Elizabeth Palmer Peabody*, 318; *SR*, Nov. 24, 1907; Cyrus Woodman to Andrew, Oct. 12, 1865, Andrew Papers, MHS.
13. *BDA*, Aug. 23, 29, 31, Sept. 2, 4 (quote), 5, 1865; *Lib*, Sept. 8, 1865; William F. Milton Arny to Andrew, July 11, 1865, Andrew Papers, MHS. Arny was the secretary of the New Mexico territory and sent Andrew the pistol John Brown carried in Kansas.
14. Pearson, *Andrew*, 2:250–51; *BDA*, Sept. 5, 8, 9, 11, 20, 21, 1865; Andrew to Sumner, July 31, 1865, Andrew to S. G. Howe, Aug. 7, 1865, Ellen Starbucks to Anne A. Andrews, Aug. 9, 1865, Andrew to Frank Howe, Aug. 9, 1865, Andrew Papers, MHS; *NI*, Sept. 7, 1865; *BP*, Sep. 8, 9, 1865; Cochrane, *The History of Brown University*, 339; Stahr, *Stanton*, 460–61. It was during September when a fabricated story found its way into the press that Seward solicited Andrew's advice on a recent draft of the Mississippi constitution that Provisional-Governor William L. Sharkey sent to Johnson for approval. Johnson apparently counseled Sharkey that to disarm the Northern adversaries, he should extend the elective franchise "to all persons of color who can read the constitution of the United States in English, and write their names, and to all persons of color who own real estate valued at not less than two hundred and fifty dollars." This, he told Sharkey, he could do with "perfect safety" and that it would place the Southern states "in reference to free persons of color, upon the same basis with the free states." As the story went, when the Mississippi convention closed without complying with Johnson's request, Seward sent Andrew the unamended draft. Since Massachusetts was the "only 'anti-slavery' state when the Union was formed," he wanted to know if the constitution was satisfactory to his state since Commonwealth legislators had the right to decide on the new constitution "which the wisdom, virtue and valor of your state have forced the less enlightened state of Mississippi to adopt." Andrew allegedly sent a copy to Garrison with a note that read since "you started the grand 'anti-slavery enterprise,' thirty years ago, and, even more than John Brown or Abraham Lincoln, are its prophets and embodiment," he asked Garrison to examine the constitution and reject or ratify. The abolitionist confessed that while the constitution did not fully embody his ideas it was "best perhaps not to 'crowd the mourners,' just now," and therefore he consented to ratify it, with the assurance that the Freedman's Bureau would prepare the freedmen for amalgamation and extermination, "and thus close up the great work forever." Had these letters not been forgeries, they might have stirred considerably more debate. McNeily, "From Organization to Overthrow of Mississippi's Provisional Government, 1865–1868," 9–11; *NYT*, Oct. 10, 1865, reported that this correspondence was published in the *Louisville Democrat* without stating where it was procured.
15. Oramel Martin to Andrew, Sept. 18, 1865, Elizabeth Peabody to Andrew, Sept. 18, 1865,

454—NOTES TO PAGES 320-323

C. M. Wright to Andrew, Sept. 21, 1865, Andrew to Edward Everett Hale, Oct. 11, 1865, James Alexander Hamilton to Andrew, Sept. 21, 1865, Adam Gurowski to Andrew, Sept. 22, 1865, Frank Bird to Andrew,Sept. 30, 1865, Andrew Papers, MHS; *BDA*, Sept. 11, 15, 28, Oct. 7, 12, 1865; Andrew to William Claflin, Sept. 13, 1865, Massachusetts Governor, Letters Official, MSA; Pearson, *Andrew*, 2:258–59; *Report of Auditor of Accounts of the Commonwealth of Massachusetts*, 94; *The Phrenological Journal and Life Illustrated*, 5. Andrew dedicated his last months in office to broadening his executive influence. At some point in the last year, he hired Ellen F. Starbuck as a confidential clerk to the military secretary in the State House. She may have been the first female to work in a Bay State governor's office.

16. *BDA*, Sept. 29, 1865.

17. Andrew D. White to Ezra Cornell, Oct. 5, 1865, Andrew to Era Cornell, Oct. 2, 1865, Ezra Cornell Correspondence, Cornell Papers, CUL; Thomas Cooley to Andrew D. White, Sept. 20, 1865, White Papers, CUL; *CaRep*, Nov. 1, 1865; Ezra Cornell to Andrew, Oct. 5, 1865, Andrew to W. D. Holmes, Oct. 18, 1865, James A. Hamilton to Andrew, Oct. 6, 1865, Forbes to Andrew, Oct. 7, 1865, Andrew to Henry Ware, Sept. 30, 1865, Andrew Papers, MHS; *BDA*, Sept. 20, 30, Oct. 4, 5, 10, 1865; *BP*, Sept. 30, 1865; Altschuler, *Andrew D. White*, 63–64; *CH*, Oct. 6, 1865; *Transactions of the New-York State Agricultural Society, 1865*, 36.

18. Richards, Elliott, and Hall, *Julia Ward Howe*, 1:231–33; Pearson, *Andrew*, 2:250; Grant, *Private Woman, Public Person*, 160; Andrew to W. D. Holmes, Oct. 18, 1865, Walter Chipman to Andrew, Sept. 15, 1865, Andrew Papers, MHS; *BDA*, Sept. 20, 30, Oct. 4, 5, 10, 1865; *BP*, Sept. 30, 1865; Altschuler, *Andrew D. White*, 63–64.

19. William Storer How to Andrew, Sept. 25, 1865, John Parkman to Andrew, Oct. 24, 1865, Andrew Papers, MHS; *Lib*, Sept. 22, 1865; *BDA*, Aug. 19, Oct. 3, 5, 1865; *SR*, Nov. 16, 1865; "Constitution and Membership of the American Association for the Promotion of the Social Science, October 4, 1865"; *NYT*, Nov. 20, 1867; Wagner, *The "Miracle Worker*," 14, 16, 20, 21; Pearson, *Andrew*, 2:247, 266–72.

20. Powell, "The American Land Company and Agency," 293–98; Edward Wild to Andrew, July 3, 1865, Andrew Papers, MHS; *BDA*, Oct. 6, 1865.

21. *BDA*, Oct. 6, 1865; *Acts and Resolves Passed by the General Court of Massachusetts in the Year 1865*, 597; *Documents Printed by the Order of the Senate of the Commonwealth of Massachusetts during the Session of the General Court, 1865*, 32; Cyrus Woodman to Andrew, Oct. 12, 1865, Andrew Papers, MHS; Powell, "The American Land Company," 296–308.

22. *VC*, Jan. 27, 1866; Powell, "The American Land Company," 296–308; Forbes to Andrew, Oct. 4, 1865, Stearns to Andrew, Nov. 14, 1865, Worthington Snethen to Andrew, Oct. 13, 1865, Frank Howe to Andrew, Oct. 11, 12, 13, 1865, Andrew to Frank P. Blair, Sr., Apr. 12, 1865, William Clifford to Andrew, Sept. 27, 1865, Andrew to E. S. Tobey, n.d., 1865, Andrew to Stearns, Nov. 6, 1865, Andrew to Frank Howe, Oct. 14, 1865, Andrew to Howe, Mar. 10, 1866, *American Land Company and Agency, Circular No. 2* (1866), Andrew Papers, MHS; Heller, *Portrait of an Abolitionist*, 203–4; *BDC*, Oct. 14, 1865; Niven, *Salmon P. Chase Papers*, 1:593–94; *BDA*, Sept. 30, Nov. 17, 1865, Jan. 31, 1866;. Worthington G. Snethen was the Maryland Agent for Andrew's Land Company.

23. Andrew to Conway, Dec. 9, 1865, E. Augusta Rupell to Andrew, Oct. 8, 1865, L. W. Winchester to Andrew, Oct. 9, 1865, John F. Severance to Andrew, Nov. 27, 1865, Andrew Papers, MHS; Schouler, *A History of Massachusetts in the Civil War*, 642–43; Pearson, *Andrew*, 2:269; Powell, "The American Land Company," 293–308; Cimbala and Miller, *The Freedman's Bureau and Reconstruction*, 193–213; Knight, "The Rost Home Colony: St. Charles Parish, Louisiana," 214–20.

24. Andrew to Francis C. Barlow, Jan. 16, 20, 1866, Andrew to Thomas W. Conway, Dec. 9, 1865, Andrew to Andrew Johnson, June 1, 1866, Dudley to Andrew, July 31, 1867, Andrew to Hermann Bokum, Nov. 30, 1865, Andrew to Sumner, Nov. 21, 1865, Andrew to William Burt, Nov. 17, 1865, Andrew to John Binney, Sept. 10, 1867, Andrew to

Frank P. Blair, Sr., Apr. 12, 1866, Edward A. Wild to Andrew, Oct. 15, 1865, Andrew Papers, MHS; Alexander H. Bullock to Henry Ware, Nov. 18, 1865, Ware to Bullock, Nov. 22, 1865, Ware Family Papers, MHS; Cimbala and Miller, *The Freedman's Bureau and Reconstruction*, xiii–xxxi; Pearson, *Andrew*, 2:270–71; Powell, "The America Land Company," 298–308; McFeely, *Yankee Stepfather*, 250–54; BDA, Oct. 18, 1865; Foner, *Reconstruction*, 164–75.

25. LDC, Oct. 4, 1865; BDA, Oct. 4, 1865; BP, Oct. 9, 1865; Frank Howe to Andrew, Oct. 13, 14, 1865, Sarah B. Shaw to Andrew, Oct. 20, 1865, Andrew to Thomas W. Conway, Dec. 9, 1865, Andrew to Francis C. Barlow, Jan. 16, 20, 1866, Andrew to Andrew Johnson, June 1, 1866, Andrew Papers, MHS; Abbott, "A Yankee Views the Organization of the Republican Party in South Carolina," 244–50; *The Monument to Colonel Robert Gould Shaw*, 7–13; Rennella, *The Boston Cosmopolitans*, 134; Blatt, Brown, and Yacovone, *Hope and Glory*, 52–93.

26. "Constitution and Membership of the American Association for the Promotion of the Social Science, October 4, 1865," 106–8; Frank B. Sanborn, Sept. 27, Nov. 24, 1865, Sarah B. Shaw to Andrew, Oct. 20, 1865, Andrew Papers, MHS; BDA, Oct. 18, 1865; NYT, Nov. 20, 1867; Pearson, *Andrew*, 2:272.

27. SR, Nov. 16, 1865: LDC, Nov. 9, 1865; BDA, Oct. 21, 27, Nov. 1, 4, 9, 1865; BET, Nov. 8, 1865; Piper, *Facts and Figures Concerning the Hoosac Tunnel*, 1–54; Black, *Buried Dreams*; Foner, *Reconstruction*, 190–248.

28 Palmer, *Selected Letters of Charles Sumner*, 2:339–41; Andrew to Sumner, Nov. 21, 1865, Sumner Papers, HU; McKitrick, *Andrew Johnson and Reconstruction*, 229; BDA, Oct. 18, Nov. 29, Dec. 25, 1865; PI, Aug. 28, 1865; NYT, Sept. 3, 1865; BDE, Dec. 23, 1865; *Congressional Globe*, 39th Congress, Senate Ex. Doc. 1st session, No. 2; Bancroft, *Speeches, Correspondences, and Political Papers of Carl Schurz*, 1:279–359; White, *The Republic for Which It Stands*, 51–55; Foner, *Reconstruction*, 179–241.

29. On Fields' quotes, see Fields, *James T. Fields*, 137; Donald, *Charles Sumner and the Rights of Man*, 235–36; BDA, Nov. 9, 1865; Lib, Dec. 1, 1865; BaDC, Nov. 9, 1865; PI, Nov. 8, 1865; Sumner to Andrew, Nov. 22, 1865, Stanton to Andrew, Nov. 3, 1865, George Luther Stearns to Andrew, Nov. 6, 1865, Andrew Papers, MHS; Pearson, *Andrew*, 2:272–76

30. Donald, *Charles Sumner and the Rights of Man*, 235–36; BDA, Nov. 9, 1865; Lib, Dec. 1, 1865; BaDC, Nov. 9, 1865; PI, Nov. 8, 1865; Sumner to Andrew, Nov. 22, 1865, Stanton to Andrew, Nov. 3, 1865, George Luther Stearns to Andrew, Nov. 6, 1865, Andrew Papers, MHS; Pearson, *Andrew*, 2:272–76.

31. Palmer, *Selected Letters of Charles Sumner*, 2:333–46; Donald, *Charles Sumner and the Rights of Man*, 235; BDC, Nov. 25, 1865, Sumner to Stanton, Nov. 5, 1865, Stanton Papers, LC; BET, Nov. 7, 1865; Stahr, *Stanton*, 462–63, 636; Lib, Dec. 1, 1865.

32. Palmer, *Selected Letters of Charles Sumner*, 2:344–45.

33. William L. Burt to Andrew, Nov. 10, 14, 1865, S. F. Wetmore to Andrew, Nov. 14, 1865, George Stearns to Andrew, Nov. 14, 1865, Andrew Papers, MHS.

34. Sumner to Andrew, Nov. 21?, 1865, Sumner Papers, HU; Palmer, *Selected Letters of Charles Sumner*, 2:345–46; BDA, Nov. 13, 14, 16, 1865; BP, Nov. 13, 14, 1865; Worthington Snethen to Andrew, Nov. 14, 25, 1865, Sumner to Andrew, Nov. 21, 1865, Andrew Papers, MHS.

35. Andrew to Sumner, November 21, 1865, Sumner Papers, HU; Palmer, *Selected Letters of Charles Sumner*, 2:345–46; Foner, *Reconstruction*, 241.

36. Andrew to Sumner, Nov. 21, 1865, Sumner to Andrew, Nov. 24, 1865, Sumner Papers, HU; Pearson, *Andrew*, 2:274–75.

37. Sumner to Andrew, Nov. 24?, 1865, Andrew Papers, MHS; Palmer, *Selected Letters of Charles Sumner*, 2:345–46; Pearson, *Andrew*, 2:272–76; Donald, *Charles Sumner and the Rights of Man*, 235–36.

38. Andrew's remarks at the Twelfth Baptist Church, Nov. 19, 1865, Jay R. Pember to Andrew, Nov. 1, 1865, Andrew Papers, MHS; BDA, Dec. 1, 1865.

39. *BDA*, Nov. 20, 1865.

40. *NI*, Nov. 24, 1865, *ArkG*, Dec. 14, 1865.

41. Bokum, *The Testimony of a Refugee from East Tennessee*; *SR*, Apr. 27, 1904; Andrew to Hermann Bokum, Nov. 30, 1865, Andrew Papers, MHS; Pearson, *Andrew*, 2:281–82; Hamrogue, "John A. Andrew," 228–29.

42. *Testimony Taken by The Joint Select Committee*, 1:93; Foner, *Reconstruction*, 199–209; Andrew to Stearns, Nov. 6, 1865, Andrew to Sumner, Nov. 21, 1865, Andrew to Francis H. Pierpont, Nov. 27, 1865, S. F. Wetmore to Andrew, Nov. 20, 1865, Andrew Papers, MHS; White, *The Republic for Which It Stands*, 53–55. Had he lived, he might have appreciated Governor Parsons answers to questions posed by Michigan congressman Austin Blair (and former Civil War governor) on the conditions of affairs in the Southern States in 1872. "We had, in 1865, a white man's government in Alabama," declared Governor Parsons, "but we lost it." When Blair responded that the reason for this loss was that certain Northern men insisted that African Americans be allowed to vote because they would vote the Republican ticket, Parsons replied: "I don't know about that: but I felt very well persuaded that the true policy for us was to have at once taken the negro right under the protection of the laws as we do our wives and children. When they became free . . . if the law did not protect them there was no protection for them. We did not do that, however, but undertook to make negro codes . . . and undertook to so reconstruct them as to make their freedom a curse rather than a blessing. That is the great blunder we made." Andrew had forecasted as much, but in 1865 he was more hopeful, and never lived to see the complete breakdown of Johnson's administration.

43. Shotwell, *Life of Charles Sumner*, 535–36; *BDA*, Dec. 6, 1865; Palmer, *Selected Letters of Charles Sumner*, 2:352–53; Donald, *Charles Sumner and the Rights of Man*, 237–38; Trefousse, *Thaddeus Stevens*, 174–88; Foner, *Reconstruction*, 202–240; S F. Wetmore to Andrew, Nov. 20, 1865, Andrew Papers.

44. *BDA*, Dec. 6, 1865; Donald, *Sumner and the Rights of Man*, 237–38; Trefousse, *Thaddeus Stevens*, 174–88; Foner, *Reconstruction*, 202–24; Abbott, *Cobbler in Congress*, 158–60.

45. Andrew to Dear Sir, Dec. 26, 1865, Andrew Papers, MHS; Abzug and Maizlish, *New Perspectives on Race and Slavery in America*, 107; Pearson, *Andrew*, 2:264–65, 270; William L. Burt to Andrew, May 24, 1866, Andrew Papers, MHS; Donald, *Charles Sumner and the Rights of Man*, 242–43; Palmer and Ochoa, *The Selected Papers of Thaddeus Stevens*, 2:86; Trefousse, *Thaddeus Stevens*, 183.

46. *SR*, Jan. 8, 1866.

47. Schouler, *A History of Massachusetts in the Civil War*, 632; Donald, *Charles Sumner and the Rights of Man*, 243; *SR*, Jan. 8, 1866; *BDA*, June 19, 1865; Pearson, *Andrew*, 2:265.

48. *SR*, Jan. 8, 1866; *BDA*, Dec. 26, 1865; Higginson, *Massachusetts in the Army and Navy*, 1:147–54; *Annual Report of the Adjutant-General of the Commonwealth of Massachusetts, 1866*, 87–90; *BDA*, Dec. 23, 1865; Browne, *Sketch of the Official Life of John A. Andrew*, 156; *BP*, Dec. 23, 1865; Hoar, *Book of Patriotism*, 352–54; Preble, *Our Flag*, 432–36.

49. Higginson, *Massachusetts in the Army and Navy*, 1:147–54; *Annual Report of the Adjutant-General of the Commonwealth of Massachusetts, 1866*, 87–90; *BDA*, Dec. 23, 1865; Browne, *Sketch of the Official Life of John A. Andrew*, 156; *BP*, Dec. 23, 1865; Hoar, *Book of Patriotism*, 352–54; Preble, *Our Flag*, 432–36.

50. *BDA*, Sept. 18, 1884, Oct. 1, 1879.

51. Charles Francis Adams to Andrew, Oct. 13, 1865, Harrison Ritchie to Andrew, Dec. 21, 1865, Andrew Papers, MHS.

52. George W. Curtis to Andrew, Nov. 7, 1865, Andrew Papers, MHS.

53. *TC*, Dec. 22, 1865.

54. Schouler, *A History of Massachusetts in the Civil War*, 670.

55. John Murray Forbes to Andrew, Dec. 15, 1865, Andrew Papers, MHS.

56. Newspaper clippings, Andrew Papers, BowC.

57. *VW*, Jan. 17, 1883; *NDH*, Aug. 2, 1868.

58. Calvin E. Stowe to Andrew, Dec. 19, 1865, Andrew Papers, MHS.
59. *Lib*, Dec. 29, 1865; *PDEB*, Dec. 19, 1865; Stewart, *William Lloyd Garrison at Two Hundred*, 1–11; Mayer, *All on Fire*, 594–803.
60. John Binney to Andrew, Dec. 27, 1865, W. F. [MaArny] to Andrew, Oct. 8, 1865, Robert Rantoul to Andrew, Dec. 20, 1865, Bulloch to Andrew, Dec. n.d., 1865, Andrew Papers, MHS; Graf and Haskins, eds., *The Papers of Andrew Johnson*, 9–10:510–13; *BDA*, Oct. 27, 1882.

CHAPTER 23: WORKING FOR THE AGES

1. *BDA*, Jan. 2, 1866; Donald, *Charles Sumner and the Rights of Man*, 242–44; Shotwell, *Life of Charles Sumner*, 536–38; George L. Stearns to Andrew, Jan. 1, 1866, Andrew Papers, MHS.
2. *BDA*, Jan. 4, 6, 1866; *BP*, Jan. 6, 1866; *BET*, Apr. 11, 1868, Andrew Papers, BowC; Bowen, *Massachusetts in the War*, 19, 83; Comey, *A Legacy of Valor*, 240; Golay, *A Ruined Land*, 310–11; Schouler, *A History of Massachusetts in the Civil War*, 647–48, 651–53; Andrew, *Valedictory Address of His Excellency John A. Andrew to the Two Branches of the Legislature of Massachusetts, January 4, 1866*, 3–42; Pearson, *Andrew*, 2:256–57. Andrew drafted a *Special Message* on the state's financial and accounting affairs and took his formal leave of the official station he had occupied for the last five years. He was careful to acknowledge the services of Mrs. Harrison Gray Otis, the daughter of a Boston merchant, William H. Boardman, but had also been married to the eldest son of Honorable Harrison Gray Otis, who was indispensable in supervising donations to the soldiers and her involvement in the New England Women's Auxiliary Association, and many of the funds were still being distributed to the families of soldiers. What started in Boston soon grew into a statewide benevolent movement to establish a Soldiers' Fund Society, the object of which was to secure and hold funds for the future needs of families.
3. *SR*, Jan. 5, 1866; *BDA*, Jan. 4, 5, 1866, June 1, 1893; *BP*, Jan. 5, 1866; Levi Lincoln to Andrew, Jan. 2, 27, 1866, Andrew Papers, MHS; Hamrogue, "John A. Andrew," 247.
4. Andrew, *Valedictory Address of His Excellency John A. Andrew to the Two Branches of the Legislature of Massachusetts, January 4, 1866*, 7; *SR*, Jan. 5, 1866; Pearson, *Andrew*, 2:277–78; *LDC*, Jan. 5, 1866; Wiecek, *The Sources of Antislavery Constitutionalism in America*, 106–249; Lerche, "Congressional Interpretations of the Guarantee of a Republican Form of Government during Reconstruction," 192–211; Oakes, *Freedom National*, 456–92.
5. Andrew, *Valedictory Address of His Excellency John A. Andrew to the Two Branches of the Legislature of Massachusetts, January 4, 1866*, 12, 15.
6. Andrew, *Valedictory Address of His Excellency John A. Andrew to the Two Branches of the Legislature of Massachusetts, January 4, 186617.
7. Andrew, *Valedictory Address of His Excellency John A. Andrew to the Two Branches of the Legislature of Massachusetts, January 4, 186630–36*; Donald, *Charles Sumner and the Rights of Man*, 244–45. To remedy the apportionment problem caused by the end of the three-fifths amendment that allowed slaves to be counted for apportionment, Sumner proposed that representation be proportional to the number of qualified voters and not to total population. He introduced the idea when Congress convened in December and some radical congressmen were aghast that we were committed to a proposal that permitted southerners to disfranchise African Americans if they were willing to have reduced representation in Washington. Andrew understood that such a proposition would reduce the number of Massachusetts representatives given the loss of population and disproportionate number of women and unnaturalized aliens who would no longer be included in apportionment counts for congressional representation.
8. Donald, *Charles Sumner and the Rights of Man*, 244–45; Andrew, *Special Message of His Excellency John A. Andrew to the Two Branches of the Legislature of Massachusetts, January 3, 1866*; Andrew, *Valedictory Address of His Excellency John A. Andrew to the Two Branches*

of the Legislature of Massachusetts, January 4, 1866, 7–36; Grimké, *The Ballotless Victim of One-Party Governments*, 7–9.

9. Andrew, *Valedictory Address of His Excellency John A. Andrew to the Two Branches of the Legislature of Massachusetts, January 4, 1866*, 11; BDA, Jan. 4, 1866, Oct. 31, 1867; Chandler, *Memoir*, 239–98; McKitrick, *Andrew Johnson and Reconstruction*, 214–15, 233–36; Hamrogue, "John A. Andrew," 242; Foner, *Reconstruction*, 241–42; Pearson, *Andrew*, 2:261.

10. SR, Feb. 17, 1871; Andrew, *Valedictory Address of His Excellency John A. Andrew to the Two Branches of the Legislature of Massachusetts, January 4, 1866*, 30–36.

11. Andrew, *Valedictory Address of His Excellency John A. Andrew to the Two Branches of the Legislature of Massachusetts, January 4, 1866*, 30–36.

12. SR, June 14, 1887; Nov. 1, 1867; Pearson, *Andrew*, 2:286–87; Chamberlain, "Reconstruction in South Carolina," 473–84; BDA, Jan. 8, 10, 1865; LDC, Jan. 26, 1866.

13. Pearson, *Andrew*, 2:290.

14. SR, Jan. 19, 1866; Pearson, *Andrew*, 2:286–87.

15. Norton to Andrew, Jan. 19, 1865, Andrew Papers, MHS; Pearson, *Andrew*, 2:288–89.

16. Annie Fields to Andrew, Jan. 12, 1866, Andrew Papers, MHS.

17. LDC, Jan. 6, 1866; BET, Jan. 6, 1866.

18. BDA, Jan. 4, 1866; LDC, Jan. 23, 1866.

19. LDC, Jan. 23, 1866.

20. BDA, Jan. 5, Feb. 3, 1866; VW, Jan. 19, 1866; BET, Jan. 22, 1866; NI, Jan. 23, 1866, June 10, 1868; NHS, Feb. 9, 1866; Chandler, "Memoir of the Hon. John Albion Andrew," 59.

21. John Binney to Andrew, Jan. 16, 1866, Cyrus Woodman, Jan. 16, 1866, Joseph B. Spear, Jan. 26, 1866, Andrew Papers, MHS.

22. SR, Jan. 8, 19, 1866.

23. Thomas C. Upham to Andrew, Feb. 14, 1866, Andrew Papers, MHS.

24. McKitrick, *Andrew Johnson and Reconstruction*, 230–31.

25. HW, Jan. 20, 1867.

26. Charles Eliot Norton to Andrew, Jan. 19, 1866, Andrew Papers, MHS.

27. BP, Jan. 19, 1866.

28. HW, Feb. 18, 1888; Hughes, *Reminiscences of John Murray Forbes*, 3:29–30; BDA, Apr. 6, 1867; Foner, *Reconstruction*, 230–37, 270–71.

29. Rufus Saxton to Andrew, Feb. 5, 1866, Andrew Papers, MHS.

30. BDA, Jan. 30, Feb. 5, 1866.

31. Palmer, *Selected Letters of Charles Sumner*, 2:355–58; Donald, *Charles Sumner and the Rights of Man*, 245–47; Sumner to Woodman, Mar. 18, 1866, Woodman Papers, MHS; NYT, Feb. 15, 1866; BDA, Feb. 6, 7, 1866; Baum, *Civil War Party System*, 104–6; Browne, *Sketch of the Official Life of John A. Andrew*, 167–200; Chandler, *Memoir*, 239–45; Andrew, *Valedictory Address of His Excellency John A. Andrew to the Two Branches of the Legislature of Massachusetts, January 4, 1866*; Bowen, *Massachusetts in the War*, 83; Andrew to Clarke, Jan. 1, 1866, Clarke Papers, HU; *Congressional Globe*, 39th Congress, 1st session, 534–87; Bellesiles, *Inventing Equality*.

32. Andrew to Frank Howe, Mar. 10, 1866, Hermann Bokum to Andrew, Mar. 30, 1866, Howe to Andrew, Feb. 5, 1866, Andrew Papers, MHS; McKitrick, *Andrew Johnson and Reconstruction*, 236.

33. Cyrus Woodman to Andrew, Jan. 16, 1866, Francis J. Child to Andrew, Jan. 24, 1866, Andrew Papers, MHS; Bellesiles, *Inventing Equality*, 173–78.

34. Andrew to Frank Blair, Sr., Mar. 11, 18, Apr. 12, 1866, Montgomery Blair to Andrew, Mar. 13, 1866, Frank P. Blair, Sr., to Andrew, Mar. 11, 1866, Andrew to Edward Atkinson, Mar. 26, 1866, Alexander H. Bullock to Andrew, May 28, 1866, Andrew to Bullock, May 28, 1866, Andrew Papers, MHS; McKitrick, *Andrew Johnson and Reconstruction*, 237; Smith, *The Francis Preston Blair Family*, 2:332–33.

35. Andrew to Frank P. Blair, Sr., Mar. 8, 1866, Andrew to Francis C. Barlow, Jan. 16, 20, 1866, Andrew to William L. Burt, Jan. 21, 1866, Horace Greeley to Andrew, Apr. 12, 1866, Charles Gilmore to Andrew, Apr. 11, 1866, Andrew Papers, MHS; *SR*, Jan. 19, 1866; Pearson, *Andrew*, 2:287, 314; Hamrogue, "John A. Andrew," 216–19, 234–36; McKitrick, *Andrew Johnson and Reconstruction*, 237; Andrew to Cyrus Woodman, Apr. 23, 1864, Mar. 21, 1866, Woodman Papers, SHSW.

36. Andrew to Frank Howe, Mar. 10, 1866, [Thouson W. Gowan] to Capt. W. L. Bingham in care of Andrew, Feb. 26, 1866, Joseph B. Spear to Andrew, Mar. 3, 1866, Howe to Andrew, Mar. 13, 1866, Andrew to Frank P. Blair, Sr., Mar. 18, 26, 1866, Andrew to Frank P. Blair, Sr., Apr. 12, 1866, Andrew Papers, MHS; Wilson, *The Crusader in Crinoline*, 524; Andrew, *To the Voters of Massachusetts*, 6; Voegeli, "A Rejected Alternative," 765–90; Hamrogue, "John A. Andrew," 236.

37. Andrew to William M. Stewart, Mar. 20, 1866, Stewart to Andrew, Mar. 17, 1866, Andrew to Frank P. Blair, Sr., Mar. 18, 1866, Andrew to Frank P. Blair, Sr., Mar. 18, Apr. 12, 1866, Frank P. Blair, Sr., to Andrew, Mar. 11, 1866, Montgomery Blair to Andrew, Mar. 13, 1866, Andrew to Edward Atkinson, Mar. 26, 1866, Alexander H. Bullock to Andrew, May 28, 1866, Andrew to Bullock, May 28, 1866 Andrew Papers, MHS; *BDA*, Mar. 17, 26, 1866; Brown, *Reminiscences of Senator William M. Stewart*, 216–17, 233; *Congressional Globe*, 30th Congress, 1st session, part 2, 1865–1866, 1754; Foner, *Reconstruction*, 245; McKitrick, *Andrew Johnson and Reconstruction*, 341; Hamrogue, "John A. Andrew," 248–49; Smith, *The Francis Preston Blair Family*, 2:332–33.

38. *BDA*, Mar. 26, 1866; *LDC*, Mar. 26, 1866.

39. Brown, *Reminiscences of Senator William M. Stewart*, 217–18; Andrew to William M. Stewart, Mar. 20, 1866, Stewart to Andrew, Mar. 17, 1866, Andrew to Frank P. Blair, Sr., Mar. 18, 1866, Andrew to Francis P. Blair, Sr., Mar. 18, Apr. 12, 1866, Frank P. Blair, Sr., to Andrew, Mar. 11, 1866, Montgomery Blair to Andrew, Mar. 13, 1866, Andrew to Edward Atkinson, Mar. 26, 1866, Alexander H. Bullock to Andrew, May 28, 1866, Andrew to Bullock, May 28, 1866, Andrew Papers, MHS; *BDA*, Mar. 26, 1866; Hamrogue, "John A. Andrew," 248–49; Smith, *The Francis Preston Blair Family*, 2:332–33.

40. Hughes, *Letters (Supplementary) of John Murray Forbes*, 3:66–68.

41. Browne, *Sketch of the Official Life of John A. Andrew*, 66–67; *NYT*, Aug. 12, 1865; Andrew to Frank P. Blair, Sr., Apr. 23, 1866, Andrew to John A. Poor, May 30, 1866, Jan. 7, 1867, John A. Poor to Andrew, Dec. 31, 1865, Andrew to Chandler, Apr. 3, 1866, Andrew to John Reed, Apr. 18, 1866, Andrew to Israel D. Andrew, Apr. 23, 1866, Andrew to Gov. Bullock, May 15, 1866, Robert Dale Owen to Andrew, Apr. 5, 1866, John Poor to Andrew, Apr. 7, 10, 1866, William S. King to Andrew, Apr. 26, 30, 1866, Joseph B. Spear to Andrew, Apr. 28, May 10, 1866, and Papers Related to the American and European Railway, Apr. and May 1866, Andrew Papers, MHS; *Memorial of the European and North American Railway Company*, 2–9; Roth and Divall, *From Rail to Road and Back Again*, 3; Hamrogue, "John A. Andrew," 240–41.

42. *TC*, Jan. 26, Mar. 9, Apr. 5, 6, May 11, 1866; *NYT*, Mar. 23, 1866; *NI*, Apr. 16, 1866; *BDA*, Mar. 1, 29, 31, Apr. 5, 14, 1866; McKivigan, *Forgotten Firebrand*, 95–97; Thomas [Greenwood] to Andrew, Jan. 12, 1866, William S. King to Andrew, Mar. 7, 1866, Andrew Papers, MHS; Andrew, *Address of His Excellency Alexander H. Bullock to the Honorable Council on the Opinion of Presenting the Case of Edward W. Green, February 27, 1866*.

43. *LDC*, Apr. 14, 1866; *BDA*, Mar. 1, 29, 31, Apr. 5, 14, 1866; *NI*, Apr. 16, 1866; Peleg W. Chandler to Andrew, Apr. 16, 1866, Green to Andrew, Mar. 10, 1866, Andrew Papers, MHS; McKivigan, *Forgotten Firebrand*, 95–97; Redpath, *Shall We Suffocate Ed. Green*.

CHAPTER 24: POSTWAR YANKEE

1. *BDA*, Apr. 30, 1866.

2. Prentice, *The Life of Gilbert Haven*, 311–12.

3. Pearson, *Andrew*, 2:292–94; Stearns to Andrew, Apr. 27, 1866, Andrew Papers, MHS; Stowe, *Lives and Deeds*, 331.

4. Clarke, *Memorial and Biographical Sketches*, 28–29; BDA, Mar. 7, Sept. 28, 1865; Pearson, *Andrew*, 2:294–95.

5. James M. Pierce to Andrew, Apr. 16, 1866, Andrew Papers, MHS.

6. Pearson, *Andrew*, 2:295–96; BDA, Apr. 20, 1866; Chandler, *Memoir*, 41–65. Andrew's biographer, Pearson lists no sources for his observations. See also Helen Pendleton to Andrew, May 18, 1866, Andrew to A. S. Packard, Mar. 30, 1866, Andrew Papers, MHS.

7. Browne, *Sketch of the Official Life of John A. Andrew*, 142; Pearson, *Andrew*, 2:296–97; Andrew to Charles G. Loring, Jan. 16, 1866, Loring Papers, HU; Andrew to Frank P. Blair, Sr., Apr. 23, 1866, Blair-Lee Family Papers, PU; Adam Gurowski to Alexander Hamilton Rice, Feb. 25, 1866, Abraham Lincoln Miscellaneous Manuscripts, UC; [. . .] to Andrew, Nov. 6, 1866, Andrew Papers, MHS.

8. "President Eliot and M.I.T.," 430–31; Rogers, *Life and Letters of William Barton Rogers*, 2:41, 74–75, 142, 167, 187–88; Pearson, *Andrew*, 2:295–97; *Proceedings of the Thursday-Evening Club*, 6–20; King, *Kings Handbook of Boston*, 229; Shand-Tucci, *MIT*, 122, 123; O'Conner, *Civil War Boston*, 141–42; James Hamilton to Andrew, Apr. 30, 1866, W. R. Nail to Andrew, May 18, 1866, Andrew Papers, MHS; Morse, *Life and Letters of Oliver Wendell Holmes*, 1:243; Hale, *James Russell Lowell and His Friends*, 202; Story and Emerson, *Ebenezer Rockwood Hoar*, 313–16; Allardt and Gilman, *The Journals and Miscellaneous Notebooks of Ralph Waldo Emerson*, 15:49–50.

9. Stowe, *Lives and Deeds*, 331; Harwood, *Life and Letters of Austin Craig*, 270; BDA, Sept. 28, 1865; TI, Sept. 27, 1865; SR, Nov. 24, 1907; Ronda, *Letters of Elizabeth Palmer Peabody*, 318.

10. Hughes, *Reminiscences of John Murray Forbes*, 3:30–35; Forbes to Andrew, June 8, 1866, Joseph B. Speer to Andrew, Apr. 28, 1866, Seward to Andrew, Dec. 12, 1866, Andrew to Seward, Dec. 14, 1866, James A. Hamilton to Andrew, Aug. 2, 1866, Andrew Papers, MHS; NYT, Jan. 25, 1866, Apr. 24, Mar. 27, 31, Nov. 27, 1866; June 26, 1868; *Index to the Senate Executive Documents for the First Session of the Thirty-Ninth Congress*, 23–24; NYT, Jan. 25, 27, 1866; BDA, Jan. 25, Mar. 20, Apr. 20, 1866; NI, May 2, 1866; BDWC, May 7, 1866.

11. U.S. Congress Committee on Foreign Relations, *Compilation of Reports of Committee*, 3; Balch, *Report of the Case of the Steamship Meteor*, 1:1–587; BDA, July 16, Sept. 13, 1866; NI, Dec. 13, 1866; Andrew to Forbes, Aug. 5, 1866, H. S. Wahl to Andrew, Sept. 24, 1866, Forbes to Andrew, July 8, 10, 1867, Andrew Papers, MHS; NYT, Mar. 24, 1866.

12. Forrester to Edith, July 12, 1866, Forrester to Mama, July 16, 1866, James Speer to Andrew, July 11, 1866, William L. Burt to Andrew, June 13, 1866, Moses Swester to Andrew, June 18, 1866, John Trumble to Andrew, June 25, 1866, Miss Laurens to Andrew, June 27, 1866, Frederick Smith to Andrew, July 6, 1866, James B. Clark to Andrew, July 3, 1866, Horatio Woodman to Andrew, July 17, 1866, Andrew Papers, MHS.

13. Pearson, *Andrew*, 2:298–99; Andrew to Charles G. Loring, Aug. 25, Sept. 24, 1866, Loring Papers, HU; Andrew to Frank P. Blair, Sr., May 25, 1866, Blair-Lee Family Papers, PU; Andrew to Clarke, Sept. 20, 1866, Clarke Papers, HU; Nason, *Discourse*, 43–58; BDA, Aug. 2, 1866; William S. King to Andrew, July 20, 1866, Joseph Speers to Andrew, July 20, 1866, Miss Drummond to Andrew July 21, 1866, Andrew Papers, MHS; Howe to Andrew, Aug. 6, 8, 1866, Andrew Papers, MHS.

14. Palmer, *Selected Letters of Charles Sumner*, 2:377–79; Bird to Andrew Aug. 3, 1866, Andrew Papers, MHS In his personal papers, Edward Kinsley provides some insight into the reconciliation between Andrew and Sumner that had to do with Sumner's support of General George L. Andrews' candidacy for a position as a United States marshal. See "Andrew and Sumner," Kinsley Papers, UMass.

15. BDA, Aug. 2, 22, 1866; LDC, Aug. 2, 10, 1866; BET, Aug. 2, 1866; NI, Sept. 8, 1866; Dillinger Smith to Andrew, June 14, 1866, see unidentified letter to Andrew, July 1866,

John Williams to Andrew, Aug. 7, 1866, James G. Blaine to Andrew, Aug. 7, William S. King to Andrew, Aug. 8, 1866, Andrew Papers, MHS; Foner, *Reconstruction*, 262–65; Abbott, *Cobbler in Congress*, 186–87.

16. Edward Atkinson to Andrew, Sept. 16, 23, 1866, Andrew Papers, MHS; Hamrogue, "John A. Andrew," 250; *NYT*, July 12, 1866.

17. Andrew to Thomas Dawes Eliot, Oct. 6, 1866, Andrew Papers, BA; Andrew to Atkinson, Sept. 20, 1866, Atkinson Papers, MHS; Hamrogue, "John A. Andrew," 250.

18. *NYH*, Sept. 4, 5, 6, 7, 1866; Stebbins, *A Political History of the State of New York*, 91; *BDA*, Sept. 6, 8, 11, 1866; *LDC*, Sept. 8, 1866; *FLIN*, Sept. 29, 1866; *BDWC*, July 31, 1866; *PI*, Sept. 5, 1866; Andrew to William S. King, Aug. 13, 1866, J. M. S. Williams to Andrew, Aug. 20, 1866, James A. Hamilton to Andrew, Aug. 27, 1866, Forbes to Andrew, Aug. 29, 1866, Charles Wright to Andrew, Aug. 31, 1866, G. S. Hillard to Andrew, Aug. 24, 1866, Theophilus P. Chandler to Andrew, Sept. 13, 1866, Frank Howe to Andrew, Sept. 13, 1866, Edward Atkinson to Andrew, Sept. 16, 23, 1866, James A. Hamilton to Andrew, Sept. 18, 1866, Andrew Papers, MHS; Foner, *Reconstruction*, 265–70.

19. *BDA*, Sept. 6, 8, 11, 1866; *LDC*, Sept. 8, 1866; *FLIN*, Sept. 29, 1866; *BDWC*, July 31, 1866; *PI*, Sept. 5, 1866; Andrew to William S. King, Aug. 13, 1866, J. M. S. Williams to Andrew, Aug. 20, 1866, James A. Hamilton to Andrew, Aug. 27, 1866, Forbes to Andrew, Aug. 29, 1866, Charles Wright to Andrew, Aug. 31, 1866, G. S. Hillard to Andrew, Aug. 24, 1866, Theophilus P. Chandler to Andrew, Sept. 13, 1866, Frank Howe to Andrew, Sept. 13, 1866, Edward Atkinson to Andrew, Sept. 16, 23, 1866, James A. Hamilton, Sept. 18, 1866, Andrew Papers, MHS; Foner, *Reconstruction*, 265–70.

20. Pearson, *Andrew*, 2:300–301; Andrew, *An Address Delivered at Brattleborough, Vermont*; Samuel B. Ward to Andrew, Oct. 9, 1866, Andrew Papers, MHS.

21. *BDA*, Sept. 26, 27, 1866; Alfred Andrew to Forrester Sept. 24, 1866, Andrew Papers, MHS.

22. *BDA*, Sep. 17, 26, 27, 28, 1866; Andrew to Stearns, Sept. 14, 1866, Andrew Papers, MHS.

23. Burnham, "Hon. John Albion Andrew," 1–12; *Report of the Select Committee to Investigate the Alleged Credit Moblier Bribery*, 374; Anderson and Moss, *Facts of Reconstruction*, 150; Nason, *Discourse*, 13; Pearson, *Andrew*, 2:302; Browne, "Governor Andrew," 267; Schutz, *A Noble Pursuit*, 21–39; Burnham, "John Albion Andrew," 1–12; Nason, *Discourse*, 57; *BDA*, Apr. 25, 1864; Edmund F. Slafter to Andrew, Jan. 8, 1866, Leonard Grimes to Andrew, May 24, 1866, Charles Lowe to Andrew, May 30, 1866, William Duane to Andrew, July 31, 1866, Edward E. Hale to Andrew, Aug. 20, 1866, Andrew Papers, MHS.

24. *BDA*, Jan. 8, 1867; James Terwilliger to Andrew, Oct. 5, 1866, Edward Atkinson to Andrew, Oct. 8, 1866, John Hamilton to Andrew, Oct. 9, 1866, James H. Lightner to Andrew, Oct. 12, 1866, John Grubb to Andrew, Oct. 12, 1866, Andrew Papers, MHS.

25. *BDJ*, Dec. 24, 1866; *LLA*, Dec. 7, 1867; *BDA*, Jan. 8, 1867; Schwartz, *Samuel Gridley Howe*, 282; Pearson, *Andrew*, 2:299; Andrew to Wiliam M. Hayes, Nov. 13, 1866, James Freeman Clarke to Andrew, Sept. 19, 1866, Feb. 21, 1867, S. G. Howe to Andrew, Feb. 19, 1867, Andrew Papers, MHS; Hamrogue, "John A. Andrew," 251; Trent, *The Manliest Man*, 246; *NI*, Jan. 6, 1868; Palmer, *Selected Letters of Charles Sumner*, 2:389.

26. *BDA*, Oct. 13, Nov. 2, 3, 6, 7, 22, 1866; *NA*, June 2, 1866; Edward H. Hooper to Andrew, Oct. 24, 1866, Andrew Papers, MHS; *FC*, Nov. 15, 1866; "Charles L. Mitchell"; Schneider, *Boston Confronts Jim Crow*, 15.

27. Hughes, *Reminiscences of John Murray Forbes*, 3:24–30; *BDA*, Apr. 6, 1867; May 31, 1875; *NHS*, Mar. 8, 1868; *LDC*, May 25, 1865, Nov. 4, 1867; Andrew was a close reader of the *Annual Report of the Board of Inspectors of the Massachusetts State Prison*, 1865; Foner, *Reconstruction*, 270–71.

28. *Alabama Official and Statistical Register*, 149; Harlan and Smock, *Booker T. Washington Papers*, 12:254; *WB*, Feb. 15, 1913; *TF*, Mar. 1, 1913; *ST*, Mar. 1, 1913; *PC*, Oct. 14, 1911. The Tuskegee Institute Trustees honored the former governor by allowing their hospital to be renamed the John A. Andrew Memorial Hospital. The original building opened

in 1892 as the Institute Hospital and Nurse Training School, but when it was donated to the Institute in 1911, Andrew's granddaughter Elizabeth Andrew Mason, whose deceased husband Charles E. Mason was a trustee, donated the funds necessary to remodel and outfit it as a modern hospital. The Masons were donors to African American education, and in 1913, gifted the Institute with $55,000 for the building and equipment

29. Edward Atkinson to Andrew, Dec. 9, 1866, William Burt to Andrew, May 10, 1866, Andrew to Burt, May 11, 1866, Joseph Speer to Andrew, May 10, 1866, Atkinson Papers, MHS; Palmer, *Selected Letters of Charles Sumner*, 2:386-88; BDC, Dec. 29, 1866; Foner, *Reconstruction*, 271-72; O'Toole and Quigley, *Boston's Histories*, 116; Andrew to Clarke, Dec. 19, 1866, Clarke Papers, Additional Correspondence, HU.

30. NHS, Dec. 21, 1866; BDA, Dec. 14, 17, 1866; LDC, Dec. 17, 1866:

31. William E. Chandler to Andrew, Dec. 12, 14, 1866, William Seward to Andrew, Dec. 12, 14, 1866, Andrew to William E. Chandler, Dec. 14, 1866, Andrew to Seward, Dec. 14, 1866, Andrew Papers, MHS; BDA, Dec. 17, 1866; LDC, Dec. 17, 1866.

32. Headley, *Massachusetts in the Rebellion*, 28; Browne, "Governor Andrew," 267; Schutz, *A Noble Pursuit*, 21-39; Burnham, "Hon. John Albion Andrew," 1-12; Nason, *Discourse*, 42-58. On the mid-afternoon of January 2, 1867, Andrew presided over the twenty-second annual meeting of the New England Historic-Genealogical Society, see Andrew, *An Address Delivered Before the New England-Genealogical Society*; BDA, Nov. 2, 1867; Andrew Scrapbooks 12, 13, Andrew Papers, MHS.

33. Fields, *James T. Fields*, 142; Henry Lee, Jr., to Andrew, Jan. 1, 1867, John Jeffries to Andrew, Jan. 1, 1867, Anson Hooker to Andrew, Jan. 1, 1867, Menu for the Dinner, Warden Gideon Haynes to Andrew, Jan. 7, 1866, Charles Whipple to Andrew, Jan. 9, 1867, Andrew Papers, MHS.

34. Andrew to Montgomery Blair, Jan. 7, 1867, Andrew Papers, MHS; Pearson, *Andrew*, 2:315; Foner, *Reconstruction*, 213.

35. Forbes to Andrew, Feb. 12, 1867, Andrew to William Pitt Fessenden, Jan. 8, 1867, Edward Everett Hale to Andrew, Jan. 15, 1867, Samuel Gridley Howe to Andrew, Jan. 30, 1867, William L. Burt to Andrew, Feb. 21, 1867, Francis B. Crownshield, Apr. 1, 1867, Andrew Papers. MHS; BDA, Jan. 23, 1867; Foner, *Reconstruction*, 272-73.

36. Anna Lowell to Andrew, Mar. 7, 9, 1867, Marvin H. Bovee to Andrew, Feb. 17, 1867, The Essex Institute Membership Certificate, Feb. 5, 1867, Boston Conservatory of Music List of Official Reference, see the Monthly statement in April 1867, Andrew Papers, MHS; Cimbala and Miller, *The Great Task Remaining Before Us*, 95; Greenwood, *First Fruits of Freedom*, 124; *Documents Printed by the Order of the Senate of the Commonwealth of Massachusetts*, 1867, 162, 163; Harrison, *Washington during Civil War and Reconstruction*, 97; BDA, Jan. 15, Mar. 28, 1867, LDC, Jan. 17, 1867; BDWC, Feb. 11, 1867; CDH, Feb. 11, 1867.

37. Anna Lowell to Andrew, Mar. 7, 9, 1867, Marvin H. Bovee to Andrew, Feb. 17, 1867, The Essex Institute Membership Certificate, Feb. 5, 1867, Boston Conservatory of Music List of Official Reference, see the Monthly statement in April 1867, Andrew Papers, MHS; Cimbala and Miller, *The Great Task Remaining Before Us*, 95; Greenwood, *First Fruits of Freedom*, 124; *Documents Printed by the Order of the Senate of the Commonwealth of Massachusetts*, 1867, Apr. 1867, Senate No., 162, 163; Harrison, *Washington during Civil War and Reconstruction*, 97; BDA, Jan. 15, Mar. 28, 1867, LDC, Jan. 17, 1867; BDWC, Feb. 11, 1867; CDH, Feb. 11, 1867.

38. LDC, Feb. 19, 1867; ZHWJ, Apr. 12, 1865, Feb. 6, 1867; BDJ, Jan. 31, 1867; Browne, *Sketch of the Official Life of John A. Andrew*, 58-62; Pearson, *Andrew*, 2:306-3; Chandler, *Memoir*, 113-16; Arthur L. Perry to Andrew, Feb. 26, 1867, Andrew Papers, MHS; Andrew, *The Errors of Prohibition*, 8-38, 147; Murray, *Prohibition vs. License*, 1-32; newspaper clippings, Andrew Papers, BowC; BDA, Nov. 4, 1867; Haven and Russell, *Father Taylor*,

265-70; Murray, *Prohibition vs. License*, 1-32; newspaper clippings, Andrew Papers, BowC; Baum, *Civil War Party System*, 128-29.

39. Browne, *Sketch of the Official Life of John A. Andrew*, 58-62; Pearson, *Andrew*, 2:306-7; Chandler, *Memoir*, 113-16; Arthur L. Perry to Andrew, Feb. 26, 1867, Andrew Papers, MHS; Andrew, *The Errors of Prohibition*, 147; Murray, *Prohibition vs. License*, 1-32; newspaper clippings, Andrew Papers, BowC; *BDA*, Nov. 4, 1867.

40. Andrew, *The Errors of Prohibition*, 8-38; E. F. (of the Boston DA) to Andrew, Mar. 6, 1867, Andrew Papers, MHS; Pearson, *Andrew*, 2:308; Haven and Russell, *Father Taylor*, 265-70; Murray, *Prohibition vs. License*, 1-32; Andrew, *The Errors of Prohibition*, 147; newspaper clippings, Andrew Papers, BowC; Baum, *Civil War Party System*, 128-30; *BDA*, Nov. 4, 1867.

41. Andrew, *The Errors of Prohibition*, 55-65.

42. *HW*, June 8, 29, Sept. 4, 1867; *ZHWJ*, Apr. 17, 1867; James A. Bolles to Andrew, Apr. 4, 1867, Albert Otis to Andrew, Apr. 17, 1867, J. W. Wetherell to Andrew, Apr. 17, 1867, William Rogers to Andrew, Apr. 22, 1867, Forbes to Andrew, Apr. 25, 1867, Joseph Speer to Andrew, Apr. 29, 1867, Andrew Papers, MHS; *CAdv*, June 6, 1867; "Boston Science," 290; Pearson, *Andrew*, 2:309; *Senator Wilson's Speech on Prohibition*; Andrew, *The Errors of Prohibition*, 1-148; newspapers clippings, Andrew Papers, BowC; Baum, *Civil War Party System*, 128-29; Donald, *Charles Sumner and the Rights of Man*, 343; Scharnhorst, *Kate Field*, 194; Chandler, *Memoir*, 58-64; *BDA*, Nov. 4, 1867; Prentice, *The Life of Gilbert Hall*, 205.

43. *ZHWJ*, May 8, 1867; Murray, *Prohibition vs. License*, 1-32.

44. *BDA*, Apr. 1, 8, May 11, 22, 1867.

45. Fields, *John T. Fields*, 159; Chandler, *Memoir*, 58-64; Pearson, *Andrew*, 2:310.

EPILOGUE: CHILDREN WILL CALL YOU BLESSED

1. *BDA*, Apr. 6, 1867, May 31, 1875; *NHS*, Mar. 8, 1868; *LDC*, May 25, 1865, Nov. 4, 1867.

2. Heller, *Portrait of an Abolitionist*, 213; *BDA*, Apr. 12, 13, 1867; *LDC*, Apr. 12, 13, 1867; *BDJ*, Apr. 12, 1867; Johnson, "George L. Stearns," 611-22; *ZHWJ*, Apr. 24, 1867; *VC*, Apr. 20, 1867.

3. Andrew to William Schouler, May 19, 1867, newspaper clippings, Andrew Papers, BowC; Pearson, *Andrew*, 2:303; Andrew to Charles G. Loring, Aug. 25, Sept. 24, Dec. 31, 1866, Loring Papers, HU; Andrew to Clarke, Dec. 7, 19, 1866, Clarke Papers, HU; Andrew referred him to P. W. Chandler's work on the Gospels, he must have had an advanced copy of the book that became *Observations on the Authenticity of the Gospels*; Hatch, *John Surratt*, 137; *BDA*, June 3, 5, 1865; Pearson, *Andrew*, 2:302; *NYEP*, May 23, 1867; *WSJ*, May 24, 1867; *CCom*, May 23, 1867; Browne, *Sketch of the Official Life of John A. Andrew*, 103; Abbott, *Cotton and Capital*, 256; Forbes to Andrew, June 4, 1867, Andrew Papers, MHS.

4. *BDA*, Apr. 30, May 16, 1867, July 4, Sept. 16, 1868, Apr. 23, 1869; *NA*, May 16, 1867; *NYOC*, May 23, 1867; *NHS*, May 17, 1867; Hale, *James Freeman Clarke*, 44; Pearson, *Andrew*, 2:303.

5. *BDA*, May 31, June 13, 1867; *CDH*, May 22, 1867.

6. *PAG*, June 20, 1867; *NI*, June 12, 1867; Abbott, *Cobbler in Congress*, 192-94; Hughes, *Reminiscences of John Murray Forbes*, 3:92-93, 96-97; *BDC*, June 15, 22, July 20, 1867; *RE*, June 13, 14, 15, 1867; *NA*, June 20, 1867; Pearson, *Andrew*, 2:319.

7. Abbott, *Cobbler in Congress*, 192-94; Pearson, *Andrew*, 2:319; Hughes, *Reminiscences of John Murray Forbes*, 3:92-93, 96-97; *BDC*, June 15, 22, July 20, 1867; *RE*, June 13, 14, 15, 1867; *NA*, June 20, 1867; *NI*, June 12, 1867.

8. Cyrus Woodman to Andrew, Aug. 13, 1867 (and Jan. 16, 1866), Eliza to Husband, July 5, 1867, Forrester to Papa, July 17, 1867, Andrew Papers, MHS; Chandler, *Memoir*, 58-59; Pearson, *Andrew*, 2:324-25; Graf and Haskins, *The Papers of Andrew Johnson*, 12:316;

Documents of the City of Boston for the Year 1867, 2:3-25; *VC,* June 29, 1867; *BDA,* June 24, July 22, 30, 1867; *NA,* June 24, 1867.

9. Dudley to Andrew, July 31, 1867, Andrew Papers, MHS; Abbott, "A Yankee Views the Organization of the Republican Party in South Carolina," 244-50; Simkins and Woody, *South Carolina During Reconstruction,* 89; *NYT,* July 31, 1867; *SR,* Mar. 19, 1913; Oertel, *Harriet Tubman,* 152.

10. Lydia Maria Child to Andrew, Aug. 8, 1867, Andrew Papers, MHS; Whittier, *Letters of Lydia Maria Child,* xiii-xiv.

11. Varon, *Southern Lady, Yankee Spy,* 9-52, 253-54; Furgurson, *Ashes of Glory*; Ryan, *A Yankee Spy in Richmond,* 1-24; *SSH,* Aug. 27, 1882; *WT,* June 29, 1902; Elizabeth Van Lew to Andrew, Jan. 5, 1866, Andrew Papers, MHS. Van Lew wrote Andrew several letters from January 1866 until his death in October 1867.

12. Van Lew to Andrew, Jan. 5, May 5, June 11, 28, 29, July 5, 1866, Andrew Papers, MHS; *SSH,* Aug. 27, 1882; *NYT,* Dec. 17, 1911; Varon, *Southern Lady, Yankee Spy,* 206; Miller, *Harvard's Civil War,* 96-97, 444.

13. Allen, *Westboro' State Reform School Reminiscences,* 179; Ryan, *A Yankee Spy in Richmond,* 1-24; Van Lew to Andrew, June 22, Aug. 6, 17, 1866, Andrew Papers, MHS; Varon, *Southern Lady, Yankee Spy,* 4, 5, 205-7.

14. W. Raymond Lee to Andrew, Jan. 22, 27, 31, 1867, Van Lew to Andrew, Nov. 5, 1866, Andrew Papers, MHS; Varon, *Southern Lady, Union Spy,* 228; Miller, *Harvard's Civil War,* 444.

15. Lee to Andrew, Jan. 27, 31, 1867, Van Lew to Andrew, Apr. 1, 27, 25, June 1, 22, 23, 26, 30, July 5, 10, 29, Oct. 26, 1867, John Van Lew to John Murray Forbes, July 2, 1867, Forbes to Andrew, July 3, 5, Aug. 11, 15, 1867, Andrew to Forbes, Aug. 16, 1867, Andrew Papers, MHS; Varon, *Southern Lady, Yankee Spy,* 206-7.

16. John O. Fiske to Andrew, July 19, 1867, Harvard Board of Overseers, July 17, 1867 (Andrew had also been elected as an Honorary Member of the Delta Kappa Epsilon Society), Charles Wheeler to Andrew, July 28, 1867, Stone and Crapo to Andrew, Sept. 7, 1867, Andrew Papers, MHS; *BDA,* Aug. 6, 7, 8, 9, 10, 1867; *BDWC,* Aug. 2, 1867.

17. Nason, *Discourse,* 47; *NYT,* June 23, 1875; *LDC,* Oct. 8, 1864; William L. Burt to Andrew, July 21, 1867, Cyrus Woodman to Andrew, Aug. 13, 1867, Andrew Papers, MHS; *BDA,* Aug. 9, 1867.

18. Forbes to Andrew, Aug. 16, 23, 1867, Office of the Secretary of the Board of Overseers, Harvard College, July 17, 1867, Andrew Papers, MHS; Andrew to Col. John Wetherell, Apr. 19, 1867, Andrew Papers, AAS; *BDA,* Aug. 14, 15, Sept. 3, 4, 1867; Hatch, *John Surratt,* 137; *BDA,* June 3, 5, 1865; *NYEP,* May 23, 1867; *WSJ,* May 24, 1867; *CCom,* May 23, 1867; Browne, *Sketch of the Official Life of John A. Andrew,* 103.

19. John Binney to Andrew, Sept. 7, Andrew to Binney, Sept. 10, 1867, Andrew Papers, MHS; Howard, *Religion and the Radical Republican Movement,* 107; Pearson, *Andrew,* 2:320.

20. Andrew to Binney, Sept. 10, 1867, Andrew Papers, MHS Pearson, *Andrew,* 2:322-23; *BET,* Dec. 19, 1867; Abzug and Mailish, *New Perspectives on Race and Slavery in America,* 107-9.

21. Andrew to Binney, Sept. 10, 1867, Andrew Papers, MHS Pearson, *Andrew,* 2:322-23; *BET,* Dec. 19, 1867; Abzug and Mailish, *New Perspectives on Race and Slavery in America,* 107-9.

22. White, *The Life of Lyman Trumbull,* 307.

23. Albert G. Browne, Jr., to Andrew, Oct. 22, 1867, H. Sidney Everett to Andrew, n.d., 1867, B. H. Channing to Andrew, Oct. 11, 1867, E. C. Thomas to Andrew, Oct. 15, 1867, Andrew Papers, MHS; *BDA,* Aug. 16, 22, Sept. 3, 4, 7, Nov. 19, 1867; *NI,* Sept. 5, 1867; *NA,* Oct. 11, 1867; *LDC,* Nov. 8, 30, 1867; Stearns, *Cambridge Sketches,* 260-62.

24. Browne, *Sketch of the Official Life of John A. Andrew,* dedication page, this work came from his article in the *North American Review*; also printed in *BDWC,* Oct. 31, 1872; *NE,* Nov. 7, 1872; *BDA,* Feb. 7, 1868; *NYT,* Feb. 8, 1868; Pearson, *Andrew,* 2:329; *SR,* Nov. 1,

1867; J. H. Chapin to Andrew, Oct. 3, 1867, John Fitch to Andrew, Oct. 5, 1867, Andrew Papers, MHS.

25. Chandler, *Memoir*, 65; Pearson, *Andrew*, 2:326; *BDJ*, Oct. 31, Nov. 1, 2, 1867, he left his wife and family an insurance policy worth $10,000. See also the folders in the Andrew Family Papers that relate to the burial details associated with Andrew's funeral, Cyrus Woodman to Andrew, Oct. 2, 5, 9, 1867, John D. Andrews to Andrew, Oct. 3, 7, 1867, Henry Hyde to Andrew, Oct. 29, 1867, Andrew Papers, MHS; Andrew to Charles G. Loring, Aug. 14, 1867, Loring Papers, HU; *BC*, Oct. 31, 1867; *BDA*, Nov. 7, 1867; *TC*, Nov. 7, 1867; *SR*, Nov. 1, 1867; *Boston Medical and Surgical Journal*, as reported in the *LDC*, Nov. 25, 1867.

26. Simon, *The Papers of Ulysses S. Grant*, 18:359.

27. Fields, *John T. Fields*, 152.

28. Lowell to Field, Oct. 31, 1867, Andrew Papers, MHS.

29. Prentice, *The Life of Gilbert Haven*, 312; Daniels, *Graduated with Honor*, 64.

30. Fields, *John T. Fields*, 152.

31. Clarke, *Memoir*, 55; *BDA*, Nov. 2, 4, 6, 27, 1867; *BDG*, July 27, 1914; Schmidt, *The Life and Works of John Knowles Paine*, 74-75; Winthrop and Aspinwall, "November Meeting," 85-92; *SR*, Nov. 4, 1867; *LDC*, Nov. 1, 13, 1867.

32. *SR*, Nov. 4, 1867; *LDC*, Nov. 4, 1867; *BDA*, Dec. 5, 1867; *NYTrib*, Oct. 31, 1867.

33. *SR*, Nov. 1, 4, 1867; *LDC*, Nov. 4, 1867; *BDA*, Dec. 5, 1867; Robinson, "Warrington" Pen-Portraits, 414; Griffin, People and Politics Observed by a Massachusetts Editor, 139-40; Pearson, Andrew, 2:237; Schouler, A History of Massachusetts in the Civil War, 216-19.

34. Pearson, *Andrew*, 2:327-30; Robinson, *"Warrington" Pen Portraits*, 414; *SR*, Nov. 1, 4, 1867.

35. *SR*, Nov. 1, 1867; Robinson, *"Warrington" Pen-Portraits*, 414; Griffin, *People and Politics Observed by a Massachusetts Editor*, 139-40; Pearson, *Andrew*, 2:327; Schouler, *A History of Massachusetts in the Civil War*, 216-19.

36. Burnham, "Hon. John Albion Andrew," 1-12; *BDJ*, Nov. 2, 1867; Weeks, *Prominent Families of New York*, 319.

37. Chandler, *Memoir*, 68-69.

38. Nason, *Discourse*, 52.

39. Chandler, *Memoir*, 66-67.

40. Charles Whipple to Mrs. Andrew, Nov. 7, 1867, Andrew Papers, MHS.

41. Chandler, *Memoir*, 121.

42. *LDC*, Nov. 13, 1867.

43. Woodman to Mrs. Andrew, Nov. 10, 1867, Andrew Papers, MHS.

44. Usher, "Cyrus Woodman," 400.

45. *HW*, Nov. 16, 1867.

46. John Van Lew to Eliza Andrew, Nov. 18, 1867, Andrew Papers, MHS.

47. Gollin, *Annie Adams Fields*, 138-39, 338; Stowe, *Lives and Deeds*, 335-37; *BWFP*, Nov. 8, 1867; Hedrick, *Harriet Beecher Stowe*, 337.

48. Stowe, *Lives and Deeds*, 335; Harriet Beecher Stowe to James Fields, Feb. ?, 1868?, and Feb. 16, 1868, Thomas Fields Papers, THL; *BWFP*, Nov. 8, 1867; Hedrick, *Harriet Beecher Stowe*, 337; Gollin, *Annie Adams Fields*, 338. Gollin writes that when Andrew's brother Isaac complained about inaccuracies in Stowe's sketch, she told Fields she had done her best with the material she had been given and the few anecdotes she had picked up on her own, but planned to ask Whipple, what corrections she should make before her book, *Men of Our Times* appeared.

49. Stowe, *Lives and Deeds*, 2:326; *WR*, Jan. 2, 1868; Adams and Foster, *Heroines of Modern Progress*, 195; *BDA*, Jan. 3, 1871.

50. *NYT*, Oct. 31, 1867; *BDA*, Nov. 2, 5, 27, 1867; *BET*, Nov. 2, 9, 1867; newspaper clippings, Andrew Papers, BowC; *TC*, Feb. 25, 1897.

51. *BI*, Nov. 13, 1867.

52. *BP*, Nov. 9, 1867.

53. Hedge, "John Albion Andrew," 435; *BDA*, Oct. 31, 1867; *TI*, Nov. 7, 1867; Hamrogue, "John A. Andrew," 252; *Appleton's Journal of Literature, Science, and Art*, 441; MPNEJA, Nov. 6, 1869; Mount Auburn Cemetery Internment Records, Nov. 2, 1867, *Mount Auburn Cemetery; NYCO*, Nov. 7, 1867; Pearson, *Andrew*, 2:329-30.

54. Clarke, *Memoir*, 55; *BDA*, Nov. 27, 1867; *BDG*, July 27, 1914; Schmidt, *The Life and Works of John Knowles Paine*, 74-75; Meeting of Colored Citizens of Boston, Nov. 6, 1867, Andrew Papers, MHS; Winthrop and Aspinwall, "November Meeting," 85-92; *SR*, Nov. 4, 1867; *LDC*, Nov. 1, 13, 1867.

55. Adams and Foster, *Heroines of Modern Progress*, 195; *BDA*, Jan. 3, 1871.

56. *WR*, Jan. 2, 1868; Adams and Foster, *Heroines of Modern Progress*, 195; *BDA*, Jan. 3, 1871.

57. *BDA*, Nov. 27, 1867; Whipple, *Eulogy on John Albion Andrew*, 35-36; *LDC*, Nov. 29, 1867; Trent, *The Manliest Man*, 233; *DJM*, Dec. 7, 1867.

58. *LDC*, Nov. 20, 1867; *NI*, Nov. 18, 1867; *SFDEB*, Feb. 24, 1871; *BI*, Nov. 20, 1867; *NA*, Nov.14, 1867; *NHS*, Nov. 15, 1867; Fields, *John T. Fields*, 152.

59. Stephenson, *Addresses and Papers*, 18-23; Bowen, *Massachusetts in the War*, 983; *MPNEJ*, Nov. 6, 1869; *BDG*, Dec. 5, 1908; newspaper clippings, Andrew Papers, BowC; *SR*, Feb. 15, 1871; *BDA*, Feb. 14, 1871; *NYT*, Nov. 1, 1869; *LDC*, Nov. 1, 1869, Mar. 14, 1872. Butler contributed to the Andrew fund, see *BDA*, Sept. 26, 1871.

60. Stephenson, *Addresses and Papers*, 18-23; *HJ*, May 13, 2010; Bowen, *Massachusetts in the War*, 983; *Appleton's Journal of Literature, Science, and Art*, 441; John A. Andrew Monument Association, *A Memorial Volume*, 48-50; Bouve, et al., *History of the Town of Hingham, Massachusetts*, 1:347; *TI*, Nov. 11, 1875; Thomas Ball to Norcross, Dec. 13, 1869, Oct. 17, Nov. 7, 1870, Nov. 7, Feb. 28, Mar. 7, May 1, 1871, Ball Papers, MHS.

61. John A. Andrew Monument Association, *A Memorial Volume*, 20-40; *HJ*, May 13, 2010; Bouve, et al., *History of the Town of Hingham, Massachusetts*, 1:347; Bowen, *Massachusetts in the War*, 983; Stephenson, *Addresses and Papers*, 18-23; *TI*, Nov. 11, 1875; *BDA*, Oct. 9, 1876; *LDC*, Oct. 13, 1875; *FLIN*, Oct. 30, 1875.

62. *Appleton's Journal of Literature, Science, and Art*, 441; MPNEJA, Nov. 6, 1869.

63. *Appleton's Journal of Literature, Science, and Art*, 441; MPNEJA, Nov. 6, 1869; Pearson, *Andrew*, 2:239-30; Hamrogue, "John A. Andrew," 252.

64. John A. Andrew Monument Association, *A Memorial Volume*, 20-40; *HJ*, May 13, 2010; Bouve, et al., *History of the Town of Hingham, Massachusetts*, 1:347; Bowen, *Massachusetts in the War*, 983; Stephenson, *Addresses and Papers*, 18-23; *TA*, Jan. 1, 1879; *TI*, Nov. 11, 1875; *BDA*, Oct. 9, 1875; *LDC*, Oct. 13, 1875; *FLIN*, Oct. 30, 1875.

65. *NYT*, 16 Apr. 16, 1904, Oct. 30, 1881; *BI*, Nov. 13, 1867; MPNEJA, Nov. 6, 1869; Browne, *Sketch of the Official Life of John A. Andrew*, 71-72; *NWCA*, Aug. 28, 1907; *Appleton's Journal of Literature, Science, and Art*, 441; Stephenson, *Addresses and Papers*, 18-23; *HJ*, May 13, 2010; Hamrogue, "John A. Andrew," 250-52; *SR*, Feb. 15, 1871.

66. Blight, *Race and Reunion*, 194-95; Cimbala and Miller, *Union Soldiers and the Northern Home Front*, 456; *BDG*, June 26, 1887.

67. *BDA*, June 1, 1897; Blight, *Race and Reunion*, 338-42; Du Bois, *Black Reconstruction in America*, 110; *BET*, June 1, 1897; Harlan and Smock, *The Booker T. Washington Papers*, 4:285-86; Washington, *Up from Slavery*, 148-49; *NA*, June 1, 1897; *VW*, June 9, 1897.

BIBLIOGRAPHY

Manuscript Collections
(with Abbreviations)

AMERICAN ANTIQUARIAN SOCIETY, WORCESTER, MA (AAS)
Manuscript Collections
  John A. Andrew
  Ammi R. Bradbury
  John Walcott Wetherell

BOSTON ATHENAEUM, BOSTON, MA (BA)
  John Andrew

BOSTON PUBLIC LIBRARY, BOSTON, MA (BPL)
Special Collections
  Anti-Slavery Collection
  Chamberlin Collection of Autographs
  William Lloyd Garrison
  Thomas W. Higginson
  MS 24
  MS 2813
  MS 6000
  MS 6003
  Frank Sanborn

BOWDOIN COLLEGE, BRUNSWICK, ME (BOWC)
George J. Mitchell Department of Special Collections and Archives,
     Hawthorne-Longfellow Library
  John Andrew
  John A. Andrew Monument Association
  Alumni Biographical Files
  Autograph Album of Jordan G. Ferguson
  Chandler Family

Matriculation Logbook, 1802–67
Records of the Praying Circle

COLUMBIA UNIVERSITY, NEW YORK, NY (CU)
Rare Book and Manuscript Library
John Brown

CONCORD FREE PUBLIC LIBRARY, CONCORD, MA (CFPL)
Special Collections
John Shepard Keyes

CONNECTICUT HISTORICAL SOCIETY, HARTFORD, CT (CHS)
John Andrew

CORNELL UNIVERSITY, ITHACA, NY (CUL)
Rare Books and Manuscripts
Ezra Cornell
Andrew White

DARTMOUTH COLLEGE, HANOVER, NH
Rauner Special Collections Library
John A. Andrew

DUKE UNIVERSITY, DURHAM, NC (DU)
David M. Rubenstein Rare Book and Manuscript Library
Charles Russell Lowell and Charles Henry Dalton
Charles Sumner
Edward Wilkinson

HARVARD UNIVERSITY, CAMBRIDGE, MA (HU)
Houghton Library
John A. Andrew
John Prescott Bigelow
Francis William Bird
Robert Carter
David Clapp
William Warland Clapp
James Freeman Clarke
James Freeman Clarke, Additional Correspondence
Ralph Waldo Emerson
Charles Greely Loring
Wendell Phillips
Charles Sumner

THE HUNTINGTON LIBRARY, ART MUSEUM, AND BOTANICAL
    GARDENS, SAN MARINO, CA (THL)
Thomas Fields

KENT STATE UNIVERSITY, KENT, OH (KSU)
Special Collections and Archives
Slack Papers

LIBRARY OF CONGRESS, WASHINGTON, D.C. (LC)
Adams Family Papers
Nathaniel P. Banks
Clara Barton
Blair Family

Caleb Cushing
Edward Kinsley
Charles Kline
Abraham Lincoln
Edwin M. Stanton
Edwin O. Wentworth
Henry Wilson
Charles H. Woodwell

LIBRARY OF VIRGINIA, RICHMOND, VA (LV)
Special Collections
Samuel E. Sewall and John A. Andrew, Argument on Behalf of Thaddeus Hyatt
Pierpont Executive Papers

MASSACHUSETTS HISTORICAL SOCIETY, BOSTON, MA (MHS)
Charles Amory Family
John A. Andrew
John A. Andrew Account Book
John A. Andrew Family
John Andrew Letterbooks
Annual Reports of the Boston Port Society and Seaman's Aid Society
Edward Atkinson
Thomas Ball
Francis W. Bird
Boston Anti-Man Hunting League
Boston Vigilance Committee
Brown Family
David Clapp
Charles Bowers
James Freeman Clarke
George Collamore
Charles Henry Dalton
Dana Family
Charles Barnard Fox
Edward Waldo Emerson
Ralph Waldo Emerson
Timothy Emerton
George Gordon
Francis Jackson
Letters Received by Samuel Gridley Howe
Lee Family
Francis L. Lee
Moses Moody Ordway
Oregon Territory
John D. Parsons
Perry-Clarke Collection
Records of the 54th Regiment
Henry Sturgis Russell
William Schouler
Benjamin Seaver
Letters to Robert G. Shaw
The Return of the Standards
George Francis Train
Ware Family

Henry F. Wellington
Charles Frederick Winslow
Horatio Woodman

MASSACHUSETTS JUDICIAL ARCHIVES, BOSTON, MA (MJA)
Boston Municipal Court Criminal Records
Suffolk County Court of Common Pleas Records

MASSACHUSETTS STATE ARCHIVES, BOSTON, MA (MSA)
Abstract of Votes for Plymouth District
Executive Department, Letters Received
Massachusetts Governor, Letters Official, 1861–1925, RG GO1
Suffolk County Supreme Judicial Court Records

MOUNT AUBURN CEMETERY, CAMBRIDGE, MA
Mount Auburn Cemetery Internment Records

NATIONAL ARCHIVES AND RECORDS ADMINISTRATION, WASHINGTON, D.C. (NARA)
Letters Received, 1863–1864
Records of the Adjutant General's Office, 1762–1984, RG 94
Records of the Division of Appointments, RG 56
Telegrams Received by the Secretary of War, RG 107

NEW ENGLAND HISTORIC GENEALOGICAL SOCIETY, BOSTON, MA
William Foster

NEW YORK HISTORICAL SOCIETY, NEW YORK, NY
John A. Andrew

PEABODY ESSEX MUSEUM, PEABODY, MA (PEM)
Phillips Library
John A. Andrew

PRINCETON UNIVERSITY, PRINCETON, NJ (PU)
Special Collections
Blair-Lee Family Papers

RUTHERFORD B. HAYES PRESIDENTIAL LIBRARY AND MUSEUM, FREMONT, OH (RBHPL)
William Claflin

THE PIERPONT MORGAN LIBRARY AND MUSEUM, NEW YORK, NY (TPML)
Special Collections Department
John A. Andrew
Literary and Historical

STATE HISTORICAL SOCIETY OF WISCONSIN, MADISON, WI (SHSW)
Cyrus Woodman

THE STATE LIBRARY OF MASSACHUSETTS, BOSTON, MA
Special Collections
Rowse R. Clarke

UNIVERSITY OF CHICAGO, CHICAGO, IL (UC)
Hanna Holborn Gray Special Collections Research Center
Abraham Lincoln Miscellaneous Manuscripts
William E. Barton Collection of Lincolniana

UNIVERSITY OF MASSACHUSETTS, AMHERST, AMHERST, MA (UMASS)
Robert S. Cox Special Collections & University Archives Research Center
Edward Kinsley

UNIVERSITY OF VIRGINIA, CHARLOTTESVILLE, VA
Benjamin F. Hutchinson
Jesse Calvin Spaulding

VIRGINIA TECH, BLACKSBURG, VA (VT)
Special Collections and University Archives, Newman Library
Stearns Family

Periodicals
(with Abbreviations)

The Aldine, The Art Journal of America (TA)
Alexandria Gazette (AG)
The American Magazine of Useful and Entertaining Knowledge (TAMUEK)
American Railway Times (ART)
Arkansas Gazette (ArkG)
Baltimore Daily Commercial (BaDC)
Bangor Daily Whig and Courier (BDWC)
Barre Gazette (BG)
Boston Atlas (BA)
Boston Bee (BB)
Boston Chronotype (BChr)
Boston Courier (BC)
Boston Daily Advertiser (BDA)
Boston Daily Commonwealth (BDC)
Boston Daily Globe (BDG)
Boston Daily Journal (BDJ)
Boston Daily Times (BDT)
Boston Daily Whig (BDW)
Boston Evening Transcript (BET)
Boston Herald (BH)
Boston Investigator (BI)
Boston Observer (BO)
Boston Pilot (BoPil)
Boston Post (BP)
The Boston Quarterly Review (TBQR)
Boston Recorder (BR)
Boston Saturday Evening Gazette (BSEG)
Boston Semi-Weekly Advertiser (BSWA)
The Boston Statesman (TBS)
Boston Traveler (BT)
Boston Weekly Journal (BWJ)
Broad Axe (BrAx)
Brunswick Telegraph (BrT)
Buffalo Express (BE)
Burlington Weekly Free Press (BWFP)
Cambridge Chronicle (CC)
Carlisle Herald (CH)

Cazenovia Republican (CaRep)
Chattanooga Daily Gazette (CDG)
Chicago Eagle (CE)
Christian Advocate (CAdv)
Christian Advocate and Journal (CAJ)
Christian Inquirer (CI)
The Christian Mirror (TCM)
The Christian Recorder (TCRec)
Christian Reflector (CR)
The Christian Register (TCR)
The Christian Union (TCU)
Christian Watchman and Reflector (CWR)
Cincinnati Commercial (CCom)
Cincinnati Daily Enquirer (CDE)
Cincinnati Weekly Herald and Philanthropist (CWHP)
The Circular (Brooklyn, NY) (TCir)
Cleveland Daily Herald (CDH)
Colored American (CA)
The Congregationalist (TC)
The Crisis (TCri)
Daily Inter-Ocean (DIO)
Daily Pittsburgh Gazette (DPG)
The Dial (TD)
Dwights Journal of Music (DJM)
Eastern Argus (EA)
Eastern State Journal (White Plains, NY) (ESJ)
Emancipator and Free American (EFA)
Emancipator and Republican (ER)
Every Other Saturday (EOS)
Frank Leslie's Illustrated Newspaper (FLIN)
Frederick Douglass Monthly (FDM)
Frederick Douglass' Paper (FDP)
Freedom's Champion (FC)
The Freeman (TF)
Friends Review (FR)
Harpers Weekly (HW)
Harrisburg Morning Telegraphy (HMT)
Hartford Press (HP)
Hingham Journal (HJ)
The Huntress (TH)
The Independent (New York) (TI)
Lawrence (MA) Sentinel (LS)
Leesburg Genius of Liberty (LGL)
The Liberator (Lib)
The Literary World (TLW)
Littell's Living Age (LLA)
Lowell Daily Citizen (LDC)
Maine Farmer (MF)
Massachusetts Ploughman and New England Journal of Agriculture (MPNEJA)
Milwaukee Daily Sentinel (MDS)
Monthly Law Reporter (MLR)
The Nation (TN)
National Anti-Slavery Standard (NASS)

National Era (NE)
National Intelligencer (NI)
National Police Gazette (NPG)
National Reflector (NaR)
National Republican (NRep)
Newark Daily Advertiser (NDA)
New Bedford Evening Standard (NBES)
New Bedford Mercury (NBM)
Newburyport Daily Herald (NDH)
New Hampshire Statesman (NHS)
New York Age (NYA)
New York Daily Times (NYDT)
New York Evangelist (NYE)
New York Evening Post (NYEP)
New York Herald (NYH)
New York Journal of Commerce (NYJC)
New York Observer and Chronicle (NYOC)
New York Spectator (NYS)
New York Sun (NYSun)
New York Times (NYT)
New York Tribune (NYTrib)
Niles Weekly Register (NWR)
North American (NA)
North Star (NS)
Northwestern Christian Advocate (NWCA)
Outlook (OL)
Philadelphia American and Gazette (PAG)
Philadelphia Daily Evening Bulletin (PDEB)
Philadelphia Inquirer (PI)
Philadelphia Press (PP)
Pittsburgh Courier (PC)
Pittsfield Berkshire County Eagle (PBCE)
Pittsfield Sun (PS)
Plaindealer (Plain)
Plymouth Rock (PlyR)
Portland Journal and Inquirer (PJI)
Portland Press Herald (PPH)
The Prairie Farmer (TPF)
Prisoner's Friend (PF)
Providence Daily Journal (PDJ)
Providence Evening News (PEN)
Puritan Recorder (PR)
Raleigh Register (RR)
Richmond Enquirer (RE)
San Francisco Daily Evening Bulletin (SFDEB)
Savannah Daily News and Herald (SDNH)
Savannah Tribune (ST)
Saturday Evening Post (SEP)
Syracuse Sunday Herald (SSH)
Springfield Republican (SR)
The Standard (TS)
Trumpet and Universalist Magazine (TUM)
Vermont Chronicle (VC)

Vermont Watchman (VW)
Virginia Sentinel (VS)
Washington Bee (WB)
Washington Times (WT)
Watchman and Reflector (WR)
Weekly Anglo-American (WAA)
Weekly Register Call (*Central City, CO*) (WRC)
Wisconsin State Journal (WSJ)
The Woman's Journal (TWJ)
Worcester Spy (WS)
Worcester Transcript (WTran)
The Youth's Companion (TYC)
Zion's Herald and Weekly Journal (ZHWJ)

Primary Published Works

Abbott, Jacob. *New England and Her Institutions, By One of Her Sons.* London: Seeley and Burnside, 1835.
Acts and Resolves Passed by the General Court, 1854–66. Boston: State Printers, 1866.
Acts and Resolves Passed by the General Court of Massachusetts, 1858. Boston: William White, 1858.
Acts and Resolves Passed by the General Court of Massachusetts in the Year 1859. Boston: William White, 1859.
Acts and Resolves Passed by the General Court of Massachusetts in the Year 1861. Boston: William White, 1861.
Acts and Resolves Passed by the General Court of Massachusetts in the Year 1865. Boston: Wright and Potter, 1865.
Acts and Resolves Passed by the General Court of Massachusetts in the Year 1866. Boston: Wright and Potter, 1866.
Acts and Resolves Passed by the General Court of the Commonwealth of Massachusetts, 1862. Boston: William White, 1862.
Acts and Resolves Passed by the Legislature of Massachusetts, 1843. Boston: Dutton and Wentworth, 1843.
Adams, Charles Francis, ed. *Memoirs of John Quincy Adams.* 12 vols. Philadelphia: J. B. Lippincott, 1877.
———. *Richard Henry Dana: A Biography.* 2 vols. Boston: Houghton Mifflin, 1890.
Adams, Elmer Cleveland, and Warren Dunham Foster. *Heroines of Modern Progress.* New York: Sturgis and Walton, 1913.
Alabama Official and Statistical Register. Montgomery: Brown Printing, 1915.
Allardt, Linda, and William Henry Gilman, eds. *The Journals and Miscellaneous Notebooks of Ralph Waldo Emerson.* 10 vols. Cambridge: Belknap Press of Harvard University Press, 1982.
Allen, John Addison. *Westboro' State Reform School Reminiscences.* Boston: Lockwood, Brooks, 1877.
Alvord, J. W. *Third Semi-Annual Report on Schools for Freedmen, January 1, 1867.* Washington, D.C.: Government Printing Office, 1867.
American Academy of Arts and Science Proceedings 28 (May 1892–May 1893): 310–17.
American Congregational Year-Book, for the Year 1858. New York: American Congregational Union, 1858.
American Quarterly Register and Magazine 3 (Dec. 1849): 309–26.
Anderson, Mary Crow, ed. *Two Scholarly Friends: Yates Snowden-John Bennett Correspondence, 1902–1932.* Columbia: University of South Carolina Press, 1993.
Andrew, John A. *Addresses of His Excellency Governor John A. Andrew, Hon. Edward Everett,*

Hon. B. F. Thomas and Hon. Robert C. Winthrop Delivered . . . August 27, 1862. Boston: J. E. Farwell, 1862.

———. Address of His Excellency John A. Andrew to the Two Branches of the Legislature of Massachusetts, January 3, 1862. Boston: William White, 1862.

———. Address of His Excellency John A. Andrew to the Two Branches of the Legislature of Massachusetts, January 9, 1863. Boston: William White, 1863.

———. Address of His Excellency John A. Andrew to the Two Branches of the Legislature of Massachusetts, January 8, 1864. Boston: Wright and Potter, 1864.

———. Address of His Excellency John A. Andrew to the Two Branches of the Legislature of Massachusetts, January 6, 1865. Boston: Wright and Potter, 1865.

———. Address of the Committee Appointed by a Public Meeting Held at Faneuil Hall, September 24, 1846, for the Purpose of Considering the Recent Case of Kidnapping from Our Soil, and of Taking Measures to Prevent the Recurrence of Similar Outrages. Boston: White and Potter, 1846.

———. An Address Delivered at Brattleborough, Vermont, by Invitation of the Agricultural Society of Vermont, September 6, 1866. Boston: Wright and Potter, 1866.

———. An Address Delivered before the New England Agricultural Society on Hampden Park, Springfield, Mass., September 9, 1864. Boston: Wright and Potter, 1864.

———. An Address Delivered before the New England Historic-Genealogical Society . . . January 2, 1867. Boston: David Clapp and Son, 1867.

———. An Address on the Occasion of Dedicating the Monument to Ladd and Whitney Members of the Sixth Regiment, M.V.M., Killed at Baltimore, Maryland, April 19, 1861. Boston: Wright and Potter, 1865.

———. An Address to the Graduating Class of the Medical School in the University a Cambridge, Wednesday, March 9, 1864. Boston: Ticknor and Fields, 1864.

———. Answers of the Governor of Massachusetts to Inquiries Respecting Certain Emigrants Who Have Arrived in This Country from Europe and Who Are Alleged to Be Illegally Enlisted in the Army of the United States. Washington, D.C.: Government Printing Office, 1864.

———. The Errors of Prohibition: An Argument Delivered in the Representatives' Hall, Boston, April 3, 1867. Boston: Ticknor and Fields, 1867.

———. Governor Andrew's Opinion in the Case of Edward W. Green. Boston: 1866.

———. History of Ida May. Boston: J. S. Potter, 1855.

———. Special Message of His Excellency John A. Andrew to the Two Branches of the Legislature of Massachusetts, January 3, 1866. Boston: Wright and Potter, 1866.

———. To the Voters of Massachusetts: Governor Andrew's Letter of Acceptance. Boston: George C. Randy and Avery, 1862.

———. Valedictory Address of His Excellency John A. Andrew, January 5, 1866. Boston: Wright and Potter, 1866.

Angell, James B. "The Recall of Ministers." Forum 6 (Jan. 1889): 486–97.

Annual Announcement of Lectures in the Atlanta Medical College, for the Session of 1857. Atlanta: C. R. Hanleiter, 1856.

Annual Report of the Adjutant-General of the Commonwealth of Massachusetts, 1861. Boston: William White, 1861.

Annual Report of the Adjutant-General of the Commonwealth of Massachusetts, 1864. Boston: Wright and Potter, 1865.

Annual Report of the Adjutant-General of the Commonwealth of Massachusetts, 1866. Boston: Wright and Potter, 1867.

Annual Report of the Board of Inspectors of the Massachusetts State Prison, 1865. Boston: Wright and Potter, 1866.

Annual Report of the Maine Temperance Society, January 23, 1833. Belfast: Printed for the Society, 1833.

Appleton's Journal of Literature, Science, and Art 14 (Oct. 1875): 441.

Bacon, Georgeanna Woolsey, and Eliza Woolsey Howland, eds. *Letters of a Family during the War for the Union, 1861–1865.* 2 vols. New Haven, CT: Privately Printed, 1899.

Balch, Francis V., ed. *Report of the Case of the Steamship Meteor.* Boston: Little, Brown, 1869.

Bancroft, Frederic, ed. *Speeches, Correspondences, and Political Papers of Carl Schurz.* New York: McClure, 1908.

Bancroft, Frederic, and William A. Dunning, eds. *The Reminiscences of Carl Schurz.* 3 vols. New York: McClure, 1908.

Barrows, Elizabeth A. *A Memorial of Bradford Academy.* Boston: Congregational S. S. and Publishing Society, 1870.

Bartlett, David W. *The Life and Public Services of Hon. Abraham Lincoln.* New York: Derby and Jackson, 1860.

Barton, William E. *The Life of Clara Barton: Founder of the American Red Cross.* 2 vols. Boston: Houghton Mifflin, 1922.

Basler, Roy P., ed. *The Collected Works of Abraham Lincoln.* 8 vols. New Brunswick, NJ: Rutgers University Press, 1953.

Beatley, Clara Bancroft. "Memorial Day and the John A. Andrew Centenary." *Christian Register* 14 (May 9, 1918): 450–56.

"Benjamin F. Butler." *American Phrenological Journal* 39 (May 1864): 39–42.

Berlin, Ira, et al., eds. *Freedom: A Documentary History of Emancipation, 1861–1867.* 3 vols. New York: Cambridge University Press, 1982.

Bird, Francis William. *Francis William Bird: A Biographical Sketch.* Boston: Privately Printed, 1897.

Bokum, Hermann. *The Testimony of a Refugee from East Tennessee.* Philadelphia: Union League, 1863.

"Boston Science." *Herald of Health* (9 June 1867): 290.

Boteler, Alexander R. "Recollections of the John Brown Raid: By a Virginian Who Witnessed the Fight." *Century Illustrated Magazine* 26 (July 1883): 399–416.

Boutwell, George S. *Emancipation: Its Justice, Expediency and Necessity, as a Means of Securing a Speedy and Permanent Peace.* Boston: Wright and Potter, 1861.

——. *Reminiscences of Sixty Years in Public Affairs.* 2 vols. New York: McClure, Phillips, 1902.

Bovee, Marvin Henry. *Reasons for Abolishing Capital Punishment.* Chicago: Lakeside Printing, 1873.

Bouve, Thomas, et al. *History of the Town of Hingham, Massachusetts.* 3 vols. Hingham, MA: Hingham Historical Society, 1893.

Bowditch, Vincent, ed. *Life and Correspondence of Henry Ingersoll Bowditch.* 2 vols. Boston: Houghton Mifflin, 1902.

"Bowdoin College," *Scribner's Monthly* 12 (May 1876): 47–61.

"Bowdoin College," *TAMUEK,* Mar. 1, 1837.

Bowen, James L. *Massachusetts in the War, 1861–1865.* Springfield, MA: Clark W. Bryan, 1889.

Bowditch, Vincent, ed. *Life and Correspondence of Henry Ingersoll Bowditch.* Boston: Houghton Mifflin, and Company, 1902.

Bradford, Sarah Hopkins. *Scenes in the Life of Harriet Tubman.* Auburn, NY: W. J. Moses Printer, 1869.

Brockett, Linus Pierpont. *The Life and Times of Abraham Lincoln Sixteenth President of the United States.* Philadelphia: Bradley, 1865.

Brooks, Noah. *Washington in Lincoln's Time.* New York: Century, 1896.

Brown, George Rothwell, ed. *Reminiscences of Senator William M. Stewart of Nevada.* New York: Neale, 1908.

Browne, Albert G., Jr. "Governor Andrew." *North American Review* 106 (Jan. 1868): 249–76.

——. *Sketch of the Official Life of John A. Andrew as Governor of Massachusetts.* New York: Hurd and Houghton, 1868.

Bruce, George A. *The Twentieth Regiment of Massachusetts Volunteer Infantry, 1861–1865*. Boston: Houghton Mifflin, 1906.

Buchanan, James Henry, ed. *The Messages of President Buchanan*. New York: Published by the Author, 1888.

Bulletins for the Constitutional Convention, 1917–1918. 2 vols. Boston: Wright and Potter, 1919.

———. *Address of His Excellency Alexander H. Bulloch to the Honorable Council on the Opinion of Presenting the Case of Edward W. Green, February 27, 1866*. Boston: Wright and Potter, 1866.

Burlingame, Michael, ed. *At Lincoln's Side: John Hay's Civil War Correspondence and Selected Writings*. Carbondale: Southern Illinois University Press, 2000.

———, ed. *Lincoln Observed: Civil War Dispatches of Noah Brooks*. Baltimore: Johns Hopkins University Press, 1998.

Burlingame, Michael, and John R. Turner Ettlinger, eds. *Inside Lincoln's White House: The Complete Civil War Diary of John Hay*. Carbondale: Southern Illinois University Press, 1997.

Burnham, Roderick H. *Genealogical Records of Henry and Ulalia Burt, the Emigrants Who Settled at Springfield, Mass., and Their Descendants Through Nine Generations*. Warwick, NY: Published by Miss Elizabeth Burt, 1892.

Burnham, Samuel. "Hon. John Albion Andrew." *New England Historic-Genealogical Register* (1869): 1–15.

Butler, Benjamin Franklin. *Butler's Book: Autobiography and Personal Reminiscences of Major-General Benjamin F. Butler*. Boston: A. M. Thayer, 1892.

Cabot, James Elliot. *Letter to the Governor of Massachusetts on Occasion of His Late Proclamation of August 20, 1861*. Boston: A. K. Loring, 1861.

Carpenter, Frank B. "How Lincoln Was Nominated." *Century Illustrated Magazine* 24 (Oct. 1888): 853–59.

"The Case of Anthony Burns." *MLR* 7 (Aug. 1854): 181–211.

"The Case of Thomas Sims," *MLR* 14 (May 1851): 1–16.

Catalogue of the Officers and Students of Bowdoin College and the Medical School of Maine, 1834. Brunswick: Press of Joseph Griffin, 1834.

Catalogue of the Officers and Students of Bowdoin College and the Medical School of Maine, 1836. Brunswick: Press of Joseph Griffin, 1836.

Catalogue of the Officers and Students of Bowdoin College and the Medical School of Maine, 1837. Brunswick: Press of Joseph Griffin, 1837.

Celebration by the Colored People's Educational Monument Association in Memory of Abraham Lincoln: On the Fourth of July, 1865 in the Presidential Grounds, Washington, D.C. Washington, D.C.: McGill and Witherow, 1865.

Ceremonials at the Unveiling of the Statue of Gov. John A. Andrew at the State House, Tuesday, February 14, 1871. Boston: Wright and Potter, 1871.

Chadwick, John White, ed. *A Life for Liberty: Anti-Slavery and Other Letters of Sallie Holley*. New York: G. P. Putnam's Sons, 1899.

Chamberlain, Daniel H. "Reconstruction in South Carolina." *Atlantic Monthly* 87 (1901): 473–84.

Chandler, Charles L. "Two Letters from Kansas, 1855–1856." *Mississippi Valley Historical Review* 29 (June 1942): 77–79.

Chandler, Horace P., ed. *Every Other Saturday: A Journal of Select Reading, New and Old*. 3 vols. Boston: Every Other, 1884.

Chandler, Peleg Whitman. *Memoir of Governor Andrew: With Personal Reminiscences*. Boston: Robert Brothers, 1881.

———. "Memoir of the Hon. John Albion Andrew, LL.D." *Proceedings of the Massachusetts Historical Society* 18 (1880–1881): 59.

Channing, William Ellery. *Memoir of William Ellery Channing*. 3 vols. Boston: W. M. Crosby and H. P. Nichols, 1848.

"Charles L. Mitchell," *The Crisis*, 58 (Mar. 1951): n.p.

Charles Sumner, His Complete Works. 20 vols. Boston: Lee and Shepard, 1900.

CIS Index to Presidential Executive Orders & Proclamations, Part 1: April 30, 1789 to Mar. 4, 1921, George Washington to Woodrow Wilson. Washington, D.C.: Congressional Information Service, 1987.

Clarke, James Freeman. *Anti-Slavery Days: A Sketch of the Struggle Which Ended in the Abolition of Slavery in the United States.* New York: John W. Lovell, 1883.

———. *Memorial and Biographical Sketches.* Boston: Houghton, Osgood, 1878.

Clarke, George Faber. *History of the Temperance Reform in Massachusetts, 1813-1883.* Boston: Little, Brown, 1866.

Cobbe, Frances Power, ed. *The Collected Works of Theodore Parker.* London: Trübner, 1864.

Collier, John S., and Bonnie B. Collire, eds. *Yours for the Union: The Civil War Letters of John W. Chase, First Massachusetts Light Artillery.* New York: Fordham University Press, 2004.

Comey, Richard, ed. *A Legacy of Valor: The Memoirs and Letters of Captain Henry Newton Comey, 2nd Massachusetts Infantry.* Knoxville: University of Tennessee Press, 2004.

Congdon, Charles Taber. *Reminiscences of a Journalist.* Boston: James R. Osgood, 1880.

"Constitution and Membership of the American Association for the Promotion of the Social Science, October 4, 1865." *The Radical* (Sept. 1866): 16–108.

Copeland, Robert Morris. *Statement of R. Morris Copeland, Asst. Adjutant General and Major of Volunteers.* Boston: Prentiss and Deland, 1864.

Craft, Ellen, and William Craft. *Running a Thousand Miles for Freedom; or, the Escape of William an Ellen Craft from Slavery.* London: William Tweedie, 1860.

Cramer, Jeffrey S. *"I to Myself": An Annotated Selection from the Journal of Henry David Thoreau.* New Haven: Yale University Press, 2007.

Cudworth, Warren H. *History of the First Regiment Massachusetts Infantry.* Boston: Walker, Fuller, 1866.

Curtis, George William, ed. *The Correspondence of John Lothrop Motley.* New York: Harper and Brothers, 1889.

Dana, Richard Henry, Jr. *Two Years before the Mast: A Personal Narrative of Life at Sea.* Boston: Harper and Brothers, 1840.

Dana, Richard Henry, III, ed. *Richard Henry Dana, Jr.: Speeches in Stirring Times and Letters to a Son.* Boston: Houghton Mifflin, 1910.

Daniels, William H., ed. *Graduated with Honor: Memorials of Gilbert Haven, Bishop of the Methodist Episcopal Church.* Boston: B. B. Russell, 1880.

Dean, Franklin H. "Undercurrents of the Great Rebellion." *The Hyde Park Historical Record.* Hyde Park, MA: The Hyde Park Historical Society, 1909.

Deane, Charles. "Memoir of Cyrus Woodman, A.M." *New-England Historical and Genealogical Register* 43 (Oct. 1889): 345.

Decisions of Hon. Peleg Sprague in Admiralty and Maritime Causes in the District Court of the United States for the District of Massachusetts, 1841-1861. Philadelphia: T & J. W., 1861.

Depew, Chauncey M. *The Library of the Oratory, Ancient and Modern.* 9 vols. New York: A. L. Fowle, 1902.

Dircks, Will H., ed. *Essays and Other Writings of Henry Thoreau.* London: Walter Scott, 1891.

Documents of the City of Boston for the Year 1867. Boston: Alfred Mudge and Son, 1868.

Documents Printed by the Order of the Senate of the Commonwealth of Massachusetts, 1867. Boston: Wright and Potter, 1867.

Documents Printed by the Order of the Senate of the Commonwealth of Massachusetts during the Session of the General Court, 1865. Boston: Wright and Potter, 1865.

Dole, Frederick Howard. *Sketches of the History of Windham, Maine, 1734-1935.* Westbrook, ME: H. S. Cobb, 1935.

Du Bois, W. E. B. *Black Reconstruction in America: An Essay Toward a History of the Part Which Black Folk Played in the Attempt to Reconstruct Democracy in America, 1860-1880.* New York: Harcourt, Brace, 1935.

Duncan, Russell, ed. *Blue-Eyed Child of Fortune: The Civil War Letters of Colonel Robert Gould Shaw*. Athens: University of Georgia Press, 1992.

"Education and Literary Institutions: May 1833." *American Quarterly Register* 4 (May 1833): 273.

Egle, William E. *Andrew Gregg Curtin: His Life and Services*. Philadelphia: Thompson, 1896.

Eleventh Annual Report of the Massachusetts School for the Idiotic and Feeble-Minded Youth. Boston: William White, 1858.

Ellis, Arthur Blake. *George S. Hale, A. M.: A Memoir*. Cambridge, MA: University Press, 1899.

Ely, Alfred. *Journal of Alfred Ely, A Prisoner of War in Richmond*. New York: D. Appleton, 1862.

The Emancipation League. *Facts Concerning the Freedom. Their Capacity and Their Destiny*. Boston: Press of Commercial Printing House, 1863.

Emerson, Edward Waldo. *The Early Years of the Saturday Club, 1855–1870*. Boston: Houghton Mifflin, 1918.

Emerson, Edward Waldo, and Waldo Emerson Forbes, eds. *Journals of Ralph Waldo Emerson, with Annotations*. 15 vols. Boston: Houghton Mifflin, 1909–1914.

Emerson, Ralph Waldo, W. H. Channing, and J. F. Clarke, eds. *Memoirs of Margaret Fuller Ossoli*. 2 vols. Boston: Robert Brothers, 1884.

Emery, George. "Cyrus Woodman: A Memoir Read before the Maine Historical Society, November 21, 1889." *Collections and Proceedings of the Maine Historical Society* 1 (1890): 113–24.

Emilio, Luis F. *A Brave Black Regiment: The History of the Fifty-fourth Regiment of Massachusetts*. Boston: Boston Book, 1894.

Ewer, James Kendell. *The Third Massachusetts Cavalry in the War for the Union*. Boston: Historical Commission of the Regimental Association, 1903.

Fairbanks, Lorenzo Sayles. *The Laws of the Commonwealth of Massachusetts Relating to Marriage and Divorce*. Boston: Soule and Bugbee, 1882.

Fair-Play. *The True State of the American Question: Reply to Mr. Thurlow Weed*. London: Robert Hardwicke, 1862.

Fields, Annie, ed. *James T. Fields: Biographical Notes and Personal Sketches*. Boston: Houghton Mifflin, 1882.

Folsom, Charles F. "Henry Ingersoll Bowditch." *American Academy of Arts and Sciences, Boston Proceedings* 28 (May 1892–May 1893): 310–32.

Ford, Andrew Elmer. *The Story of the Fifteenth Regiment Massachusetts Volunteer Infantry in the Civil War, 1861–1864*. Clinton, MA: Press of W. J. Coulter, 1898.

Ford, Worthington C., ed. *A Cycle of Adams Letters, 1861–1865*. 2 vols. Boston: Houghton Mifflin, 1920.

———, ed. *Letters of Henry Adams*. Boston: Houghton Mifflin, 1930.

———, ed. "Sumner's Letters to Governor Andrew, 1861." *Proceedings of the Massachusetts Historical Society* 60 (Apr. 1927): 223–33.

———, ed. *War Letters, 1862–1865 of John Chipman Gray and John Codman Ropes*. Boston: Houghton Mifflin, 1927.

Forty-Second Annual Report of the Executive Committee of the Children's Mission to the Children of the Destitute in the City of Boston. Boston: Rooms of the Children's Mission, 1891.

"Frank E. Howe." *The Portrait Monthly*. New York: T. B. Leggett, 1864.

"The Free Soil Party and the Late Election." *Massachusetts Quarterly Review* 2 (Dec. 1849): 105–27.

Fuller, Richard Frederick. *Recollections of Richard Frederick Fuller*. Boston: Printed Privately, 1936.

Garrison, Wendell Phillips, and Francis Jackson Garrison. *William Lloyd Garrison, 1805–1879: The Story of His Life Told By his Children*. 4 vols. Boston: Houghton Mifflin, 1894.

General Catalogue of Bowdoin College and the Medical School of Maine, 1794–1912. Brunswick, ME: Published by the College, 1912.

General Laws and Resolves Passed by the Legislature of Massachusetts During the Session of 1865. Boston: Wright and Potter, 1866.

Gienapp, William E., and Erica L. Gienapp, eds. The Civil War Diary of Gideon Welles: Lincoln's Secretary of Navy. Champaign-Urbana: University of Illinois Press, 2014.

Giesberg, Judith Ann, and Randall M. Miller, eds. Women and the American Civil War: North-South Counterpoints. Kent: Kent State University Press, 2018.

Goodall, Henry H. "The Massachusetts Agricultural College." New England Magazine 3 (Sept. 1890–Feb. 1891): 224–31.

Gooding, James Henry, ed. On the Altar of Freedom: A Black Soldier's Civil War Letters from the Front. Amherst: University of Massachusetts Press, 1991.

Goodrich, Frank B. A Tribute Book. New York: Derby and Miller, 1865.

Graf, LeRoy P., and Ralph W. Haskins, eds. The Papers of Andrew Johnson. 16 vols. Knoxville: University of Tennessee Press, 1967–2000.

Grant, Mary Hetherington, ed. Private Woman, Public Person: An Account of the Life of Julia Ward Howe from 1819 to 1868. Brooklyn: Carlson, 1994.

Gray, Horace, Jr. Reports of Cases Argued and Determined in the Supreme Judicial Court of Massachusetts. 16 vols. Boston: Little, Brown, 1866.

Gray, Jane Loring, ed. Letters of Asa Gray. Boston: Houghton Mifflin, 1894.

Griffin, Solomon B. People and Politics Observed by a Massachusetts Editor. Boston: Little, Brown, 1923.

Griffis, William Elliot. Charles Carleton Coffin, War Correspondent, Traveller, Author, and Statesman. Boston: Estes and Lauriat, 1898.

Grimké, Archibald H. The Ballotless Victim of One-Party Governments. Washington, D.C.: Published by the American Negro Academy, 1913.

Gurowski, Adam. Diary from March 4, 1861, to November 12, 1862. Boston: Lee and Shepard, 1862.

Guthrie, James. Camp-Fires of the Afro-American. Philadelphia: Afro-American, 1899.

Hale, Edward Everett, ed. James Freeman Clarke: Autobiography, Diary, and Correspondence. Boston: Houghton Mifflin, 1891.

———. James Russell Lowell and His Friends. Boston: Houghton Mifflin, 1899.

———. The Story of Massachusetts. Boston: D. Lothrop Company, 1891.

———. The Story of the Battle Hymn of the Republic. New York: Harper and Brothers, 1916.

Hallowell, Norwood P. "The Negro as a Soldier in the War of the Rebellion." Papers of the Military Historical Society of Massachusetts 13 (1913): 301.

———. "The Negro as Soldier." In Selected Letters and Papers of N. P. Hallowell. Petersborough, NH: Richard R. Smith, 1963.

Halstead, Murat, ed. Caucuses of 1860: A History of the National Political Conventions of the Current Presidential Campaign. Columbus: Follett, Foster, 1860.

Hamilton, James Alexander. Reminiscences of James A. Hamilton. New York: Charles Scribner, 1869.

Hamilton, Luther, ed. Memoirs, Speeches, and Writings of Robert Rantoul, Jr. Boston: John P. Jewett, 1854.

Harlan, Louis R., and Raymond W. Smock, eds. Booker T. Washington Papers. 14 vols. Urbana: University of Illinois Press, 1972–89.

Harris, Thomas L. The Trent Affair. Indianapolis: Bowen-Merrill Company, 1896.

Harris, William C. Prison Life in the Tobacco Warehouse at Richmond. Philadelphia: George W. Childs, 1862.

Harrison, Frederick G. Biographical Sketches of Preeminent Americans. Boston: W. W. Walker, 1893.

Hartman, Lee Foster, and Thomas Bucklin Wells. "John Albion Andrew of Massachusetts by a Member of his Church." Harper's New Monthly Magazine 36 (Dec. 1867–May 1868): 324–28.

Harwood, William Sumner. Life and Letters of Austin Craig. New York: Fleming H. Revell Company, 1908.

Haven, Gilbert, and Thomas Russell. *Father Taylor, the Sailor Preacher*. Boston: B. B. Russell, 1872.

Hayden, Lewis. *Caste among Masons: Address before Prince Hall Grand Lodge*. Boston: Edward S. Coombs, 1866.

Headley, Phineas Camp. *Massachusetts in the Rebellion: A Record of the Historical Position of the Commonwealth and the Services of the leading Statesmen, the Military, the Colleges, and the People, in the Civil War of 1861–1865*. Boston: Walker, Fuller, 1866.

Hedge, Frederic H. "John Albion Andrew." *Monthly Religious Magazine* 38 (Dec. 1867): 435.

Helper, Hinton Rowan. *Impending Crisis of the South*. New York: A. B. Burdick Publishers, 1857.

Higginson, Thomas Wentworth. *Army Life in a Black Regiment*. Boston: Fields, Osgood, 1870.

———. *Massachusetts in the Army and Navy During the War of 1861–1865*. 2 vols. Boston: Wright and Potter, 1896.

Hines, Harvey Kimball. *Illustrated History of the State of Washington*. Chicago: Lewis, 1893.

Hinsdale, Burke Aaron. *Horace Mann and the Common School Revival in the United States*. New York: Charles Scribner's Sons, 1898.

"Historical Notices of Thomas Fuller and his Descendants, with a Genealogy of the Fuller Family." *New-England Historical and Genealogical Register* 12 (Oct. 1859): 351–60.

Hoar, George Frisbie. *Book of Patriotism*. Boston: Hall and Locke, 1902.

The Hoosac Tunnel and Troy Greenfield Railroad, 1862–1863. Boston: Wright and Potter 1863.

Howe, Henry Warren. *Passages from the Life of Henry Warren Howe: Consisting of Diary and Letters Written During the Civil War, 1861–1865*. Lowell, MA: Courier-Citizen Co. Printers, 1899.

Howe, Julia Ward. "The Great Agitation. IV. Recollections of the Antislavery Struggle." *Cosmopolitan* 7 (July 1889): 278–88.

———. *Reminiscences 1819–1899*. Boston: Houghton Mifflin, 1900. Reprinted by New American Library, 1969.

———. "Reminiscences of Julia Ward Howe." *Atlantic Monthly* 83 (May 1899): 701–12.

———. "What Life Means to Me." *Cosmopolitan* 41 (July 1906): 285–89.

Hubbell, George Allen. *Horace Mann: Educator, Patriot, and Reformer*. Philadelphia: William F. Fell, 1910.

Hughes, Sarah Forbes, ed. *Letters (Supplementary) of John Murray Forbes*. Boston: George H. Ellis, 1905.

———, ed. *Reminiscences of John Murray Forbes*. 3 vols. Boston: George H. Ellis, 1902.

Index to the Executive Documents Printed by Order of the Senate of the United States, First and Second Sessions, Thirty-Fourth Congress, 1866–56. 2 vols. Washington, D.C.: A. O. P. Nicholson, 1856.

Index to the Senate Executive Documents for the First Session of the Thirty-Ninth Congress of the United States of America, 1866. Washington, D.C.: Government Printing Office, 1866.

Index to the Reports of the Committees of the Senate of the United States, for the Second Session of the Forty-Second Congress, 1871–'72. Washington, D.C.: Government Printing Office, 1872.

"Intelligence: New Religious Newspaper." *Monthly Miscellany of Religion and Letters* 8 (Feb. 1843): 125.

"James Freeman Clarke to Mr. Shippen, July 13, 1886." *Unitarian: A Monthly Magazine of Liberal Christianity* 1 (Aug. 1886): 221.

John A. Andrew Monument Association. *Memorial Volume Containing the Exercises at the Dedication of the Statue of John A. Andrew at Hingham, October 8, 1875*. Boston: John A. Andrew Monument Association. 1875.

Johnson, Arnold Burges. "Charles Sumner." *Cosmopolitan* 3 (1887): 146–47.

Johnson, Elmer H., ed. *The Professional Convict's Tale: The Survival of John O' Neill In and Out of Prison*. Carbondale: Southern Illinois University Press, 2007.

Johnson, Samuel. "George L. Stearns." *The Radical* (June 1867): 611–22.

Jordan, F. "The Occupation of Fort Sumter, and Hoisting the Old Flag Thereon, April 14,

1865." *United Service: A Quarterly Review of Military and Naval Affairs* 14 (Nov. 1895): 406–26.

Journal of the House of Representatives of the Commonwealth of Massachusetts, 1855. Boston: William White, 1855.

Julian, George W. "Political Recollections and Notes." *International Review* 1 (Oct. 1882): 321.

King, Moses. *Kings Handbook of Boston, 1881.* Cambridge: Moses King, 1881.

Langston, John Mercer. *From the Virginia Plantation to the National Capital.* Hartford: American, 1894. Reprint 1969.

"Letter from Gov. Andrew," *Old and New* 3 (Feb. 1871): 211–13.

"Letter of John A. Andrew." *Proceedings of the Massachusetts Historical Society* 49 (Oct. 1915–June 1916): 2.

Lincoln, George, and Fearing Burr. *The Town of Hingham in the Late Civil War, with Sketches of Its Soldiers and Sailors.* Hingham: Published by Order of the Town, 1876.

List of the Executive and Legislative Departments of the Government of the Commonwealth of Massachusetts, 1862. Boston: William White, 1862.

Livermore, George. *An Historical Research Respecting the Opinions of the Founders of the Republic on Negroes as Slaves, as Citizens, and as Soldiers.* Boston: A Williams, 1862.

Livingston, John. *Biographical Sketches of Distinguished Americans, Now Living.* New York: Broadway, 1853.

"Locomotive Traction." *The Engineer* 14 (July–Dec. 1862): 4.

Long, John Davis. *After-Dinner and Other Speeches.* Boston: Houghton Mifflin, 1895.

Longfellow, Samuel, ed. *Life of Henry Wadsworth Longfellow.* 3 vols. Boston: Ticknor, 1886.

Longley, Max. *For the Union and the Catholic Church: Four Converts in the Civil War.* Jefferson, NC: McFarland, 2015.

Lucid, Robert F., ed. *The Journal of Richard Henry Dana, Jr.* 3 vols. Cambridge: Harvard University Press, 1968.

Lunt, George. *The Origin of the Late War: Traced from the Beginning of the Constitution to the Revolt of the Southern States.* New York: D. Appleton, 1866.

Macleôd, Norman, ed. *Good Works for 1864.* London: Publishing Office, 1864.

Maine Minutes: General Conference and Maine Missionary Society 1892: General Conference of the Congregational Churches in Maine 66 (1892): 111–12.

Mann, Jonathan B. *The Life of Henry Wilson, Republican Candidate for Vice-President.* Boston: James R. Osgood, 1872.

Marshall, Jessie Ames, ed. *Private & Official Correspondence of Gen. Benjamin F. Butler, during the Period of the Civil War.* 5 vols. Norwood, MA: Plimpton Press, 1917.

"Massachusetts Agricultural College: Industrial Education is the Price of Industrial Supremacy." *Scribner's Monthly* 12 (Oct. 1876): 836–49.

"The Massachusetts Board of State Charities, and the Westborough Reform School." *Christian Examiner* 83 (1867): 118.

Massachusetts House of Representatives, House Report, No. 167. Boston: State Printers, 1855.

Massachusetts Senate Documents, 1861. Boston: William White, 1861.

Massachusetts Senate Documents, 1862. Boston: William White, 1862.

The Massachusetts Teacher; A Journal of School and Home Education. Boston: Mass. Teachers' Association, 1865.

McClellan, George B. *McClellan's Own Story: The War for the Union.* New York: Charles L. Webster, 1887.

McClure, Alexander Kelly. *Abraham Lincoln and Men of War-Times.* Philadelphia: Time, 1892.

McClure, Colonel Alexander. *Recollections of Half a Century.* Salem, MA: Salem Press, 1902.

McMaster, John Bach. "The Riotous Career of the Know Nothings." *Forum* (July 1894): 524–37.

McNeily, John Seymore. "From Organization to Overthrow of Mississippi's Provisional Government, 1865–1868." In *Publications of the Mississippi Historical Society*, edited by Dunbar Rowland, 9–403. Jackson: Mississippi Historical Society, 1916.

Mellen, Grenville. "The Marty's Triumph, the Buried, and Other Poems," *American Quarterly Review* (Sept. 1, 1837): 194–98.

Memorial Biographies of the New England Historic Genealogical Society, 1845–1852. 9 vols. Boston: Published by the Society, 1880.

Memorial of the European and North American Railway Company to the Legislature of Massachusetts, January 1865. Boston: Wright and Potter, 1865.

A Memorial of the Hon. Charles Allen from His Children. Cambridge: Press of John Wilson and Son, 1870.

Merriam, George S. *The Life and Times of Samuel Bowles.* 2 vols. New York: Century, 1885.

Merrill, Walter M., and Louis Ruchames, eds. *The Letters of William Lloyd Garrison.* 6 vols. Cambridge: Belknap Press of Harvard University Press, 1981.

Meyer, Howard N. *Colonel of the Black Regiment: The Life of Thomas Wentworth Higginson.* New York: W. W. Norton, 1967.

Miner, Alonzo Ames, and R. C. Pitman. *Shall Criminals Sit on the Jury: A Review of Governor Andrew's Veto.* Boston: Massachusetts Temperance Alliance, 1865.

Minutes of the General Conference of Maine at Their Annual Meeting in Gorham, June 1828. Portland: Shirley and Hyde, 1828.

The Monument to Colonel Robert Gould Shaw: Its Inception, Completion, and Unveiling, 1865–1897. Boston: Houghton Mifflin, 1897.

Moore, Frank, ed. *The Rebellion Record: A Diary of Events with Document, Narratives, Illustrative Incidents, Poetry, Etc.* 9 vols. New York: G. P. Putnam, 1862.

Moore, John Bassett, ed. *The Works of James Buchanan.* 11 vols. Philadelphia: Lippincott, 1910.

Morison, John Hopkins. *A Sermon Preached at the Installation of Rev. George W. Briggs as Pastor of the First Church in Salem, by Rev. Mr. Morison of Milton.* Salem: Gazette Press, 1853.

Morse, John Torrey, Jr., ed. *Life and Letters of Oliver Wendell Holmes.* 2 vols. Cambridge: Printed at the Riverside Press, 1896.

——, ed. *Memoir of Colonel Henry Lee: With Selections from His Writings and Speeches.* Boston: Little, Brown, 1905.

Mott, Wesley T. "The Eloquence of Father Taylor: A Rare 1846 Eyewitness Report." *New England Quarterly* 70, no. 1 (Mar. 1997): 102–13.

Murray, William Henry Harrison. *Prohibition vs. License: A Review of Ex-Gov. Andrew's Argument for License.* New York: John J. Reed Printer, 1867.

Nason, Elias. *Discourse Delivered before the New England Historic-Genealogical Society, Boston, April 2, 1868, on the Character and Life of the Hon. John Albion Andrew, LL.D.* Boston: New England Historic-Genealogical Society, 1868.

Nason, Elias, and Thomas Russell. *The Life of Henry Wilson.* Boston: B. B. Russell, 1876.

Nicolay, John G., and John Hay, eds. *Complete Works of Abraham Lincoln.* 12 vols. New York: Francis D. Tandy, 1905.

Niven, John, ed. *The Salmon P. Chase Papers.* 5 vols. Kent: Kent State University Press, 1993.

"Obituary Notice for Henry Holton Fuller." *MLR* 6 (Oct. 1852): 354–60.

Olsavsky, Jesse Joseph. "Fire and Sword Will Affect More Good: Runaways, Vigilance Committees, the Rise of the Revolutionary Abolitionism: 1835–1860." PhD diss., University of Pittsburgh, 2019.

"Open Letters." *Century Magazine* 47 (Nov. 1893): 637.

The Opinion of Judge Story in the Case of William Allen vs. Joseph McKeen; Treasurer of Bowdoin College. Boston: Office of the Daily Advertiser and Patriot, 1833.

Palmer, Beverly Wilson, ed. *The Selected Letters of Charles Sumner.* Boston: Northeastern University Press, 1990.

Parker, Francis Jewett. *The Story of the Thirty-Second Regiment Massachusetts Infantry.* Boston: C. W. Calkins, 1880.

Parker, Theodore. *The Boston Kidnapping: A Discourse to Commemorate the Rendition of Thomas Simms, Delivered of the First Anniversary Thereof, April 12, 1852, Before the*

Committee of Vigilance, at the Melodeon in Boston. Boston: Crosby, Nicholas, 1852. Reprinted by Arno Press, 1969.

———. *Ten Sermons of Religion.* Boston: Crosby, Nichols, 1853.

Parsons, Theophilus. *Re-organization of the Rebel States, Public Meeting in Faneuil Hall, June 21, 1865.* Boston: S. N., 1865.

Pattee, William Sullivan. *Illustrative Cases in Reality.* Philadelphia: T. and J. W. Johnson, 1986.

Peabody, Andrew P. *Memoir of James Freeman Clarke.* Cambridge: John Wilson and Son, 1889.

Phillips, Wendell. *Disunion: Two Discourses at Music Hall on January 20ᵗʰ and February 17, 1861.* Boston: Robert F. Walcott, 1861.

Phrenological Journal and Life Illustrated 55 (July 1872): 5.

Pickard, John B., ed. *The Letters of John Greenleaf Whittier.* 3 vols. Cambridge: Belknap Press of Harvard University Press, 1975.

Pickard, Samuel Thomas. *Life and Letters of John Greenleaf Whittier.* 2 vols. Boston: Houghton Mifflin, 1894.

Pierce, Edward Lillie, ed. *Memoirs and Letters of Charles Sumner.* 4 vols. London: Sampson Low, Marston, Searle, and Rivington, 1878.

Pierce, Josiah. *An Address Delivered on the Twenty-sixth of May, the Centennial Anniversary of the Settlement of Gorham.* Portland: Charles Day, 1836.

Piper, John J. *Facts and Figures Concerning the Hoosac Tunnel.* Fitchburg: John J. Piper Printer, 1866.

Pittman, A. A., and R. C. Miner. *Shall Criminals Sit on the Jury: A Review of Governor Andrew's Veto.* Boston: Published by the Massachusetts Temperance Alliance, 1865.

The Poetical Works of Lord Byron, Complete. London: John Murray, 1867.

Preble, George Henry. *Our Flag: Origin and Progress of the Flag of the United States.* Albany, NY: Joel Munsell, 1872.

Private and Special Statutes of the Commonwealth of Massachusetts from the Year 1780, to the Close of the Session of the General Court, 1805. 3 vols. Boston: Manning and Loring, 1805.

Proceedings of the First Three Republican National Conventions of 1856, 1860 and 1864. Minneapolis: Harrison and Smith, 1893.

Proceedings of the National Convention of Colored Men, Held in the City of Syracuse, N.Y., October 4, 5, 6, and 7, 1864. Boston: J. S. Rock and Geo. L. Ruffin, 1864.

Proceedings of the Thursday-Evening Club, on the Occasion of the Death of Hon. Edward Everett, 1865. Boston: Wilson and Son, 1865.

Proceedings of the Twenty-Second Annual Meeting of the Association for the Support of the Warren Street Chapel, 1859. Boston: Geo C. Rand and Avery, 1859.

Putnam, Elizabeth C. "Massachusetts State Care of Children." *Survey* 13 (Oct. 1904–Mar. 1905): 360–61.

———, ed. *Memoirs of the War of '61: Colonel Charles Russell Lowell, Friends and Cousins.* Boston: Press of George H. Ellis, 1920.

Randolph, Peter. *From Slave Cabin to the Pulpit: The Autobiography of Rev. Peter Randolph.* Boston: James H. Earle Publishers, 1893.

Redpath, James. *Shall We Suffocate Ed. Green?* Boston: J. Redpath, 1864.

"The Removal of Judge Loring," *MLR* 18 (May 1855): 1–17.

Reno, Conrad, ed. *Memoirs of the Judiciary and the Bar of New England for the Nineteenth Century.* 2 vols. Boston: Century Memorial, 1901.

Report of Auditor of Accounts of the Commonwealth of Massachusetts. Boston: Wright and Potter, 1865.

Report of the Boston Society for Aiding Discharged Convicts. Boston: William White, 1857.

Report of the Select Committee of the Senate Appointed to Inquire into the Late Invasion and Seizure of the Public Property at Harper's Ferry, 36 Congress, 1ˢᵗ Session. Washington, D.C.: Government Printing Office, 1860.

Report of the Select Committee to Investigate the Alleged Credit Mobilier Bribery: Made to the House of Representatives, Feb. 18, 1873. Washington, D.C.: Government Printing Office, 1873.

Reports of Cases Determined in the Circuit Court of the United States for the First Circuit. 3 vol. Boston: Little, Brown, 1878.

Report on the Hoosac Tunnel and Troy and Greenfield Railroad by the Joint Standing Committee of 1866. Boston: Wright and Potter, 1867.

Reports of Controverted Elections in the Senate and House of Representatives of the Commonwealth of Massachusetts from 1853–1885. Boston: Wright & Potter, 1886.

Reunion of the Free-Soilers of 1848, at Downer Landing, Hingham, Mass., August 9, 1877. Boston: Albert J. Wright, 1877.

Richards, Laura E., ed. *Letters and Journals of Samuel Gridley Howe.* 2 vols. Boston: Dana Estes, 1909.

Richards, William C. *Great in Goodness: A Memoir of George N. Briggs.* Boston: Gould and Lincoln, 1866.

Ripley, C. Peter, et al., eds. *The Black Abolitionist Papers.* 5 vols. Chapel Hill: University of North Carolina Press, 1992.

Robinson, Harriet H., ed. *"Warrington" Pen Portraits: A Collection of Personal and Political Reminiscences from 1848 to 1876, from the Writings of William S. Robinson.* Boston: Lee and Shepard Publishers, 1877.

———. "William S. Robinson ('Warrington')." *New England Historical and Genealogical Register* 39 (Oct. 1855): 313–25.

Robinson, William S. *A Conspiracy to Defame John A. Andrew Being a Review of the Proceedings of Joel Parks, Linus Child and Leverett Saltonstall, at the People's Convention Held in Boston, Oct. 7, 1862.* Boston: Wright and Potter, 1862.

Rogers, Emma, ed. *Life and Letters of William Barton Rogers.* 2 vols. Boston: Houghton Mifflin, 1896.

Ronda, Bruce A., ed. *Letters of Elizabeth Palmer Peabody: American Renaissance Woman.* Middletown, CT: Wesleyan University Press, 1984.

Ropes, Hannah Anderson. *Six Months in Kansas: By a Lady.* Boston: John P. Jewett, 1856.

Roth, Ralf, and Colin Divall, eds. *From Rail to Road and Back Again: A Century of Transport Competition and Interdependency.* London: Ashgate, 1915.

Ruschenberger, Surgeon William. "Naval Staff Rank." *United States Service Magazine* 3 (Apr. 1865): 356–70.

Rusk, Ralph L., ed. *The Letters of Ralph Waldo Emerson.* 6 vols. New York: Columbia University Press, 1939.

Russell, Thomas, and Elias Nason. *The Life and Public Services of Hon. Henry Wilson.* Boston: B. B. Russell, 1872.

Ryan, David D. *A Yankee Spy in Richmond: The Civil War Diary of "Crazy Bet" Van Lew.* Mechanicsburg, PA: Stackpole Books, 1996.

Samuels, Ernest, ed. *Henry Adams, Selected Letters.* Cambridge: Belknap Press of Harvard University Press, 1992.

Sanborn, Frank B. "Comment by a Radical." *Century Illustrated Magazine* 26 (July 1883): 416–18.

———. *Dr. S. G. Howe: The Philanthropist.* New York: Funk and Wagnalls, 1891.

———, ed. *The Public Charities of Massachusetts during the Century Ending Jan. 1, 1876.* Boston: Wright and Potter, 1876.

———, ed. *Recollections of Seventy Years.* 2 vols. Boston: Gorham Press, 1909.

———, ed. *Reports on the Status of Paupers in Massachusetts, 1858–1863.* Boston: Wright and Potter, 1865.

"Sanborn's Case." *MLR* 23 (May 1860): 7–20.

Sanger, George P., ed. *The Statutes at Large, Treaties and Proclamations of the United States of America from December 5, 1859, to March 3, 1863.* Boston: Little, Brown, 1863.

Sargent, Horace Binney. *Memorial Address Delivered before the John Albion Andrew Monument Association at Hingham, October 8, 1875*. Boston: Press of Rockwell and Churchill, 1875.

———. *The Return of the Standards: To His Excellency John A. Andrew, Who Suggested the First Provision of Two Thousand Soldiers' Overcoats in the Winter*. Boston, 1866.

Scharnhorst, Gary. *Kate Field: The Many Lives of a Nineteenth-Century American Journalist*. Syracuse: Syracuse University Press, 2008.

Schouler, William. *A History of Massachusetts in the Civil War*. Boston: E. P. Dutton, 1868.

Sears, Stephen W., ed. *The Civil War Papers of George B. McClellan: Selected Correspondence, 1860–1865*. New York: Da Capo Press, 1992.

Second Annual Report of the Boston Society for Aiding Discharged Convicts. Boston: White and Potter, 1848.

Seguin, Edward. *Idiocy and Its Treatment by the Physiological Method*. New York: William Wood, 1866.

Seilhamer, George O. *History of the Republican Party*. 3 vols. New York: Judge, n.d.

"Selections from Charles Francis Adams Correspondence." *Proceedings of the Massachusetts Historical Society* 55 (Oct. 1911–June 1912): 94.

The Senate of the Commonwealth of Massachusetts During the Session of the General Court, 1844. Boston: Dutton and Wentworth, 1844.

Senator Wilson's Speech on Prohibition, Tremont Temple, April 15, 1867. Boston: Mass. Temperance Alliance, 1867.

Shackelford, George G., ed. "From the Society's Collections: Attorneys Andrew of Boston and Green of Richmond Consider the John Brown Raid." *The Virginia Magazine of History and Biography* 60, no. 1 (Jan. 1952): 89–114.

Shannon, Fred Albert. *The Organization and Administration of the Union Army, 1861–1865*. Cleveland: Arthur H. Clarke, 1928.

Shapiro, Samuel. "The Rendition of Anthony Burns." *Journal of Negro History* 44, no. 1 (Jan. 1959): 34–51.

Shillaber, Benjamin P. "Experiences during Many Years." *New England Magazine* 9 (Sept. 1893–94): 628.

Shoemaker, Henry W. *The Last of the War Governors*. Altoona, PA: Altoona Tribune, 1916.

Shotwell, Walter Gaston. *Life of Charles Sumner*. New York: Thomas Y. Crowell, 1910.

Shrady, George Frederick. *Medical Record: A Weekly Journal of Medicine and Surgery* 40 (July 4, 1891–Dec. 26, 1891): 626.

Siebert, Wilbur Henry. *The Vigilance Committee of Boston: A Paper Read in the Council Chamber of the Old State House at a Meeting of the Bostonian Society*. Boston, 1953.

Simon, John Y., ed. *The Papers of Ulysses S. Grant*. 31 vols. Carbondale: Southern Illinois University Press, 1967–1999.

Simpson, Brooks D., and Jean Berlin, eds. *Sherman's Civil War: Selected Correspondence of William T. Sherman, 1860–1865*. Chapel Hill: University of North Carolina Press, 1999.

Smalley, George W. "Memoirs of Wendell Phillips." *Harper's Magazine* 94 (June 1894): 137–45.

Smyth, Egbert Coffin. *Three Discourses Upon the Religious History of Bowdoin College during the Presidents McKeen, Appleton, & Allen*. Brunswick: J. Griffin, 1858.

Speeches of John A. Andrew at Hingham and Boston, His Testimony before the Harper's Ferry Committee of the Senate, in Relation to John Brown, also the Republican Platform and Other Matters. Boston: Order of the Republican State Committee, 1860.

Speech of Hon. Robert C. Winthrop, Delivered at the Ratification Meeting in Music Hall, Sept. 25, 1860. Boston, 1860.

Spurgeon, Charles H. *Broad Churchism*. London: Houlston and Wright, 1866.

Stackpole, J. L. "The Early Days of Charles Sumner." *American Law Review* 13 (Apr. 1879): 405–18.

Stearns, Frank Preston. *Cambridge Sketches*. Philadelphia: J. B. Lippincott, 1905.

———. *The Life and Public Services of George Luther Stearns*. Philadelphia: J. B. Lippincott, 1907.

Stephenson, Luther, Jr. *Address and Papers*. Togus, ME, 1885.

Stone, Eben F. "Sketch of John Albion Andrew, Paper Read before the Essex Institute, December 2, 1889." *Historical Collections of the Essex Institute* 27 (Jan.–Mar. 1890): 1–30.

Story, Moorfield, and Edward Waldo Emerson. *Ebenezer Rockwood Hoar: A Memoir.* Boston: Houghton Mifflin, 1911.

Stowe, Harriet Beecher. *The Lives and Deeds of Our Self-Made Men.* 2 vols. Hartford: Worthington, Dustin, 1872.

Sumner, Charles, ed. *The Works of Charles Sumner.* 2 vols. Boston: Lee and Shepard, 1875.

Tarbell, Ida. *The Life of Abraham Lincoln.* 2 vols. New York: S. S. McClure, 1895.

Testimony Taken by the Joint Select Committee to Inquire into the Condition of Affairs in the Late Insurrectionary States, Alabama, Report of Committees of the House of Representatives for the Second Session of the Forty-Second Congress, 1871–1872. 4 vols. Washington, D.C.: Government Printing Office, 1872.

Thomas, John Wesley. "The Conversational Club." *New England Quarterly* 16, no. 2 (June 1943): 296–98.

———. *James Freeman Clarke: Apostle of German Culture to America.* Boston: J. W. Luce, 1949.

Transactions of the New-York State Agricultural Society, 1865. Albany: Cornelius Wendell, 1865.

Trial and Execution of Washington Goode. Boston: Skinner's Publications Rooms, 1849.

Trial of Orrin De Wolfe for the Murder of Wm. Stiles at Worcester, Jan. 14, 1845, Including Its Confession. Worcester: Thomas Dew Jr., 1845.

The Trial of Theodore Parker for the Misdemeanor of a Speech in Faneuil Hall Against Kidnapping before the Circuit Court of the United States, April 3, 1854. Boston: Published for the author, 1855.

Trial of Thomas Sims on an Issue of Personal Liberty, Arguments of Robert Rantoul, Jr. and Charles G. Loring with the Decision of George T. Curtis, Boston, April 7–11, 1851. Boston: Wm. S. Damrell, 1851.

Trudeau, Noah Andre, ed. *Voices of the 55th: Letters from the 55th Massachusetts Volunteers, 1861–1865.* Dayton, OH: Morningside, 1996.

Twentieth Annual Report of the Boston Port Society for the Year 1848–9. Boston: Eastburn Press, 1849.

Twenty-eighth Annual Report of the American Anti-Slavery Society 1861. New York: American Anti-Slavery Society, 1861.

Underwood, Francis Henry. *James Russell Lowell: A Biographical Sketch.* Boston: James R. Osgood, 1882.

United States Magazine and Democratic Review 29 (July 1851): 72.

Upton, Emory. *The Military Policy of the United States.* Washington, D.C.: Government Printing Office, 1904.

U.S. Congress Committee on Foreign Relations. *Compilation of Reports of Committee, 1789–1901, First Congress, First Session, to Fifty-sixth Congress, Second Session.* Washington, D.C.: Government Printing Office, 1901.

U.S. Statutes at Large, Treaties, and Proclamations of the United States. Boston: Little, Brown, 1866.

U.S. War Department. *Preliminary Report Touching the Condition and Management of Emancipated Refugees Made to the Secretary of War by the American Freedman's Inquiry Commission, June 30, 1863.* New York: J. F. Trow, 1863.

U.S. War Department. *War of Rebellion: A Compilation of the Official Records of the Union and Confederate Armies.* 128 vols. Washington, D.C.: Government Printing Office, 1880–1901. (Abbreviated as OR throughout text.)

Wall, Caleb Arnold. *Reminiscences of Worcester.* Worcester, MA: Tyler and Seagrave, 1877.

"War Letters of Charles P. Bowditch." *Massachusetts Historical Society Proceedings* 57 (1923–24): 415–16.

Warner, Oliver, ed. *Abstract of the Census of Massachusetts, 1865.* Boston: Wright and Potter, 1867.

Washington, Booker T. *Up from Slavery: An Autobiography.* New York: Doubleday, Page, 1907.

Weeks, Lyman H. *Prominent Families of New York.* New York: Historical Company, 1898.

Weiss, John, ed. *Life and Correspondence of Theodore Parker*. 2 vols. New York: D. Appleton, 1864.

Welles, Gideon. *Lincoln and Seward*. New York: Sheldon, 1874. Reprinted by Massachusetts Historical Society, 1979.

Wesley, Dorothy Porter, and Constance Porter Uzelac, ed. *William Copper Nell: Nineteenth-Century African American Abolitionist, Historian, Integrationist: Selected Writings from 1832–1874*. Baltimore: Black Classic Press, 2002.

Wheelwright, Edmund M. "Hon. John Forrester Andrew, L.L.B." *Publications of the Colonial Society of Massachusetts* 3 (1897): 351–52.

Whipple, Edwin P. *Eulogy on John Albion Andrew*. Boston: Alfred Mudge and Son, 1867.

White, Horace. *The Life of Lyman Trumbull*. Boston: Houghton Mifflin, 1913.

Whittier, John Greenleaf, ed. *Letters of Lydia Maria Child*. Boston: Houghton Mifflin, 1883.

Williams, George D. *A History of the Negro Troops in the War of the Rebellion, 1861–1865*. New York: Harper and Brothers, 1888.

Wilson, Forrest. *The Crusader in Crinoline: The Life of Harriet Beecher Stowe*. Philadelphia: J. B. Lippincott, 1941.

Wilson, Henry. *History of the Rise and Fall of the Slave Power in America*. 2 vols. Boston: Houghton Mifflin, 1884.

——. *Senator Wilson's Speech on Prohibition in Tremont Temple, April 15, 1867*. Boston: Massachusetts State Temperance Alliance, 1867.

Wiltse, Charles M., and Michael J. Birkner, eds. *The Papers of Daniel Webster*. 7 vols. Hanover, NH: University Press of New England, 1974–1983.

Winthrop, John C., and Thomas Aspinwall. "November Meeting. John A. Andrew; Donations to the Library; Letters from John Adams." *Proceedings of the Massachusetts Historical Society* 10 (1867–1869): 85–92.

Winthrop, Robert C., Jr. *A Memoir of Robert C. Winthrop*. Boston: Little, Brown, 1897.

Winthrop, Robert C., and Thomas Aspinwall. "November Meeting. Death of John A. Andrew; Donations to the Library; Letter from John Adams." *Proceedings of the Massachusetts Historical Society* 10 (1867–1869): 85–92.

"The Yacht Wanderer, G. B. Lamar." MLR 23 (July 1860): 139–50.

The Year-Book of the Unitarian Congregational Churches for 1892. Boston: American Unitarian Association, 1892.

Yerrinton, James M. W. *Report of the Case of George C. Hersey, Indicted for the Murder of Betsy Frances Tirrell*. Boston: A. Williams, 1862.

Secondary Sources

Aamodt, Terrie Dopp. *Righteous Armies, Holy Cause: Apocalyptic Imagery and the Civil War*. Macon, GA: Mercer University Press, 1986.

Abbott, Richard H. *Cobbler in Congress: Life of Henry Wilson, 1812–1875*. Lexington: University Press of Kentucky, 1972.

——. *Cotton and Capital: Boston Businessmen and Antislavery Reform*. Amherst: University of Massachusetts Press, 1991.

——. "Massachusetts and the Recruitment of Southern Negroes, 1863–1865." *Civil War History* 14, no. 3 (Sept. 1968): 197–210.

——. "A Yankee Views the Organization of the Republican Party in South Carolina." *South Carolina Historical Magazine* 85, no. 3 (July 1984): 244–50.

Abel, E. Lawrence. *A Finger in Lincoln's Brain: What Modern Science Reveals about Lincoln, His Assassination, and Its Aftermath*. Santa Barbara, CA: Praeger, 2015.

Abzug, Robert H., and Stephen E. Maizlish, eds. *New Perspectives on Race and Slavery in America: Essays in Honor of Kenneth M. Stampp*. Lexington: University Press of Kentucky, 1986.

Adams, George M., ed. *Memorial Biographies of the New-England Historic and Genealogical Society*. 9 vols. Boston: Published by the Society, 1905.

Alt, William E., and Betty L. Alt. *Black Soldiers, White Wars: Black Warriors from Antiquity to the Present.* Westport, CT: Praeger, 2002.

Altschuler, Glenn C. *Andrew D. White: Educator, Historian, Diplomat.* Ithaca: Cornell University Press, 1979.

Amestoy, Jeffrey L. *Slavish Shore: The Odyssey of Richard Henry Dana Jr.* Cambridge: Harvard University Press, 2015.

Anbinder, Tyler. *Nativism & Slavery: The Northern Know Nothings & the Politics of the 1850s.* New York: Oxford University Press, 1992.

Anderson, Eric, and Alfred A. Moss, eds. *Facts of Reconstruction: Essays in Honor of John Hope Franklin.* Baton Rouge: Louisiana State University Press, 1991.

Archer, Richard. *Jim Crow North: The Struggle for Equal Rights in Antebellum New England.* New York: Oxford University Press, 2017.

Bailey, Brigitte, Katheryn P. Viens, and Conrad Edick Wright, eds. *Margaret Fuller and Her Circles.* Durham: University of New Hampshire Press, in association with the Massachusetts Historical Society, 2013.

Barton, William Eleazer. *The Life of Abraham Lincoln.* 2 vols. Indianapolis: Bobbs-Merrill, 1925.

Basbanes, Nicholas A. *Cross of Snow: A Life of Henry Wadsworth Longfellow.* New York: Knopf, 2020.

Baum, Dale. *Civil War Party System: The Case of Massachusetts, 1848–1876.* Chapel Hill: University of North Carolina Press, 1984.

Bellesiles, Michael A. *Inventing Equality: Reconstruction the Constitution in the Aftermath of the Civil War.* New York: St. Martin's Press, 2020.

Belohlavek, John M. *Broken Glass: Caleb Cushing and the Shattering of the Union.* Kent: Kent State University Press, 2005.

Belz, Herman. "Law, Politics, and Race in the Struggle for Equal Pay During the Civil War." *Civil War History* 22 (Sept. 1976): 197–222.

Bergeson-Lockwood, Millington W. "'We Do Not Care Particularly about the Skating Rinks': African American Challenges to Racial Discrimination in Places of Public Amusement in Nineteenth-Century Boston, Massachusetts." *Journal of the Civil War Era* 5, no. 2 (June 2015): 254–88.

Berlin, Ira, Barbara J. Fields, Steven F. Miller, Joseph P. Reidy, and Leslie S. Rowland. *Slaves No More: Three Essays on Emancipation and the Civil War.* New York: Cambridge University Press, 1992.

Berlin, Ira, Joseph P. Reidy, and Leslie S. Rowland, eds. *Freedom's Soldiers: The Black Military Experience in the Civil War.* New York: Cambridge, 1998.

Black, Andrew. *Buried Dreams: The Hoosac Tunnel and the Demise of the Railroad Age.* Baton Rouge: Louisiana State University Press, 2021.

Blackett, R. J. M. *The Captive's Quest for Freedom: Fugitives Slaves, the 1850 Fugitive Slave Law and the Politics of Slavery.* New York: Cambridge University Press, 2018.

Blatt, Martin H., Thomas J. Brown, and Donald Yacovone, eds. *Hope and Glory: Essays on the Legacy of the 54th Massachusetts Regiment.* Amherst: University of Massachusetts Press in association with Massachusetts Historical Society, 2001.

Blight, David W. *Frederick Douglass: Prophet of Freedom.* New York: Simon and Schuster, 2018.

———. *Race and Reunion: The Civil War in American Memory.* Cambridge: Harvard University Press, 2001.

Blue, Frederick J. *The Free Soilers: Third Party Politics, 1848–1854.* Urbana: University of Illinois Press, 1973.

Bogue, Alan G. *The Earnest Men: Republicans of the Civil War Senate.* Ithaca: Cornell University Press, 1961.

Breault, Judith Colucci. *The World of Emily Howland: Odyssey of a Humanitarian.* Millbrae, CA: Les Femmes, 1976.

Brock, Jared A. *The Road to Dawn: Josiah Henson and the Story That Sparked the Civil War.* New York: Hachette Book Group, 2018.

Brock, Peter, *Pacifism in the United States: From the Colonial Era to the First World War*. Princeton: Princeton University Press, 1968.

Brooke, John L. *"There Is a North": Fugitive Slaves, Political Crisis, and Cultural Transformation in the Coming of the Civil War*. Amherst: University of Massachusetts Press, 2019.

Brooks, Corey M. *Liberty Power: Antislavery Third Parties and the Transformation of American Politics*. Chicago: University of Chicago Press, 2016.

Brown, George S. *Yarmouth, Nova Scotia: Sequel to Campbell's History*. Boston: Rand Avery Company, Printers, 1888.

Bryant, James K., II. *The 36th Infantry United States Colored Troops in the Civil War: A History and Roster*. Jefferson, NC: McFarland, 2012.

Buehrens, John A. *Conflagration: How the Transcendentalists Sparked the American Struggle for Racial, Gender, and Social Justice*. Boston: Beacon Press, 2020.

Buescher, John Benedict. *The Remarkable Life of John Murray Spear: Agitator for the Spirit Land*. Notre Dame, IN: Notre Dame University Press, 2006.

Bundy, Carol. *The Nature of Sacrifice: A Biography of Charles Russell, Jr., 1835–64*. New York: Farrar, Straus and Giroux, 2005.

Burlingame, Michael. *Abraham Lincoln: A Life*. 2 vols. Baltimore: Johns Hopkins University Press, 2008.

——. "New Light on the Bixby Letter." *Journal of the Abraham Lincoln Association* 16, no. 1 (Winter 1995): 59–71.

Burnette, Patricia B. *James F. Jaquess: Scholar, Soldier and Private Agent for President Lincoln*. Jefferson, NC: McFarland, 2013.

Bushman, Richard L., Neil Harris, David Rothman, Barbara Miller Solomon, and Stephan Thernstrom, eds. *Uprooted Americans: Essays to Honor Oscar Handlin*. Boston: Little, Brown, 1979.

Calonius, Erik. *The Wanderer: The Last American Slave Ship*. New York: St. Martin's Press, 2006.

Capper, Charles, and Conrad Edick Wright, eds. *Transient and Permanent: The Transcendentalist Movement and Its Context*. Boston: Massachusetts Historical Society, 1999.

Carmichael, Orten H. *Lincoln's Gettysburg Address*. New York: Abingdon Press, 1917.

Carroll, Bret E. *Spiritualism in Antebellum America*. Bloomington: Indiana University Press, 1997.

Casstevens, Francis H. *Edward A. Wild and the African Brigade in the Civil War*. Jefferson, NC: McFarland, 2003.

Castel, Albert. "The Fort Pillow Massacre: A Fresh Examination of the Evidence." *Civil War History* 4, no. 1 (1958): 37–50.

Celebration of the One Hundred and Fiftieth Anniversary of Gorham, Maine. Portland: B. Thurston, 1886.

Chadwick, John W. *Theodore Parker, Preacher and Reformer*. Boston: Houghton Mifflin, 1900.

Chalfant, Edward. *Both Sides of the Ocean: A Biography of Henry Adams, His First Life, 1838–1862*. Hamden, CT: Archon Books, 1994.

Cheek, William, and Aimee Lee Cheek. *John Mercer Langston and the Fight for Black Freedom, 1829–1865*. Urbana: University of Illinois Press, 1996.

Chirhart, Ann Short, and Betty Wood, eds. *Georgia Women: Their Lives and Times*. Athens: University of Georgia Press, 2009.

Cimbala, Paul Alan, and Randall M. Miller, eds. *The Freedman's Bureau and Reconstruction: Reconsiderations*. New York: Fordham University Press, 2010.

——, eds. *The Great Task Remaining Before Us: Reconstruction as America's Continuing Civil War*. New York: Fordham University Press, 2010.

——, eds. *Union Soldiers and the Northern Home Front*. New York: Fordham University Press, 2002.

Cimprich, John, and Robert C. Mainfort, Jr. "Fort Pillow Revisited: New Evidence about an Old Controversy." *Civil War History* 28, no. 4 (1982): 293–306.

Clinton, Catherine. *Harriet Tubman: The Road to Freedom*. New York: Little, Brown, 2004.

Cochrane, Walter. *The History of Brown University, 1764–1914*. Providence: Published by Brown University, 1914.

Coddington, Ronald S. *Faces of the Civil War: An Album of Union Soldiers and Their Stories*. Baltimore: Johns Hopkins University Press, 2004.

Coles, David J. "Far from Fields of Glory: Military Operations in Florida during the Civil War, 1864–1865." PhD diss., Florida State University, 1996.

Collison, Gary. *Shadrach Minkins: From Fugitive Slave to Citizen*. Cambridge: Harvard University Press, 1997.

———. "'This Flagitious Offense': Daniel Webster and the Shadrach Rescue Cases, 1851–1852." *New England Quarterly* 68, no. 4 (Dec. 1995): 609–25.

Congressional Globe. Washington, D.C.: Government Printing Office, 1861–1865.

Cook, Robert J. *Civil War Senator: William Pitt Fessenden and the Fight to Save the American Republic*. Baton Rouge: Louisiana State University Press, 2011.

Cooke, George Willis. *Unitarianism in America: A History of Its Origins and Development*. Boston: American Unitarian Association, 1902.

Cornish, Dudley Taylor. *The Sable Arm: Negro Troops in the Union Army, 1861–1865*. New York: W. W. Norton, 1966.

Coulter, E. Merton. "Robert Gould Shaw and the Burning of Darien, Georgia." *Civil War History* 5, no. 4 (1959): 363–73.

Cox, LaWanda. *Lincoln and Black Freedom: A Study in Presidential Leadership*. Columbia: University of South Carolina Press, 1994.

Cozzens, Peter, *Shenandoah 1862: Stonewall Jackson's Valley Campaign*. Chapel Hill: University of North Carolina Press, 2008.

Cullen, James B., ed. *The Story of the Irish in Boston*. Boston: James B. Cullen, 1889.

Cumbler, John T. *From Abolition to Rights for All: The Making of a Reform Community in the Nineteenth Century*. Philadelphia: University of Pennsylvania Press, 2008.

Dalton, Cornelius, John Wirkkala, and Anne Thomas, eds. *Leading the Way: A History of the Massachusetts General Court, 1629–1980*. Boston: Office of the Massachusetts Secretary of State, 1984.

David, William Thomas. *Bench and Bar of the Commonwealth of Massachusetts*. 2 vols. Boston: Boston History, 1895.

Davis, John Stuart. "Liberty Before Union: Massachusetts and the Coming of the Civil War." PhD diss., University of Massachusetts, 1975.

Deese, Helen R., ed. *Daughter of Boston: The Extraordinary Diary of a Nineteenth-Century Woman Caroline Healey Hall*. Boston: Beacon Press, 2005.

DeLombard, Jeannine Marie. *Slavery on Trial: Law, Abolitionism, and Print Culture*. Chapel Hill: University of North Carolina Press, 2007.

Dickerson, Donna. *Margaret Fuller: Writing a Woman's Life*. New York: St. Martin's Press, 1993.

Doherty, William W. "The Republican Party in Massachusetts." *New England Magazine* 48 (Jan. 1913): 505–15.

Doherty, William. "The Republican Party in Massachusetts." *New England Magazine* 49 (Mar. 1913): 21–35.

Donald, David Herbert. *Charles Sumner and the Coming of the Civil War*. New York: Knopf, 1960.

———. *Charles Sumner and the Rights of Man*. New York: Knopf, 1970.

———. *Lincoln*. New York: Simon and Schuster, 1995.

Dowling, Linda C. *Charles Eliot Norton: The Art of Reform in Nineteenth-Century America*. Hanover, NH: University of New England Press, 2007.

Dray, Philip. *There Is Power in a Union: The Epic Story of Labor in America*. New York: Anchor Books, 2011.

Duberman, Martin. *Charles Francis Adams, 1807–1886*. Boston: Houghton Mifflin, 1961.

———. "Some Notes on the Beginnings of the Republican Party in Massachusetts." *New England Quarterly* 34, no. 3 (Sept. 1961): 364–70.

Dubois, Laurent. *Haiti: The Aftershocks of History*. New York: Henry Holt, 2012.

Egerton, Douglas R. *Thunder at the Gates: The Civil War Regiments That Redeemed America.* New York: Basic Books, 2016.

———. *The Wars of Reconstruction: The Brief, Violent History of America's Most Progressive Era.* New York: Bloomsbury Press, 2014.

Eicher, David J. *The Longest Night: A Military History of the Civil War*. New York: Simon and Schuster, 2001.

Eliot, Charles W. "President Eliot and M.I.T." *Technology Review* 22 (Jan. 1920): 430–31.

Eliot, Samuel Atkins, ed. *Heralds of a Liberal Faith: The Preachers*. 3 vols. Boston: American Unitarian Association, 1910.

Engle, Stephen D. *Gathering to Save a Nation: Lincoln and the Union's War Governors*. Chapel Hill: University of North Carolina Press, 2016.

———. "Shaping the Contours of Federalism: The American Civil War and the Negotiation of Nation-State Power." *Journal of Federal History* 11 (2019): 83–108.

———. "'Under Full Sail': John Andrew, Abraham Lincoln, and Standing by the Union." *Massachusetts Historical Review* 19 (2017): 43–81.

Escot, Paul. *The Worst Passions of Human Nature: White Supremacy in the Civil War North* Charlottesville: University Press of Virginia, 2020.

Faulkner, Carol. *Women's Radical Reconstruction: The Freedman's Aid Movement*. Philadelphia: University of Pennsylvania Press, 2004.

Finkelman, Paul, ed. *His Soul Goes Marching On: Responses to John Brown and the Harpers Ferry Raid*. Charlottesville: University Press of Virginia, 1995.

———. *Race and Law Before Emancipation*. New York: Garland, 1992.

———. *Slavery in the Courtroom*. Union, NJ: Lawbook Exchange, 1998.

Fischer, Leroy. *Lincoln's Gadfly: Adam Gurowski*. Norman: University of Oklahoma Press, 1964.

Flower, Frank Abial. *History of the Republican Party*. Springfield, IL: Union, 1884.

Foner, Eric. *The Fiery Trial: Abraham Lincoln and American Slavery*. New York: W. W. Norton, 2010.

———. *Free Soil, Free Labor, Free Men: The Ideology of the Republican Party Before the Civil War.* New York: Oxford University Press, 1970. Reprint 1995.

———. *Reconstruction: America's Unfinished Revolution, 1863–1877*. New York: HarperCollins, 1988.

Formisano, Ronald. *For the People: American Populist Movements from the Revolution to the 1850s*. Chapel Hill: University of North Carolina Press, 2008.

———. *Transformation of Political Culture: Massachusetts Parties, 1790s–1840s*. Charlottesville: University Press of Virginia, 1983.

Frank, Joseph Allen. *With Ballot and Bayonet: The Political Socialization of American Civil War Soldiers*. Athens: University of Georgia Press, 1998.

Freeman, Joanne B. *Field of Blood: Violence in Congress and the Road to Civil War*. New York: Farrar, Straus and Giroux, 2018.

Fuess, Claude M. *The Life of Caleb Cushing*. 2 vols. New York: Harcourt, Brace, 1923.

Furgurson, Ernest. *Ashes of Glory: Richmond at War*. New York: Knopf, 1996.

———. *Freedom Rising: Washington in the Civil War*. New York: Random House, 2005.

Galluzzo, John J. *Looking Back at South Shore History: From Plymouth to Quincy Granite*. Charleston, SC: History Press, 2013.

Gamble, Richard M. *A Fiery Gospel: The Battle Hymn of the Republic and the Road to Righteous War*. Ithaca: Cornell University Press, 2019.

Gara, Larry. "Cyrus Woodman: A Biography." PhD diss., University of Wisconsin, 1953.

———. *Westernized Yankee: The Story of Cyrus Woodman*. Madison: State Historical Society of Wisconsin, 1956.

Garner, Stanton. *The Civil War World of Herman Melville*. Kansas City: University Press of Kansas, 1993.

Gatell, Frank Otto. "Conscience and Judgment: The Bolt of the Massachusetts Conscience Whigs." *The Historian* 21, no. 1 (1958): 18–45.

Geary, James W. *We Need Men: The Union Draft in the Civil War*. Dekalb: Northern Illinois University Press, 1991.

Geldard, Richard G. *God in Concord: Ralph Waldo Emerson's Awakening to the Infinite*. New York: Larson Publications, 1999.

Gienapp, William E. "The Crime Against Sumner: The Canning of Charles Sumner and the Rise of the Republican Party." *Civil War History* 25, no. 3 (Sept. 1979): 218–45.

———. "Nativism and the Creation of a Republican Majority in the North before the Civil War." *Journal of American History* 72, no.3 (Dec. 1985): 529–59.

———. *The Origins of the Republican Party, 1852–1856*. New York: Oxford University Press, 1987.

Gilbert, Kevin Lee. "The Ordeal of Edward Greeley Loring: Fugitive Slavery, Judicial Reform, and the Politics of Law in 1850s Massachusetts." PhD diss., University of Massachusetts Amherst, 1997.

Glatthaar, Joseph T. *Forged in Battle: The Civil War Alliance of Black Soldiers and White Officers*. Baton Rouge: Louisiana State University Press, 1990.

Glymph, Thavolia. *The Women's Fight: The Civil War's Battle for Home, Freedom, and Nation*. Chapel Hill: University of North Carolina Press, 2020.

Golay, Michael. *A Ruined Land*. New York: Wiley, 2001.

Gollin, Rita K. *Annie Adams Fields: Woman of Letters*. Amherst: University of Massachusetts Press, 2002.

Goodheart, Adam. *1861: The Civil War Awakening*. New York: Vintage Books, 2012.

Goodwin, Doris Kearns. *Team of Rivals: The Political Genius of Abraham Lincoln*. New York: Simon and Schuster, 2005.

Gosse, Van. *The First Reconstruction: Black Politics in America from the Revolution to the Civil War*. Chapel Hill: University of North Carolina Press, 2021.

Grant, Susan-Mary. *Oliver Wendell Holmes, Jr.: Civil War Soldier, Supreme Court Justice*. New York: Routledge, 2016.

Green, Michael S. *Freedom, Union, and Power: Lincoln and His Party during the Civil War*. New York: Fordham University Press, 22004

Greenwood, Andrea, and Mark W. Harris. *An Introduction to the Unitarian and Universalist Traditions*. New York: Cambridge University Press, 2011.

Greenwood, Janette Thomas. *First Fruits of Freedom: The Migration of Former Slavs and Their Search for Equality in Worcester, Massachusetts, 1862–1900*. Chapel Hill: University of North Carolina Press, 2009.

Griffin, Joseph. *History of the Press of Maine*. Brunswick: From the Press, 1872.

Grodzins, Dean. "'Slave Law' versus 'Lynch Law' in Boston: Benjamin Robbins Curtis, Theodore Parker, and the Fugitive Slave Crisis, 1850–1855." *Massachusetts Historical Review* 12 (2010): 1–33.

Guilmette, Ronald J. *The First to Serve: The Massachusetts State Police's Ten-Year War Against Liquor Shops, Gambling, and Place of Ill Fame*. Morrisville, NC: Lulu Press, 2018.

Hack, Daniel. *Reaping Something New: African American Transformations of Victorian Literature*. Princeton: Princeton University Press, 2017.

Hall, Matthew Lee. "Coverage of the Prohibition Issue in Selected Massachusetts Newspapers, 1851–1855." PhD diss., Southern Connecticut University, 2011.

Hamrogue, John M. "John A. Andrew: Abolitionist Governor, 1861–1865." PhD diss., Fordham University, 1974.

Hancock, Scott. "The Elusive Boundaries of Blackness: Identity Formation in Antebellum Boston." *Journal of Negro History* 8, no. 2 (Spring 1999): 115–29.

Handlin, Oscar. *Boston's Immigrants, 1790–1880. A Study in Acculturation*. Cambridge: Harvard University Press, 1941.

Harrington, Fred Harvey. *Fighting Politician: Major General N. P. Banks*. Philadelphia: University of Pennsylvania Press, 1948.

———. "Nathaniel Prentiss Banks: A Study in Anti-Slavery Politics." *New England Quarterly* 9, no. 4 (Dec. 1936): 626–54.

Harris, Sheldon H. "Mutiny on Junior." *American Neptune* 21 (1961): 110–29.

Harris, William C. *Lincoln and the Union Governors*. Carbondale: Southern Illinois University Press, 2013.

Harrison, Robert. *Washington during Civil War and Reconstruction: Race and Radicalism*. New York: Cambridge University Press, 2011.

Harrold, Stanley. *American Abolitionism: Its Direct Political Impact from Colonial Times into Reconstruction*. Charlottesville: University Press of Virginia, 2019.

Hatch, Frederick. *John Surratt: Rebel Lincoln Conspirator, Fugitive*. Jefferson, NC: McFarland, 2016.

Hatch, Louis Clinton. *The History of Bowdoin College*. Portland: Loring, Short, and Harmon, 1927.

Hawley, Elizabeth. *The Olden Time Stories for Betty*. Bloomington, IN: Xlibris, 2005.

Hearn, Daniel Allen. *Legal Executions in New England: A Comprehensive Reference, 1623–1960*. Jefferson, NC: McFarland, 1999.

Heller, Charles E. *Portrait of an Abolitionist: A Biography of George Luther Stearns, 1809–1867*. Westport, CT: Greenwood Press, 1996.

Hedrick, Joan. *Harriet Beecher Stowe: A Life*. New York: Oxford University Press, 1994.

History of Penobscot County, Maine: The Annals of Bangor, 1769–1882. Cleveland: Williams, Chase, 1882.

Hollandsworth, James G. *Pretense of Glory: The Life of General Nathaniel P. Banks*. Baton Rouge: Louisiana State University Press, 1998.

Holloran, Peter C. *Boston's Wayward Children: Social Services for Homeless Children 1830–1930*. Rutherford, NJ: Fairleigh Dickinson University Press, 1989.

Holt, Michael F. *The Rise and Fall of the American Whig Party: Jacksonian Politics and the Onset of the Civil War*. New York: Oxford University Press, 1999.

Holzer, Harold. *Lincoln, President Elect: Abraham Lincoln and the Great Secession Winter, 1860–1861*. New York: Simon and Schuster, 2008.

Holzer, Harold, Craig Symonds, and Frank J. Williams, eds. *Exploring Lincoln: Great Historians Reappraise Our Greatest President*. New York: Fordham University Press, 2015.

Horton, James Oliver, and Lois E. Horton. *Black Bostonians: Family Life and Community Struggle in the Antebellum North*. New York: Holmes and Meier, 1979.

Howard, Victor B. *Religion and the Radical Republican Movement, 1860–1870*. Lexington: University Press of Kentucky, 1990.

Howe, David Walker. *The Political Culture of the American Whigs*. Chicago: University of Chicago Press, 1979.

———. *What Hath God Wrought: The Transformation of America, 1815–1848*. New York: Oxford University Press, 2007.

Howe, Mark De Wolfe. *Boston: The Place and the People*. New York: Macmillan, 1912.

———. *Justice Oliver Wendell Holmes: The Proving Years, 1870–1882*. Cambridge: Belknap Press of Harvard University Press, 1963.

Hudson, Lynn Maria. *The Making of "Mammy Pleasant": A Black Entrepreneur in Nineteenth-Century San Francisco*. Urbana: University of Illinois Press, 2003.

Humez, Jean M. *Harriet Tubman: The Life and the Life Stories*. Madison: University of Wisconsin Press, 2003.

Hurd, Duane Hamilton. *History of Worcester County, Massachusetts*. Boston: C. F. Jewett, 1879.

———. *History of Plymouth, Massachusetts*. Philadelphia: J. W. Lewis, 1884.

Jackson, Kellie Carter. *Force and Freedom: Black Abolitionists and the Politics of Violence*. Philadelphia: University of Pennsylvania Press, 2019.

Johnson, Franklin. *The Development of State Legislation Concerning the Free Negro*. New York: Arno Press, 1919.

Jones, Jacqueline. *No Right to an Honest Living: The Struggles of Boston's Black Workers in the Civil War Era*. New York: Basic Books, 2023.

Jordan, Jim. "Charles Augustus Lafayette Lamar and the Movements to Reopen the African Slave Trade." *Georgia Historical Quarterly* 93, no. 3 (Fall 2009): 247–90.

Kahan, Paul. *Amiable Scoundrel: Simon Cameron, Lincoln's Scandalous Secretary of War*. Lincoln: University of Nebraska Press, 2016.

Kantrowitz, Stephen. *More Than Freedom: Fighting for Black Citizenship in a White Republic, 1829–1889*. New York: Penguin Press, 2012.

———. "A Place for 'Colored Patriots': Crispus Attucks among the Abolitionists, 1842–1863." *Massachusetts Historical Review* 11 (2009): 96–117.

Karcher, Carolyn L. *The First Woman in the Republic: A Cultural Biography of Lydia Maria Child*. Durham, NC: Duke University Press, 2012.

Keith, LeeAnna. *When It Was Grand: The Radical Republican History of the Civil War*. New York: Hill and Wang, 2020.

Knickerbocker, Wendy. *Bard of Bethel: The Life and Times of Boston's Father Taylor*. Newcastle: Cambridge Scholars Publishing, 2014.

Knight, Michael F. "The Rost Home Colony: St. Charles Parish, Louisiana." *Prologue* 33, no. 3 (Fall 2001): 214–20.

Kritzberg, Barry. "Thoreau, Slavery, and Resistance to Civil Government." *Massachusetts Historical Review* 30, no. 4 (Winter 189): 535–65.

LaBarre, Steven M. *The Fifth Massachusetts Colored Cavalry in the Civil War*. Jefferson, NC: McFarland, 2016.

Langsdorf, Edgar. "Thaddeus Hyatt in Washington Jail." *Kansas Historical Quarterly* 9, no. 3 (Aug. 1940): 225–39.

Larson, Kate Clifford. *Bound for the Promised Land: Portrait of an American Hero*. New York: Random House, 2004.

Laurie, Bruce. *Beyond Garrison: Antislavery and Social Reform*. New York: Cambridge University Press, 2005.

Leonard, Elizabeth D. *Benjamin Franklin Butler: A Noisy, Fearless Life*. Chapel Hill: University of North Carolina Press, 2022.

Lepore, Jill. "How Longfellow Woke the Dead." *American Scholar* 80, no. 2 (Spring 2011): 33–46.

Lerche, Charles O., Jr., "Congressional Interpretations of the Guarantee of a Republican Form of Government during Reconstruction." *Journal of Southern History* 15, no. 2 (May 1949): 192–211.

Lerner, Gerda. *The Grimké Sisters from South Carolina: Pioneers for Woman's Rights and Abolition*. New York: Oxford University Press, 1998.

Levesque, George A. *Black Boston: African American Life and Culture in Urban America, 1750–1860*. New York: Garland Publishing, 1994.

———. "White Bureaucracy, Black Community: The Contest Over Local Control of Education in Antebellum Boston." *Journal of Educational Thought* 11 (Aug. 1977): 140–55.

Lewis, Katherine B., ed. *History of Gorham, ME., by Hugh D. McLellan*. Portland: Smith and Sale, Printers, 1903.

Link, William A., and James J. Broomall, eds. *Rethinking American Emancipation: Legacies of Slavery and the Quest for Black Freedom*. New York: Cambridge University Press, 2016.

Litwack, Leon F. *Been in the Storm So Long: The Aftermath of Slavery*. New York: Knopf, 1979.

Lowenstein, Roger. *Ways and Means: Lincoln and His Cabinet and the Financing of the Civil War*. New York: Penguin Press, 2022.

Luce, Robert. *Legislative Problems: Development, Status, and Trend of the Treatment and Exercise of Lawmaking Powers*. Clark, NJ: Lawbook Exchange, 2006.

Luskey, Brian P. *Men Is Cheap: Exposing the Frauds of Free Labor in Civil War America*. Chapel Hill: University of North Carolina Press, 2020.

Luthin, Reinhard H. "Abraham Lincoln and the Massachusetts Whigs in 1848." *New England Quarterly* 14, no. 4 (Dec. 1941): 619–32.

MacCarthy, Esther. "The Home for Aged Colored Women, 1861–1944." *Historical Journal of Massachusetts* 21, no. 1 (Winter 1993): 55–73.

Maltz, Earl M. *Fugitive Slave on Trial: The Anthony Burns Case and Abolitionist Outrage.* Lawrence: University Press of Kansas, 2010.

Manning, Chandra. *Troubled Refuge: Struggling for Freedom in the Civil War.* New York: Knopf, 2016.

Marvel, William. *Burnside.* Chapel Hill: University of North Carolina Press, 1991.

———. *Lincoln's Autocrat: The Life of Edwin Stanton.* Chapel Hill: University of North Carolina Press, 2015.

Mason, Matthew. *Apostle of Union: A Political Biography of Edward Everett.* Chapel Hill: University of North Carolina Press, 2016.

Masur, Kate. "African American Delegation to Abraham Lincoln: A Reappraisal." *Civil War History* 56, no. 2 (June 2010): 117–44.

———. *An Example for All the Land: Emancipation and the Struggle over Equality in Washington, D.C.* Chapel Hill: University of North Carolina Press, 2010.

———. *Until Justice Be Done: America's First Civil Rights Movement, from the Revolution to Reconstruction.* New York: W. W. Norton, 2021.

Masur, Louis P. *Lincoln's Hundred Days: The Emancipation Proclamation and the War for the Union.* Cambridge: Harvard University Press, 2021.

Mayer, Henry. *All on Fire: William Lloyd Garrison and the Abolition of Slavery.* New York: W. W. Norton, 2008.

McCaughy, Robert A. *Josiah Quincy: The Last Federalist.* Cambridge: Harvard University Press, 1974.

McClintock, Russell. *Lincoln and the Decision for War: The Northern Response to Secession.* Chapel Hill: University of North Carolina Press, 2008.

McDougall, Marion Gleason. *Fugitive Slaves: 1619–1865.* Boston: Ginn, 1891.

McFeely, William S. *Yankee Stepfather: General O. O. Howard and the Freedmen.* New Haven: Yale University Press, 1968.

McGraw, Robert F. "Minutemen of '61: The Pre-Civil War Massachusetts Militia." *Civil War History* 15, no. 2 (June 1969): 101–15.

McKay, Ernest A. "Henry Wilson and the Coalition of 1851." *New England Quarterly* 36, no. 3 (Sept. 1963): 338–57.

McKitrick, Eric. *Andrew Johnson and Reconstruction.* Chicago: University of Chicago Press, 1960.

McKivigan, John R. *Forgotten Firebrand: James Redpath and the Making of Nineteenth-Century America.* Ithaca: Cornell University Press, 2008.

———, ed. *The Frederick Douglass Papers.* Series 3, Volume 2. New Haven: Yale University Press, 2009.

McNamara, Daniel George. *The History of the Ninth Regiment, Massachusetts Volunteer Infantry, June, 1861–June, 1864.* New York: Fordham University Press, 2000.

McPherson, James M. *Marching Toward Freedom: Blacks in the Civil War, 1861–1865.* New York: Facts on File, 1994.

———. *The Negro's Civil War: How American Blacks Felt and Acted During the War for the Union.* New York: Random House, 1965.

———. *The Struggle for Equality: Abolitionists and the Negro in the Civil War and Reconstruction.* Princeton: Princeton University Press, 1964.

Mendelsohn, Jack. *Channing, the Reluctant Rebel: A Biography.* Boston: Little, Brown, 1971.

Mendez, James G. *A Great Sacrifice: Northern Black Soldiers, Their Families, and the Experience of Civil War.* New York: Fordham University Press, 2019.

Meneely, A. Howard. *The War Department: A Study in Mobilization and Administration.* New York: Columbia University Press, 1928.

Merrill, Louis Taylor. "General Benjamin F. Butler in the Presidential Campaign of 1864." *Mississippi Valley Historical Review* 33, no. 4 (Mar. 1947): 537–70.

Mezurek, Kelly D. *For Their Own Cause: The 27th United States Colored Troops.* Kent: Kent State University Press, 2016.

Michener, Roger. "Rivals and Partners: Early Literary Societies at Bowdoin College." *Journal of Library History* 10, no. 3 (July 1975): 214–30.

Milano, Andrew J. "The Copperhead Regiment: the 20th Massachusetts Volunteer Infantry." *Civil War Regiments: A Journal of the American Civil War* 2, no. 1 (1993): 31–63.

Miller, Edward A. *Lincoln's Abolitionist General: The Biography of David Hunter.* Columbia: University of South Carolina Press, 1997.

Miller, Richard F. "Brahmin Janissaries: John A. Andrew Mobilizes Massachusetts' Upper Class for the Civil War." *New England Quarterly* 75, no. 2 (June 2002): 204–34.

———. *Harvard's Civil War: A History of the Twentieth Massachusetts Volunteer Massachusetts Infantry.* Hanover, NH: University Press of New England, 2005.

———, ed. *States at War: A Reference Guide for Connecticut, Maine, Massachusetts, New Hampshire, Rhode Island, and Vermont.* 6 vols. Hanover, NH: University of New England, 2012.

———. "The Trouble with Brahmins: Class and Ethnic Tensions in Massachusetts' 'Harvard Regiment.'" *New England Quarterly* 76, no. 1 (Mar. 2003): 38–72.

Miller, William Lee. *President Lincoln: The Duty of a Statesman.* New York: Random House, 2008.

Mitchell, Mary Niall. "The Real Ida May: A Fugitive Tale in the Archives." *Massachusetts Historical Review* 15 (2013): 54–88.

Mitchell, Wilmot Brookings, ed. *Elijah Kellogg: The Man and His Work.* Boston: Lee and Shepard, 1903.

Montgomery, David. *Beyond Equality: Labor and the Radical Republicans, 1862–1872.* Urbana: University of Illinois Press, 1981.

Morgan-Owens, Jessie. "The Enslaved Girl Who Became America's First Poster Child." *Smithsonian* 49 (Mar. 2019): 8.

———. *Girl in Black and White: The Story of Mary Mildred Williams and the Abolition Movement.* New York: W. W. Norton, 2019.

Muldoon, James B. *You Have No Courts with Any Sure Rule of Law: The Saga of the Supreme Judicial Court of Massachusetts.* Lookout Hill Press, 1992.

Mulkern, John R. *The Know-Nothing Party in Massachusetts: The Rise and Fall of a People's Movement.* Boston: Northeastern University Press, 1990.

Murdock, Eugene Converse. *Patriotism Limited, 1862–1865: The Civil War Draft.* Kent: Kent State University Press, 1967.

Murray, Williamson, and Wayne Wei-Sian Hsieh. *A Savage War: A Military History of the Civil War.* Princeton: Princeton University Press, 2016.

Myers, Mildred D. *Miss Emily: Emily Howland, Teacher of Freed Slaves, Suffragist, and Friend of Susan B. Anthony and Harriet Tubman.* Charlotte Harbor, FL: Tabby House, 1998.

Nagel, Paul C. *Descent from Glory: Four Generations of the John Adams Family.* Cambridge: Harvard University Press, 1983.

Nash, Howard P. *Stormy Petrel: The Life and Times of General Benjamin F. Butler.* Rutherford, NJ: Fairleigh Dickinson University Press, 1969.

Neal, John. *Portland Illustrated.* Portland: W. S. Jones Publishers, 1874.

Nevins, Allan. *The Emergence of Lincoln.* 2 vols. New York: Charles Scribner's, 1950. 2:258.

———. *Ordeal of the Union.* 8 vols. New York: Charles Scribner's Sons, 1947.

Nichols, Roy F. *Blueprints for Leviathan: American Style.* New York: Atheneum, 1963.

Niven, John. *Salmon P. Chase: A Biography.* New York: Oxford University Press, 1995.

Nolan, Dick. *Benjamin Franklin Butler: The Damnedest Yankee.* Novato, CA: Presidio Press, 1991.

"Notes. Rights Under a Theatre Ticket." *Harvard Law Review* 14 (Feb. 1901): 455–56.

Oakes, James. *Freedom National: The Destruction of Slavery in the United States, 1861–1865.* New York: W. W. Norton, 2014.

Oates, Stephen B. *A Woman of Valor: Clara Barton and the Civil War*. New York: Free Press, 1994.
———. *To Purge This Land with Blood: A Biography of John Brown*. New York: Harper and Row, 1970.
Ochiai, Akiko. "The Port Royal Experient Revisited: Northern Visions of Reconstruction and the Land Question." *New England Quarterly* 74, no. 1 (Mar. 2001): 94–117.
O'Conner, Thomas H. *Boston Irish: A Political History*. New York: Little, Brown, 1997.
———. *Civil War Boston: Home Front and Battlefield*. Boston: Northeastern University Press, 1997.
———. *Lords of the Loom: The Cotton Whigs and the Coming of the Civil War*. New York: Charles Scribner's Sons, 1968.
Oertel, Kristen T. *Harriet Tubman: Slavery, the Civil War, and Civil Rights in Nineteenth-Century America*. New York: Taylor and Frances, 2015.
Öfele, Martin W. *German-Speaking Officers in the United States Colored Troops, 1863–1867*. Gainesville: University Press of Florida, 2004
Okker, Patricia. *Our Sisters: Sarah J. Hale and the Tradition of Nineteenth-Century American Women Workers*. Athens: University of Georgia Press, 1995.
O'Toole, James M. *Passing for White: Race, Religion, and the Healy Family, 1820–1920*. Amherst: University of Massachusetts Press, 2002.
O'Toole, James M., and David Quigley, ed. *Boston's Histories: Essays in Honor of Thomas H. O'Conner*. Boston: Northeastern University Press, 2004.
Packard, Alpheus Spring, ed. *History of Bowdoin College with Biographical Sketches of Its Graduates from 1806 to 1879 by Nehemiah Cleaveland*. Boston: James Ripley Osgood, 1882.
Palmer, Beverly Wilson, and Ochoa, Holly Byers, eds. *The Selected Papers of Thaddeus Stevens*. 2 vols. Pittsburgh: University of Pittsburgh Press, 1998.
Paludan, Phillip Shaw. *The Presidency of Abraham Lincoln*. Lawrence: University Press of Kansas, 1994.
Payne, Charles M., and Adam Green, eds. *Time Longer than Rope: A Century of African American Activism, 1850–1950*. New York: New York University Press, 2003.
Peck, Charles. "John Van Buren: A Study in By-Gone Politics." *Magazine of American History* 17 (Jan–June 1887): 328.
Pearson, Henry Greenleaf. *An American Railroad Builder: John Murray Forbes*. Boston: Houghton Mifflin, 1911.
———. *The Life of John Andrew Governor of Massachusetts, 1861–1865*. 2 vols. Boston: Houghton Mifflin, 1904.
Perley, Sidney. *History of Boxford, Essex County, Massachusetts*. Boxford: Published by the author, 1880.
Peterson, Mark. *The City-State of Boston: The Rise and Fall of an Atlantic Power, 1630–1865*. Princeton: Princeton University Press, 2019.
Petry, Ann. *Harriet Tubman: Conductor on the Underground Railroad*. New York: Thomas Y. Crowell, 1955.
Pierce, Josiah. *A History of the Town of Gorham, Maine*. Portland: Foster and Cushing, and Bailey and Noyes, 1862.
Potter, David M. *The Impending Crisis, 1848–1861*. New York: Harper and Row, 1976.
Powell, Lawrence N. "The American Land Company and Agency: John A. Andrew and the Northernization of the South." *Civil War History* 21, no. 4 (Dec. 1975): 293–308.
Prentice, George. *The Life of Gilbert Haven: Bishop of the Methodist Episcopal Church*. New York: Phillips and Hunt, 1883.
Pryor, Elizabeth Brown. *Clara Barton, Professional Angel*. Philadelphia: University of Pennsylvania Press, 1987.
Randall, James G. *Lincoln the President*. 2 vols. New York: Dodd, Mead, 1945.
Rayback, Joseph G. *Free Soil: The Election of 1848*. Lexington: University Press of Kentucky, 1970.

"Recent Decisions. Theatres and Shows. Right to Admission. Right to Dramatic Critic." *Virginia Law Review* 3, no. 7 (Apr. 1916): 561–62.

Redkey, Edwin S., ed. *Grand Army of Black Men*. New York: Cambridge University Press, 1992.

Reid, Richard M. *Freedom for Themselves: North Carolina's Black Soldiers in the Civil War Era*. Chapel Hill: University of North Carolina Press, 2008.

———. "Raising the African Brigade: Early Recruitment in Civil War North Carolina." *North Carolina Historical Review* 70, no. 3 (July 1993):266–97.

Reidy, Joseph P. *Illusions of Emancipation: The Pursuit of Freedom and Equality in the Twilight of Slavery*. Chapel Hill: University of North Carolina Press, 2019.

Remini, Robert V. *Daniel Webster: The Man and His Time*. New York: W. W. Norton, 1997.

———. *The House: The History of the House of Representatives*. New York: Smithsonian Books with HarperCollins, 2006.

Renehan, Edward. *The Secret Six: The True Tale of the Men Who Conspired with John Brown*. Columbia: University of South Carolina Press, 1997.

Rennella, Mark. *The Boston Cosmopolitans: International Travel and American Arts and Letters*. New York: Palgrave Macmillan, 2008.

Reynolds, David S. *John Brown Abolitionist: The Man Who Killed Slavery, Sparked the Civil War, and Seeded Civil Rights*. New York: Knopf, 2005.

Reynolds, Robert Lester. "Benevolence on the Home Front in Massachusetts during the Civil War." PhD diss., Boston University, 1970.

Rhea, Gordon C. *Stephen A. Swails: Black Freedom Fighter in the Civil War and Reconstruction*. Baton Rouge: Louisiana State University Press, 2021.

Rhodes, James Ford. *History of the Civil War from the Compromise of 1850 to the McKinley-Bryan Campaign of 1896*. New York: Harper and Brothers, 1900.

———. *History of the United States*. 8 vols. New York: Macmillan, 1900–1919.

Richards, Laura Elizabeth Howe, Florence Howe Hall, and Maud Howe Elliott, eds. *Julia Ward Howe, 1819–1910*. 2 vols. Boston: Houghton Mifflin Company, 1915.

Richardson, Robert D. *William James: In the Maelstrom of American Modernism*. Boston: Houghton Mifflin, 2006.

Robboy, Stanley J., and Anita W. Robboy. "Lewis Hayden: From Fugitive Slave to Statesman." *New England Quarterly* 46, no. 4 (Dec. 1973): 591–613.

Rogers, Alan. *Murder and the Death Penalty in Massachusetts*. Amherst: University of Massachusetts Press, 2008.

Rose, Sarah F. *No Right to Be Idle: The Invention of Disability, 1840s–1930s*. Chapel Hill: University of North Carolina Press, 2017.

Rose, Willie Lee. *Rehearsal for Reconstruction: The Port Royal Experiment*. Athens: University of Georgia Press, 1999.

Sandburg, Carl. *Abraham Lincoln: The Prairie Years and the War Years*. One-volume ed. New York: Harcourt, 2002.

———. *Abraham Lincoln: The War Years*. 4 vols. New York: Harcourt, Brace, 1939.

Saunders, Judith P. "The People's Party in Massachusetts during the Civil War." PhD diss., Boston University, 1970.

Schmidt, John C. *The Life and Works of John Knowles Paine*. Ann Arbor: UMI Research Press, 1980.

Schneider, Mark R. *Boston Confronts Jim Crow, 1890–1920*. Boston: Northeastern University Press, 1997.

Schutz, John A. *A Noble Pursuit: The Sesquicentennial History of the New England Historic Genealogical Society, 1845–1995*. Boston: New England Historic Genealogical Society, 1995.

Schwartz, Harold. *Samuel Gridley Howe: Social Reformer, 1801–1876*. Cambridge: Harvard University Press, 1956.

Sears, Stephen W. ed. *George B. McClellan: The Young Napoleon*. New York: Ticknor and Fields, 1988.

Sernett, Milton C. *Harriet Tubman: Myth, Memory, and History.* Durham: Duke University Press, 2007.

Sewell, Richard. *Ballots for Freedom: Antislavery Politics in the United States, 1837–1860.* New York: Oxford University Press, 1976.

Shand-Tucci, Douglas. *MIT: An Architectural Tour.* New York: Princeton Architectural Press, 2016.

Showalter, Elaine. *The Civil Wars of Julia Ward Howe.* New York: Simon and Schuster, 2016.

Siebert, Wilbur H. "The Underground Railroad in Massachusetts." *Proceedings of the American Antiquarian Society* 45 (1936): 86.

Simkins, Francis B., and Robert H. Woody. *South Carolina During Reconstruction.* Chapel Hill: University of North Carolina Press, 1932.

Sinha, Minisha. "The Caning of Charles Sumner: Slavery, Race, and Ideology in the Age of the Civil War." *Journal of the Early Republic* 23, no. 2 (Summer 2003): 233–62.

———. *The Slave's Cause: A History of Abolition.* New Haven: Yale University Press, 2016.

Smith, Adam I. P. *The Stormy Present: Conservatism and the Problem of Slavery in Northern Politics, 1846–1865.* Chapel Hill: University of North Carolina Press, 2017.

Smith, John David, ed. *Black Soldiers in Blue: African American Troops in the Civil War Era.* Chapel Hill: University of North Carolina Press, 2002.

———. *Lincoln and the U.S. Colored Troops.* Carbondale: Southern Illinois University Press, 2013.

Smith, William Ernest. *The Francis Preston Blair Family in Politics.* 2 vols. New York: Macmillan, 1933.

Stahr, Walter. *Seward: Lincoln's Indispensable Man.* New York: Simon and Schuster, 2012.

———. *Stanton: Lincoln's Secretary of War.* New York: Simon and Schuster, 2017.

Stange, Douglas C. *Patterns of Antislavery Among American Unitarians, 1831–1860.* Cranbury, NJ: Associated University Presses, 1977.

Stebbins, Homer A. *A Political History of the State of New York, 1865–1869.* New York: Columbia University, 1913.

Stephens, George, and Donald Yacovone, ed. *A Voice of Thunder: A Black Soldier's Civil War.* Urbana: University of Illinois Press, 1998.

Stewart, James B. *Wendell Phillips: Liberty's Hero.* Baton Rouge: Louisiana State University Press, 1986.

———, ed. *William Lloyd Garrison at Two Hundred: History, Legacy, and Memory.* New Haven: Yale University Press, 2008.

Strangis, Joel. *Lewis Hayden and the War Against Slavery.* North Haven, CT: Linnet Books, 1999.

Stratton, Julius Adams, and Loretta H. Mannix. *Mind and Hand, The Birth of MIT.* Cambridge: MIT Press, 2005.

Sweeny, Kevin. "Rum, Romanism Representation, and Reform: Coalition Politics in Massachusetts, 1847–1853." *Civil War History* 22, no. 2 (June 1876): 116–37.

Taaffe, Stephen R. *Commanding the Army of the Potomac.* Lawrence: University Press of Kansas, 2006.

Tap, Bruce. *Over Lincoln's Shoulder: The Committee on the Conduct of the War.* Lawrence: University Press of Kansas, 1998.

Taylor, Brian. *Fighting for Citizenship: Black Northerners and the Debate over Military Service in the Civil War.* Chapel Hill: University of North Carolina Press, 2020.

Taylor, Karen C. *Legendary Locals of Beacon Hill Massachusetts.* Arcadia, SC: Legendary Locals, 2014.

Taylor, Stephen. "Progressive Nativism: The Know Nothing Party in Massachusetts." *Historical Journal of Massachusetts* 28 (2000): 167–84.

Tewell, Jeremy J. *A Self-Evident Lie: Southern Slavery and the Threat to American Freedom.* Kent: Kent State University Press, 2014.

Tharp, Louise Hall. *Three Saints and a Sinner.* Boston: Little, Brown, 1956.

Thomas, Benjamin P. *Abraham Lincoln: A Biography.* New York: Knopf, 1952.

Thomas, Benjamin P., and Harold M. Hyman. *Stanton: The Life and Times of Lincoln's Secretary of War*. New York: Knopf, 1962.

Traub, James. *John Quincy Adams: Militant Spirit*. New York: Basic Books, 2016.

Trefousse, Hans L. *Andrew Johnson: A Biography*. New York: W. W. Norton, 1989.

———. *Ben Butler: The South Called Him Beast!* New York: Twayne, 1957.

———. *Thaddeus Stevens: Nineteenth-Century Egalitarian*. Chapel Hill: University of North Carolina Press, 1997.

Trent, James W., Jr. *The Manliest Man: Samuel Gridley Howe and the Contours of Nineteenth-Century American Reform*. Amherst: University of Massachusetts Press, 2012.

Underwood, Francis H. *Henry Wadsworth Longfellow: A Biographical Sketch*. Boston: Houghton Mifflin, 1984.

Usher, Ellis B. "Cyrus Woodman: A Character Sketch." *Wisconsin Magazine of History* 2, no. 4 (June 1919): 393–412.

Varon, Elizabeth. *Southern Lady, Yankee Spy: True Story of Elizabeth Van Lew, A Union Agent in the Heart of the Confederacy*. New York: Oxford University Press, 2003.

Villard, Oswald Garrison. *John Brown, 1800–1859*. Boston: Houghton Mifflin, 1910.

Voegeli, Jacque V. "A Rejected Alternative: Union Policy and the Relocation of Southern 'Contrabands' at the Dawn of Emancipation." *Journal of Southern History* 69, no. 4 (Nov. 2003): 765–90.

Vorenberg, Michael. *Final Freedom: The Civil War, the Abolition of Slavery, and the Thirteenth Amendment*. New York: Cambridge University Press, 2001.

Wagner, David. *The "Miracle Worker" and the Transcendentalist: Annie Sullivan, Frank Sanborn, and the Education of Helen Keller*. New York: Paradigm Publishers, 2012.

Ware, Edith Ellen. *Political Opinion in Massachusetts during the Civil War and Reconstruction*. New York: Columbia University Studies in History, Economics, and Public Law, 1916.

Warren, Gorden H. *Fountain of Discontent: The Trent Affair and Freedom of the Seas*. Boston: Northeastern University Press, 1981.

Washington, Margaret. *Sojourner Truth's America*. Urbana: University of Illinois Press, 2009.

Weber, Thomas. *The Northern Railroads in the Civil War, 1861–1865*. Bloomington: Indiana University Press, 1952.

Weeden, William B. *War Government, Federal and State, 1861–1865*. Boston: Houghton Mifflin, 1906.

Wells, Jonathan Daniel. *Blind No More: African American Resistance, Free-Soil Politics, and the Coming of the Civil War*. Athens: University of Georgia Press, 2019.

Wells, Tom H. *The Slave Ship Wanderer*. Athens: University of Georgia Press, 1967.

Wesley, Charles J. *Ohio Negroes in the Civil War*. Columbus: Ohio State University Press, 1962.

Westwood, Howard C. "The Cause and Consequence of a Union Black Soldier's Mutiny and Execution." *Civil War History* 31, no. 3 (Sept. 1985): 222–36.

———. "Generals David Hunter and Rufus Saxton and Black Soldiers." *South Carolina Historical Magazine* 86 (1985): 165–81.

White, Arthur O. "Antebellum School Reform in Boston: Integrationists and Separatists." *Phylon* 34, no. 2 (1973): 203–17.

White, Jonathan W. *Midnight in America: Darkness, Sleep, and Dreams during the Civil War*. Chapel Hill: University of North Carolina Press, 2017.

White, Richard. *The Republic for Which It Stands: The United States during Reconstruction and the Gilded Age, 1865–1896*. New York: Oxford University Press, 2017.

Wickenden, Dorothy. *The Agitators: Three Friends Who Fought for Abolition and Women's Rights*. New York: Scribner, 2021.

Wiecek, William M. *The Sources of Antislavery Constitutionalism in America, 1760–1848*. Ithaca: Cornell University Press, 1977.

Wilentz, Sean, ed. *The Best American History Essays on Lincoln*. New York: Palgrave Macmillan, 2009.

————. *The Rise of American Democracy: Jefferson to Lincoln.* New York: W. W. Norton, 2006.

Williamson, Harold F. *Edward Atkinson: The Biography of an American Liberal.* Boston: Old Corner Book Store, 1934.

Wills, Gary. *Lincoln at Gettysburg: The Words that Remade America.* New York: Simon and Schuster, 2012.

Wilson, Keith P. *Campfires of Freedom: The Camp Life of Black Soldiers during the Civil War.* Kent: Kent State University Press, 2002.

Wilson, Joseph T. *The Black Phalanx.* New York: Da Capo Press, 1994.

Wirzbicki, Peter. "Black Transcendentalism: William Cooper Nell, the Adelphic Union, and the Black Abolitionist Tradition." *Journal of the Civil War Era* 8, no. 2 (June 2018): 269–90.

Winsor, Justin. *The Memorial History of Boston, Including Suffolk County, Massachusetts, 1630–1880.* 4 vols. Boston: James R. Osgood, 1881.

Witt, John Fabian. *Lincoln's Code: The Laws of War in American History.* New York: Free Press, 2013.

Woodson, Carter G. *The History of the Negro Church.* Washington, D.C.: Associated Publishers, 1921.

Zebley, Kathleen Rosa. "God and Liberty: The Life of Charles Wesley Slack." MA thesis, Kent State University, 1992.

INDEX

Note: Page references in *italics* refer to figures.

Abbott, Edward, 214
Abbott, Henry, 283
Abbott, Josiah, 87, 88
abolitionism: Andrew's Civil War goal for, 158–61, 169, 187–90; Andrew's early Boston exposure to, 24–29, 31–38; antislavery vs. abolition, 42; *Dred Scott v. Sandford* decision and reaction, 85–99; elections of 1860 and rhetoric about, 118–34; Emancipation Proclamation issued by Lincoln, 214, 219–27; and Fugitive Slave Law, 53–68; House of Representatives gag rule on slavery, 25; Human Rights meeting (Faneuil Hall, October 1843), 33; John Brown at Harpers Ferry, 107–17; John Quincy Adams on, 1–4, 9; and Latimer Law, 31–34, 58; Maryland, slavery abolished by, 293; and Massachusetts school integration, 76–78, 190; Missouri, slavery abolished by, 299; New York State, abolitionist voters in, 258; and Republican Party's rise in Massachusetts, 70–72, 78–84; "slavery has no business to exist *any where*" (Andrew), 101; *Uncle Tom's Cabin* and public opinion, 59–60; Whig Party and Free-Soil Party inception, 39–52; women abolitionists' antislavery petition (1837), 27. *See also* Brown, John; Civil War; Emancipation Proclamation
Act in Aid of the Families of Volunteers (Massachusetts), 166
Adams, Charles Francis, Jr., 221, 304, 332

Adams, Charles Francis, Sr.: Andrew's introduction to, 4; and Civil War mobilization, 164; Congress election of, 101; events leading to Civil War, 137, 141–43, 145–46; and Free-Soil Party inception, 40, 44, 45, 47–48; on Fugitive Slave Act, 54–55; son of, as commissioned officer, 168
Adams, John Quincy, 1–4, 9, 25, 42, 46, 47
Adams, John Quincy, II, 168
Adams, John Quincy, Jr., 359
Adams, Samuel, 135, 170, 375, 376
The Adventures of Gil Blas (Lesage), 9
African Americans: Andrew on postwar civil rights protections, 326, 329–30, 337–47; havens suggested for freed slaves, outside United States, 212; in Massachusetts legislature, 149; race riots (Memphis and New Orleans), 354, 368; suffrage debate, 313, 330–31, 335, 338–39, 342–44, 346–47; Thirteenth Amendment, 273, 280, 299–302, 324–25. *See also* abolitionism; slavery; *individual names of African American leaders*
African American troops: authorization of, 147, 149, 160, 196, 205–6, 220, 235–41; Bureau of Colored Troops, 248, 255; commissioned officers of, 254; Fifth Massachusetts Cavalry, 254, 304, 318; Fifty-fifth Regiment (Massachusetts), 260, 288, 357; First and Third Infantry of New Orleans Corps d'Afrique, 247; First South Carolina regiment, 217, 232, 234,

African American troops (continued)
239; Fort Pillow massacre, 272; Louisiana Native Guards, 271–72; and national
conscription, 242–46; pay disparity and
recruitment problems, 253–57, 263–79,
280, 301; recruitment in southern states,
289; salaries of, 236, 239–41; Second
Regiment of Cavalry, 233; Third South
Carolina Colored Infantry, 248, 267;
treatment of, 318; Twenty-fifth Corps,
304, 309; United States Colored Troops,
249; white soldiers' prejudice toward,
283–84, 291; William Walker's execution,
267, 275. See also Fifty-fourth Regiment
Agassiz, Louis, 55, 102
Alabama, capitalist support sought, 324–25
alcohol legislation (Massachusetts), 70,
308, 361–64, 408n30
Allen, Charles, 49, 141, 351
Allen, William, 15
Alley, John, 197
Altoona, governors' meeting in Providence,
212–22, 431n42
American Anti-Slavery Society, 14, 19,
59–60, 263
American Association for the Promotion of
the Social Science, 323
American Land Company and Agency, 322
American Missionary Association, 164, 223
American Party. See Know Nothing Party
American Peace Society, 18, 131
American Tract Society, 158
American Unitarian Association, 356–57
Amistad (ship), 1, 31
Anderson, Robert, 305
Andrew, Charles Albion (son), 51
Andrew, Edith (daughter), 63
Andrew, Elizabeth Loring (daughter), 60
Andrew, Eliza Jones Hersey (wife), 50–51,
60, 75, 175, 244, 290–91, 321, 352–54, 372,
374–76
Andrew, Henry Hersey (son), 98
Andrew, Isaac Watson (brother), 6, 9, 10,
12, 24, 50, 372–73, 416n48
Andrew, John Albion: as abolitionist, 1–4, 9;
agricultural fairs enjoyed by, 170, 256, 287,
320–21, 356; birth of children, 51, 63, 98; at
Bowdoin, 14–23; characterization of, 17,
22–23, 26, 168–77, 185–86; courtship and
wedding to Eliza, 50–51; death and legacy
of, 372–83; death of son, 51; early law
career, 27–28; early life of, 5–11; education
of, 7, 8, 11–13, 24–27; family finances of,

254–55, 258–62; on Harvard board of
overseers, 314, 370; health problems of,
71, 132, 264, 290–91, 295–96, 312, 348, 350,
354–56; homes of, 75, 369, 373; photos of,
198, 210; physical description of, 1, 12,
28, 382; statue of, 380, 381–83. See also
abolitionism; Civil War
Andrew, John Albion, causes and charitable
work: and Barton's nursing activism,
193; and family finances, 254–55, 258–62,
348; and Freedman's Commission, 193;
Home for Aged Colored Women, 118–19;
as priority, 26, 44, 49, 208, 261–62;
Samuel Gridley Howe on, as "poor
man's lawyer," 106; for soldiers and
families, 182–83. See also abolitionism;
capital punishment; prison reform and
prisoners' welfare; women's rights;
individual names of charity organizations
Andrew, John Albion, law career: Buffalo
(British brig) case of, 75–76; on capital
punishment, 36–38, 419n12; former
client hired by, 138–39; Free State
officers (Kansas) case, 402n28; fugitive
slaves defended by, 72–76, 105–6; Henry
H. Fuller-Andrew partnership, 26–29,
34–37; Garron case, 400n5; income
from, 44, 51; and John Brown's Harpers
Ferry raid, 107–17; legal education and
apprenticeship, 24–27; maritime cases,
75–76, 123–24; poor clients' championed
by, 29, 34; post-legislative commitment,
return to, 97–98, 100–106; return to,
after governorship, 323, 329, 332, 339–44,
350–64, 365–72; Sanborn ("secret
six") defended by, 119; on school
desegregation, 76–78; Suffolk County
bar admission, 27; Sweet case, 89–90;
in Theophilius Parsons Chandler law
practice, 37. See also capital punishment;
prison reform and prisoners' welfare
Andrew, John Albion, political career:
Alexander Bullock as gubernatorial
successor, 323; Bowdoin's American
Peace Society, 18, 131; cabinet positions
proposed for, 293, 300–301, 303; Civil
War, militias called, 148–55; Civil War and
emancipation goal of, 158–61, 169, 187–90,
195–96, 200–203; Civil War leadership of,
168–77, 185–86; Civil War mobilization by,
156–67, 184; Civil War preparedness, 135–
47, 148–49; on commissioning of officers
in Massachusetts, 161–62; concern for

constituents, 332–33; freedom souvenirs given to, 284, 295; gubernatorial election, first (1860), 122–28; gubernatorial elections, subsequent (1861–1866), 171, 174, 177, 190–91, 218–27, 228–30, 259, 285, 289–96; judgeship declined by, 102–3, 119; last months as governor, 315–34; at Lewis Hayden's home on Thanksgiving Day, 260; and Lincoln's nomination (1860), 120–22, 410–11n8; as Massachusetts Sixth Ward legislator, 87–99; and Republican Party's rise in Massachusetts, 67, 70–72, 78–79; on state vs. military authority, 169, 173–77, 179–83; and support by elite families, 145, 162; and Tubman, 248–52; valedictory address, 335–39; violent threat made to, 307; Washington trips of, 132–33, 175–77, 181–82, 280–83, 287–88; Whig Party and Free-Soil Party inception, 39–52; Whig Party joined by, 28, 38; Windham visits, 203, 370
Andrew, John Albion, religious interests of: Methodist Bethel mission attendance of, 31; as Unitarian, 1, 16, 22, 23, 29–30. See also Clarke, James Freeman; Grimes, Leonard; Twelfth Baptist Church; Unitarianism
Andrew, John Albion, written works/speeches: at Boxford (Massachusetts) lyceum, 49–50; Fifty-fourth presented regimental colors, 268–69; General Court address, 298; "History of Ida May" (broadside), 74–75; holiday proclamation (1861), 178–79; "Hymn to Peace" (poem), 18; inaugural addresses, 132, 134, 136, 138, 184, 229–30, 233, 265; Lincoln Memorial Association speech, 363–64; Methodist Camp Meeting Association sermon, 209–11; public letters for call to arms, 197–99; "The Road to Honor" (Commencement Day poem, 1836), 21; Springfield address, 287; valedictory address, 335–39; voluminous correspondence of, 202; "Wetmore" letter, 235
Andrew, John Forrester (son), 51, 351, 354, 366
Andrew, Jonathan (father), 5–9, 11, 17, 24, 51
Andrew, Nancy Alfreda (sister), 6, 24, 50
Andrew, Nancy Pierce (mother), 5–9, 13
Andrew, Sarah Elizabeth (sister), 6, 7, 24, 50, 320
Andrews, Dean, 22
Andrews, Jacob, 279

Andrews, John D., 148, 173, 204, 206, 215, 216
Antioch College, 320
An Appeal in Favor of That Class of Americans Called Africans (L. M. Child), 10–11
Appeal to the Colored Citizens of the World (D. Walker), 10
Appleton, Nathan, 47
Army of the Potomac, and McClellan, 165. See also McClellan, George
Aspinwall, William, 52
Astor House "ruse," 202–6
Athenaean Society, 17–18, 33–34, 50
Atkinson, Edward, 301, 355, 358
Atlantic Monthly, mission of, 396n6

Baker, Almira P., 8
Baker, Nathaniel, 316
Banks, Nathaniel: additional soldiers needed by, 197–99; on Andrew's leadership, 374; as Department of the Gulf commander, 226; on emancipation as wartime measure, 180; gubernatorial elections, 88, 90, 95–96, 99, 101, 102, 106, 123–25, 130, 132; gubernatorial power of, 135–36; Hoosac railroad tunnel, 170; House speakership, 79–80, 83; and Massachusetts militia, 139; Massachusetts Republican convention chaired by, 78; as Massachusetts speaker of the house, 58
Barker, Fordyce, 22
Barker, Thomas, 273
Barlow, Francis C., 437n3
"The Barnstable Ball" (J. W. Howe), 321
Barton, Clara, 193
Batchelder, James, 63
Bates, Edward, 257, 272–73, 276, 293
"Battle Hymn of the Republic" (song, J. W. Howe), 176
Beach, Erasmus D., 129
Beale, Arthur, 382
Beatley, Clara Bancroft, 13
Beecher, Henry Ward, 11, 312, 324–25, 357
Bell, Luther, 269
Bell, Prudence, 73, 74
Bennett, Augustus, 267
Bertonneau, Arnold, 271
Bethel Chapel, 103, 331
Betts, Samuel, 353
Bigelow, Andrew, 118
Bigelow, John, 262
Bingham, Caleb, 8
Bingham, John, 343

Binney, John, 330, 333–34, 341, 370–71
Bird, Francis William "Frank": on Andrew
as Seward's replacement, 293; Andrew
praised by, 297; Andrew's gubernatorial
election (1860), 119, 125, 130; on
Andrew's reaction to bounty loan,
270–71; Andrew's reliance on, 239; and
Andrew's return to private life, 340,
348, 354; on Andrew's war leadership,
171; "Bird Club" of, 48, 60, 168–69; on
capital punishment, 308, 309; *Dred Scott
v. Sandford* decision and reaction, 88,
95, 99; on emancipation as wartime
measure, 189, 190; and Emancipation
Proclamation plans, 224; enlistment/
conscription strategies debated, 195;
events leading to Civil War, 137–38,
142, 146; and Free-Soil Party inception,
47, 48; "Honest Man's Ticket" of,
83–84; and John Dix, 433n57; Lincoln's
cabinet change, 234; Massachusetts state
legislature election, 55
Birney, James G., 28
Bixby, Lydia, 294
Blair, Francis, Sr.: on Andrew appointment
to cabinet, 300; Andrew on emancipation as wartime measure, 188; on
Andrew's return to private life, 345–46;
enlistment/conscription strategies
debated, 194, 203; and governors' meeting in Altoona, 217, 222; Harvard address
by, 314; on Maryland's abolished slavery,
293; and Sumner's recovery, 81–82
Blair, Montgomery: on Andrew's aboli-
tionist goal for war, 159; appointed to/
resigned from Lincoln's cabinet, 143,
154, 292; and Benjamin Butler, 169; and
Frémont, 167; and Georgia raid, 250;
and John Brown's defense, 108, 114; and
Johnson administration, 345, 359, 371;
and Tubman, 249
Blair House, 403n35
Blake, J. Vila, 254
Blanchard, Mary, 65
"Bleeding Kansas," 81, 83
Blodgett, Mrs. (boardinghouse owner), 26
Board of State Charities of Massachusetts,
309
Boker, George, 252
Bokum, Hermann, 328
Bolles, John, 224
Bond, Elias, 20–21
Booth, Edwin, 306

Booth, John Wilkes, 306, 307, 365
Boston Anti-Man Hunting League, 71
Boston Pilot (Irish newspaper), on African
American troops, 245
Boston Port Society, 31, 102
Boston Post, on "Emancipation: The Cure
for the Rebellion" (Sumner), 171
Boston Society for Aiding Discharged
Convicts, 38
Boston Temporary Home for the Destitute,
47
Boston Vigilance Committee: Andrew's
fundraising for fugitives, post-legislative
commitment, 102, 106; Andrew's rec-
ognition for, 42; and Boston Anti-Man
Hunting League, 71; and Botts family,
72; *Dred Scott v. Sandford* decision and
reaction, 89; and Fugitive Slave Act, 54,
56, 57, 63, 66
Boteler, Alexander, 107
Botts, Elizabeth, 73
Botts, Mary, 73–75
Botts, Seth (aka Henry Williams), 72–75, 114
bounty loan, 270–71
Boutwell, George, 102, 154, 155, 158, 166, 172,
189, 323
Bowditch, Charles, 164
Bowditch, Henry Ingersoll: as abolitionist,
2–4; African American soldiers recruited,
236; and Andrew's early abolitionist
stance, 27, 33; and Andrew's return to
private life, 361; and Boston Anti-Man
Hunting League, 71; and Boston Society
for Aiding Discharged Convicts, 38; and
Civil War mobilization, 164; enlistment/
conscription strategies debated, 205–6;
on school desegregation, 77; on soldiers'
pay, 223
Bowdoin College: American Peace Society,
18, 131; Andrew's education at, 14–23;
charter of, 388n2; in 1830s, 18; and Gor-
ham Academy, 11–13, 15; "illustrious class
of '37" reunion, 369–70; and Mellen, 8;
William Allen v. Joseph McKeen, 15
Bowen, James, 149, 236
Bowers, Charles, 158
Bowles, Samuel, 127, 372
Bradbury, Ammi, 17
Bradbury, James, 369
Bradford, William, 220, 316
Breckinridge, John, 83, 129
Bridgton Academy, 8–9
Britain: British Emancipation Day, 122;

British Royal Commission on Capital Punishment, 360; British West Indies slaves' liberation, 106; neutral Civil War stance of, 182
Broad Street Riot (Boston, 1837), 24
Brooks, Noah, 300
Brooks, Preston, 80–81
Brough, John, 287
Broughton, Nicholson, 158
Brown, George, 151
Brown, John: on antislavery commitment, 25; election rhetoric about (1860), 118–19, 127, 131; execution and martyrdom of, 112–17; execution anniversary and rhetoric about, 139; execution site of, 321; Harpers Ferry raid events, 107–12; "John Brown's Body" (song), 160, 176, 304–5; Kansas abolitionist fight of, 81–84, 87–88; legacy of, 383; marble bust of, 378; prosecutor of, 195; sanity questioned, 408n29; Senate inquiry, 114–17, 410n4
Brown, John M., 42
Brown, Oliver, 107
Brown, Owen, 107
Brown, Watson, 107
Brown, William, 105
Brown, William Wells, 227, 278
Browne, Albert, Jr.: on Andrew's family life, 351–52; in Andrew's law office, 64; on Andrew's post-gubernatorial role, 372; on Andrew's proclamation (1861), 178; on Andrew's prohibition case, 362; as military secretary to Andrew, 158; on militia left in Massachusetts, 250; as private secretary to Andrew, 138; and Salmon P. Chase, 295; on war conditions in southern states, 289–90; in Washington, 242, 303
Browne, John, 38
Bruce, Frederick, 319, 378
Bryant, William Cullen, 286, 362
Buchanan, James, 83–84, 85, 101, 104, 133, 146, 315
Buckingham, Catharinus, 203
Buckingham, William, 216, 219
Buell, Don Carlos, 188
Bullock, Alexander, 224, 320, 323, 339–40, 347–48, 351
Bullock, William, 162
Bunting, John, 80
Bureau of Colored Troops, 248, 255
"Buried with his Niggers" (Boker), 252
Burlingame, Anson, 101, 127, 319

Burnham, George P., 408n30
Burns, Anthony, 63–66, 75, 91, 245
Burns, Robert, 7
Burnside, Ambrose, 193, 226
Burt, William, 65, 75, 106, 161, 301, 373
Butler, Ambrose, 80
Butler, Benjamin: and Andrew's dispute on commissioning of soldiers, 169, 173–77; Andrew's gubernatorial election (1860), 129; and Civil War mobilization, 156, 163, 164, 167; and emancipation as wartime measure, 180, 184–88; and Emancipation Proclamation plans, 226; events leading to Civil War, 147; and Maryland secession threat, 155; Massachusetts brigade led by, 150–51; Plumer case, 103–4; and Tubman, 248; vice presidency consideration, 278
Butts, Brian J., 429n12
Byron, George Gordon (Lord), 153, 266

Cabot, Frederick, 33
Cabot, James, 165–66
Cailloux, Andre, 247
Calhoun, John, 61
Cameron, Simon: and Andrew's war leadership, 169, 174, 175, 177; and Civil War mobilization, 158, 159, 160, 164, 165; on emancipation as wartime measure, 180, 185, 188; events leading to Civil War, 143; as Lincoln's secretary of war, 149–50, 154, 155
Campbell, Archibald, 155
capital punishment: Andrew's expertise recognized, 360; Andrew's opposition to, 36–38, 419n12; Goode's trial, 52; Green case, 308–9, 321, 348–49, 350; Hersey case, 429n7; William Lloyd Garrison on, 70–71; William Walker's execution by Union army, 267, 275
Carleton, Silas, 119
Carter, Robert, 60
Cass, Lewis, 47
Catholics, immigration of, 69–70
Chamberlain, Joshua, 369
Chandler, Charles, 103, 201, 208
Chandler, Peleg Whitman: Andrew in Maine with, 367; and Andrew's early law career, 26–28, 37; on Andrew's legacy, 375, 377; and Andrew's parents, 5, 6; and Andrew's war leadership, 170, 173; enlistment/conscription strategies debated, 195; events leading to Civil War,

Chandler, Peleg Whitman (*continued*) 136, 141; and Free-Soil Party inception, 44, 50

Chandler, Theophilus Parsons, 37, 44, 50, 80, 95, 141, 144, 187–88, 312

Chandler, William, 359

Channing, Walter, 38

Channing, William Ellery, 25, 36, 316

Channing, William Francis, 33

Chase, John, 201

Chase, Salmon P.: Andrew on emancipation enactment, 233; cabinet withdrawal of, 268; and Civil War funding, 159; enlistment/conscription strategies debated, 193; on equal pay, 280; events leading to Civil War, 139, 143; and John Brown, 88; John Greenleaf Whittier on, 368; presidential ambition, 285; presidential election (1860), 119; retirement from cabinet, 282, 292; as Supreme Court chief justice, 295, 370

Cheney, Ednah, 248

Child, Francis, 345

Child, Linus, 361

Child, Lydia Maria, 10–11, 52, 368

Choate, Joseph, 352–53

Choate, Rufus, 37

Christian Register, Unitarian mission of, 31, 34

Christian World: Andrew as editor of, 43; James Freeman Clarke as editor of, 45; Unitarian mission of, 31, 34

Church of the Disciples, 29–31, 34, 47. *See also* Clarke, James Freeman

Chute, John, 5

citizenship: *Dred Scott v. Sandford*, 85–99; Fourteenth Amendment, 343–45, 347; and immigrants, 69–72, 155, 194

Civil War: Andrew on prisoners of war, 174, 256, 288, 302; and Andrew's emancipation goal, 158–61, 169, 187–90, 195–96, 200–203; Andrew's leadership during, 168–77, 185–86; casualties of, Andrew on, 173; contractors, 168, 170; draft, governors in control of, 207–11; draft incentives and equal pay problems, 253–57, 267–68, 271–78, 280, 301; draft/recruitment strategies debated, 192–206, 242–46; Emancipation Proclamation issued by Lincoln, 214, 219–27; European soldiers in, 369; events leading to, 135–47; governors' meetings in Providence and Altoona, 212–22, 431n42; Grand

Review ceremony, 310–11; Lee's surrender, 302, 304–6, 309; Massachusetts mobilization for, 148–55, 156–67, 184; mobilization for, 156–67; prisoners of war, 174; Return of the Flags (Massachusetts) ceremony, 331–32; soldiers' pay, late/missing, 223; South Carolina's secession, 133–34; wounded and dead, treatment of, 223. *See also* African American troops; Reconstruction

Civil War, battles: Antietam, 218, 219, 223, 225, 229, 370; Antietam commemoration, 370; Ball's Bluff, 172–74, 179, 259, 369; Bull Run, First, 163–65, 169, 172; Bull Run, Second, 214–16; Cedar Creek, 361; Chancellorsville, 243, 247; Chickamauga, 258; Cold Harbor, 278; of the Crater, 283; Fort Sumter, 148, 155, 272; Fort Sumter, commemoration, 3–5; Fort Wagner, 252, 254, 277; Fredericksburg, 229–30, 265, 317; Gettysburg, 251, 274; Glendale, 201; Hampton Roads, 193; Manassas, 163; Petersburg, 283; Seven Days, 204; Seven Pines, 201; Shenandoah Valley campaign, 288–89; Shiloh, 195; South Mountain, 238; Stones River, 234; Vicksburg, 247, 251; of the Wilderness, 274, 283

Claflin, William, 118, 125, 300

Clapp, George, 88

Clapp, William, 246

Clark, Augustus, 309–10

Clark, John, 73

Clarke, James Freeman: on Andrew's concern for constituents, 332; on Andrew's legacy, 374; and Andrew's return to private life, 351, 363–64; and Andrew's war leadership, 175–76; and Boston Anti-Man Hunting League, 71; on capital punishment, 37; church contributions sought by, 261; and Church of the Disciples, 29–31, 34, 47; emancipation enactment, 231; events leading to Civil War, 139, 140, 144; and Free-Soil Party inception, 45, 46, 51–52; on Fugitive Slave Law, 55, 56, 65, 66; Home for Aged Colored Women, 118; photo, 35; at reception for Bertonneau and Roudanez, 271; on Seward, 290

Clarke, Lillian, 34

Clay, Henry, 14–15, 53, 54, 61

Clifford, John, 142

Coffin, Charles, 159

Collamore, Horace, 61

The Columbian Orator (C. Bingham), 8
Combahee Raid, 249–50
Comins, Linus B., 146
Committee of One Hundred, 154
Commonwealth (journal), inception of, 55, 60, 65, 398n20
Commonwealth v. John Hunt & Others (1842), 36
Compromise of 1850, 53–59
"Conditions of a Restored Union" (sermon, Beecher), 324
Condon, Charles T., 48
Congress, U.S.: Crittenden-Johnson Resolution, 168, 169, 179; Fort Pillow massacre investigation, 272; Fugitive Slave Act, 33, 54, 56, 57, 63, 66; House of Representatives and gag rule on slavery (1837), 25; Kansas-Nebraska Act, 62–68; on Lincoln's war management, 179; Militia Act, 205–6, 207, 227, 239; Second Confiscation Act, 205–6, 272–73. *See also* Fugitive Slave Law; *individual names of political parties*; *individual names of representatives*; *individual names of senators*
Constitution, U.S.: Fourteenth Amendment, 343–45, 347; Thirteenth Amendment, 273, 280, 299–302, 324–25
contraband policy, 164, 173, 179–80, 194–97, 200–202, 205–6
Conversational Club, 46
Converse, Frank, 308
Conway, Thomas, 322
Copeland, Robert, 180, 200
Copperheads, 270, 292
Cornell, Ezra, 320
"Cornerstone of the Confederacy" (speech, Stephens), 346
Cornhill Coffeehouse, 33, 48, 56
Cornwell, John, 73
cotton industry, northern support of, 14, 38
Coutrell, Madame, 256
Cowdin, Robert, 158
Cowper, William, 7–8
Craft, William and Ellen, 54
Crandall, H. Burr, 119
Cretan rebels, Samuel Gridley Howe's support of, 356
Crittenden-Johnson Resolution (1861), 168, 169, 179
Crowninshield, Francis, 141, 151
Cummings, Asa, 10
Curiosity (C. Sprague), 12
Curtin, Andrew, 202, 215, 217, 219–20, 250

Curtis, Benjamin, 86
Curtis, George Ticknor, 56, 134, 287, 332
Cushing, Caleb, 91–92, 94–98, 132, 153
Cushing, Luther S., 37
Cushman, Barzillai, 8

Daily Advertiser (Boston), on Republican Party's rise, 78–79, 83
Daily Citizen (Lowell, Massachusetts), on Andrew's gubernatorial nomination, 129
Dale, William, 161
Dall, Caroline Healey, 163, 415n21
Dalton, Charles, 158
Dana, Charles, 372
Dana, Richard Henry, Jr.: and Andrew's early law career, 27, 37; on Andrew's legacy, 376, 377; enlistment/conscription strategies debated, 199; and Free-Soil Party inception, 44; and Fugitive Slave Law, 56, 58, 59, 62–64, 66; on political rights of freed slaves, 312
Davis, Charles, 56
Davis, Henry, 268, 282
Davis, Isaac, 174
Davis, Jefferson, 147, 226, 248, 289, 304
Davis, Woodbury, 290
Dawes, Henry, 101, 124, 127, 171, 340
Day, Joseph, 161
Dayton, William, 82
Democratic Party: and Free-Soiler Party inception, 47–49; Fugitive Slave Law and politics of fugitive hunting, 58–61
Derby, George, 372
Desmarteau, Alexander, 419n12
Devens, Charles, Jr., 172, 221, 313–14
Devereux, Charles, 235
De Wolf, Orinn, 36
The Dial (journal), and Margaret Fuller, 28
Dickens, Charles, 364
Dickinson, Daniel, 190
Dix, James, 126–27
Dix, John, 223–25, 433n57
Dodge, John, 122
Donelson, Andrew, 83
Douglas, Stephen A., 62, 66, 80, 100, 120, 129
Douglass, Charles, 244
Douglass, Frederick: on capital punishment, 52; and Educational Commission for the Freedmen, 231; at "Great Jubilee" meeting, 305; and John Brown, 107–8; *Narrative of the Life of Frederick, An American Slave*, 38; on pay equity and protection of Black prisoners of war, 256–57;

Douglass, Frederick (*continued*)
  postwar July Fourth celebration letter
  of, 316; on recruitment, 277; on runaway
  female slave, 54–55; sons' enlistment,
  244; and William Lloyd Garrison, 60
Douglass, Lewis, 244, 252
Dow, Neal, 27
Downing, George, 241
Draper, Alonzo, 238–39
Dred Scott v. Sandford (1857), 85–99, 134
Dudley, Elbridge, 367–68
Durant, Henry, 65
Dwight, Louis, 38

Early, Jubal, 283, 289
Edloe, Carter H., 45
education: Andrew on schools for former
  slaves, 321, 358, 360–61, 366; Massachu-
  setts school integration, 76–79, 190
Eliot, Thomas Dawes, 355, 357
Ellis, Charles, 65
Ellis, Matthias, 61
Ellms, Belinda, 366
Emancipation League, 187–90
Emancipation Proclamation, 228–35, 273.
  See also Freedman's Bureaus
Emerson, George, 51
Emerson, Ralph Waldo: as abolitionist, 3,
  4; on Edwin Stanton, 185; events leading
  to Civil War, 139; and Free-Soil Party
  inception, 52; and Fugitive Slave Law, 55,
  58; at George Stearns's funeral, 365; and
  transcendentalism, 28, 29
Emerton, Timothy, 220
Emery, John, 214
Emigrant Aid Company, 88
Essex Institute, 360
Eustis, Henry, 193
Evans, George, 246
Evarts, William, 352–53, 376
Everett, Edward: on Andrew's popularity,
  190; and Civil War mobilization, 152,
  164; death of, 299; events leading to Civil
  War, 135, 141; on Livermore's lecture,
  211; speeches of, 283, 289; statue of, 371;
  Thursday Evening Club of, 266; Wilson
  as U.S. Senate replacement, 70

Farnsworth, Sibyl Ann, 8
Faye, Richard, 130
Felton, Cornelius, 157
Ferguson, Jordan G., 17
Fessenden, William Pitt, 119, 190, 267

Field, David, 285
Fields, Annie, 341, 352, 364, 377, 381
Fields, James, 325, 341, 352, 359, 364, 373–74,
  381
Fifty-fourth Regiment (Massachusetts):
  in battle, 247–48, 252; formation of,
  238, 242–46; pay disparity, 260, 269–71;
  regimental colors presented to, 268–69;
  return to Massachusetts, 319; Robert
  Gould Shaw's memorial, 323
Fillmore, Millard, 56, 83
Fiske, John, 369
Fletcher, Francis, 196
Fletcher, Thomas, 299
Flowers, Jack, 284, 295
Forbes, John Murray: African American
  cavalry organized by, 254; African
  American soldiers recruited, 235, 236,
  237; on Andrew for cabinet post, 293;
  on Andrew's finances, 258, 348; and
  Andrew's gubernatorial election (1860),
  133; on Andrew's post-gubernatorial
  role, 300–301, 303, 332, 348, 350, 352–
  53, 358, 365, 369, 370; and Andrew's war
  leadership, 168, 170; on Black suffrage,
  342–43; and Civil War mobilization,
  153, 158, 159, 161; and Edwin Stanton,
  185; enlistment/conscription strategies
  debated, 195–96; events leading to Civil
  War, 135–36, 141, 142; at Fort Monroe,
  150; on Grand Review, 310–11; and
  Lincoln's reelection bid, 286, 287; in
  New York City, 186; on recruitment of
  African American troops, 281
Forbes, Robert, 353
Forney, John, 302
Forrest, Nathan Bedford, 272
Forrester, John, 24
Fort Pillow massacre, 272
Foster, Charles, 241, 248
Foster, Dwight, 288
Foster, John, 277
Fourteenth Amendment, 343–45, 347
Fox, Charles, 173, 196
Fox, Gustavus, 186
Freedman's Bureaus, 230, 273, 293, 301, 321,
  327, 343, 344, 357, 361
Freedman's Commission, 193
Freedman's Inquiry Commission, 216, 273
Freedman's Union Commission, 357
Free-Soil Party: Fugitive Slave Law and
  politics of fugitive hunting, 58–61;
  inception, 394n20

Frémont, John, 82, 83, 166–67, 180, 195–96, 274, 278
French, Jonas, 130, 161
Fry, James, 251
Fugitive Slave Act (1793), 33, 54, 56, 57, 63, 66
Fugitive Slave Law (1850): and Compromise of 1850, 53–58; *Dred Scott v. Sandford* decision and reaction, 94, 98; and James Mason, 114–17, 181–82; and Kansas-Nebraska Act, 62–68; politics of fugitive hunting, 58–61; repeal of, 284; Republican Party on, 101; and Republican Party's rise in Massachusetts, 72, 73, 76, 77–78
Fuller, Arthur, 317
Fuller, Henry H., 26–29, 34–37, 61
Fuller, Margaret, 28, 29
Fuller, Richard Frederick, 37

Gardner, Henry J., 17, 28, 66, 70, 77–79, 83, 87, 131, 153
Garfield, James, 319
Garrison, George, 253, 263
Garrison, William Lloyd: on African American troops, 239; on Andrew for cabinet post, 292; and Andrew's abolitionist views, 39–40, 45; and Andrew's gubernatorial election (1860), 122–23, 128; and Andrew's return to private life, 357; Anti-Slavery Society lecture of, 14; British West Indies slaves' liberation, 106; on capital punishment, 37, 70–71; *Dred Scott v. Sandford* decision and reaction, 85, 86; on emancipation enactment, 231–32, 243, 245; on Emancipation Proclamation, 221; at Fort Sumter ceremony, 306; and Fugitive Slave Law, 54, 55, 59–60, 63; Fugitive Slave Law burnt by, 72; at George Stearns's funeral, 365; on governors' meetings, 212; and *Liberator* mission, 10, 25, 27, 85; and *Liberator* publication ended, 333; retirement of, 333; son's enlistment, 253; tribute to, 371
Garron, Ebenezer, 400n5
Gaskins, Maria, 105–6
Gay, Sydney, 287
George (enslaved man), 2–4, 40
George III (king of England), 15
Gerry, Elbridge, Jr., 3
Gerry, Elbridge, Sr., 3
Gibbs, Oliver, 267–68
Gillet, Frederick, 211
Gillmore, Quincy, 247, 260
Githel, John, 76

Godwin, Parke, 375
Goode, Washington, 52
Goodrich, John, 129, 141, 146, 417n51
Gorham Academy, 15
Gould, Charles, 215–16
Gould, Thomas, 381, 382
"gradualists," 25
Grant, Ulysses S.: Andrew on, 370–71; and Elizabeth Van Lew, 368; and end of Civil War, 303, 309; enlistment/conscription strategies debated, 192, 195; leadership of, 283; at Old South Church service, 318; overland campaign, 278; presidential campaign of, 372; promotion to Union army command, 266; at Vicksburg, 251
Gray, James, 31–33
Gray, John, Jr., 269
Gray, William, 152
Great Britain. *See* Britain
"Great Jubilee" meeting, 305
Greeley, Horace, 67, 212, 286, 316, 371
Greely, Phillip, Jr., 28
Green, Edward, 308–9, 321, 348–49, 350
Green, Harriet, 211, 429n12
Grimes, Leonard: African American soldiers recruited, 236; and Andrew's election to Massachusetts legislature, 87; on Andrew's legacy, 374, 377; Andrew's plan for legislative captain appointment, 263, 278; and Andrew's return to private life, 357; Andrew's worship at church of, 173; and Civil War inception, 149; and emancipation enactment, 231, 232; on equal pay, 255; and Free-Soil Party inception, 42, 45; and Fugitive Slave Law, 54, 55, 57, 63, 66; Home for Aged Colored Women, 118; at Lincoln's funeral, 307; photo, 32; and Sweet case, 89, 90; Twelfth Baptist Church led by, 31
Grimké, Angelina, 27
Grimké, Sarah, 27
Gurney, William, 278
Gurowski, Adam: and Andrew's war leadership, 175, 185–86; on emancipation, 215, 216, 225; enlistment/conscription strategies debated, 192, 199, 202–6; on equal pay, 275; on governors' meetings, 208

Haiti, diplomatic recognition of, 190–91, 194, 426n43
Hale, Charles, 120, 263

Hale, George, 275–76, 365
Hale, John, 60–61, 65
Hall, Florence Howe, 97
Halleck, Henry, 188, 196, 206, 207, 283
Hallett, Benjamin, 75
Hallowell, Edward, 237–38, 240, 277–78
Halstead, Murat, 120
Hamilton, James Alexander, 179, 219–20, 298, 305
Hamilton, John, 216
Hancock, John, 135
Hannum, James W., 2
Hansen, Josiah, 71
Harper's Weekly: on African American enlistment, 263; on Lincoln Memorial Association speech (Andrew), 363–64
Harrison, Frederick, 98
Harrison, Samuel, 271
Harvard, Andrew on board of overseers, 314, 370
Harvard Law School, 66
Hatch, Louis Clinton, 22
Haven, Gilbert, 5, 349, 363, 374
Hawthorne, Nathaniel, 55, 175
Hay, John, 294
Hayden, Lewis: on African American enlistment, 226–27; African American soldiers recruited, 236; Andrew at home of, on Thanksgiving Day, 260; and Andrew's election to Massachusetts legislature, 87, 88, 90; and Andrew's return to private life, 357; and Andrew's valedictory address, 335; and Civil War inception, 149; on emancipation enactment, 231; on equal pay, 255; events leading to Civil War, 147; and Free-Soil Party inception, 42; and Fugitive Slave Law, 54, 55–58, 63–64; gavel gift sent to, 295–96; and Know Nothings, 70; photo, 43; recruitment by, 262, 264–65, 274; on school desegregation, 76–77
Haynes, Gideon, 296, 309
Hazewell, Charles Creighton, 96
Hedge, Frederic, 378
Henshaw, Daniel, 222
Herbert, William, 103
Hersey, George C., 429n7
Higginson, Thomas Wentworth, 27, 57, 63–64, 65, 107–8, 217, 232, 249, 332
Hildreth, Richard, 3
Hillard, George S., 37, 44, 376
"History of Ida May" (broadside, Andrew), 74–75

Hitchcock, Alfred, 193
Hoadley, John, 440n35
Hoar, Ebenezer Rockwood, 120, 158
Hobart, Aaron, 61
Hodges, Edgar, 52
Holloway, Joseph, 270
Holmes, Isabella, 72
Holmes, William and Mary, 105
Home for Aged Colored Women, 118–19
Hooker, Joseph, 201, 208, 235, 243, 248
Hooper, Samuel, 282, 307, 320, 355
How, William, 321
Howard, Charles, 361
Howard, Jacob, 343
Howard Industrial School for Colored Persons, 361
Howe, Frank: American Land Company and Agency, 322; and Andrew's return to private life, 354; on Andrew's sermon (1862), 211; and Andrew's war leadership, 168; and Civil War mobilization, 166; on emancipation as wartime measure, 184–87; and Lee's surrender, 305, 306; and Lincoln's reelection bid, 286, 287, 290, 292, 293, 295
Howe, Henry Warren, 187
Howe, Julia Ward: and Andrew's early abolitionist stance, 27; on Andrew's early life, 5; and Andrew's return to private life, 321, 352; and Andrew's war leadership, 170, 175–76; "The Barnstable Ball," 321; "Battle Hymn of the Republic," 176, 373; on emancipation enactment, 243; events leading to Civil War, 140, 145–46; and Free-Soil Party inception, 46, 47, 394n20; "I Stood Before His Silent Grave," 378–79
Howe, Samuel Gridley: as abolitionist, 2–4; on Andrew as "poor man's lawyer," 106; and Andrew's early abolitionist stance, 27; and Andrew's early law career, 37, 38; and Andrew's gubernatorial election (1860), 117, 130; and Andrew's return to private life, 352, 356; and Andrew's war leadership, 168, 175; and Boston Anti-Man Hunting League, 71; charitable causes, 309; and Civil War inception, 148; *Dred Scott v. Sandford* decision and reaction, 94; and Emancipation League, 189; events leading to Civil War, 146; and Free-Soil Party inception, 40, 44, 46, 47, 51; and Fugitive Slave Law, 55; and

John Brown's Harpers Ferry raid, 107–8; on problem of incarcerated girls, 309; and Robert Gould Shaw's memorial, 323; on war and sanitation need, 158
Howland, Emily, 138
Hoyt, George, 108–9, 408n29
Hubbard, Samuel, 2
Hunter, David, 195–96, 197, 216–17, 242–43, 247–50, 437n3
Huntington, Asahel, 361
Hyatt, Thaddeus, 410n4
"Hymn to Peace" (Andrew), 18

Ida May (Langdon), 74
"immediatists," 25
immigration: Know Nothings on, 69–72; and militia policy, 155; and voting, 194
Ingersoll, Charles, 73, 268

Jackson, Andrew, 8, 14–15, 47, 137
Jackson, Edmund, 77
Jackson, Francis, 3, 4, 36–37, 139
Jackson, Thomas "Stonewall," 196–97
Jacob, Frederic, 12
Jaquess, James F., 447n46
Jay, John, Jr., 375
Jefferson, Thomas, 102
jobs for former slaves, Andrew on, 227, 228–35, 321–22, 371
John A. Andrew Memorial Hospital, 461–62n28
"John Brown's Body" (song), 176, 245
Johnson, Andrew: Andrew considered for cabinet of, 370, 371; Andrew's withdrawal of support for, 345; behavior of, 302, 450n23; Boston visit by, 366; Confederate rebels pardoned by, 337; impeachment of, 360; presidency assumed by, 311–14, 319, 325–27, 329–30; racism of, 290, 326; on Reconstruction, 354–56, 359; "swing around the circle" speaking campaign, 357–58; vice presidency, 278
Johnson, Frederick, 256
Jones, Edward, 150
Jones, Jacqueline, 393–94n16
Jones, William, 82–84
Justice and Expediency; or Slavery Considered with a View to its Rightful Remedy, Abolition (J. G. Whittier), 10

Kansas: John Brown and freedom fighters in, 81–84, 87–88, 115, 116, 402n28;

Kansas-Nebraska Act (1854), 62–68; pro-slavery attack in, 79–81
Kazinski, Louis, 75–76
Kellogg, Elijah, 12
Keyes, John, 120
Kimball, Moses, 132, 412–13n45
Kinsley, Edward, 213–14, 273, 277
Knight, Nehemiah, 216
Know Nothing Party, 69–72, 77–79, 83–84

labor unions, Commonwealth v. John Hunt & Others, 36
Ladd, Luther, 313
Lamar, Charles, 124
Langdon, Mary, 74
Langston, John, 280
Latimer, George, 31–33
Latimer, Rebecca, 31
Latimer Journal and North Star (abolitionist newspaper), founding of, 33
Latimer Law (1843), 31–34, 58
Lawrence, Abbott, 47
Lawrence, Amos, 127, 129, 141
Law Reporter (magazine), founding of, 37
League of Freedom, 54
Lee, Henry, Jr., 138, 140, 142, 156, 177, 250, 255, 285, 323
Lee, Robert E.: Burnside's offensive, 226; and John Brown's Harpers Ferry raid, 107; march north by (1862), 216–18; surrender of, 302, 304–6, 309. See also Civil War, battles
Lee, William, 195, 369
Lenox, Charles, 277
Lesage, Alain-René, 9
Liberator: antislavery mission of, 10, 25, 27; masthead change (1857), 85; publication ended, 333; William Lloyd Garrison on capital punishment, 70–71. See also Garrison, William Lloyd
Liberia, diplomatic recognition of, 190–91
Lieber, Francis, 314
Lincoln, Abraham: and Andrew on state vs. military authority, 169, 174, 177; Andrew on war policy of, 171, 173; Andrew's Washington meetings with, and administration, 132–33, 175–77, 181–82, 280–83, 287–88; assassination of, 306–14, 365–66; cabinet change forced by Republicans, 229, 234; and Civil War inception, 155; and Civil War mobilization, 156, 159, 160, 162, 165–67; and dog bite story, 447n44; on emancipation as wartime measure,

Lincoln, Abraham (*continued*)
179, 181, 183–88, 190–91; emancipation enactment, 228, 230, 231, 234;
Emancipation Proclamation issued by,
214, 219–27; enlistment/conscription
strategies debated, 194, 197, 199–206,
242–46; on equal pay, 253–57, 267–68,
271–78; Gettysburg Address, 260,
275; Grant promoted by, 266; Harriet
Beecher Stowe on, 377; and Hunter,
247; inaugural addresses, 146, 302,
328, 337; and Jaquess, 447n46; Julia
Ward Howe on, 378; legacy of Andrew's
influence on, 298; presidential election
(1860), 100, 120–22, 125, 129, 131, 133,
410–11n8; presidential election (1864),
274, 278, 283, 285–86, 289, 292–96;
presidential transition and inauguration of, 140, 142–43, 144, 146; Proclamation of Amnesty and Reconstruction,
260; Reconstruction plans, 260, 282,
326; recruitment returned to governors, 258; and Thirteenth Amendment,
300
Lincoln, Frederic, Jr., 365
Lincoln, Mary Todd, 187
Lincoln Memorial Association, 363–64
Litchfield, James, 313
Livermore, George, 211, 239
Logan, William, 277
Longfellow, Henry Wadsworth: as
abolitionist, 4; on Botts family emanci-
pation, 74; at Bowdoin, 15, 16; and Civil
War inception, 153; on Fifty-fourth Reg-
iment deployment, 245; and Fugitive
Slave Law, 55; and Gorham Academy, 11;
Outre-Mer, 15; "Paul Revere's Ride," 137;
and Sumner, 79
Loring, Charles, 57, 138
Loring, Edward G., 37, 63–66, 72, 78, 91–92,
94–95, 98, 279
Loring, Ellis Gray, 36, 37, 71
Loring, George, 133
Lovejoy, Elijah, 25
Lovejoy, Joseph Cammett, 72
Lowell, Anna, 360–61
Lowell, Charles, 201, 233
Lowell, Charles, III, 238
Lowell, Charles, Jr., 158, 351, 361
Lowell, James Russell, 55, 373
Lucas, Augustina, 419n12
L'Union (French-English newspaper),
founding of, 271

Lunt, George, 127
Lyman, John, 398n20

Macy, George, 180
Magoffin, Beriah, 176
Mahan, John, 259
Maine, District of: Andrew's early life in,
5–11; "mock mustering" protest (1837), 19
manifest destiny, 37
Mann, Horace, 37, 315–16, 319, 321
Marino Faliero, Doge of Venice (Byron), 266
Marsh, Robert, 86–87
Marshall, James, 161
Martin, John, 164
Maryland: constitutionally abolished
slavery, 293; secession threat, 142–44,
151, 155
Mason, Charles E., 462n48
Mason, Elizabeth Andrew, 462n48
Mason, James, 114–17, 133–34, 181–82
Massachusetts: Act in Aid of the Families of
Volunteers, 166; alcohol legislation, 70,
308, 361–64, 408n30; Andrew's speech
to General Court, 298; Boston North
End riot, 251; Civil War mobilization
by, 156–67, 184; Civil War preparedness
by, 135–47, 148–49; commissioning of
officers, 161–62; draft in, 251–52; Fugitive
Slave Law and politics of fugitive
hunting, 58–61; General Court's role,
135, 136; gubernatorial role, antebellum
period, 135; Hoosac railroad tunnel plan,
170; judgeship declined by Andrew,
102–3; and Maine as district of, 5;
militias called for Civil War, 148–55; navy
members of, 165, 281; "overcoat march,"
162; Personal Liberty Law, 77–78, 82,
96–98, 132, 134, 136–37, 139; Return of the
Flags ceremony, 331–32; Sixth Regiment
attacked by pro-secession mob, 151, 313;
Thirteenth Amendment ratified by, 300;
Thirtieth Massachusetts regiment, 187;
Twentieth Massachusetts (Harvard
Regiment), 172; Worcester as soldiers'
transfer point, 303. *See also* abolitionism;
Andrew, John Albion, political career
Massachusetts Anti-Slavery Society, 3–4,
72, 91–92, 139
Massachusetts Institute of Technology,
Andrew as trustee, 356
Massachusetts in the War (Bowen), 236
Massachusetts School for Idiotic and
Feeble-Minded Youth, 51, 102

Massachusetts Society for the Abolition of Capital Punishment, 36–37, 52, 70

May, Samuel, Jr., 45, 231

McClellan, George: Andrew on political/military views of, 174–75; as Army of the Potomac chief, 165; and enlistment/conscription strategies debated, 192, 194, 195, 199, 201, 203–5; military review in Virginia (1861), 176; recall/reinstatement of, 207, 214–18, 222, 226; on state vs. military authority, 180–81, 186; and Virginia mobilization, 188

McCrea, Julian, 86–87

McCrea v. Marsh (1858), 86–87, 102

McCulloch, Hugh, 358–59

McDowell, Irvin, 163, 165, 197

McFarland, Charles, 151

McKaye, James, 230

McKim, James, 230

McLellan, George W., 120

Meade, George, 251, 317

Mellen, Grenville, 8

Merriam, Francis, 248

CSS *Merrimack*, 193

Metcalf, Theron, 82–83, 106

Meteor (steamship), 352–53

Methodist Bethel mission, 31

Methodist Camp Meeting Association, 209

Mexican American War, 1–2, 39, 40, 43, 45, 46, 53

Militia Act (1862), 205–6, 207, 227, 239

Milton, John, 132, 153

Miner, Alonzo, 361

Minkins, Shadrach, 56, 58–59

Mississippi, constitution of, 453n14

Missouri: Civil War status of, 166–67; Missouri Compromise, 62, 66; slavery abolished by, 299

Mitchell, Charles, 357

USS *Monitor*, 193

Montgomery, James, 249–50

Moore, Thomas, 7

Morgan, Edwin, 82, 166, 202–3, 286, 301

Morris, Robert, 56, 63, 76–77, 147, 227

Motley, John, 295, 314

Müller, Heinrich, 238

Mussey, Reuben, Jr., 264

Nason, Elias, 7, 8, 375

Nason, Reuben, 11

National Union Party, 278, 286, 288, 290, 354–55

Neale, Christopher, 72, 73

Nell, William Cooper: African American soldiers recruited, 236; on Andrew's legacy, 377; Andrew's Massachusetts legislature election, 87, 91; Andrew's tribute by, 278–79; on emancipation enactment, 231; on equal pay, 255; on Fifty-fourth Regiment formation, 245; and Free-Soil Party inception, 45; and Latimer laws, 31–33; on school desegregation, 77

New Bedford Copper Company, 440n35

New England Convention of Colored People, 327

New England Historic-Genealogical Society, 356, 359

New England Refugees' Aid Society, 299

New England Women's Auxiliary Association Supply Department, 152

Newman, Samuel Phillips, 18

New York State, abolitionist voters in, 258

Niagara (ship), 2, 4

Niles, John Milton, 397n9

Norcross, Otis, 374

No Right to an Honest Living (J. Jones), 393–94n16

North Star, 78

Norton, Charles Eliot, 340–41, 342

Nouse, Amos, 413n45

Olden, Charles, 202

"The Old Oaken Bucket" (Woodworth), 125–26

Oliver, John, 82

Otis, James, 376

Otis, Mrs. Harrison Gray, 457n2

Ottoman (brig), 2–4, 40, 41

Outre-Mer (Longfellow), 15

"overcoat march," 162

Owen, Robert, 230

Packard, Alpheus Spring, Sr., 22, 287

Paine, Henry, 257, 259, 292

Paine, John Knowles, 378

Paine, Robert, 120

Palfrey, Francis, 172, 180

Palfrey, John G., 55, 398n20

Parker, Edward, 63

Parker, Francis, 197–98

Parker, Theodore: as abolitionist, 4; Andrew's correspondence with, 106; and Andrew's early abolitionist stance, 27; *Dred Scott v. Sandford* decision and reaction, 88, 97; events leading to Civil War, 140; and Free-Soil Party inception,

Parker, Theodore (*continued*)
46, 48; and Fugitive Slave Law, 57, 65;
and John Brown's Harpers Ferry raid,
107–8; "Of Justice and the Conscience"
(sermon), 64; "Some Thoughts on the
Progress of America" (speech), 64; "The
Transient and Permanent in Christianity" (sermon), 34
Parsons, John, 259
Parsons, Lewis, 324–25, 456n42
"Paul Revere's Ride" (Longfellow), 137
Peabody, Elizabeth, 320
Peabody, George, 361
Peace Convention, 140–41, 145
Pearson, John H., 2–3
Peirce, Richard, 161
Pennsylvania, need for defense, 250
People's Party, 218, 221, 257
Personal Liberty Law (Massachusetts),
77–78, 82, 96–98, 132, 134, 136–37, 139
Peucinian Society, 17–18
Phillips, Stephen C., 4, 142
Phillips, Wendell: as abolitionist, 4; and
Andrew's early abolitionist stance, 27;
and Andrew's early law career, 36, 37; on
Andrew's suffrage stance, 358; *Dred Scott
v. Sandford* decision and reaction, 92,
97; events leading to Civil War, 139–40;
and Free-Soil Party inception, 45, 52; and
Fugitive Slave Law, 57, 61, 65; and John
Brown, 409n44; and Lincoln's nomination (1860), 119; and Lincoln's reelection,
274, 278; speaking eloquence of, 101
Pierce, Albion K., 5
Pierce, Edward, 138, 159, 193, 252, 357
Pierce, Franklin, 60–61, 63, 65, 80, 83
Pierce, Henry L., 48
Pierce, James, 351
Pierpont, Francis, 442n22
Pierson, Charles, 174
Pike, Richard, 21
Plumer, Cyrus, 103–4
Pope, John, 207, 214–16
popular sovereignty, 47, 83
population statistics: African Americans
in Massachusetts (1860), 240; African
Americans in Union army (February
1864), 266; apportionment problem,
457n7; Boston (1837), 26; Boston (1850),
56; Massachusetts, females to males
ratio, 413–14n7
"The Prayer of Twenty Millions" (Greeley),
212

Prentiss, Henry, 71
Prentiss, Sargent, 211
prison reform and prisoners' welfare:
Andrew on imprisonment of poor,
332–33; Andrew on prisoners of war,
174, 256, 288, 302; Andrew's devotion
to, 29, 54, 296, 371; Boston Society for
Aiding Discharged Convicts, 38; and
debtors, 90; Frederick Douglass on
protection of Black prisoners of war,
256–57; incarcerated girls' treatment,
309; *Prisoner's Friend* on, 36, 392n31;
and racial prejudice, 52. *See also* capital
punishment
Proclamation of Amnesty and Reconstruction (Lincoln), 260
prohibition legislation (Massachusetts),
70, 308, 361–64, 408n30
Providence, governors' meeting in
Providence, 212–22
Provost, Nelson, 103
Putnam, William, 172

Quincy, Eliza, 266
Quincy, Josiah, Jr., 51, 62–63, 83, 154, 283, 320
Quint, Alonzo, 332

race riots (Memphis and New Orleans),
354, 368
railroads and railway authorities: African
Americans allowed on streetcars, 284;
and Andrew's transatlantic shipping
plans, 348, 351; Hoosac railroad tunnel,
170; Union Pacific Railroad, 356
Randolph, John, 63
Randolph, Peter, 45–46, 393–94n16
Rantoul, Robert, Jr., 36, 52, 57, 375
Raymond, Henry, 286
Read, Samuel, 255, 256
Reconstruction: Andrew Johnson on,
311–14, 319, 354–56, 359; Andrew's
disagreement with Sumner about, 324–
31, 338, 354; Andrew's plans for schools
and jobs, 227, 228–35, 321–22, 371; Cyrus
Woodman on fighting "good fight" of,
345; Lincoln's 10 percent proposal, 260,
282, 326
Redpath, James, 349
Reed, John, 161, 170
Remond, Charles Lenox, 45, 231
Republican Party: inception of, 67, 69–70,
403n36; and Know Nothing Party, 70–72;
Lincoln's nomination (1860), 120–22,

410–11n8; Massachusetts rise of, 67, 69–84; presidential election (1864), 274, 278; radical Republicans and Frémont's nomination, 278; radical Republicans on emancipation, 148–49; radical Republicans on Lincoln's war management, 179; radical Republicans on Reconstruction, 325–31

Return of the Flags (Massachusetts), 331–32

"The Return of the Standards" (Sargent), 417n6

Revere, Edward, 195

Revere, Paul, 195

Ricketson, Daniel, 274

Ricketson, Joseph, 274

Riley, Hugh, 300

Ritchie, Harrison, 158, 161, 168, 202, 440n35

Ritchie, John, 144

Robinson, William S. "Warrington," 48, 123, 125, 127, 141, 152, 222, 374–75

Rock, John, 290

Rockwell, Julius, 78

Rogers, Emma, 352

Rogers, John, 378

Rogers, William, 128, 157, 207, 352

Ropes, Hannah Anderson, 80, 81

Roudanez, Jean Baptiste, 271

Roudanez, Louis Charles, 271

Russell, Charles, 309

Russell, Edward, 182

Russell, Henry, 221

Russell, Le Baron, 224, 225, 229–30

Russell, Thomas, 105

Saint-Gaudens, Augustus, 383

Sanborn, Frank, 4–5, 55, 97, 107–8, 119–20, 130, 309, 323

Sargent, Horace, 138, 156–57, 168, 192–93, 225, 417n6

Saturday Evening Gazette, on African American troops, 246

Saxton, Rufus, 217, 224, 232, 233, 284, 290, 343

Schmitt, George, 172

Schouler, William: as adjutant general of Massachusetts, 259; on African American troops, 242, 246; and Alexander Bullock, 323; on Andrew's correspondence, 202; on Andrew's gubernatorial legacy, 332; on Cape Cod, 321; events leading to Civil War, 139; post–Civil War reports, 316; travel to soldiers in field, 289, 291, 294

Schurz, Carl, 324

Scott, Winfield, 45, 59–61, 142, 144, 154, 156, 163, 165

Seaver, Benjamin, 65

Second Confiscation Act (1862), 205–6, 272–73

"secret six," 107, 110

"Seventh of March Speech" (Webster), 54, 315

Sewall, Samuel Edmund, 2, 57, 120

Seward, William Henry: Andrew asked to represent United States in England, 359; and Andrew in Annapolis, 175; Andrew on, 185, 186, 188, 353; and Andrew on commissioning of soldiers, 174; and Bird, 189; and Britain's Civil War stance, 182; enlistment/conscription strategies debated, 200, 202–3, 206; events leading to Civil War, 140; and Lincoln's cabinet change, 229; and Lincoln's reelection bid, 285, 290; and presidential election (1860), 119, 120–22, 125, 410–11n8; pressure to leave cabinet, 292, 293; slavery's future in and as, 79; on Surratt case, 365

Seymour, Horatio, 230, 284–85, 447n46

Seymour, Truman, 277

"Shall We Suffocate Ed. Green" (Redpath), 349

Sharkey, William L., 453n14

Shaw, Francis, 237–38

Shaw, Lemuel, 36, 52, 57, 89, 120

Shaw, Robert Gould, 180, 237–38, 243, 244, 250, 252–53, 268, 323, 383

Sherburn, Mary, 208

Sheridan, Philip, 289

Sherman, Thomas, 165, 169

Sherman, William T., 281, 286–88, 294, 296, 303, 310–11

Sickles, Daniel, 321

Sidwell, J. A., 120

Simpson, William, 279

Sims, Thomas, 56–58, 59

Six Months in Kansas by a Lady (Ropes), 81

Slack, Charles W., 55, 77

slavery: asylum for freed slaves, 223; enslaved people as soldiers for north (contraband policy), 164, 173, 179–80, 194–97, 200–202, 205–6; manifest destiny concept, 37; slave collar torture of slaves, 255, 255–56; slave states in Union at time of Civil War, 166–67, 179–80; and Turner, 14. *See also* abolitionism

Slidell, John, 181–82
Smalley, George, 272
Smith, A. D., 250
Smith, Gerrit, 88, 107–8, 370
Smith, Henry, 306
Smith, Increase, 138
Smith, Joshua, 323
Snethen, Worthington, 293
Snowden, Samuel, 72
Soldiers' Fund Society, 457n2
Soldiers' Rest (Worcester), 303
South Carolina, secession of, 133–34
Southern Loyalist Convention, 355
Spear, Charles, 36, 38, 52, 392n31
Spear, John Murray, 36, 392n31
Spear, Joseph, 138–39
Speed, James, 293
Spooner, Lysander, 409n44
Spooner, Nathaniel, 105–6
Spooner, William, 361
Sprague, Charles, 12
Sprague, Peleg, 76
Sprague, William, 215–16
Stanley, Charles Henry, 75
Stanly, Edward, 200
Stanton, Edwin: on African American
   recruitment, 266; on African American
   troops, 235–36, 239, 241–43, 246; cabinet
   resignation of, 372; and emancipation
   enactment, 229–30; on emancipation
   issue, 185–88; on end of Civil War, 304;
   and enlistment/conscription strategies
   debated, 194–95, 196–205, 427–28n23;
   on equal pay, 255, 257, 271, 272, 276–77,
   301; events leading to Civil War, 142;
   governors' meetings and Emancipation
   Proclamation, 207, 213, 216–17, 224,
   225, 227; as incoming War Department
   secretary, 185; on recruitment and
   draft, 250, 253, 254; on recruitment
   quotas, 274; on Union's restoration,
   324, 325
Stanton, Elizabeth Cady, 263
Starbuck, Ellen F., 454n15
State Liquor Agency (Massachusetts),
   408n30
Stearns, Frank Preston, 28
Stearns, George: as abolitionist, 28, 55; on
   African American troops, 236, 239–40,
   243–44, 246; American Land Company
   and Agency, 322; on Andrew's appointment to cabinet, 300; and Andrew's
   gubernatorial election (1860), 130,

132–33; on Andrew's return to private
   life, 350; death of, 365; and emancipation
   enactment, 232; and Emancipation
   League, 189; and John Brown, 88; and
   John Brown's Harpers Ferry raid, 107–8;
   legacy of, 383; on Pennsylvania's need
   for defense, 250
Stearns, Isaac, 282
Stearns, Mary, 232
Stearns, Oliver, 51
Stearns, William, 265
Stephens, Alexander, 346
Stephenson, Luther, Jr., 381–82
Stevens, John, Jr., 216
Stevens, Thaddeus, 183, 275, 329–30, 343,
   345, 435n28
Stewart, William, 347–48
Stone, Charles, 172, 180–81
Stone, Eben, 96, 98, 100–101, 125
Stone, James W., 48
Stone, Thomas Treadwell, 8–9
Story, Joseph, 15, 31, 33
Stowe, Calvin, 11
Stowe, Harriet Beecher, 5–7, 59–60, 104,
   328, 333, 352, 377
Stowell, Martin, 65
Stuart, Jeb, 107
Sturgis, James, 260
suffrage: of African Americans, 313, 330–31,
   335, 338–39, 342–44, 346–47; of women,
   344
Sumner, Charles: as abolitionist, 4; Afri-
   can American soldiers recruited, 236;
   on African Americans riding streetcars,
   284; and Andrew's appointment to
   cabinet, 301; Andrew's correspondence
   with, 177; Andrew's disagreement
   with, 324–31, 338, 354; and Andrew's
   early abolitionist stance, 27; and
   Andrew's early law career, 37; and
   Andrew's gubernatorial election (1860),
   125, 126, 130, 131–33; beating of, in
   Congress, 80–82, 84; and Botts family's
   emancipation, 72–75, 114; and Civil
   War inception, 150, 152; and Civil War
   mobilization, 162–63, 165; considered
   for Seward's replacement, 293; "The
   Crime against Kansas" (speech), 80,
   97; *Dred Scott v. Sandford* decision and
   reaction, 85, 86, 90–92, 94, 95, 98–99;
   elections of, 218, 221, 222; "Emancipation: The Cure for the Rebellion," 171;
   and emancipation as wartime measure,

180, 181, 183–85, 190–91; and emancipation enactment, 229–30; and Emancipation Proclamation, 214; enlistment/conscription strategies debated, 194, 195–97, 199–200; on equal pay, 263, 266–67, 271, 272, 274–77; events leading to Civil War, 136, 138, 139–42, 145; on Field, 285; on Fourteenth Amendment, 343–44; and Free-Soil Party inception, 40, 44, 47–49; and Fugitive Slave Law, 55, 57–60, 61, 62, 67–69; John Greenleaf Whittier on, 368; and Johnson presidency, 311; in Johnson's cabinet, 345; and Julia Ward Howe, 378; legacy of, 339; Lincoln cabinet appointment, 146; and Motley, 295; on national conscription, 242; at Old South Church service, 318; photo, 41; and Republican Party's rise in Massachusetts, 67–68, 70, 72–82, 84; retirement rumors, 360; and Robert Gould Shaw's memorial, 323; and Salmon P. Chase, 282; and school desegregation, 76–79
Surratt, John H., 365–66
Surratt, Mary, 365
Suttle, Charles, 63
Swails, Stephen, 277–78, 302, 444n46
Sweet, Betty, 89–90
Sweet, Lewis, 89

Taney, Roger B., 85–87, 93
Tappan, Arthur and Lewis, 14
The Task (Cowper), 7–8
Taylor, Edward Thompson, 31, 357, 374, 378
Taylor, Zachary, 47, 49, 53
Telegraph (Boston), 74, 77
temperance movement, 7, 10, 12
Thayer, Eli, 101
Thayer, William, 361
Thirteenth Amendment, 273, 280, 299–302, 324–25
Thomas, Lorenzo, 236
Thomas, Seth, 63
Thomas H. Thompson (ship), 45
Thompson, George, 19–21, 20, 268, 273, 357, 365
Thoreau, Henry David, 52, 72
Tilton, Theodore, 260–61
Timrod, Henry, 375
Tirrell, Betsy Frances, 429n7
Tod, David, 217
Tolson, James, 72–73
transcendentalism, 4, 28–30, 46

"The Transient and Permanent in Christianity" (sermon, T. Parker), 34
Tubman, Harriet, 247–52, 273
Tucker, Hilary, 246
Turner, Nat, 10, 14
Twelfth Baptist Church: Andrew as Sunday School teacher, 31, 327; Andrew honored at, 278–79; Andrew's attendance, 31; Andrew's tribute by, 278–79; as "Church of the Fugitive Slaves," 77; and Underground Railroad, 31, 42. See also Grimes, Leonard
Tyler, John, 37

Uncle Tom's Cabin (H. B. Stowe), 328
Underground Railroad: Andrew's support of, 4; and Fugitive Slave Law, 54, 56; and Hayden, 226; and Tubman, 247–52, 273; and Twelfth Baptist Church, 31, 42
Union Club of Boston, 259, 285
Union Leagues, 263, 366
Union Pacific Railroad, 356
Unitarianism: American Unitarian Association, Andrew on executive committee, 356–57; Andrew's membership in, 1; Brunswick (District of Maine) church, 16, 22, 23; on capital punishment, 308–9; Church of the Disciples, 29–31, 34, 47; first national convention, 305; newspapers of, 31, 34; Unitarian Festival (Boston, 1866), 366. See also Andrew, John Albion, religious interests of; Clarke, James Freeman
Upham, Thomas Cogswell, 18, 342

Van Buren, John, 60
Van Buren, Martin, 47–48
Van Lew, Elizabeth, 368–69
Van Lew, John, 368, 376–77
Vigilance Committee (Boston), 3–4
Virginia: McClellan's military review in (1861), 176; secession of, 164
Von Liebig, Justus, 362

Wade, Benjamin, 268, 282
Walbridge, Hiram, 160
Walker, Amasa, 47
Walker, David, 10
Walker, William, 267, 275
Wallcut, Robert F., 36, 37
Walley, Samuel, 78
Wanderer (yacht), 123–24
Ward, Samuel, 186

War Department. *See* Cameron, Simon; Stanton, Edwin

Ware, Henry, 280–81, 289, 309, 340

Warner, Oliver, 147

Warren Street Chapel Association, 102

Washburn, Israel, Jr., 215–16, 219

Washington, Booker T., 383

Washington, George, 343

Waters, Richard, 141

Webb, Seth, Jr., 120

Webster, Daniel: and Clay, 54; law career of, 15, 37; on Mexican American War, 40; Senate retirement of, 61; on slave-catching, 57, 58; statue of, 102, 266, 315–16; on Union as "inseparable," 150

Weed, Thurlow, 202–3, 216, 300

Weitzel, Godrey, 304

Welles, Gideon, 143, 292

Wentworth, Edwin, 239

Wetmore, Prosper, 216

Whidden, Benjamin, 425n43

Whig Party: Andrew's early membership in, 28, 38; Clay's founding of, 14–15; and Free-Soil Party inception, 39–52; Fugitive Slave Law and politics of fugitive hunting, 58–61

Whipple, Charles, 375–76

Whipple, Charlotte, 175

Whipple, Edwin Percy, 5–6, 145, 175, 185, 378

White, Andrew, 320

Whiting, William, 239, 253

Whitney, Addison, 313

Whittier, Hannah, 8

Whittier, John Greenleaf, 10, 37, 55, 144, 153, 178, 365, 368

Wicker, Rachel, 288

Wightman, Joseph, 139–40, 200

Wild, Edward, 238, 254, 318

Wilder, Charles, 223–24

Wilkes, Charles, 181–82

William Allen v. Joseph McKeen (1833), 15

Williams, George, 263

Williams, John, 216

Williams and Everett Gallery (Boston), 256

Wilmot, David, 2, 39, 54

Wilson, Henry: American Missionary Association meeting (1862), 224; Andrew considered for Senate position

of, 292; and Civil War inception, 149, 150; and Civil War mobilization, 158; elected Massachusetts governor, 70; on emancipation as wartime measure, 183, 184; on end of Civil War, 305; enlistment/conscription strategies debated, 197, 242; on equal pay, 266–67; as Free-Soiler, 69–70, 81; and Free-Soil Party inception, 47; and Fugitive Slave Law, 58, 68; and "Honest Man's Ticket" of Bird, 83; John Greenleaf Whittier on, 368; Lincoln cabinet appointment, 146; at Old South Church service, 318; speaking popularity of, 101; and Sumner, 81; and Union Leagues, 366

Winslow, Charles, 126–27, 128, 134, 155

Winthrop, John, 170

Winthrop, Robert C., 40, 59, 358

Wirt, William, 276

Women's National Loyal League, 263

women's rights: Andrew on, 299; Andrew on divorced women's rights, 309; Andrew on emigration west by single women, 318; Andrew on women's status, 299; suffrage, 344

Woodman, Cyrus: American Land Company and Agency, 322; Andrew's early friendship with, 13, 24, 26–27, 29, 30, 101–3; on Andrew's finances, 258; and Andrew's gubernatorial election (1860), 122; on Andrew's legacy, 376; on Andrew's speech to General Court, 298; Andrew's travels with, 366–67; at Bowdoin, 17, 21; early law career of, 23; events leading to Civil War, 144; and Free-Soil Party inception, 42–44, 50; and presidential election (1860), 119; on Reconstruction and fighting "good fight," 345

Woodman, Horatio, 34, 284, 344, 423n27

Woodwell, Charles, 232

Woodworth, Samuel, 125–26

Wool, John, 154

Wright, Elizur, 55, 56

Wright, Mrs. Francis, 152

Wyman, Powell, 201

Yates, Richard, 286, 287